THE INDEPENDENT SCHOOLS GUIDE 2013

EIGHTEENTH EDITION

THE INDEPENDENT SCHOOLS GUIDE 2013

St Paul's Cathedral School, London, Winner of *The Independent Schools Guide* Profile Image Competition

A fully comprehensive guide to independent education in the United Kingdom

CONSULTANTS SINCE 1873

The global experts in British Independent education

LONDON   PHILADELPHIA   NEW DELHI

First published in Great Britain in 1995 by Kogan Page Limited
This eighteenth edition published in 2013

120 Pentonville Road
London N1 9JN
United Kingdom
www.koganpage.com

1518 Walnut Street, Suite 1100
Philadelphia PA 19102
USA

4737/23 Ansari Road
Daryaganj
New Delhi 110002
India

British Library Cataloguing in Publication Data

A CIP record for this book is available from the British Library

ISBN   978 0 7494 6418 9
E-ISBN   978 0 7494 6419 6

Typeset by Graphicraft Limited, Hong Kong
Print production managed by Jellyfish
Printed and bound in Great Britain by Ashford Colour Press Ltd, Gosport

Contents

Acknowledgements

The Independent Schools Guide is the result of many, many hours, weeks and indeed months of work by editors, proofreaders, designers, data administrators, publishing professionals, educationalists and friends of Gabbitas. The guide you see today is the result of generations of experience, a good helping of insight and heaps of industrious lucubration.

For those who have already glanced at the contents, the next acknowledgements will come as no surprise. Additional editorial contributions from Peter Dix, Hilary Moriarty, Sarah Bellotti, James Wardrobe, Durrell Barnes, Fergus Rose, Towry Ltd and Dr Wendy Piatt, are all included with thanks.

Special thanks also go to the parent company of Gabbitas, Prospects Services and in particular Ray Auvray, Executive Chairman – whose support is greatly appreciated.

It would be entirely remiss not to mention the contributions from independent schools. A particular mention goes to St Paul's Cathedral School, as their entry won first place in this year's profile image competition. Thanks also go to Blundell's for kind permission to reproduce the image used on the cover.

We must not forget all the heads and school contacts who have so promptly provided information in the making of this new eighteenth edition. The many educational associations and organizations that add to the rich, characteristic idiosyncrasies of the independent sector are also owed a debt of gratitude for the useful information they provide.

Thank you.

Foreword

Welcome to the eighteenth edition of
The Independent Schools Guide

The first Gabbitas schools guide appeared in 1924 (then simply entitled *Schools*). The modest publication with thin glossy paper, tiny print and dubiously reproduced monochrome images has been reincarnated, year on year through many an event, not least World War II, bringing invaluable information and guidance to generations of parents.

The guide has, as you will see, evolved immeasurably since the first edition and represents a great departure from more recent editions. Introductions such as full-colour, new editorial contributors and an intuitively arranged directory make for an imminently accessible, contemporary guidebook.

Independent schools have, similarly, seen many a change. There has been a conspicuous shift towards co-education, with only 20 per cent of schools now single sex. Exclusive full boarding schools are in the minority, with day boarding schools growing in number. Adapting to changing attitudes, flexi-boarding and weekly boarding are also much more widespread.

International intake is more evident than ever with as many as 23,000 overseas pupils in attendance throughout the sector. See the section entitled 'Coming from Overseas' for those living outside the UK contemplating British independent schools.

The curriculum has, of course, changed since the first edition. Throughout the years we have seen the O-level then the CSE discontinued, giving way to the GCSE and its many revised versions. Of course, we are now anticipating the English Baccalaureate. In recent years, the IB has featured prominently and independent educationalists have established teaching of the IGCSE and Pre-U. In response to calls for greater differentiation amongst top-grade students, the A* grade has appeared, first for GCSE and more recently for A-level.

A defining characteristic of independent schools, however, remains unmoved by trends... that is the quality of education provided. Independent senior schools, now as ever, produce some of the very best academic results, a fact that sees them frequently featured at the top of league tables, statistical methodologies allowing.

As the independent sector has seen many a development, there is manifest need for an accurate record of schools and for guidance when choosing between them. *The Independent Schools Guide* now in its eighteenth edition provides this and a great deal more, collated in a creatively designed reference format.

About *The Independent Schools Guide*

Within the pages readers are advised by The Global Experts in British Independent Education – Gabbitas. The consultants introduce and explain all pertinent aspects of independent education and offer invaluable guidance for those preparing for and selecting independent schools.

The Independent Schools Guide provides comprehensive coverage with circa 2,000 school entries and is equally well suited to parents with nascent children, planning for day nursery and pre-prep induction, as to seniors and their families preparing for boarding schools, independent sixth forms and colleges. Visit the online accompaniment to the guidebook at www.independentschoolsguide.com.

About Gabbitas

Established in 1873, Gabbitas is uniquely placed to offer independent expertise. Each year the consultants provide personal advice and guidance to thousands of parents and pupils the world over, at all stages of education. Advice and guidance covers:

- choosing the right independent school (pre-prep, prep and senior);
- educational assessment;
- sixth form options – including A levels, IB, Cambridge Pre-U and vocational courses;
- university and degree choices, also UCAS applications;
- alternatives to university;
- careers assessment and guidance, job searching and interview technique.

Gabbitas also advises on transferring to the British education system and offers AEGIS-accredited guardianship services for overseas pupils at UK boarding schools. To find out more contact us at:

GABBITAS EDUCATION
Norfolk House
30 Charles II Street
London SW1Y 4AE
Tel: +44(0)20 7734 0161
Fax: +44(0)20 7437 1764
E-mail: info@gabbitas.co.uk
Website: www.gabbitas.co.uk

How to Use the *Guide*

About independent schools

The first part of this *Guide* offers extensive information about independent schools, examinations, fee-planning, scholarships and bursaries as well as guidance on choosing a school.

Researching individual schools

The main index at the back gives all page references for each school.

Selecting schools

If you are looking for a school in a specific area, turn to the directory section (Part 2), which is arranged geographically by town and county. Schools in London are listed under their postal areas. Each entry gives the name, postal address, and website of the school, together with the age range of pupils accepted.

Schools that have an asterisk also appear in the School Profiles section (Part 3), where select schools provide more detailed information. These schools also have a map reference to show their exact location. The Schools by Category section (Part 4) also contains a number of schools listed with details of their particular characteristics.

For further references, for example to find out whether a school offers scholarships, turn to the appropriate index in Part 5.

Scholarships, bursaries and reserved entrance awards

Many schools offer scholarships for children with a particular talent, bursaries where there is financial hardship or reserved entrance awards for children with a parent in a specific profession such as the clergy or HM Forces. Part 5 contains a complete list of schools, by county, that offer such awards. This section is necessarily only a brief guide to awards available. More specific information can be obtained from individual schools.

Religious affiliation

The index in Part 5 provides a full list of schools under appropriate headings.

Single-sex schools

For a complete list of single-sex schools, turn to Part 5.

Boarding schools

Schools with boarding provision generally offer full, weekly or flexi-boarding options. Some Sixth Form Colleges, with no residential facilities, may offer accommodation with host families. The number of boarders is shown in the entries in Part 2. For an index of boarding provision by county, see Part 5.

Dyslexia

Most schools offer help, in varying degrees, for pupils with dyslexia. A list of schools registered with CReSTeD (Council for the Registration of Schools Teaching Dyslexic Pupils) appears in Part 5.

English as a foreign language

Most independent schools offer assistance to overseas pupils who require special English language tuition. A list of schools, arranged by county, appears in Part 5.

Schools accredited by the Independent Schools Council

Part 5 contains an index of schools in membership of the associations listed below, which together form the Independent Schools Council (ISC). A satisfactory inspection report by the Independent Schools Inspectorate is a requirement for any school wishing to join one of these associations and for its continued accreditation as a member. For more information on the inspection of independent schools, see Part 1.1.

Headmasters' and Headmistresses' Conference (HMC)

Girls' Schools Association (GSA)

Society of Heads

Independent Association of Prep Schools (IAPS)

Independent Schools Association (ISA)

Other associations that are constituent members of ISC but not covered by the index are the Association of Governing Bodies of Independent Schools (AGBIS), the Independent Schools Bursars' Association (ISBA) and the Council of British International Schools (COBIS).

The Independent Schools Guide online

Remember that you can search for schools at www.independentschoolsguide.com.

PART ONE

THE INDEPENDENT SECTOR AND INDEPENDENT SCHOOLS

www.independentschoolsguide.com

The Independent Schools Guide Profile Image Competition 2012 1st runner up

Cameron House School

See winning entry from St Paul's Cathedral School
on the back cover

The independent sector and independent schools

Independent schools are largely self-governing and are not required to comply with all legislation covering schools maintained by the state. Under the Education Act 2002 all schools in England must be registered with the Department for Education (DfE), in Wales the Department for Children, Education, Lifelong Learning and Skills (DCELLS). In accordance with the Education Scotland Act 1980, independent schools in Scotland are registered by the Scottish government. However, independent schools throughout the UK receive little or no direct state funding and are free from much central and local government control.

Independent sector – defining terms

There is quite some discourse about the appropriate defining and descriptive language for schools in the sector. The term 'private school', although referring specifically to privately owned schools, is used to indicate schools free from government control. Although used more often in previous years, it is still relevant for today's parents.

A phrase frequently voiced by those familiar with independent education is 'fee paying schools'. This figurative saying includes reference to school fees paid to schools.

Another term, 'public school', is well known and generally refers to old established schools in membership of the Headmasters' and Headmistresses' Conference (HMC). As many of these date back to the days when education was a luxury chiefly provided by private tutors, the term 'public school' was used to indicate a school which the public could attend.

Gabbitas consultants tend to use the term 'independent school', which is in line with the current customs of teachers, the DfE and parents. As you read on you will see that it is also used throughout *The Independent Schools Guide*.

School organizational structures and management

Most independent schools are run as charitable trusts under a board of governors. Schools with charitable status are effectively non-profit-making concerns; surplus funds are allocated at the discretion of the governors. Often they are invested in new facilities or in scholarships or bursaries. A few schools are still privately owned.

The board of governors is the policy-making body for the school. It is responsible for the appointment of the head, allocation of finances and major decisions affecting the school and its development. Governors give their time voluntarily, often contributing professional expertise in education, business, finance, marketing or other areas relevant to the management of the school. The board commonly includes a number of parent-governors who have children at the school.

Day-to-day responsibility for the running of the school is delegated to the head, who is accountable to the board of governors, with support from one or more deputy heads. Other key figures include the bursar, who is responsible for the school's financial management, the director of studies, who manages the curriculum, timetable, examinations and other academic matters, and the registrar, who is responsible for admissions and arrangements for parents to visit the school. Further details of independent school staff and contacts can be found at the end of Part 1.2.

Independent sector – number of schools

Independent schools in the UK represent approximately 7 per cent of all schools. Most of the 2,000 or so independent schools are to be found in England, with a small proportion located in Scotland, Wales and Northern Ireland.

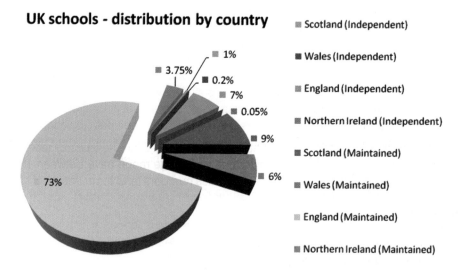

UK schools - distribution by country

- 1% — Scotland (Independent)
- 3.75% — Wales (Independent)
- 0.2% — England (Independent)
- 7% — Northern Ireland (Independent)
- 0.05% — Scotland (Maintained)
- 9% — Wales (Maintained)
- 6% — England (Maintained)
- 73% — Northern Ireland (Maintained)

Details of independent schools in each of the regions of the UK and some schools in mainland Europe are included in Parts 2 and 3.

Different schools, different styles

The independent sector includes schools of many different styles and philosophies, including both the traditional and the more liberal. Each is unique, with its own ethos and culture. Sizes can vary greatly, from small schools with less than 100 pupils to much larger-intake schools catering for up to 2,000 pupils. Some are based in towns or cities while others, including many boarding schools, are located in the countryside. Many are co-educational and others are single-sex, although it is not uncommon for boys' and girls' schools to co-educate for specific age ranges, eg for pre-prep or sixth form. International pupil intake is a characteristic of some independent schools. Boarding schools, for example, tend to attract significant numbers of overseas pupils and there are a few schools (international schools and international study centres) primarily for international pupils.

Education for all

Your child's academic needs are a high priority. Independent schools are not only for the most academically gifted children, although there is always some form of selection. The most selective accept only pupils capable of keeping pace with a fast-moving curriculum but there are many others catering for a wider range of ability. Some, for example, specialize in educating those in need of more individual attention in a less academic environment. Good independent schools enable pupils, whatever their academic ability, to achieve their best. Their success in helping children to fulfil their potential is evident from the excellent examination results reported each year.

Development of strengths and interests

Pupils are encouraged to develop their strengths outside, as well as inside, the class-room, ensuring that special talents in music, drama, art or sport, are nurtured. They provide a range of extra-curricular activities that inspire enthusiasm for a great many wider interests.

Small classes and individual attention

Small class sizes and close individual attention are prime characteristics of the sector. Generally, classes for children at the lower end of the age range have between 15 and 20 pupils. At senior school, GCSE (or IGCSE) class numbers tend to be between 12 and 18. Independent school sixth forms offer the opportunity for more attentive tuition still, with between 4 and 12 pupils in a class.

Traditional values and personal growth

Much emphasis is placed on the traditional values of tolerance and consideration for others and on personal development within a secure, disciplined environment. Pupils normally have a personal tutor who, as part of an experienced team, monitors progress and personal welfare throughout their time at school.

Excellent teachers and facilities

The independent sector often appeals to teachers at the height of their profession. Academic traditions and greater educational liberty draw those with a dedication to education and young people's learning. Many schools also offer unparalleled facilities for teaching, accommodation, sports and all aspects of school life, complementing the quality of teaching.

Following this brief introduction to the independent offering, we turn to the personal matter of selecting the right school for your child.

Choosing an independent school

Peter Dix, Former Head of Port Regis, provides advice and guidance on choosing a school for your child

Choosing the right school(s) for one's children is likely to be the most important decision parents will make for them, so it is vital to do all that is possible to get it right.

Beginning your research

If you plan to send your children locally and have some familiarity with your school options, it is never too early to engage purposefully with your research. If you are moving to a new part of the country, however, or have recently done so, you have even more work to do, so get cracking now! Often parents are torn as to whether they should find the house or the school first: my resounding advice is choose the right school and let the house follow, even if, as is so often the case, you have to rent for a while before you settle on your choice of house. The school is by far the more important consideration!

Entering schools – appropriate stages

Changing schools at 15 or 17 is not generally recommended because of the likely disruption to GCSE or A level studies, particularly if the move means a change to a different examination syllabus. If a move has to be made after age 13, it may be best to wait until after GCSEs or their equivalent have been completed.

School selection

You will, no doubt, start off by establishing your parameters: location (which, for boarding schools, will include proximity to airports, the country cottage, grandparents and so on); fee levels; co-ed or single-sex; style (highly academic, more all-round; traditional, more contemporary; campus or urban ...) and what facilities and emphasis there may be for your child's particular interests and talents. I would strongly advise you, though, not to be too exclusive in all this. You may just find, for example, that a more forward-looking co-ed school really appeals despite your assumption that traditional single-sex is what you are looking for. In other words, make sure you have a long preliminary list of possible schools that includes a few outside your template.

A vital consideration when choosing an independent school is when to register and enrol your child. The independent sector provides schooling for all age ranges. Entry stages are shown below:

Independent school entry age by school type

Entry age	School type
2–7/8	Nursery or pre-preparatory school
7/8–13	Preparatory school
11/13–16/18	Senior school
16–18	Sixth form

Sources of useful information

I am sure you will be chatting to your friends and neighbours, and may also consider using an educational consultancy, to identify target schools. You should then have a look at the websites of any contenders to make sure that each school is offering more or less what you are looking for and then phone the school – much better than writing or going via the website's 'Contact Us' link – and ask for a prospectus and the current school magazine (plus any other such material they may have available). You should also go onto the Independent Schools Inspectorate (ISI) website (www.isi.net) and read the latest inspection report of each one, and do the same on the Ofsted site (www.ofsted.gov.uk) for the pastoral reports on schools that have boarding provision (more details on schools inspections can also be found later in this guide). As the independent sector consists of uniformly good to excellent schools, expect these inspection reports to glow ... but look for small points of difference, which can prove very revealing. I suspect you will then find yourself drawing up a long list of half a dozen or so schools, which, as you refine the process, you reduce to two or three for your short list.

Misleading league tables

Do not be over-exercised about league table positions. These tell you quite a lot about the selectivity of a school and very little about what the school will do for your child. They also indicate levels of attainment in a school (where the pupils are) but nothing about degrees of achievement (how far they have travelled to get there or, to put it another way, the all-important 'value-added'). Remember too that more and more senior schools, including many of the most academically prestigious, are refusing to cooperate with the league-table industry (which has now been largely discredited) and that most of the best prep schools don't even do the National Curriculum tests on which their league tables are based.

Keeping your options open

You may well be looking in the first instance for a prep school, perhaps with a pre-prep and nursery attached. London day schools are often in heavy demand and you may be confronted by an entrance test of some sort, irrespective of the age of the child. Such a process can prove stressful for the parents and equally so for the child – but only if the parents let that happen. I strongly advise you not to tell a child that the rest of his or her life depends on the outcome! This will almost certainly lead to underperformance. If a place is not offered, don't worry; there are dozens and dozens of terrific schools available. It may all just take a little longer as you cast your net wider.

More than a purely academic consideration

You may feel, as many do, that education is about much more than merely the academic and that having a narrow focus on this is not the best way to educate children. All schools, I believe, but especially prep schools, have a responsibility to provide an education that is also moral, spiritual, emotional, physical and cultural to prepare children for what awaits them at the next stage of their education and for life in the outside world. My advice would be to look for a school that does not sell itself exclusively, or even mainly, on exam results but seeks instead to nurture rounded and civilized children who develop an attitude to work based on self-motivation and enthusiasm. The best schools are those that enrich children's outlook on life, encouraging critical thinking and intellectual curiosity, as well as introducing them to the history and range of language, ideas and civilizations. The appreciation of art, music, poetry and much else is an important part of what it is to be educated, and all of this should be embodied in the school's approach to education. I have always felt it important that children at school strive to engage enthusiastically with things outside the classroom and to develop the sort of considerate and decent conduct towards others that produces rounded and emotionally literate people. This general competence should sit comfortably and effectively alongside academic ability, and so I feel you should strive to find a school that has such an educational agenda.

Entry procedures

Most prep schools will have a more informal admissions process, with any entrance test not much more than a procedure for making sure the children can access the Common Entrance curriculum (which is followed by a large number of such schools) or the less demanding National Curriculum (which is also offered by state schools). Schools will also be looking for a good 'fit' of child (and parents!) to school, and so it is standard procedure for the family to visit the schools as part of the application process.

The entry requirements for senior independent schools are often more demanding, with the better-known ones operating admissions procedures that require (sometimes quite significant) academic potential to be proven. This may take the form of a full-blown entrance exam covering up to seven subjects, almost inevitably the Common Entrance exam or a less comprehensive but equally searching assessment, which usually consists of an IQ test of some sort (increasingly often taken on computer), an interview and a report from the child's current school. Parents should, of course, look into all of these options and procedures as part of their research, and the junior school heads will always be extremely helpful in the process. Candidates from overseas, who have not been following the same curriculum as their UK counterparts, will nearly always find senior schools offering a different and more appropriate form of entrance assessment. The schools will advise.

Visiting schools

And so to your all-important visit to the schools. I do have some reservations about the usefulness of open days. They are by definition rather artificial marketing exercises where schools roll out their best teachers and pupils to impress and steer parents to what they want them to see. There are also likely to be limited opportunities for one-to-one discussions with heads and other senior staff. Given the choice, I would visit on any ordinary day and get an impression of the school in action without the razzmatazz and make sure I had appointments to meet certain staff. If you can do both, however, go for it, because you will then at the very least see what the school is like when it is really making an effort and be able to make judgements from that, especially in comparison with a normal day! If you have the choice, try to visit senior schools in the first half of the Autumn or Summer terms, and avoid the second half of the Summer one when schools are in full exam (or worse, post-exam) mode. Prep schools can be visited comfortably at any time. Schools look best in good weather, but perhaps it is better to see them in the wet and gloom when you are less likely to be seduced by the look of the place!

Finding the human dimension

On any visit, please look out for the human dimension of the school. Look at the faces of the children as you walk around (are they bright-eyed and happy?) Watch how the pupils interact with one another and the staff (is that the tone and style of relationship you want?) Is there recent and lively work on display round the school? Is there evidence of attention to detail (notices pinned neatly on boards; little or no litter around; reasonably tidy changing-rooms ... because negatives here can betray a rather casual attitude in general)? How efficiently has your communication been handled? Is the atmosphere purposeful, friendly, warm and, particularly where young children are involved, is there a sense of fun? Small word: massive importance! Most of all though, does it feel right? Does the school reflect your own values and will it reinforce these in your child when you are not there? Do not sign up to any school or boarding house until you are satisfied that you (and, in most cases, your child) are happy with all this.

Touring the school

Your visit will always include a tour, and each school will have its own style of doing things. Here is your chance, whoever is showing you round, of seeing the school in action and getting a real feel for how the school manages things that you feel are important. At the heart of every school is the classroom lesson, and what happens in the classroom should be one of your main criteria in choosing a school. You should insist on visiting some classes in action and just hope it is not one of those silly schools that think prospective parents would rather see the lesson freeze to a standstill, with children suddenly standing and looking awkwardly at you (and vice versa) when you walk in. If this does happen, I suggest you say hello to the teacher and pupils and ask the teacher to carry on … and then watch what happens! You will have your own ideas about how lessons should be conducted, but I do not think it is good practice to have children sitting passively in front of a teacher who drones on and on without involving them in active learning. The only sound in the world to beat the purr of happy parents is the hum of children engaged enthusiastically in learning (and the former is likely to follow the latter)! A good lesson will have some traditional whole-class delivery from the teacher with hands up and the like from the children; some individual written work performed in silence by the children; but also some grouping of the children where they spark off one another … without undue noise and general mayhem! Good teachers teach on the edge some of the time to create excitement in their lessons and an enthusiasm for learning. Bad teachers grip their classes either so tightly that any spark is obliterated or so slackly that conflagration ensues! Your instinct and common sense will help you decide whether what is happening in a class when you visit is inspiring the children or not. You will also quickly get a feel for the teacher–pupil chemistry as well as the extent to which the environment of the classrooms is likely to be helping or hindering the pupils' learning. This is your chance to glance over children's shoulders at their books and to have a look at what is on the walls. The corridors too should be bright and covered with examples of recent work. Frown at any displays that are more than a term old. Insist too on going off-piste on your tour. Ask (courteously, of course) to peep behind doors that are closed, and make sure you stop and talk to passing pupils and teachers, who have not been specifically briefed to impress you!

Trusting your own judgement

Of course, different schools suit different children, but above all else please be guided by your gut-feeling when you are choosing a school. When buying a house, the estate agent's details about size of sitting room or type of kitchen, which you thought were so important, will often go out the window in favour of the strong intuitive sense you have when you walk into a house that just feels right – so too with schools. Do not be over-impressed by glossy prospectuses or smooth-talking staff. They may have a wonderful new music school, for example, but talk to pupils about how it is used and whether it is making a difference to the school's music. Is the head of Music dynamic and inspirational? Good facilities are not the defining feature of good schools – and any head would rather have good staff than good facilities – but the best schools have both.

The head and house staff

The head is a really key figure in any school (particularly, perhaps, in a junior school), with much of the ethos, character and style determined by him or her, and in a boarding school the housemaster/mistress is also extremely important. You may well want to know how much longer the head is likely to be at the school and how many years the housemaster/mistress has on his or her contract, but I would not let this be the overriding concern. The independent sector is full of talented and ambitious staff, and these good schools will always find good replacements! Details of other important independent school contacts appear later in Part 1.2.

Questions to ask the head

Ask the head searching questions about things academic and look at some pupils' books if you can, and check that they are being marked positively and thoroughly. There will also be any number of other things you will want to ask during your interview, so make a list before you go! You should certainly enquire as to the destinations of leavers – this will give you a steer on the academic levels achieved as well as the ambitions of the schools – and you will also doubtless want to know about how well the school can sustain and develop your child's interests and talents in various things like sport, art, drama, music and technology. Ask for evidence and do not allow yourself to be fobbed off with bland assurances. You may want to know about religious observance as well as the cultural mix of the school. You will probably want to understand how inclusive the school's selection policies are: are there sports teams for everyone or just the superstars; can anyone be in the play, or is it always reserved for the thespians; will your child's artwork ever go on view; and will his or her enthusiastic but comparatively modest scrapings on the violin ever be heard in the recital hall?

I would turn my back on any school that was interested more in obviously talented children than in the others. Satisfy yourself that your child will not disappear between the cracks and make as sure as you possibly can that he or she will enjoy being there and will really get something out of the experience over and above certain grades at the end of the process. The child is the father of the man, and you have a golden opportunity to ensure he inherits the value of the opportunities that an independent school provides.

A word or two on boarding

There is detailed advice about boarding schools later in Part 1.2 but allow me just a word or two here. While every school in the country, boarding or day, has a loose-limbed group or two, there tends to be much more overview of social interaction in a boarding school than is possible in a day school, where any bullying is more likely to happen outside the school gates and/or electronically. Good boarding schools can monitor the latter issue pretty effectively too, and the same applies to sex and drugs. These things are much more likely to swirl around outside school ... not least at parties! While there are no guarantees in these things, if you are considering a boarding school for your child, there is an excellent chance nowadays that things will work out well ... but you do need to trust the school and not interfere over every minor issue. A good school will employ excellent communication with parents, especially perhaps those who live overseas, and as long as any queries or concerns you have about your child are responded to promptly and reassuringly, you should let go and thank goodness that such wonderful boarding schools are now available to people just like you.

Involving your children in the decision

One might well ask these days who is actually doing the choosing – the parents or the child? Even at the prep school stage, children are becoming more and more involved in the decision (as, one might venture, parents become more and more indulgent!). I do think children should have a say, especially when the senior school is being chosen, but I do not think they should drive the process. Too often they can, in their lack of experience, be over-impressed or otherwise swayed by relatively unimportant considerations. I was shocked (and not a little upset) a year or two ago when a parent told me they had chosen Port Regis for their son, not as a result of my scintillating sales pitch, or my wife's dazzling charm or the fabulous reputation of the rugby team, but rather because he had seen several Manchester United posters on the dormitory walls and so had insisted that this should be his school! My advice would be to make the decision yourselves but to take the child along in this with you, using your powers of persuasion to let him or her see that, while he or she may have preferred another, this will be the one that will suit him or her best ... even if Chelsea posters predominate! Do not, however, persist with a choice towards which he or she is furiously hostile. It will end in tears.

An invaluable investment

Finally, the independent schools sector in the UK is full of world-class schools and it is quite properly the envy of the rest of the world. You need only look at the thousands of pupils who are sent over to the UK by their parents from almost any country you can think of to take advantage of what our schools have to offer. We are uniquely privileged to have them on our own doorstep. Yes, they can be expensive, but, if you are able to meet the costs (and the least expensive are no more than £6,000 a year, and there is also generous bursarial help available at every school), you will find you have made the most valuable investment of your life, with the dividend being repaid many times over for years and years to come. Good luck with your choice!

Hilary Moriarty, Director of the Boarding Schools' Association, explains the changing character of boarding education and what parents should now expect

Hands up if you think boarding schools are great for education but boarding itself is not likely to be great. Keep your hand up if that translates into big dormitories, possibly with the windows wide open and great draughts of cold air billowing the thin curtains between the iron beds, no privacy, communal bathrooms with 20 or more sinks, big common rooms where bullied children are ignored, bleak dining rooms serving dismal plates of unappetizing food and in general a tough, Spartan regime that no one in their right minds would contemplate for a beloved child. And – quite simply – no child in his or her right mind would agree to attend.

Now put your hand down and let me tell you a little about modern boarding, about boarding schools in 21st-century Britain, and about why, increasingly, a boarding education is the perfect choice for children and young people today.

Why and how have boarding schools changed so much?

The question of why?

'Why?' is easy to answer: because changing the product for a changing market was essential. Change was not necessary while the old market was constant – colonial or aristocratic families, happy to send their children to the schools the parents themselves (usually Dad) had attended, pragmatic about separation, convinced of the value of a stiff upper lip in the youngest child, seeing school as a place where a child was not only educated but also toughened up for a future serving an empire. At least one boarding school to my knowledge has on its walls portraits of no fewer than seven old boys awarded VCs. That was service with honour and distinction, and under fire.

But all the certainties of a constant market collapsed in the latter half of the 20th century – we learnt more about child development and psychology and fewer parents wanted prolonged separation from their children. If parents were sent abroad, they expected children to go too. And overseas, high-quality international schools sprang up to cater for such children on the spot.

The cost of running boarding schools rose and fees marched inexorably beyond the range of many families. So schools themselves had to change.

How did they change?

Many took day pupils, original all-boys schools went co-ed, boarding itself had to be better, or it would not survive at all. The best way to be better was to get closer to what parents wanted. So boarding schools moved towards more comfort and less separation. More access and less distance. Less toughening up of young children and more recognition of the value of nurturing young people. Less discipline, more happiness. More pastoral care, and more recognition that schools are actually all about pastoral care. Boarding school heads began to adopt new philosophies: an unhappy child will not thrive; children prosper if they are happy; happy schools attract more pupils. A positive, virtuous circle, with the child at the very heart of the school and all that it accomplishes, became the boarding paradigm.

Boarding schools – statistics

About 13 per cent of all independent school pupils are boarders and in the region of 700 schools, including single-sex and co-educational schools, offer boarding places. Relatively few schools are for boarders only as most also admit a significant number of day pupils.

Boarding staff – changing practices

Improvements in the quality of the pastoral care practices of those at the sharp end of residential provision have contributed to the transformation of boarding schools over the past 15 years. The Boarding Schools Association (BSA), amongst other bodies, has contributed to the development of quality care practices for children at boarding school through its Professional Development and Training. The specialist care provided by house-masters and house-mistresses has come on a great deal and is a strength of the modern boarding experience – especially so for pupils who are often some distance from home.

What you see is what you get (boarding facilities)

Let's think about the home comforts first. In the past several years, independent boarding schools have spent in the region of £100 million on boarding accommodation. They have refurbished listed buildings and built new if necessary. Boarding accommodation really is comfortable now.

Bedrooms

While psychologists advise that younger boarders should share bedrooms in threes or fours so that they can forge friendships and ward off those inevitable pangs of homesick-ness in the early days, older pupils increasingly find that their bedrooms are singles or doubles, often with en suite facilities. Schools recognize that privacy matters – oh the bliss of your own shower – and parents and pupils alike seek the quiet study space which is more likely if your room mate is not playing heavy metal until late at night.

Common rooms and kitchens

Common rooms, and the small kitchens in which snacks are made both early and late, are comfortable spaces, probably warmer and more convivial than those their occupants will find at university halls of residence in due course.

Recreational facilities

With such facilities, schools seek to create the 'Wow!' factor. Really attractive bedrooms, warm and comfortable, are very important to pupils as well as to their mums and dads.

Schools are also competing to feature in the conversation in the car – 'But I really loved the one where ...' and it might be the Olympic-sized swimming pool, or the near-professional theatre, or the really cool library created with metal mezzanine floors out of the old gym after the new sports hall had been built.

These recreational spaces, plus the courts and the pitches and the astro-turfs and now the riding schools, are a major part of marketing not just a school but boarding itself. Many day schools also have such facilities, but cater only for a day population that is trudging home by tea-time.

Increased opportunity in the boarder's day

But boarding days are long and of course it's not just about studying in a pleasant room. Boarders still have hours at their disposal – hours for supervised prep, so it is thoroughly done, but also hours for music practice and joining a choir or orchestra, for an impromptu five-aside match or a game of volley-ball. For all the things, in fact, which a modern parent would want them to be doing but may not have time to organize or transport to and from.

Day schools with boarding (day boarders)

Even when a school has a large day population and a relatively small number of boarders, many would say that boarding is at the heart of their operation. Keeping boarders occupied, engaged and interested, happy with their term-time lives, is vital even when there are relatively few of them!

At school, in touch

There was a time when a boarding school really was something of a closed and often remote world. That is infinitely less so today. British parents are increasingly likely to choose a boarding school for their child that is within an hour and a half of home. Some boarders have even grumped gently that they went to boarding school and that Mum and Dad seemed to follow! Parents make huge efforts to get to concerts, productions and matches, as well as speech days and carol services. There is also a real recognition on the part of schools that they are in a living, working partnership with parents to ensure the best for the child, and parental support is always valued.

Writing home, or is that facebooking and tweeting home?

For all boarders, but of most interest to international pupils, boarding has been transformed by the online revolution. Fewer and fewer pupils actually write home: while it's always lovely to get a handwritten letter or card, 'snail mail' has been completely overtaken by e-mail, texts and of course by the growing range of social media websites available. And how fast and effective! A great test result can be relayed to Mum on the far side of the world at break-time; an evening e-mail (tweet or status update) can keep child and parent in touch every single day.

Schools will be mindful of their responsibility to protect children from the worst effects and possible dangers of the internet, and details will be in their policy statements for parents to inspect. Expect greater supervision of younger boarders – prep schools in particular work with parents to ensure that they are happy about their child's access to the internet and to mobile phones. But oh what a change for a child to have a phone at school – how good that the days are gone when a worried parent might call the one phone on a long corridor when the child was never available.

Accessibility: a defining feature of today's boarding

Accessibility, in fact, might be the biggest difference between boarding then and boarding now: whatever the distance, a boarder now is never, really, that far away. And it's really useful to be able to e-mail a houseparent if you're worried. However, with so many means of keeping in touch with boarders available, parents should keep in mind that it can sometimes be advisable to reduce contact with children if they are having problems settling in. Although difficult, this can help by giving time and freedom for new relationships to develop.

Full, weekly and flexi-boarding options

Changing the pattern of boarding itself has been another response from schools to the needs of modern families. In many boarding schools, there is a 'mixed economy' of boarders who may be 'full', ie go home or to guardians one weekend in three, or 'weekly', ie are in school from Monday to Friday (or Sunday night to Saturday lunchtime if the school has lessons on Saturday) and go home every weekend, or 'flexi', ie stay sometimes.

Flexi-boarding

Flexi-boarding really can be as various as the parents wish and the school finds workable, and is particularly popular for younger pupils: some children stay for one or two nights a week on a regular basis; others stay occasionally, perhaps for a concert or trip night, or when parents are called away unexpectedly. Flexi-boarders who find they like it often grow into weekly boarders, with both children and parents recognizing that homesickness was not, after all, the enormous problem it might have been, and school journeys can usefully disappear, with time better spent all round.

Prospective full boarders – weekend population

For international pupils or for British children with parents abroad, it is probably wise to be sure that the school of your choice has a substantial weekend population. There is more likely to be plenty to do if a lot of the boarders are still on site than if most have gone home. Ask for details at interview, such as, 'Exactly how many boarders of my daughter's age were in last weekend?'

Tell me everything! (Researching boarding options online)

The internet revolution allows parents an intimate view of any school they are considering for their child. What does their website look like? Do you like the feel of it? Does it have videos? Do these look like people you could get along with? You can learn all that from the comfort of your chair and without the school even knowing you're looking.

Boarding school inspections

Boarding at all English schools is inspected by Ofsted (although the responsibility is set to move to the ISI for independent schools' boarding inspection) and their reports are available on the Ofsted website as well – probably – as on the school's own. Check them out. They're about 12 pages long and they rate a school's boarding as Outstanding, Good, Satisfactory or Inadequate. For further details see Part 1.6 on inspections.

Things to ask when visiting a boarding school

When you visit, ask to be toured by a pupil – this is usual, so don't be afraid to ask. And ask them what it's really like. What is the worst meal of the day? What is the best thing for them about being a boarder? What goes on at weekends? On that subject, check with the head how many activities are included in the fees and how many would be pay-for extras.

Questions for prospective boarders' parents

Where is the school? How good are the transport connections?

If you're coming from overseas, where's the nearest airport? Which airlines fly into there and are flights expensive?

How much does a journey from school to airport cost if your child is flying alone? Does the school run a minibus service to airports?

If overseas, have you arranged a guardian family for your child when he or she can't get home?

Nice to have grandparents or relatives reasonably close, but, in general, don't rely on work colleagues to be guardians – it can be quite an undertaking.

If your child will be a full boarder, not going home at weekends, how many other boarders of his or her age are likely to be on the premises at the same time?

How full a programme of activities operates at weekends, and which are included in the fees and which are paid-for extras? And is it always just shopping or cinemas?

What activities are provided in the evening? The prospectus may say there are choirs and bands and debating and Scrabble clubs, but all will depend on staff – do these activities really happen and happen regularly?

Does the school have a good counselling service? If a child is lonely or upset or homesick, who will notice, who will help?

If the child is an international pupil needing help with English language, who decides how much help, and what will it cost?

For an older pupil, how does the school arrange visits to universities so that the pupil makes an informed choice if applying to university?

How good is the food – really, every evening and every weekend? How much do pupils contribute to any debates about food?

Does the school let out its premises at weekends and does this have an impact on the boarders' lives?

Additional school selection considerations

Courses and qualifications offered

Do research the qualifications and courses available at the schools that interest you. Independent schools in England and Wales are not required to teach the National Curriculum or to use the National Tests, which are compulsory for state-maintained schools. However, since most are preparing pupils for public examinations, they generally do follow the National Curriculum, complementing it with additional options or areas of study as desired. Independent schools in Scotland are free to form their own curriculum policy but, like maintained schools in Scotland, they are normally preparing pupils for Standard and Higher examinations. Most senior schools in England and Wales are preparing pupils for the General Certificate of Secondary Education (GCSEs) or international GCSE (IGCSE), taken at 16, the Advanced Subsidiary (AS) and Advanced GCE (A2) taken in the sixth form. In Scotland pupils are prepared for Scottish National Qualifications. Find out in advance whether the schools that interest you are offering the courses appropriate for your child. For further details see Part 1.4.

Assessment and examination

Assessments and examinations may take place for each subject as frequently as each term. Many schools operate a tutorial system under which a House tutor is assigned to each pupil to monitor social and personal development as well as academic progress. Parents receive a full report at the end of each term. In some schools, mock examinations (in preparation for GCSE, AS/A2 or Scottish equivalents) are held in the spring preceding the real examinations. These are marked internally by the school and give an indication of likely performance in the summer. To ensure your son or daughter is appropriately prepared it is a good idea to find out what form assessment takes well ahead of his or her first day. Further details about examinations can also be found in Part 1.4.

Sixth form options

There are many different decisions to make regarding sixth form studies, including whether to opt for the sixth form at the current school or to look for a place at an independent college. Seniors need to be planning for sixth form study, including course choice, before completing GCSE (or equivalent) examinations. As sixth formers need to study with greater independence, senior school pupils should be reflecting on their study skills and areas for improvement before beginning their course. More details about sixth form options can be found in Part 1.7.

Education and wider activities

Aside from academic studies, independent schools place great emphasis on wider activities. Many excel in areas such as sport, where pupils can develop their talents through fixtures against other schools as well as county or national school championships. Most schools recognize, however, that not all pupils enjoy team games. Many offer more individual sports including, for example, squash, horse-riding, sailing and golf. Music, art and drama are also important aspects of the curriculum and extra-curricular activities. Many schools offer individual music lessons on a range of instruments and encourage pupils to play in the school orchestra, other music groups or to sing in the choir. Drama is often taught to a very high standard, with performances staged for public festivals as well as in school. Many schools offer preparation for examinations set by the Associated Board of the Royal Schools of Music and the London Academy of Music and Dramatic Art (LAMDA) and there may be regular trips to galleries, concerts, the theatre or the ballet. Many schools have long traditions in particular sports or performance arts, so make sure your school short list includes those that cater for your son or daughter's non-academic interests as well. School profiles, in Part 3, often include details about specialisms and provide insight into the whole educational experience provided.

Pastoral care and discipline

Many independent schools, whether boarding or day, operate a house system, which divides pupils into smaller communities to ensure a good staff:pupil ratio for pastoral care. Boarders are often accommodated in small groups with resident house staff. The housemaster or housemistress is in charge of pastoral care and will also go through the school report with each child at the end of term. House staff monitor overall progress, keep the head informed about each child and, in boarding schools, may be the first point of contact for parents. Many schools also allocate each pupil a personal tutor, who assists with educational guidance, keeps progress and welfare under constant review and can deal with issues arising on a day-to-day basis. All schools are legally obliged to provide a statement of the policy and system of care in place for pupils. They are also required to have a published policy on bullying.

Most schools keep rules simple, encouraging self-discipline and common sense in their pupils and giving praise for good behaviour. Sometimes children may contribute to a house points system, being awarded points for good work, thoughtful behaviour and for showing initiative or making a particular effort. Points might be deducted for bad behaviour. Other sanctions imposed might include limitations on leaving school premises or detention. A breach of school rules with regard to smoking or alcohol may mean suspension. Breaches involving illegal drugs may mean immediate permanent exclusion. Corporal punishment is illegal in all schools.

Religious affiliation

Spiritual growth is an important aspect of life in most independent schools, whatever their affiliation. The range includes Church of England, Roman Catholic, Quaker, Methodist, Jewish and others. Most adopt an inter-denominational approach and are happy to accept children of other faiths, but parents should check with individual schools the extent to which their child, if of a faith other than the majority of pupils, would be expected to participate in school worship. School profiles, in Part 2, show religious affiliation, and an index of schools by religious affiliation appears in Part 5.

Educational guidance and careers assessment

The value of good educational guidance cannot be overestimated, particularly in view of the complexity and variety of options now available to school leavers and the importance of making the right choice. Some schools have a well-stocked, permanently staffed careers department and a full programme of careers guidance that includes formal assessment, talks from visiting speakers and work experience opportunities. Others may have more limited resources. For parents seeking specialist guidance, an independent provider such as Gabbitas may be a useful option. For more details of the one-to-one careers assessment services visit www.gabbitas.co.uk/uk-parents-consultancy-services.

Special educational needs

Parents of children in need of extensive individual attention, usually those with specific learning difficulties such as dyslexia, will find that there is a wide range of support available in mainstream independent schools. Some may bring in a specialist teacher to assist pupils at set times during the week. Some may have specialist teachers permanently on staff. Others may run a specially staffed department or unit. Parents interested in schools that offer provision for dyslexia in some form should look out for CReSTeD registered schools indicated in the geographic schools directory in Part 2 and school profiles in Part 3; there is also an index of CReSTeD registered schools in the reference section in Part 5. More detailed information on special needs provision and special schools can be found in a separate Gabbitas publication, *Schools for Special Needs*.

Inspections and school standards

Independent schools must meet rigorous inspection criteria. Schools in membership of any of the associations that form the Independent Schools Council must conform to strict accreditation requirements and are regularly inspected by the Independent Schools Inspectorate. Other independent schools in England and Wales are inspected by Her Majesty's Inspectorate for Ofsted. Inspection reports can provide useful insight for parents before selecting a school. For more details please turn to Part 1.6 on independent school inspections.

Overseeing your child's progress

Once your son or daughter begins at a school there is a good deal of information available to help you monitor their progress. Every child receives a termly report which is sent home to parents. The results of any internal examinations are generally included in these reports. Parent's evenings are held at regular intervals at which parents are briefed on their child's progress. In addition the evening provides the opportunity for parents to discuss their child's education and any areas of concern. Invitations are also extended to attend school sporting, musical and theatrical events, whether or not their child is taking part, and sometimes to help with school projects such as fundraising activities.

School fees – general trends

As each independent school is very much an individual institution, fees can vary a great deal. It is generally the case that fees are higher the older the pupil. It is safe to expect that nurseries and pre-preps are at the lowest end of the fees scale, with prep schools being higher priced and senior and sixth form places commanding the greatest fees. Other influencing factors include accommodation type, location, gender taught, the history and reputation of a school and the bursaries and scholarships available. For further details on fees, fees planning, scholarships and bursaries please see Part 1.5.

Independent school contacts

The board of governors

The board of governors is the planning and policy-making body that controls the administration and finance of the school. Some board members may also be parents of children at the school. The governors are responsible for the appointment of the head and for all major decisions affecting the school. Governors give their time voluntarily. Many are individuals with expertise in their professional lives, for example in law or accountancy, who can contribute their knowledge for the benefit of the school.

Head

With accountability to the board of governors, the head or principal is responsible for all elements of the day-to-day management of a school. Included within this remit are appointment of staff, the administrative structure, curriculum content, and the safety and welfare of pupils. Many heads are accomplished academics who dedicate time in the week to teaching; to share their subject knowledge and to develop relationships amongst the pupil body. A good number take a lead on the marketing of their school, although more now recruit marketing directors.

Bursar

The bursar, in conjunction with the governors, is responsible for financial matters within the school. The bursar also takes charge of maintenance of the grounds, premises and buildings as well as catering arrangements.

Director of studies

Many schools have a director of studies, who is responsible for day-to-day curriculum matters, timetabling and for ensuring that staff are kept informed of new developments.

Registrar/Admissions secretary

The registrar is responsible for the admission of pupils and arrangements for parents to visit the school and meet the head. He or she also takes care of the practical aspects of registration and joining. This is the first person to contact for registration and enrolment details.

Housemaster/Housemistress

The housemaster or housemistress takes care of the welfare and overall progress of children in the house and is normally the first point of contact for parents. He or she will keep the head informed of each child's progress and may often be the first to hear of any problems. Serious issues are always referred to the head.

Subject teachers

Subject teachers are responsible for the academic progress of pupils taking their subject: Sciences, English, Latin, Mathematics, etc. They are responsible for classroom teaching and for in-class pastoral care. Subject teachers also produce a termly report for each of their students and attend parents' evenings.

Chaplain

The chaplain has a special role within school. Independent of academic or disciplinary considerations, the chaplain is responsible for the spiritual development of pupils and can often provide a sympathetic ear to children who seek guidance on issues of concern.

Matron

The matron looks after the practical aspects of boarding life, supervising and arranging laundry. Separate houses normally have their own Matron. She often knows children individually and can provide sympathy and support for those who feel homesick or upset.

Sister

The sister is a qualified nurse responsible for medical arrangements. She looks after pupils who may be admitted into the sanatorium with minor ailments and may require a few days in bed. Within a boarding school, serious medical matters are always referred to the school doctor and where necessary children will be taken to hospital.

Pupils

Independent schools encourage their pupils to take on positions of responsibility as part of school life. Senior pupils who show good sense and have contributed to the school by their achievements in academic work, musical or sporting activities, for example, may be granted suitable senior positions in recognition of their efforts. Hence an excellent sports-person may be made games captain or an outstanding chorister head of choir. Pupils with an excellent academic record or who deserve merit for other contributions may be given the post of head boy or girl. Prefects are students appointed to take responsibility for some of the daily routines in school and are encouraged to set a good example to younger pupils.

1.3

Overseas pupils and students – coming to the UK

If you live overseas, the best advice is to plan ahead as far as possible and at least a year in advance. This will give you a wider choice of school and allow you time to research all the options properly and make an informed choice. To help you, the most important aspects of coming to school in the UK are explored here.

Level of English

Most independent schools will expect your child to speak some English on arrival, although additional tuition is often available in school to improve fluency and accuracy and to ensure that your child can cope with a normal curriculum.

If your child is to board in the UK but speaks only a little or no English, he or she may benefit from a short period in one of the specialist boarding schools ('international study centres'), which prepare overseas pupils for entry into mainstream boarding schools at senior level. Detailed information on international study centres appears later in Part 1.3.

Alternatively, you may wish to arrange for your child to spend the summer at one of the UK's many language schools before joining a boarding school in September.

Academic background

If your child has been educated within the British system, it should not be difficult to join a school in the UK, although care should be taken to avoid changing schools while a pupil is in the middle of GCSE or A level studies. However, if your child has not been following a British curriculum, entry to a mainstream independent school may be less straightforward. The younger your child, the easier it is likely to be for him or her to adapt to a new school environment. Prep schools may accept overseas pupils at any stage up to the final two years, when pupils are prepared for Common Entrance exams. Senior schools, in particular, will normally look for evidence of ability and achievement comparable with pupils educated in the British system and will probably wish to test your child in English, Maths and Science before deciding whether to offer a place. Pupils wishing to enter the sixth form will probably be tested in the subjects they wish to study. Recent reports and transcripts, in translation, should also be made available to schools.

If your child has been following the International Baccalaureate (IB) programme overseas, you will find a number of schools and colleges in the UK which offer the IB. Details of IB schools and colleges can be found in Parts 2 and 3.

For schools with a broad mix of nationalities offering international curricula (often incorporating the IB) you can select from a range of international schools. More detailed information on international schools appears later in Part 1.3.

Length of stay

If your stay is relatively short and you plan to return home afterwards, you may be able to enter your child in one of the schools in the UK specifically for nationals of other countries who are based in the UK. France, Germany, Sweden, Norway, Greece and Japan are all represented. Your own embassy in London should be able to provide further details.

Boarding schools – location

If you are looking for a boarding school, try not to focus your search too narrowly. Most schools, including those in the most beautiful and rural parts of the UK, are within easy reach of major transport links and the UK is well served by air, rail and road routes. In addition, most schools will make arrangements to have your child escorted between school and the airport and vice versa.

Visiting schools

Once you have decided on the most suitable type of school, you can obtain information on specific schools. It is essential that you visit schools before making a final choice. Try to plan your visits during term time.

Independent schools set their own holidays and term dates, making it difficult to give a definitive schedule for the year at all schools. As a general guide, the academic year is divided into three terms (autumn, spring and summer), each with a half-term holiday. A generous, six-week 'summer holiday' follows the summer term.

Term/holiday	Dates
Autumn term (half-term holiday)	22 Oct–3 Nov
Christmas holiday	15 Dec–9 Jan
Spring term (half-term holiday)	11 Feb–20 Feb
Easter holiday	1 Apr–25 Apr
Summer term (half-term holiday)	28 May–5 June
Summer holiday	2 Jul–6 Sep

Questions to ask

English language support

What level of English does the school expect? Is additional support available at school? How is this organized? Is there a qualified English language teacher?

Pupil mix

International schools naturally have pupils of many different nationalities at any one time. If you are looking to enter your child into a mainstream independent school, you may wish to find out how many other pupils of your nationality attend the school and what arrangements are made to encourage them to mix with English pupils.

Pastoral care

If your child has special dietary needs or is required to observe specific religious principles, is the school willing and able to cope? Would your child also be expected to take part in the school's normal worship?

If your child speaks little English, it can be very comforting during the early days when homesickness and minor worries arise, or in the event of an emergency, to have a member of staff on hand to whom the child can speak in his or her own language. Bear in mind, however, that fewer schools are likely to have staff who speak non-European languages.

Ask about arrangements for escorting your child to and from school at the beginning and end of term. Some schools have a minibus service to take children to railway stations and airports or will arrange a taxi where appropriate.

AEGIS accredited guardianship

Most schools insist that boarding pupils whose parents live overseas have an appointed guardian living near the school who can offer a home for 'exeats' (weekends out of school), half-term breaks and at the beginning and end of term in case flights do not coincide exactly with school dates. A guardian may be a relative or friend appointed by parents, but bear in mind that the arrangement may need to continue for some years and that guardianship is a substantial commitment.

For parents with no suitable contacts in the UK, schools may be able to assist in making arrangements. Alternatively, there are independent organizations, including Gabbitas, which specialize in the provision of guardianship services. Good guardian families should offer a 'home from home', looking after the interests and welfare of your child as they would their own, providing a separate room and space for study, attending school events and parents' evenings, involving your child in all aspects of family life and encouraging him or her to feel comfortable and relaxed while away from school. Some guardianship organizations are very experienced in selecting suitable families who will offer a safe and happy home to pupils a long way from their own parents. The range of services offered and fees charged by different providers will vary, but you should certainly look for a service which:

- personally ensures that families are visited in their homes by an experienced member of staff and that all appropriate checks are made;

- takes a genuine interest in your child's educational and social welfare and progress;

- keeps in touch with you, your child, the school and the guardian family to ensure that all is running smoothly;

- provides administrative support as required and assistance with visa and travel requirements, medical and dental checks and insurance, and any other matters such as the purchase of school uniform, sports kit and casual clothes.

Parents seeking a guardianship provider may like to contact AEGIS (Association for the Education and Guardianship of International Students), of which Gabbitas is a founder member. The purpose of AEGIS is to promote best practice in all areas of guardianship and to safeguard the welfare and happiness of overseas children attending educational institutions in the UK. AEGIS aims to provide accreditation for all reputable guardianship organizations. Applicants for membership are required to undergo assessment and inspection to ensure that they are adhering to the AEGIS Code of Practice and fulfilling the Membership Criteria before full membership can be granted. For further details contact Gabbitas Guardianship on +44 (0)20 7734 0161 or visit www.gabbitas.co.uk. For further information about AEGIS, visit the website at www.aegisuk.net.

Preparing your child to come to the UK

Coming to school in a different country is an enriching and exciting experience. You can help your child to settle in more quickly by encouraging him or her to take a positive approach and to absorb the traditions and social customs of school and family life in the UK. After the first year, most children begin to feel more confident and comfortable in their surroundings, both at school and with their guardian family. A good guardianship organization will ensure that you and your child know what to expect from life in the UK, and that you are aware of the kind of behaviour and approach the school and guardian family will expect. They should be able to advise on visas, UK entry requirements and related matters, and provide support on a range of issues throughout your transition to the UK.

Where to go for help

You may be able to obtain information about schools from official sources in your own country. For detailed guidance and assistance in the UK you may wish to contact an independent educational consultancy such as Gabbitas, which can advise you on all aspects of education in the UK and transferring into the British system.

International study centres

By Sarah Bellotti, director of King's Ely International

'International study centre' (ISC) is a term used to describe a school that gives support to both the academic and linguistic needs of international pupils in an independent school setting. ISCs are usually, but not always, part of larger independent boarding schools, either existing within the school itself or separately on the same site but in a different purpose-built building.

ISCs exist to provide a supportive pastoral framework and academic environment for international pupils. For international pupils, it is often their first experience of UK schools and the study centre serves as a bridge between a pupil's education and culture and the British educational system.

What do international study centres offer?

The ISCs have reliable methods of assessing the linguistic needs of international pupils according to their age and ability. While a strong emphasis is placed on improving the pupil's English, there is a rigorous programme of academic study, including a range of curriculum subjects taught by teachers who have had specialist training in teaching pupils with English as a second language (ESL).

The ISC classroom experience

Class sizes are typically smaller than ordinary school classes – usually ranging from five up to a maximum of 12 pupils per class. The classes tend to be interactive, where pupils are encouraged to participate and teachers focus on helping them articulate their understanding. Pupils often work in pairs or in small groups to maximize their speaking and are encouraged to verbalize as much as possible. There is often a vocabulary focus to each lesson, helping the pupils build up an academic lexis that will serve for use as they further their study.

The courses on offer

Many study centres focus on intensive one- or two-year GCSE programmes where pupils, usually between the ages of 14 and 17, can study five or more subjects depending on their needs, abilities and interests. Maths and English are compulsory. Many ISCs also offer programmes of study for junior pupils, who are younger than 14, and 'Pre-GCSE programmes', which prepare pupils for GCSE subjects. In some schools, the international pupils may integrate into the mainstream school for some subjects.

Extra-curricular activities

Like all independent schools, ISCs provide international pupils with extra-curricular activities and clubs that take place after school or during lunch times. In these activities, the international pupil will often have the opportunity of mixing with the British pupils from the main school through, for example, the school orchestra or sports teams. ISCs also usually include some element of explicit instruction in the discipline and culture of British boarding school life and of British culture in the wider sense. Most offer a programme of events, excursions and trips that take the international pupils to see different places of cultural interest in the UK.

Pastoral care and boarding

Pastoral care is of particular importance for pupils who are far away from home and ISCs pay close attention to make sure that the international pupils' needs are well catered for. There is 24-hour residential care by responsible adults based on the boarding house model and an appropriate and age-specific leisure programme. Boarding houses have rigorous guidelines and are inspected regularly.

ISCs aim to host a wide variety of nationalities and their mission is to embrace and include the cultures of their international pupil bodies into their own academic and pastoral programmes, showing respect for diversity.

Destination of pupils

Most international pupils come to the UK as part of a longer educational journey, culminating in studying at a British university. However, some pupils wish to stay for just a year, to improve their English, and then slot back into their native education system. Many stay between one and two years and then move on to mainstream education, sometimes within the same school, for example studying GCSEs at the ISC and A levels/IB at the main school. Others move to a different school to complete their further education.

Accreditation

Many international study centres have been accredited by the British Council and, once accredited, are regularly inspected to ensure standards are maintained. The accreditation scheme sets overarching standards in four areas: management, resources and environment, teaching and learning, and welfare and student services. Study centres that have not been accredited by the British Council will have been accredited by other reputable accreditation boards such as the Independent Schools Council (ISC) or Council of Independent Schools (CIS). The British Association of International Schools and Colleges (BAISC) also accredits international study centres for quality assurance purposes and provides help in the form of development, training and mutual support to its members.

The international study centre pupil

Cristina Blazquez is a 13-year-old pupil from Madrid, in the Pre-GCSE group at King's Ely International.

'Last summer I was very excited and nervous because, for the first time, I would spend a whole year studying in another country, in England.

'I am studying 11 subjects, but they are not very difficult for me because the teachers make a great effort to teach us and they spend time outside of class to help us. I also get additional help from my friends to do my homework. I have joined some clubs where I have met some British students, so I can improve my English faster.

'I am sure that when I finish this year here and go back to Spain, my English will be very good.

'I have many friends from different countries and I learn interesting things about their culture and lifestyle. This is also an opportunity to get to know about life around the world.'

Liwei Zhang is a 16-year-old girl from China. She is taking the One Year Intensive GCSE course at King's Ely International.

'It is a totally new experience of studying in a different country with people from all over the world ... The school also organizes many interesting trips to other cities in England, such as Cambridge and London, which is a great experience.

'Compared to life in China, studying here is more relaxing and exciting. The diverse ways of teaching have inspired my imagination and curiosity.'

After finishing her GCSEs at King's International, Liwei will be moving to Lancing College to study A levels.

International study centres

- Bedford School Study Centre, Bedfordshire
- Box Hill International Study Centre, Surrey
- Dover College, International Study Centre, Kent
- The International Centre, Ackworth School, West Yorkshire
- International College, Sherborne School, Dorset
- International Study Centre at Kent College, Canterbury, Kent
- International Study Centre at The Royal School, Haslemere, Surrey
- King's Ely International, Cambridgeshire
- Millfield English Language School, Millfield School, Somerset
- Rossall School International Study Centre, Lancashire
- Sidcot Academic English School, Sidcot School, North Somerset
- Taunton International Study Centre, Somerset

For further details please see entries in the geographical directory in Part 2 and the school profile section in Part 3.

International schools

Fergus Rose, Senior Management Team, ACS International Schools

In a world where global mobility is increasing, the value of the international school is well understood. International schools bring together young people from many different cultures and countries, including the UK, in a motivating, educational environment where they can gain qualifications recognized the world over. As well as providing a distinctive academic experience, UK international schools enable pupils to establish lasting friendships and affinities with peers from around the world. Although a relatively small element of the UK independent education sector, international schools contribute to the diversity of schooling options available for those seeking to study in the UK.

Indubitably international

The character of an international school in the UK lies principally in its overseas pupil population, with pupils from as many as 50 different countries admitted to a particular school, and in the provision of teaching of English as an additional language. Although they share these characteristics with international study centres they offer a distinct educational option. International schools, unlike study centres, generally offer international qualifications and have no affiliation to a British boarding school (many ISCs are based on the same premises as an independent boarding school). Moreover, international schools tend to be 'straight-through' providers catering for the full range of ages from 2 to 18 – although some do specialize in teaching specific age groups such as junior or senior pupils.

The international school experience

Being involved with people from different cultures at a young age really benefits pupils later on in adult life. The multicultural experience available at international schools provides pupils with the global perspective and social skills necessary to interact successfully with a wide range of people from the UK and abroad in a variety of academic and professional environments.

The international school pupil

Izabella Kaminski-Cook is a 17-year-old pupil studying at ACS Egham International School. Izabella joined ACS Egham in the 10th grade and has had experience of international education both in Bangkok where she attended an international school following the British education system for three years and in France where she studied at a bilingual school for two years.

Izabella's school day routine is in fact fairly similar to those of school pupils across the globe, with her day consisting of four lessons, each one hour and 10 minutes in length, followed by homework and recreational activities (including music tuition for the flute and football three nights a week). Yet amongst her immediate friendship group Izabella has close friends from Britain, Holland, Brazil, Australia, America and Canada. With over 500 pupils, the school itself represents 40 countries from across the world, making the cultural diversity of pupils alongside whom Izabella studies even wider.

Izabella has found that attending school with young people from a variety of different countries and cultures has enriched her knowledge in a way that simply cannot be taught in a classroom.

'Working alongside my peers of varying nationalities has increased my cultural awareness incredibly because I have direct access to first-hand accounts of different cultures. I am able to see a wide variety of different aspects of the world through my peers and their experiences and I am also able to share my own experience.

'Studying with people of different nationalities in the classroom certainly encourages the learning process and provides an excellent preparation for life in the real world, which is culturally diverse and varied.'

In addition to learning from the experiences of her peers, Izabella also learns about cultural diversity during her course of study, by following the IB Diploma.

Izabella's overall view of her international education is very positive: 'Having studied in international schools in various countries, I have found it to be a fantastic opportunity. It is both enjoyable and cultured and allows me to constantly meet new people from different backgrounds.'

Curricula and qualifications

Many schools offer a choice of US and international qualifications, and a few also offer British qualifications. English as a foreign language, native language enrichment and university preparation courses are also frequently available.

IB, American High School Diploma and Advanced Placement

The International Baccalaureate (IB) programme is most frequently offered (see Part 1.4 for more information on the IB). However, for US expatriates who plan to return to the United States or those who wish to study in the United States in later life, many international schools offer a course based on the American High School Diploma. These pupils can also choose to meet credit requirements for graduation through regular high school courses, honours-level high school courses, Advanced Placement (AP) and/or IB courses.

AP courses are widely available for those seeking to win places at universities around the world – especially those applying for US university places; 90 per cent of US higher education institutions and many foreign institutions accept AP credits for college applications. The course is designed to expose able and motivated high school pupils to college-level academic material. Those who perform particularly well in their AP exams can increase their chances of being awarded scholarships.

English language support

For those whose first language is not English, and who are deemed to need help with their English language skills, English as an Additional Language (EAL) support is provided. For some pupils, this means regularly scheduled, small-group sessions, offered in place of some core subjects. Pupils generally take these sessions until English proficiency commensurate with their age and grade level is achieved. Many schools also offer the opportunity to take International English Language Testing System (IELTS) examinations to provide formal recognition of their English language skills.

Native language enrichment

Non-native English-speaking pupils are often encouraged to maintain their native language and cultures by participating in native language enrichment classes, often led by teachers or parents from their native countries. This gives pupils the opportunity to maintain their own cultural identity and share their experiences with peers from their native countries, whose relocation experiences may have been similar.

Accreditation

International schools established in the UK have to be registered with the appropriate government department (Department for Education, in England), as with all independent schools. International schools can apply for membership of one of the Independent Schools Council (ISC) associations, and receive inspections carried out by the Independent Schools Inspectorate (ISI) (which is monitored by Ofsted).

However, international schools are often subject to a number of additional inspections and accreditations. Those providing further education, for pupils 16 and over, can also seek accreditation from the British Accreditation Council (BAC). This is required for institutions that wish to enrol visa pupils, as visas will only be granted to pupils who have an offer from a licensed school. A number of schools also gain accreditation from the Council of International Schools (CIS), an international organization with school members throughout the world.

International schools that offer the International Baccalaureate can seek accreditation from the governing organization, The IB. The IB makes a formal school visit every five years to 'authorize' the school curriculum, and establish that its governance and philosophy are in keeping with the values of The IB.

Destination of pupils

As might be expected with international schools, pupils often go on to attend universities and higher education institutions across the globe. Many will return to their native country to continue their education, or relocate to another country to complete their global education. However, a large number of pupils from international schools in the UK choose to remain in the country for university; a true testament to the high quality education available in the UK.

1.4

UK independent school examinations and qualifications

Active initiation and introduction of courses and qualifications lead to great diversity in assessment methods used in independent schools. The IB, IGCSE and Cambridge Pre U were, for example, initially offered only in the independent sector. Independence enables schools to offer qualifications outside the national framework, adding to the breadth of options available to pupils.

For those considering independent schools with 'selective' entry policies, this section begins with the senior school entry examination – Common Entrance (CE). Attention then moves to senior school courses and qualifications ranging from GCSE and IGCSE to A levels and other sixth-form courses.

Common Entrance (CE)

The Common Entrance examination forms the basis of entry to many independent senior schools, although some schools set their own entrance exams. Traditionally it is taken by boys at the age of 13+ and by girls at the age of 11+. However, with the growth of co-education at senior level the divisions have become less sharply defined and the examinations are open to both boys and girls.

The Common Entrance papers are set centrally by the Independent Schools Examinations Board. The papers are marked, however, by the individual schools, which have their own marking schemes and set their own entry standards. Common Entrance is not an exam that candidates pass by reaching a national standard.

The content of the Common Entrance papers has undergone regular review and the Independent Schools Examinations Board has adapted syllabuses to bring them into line with Curriculum requirements.

Candidates are entered by their junior or preparatory schools. Parents whose children attend state schools should apply to the Independent School Examinations Board, ideally four months before the scheduled examination date. Some pupils may need additional coaching for the exam if they are not attending an independent preparatory school. To be eligible, pupils must normally have been offered a place by a senior school subject to their performance in the exam. Pupils applying for scholarships may be required to pass Common Entrance before sitting the scholarship exam. Candidates normally take the exam in their own junior or preparatory school.

At 11+ the Common Entrance exam consists of papers in English, Mathematics and Science, and is designed to be suitable for all pupils. Most pupils who take the exam at 13+ come from independent preparatory schools. Subjects are English, Mathematics, Science (these are compulsory); French, History, Geography, Religious Studies, German, Spanish, Latin and Greek (these are optional).

The examination for 13+ entry takes place in January and May/June. For entry at 11+ the exam is held in January. Further information on Common Entrance is available from Gabbitas or the ISEB:

The General Secretary
Independent Schools Examinations Board
The Pump House
16 Queen's Avenue
Christchurch BH23 1BZ
Tel: 01202 487538
Fax: 01202 473728
E-mail: enquiries@iseb.co.uk

General Certificate of Secondary Education (GCSE)

The GCSE forms the principal course for senior school pupils between 14 and 16 years of age. Pupils are generally required to choose GCSE subjects in year 9 before commencing their studies in year 10 at age 14. Most pupils of average ability take 9 or 10 GCSEs, including mathematics, English and science, although some may take 11 or more. Most courses are taught over two years but very able pupils may take some GCSE examinations after one year.

GCSE (Short Course) qualifications are also available and take only half the study time of a full GCSE. These are graded on the same scale as a full GCSE, covering fewer topics, and are equivalent to half. The GCSE (Short Course) can be used in various ways: to offer able pupils additional choices such as a second modern language or to offer a subject that could not otherwise be studied as a full GCSE because of other subject choices. It may also be attractive to pupils who need extra time in their studies and would be better suited to a two-year course devoted to a GCSE (Short Course) rather than a full GCSE.

All results for GCSE are graded on a scale from A* to G. Examinations generally have differentiated or tiered papers that target different ability ranges within the A*–G grade range. Many large-entry GCSE subjects are examined through a foundation tier covering grades C–G and a higher tier covering grades A*–D.

A review of the GCSE led to changes in the assessment system that affect both course work and examinations. Course work is replaced by controlled assessment in most subjects and external examination questions are revised. Controlled assessment was introduced to provide greater control in three areas: setting of tasks, task taking and task marking. Assessed task taking, for example, is carried out in a supervised environment such as the classroom to safeguard against plagiarism and undue assistance. External examinations now incorporate a number of different question styles to enable pupils to better demonstrate their knowledge, understanding and ability.

International General Certificate of Secondary Education (IGCSE)

The International General Certificate of Secondary Education (IGCSE) was originally developed for use by international schools. However, IGCSEs have since been adopted by many independent schools in the UK because they are thought to afford greater flexibility and rigour in assessment, including the capacity to stretch the more able candidates.

The IGCSE, which is marked on the same A*–G scale as the GCSE, is widely recognized by schools, universities and employers as equivalent, and provides progression to AS and A level study in the same way. There are, however, differences in the content and examination of the two qualifications, which vary by subject. Examination for the IGCSE generally has either an optional coursework component with terminal (end of course) examination or examination-only assessment.

There are two awarding bodies for IGCSEs: University of Cambridge International Examinations (CIE), which has been awarding the qualifications for over 20 years; and Edexcel, which began to award IGCSEs more recently. In addition to the differences between the IGCSE and GCSE, the content and assessment structure of the CIE and Edexcel IGCSE also vary by subject. Please contact these organizations for further information.

University of Cambridge International Examinations
1 Hills Road Cambridge CB1 2EU
United Kingdom
Tel: +44 (0) 1223 553554
Fax: +44 (0) 1223 553558

Edexcel International
One90 High Holborn
London WC1V 7BH
United Kingdom
Tel: +44 (0) 1204 770696
Fax: +44 (0) 207 190 5700

English Baccalaureate

The English Baccalaureate, while not a qualification in itself, is a performance measure for GCSE and IGCSE study that can only be achieved by gaining grade C or above in a core set of academic subjects – English, mathematics, history or geography, the sciences and a language. Introduced in 2010, the English Bacc is, as 'five Cs or above' has been for some time, a benchmark for GCSE attainment.

GCE A levels and GCE AS levels

Advanced and Advanced Subsidiary Levels are the post-16 qualifications most widely taught in UK sixth forms and tutorial colleges. A and AS levels, as they are commonly known, are also the most prevalent means of entry to higher education in the UK. Subjects offered include academic studies such as Mathematics, English Literature, Physics and Geography. Vocationally focused 'Applied A levels' are also available in subjects ranging from Art and Design to Business Studies (further details about vocational qualifications can be found later in Part 1.4).

A level subjects are generally taught over two years, typically with two units studied in the first year and a further two in the second (although most now have four modules, some do remain with six units). The first-year units make up an Advanced Subsidiary (AS) course. If these are followed in the second year by the appropriate number of A2 units (these are at a higher level than the AS units), the AS and A2 units combined represent a complete A Level course.

Pupils may take four or five AS level subjects in the first year, with the option of reducing the number to three or four A2 subjects in the second year. Advanced Subsidiary units focus on material appropriate for the first year of an A level course and are assessed accordingly. Second-year A2 modules are more demanding and are assessed at full A level standard.

Overall assessment is based on examinations and/or coursework and may be made at stages during the course (modular) or at the end of the course (linear). A synoptic component is also incorporated into these assessments to examine pupils' understanding of the course as a whole and the connections between its different elements.

An A level grade is reached by combining AS and A2 grades. AS and A levels also attract UCAS (University and Colleges Admission Service) tariff points for the purpose of university entry. Pupils who successfully complete the first-year units will be awarded an AS level. This is a qualification in its own right, although it is not enough to gain entry to university.

Passes at AS and A levels are initially graded on a scale of A to E, with the U grade (unclassified) indicating a fail. An A* is awarded for the achievement of an A grade overall with a score of at least 90 per cent, according to the Uniform Mark Scale, in the A2 units studied. Individual units can be retaken and the best attempts are used when certification is requested.

An optional extended project is available, which gives pupils the opportunity to under-take individual study in a subject of their own choosing in addition to their A level courses.

The extended project is a single piece of work, requiring a high degree of planning, preparation, research and autonomous working. It is assessed at the same level as A level but is equivalent to half an A level. The extended project is also graded from A* to E and for university entrance attracts half the UCAS tariff points of an A level.

The AQA Baccalaureate (AQA Bacc)

The AQA Baccalaureate (AQA Bacc) is a qualification that recognizes and celebrates the achievements of well-rounded students with A levels and more. Students build on core A level subjects, adding value through wider learning and enrichment activities.

The Bacc comprises: three A level subjects (students' main subject choices), independent learning through the Extended Project Qualification, personal development through Enrichment Activities such as work-related learning, community participation and personal development. Added breadth is provided for AQA Bacc students by study of an AS level in General Studies, Critical Thinking or Citizenship Studies. Final achievement is graded Pass, Merit or Distinction.

Vocational education and training

There are 116 awarding bodies for vocational education and training awards. Many of these are sector based and provide specific qualifications for their particular industry. However, there are also a number of key awarding bodies that provide a wide range of vocational qualifications across sectors and subjects. These include:

- Edexcel (offers BTEC qualifications);
- City & Guilds;
- Cambridge International Examinations;
- Oxford, Cambridge and RSA Examinations;
- AQA.

Many vocational qualifications come within the National Qualifications Framework, falling into one of two broad categories, namely Vocationally Related Qualifications and National Vocational Qualifications (NVQs). The latter are competence-based occupational qualifications and are generally taken while the candidate is in employment. The body responsible for the overall framework is the Qualifications and Curriculum Development Authority. In Scotland the equivalent body for the Scottish Vocational Qualifications framework (SVQ and GSVQ) is the Scottish Qualifications Authority.

Applied GCSEs

Pupils generally take Applied GCSE subjects alongside academic ones in years 10 and 11. These qualifications are designed for pupils who seek a course that gives a general introduction to a broad vocational area. Most Applied GCSEs are available as single and double awards (double awards are graded from A*A* to GG). Subjects available include: Applied Art and Design, Applied Business, Applied ICT, Applied Science, Engineering, Health and Social Care.

Applied A levels

Applied A levels are general qualifications set in the context of a broad vocational area. Subjects generally correspond to applied subjects available at GCSE such as Art and Design, ICT, Performing Arts and Business. Like traditional A levels, courses are usually taken over two years with the first year's study representing an AS level. Pupils are normally expected to have achieved at least four or five GCSEs at grades A* to C to undertake studies including Applied A levels. As with traditional A levels, the qualifications provide preparation for both higher education and employment.

In Scotland, General Scottish Vocational Qualifications (GSVQs) have been brought under the new National Qualifications framework. Applied A levels and GSVQs are recognized by universities as a basis for entry to higher education. As well as qualifications within the vocational framework, the awarding bodies offer a range of other qualifications. Further guidance may be obtained from schools, colleges and careers advisers. Alternatively, contact a reputable independent consultancy such as Gabbitas.

Scottish National Qualifications

Most schools in Scotland prepare pupils for Standard Grade examinations taken at 16. All pupils who stay on in education after Standard Grade follow a qualifications system which begins at one of five levels, depending on their examination results.

Access, Intermediate 1 and Intermediate 2 are progressive levels a pupil might take to gain a better grounding in a subject before going on to take one of two higher levels: Higher and Advanced Higher. The lower three levels are not compulsory for pupils with aptitude, who may move straight on to study one of the higher-level courses. With the exception of Standard Grade, each National Qualification is built on units, courses and group awards:

- National Units – these are the smallest elements of a qualification and are internally assessed; most require 40 hours of study.

- Courses – National Courses are usually taken in S5 or S6 and at college. They are made up of three units each, and are assessed internally and by examination, for which grades A–C are awarded.

- Scottish Group Awards (SGAs) – these are programmes of courses and units that cover 16 broad subject areas. An SGA can be obtained within one year, or worked towards over a longer period.

There are 75 subjects available, including Philosophy, Politics, Care; job-oriented subjects such as Travel and Tourism; and traditional ones such as Maths and English. All National Qualifications have core skills embedded in them, although it is possible to take stand-alone units, for example Problem Solving, Communication, Numeracy and Information Technology.

For further information contact the Scottish Qualifications Authority – www.sqa.org.uk.

Cambridge Pre-University Diploma

The Cambridge Pre-U Diploma is a new post-16 qualification developed by University of Cambridge International Examinations in collaboration with schools and universities. The qualification is designed to prepare pupils with the skills and knowledge required for successful progression to higher education.

Recently accredited for use within the National Qualifications framework, the Cambridge Pre-U is expected to be available at over 100 schools in the next two years. Schools generally offer the Cambridge Pre-U alongside A levels. Within the structure of the quali-fication it is possible to exchange up to two A levels for corresponding Principal Subjects.

The qualification offers opportunities for interdisciplinary study, includes independent research that builds on individual subject specialisms, and is informed by an international perspective. Pupils choose from a total of 26 Principal Subjects including Mathematics, Russian, Classical Greek and Music. To qualify for the Cambridge Pre-U Diploma, pupils must achieve passes in at least three Principal Subjects, an Independent Research Report and a Global Perspectives Portfolio.

Cambridge Pre-U is underpinned by the following educational aims:

- encouraging the development of well-informed, open- and independent-minded individuals;

- promoting deep understanding through subject specialization, with a depth and rigour appropriate to progression to higher education;

- helping learners to acquire specific skills of problem-solving, critical thinking, creativity, team-working, independent learning and effective communication;

- recognizing a wide range of individual talents and interests;

- promoting an international outlook and cross-cultural awareness.

The structure of the qualification is linear, with one set of examinations at the end of the two-year course. Achievement is reported on a scale of nine grades: D1 (Distinction 1), D2, D3, M1 (Merit 1), M2, M3, P1 (Pass 1), P2 and P3. The grade D1 reports achievement above the A level A* grade (see GCE A levels and GCE Advanced Subsidiary). The intention is to enable greater differentiation between pupils, especially at the higher end of the grading scale.

The Universities and Colleges Admission Service (UCAS) formally recognizes the Cambridge Pre-U Diploma for entry to higher education institutions in the UK. UCAS tariff points have now been attributed to the individual elements of the qualification, enabling university admissions staff to assess applications from diploma pupils. For more information please contact:

University of Cambridge International Examinations
1 Hills Road
Cambridge CB1 2EU
United Kingdom
Tel: 01223 553554
E-mail: international@cie.org.uk

The International Baccalaureate (information supplied by The International Baccalaureate®)

The International Baccalaureate is a non-profit, international educational foundation registered in Switzerland that was established in 1968. The Diploma Programme, for which the IB is best known, was developed by a group of schools seeking to establish a common curriculum and a university-entry credential for geographically mobile pupils. They believed that an education that emphasized critical thinking and exposure to a variety of points of view would encourage intercultural understanding and acceptance of others by young people. They designed a comprehensive curriculum for the last two years of secondary school that could be administered in any country and that would be recognized by universities worldwide.

Today the IB offers three programmes to schools. The Diploma Programme is for pupils aged 16 to 19 in the final two years of secondary school. The Middle Years Programme, adopted in 1994, is for pupils aged 11 to 16. The Primary Years Programme, adopted in 1997, is for pupils aged 3 to 12. The IB has in the region of 2,400 authorized schools in 129 countries. This number is fairly evenly divided between state schools and private (including international) schools.

The Diploma Programme (DP)

The Diploma Programme (DP), for pupils aged 16 to 19, is a two-year course of study. Recognized internationally as a qualification for university entrance, it also allows pupils to fulfil the requirements of their national education system. Pupils share an educational experience that emphasizes critical thinking as well as intercultural understanding and respect for others in the global community.

The DP offers a broad and balanced curriculum in which pupils are encouraged to apply what they learn in the classroom to real-world issues and problems. Wherever possible, subjects are taught from an international perspective. In economics, for example, pupils look at economic systems from around the world. Pupils study six courses (including both the sciences and the humanities) selected from the following six subject groups:

Group 1: language A1.

Group 2: (second language) language *ab initio,* language B, language A2, and classical languages.

Group 3: individuals and societies.

Group 4: experimental sciences.

Group 5: mathematics and computer science.

Group 6: the arts.

Pupils must also submit an extended essay, follow a course in theory of knowledge (TOK) and take part in activities to complete the creativity, action and service (CAS) requirement.

The assessment of pupil work in the DP is largely external. At the end of the course, pupils take examinations that are marked by external examiners who work closely with the IB. The types of questions asked in the examination papers include multiple-choice questions, essay questions, data-analysis questions and case studies. Pupils are also graded on the extended essay and on an essay and oral presentation for the TOK course.

A smaller part of the assessment of pupil work is carried out within schools by DP teachers. The work that is assessed includes oral commentaries in the languages, practical experimental work in the sciences, fieldwork and investigations in the humanities, and exhibitions and performances in the arts. Examiners check the assessment of samples of work from each school to ensure that IB standards are consistently applied. For each examination session, approximately 80 per cent of DP pupils are awarded the Diploma. The majority of pupils register for the Diploma, but pupils may also register for a limited number of Diploma subjects, for each of which they are awarded a certificate with the final grade.

The Middle Years Programme (MYP)

The Middle Years Programme (MYP), for pupils aged 11 to 16, recognizes that pupils in this age group are particularly sensitive to social and cultural influences and are struggling to define themselves and their relationships to others. The programme helps pupils develop the skills to cope with this period of uncertainty. It encourages them to think critically and independently, to work collaboratively and to take a disciplined approach to studying. The aim of the MYP is to give pupils an international perspective to help them become informed about the experiences of people and cultures throughout the world. It also fosters a commitment to help others and to act as a responsible member of the community at the local, national and international levels.

Pupils in the MYP study all the major disciplines, including languages, humanities, sciences, mathematics, arts, technology and physical education. Each of the disciplines or 'subject groups' is studied through five areas of interaction:

1 approaches to learning;

2 community and service;

3 human ingenuity;

4 environment;

5 health and social education.

The framework is flexible enough to allow a school to include subjects that are not part of the MYP curriculum but that might be required by local authorities. While the courses provide pupils with a strong knowledge base, they emphasize the principles and concepts of the subject and approach topics from a variety of points of view, including the perspectives of other cultures.

MYP teachers use a variety of tools to assess pupil progress, including oral presentations, tests, essays and projects, and they apply the assessment criteria established by the IB to pupils' work. Schools may opt for official IB certification by asking the IB to validate their internal assessment. This is often referred to as the 'moderation system'. In this process, the IB reviews samples of the schools' assessment of pupil work and checks that schools are correctly applying the MYP assessment criteria. The IB offers guidance for teachers in the form of published examples of assessment.

The Primary Years Programme (PYP)

The Primary Years Programme (PYP), for pupils aged 3 to 12, focuses on the development of the whole child, addressing social, physical, emotional and cultural needs. At the same time, it gives pupils a strong foundation in all the major areas of knowledge: mathematics, social studies, drama, language, music, visual arts, science, personal and social education, and physical education. The PYP aims to help pupils develop an international perspective – to become aware of and sensitive to the points of view of people in other parts of the world.

The PYP curriculum is organized around six themes:

1 who we are;

2 where we are in place and time;

3 how we express ourselves;

4 how the world works;

5 how we organize ourselves;

6 sharing the planet.

These themes are intended to help pupils make sense of themselves, of other people and of the physical environment, and to give them different ways of looking at the world.

Assessment is used for two purposes: to guide teaching and to give pupils an opportunity to show, in a variety of ways, what they know and what they can do. In the PYP, assessment takes many forms. It ranges from completing checklists and monitoring progress to compiling a portfolio of a pupil's work. The IB offers schools substantial guidance for conducting assessment, including a detailed handbook and professional development workshops. Pupil portfolios and records of PYP exhibitions are reviewed on a regular basis by the IB as part of programme evaluation. For further information about the IB programmes, please contact:

International Baccalaureate Programme
Route des Morillons 15
CH-1218 Grand-Saconnex
Geneva
Switzerland
Tel: +41 22 791 7740
Fax: + 41 22 791 0277
E-mail: ibhq@ibo.org
Website: www.ibo.org

Independent school fees, fees planning, bursaries and scholarships

School fees, financial planning, scholarships and bursaries are often the first consider-ations for parents who have decided upon an independent education for their child. Part 1.5 explores some of the financial components of school choice. First, the varying school fees to expect throughout the independent sector are explained.

Independent school fees

Fees differ widely depending on the types of school you are contemplating. As a general guide, in 2013 parents can expect to pay annual fees of between £5,000 and £13,000 at a preparatory day school or £13,000 to £20,000 for boarding. At senior level, fees range from about £9,000 to £18,000 at day schools, or £18,000 to £25,000+ for a boarding place.

School type	From	To
Prep day	£5,000	£13,000
Prep boarding	£13,000	£20,000
Senior day	£9,000	£18,000
Senior boarding	£18,000	£25,000+

Fees at girls, boys and co-ed schools

Fees at girls' schools tend to be marginally lower than those at boys' and co-educational schools. While day places, as you can see from the table above, tend to be less expensive than boarding places, there is quite a range. Day places at boarding schools, for instance, generally command higher fees than similar places at a day school.

Fees at independent sixth form colleges

Fees at independent sixth form colleges are usually charged per subject, with accommodation constituting a separate fee. The overall costs of tuition and accommodation for a pupil studying three subjects at A level are broadly in line with those charged at a senior boarding school.

How are fees paid?

Parents are normally asked to pay fees in three termly instalments, one at the start of each term, although some schools may offer a choice of payment methods. If you wish to move your child to another school, the present school will normally require a full term's notice in writing. If notice isn't given you may find that you are charged an additional term's fees in lieu.

Insurance policies for school fees

Many schools encourage parents to take out insurance against the risk of their child not being able to attend school, for example in the event of illness. Parents may be asked to meet additional costs during the school year for school lunches, school trips, sports kit, music lessons and similar items, so it is important to check what is and what is not included in the basic termly fee and to take account of other essentials when estimating the overall costs. Boarders will also require additional items such as bed linen and weekend wear.

Fees for international pupils

If you live overseas, bear in mind that there will be other costs associated with a boarding education in the UK. These include the costs of guardianship, travel and any specialist dental treatment, eye tests or spectacles your child may need while he or she is in the UK. Your child will also need a regular supply of pocket money. Schools discourage pupils from carrying large amounts of cash, but your child will probably want to buy music or clothes as well as small treats.

Scholarships and bursaries

If your child is exceptionally talented in a specific area, there may well be scholarship opportunities that could reduce the fees by as much as 50 per cent or possibly more. If financial hardship is an issue, bursaries may be available to help top up the shortfall. The decision to grant a bursary will be taken according to individual circumstances. Further details of the types of scholarship and bursaries available can be found later in Part 1.5.

Towry Limited – finding the fees

Your first decision is what fees you are planning to meet. Do you have a specific school or schools in mind and if so what are the fees? Hopefully you have started planning early, which means that you are unlikely to have made a final choice of school. In this case you need to work on the average or typical fees for the type of school. This can range from day preparatory to senior boarding school. If your child was born in the latter part of the year, check that you are planning for the right period, ie don't plan to provide funds a year early, leaving a gap year at the end.

Next, you need to allow for inflation. A school's major cost is teacher and other salaries, which tend to increase in line with earnings rather than prices. Historically, earnings have risen faster than prices so inflation is not something you can ignore.

The distinctive feature of planning for educational costs

This lies in the fact that you are planning for a 'known commitment'. You know that at the beginning of each term or school year you will have a bill to pay and will need to draw on your investments.

This is where the 'reward–risk' spectrum comes in. At one end, asset-backed investments offer a higher potential reward but also a degree of investment risk and potential volatility. In the longer term, such investments have been the way to achieve real growth and outpace inflation (though the past is not necessarily a guide to future performance). On the other hand, you do not want to rely on such investments if it means encashing them at the worst possible time, just after a stock market setback. Remember, because of the nature of educational planning you probably do not have any choice about when you need funds to pay a bill.

At the other end of the reward–risk spectrum are deposit accounts; just about as safe as safe can be (so long as the institution is sound), but will they keep up with inflation?

You do not need to plump for either extreme. The answer partly depends on the period over which you are investing. If you are starting soon after the birth of your child, asset-backed investment can play a larger role, giving greater potential for real growth. Nearer the time, your holdings can be switched on a phased basis into more secure investment vehicles to lock in any gains and from which you can draw during the schooling period.

An alternative approach is 'mix and match'. A mixture of asset-backed investments and more secure ones will allow you to draw from the former in years when their values are high. In other years, you can draw from the more secure investments.

Existing investments

Your strategy should take into account any existing investments or savings that may be suitable. These may not have been taken out with school fees in mind. For example, you may have started a mortgage endowment some years ago and changed to a repayment mortgage. This would free up the endowment, which could be used for school fees.

Tax-efficient investments

You can invest regular contributions or a lump sum into Individual Savings Accounts (ISAs). They are generally a good idea, especially for a higher-rate taxpayer, because the tax benefits should enhance returns. You can use ISAs for cash deposits, equities, fixed interest and commercial property investments. There is a limit on the contributions that can be made in each year, but both parents can take out an ISA.

Rather than investing in individual shares, investors nowadays more commonly use 'collective' investments like unit trusts (or open-ended investment companies – OEICs) or investment trusts. Collective funds give access to the benefits of equity investments without the investment risk inherent in investing in one or a small number of individual shares. Collective funds are a low-cost way of spreading risk by investing in a portfolio of shares, with the added advantage of professional fund management.

Investment services are now available that offer diversification across a wider range of asset classes than just equities and bonds. The allocation between asset classes should also be maintained to keep the investment in line with your objectives of meeting as much of the fees as possible without undue risk. Together, this very broad diversification and ongoing oversight of the investment should achieve an effective form of risk management.

Any existing ISAs could, of course, be used as part of your planning. Not everyone is aware that you can transfer existing ISAs from one manager to another if appropriate, so that they will better meet your current objectives.

Other investment options

A range of other investment options are available. For instance, if you will be over 55 when fees (or university expenses) are required, you may be eligible to contribute more to a pension and use the benefits towards the bills (although this will reduce the amount available to provide retirement income).

Once you have used your ISA entitlement, you can still invest in the same underlying funds and benefit from the manager's expertise, but without the tax advantages of an ISA. Insurance companies also offer a number of lump-sum investment options with a range of underlying investments and risk ratings.

Expatriate parents

If you are an expatriate or offshore investor, there are offshore versions of most of the investments described above. Important considerations are your tax position while you are offshore and, if you will be returning to the UK during the schooling period, your UK tax position.

Late planning

If you have left it late to start planning, say within five years, you could consider the following:

- Check the school's terms for payment in advance (sometimes called composition fees schemes) as these can be attractive. Ask what happens if, for whatever reason, you switch to another school.

- Consider deposit-based schemes.

- Tax-efficient investments may play a part (eg cash ISAs).

- For other deposit accounts, consider internet or postal accounts, as they often offer better rates.

- National Savings, gilts and fixed-interest securities could also be considered.

- Loan schemes may be available whereby you arrange a 'drawdown' facility secured on your house. This assumes you have some 'free equity' (the difference between the value of the house and your mortgage) and is usually set up as a second mortgage. You can then 'draw down' from the facility as and when you need to pay fees, hence you do not start paying interest sooner than necessary, keeping down the total cost. However, you should think carefully before securing other debts against your home. Your home may be repossessed if you do not keep up repayments on your mortgage.

- Because of the interest payments, loan schemes are costly, so they should be regarded as a last resort and only after you have reviewed your finances to check that there is no alternative.

The need for protection

For most families, the major resource for educational expenses is the parents' earnings. Death or prolonged illness could destroy a well-laid plan and have a terrible effect on a family's standard of living and a child's education. You should therefore review your existing arrangements (whether from a company or private scheme) and make sure you are sufficiently protected.

University expenses

Although many of the same investment considerations apply, planning needs to cover living expenses and the appropriate fees. There is a system of student loans. Although university expenses are generally not as high as school fees, they have become more onerous in recent years.

Seeking advice

Whatever your circumstances, it is sensible to take professional advice to ensure you are headed in the right direction; making inappropriate investment decisions can be very costly. You should seek an independent wealth adviser, able to advise on all investment products, who is not paid solely by commissions from sales.

'Golden' rules of educational planning

- Plan as early in the child's life as possible.

- Set out what funds you need and when you need them, and plan accordingly.

- Mitigate tax on the investments wherever possible.

- Use capital if available, particularly from grandparents.

- Take professional financial advice.

This section briefly outlines some of the considerations and investment opportunities and does not make specific or individual recommendations. There is no one answer to suit everyone as solutions depend on a number of considerations. For a strategy tailored to your individual circumstances, seek professional advice.

Towry Limited
Towry House
Western Road
Bracknell RG12 1TL
Tel: 0845 788 9933
E-mail: info@towry.com
Website: www.towry.com

Scholarships, bursaries and other awards

In addition to your own school fees investment planning, assistance may be available from scholarship, bursaries and other awards. Here we explore the various types of school fees support that can be found.

Scholarships

Many senior schools offer scholarship opportunities. These are awarded at the discretion of the school to pupils displaying particular ability or promise in academic subjects, as an all-rounder or in specific areas such as music or art. Candidates are normally assessed on the basis of their performance in an examination or audition. Scholarship examinations are normally held in the February or March preceding September entry. Pupils awarded scholarships in, for example, music or art may be required to sit the Common Entrance examination to ensure that they meet the normal academic requirements of the awarding school.

When and who are eligible?

Scholarships are normally offered at the usual entry stage or stages of a school (eg 11 or 13+ for senior). Some schools also offer awards for sixth form entry, for example for pupils who have performed particularly well in the GCSE examinations. These awards may be restricted to pupils already attending the school or may also be open to prospective entrants coming from other schools.

The value

Scholarships vary in value, although full-fee scholarships are now rarely available. Scholarships are generally awarded as a percentage of the full tuition fee to allow for inflation.

Prep school scholarships

Fewer scholarships are available at preparatory school level. Choristers are, however, a special category. Choir schools generally offer much reduced fees for choristers, well below the normal day fee. Help may also be available at senior schools, although in practice it is common for choristers to gain music scholarships at their senior schools. Information about other music awards at independent schools is available from the Music Masters' and Mistresses' Association (MMA) at www.mma-online.org.uk.

For a general guide to scholarships offered by individual schools, turn to the Scholarships index in Part 5.

Bursaries

Bursaries are intended primarily to ensure that children obtain provision suited to their needs and ability in cases where parents cannot afford the normal fees. They are awarded on the basis of financial hardship, rather than particular ability. All pupils applying for a bursary are required to demonstrate that they meet academic requirements, typically by passing Common Entrance or the school's own entry tests. The size of the award is entirely at the discretion of the school. An index of schools that offers bursaries is given in Part 5.

Reserved entrance awards

Some schools reserve awards for children with parents in a specific profession, for example in HM Forces, the clergy or in teaching. These are similar to bursaries in that the child must meet the normal entry requirements of the school, but eligibility for the award will be dependent upon fulfilment of one of the criteria stated above. Normally schools will reserve only a few places on this basis. Once a place for a specific award has been filled, it will not become available again until the pupil currently in receipt leaves the school, so the award may be available only once every five years or so.

A list of schools and brief summary of the reserved entrance awards offered by each is given in Part 5. The awards covered include those offered to children with one or both parents working in any of HM Forces, the Foreign Office, the medical profession, teaching, the clergy or as Christian missionaries.

Other awards

Schools may also offer concessions for brothers and sisters (sibling discounts) or for the children of former pupils.

If you are interested in the possibility of a scholarship or bursary or in other awards, it is a good idea to advise the schools you are interested in accordingly when you first contact them.

The GDST Scholarship and Bursary Scheme

The GDST (Girls' Day School Trust), which comprises 26 girls' schools educating over 20,000 girls, has traditionally aimed to make its schools accessible to bright, motivated girls from families who could not afford a place at a GDST school without financial assistance. It has a Scholarship and Bursary Scheme specifically designed for low-income families. Grants are only awarded at GDST schools.

Most bursaries under the scheme are awarded to girls from families with a total annual income of under £16,500, and it is unlikely that a bursary would be awarded in cases where total gross income exceeds £48,000. Bursaries are means-tested and may cover up to full fees. Scholarships, which are not means-tested, are awarded on merit and may cover up to half the fees. Most awards are available either on entry at 11 or for girls entering the sixth form. The Scheme is also designed to assist pupils already attending a GDST school whose parents face unexpected financial difficulties that could mean having to remove their daughter from the school and disrupt her education.

Awards are made at the discretion of individual school heads rather than the Trust and requests for further information should therefore be directed to the head of the school at which parents wish to apply for a place.

Other government grants

Assistance with the payment of fees is also offered to personnel employed by the Foreign and Commonwealth Office (FCO) and by the Ministry of Defence, where a boarding education may be the only feasible option for parents whose professional lives demand frequent moves or postings overseas.

The FCO termly boarding allowance is available to FCO parents on request and is reviewed annually. Parents in need of further information should contact the FCO Personnel Services Department on 020 7238 4357.

Services personnel may seek guidance from the Service Children's Education Advisory Service, which can advise on choosing a boarding school and on the Continuity of Education Allowance (formerly boarding allowance). The Continuity of Education Allowance is in the region of £4,480 per term for junior boarding pupils and £5,833 per term for senior boarding pupils. An allowance is also available for children with special educational needs. Further information may be obtained from Children's Education Advisory Service, Trenchard Lines, Upavon, Pewsey, Wiltshire SN9 6BE; Tel: 01980 618244. You may also find it helpful to visit www.army.mod.uk and www.sceschools.com.

Parents may also find it helpful to consult the list of schools offering reserved entrance awards in Part 5. Some schools may be able to supplement allowances offered by employers through a reserved entrance award offered to pupils who meet the relevant criteria, eg with a parent in HM Forces.

Grant-giving trusts

There are various educational and charitable trusts that exist to provide help with the payment of independent school fees. Usually the criteria restrict eligibility to particular groups, for example orphans, or to cases of sudden and unforeseen financial hardship. In many cases a grant may be given only to enable a child to complete the present stage of education, eg to finish a GCSE or A Level course. Applications are normally considered on an individual basis by an appointed committee. The criteria for eligibility and for the award of a grant will vary according to individual policy. In some cases several trusts may each contribute an agreed sum towards one individual case to make up the fees required. It should be noted that such trusts receive many more applications for grants than can possibly be issued and competition is fierce. Applications for financial help purely on the grounds that parents would like an independent education for their child but cannot afford it from their own resources will be rejected. Parents are advised to consider carefully before applying for an independent school place and entering a child for the entrance examination if they cannot meet the fees unaided and cannot demonstrate a genuine need, as defined by the criteria published by the awarding trust. Parents may find it helpful to consult the *Educational Grants Directory,* published by the Directory of Social Change. Charitable funding can also be sought from The Royal National Children's Foundation, Sandy Lane, Cobham, Surrey KT11 2ES; contact David Howarth or Chris Hughes on 01932 8686822.

Local Authority grants

Grants from Local Authorities are sometimes available where a need for a child to board can be demonstrated, for example where the child has special educational needs that cannot be met in a day school environment or where travel on a daily basis is not feasible. Such grants are few in number. Awards for boarding fees at an independent school may not be granted unless it can be shown that there is no boarding place available at one of the 35 state boarding schools nationwide.

Awards from Local Authorities are a complex issue. Parents wishing to find out more should contact the director of education for the Authority in which they live.

Independent school inspections

Durell Barnes, the Independent Schools Inspectorate (ISI)

Inspection reports are an important source of objective information about schools for parents and prospective parents. They have an equally important function in helping schools improve. The inspections undertaken by the Independent Schools Inspectorate (ISI), as well as reporting on schools for parents, school associations, the government and the wider community, are designed to improve the quality and effectiveness of education and welfare for pupils. Inspection should help governors and teaching staff recognize and build on strengths, improve on any weaker areas and encourage the spread of best practice throughout the independent sector.

ISI is the agency responsible for the inspection of schools in membership of the associations of the Independent Schools Council (ISC). These schools educate about 80 per cent of the pupils in independent education. ISI has also been given responsibility for inspecting registered early years settings (under 3s) in ISC schools and, since 2011, for the inspection of boarding welfare provision in ISC schools. Reports on all these aspects of provision are now available from the ISI website: www.isi.net.

Other non-association schools are inspected by Ofsted (www.ofsted.gov.uk). There are also two small inspectorates that inspect a few non-association schools: the Bridge Schools Inspectorate and School Inspection Services.

Changing inspection frameworks

Inspection frameworks have changed over the years, so you will find a variety of report formats on the ISI website, some dating back to the start of the 'first cycle' of inspections in 2000.

The current cycle began in January 2012, providing a fully integrated inspection of all education and welfare provision. The frequency of inspection will vary depending on a variety of factors, including the quality found at the school's last inspection, regulatory compliance, and whether a school has boarders or children under 3 years of age. For some schools, inspections may be up to six years apart whereas others may be every three years.

Boarding welfare and registered early years provision must be inspected every three years and shorter Intermediate Inspections take place where this does not coincide with the education inspection, to check compliance with the relevant regulations. The resulting short regulatory report is published alongside the last full inspection report on the school.

Integrated Inspection reports include a clear judgement on each aspect of the school's work at the beginning of each section. ISI applies a different framework from that used by Ofsted and has different criteria for judging school quality to reflect the different types of schools it inspects. Although both report on schools' compliance with regulatory requirements and both use a four-point scale for judgements of quality, the ISI terminology reflects its different approach. ISI reports do not provide a single overarching judgement for the school but instead give a clear judgement on each aspect of the school's work at the beginning of each section. Each of these statements will include one of the ISI 'descriptors' ('excellent', 'good', 'sound' or 'unsatisfactory'). These terms are deliberately different from Ofsted's and represent the four grades for inspection. For schools where pupils' achievement is far above that usually found, the descriptor 'exceptional' may replace 'excellent' as the top grade. For early years provision, however, ISI reports are required to use the same terminology ('outstanding', 'good', 'satisfactory' and 'inadequate') as Ofsted reports.

The criteria for judgement for Integrated Inspections can be found in the ISI Inspection Framework under 'Frequently Asked Questions'.

Who does the inspecting?

Inspection teams are led by highly trained reporting inspectors who are usually former HMI (Her Majesty's Inspectors), senior Ofsted inspectors or suitably qualified and trained former heads from independent schools with extensive relevant inspection experience. Intermediate inspections – of boarding or early years provision – are led by inspectors with specific expertise in boarding and early years respectively.

It is an important and unique feature of ISI inspections that they are, in effect, a peer review system. Team inspectors are usually serving heads or senior staff of other schools. This ensures both that judgements about schools are made by current practitioners and that the experience of inspection enables best practice to be spread throughout the sector by inspectors when they return to their own schools.

The number of inspectors on a team will vary, from two on an Intermediate Inspection of an early years setting, or of a school with a single boarding house, to 10 or more on an integrated inspection of a large school with several boarding houses or a substantial registered EYFS setting.

There is a Code of Conduct to ensure that inspectors' judgements are 'first-hand, valid, corporate, even-handed, reliable and objective'. To make their judgements, inspectors get evidence from observation of lessons, activities and boarding house life, from pupils' work and from talking to pupils, the head, staff and governors. They also analyse responses to the confidential pre-inspection parental and pupil surveys as well as performance indicators and the school's own self-evaluation and policy documents.

Once the inspection is over, the report should reach the school within four weeks and should be issued to parents within a further two weeks, at which point it is published on the ISI website.

What does inspection cover?

All Integrated Inspections have to check schools' compliance with government regulations. In addition, inspectors report on how successfully the school fulfils its own aims, on the extent to which pupils are supported to be healthy, stay safe, enjoy school and achieve good educational standards, make a positive contribution to their own and the wider community and develop skills that will contribute to their future economic wellbeing.

The six sections of the framework for Integrated Inspections

1 Characteristics of the school – including its aims, distinctive features and governance structures; its size, type, location and history; the ability of the pupils.

2 Success of the school – main findings and action points and recommendations for further improvement.

3 Quality of academic and other achievements.

4 Quality of pupils' personal development – including the spiritual, moral, social and cultural development of pupils; pastoral care; arrangements for welfare, health and safety; the quality of boarding.

5 Effectiveness of governance, leadership and management – including links with parents.

6 Effectiveness of the early years foundation stage (where relevant).

Intermediate Inspections only report on the school's compliance with the relevant statutory requirements for early years foundation stage, and/or the national minimum standards for boarding.

Where any school is found to be non-compliant, the Department for Education (DfE) will request an action plan to deal with the failings. ISI is later asked to evaluate that plan, which may include another visit to the school.

The inspection and reporting process is itself quality assured. Reports are edited by expert readers and subsequently proof-read. Schools and inspectors complete evaluations after inspections, and inspections are also evaluated by experienced senior inspectors on behalf of ISI. Finally, Ofsted monitors a proportion of ISI inspections and reports on behalf of DfE, resulting in an annual report on the work of ISI, published on the Ofsted and ISI websites.

ISI Reports

Reports can be found on the ISI website (www.isi.net). Where the most recent report is a short Intermediate Inspection report of relevant regulatory compliance only, the last full inspection report on the school remains on the ISI website. ISI aims to avoid all education jargon in reports to make them accessible to the ordinary reader.

Schools develop and change very quickly. It is important to realize, therefore, that an inspection report is, like any health check, accurate at the time it is undertaken and within the specific areas of its remit. Parents should read them in conjunction with other information, for example from the school's website, from other parents and from visiting the school, to make their own judgements about a school. It may also be helpful to ask schools what they believe has contributed to any aspect deemed excellent or outstanding, how such standards are maintained, and how schools have used inspection findings to aid their ongoing improvement.

The sixth form and beyond – parents' guide

Pupils studying for GCSEs, IGCSEs or the equivalent, like most 15 and 16-year-olds, are probably still some way from decisions about higher education and careers. At this stage there is, of course, plenty of room for the development and discussion of ideas and interests. To reach the right decisions, it is important to have an open mind about all of the options and to begin preliminary planning well in advance. This section introduces some of the most important considerations.

Making the right choices for future plans

Choosing the right sixth form course is becoming increasingly important as the options at 18 become more complex. Pupils who have given some thought to their future plans and to their own strengths and personal qualities will find it easier to identify broad potential career areas. This in turn will enable them to choose suitable sixth form and higher education options, which allow flexibility for the development of skills and personal growth. At the same time, extra-curricular activities, relevant work experience and other activities will help to build up the essential personal and practical skills sought by today's employers.

Careers advice

Good advice is essential. Some schools have excellent careers guidance programmes and materials and may also arrange talks from visiting speakers and work experience opportunities. Others may have more limited resources. Computer-based or online careers assessments are often used in schools. Such assessments are not designed to provide all the answers but rather to highlight possibilities. They should form part of a much more extensive discussion that includes consideration of academic achievements and aspirations, attitudes, interests and any special needs. Your son or daughter may also find it helpful to speak to an independent consultant, who can offer an objective view and perhaps a wider perspective of potential careers.

Sixth form options

The main options available after GCSE are: Advanced Subsidiary GCE (AS) and Advanced GCE (A2); in Scotland, National Qualifications (Highers); the International Baccalaureate (IB); and Applied A levels; although the Cambridge Pre-U is now available at some schools. The basic structure of these courses is covered in Part 1.4.

All can be used as a means of entry to British universities. The IB, as its name implies, is an international qualification and is also recognized for admissions purposes by many universities worldwide. Similarly, the Cambridge Pre-U is an international qualification that can be used for university entry. Unlike AS and A levels, however, these courses are not widely taught in the UK.

Subjects or areas of study

Is depth or breadth the most important factor? A levels offer a high degree of specialization. The IB is a demanding academic qualification but covers a wider range of subjects in less depth. A vocational course will probably have a relatively narrow focus on a particular career area such as Business, Leisure and Tourism, or Information Technology.

Course load

Most pupils take four AS subjects in the lower sixth form and continue three of these as A2s in the upper sixth form, thus emerging with three full A levels and one AS in a fourth subject. The equivalent of three A level passes is the core requirement for university entry. However, in some cases universities may ask for specific grades in certain subjects and in others they may seek an overall number of UCAS points. In this relatively uncertain climate, sixth formers should appreciate that quality is more important than quantity – in other words additional courses should not be taken if this would jeopardize the grades obtained in core subjects. If they are in any doubt about the combination of A/AS levels and grades that will be acceptable to a university, they should not hesitate to contact admissions staff or seek other forms of professional advice.

Availability

Is the required course available at your child's present school or, if not, at another school or independent college? Is living away from home an option?

Assessment method and course structure

Some pupils prefer regular assessment through submission of coursework or projects rather than exam-based assessment. Most A level courses, traditionally assessed through a final exam, now include coursework as part of the assessment – applied A levels tend to have a large coursework component. The Cambridge Pre-U Diploma includes assessed projects and final examinations. Assessment for the IB is chiefly by examination.

Academic ability

A level courses often demand a good deal of reading and the ability to write well-argued essays. In science-based subjects, abstract thinking and in some cases strong mathematical skills are important. Pupils must reflect on their areas of strength and real subject interests when selecting courses and make realistic choices based on their academic abilities.

Future plans

Pupils aiming for a specific career should check whether their preferred sixth form options are suitable. Those still undecided should choose a programme that allows some flexibility.

Which A levels?

It is natural for pupils to want to continue with subjects they enjoy. Clearly, a high GCSE result suggests that a similar result may be expected at A level. This is important, of course, but pupils must also consider whether or not their preferred combination of subjects is suitable for their higher education or career plans. It is also possible to take certain A level courses in subjects not previously studied.

Career choice

Some careers, for example engineering, medicine and architecture, demand a specific degree. This may limit, or sometimes dictate, the choice of A level subjects and pupils must be confident that they can do well in these. If career plans are undecided, it is wise to choose subjects that will leave a number of options open.

Requirements for sixth form studies

It is advisable to have achieved at least a grade B at GCSE in any subjects being considered for A level (ideally grade A in Maths, Science and Modern Languages). Some A level subjects such as Economics can be taken without any previous knowledge, but pupils should consider what skills are required, eg numerical, analytical or essay writing, and whether or not it will suit them.

Different examining bodies may assess the same subject in different ways. If your son or daughter has concerns about a final exam-based assessment, he or she might consider a syllabus that offers a modular structure and a higher degree of assessment through coursework. Remember, however, that if all the subjects chosen are assessed on this basis, the workload and the pressure to meet deadlines during the course could be very heavy.

Interest and motivation

Genuine interest is essential if a pupil is to feel motivated throughout the two-year course and achieve high grades. Pupils in a dilemma over the choice between a subject they enjoy and a subject they feel they ought to take may be well advised to opt for the former but should check that this is suitable for their future plans. Pupils who are thinking of taking up a new subject, for example Psychology, may find it helpful to read a few books on the subject to test their interest before making any decisions.

Which subject combinations?

If no specific combination is demanded, how can pupils ensure a suitable choice? At least two subjects should be complementary, ie two arts/social sciences or two sciences. It is quite common for pupils to combine arts and sciences. It should be remembered that even those career areas that do not demand specific degree courses may still require certain skills, which some A level subjects will develop better than others.

If a particular degree course does not require an A level in the subject, eg Psychology, it may be better to choose a different A level subject or perhaps a complementary option and so demonstrate a wider knowledge/skills base to university admissions tutors. This also avoids the risk of repeating the A level syllabus in the first year at university.

Other matters to consider include the timetabling constraints at school that may make a certain combination impossible, in which case pupils may have to compromise or change to a school or college with greater flexibility.

Where shall I study?

Staying on into the sixth form of the present school does have advantages, including continuity and familiarity with surroundings, staff and fellow pupils. It is not unusual, however, for pupils to change schools at 16. Some may be looking for a course, subjects or combination of subjects not available at their present school. Others may simply want a change of atmosphere or a different style of education.

If a change to a different school is sought, consider the school's academic pace and examination results, its university entry record, the criteria for entry to the sixth form and the availability of places. Other considerations include the size of the sixth form and of the teaching groups and, where appropriate, the opportunities to develop skills or pursue interests aside from A level studies. Independent sixth form colleges or tutorial colleges offer an alternative environment that can suit some pupils – more details on this option follow.

James Wardrobe, Council of Independent Education (CIFE), explains what independent sixth form colleges have to offer

Independent sixth form colleges in the UK, often still referred to as tutorial colleges, have a distinctive history. The earliest were established in the early 20th century to prepare students for Oxbridge and officer-level entry to the Armed Forces. Following the Second World War more tutorial colleges specializing in A level and O level teaching surfaced but they were still often derided as 'crammers'. The now fully accepted contemporary independent sixth form colleges are much in demand from UK and international students seeking quality in teaching and examination preparation.

Wide A level subject range

Colleges tend to offer a wider range of subjects and greater flexibility in subject combinations than traditional schools. Most allow students any combination of subjects and there are commonly over 40 AS and A level subjects to choose from! Unusual subject combinations such as Accounting, Psychology and History can be accommodated more readily and joining a college for the second year of A level (A2) is often possible. At some London colleges you will also find one-year courses (covering AS and A2 modules) and retake courses (both one-term and one-year).

Flexible GCSE courses

Although the majority of students take A levels, most colleges run equally flexible GCSE courses, usually offering more creative subjects such as Photography alongside the mainstream ones. Again, the number of subjects to choose from is generally greater than that offered by schools. One-year GCSE courses are also often available, as are standard two-year courses.

The college atmosphere and pastoral support

The college environment is famous for being more relaxed and less rules-driven than at school. There are no uniform requirements and the generally held philosophy that 'students are to be treated as adults' is evident. Nevertheless, pastoral and academic support is of a high standard. Colleges tend to succeed in balancing authority with liberty by guiding students without dictating to them. This approach enables students to grow in confidence without compromising their wellbeing and safety.

Other qualifications available

As well as A level and GCSE courses, some institutions offer one-year University Foundation courses, designed specifically for overseas students. Scottish colleges, as you would expect, tend to offer SQA courses. Most colleges also run EFL programmes, usually leading to internationally recognized qualifications such as IELTS. Some offer preparation for SATS for US university entrance. As yet, no independent sixth form colleges offer the Cambridge Pre-U and the International Baccalaureate is not widely available. Colleges do, however, offer short courses unavailable at most schools, such as intensive Easter revision courses.

Class sizes

Small classes are the norm even at GCSE level. This is especially true in less common subjects, such as Geology, Philosophy, Italian and Classical Greek. An average of just six students per class has been noted, resulting in an atmosphere similar to that of a university tutorial where all are encouraged to debate and actively engage with course topics.

Teaching at independent sixth form colleges

As a former college principal, headmaster and ISI inspector, I have observed hundreds, if not thousands, of lessons taught in prep schools, senior schools and sixth form colleges. This gamut of lessons has ranged from unsatisfactory (occasionally) to outstanding. As far as the sixth form colleges are concerned, I have frequently seen what I believe are some of the best A level practitioners in the business, who would be equally comfortable teaching in highly selective academic schools. Of course, as all good teachers do, they display great enthusiasm and passion for their subject and communicate effectively their impressive subject knowledge. However, these college tutors seem to have two added advantages. First, they are able to specialize in their subject at a particular level for a particular syllabus throughout their whole teaching timetable, thus acquiring a specific expertise; for example, one college had a Maths tutor who taught only A level Further Mathematics. Secondly, the informal, relaxed nature of the tutorial college's small-group environment enables tutors to quickly establish and maintain highly productive working relationships with students.

Teaching resources

In terms of teaching resources, as you will discover for yourself if you make a visit, all the reputable colleges have well-equipped science laboratories, IT equipment, libraries and, where such subjects are offered, art, music, drama, film and media studies facilities.

University preparation

As far as UCAS advice is concerned, in my experience college tutors know the examination and university entrance systems inside-out and pride themselves on keeping up to date on the latest admissions requirements. Some colleges run very sophisticated and targeted programmes of support for students applying for challenging university courses. These include specialist Medical Sciences programmes, with guest lectures from medical admission tutors, and tailor-made courses for potential Oxbridge, Medical, Dental and Veterinary students. Many also offer study skills and work experience programmes.

Extra-curricular activities

Most colleges offer a wide range of sporting opportunities. If sport is important to you, college staff members encourage you to continue by joining their own teams or those of associated local clubs and leisure centres. A quick glance at college websites will give you a good idea of the range of leisure activities on offer. Schemes such as the Duke of Edinburgh's Award and the Young Enterprise programme are often available.

Why consider independent sixth form college?

Students choose sixth form colleges in the independent sector for diverse reasons, but seem united by their ambition to get the best education and the best preparation they can before moving on to university. The old image of catering largely for public school expellees and drop-outs is completely out of date and was probably never that true anyway. Often students who make a change after GCSEs feel that they have outgrown the traditional school ethos and are looking for a better transition to the less regulated environment encountered at university. In recent years there have certainly been growing numbers following traditional two-year A level courses at independent colleges. Some others want to make a fresh start for their upper sixth year after studying AS levels else-where (approximately 10 per cent of the annual intake of colleges are students who have spent their lower sixth year in another school). Appropriate courses are available to them, which often revitalize higher education prospects. These courses are often ideal for students who for various reasons have missed a key part of their school education. At the annual CIFE Academic Awards Presentation, held at the House of Lords in March 2012, the Gold Award went to Poppy Waskett, a student at Lansdowne College, London, who missed three years of schooling owing to ill-health and then achieved three A*s at A level in one year, gaining a place at Oxford University.

Although only one component of their expertise, these colleges are very well equipped for those wishing to retake courses, both one-term and one-year, and the best have a remarkably consistent record for grade improvement. Some colleges have also discovered a small but growing trend for IB students to 'retake' their subjects as A levels in one year.

International students

As well as home students, you will find students from overseas who are preparing for UK universities by taking A levels, or possibly a University Foundation course. They are usually very hard-working, very focused on their academic studies and contribute a great deal to sixth form life.

Overall, this part of the independent sector, which prides itself on getting students into higher education, is booming. This is helped, in no small part, by the increasing demand from international and domestic students aspiring to take places at ever more selective universities.

Admissions procedures

All reputable colleges will expect prospective students to visit for interview. If that's impossible, most can make assessments via reports, references, etc. Interviews are not meant to be stressful – they are designed to explore what a student has done, what his or her hopes are and what, for him or her, is the best blend of courses. Students should take along their most recent school reports and examples of written work to give college staff an insight into their ability and attainment. Colleges generally offer places when they can provide the courses and support required.

Course fees

These independent colleges rely entirely on student fees to provide the high staffing levels required for small groups and individual attention. They are, therefore, by no means cheap. Colleges mostly charge according to the number, type and duration of courses taken, so the variety of possible combinations makes it difficult to give an accurate general fee. In terms of comparison, the annual fees for GCSE and A level courses are generally in line with those of a good senior independent school.

Financial support

Some colleges offer financial help and each college will have its own criteria for awarding bursaries and scholarships. It is likely that you will have to prove that you have exceptional academic promise and financial hardship. Timing is important: you should apply to the college of your choice as early as possible in the preceding academic year.

Accommodation

It is vital to have somewhere quiet, comfortable and safe to live while you study, particularly if you have to live away from home. The proportion of residential students varies from college to college. Some have accommodation on site or in college-managed dorms nearby. Most colleges have a team of host families with whom they have well-established relationships.

Choosing the right college

Finding the right college depends on the type of person and on the need. Each college has its own unique atmosphere and to know which one will best suit a student can only really be judged by visiting the college and meeting the staff. However, colleges of good reputation rely to a large extent on word-of-mouth referrals from previous students, so asking around amongst friends and older students who have actually been to a sixth form college is probably the best way to start research. Most colleges give detailed exam results and university entry success information on their websites and all the good ones will be happy to answer questions about grades achieved and student destinations.

Accreditation

All reputable colleges are inspected regularly by at least one of the following national bodies: the Independent Schools Inspectorate (ISI), the Office for Standards in Education (Ofsted) or the British Accreditation Council (BAC). Latest inspection reports can be found on their websites at www.isi.net, www.ofsted.gov.uk and www.the-bac.org. Many of the best colleges are members of the Council of Independent Education (CIFE), the president of which is Baroness Perry of Southwark. For more information visit www.cife.org.uk.

Fresh starts, successful pre-university education

The sixth form colleges, once a poor relation of the independent sector, have established themselves as reliable and successful providers of pre-university education. For senior school pupils who need a fresh start, this type of college is ideal and may well offer the precise opportunity they are seeking.

The university challenge

Despite continuing pressures on graduate employment opportunities and the introduction of increased tuition fees, higher education applications are still great in number. Higher education offers a unique range of academic, career and social opportunities. However, under-preparing for university applications can prove disastrous. 'Having made the wrong choice' is often cited as the root cause by students who do not complete their degree courses – and this can be as many as one in five.

Why does your son or daughter want to go to university? Is he or she genuinely motivated and keen to study a particular subject in depth, to qualify for a specific career and to take advantage of all the benefits that university life offers? All these reasons are valid, but some pupils may apply to university largely because they feel under pressure at home and/or at school to do so. It is important to allow time to consider options – pupils who are unsure of what to study should not rush into a decision. It may be better to take a year out and to use the additional time constructively before making a choice.

Most schools encourage pupils to begin thinking seriously about higher education soon after entering the sixth form. During the spring and summer terms of the lower sixth form pupils should be researching course and university options. Information is available from reference guides, student-focused websites and university prospectuses. Most universities organize open days where pupils can visit and talk to staff and students. Pupils and their families should use all available resources to prepare for applications. Applications are due to arrive at UCAS (the Universities and Colleges Admissions Service) in January of the year of intended enrolment. Submissions must be made by the end of June to avoid clearing. Pupils applying to Oxford, Cambridge, Medicine, Veterinary Science or Dentistry should note that their applications are required earlier, by mid-October in the year preceding planned entry.

Support and guidance from school, external advisers and parents are essential throughout this period, but the final choice of course and university lies with the pupil. It is important that he or she takes an active part in the process and comes to a well-reasoned decision. So what are the key points to consider?

Which course?

Is a specific degree necessary for a specific career? In some cases, typically medicine, yes. In many cases, however, including law, students have more flexibility. If there are no specific requirements, prospective employers will often take account of the quality of degree obtained and the reputation of the university as much as the subject studied, and will look for other skills and qualities that match their requirements. This means that students should take a subject in which they expect to do well rather than something which they may, perhaps wrongly, believe to be 'the right thing'. There are differing views on the importance of taking some career-related degree subjects, for example Business Studies or Media/Communication Studies. Some employers may prefer to employ graduates with a wider education background and train them in-house. Others may prefer applicants to be able to demonstrate practical knowledge and interest. Taking the above examples, this might include work experience with a company or involvement with the university newspaper or radio station.

Sandwich courses including work experience as part of the programme are quite prevalent. They can help employment prospects, enhance practical skills and allow students to test their interest in a particular career before committing themselves. In some cases placements may turn into permanent positions with the same employer after graduation. Some students may, however, not want to delay graduation (a sandwich course usually takes an extra year), and may dislike the disruption of a year spent in a work placement.

For those who would appreciate an extra year off-campus, many universities offer Language degrees incorporating a year spent abroad. Students on a range of other courses can also find opportunities to study abroad as part of their studies.

Foundation degrees

Foundation degrees are vocationally-focused intermediate qualifications, slightly below the level of an Honours degree. Foundation degrees take two years' full-time study, but they can also be studied part-time. They often combine work experience with the traditional academic structure of a degree course and are intended to equip students with the skills required by today's employers. Each Foundation degree is usually linked with at least one Honours degree in the same subject area, which means that those who wish to further their qualification can go on to a BA/BSc (Hons) qualification if they choose to do so. Entry to Foundation degrees is flexible in order to attract school leavers and those already in employment who are seeking to develop their skills.

Specialization

Students have, amongst others, a choice of studying one subject (single honours) or a combination (combined honours). A combined course offers more breadth and the opportunity to follow complementary studies, but almost always means a heavier workload.

For students unsure about taking a subject not studied at school or about going directly into a specialized field, for example civil engineering, a more general foundation year may be helpful.

Checking course content

Courses with the same name may be very different in content, so it is essential to read the prospectus for details. Modern language degrees, for example, vary widely in focus. Some place particular emphasis on practical language skills and an understanding of current affairs; others may have a more traditional emphasis on literature. Course titles like Communication Studies can also mean a wide variety of things.

Entry requirements

What subjects and grades does the course specify? Is the pupil likely to achieve these grades or should he or she look for a course with less stringent entry requirements? Remember that published grades are given only as a guide and may be adjusted upwards or downwards when offers are made to individual pupils. With the variety of sixth form programmes being taken, Gabbitas strongly recommends that pupils contact universities directly to find out what they may be expected to achieve. For arts A level pupils who wish to take a degree in a science-based subject such as Medicine or Engineering, one-year conversion courses are available, but pupils will be expected to have good GCSE grades in Maths and Science. Many modern language courses do not require previous knowledge, although evidence of competency in another foreign language is usually essential.

Remember too that as the A level pass rate rises, admissions tutors increasingly use AS and GCSE results as well as A level grades as an indicator of ability. The A level A* grade is now included in offers made by an increasing number of universities.

Which university?

Quality and reputation are as important for the individual course and department as for the institution as a whole. Beware of published league tables, which will not necessarily answer your questions. Find out about the career or employment destinations of recent graduates. This information may be available from the university or in one of the many published handbooks. If you have in mind a particular employer, it may be useful to contact the recruitment department to find out their views on specific universities or degree courses. If you have decided on a career area, you might similarly contact the relevant professional body. Also consider asking the university about the teaching styles, methods of assessment and the level of supervision available.

Some pupils may be attracted to a collegiate-style university such as Oxford, Cambridge or London. Others may prefer a self-contained campus where all academic, social and other facilities are available on-site. Some may prefer a big city environment; others a smaller, more rural location. Living costs are a further important, but often neglected, issue. What is the local transport like? Is a car necessary? How safe is the area after dark? How far is the campus from home? What other facilities are offered to cater for individual hobbies and interests?

There is, of course, much more to finding the right university than simply the course. Aspects such as accommodation (both on and off campus), location or availability of social activities, can generate just as much anxiety and dissatisfaction as academic worries. So it is a good idea to consider the whole offering.

The Universities and Colleges Admissions Service (UCAS) tariff point system

The UCAS tariff point system is designed to help universities and colleges set course entry requirements to select undergraduate students. Universities generally set a minimum UCAS point requirement for entry to a course or make conditional offers to pupils based on the UCAS point value of their sixth form examinations – with a certain number being required for entry. An offer will include the points accepted based on three A Levels or equivalent. Offer levels depend on the popularity of the course and can range from unconditional '0' points to '420' (three A*s) or more.

UCAS tariff points (AS and A level)

Grade	GCE A levels	AS levels
A*	140	
A	120	60
B	100	50
C	80	40
D	60	30
E	40	20

(For the UCAS point value of other qualifications such as the Cambridge Pre U and the IB please refer to UCAS.)

The UCAS tariff point system converts qualifications into UCAS points to create an objective, common currency for university admissions staff. Pupils then use the tariff to calculate their UCAS point total to find out whether they have enough to gain a place on the course of their choice. Pupils are advised that attaining the UCAS point total is not necessarily the only criterion for entry to a course.

Other things to consider when using the UCAS tariff point system

Entry requirements and conditional offers that use the UCAS tariff point system will often have certain conditions that have to be met, eg '320 points needed but with an A grade in English'.

Certain qualifications build up over different levels, with each level attracting a certain number of UCAS tariff points. The tariff point values of each level cannot be combined to create a total. Simply count the UCAS point value from the highest level attained. Examples of qualifications with levels where this applies are:

Qualifications where UCAS points are awarded at different levels

GCE Advanced Subsidiary level and GCE Advanced level
Scottish Highers and Advanced Highers
Key Skills at levels 2, 3 and 4
Speech, drama and music awards at grades 6, 7 and 8

Use of the UCAS tariff system can vary from department to department within one university or college. Therefore you should always check on the specific entry requirements for a particular course with the university or college department itself.

Not all post-16 qualifications attract tariff points and not every university or college uses the tariff when making offers. Applicants may, therefore, still be accepted onto their chosen course if their qualifications do not translate into tariff points.

Where a prospective applicant is unsure of the acceptability of a qualification, it is recommended that advice is sought from the relevant university or college before a formal application is submitted to UCAS. For pupils with overseas qualifications the government-funded body NARIC (www.naric.org.uk) can be consulted for an evaluation and to issue a comparability statement against UK qualifications.

Alternatives to university entry

Pupils who are not attracted by the idea of full-time study at university will find that there are a number of alternatives available. It is possible to study for a degree part-time by distance learning through private institutions, or if practical skills are sought, there are many short courses available in areas such as business, computer skills, marketing, PR and languages.

There are also companies and other organizations that take on young people with A levels or the equivalent and offer them part-time academic training leading to relevant professional qualifications, which can be the equivalent of a first degree or postgraduate qualification. Examples include the Armed Forces and Emergency Services, the Merchant Navy, retail, hotel and catering, IT, accountancy, estate agency and certain branches of the Law.

Finding out more

There are, of course, many other options and issues that your son or daughter may want to discuss. These might include the pros and cons of taking a year out after school and how to make the best use of it, sponsorship to help finance a degree course, presenting a well-structured and effective UCAS application, interview techniques, CV writing and job applications.

Advice should be available from your child's school. Expert, independent guidance is also available from Gabbitas for seniors and current undergraduates, including: advice on university choices and applications, changing course or university and career options. For more details please visit www.gabbitas.co.uk/careers-colleges-and-universities or contact our post-16 and higher education team, Tel: 020 7734 0161 or e-mail he@gabbitas.co.uk.

Dr Wendy Piatt expresses why seniors should contemplate studying at a Russell Group university

University offers the chance to learn – about a subject, about the world, about yourself. But before arriving for your first day at university you will have to make many choices. What subject should you choose? Where should you study it? Would it be better to study part-time or full-time? You will probably want to consider all sorts of factors, such as the course content, the teaching style, the entry requirements, and even where the institution is located.

Higher education options

The UK offers a very wide range of options for studying at higher education level and it is important to take the time to investigate what all these options are before deciding the best match for your interests, aspirations and abilities.

World-class educational setting

Russell Group universities are to be found in all four nations and in every major city of the UK. They offer a wide range of subjects at both undergraduate and postgraduate level, with teaching conducted in a setting where world-class, ground-breaking research is being undertaken. Students at Russell Group universities can choose internationally renowned courses across a range of subjects, from medical, biological and physical sciences to business, social sciences and the humanities.

The research endeavour

The size and success of the research endeavour in Russell Group universities enables them to offer a student experience where teaching and learning are enriched and informed by leading-edge, world-class research. A good example is the research by Andre Geim and Konstantin Novoselov, two Manchester University physicists, which led to the Nobel award-winning creation of graphene, the thinnest and strongest material in the world. And in the Department of Zoology in the University of Oxford, a novel IT application originally developed by Torsten Reil and Colm Massey to achieve a better understanding of animal and human motion is now incorporated in blockbuster video games such as 'Grand Theft Auto IV' and 'Star Wars: The Force Unleashed'.

Discovery and intellectual curiosity

There is a high ratio of staff to students in Russell Group universities and it can be thrilling to learn from award-winning academics like the pioneers and their teams mentioned above and to get involved in their research. The academic, personal and professional benefits of this sort of experience can be enormous. You learn the importance of thinking independently. The emphasis on active processes of discovery and intellectual curiosity develops not only specialist knowledge but the entrepreneurialism, analytical problem-solving and communication skills that are so vital for success in many careers. This is demonstrated by the fact that graduates of Russell Group universities are held in particularly high esteem by employers: in a recent survey of international graduate recruiters 11 Russell Group universities were ranked in the top 50 in the world.[†]

International connections

Their world-class status means that Russell Group institutions also have partners across the globe, including businesses and governments as well as other universities. These relationships mean that students are offered excellent opportunities to apply their skills to issues outside their university, whether through work placements, international exchange programmes or other activities.

Facilities

As well as first-rate academic facilities, Russell Group universities offer excellent facilities for a wide range of activities, from social and sporting activities to cultural resources including exceptional libraries, museums and galleries. With a wide range of public arts and science events, the universities make a major contribution to the cultural life of the UK.

Well-regarded university places

Given the high standards of teaching and learning resources, as well as the opportunities students are offered outside their formal studies, it is not surprising that Russell Group universities are amongst the most popular in the UK. Drop-out rates are very low indeed, particularly in comparison with universities even in the United States. Levels of student satisfaction at Russell Group universities are particularly notable, with 86 per cent of students reporting satisfaction with the quality of their course.

Competitive entry

With this excellence and popularity comes competition for entry, however. Far more people apply to Russell Group universities than these institutions can accept, and the vast majority have high grades – so competition for places is fierce. Because of this, you will need excellent results in A levels or equivalents in order to take up a place. It is

[†] Source: QS World Rankings – http://www.topuniversities.com/university-rankings/world-university-rankings/2011/indicator-rankings/employer-review.

advisable to be as realistic as possible during the application process and make sure that you have an 'insurance offer' or have considered other options you could pursue in the event that you don't achieve the grades you were hoping for.

Other universities

There are many other universities that are not Russell Group members. The majority tend to be more recently established, particularly after 1992 when many polytechnics became universities. Entry requirements tend to be lower than those at Russell Group institutions but offers vary depending on which faculty and course you are contemplating.

Choosing sixth form subjects

To maximize your chances of getting into the university and course of your choice, you should consider your choice of subjects at school very carefully. Many courses at university level build on knowledge gained while still at school, and so universities need to make sure that all the students they admit have prepared themselves in the best way to cope with their chosen course. Some university courses require you to have studied a specific subject prior to entry, though others may not.

Facilitating subjects

Some subjects are required or recommended more often than others for entry to courses at Russell Group institutions; these include: Mathematics and Further Maths, English, Physics, Biology, Chemistry, Geography, History and Languages. These are sometimes called 'facilitating subjects' and by choosing them at advanced level (A level) you will have a much wider range of options open to you at university.

Researching options

The best way to check your options is to find out the entry requirements of courses you are interested in studying at a particular university through the university prospectus or UCAS website.

Remember the 'extra' elements when making an application

Getting your post-16 subject choices right is an important first step towards university; working as hard as you can to get the best grades possible is the second. But academic achievement, while vitally important, is only one of several things universities will take into account when they consider your application.

Russell Group universities are constantly seeking to develop the most effective ways of identifying real potential. Our admissions tutors are skilled at reviewing a range of factors and information about candidates to identify those with the most talent and potential to excel on our courses, whatever their social or educational background.

They will also want to select students who are clearly well-motivated and passionate about their subject. The vast majority of admissions tutors use personal statements and references when assessing candidates. Some departments may interview applicants or ask them to sit additional tests, particularly for the most competitive courses like Medicine or Law.

These 'extra' elements of the admissions process are not designed to catch students out and shouldn't be seen as obstacles to get around. They are there to give candidates as many opportunities as possible to demonstrate their strengths, passion and commitment for a subject and to help the university identify a student's true potential as accurately and fairly as possible. Admissions tutors may also take into account any particular barriers a candidate may have faced during his or her education, such as spending time in care.

University and financial support

Recently there has been a considerable amount of discussion and debate about the cost of going to university in the UK, particularly in England. It is important to be aware of the financial support – usually in the form of government loans or grants and university bursaries – that is available to students entering undergraduate courses. The details of what is available to you will differ depending on whether you live in England, Scotland, Wales, Northern Ireland or elsewhere in the EU, and where your university is located.

It is really important to understand that student loans are a world away from conventional 'debt'. Graduates are only asked to start making repayments once they are have finished studying and are earning a reasonable salary. Even then, contributions are what we call 'income-contingent'; this means that graduates repay only a small proportion of their income above a certain level each month.

In addition to the loans and grants provided by the government, Russell Group universities offer a wide range of bursaries and financial aid for their students. You are strongly advised to look at the financial support pages of university websites to see what is available at different institutions. Remember, graduates, not students, are asked to make a contribution to the costs of going to university and that contribution is a sound investment. University can lead to the most satisfying careers but also offer the most amazing experiences which many people only fully appreciate once they've left.

The university experience

I relished my time at two Russell Group universities – Lincoln College, Oxford and King's College, London – so much so that I spent as long as possible being a student, first as an undergraduate and then going on to study for a Masters and a PhD! If you are contemplating going to university you are in the enviable position of embarking on one of the best experiences of your life. So make sure you find out as much as you can about what is on offer, work hard and make the most of your time when you're there, and don't forget to appreciate and enjoy the ride.

More information about the Russell Group and its member universities is available from our website: www.russellgroup.ac.uk.

PART TWO

GEOGRAPHICAL DIRECTORY

www.independentschoolsguide.com

The Independent Schools Guide Profile Image
Competition 2012 2nd runner up

Cobham Hall School

See winning entry from St Paul's Cathedral School
on the back cover

2.1

Notes on information given in the directory section

Type of school

The directory comprises schools listed within the Department for Education register of independent schools. Maintained schools, foundation schools, special schools, independent further education colleges and overseas schools are not included, unless they have a profile in Part 3.

Schools are listed by type as follows: Nursery and Pre-Prep, Preparatory, Senior, Independent Sixth Form College/Tutorial College or International Schools and International Study Centres. The highest age range admitted has been used to categorize (except in the case of International Schools and International Study Centres), eg a straight-through school of 3–18 will appear under Senior, rather than Nursery and Prep-Prep or Preparatory.

Each school is given a brief entry that provides address details, web address (where available) and age range admitted. In some cases single-sex schools take small numbers of the opposite sex within a specified age range. These are indicated where appropriate, eg: 3–18 (Girls 16–18).

Also included is colour coded information about the gender admitted, accommodation available, the presence of a sixth form, whether the IB is offered and CReSTeD registration.

Please refer to the symbol key that follows when using the directory.

SYMBOL KEY

Gender

● Girls
● Boys
● Coed

Accommodation

♠ Boarding only
♠ Boarding and Day
♠ Day and Boarding
♠ Day only

* The school has a profile in Part 3.

International Bacc.

★ Offers IB

CReSTeD

◆ Crested Registered

Has 6th Form

▲ Has 6th Form

2.2

England

BEDFORDSHIRE

NURSERY AND PRE-PREP

PILGRIMS PRE-PREPARATORY SCHOOL
● 🏠
Brickhill Drive, Bedford,
Bedfordshire MK41 7QZ
Website:
www.pilgrimpreprep.org.uk

PREPARATORY

ACORN SCHOOL
● 🏠
15 St Andrews Road, Bedford,
Bedfordshire MK40 2LL
Website: www.acornschool.net
Age Range: 2–8

BEDFORD PREPARATORY SCHOOL
● 🏠
De Parys Avenue, Bedford,
Bedfordshire MK40 2TU
Website:
www.bedfordschool.org.uk
Age Range: 7–13

CHILDREN'S MONTESSORI SCHOOL
● 🏠
Green End, Gamlingay, Sandy,
Bedfordshire SG19 3LB
Age Range: 4–9 (Nursery)

MOORLANDS SCHOOL
● 🏠
Leagrave Hall, Luton,
Bedfordshire LU4 9LE
Website:
www.moorlandsschool.com
Age Range: 2–11

POLAM SCHOOL
● 🏠
45 Lansdowne Road, Bedford,
Bedfordshire MK40 2BU
Website:
www.polamschool.co.uk
Age Range: 2–9

ST GEORGE'S
● 🏠
28 Priory Road, Dunstable,
Bedfordshire LU5 4HR
Age Range: 2–11

SENIOR

BEDFORD HIGH SCHOOL FOR GIRLS
● 🏠 ★ ▲
Bromham Road, Bedford,
Bedfordshire MK40 2BS
Website:
www.bedfordhigh.co.uk
Age Range: 7–18

BEDFORD MODERN SCHOOL
● 🏠 ▲
Manton Lane, Bedford,
Bedfordshire MK41 7NT
Website: www.bedmod.co.uk
Age Range: 7–18

BEDFORD SCHOOL
● 🏠 ★ ▲
De Parys Avenue, Bedford,
Bedfordshire MK40 2TU
Website:
www.bedfordschool.org.uk
Age Range: 7–18

DAME ALICE HARPUR SCHOOL
● 🏠 ▲
Cardington Road, Bedford,
Bedfordshire MK42 0BX
Website: www.dahs.co.uk
Age Range: 7–18

RUSHMOOR SCHOOL
● 🏠
58–60 Shakespeare Road,
Bedford, Bedfordshire
MK40 2DL
Age Range: 4–16

ST ANDREW'S SCHOOL

● ♠

78 Kimbolton Road, Bedford,
Bedfordshire MK40 2PA
Website:
www.standrewsschoolbedford.com
Age Range: 3–16 (Boys 3–7)

SCEPTRE SCHOOL

● ♠ ▲

Ridgeway Avenue, Dunstable,
Bedfordshire LU5 4QL
Age Range: 11–18

INTERNATIONAL SCHOOLS AND INTERNATIONAL STUDY CENTRES

BEDFORD SCHOOL STUDY CENTRE

● ♠

67 De Parys Avenue, Bedford,
Bedfordshire MK40 2TR
Website: www.bedfordschool.org.uk/bssc
Age Range: 10–17

BERKSHIRE

NURSERY AND PRE-PREP

BROCKHURST & MARLSTON HOUSE PRE-PREPARATORY SCHOOL

● ♠

Hermitage, Thatcham, Berkshire
RG18 9UL
Website: www.brockmarl.org.uk
Age Range: 3–6

PREPARATORY

ALDER BRIDGE SCHOOL

● ♠

Bridge House, Mill Lane,
Padworth, Reading, Berkshire
RG7 4JU
Website:
www.alderbridge.org.uk
Age Range: 3–13

THE ARK SCHOOL

● ♠

School Road, Padworth,
Reading, Berkshire RG7 4JA
Website: www.arkschool.co.uk

BROCKHURST AND MARLSTON HOUSE SCHOOLS

● ♠

Hermitage, Newbury, Berkshire
RG18 9UL
Website: www.brockmarl.org.uk
Age Range: 3–13

THE CEDARS SCHOOL

● ♠

Church Road, Aldermaston,
Berkshire RG7 4LR
Website:
www.thecedarsschool.co.uk
Age Range: 4–11

CHEAM SCHOOL

● ♠

Headley, Newbury, Berkshire
RG19 8LD
Website:
www.cheamschool.com
Age Range: 7–13

CHILTERN COLLEGE SCHOOL

● ♠

16 Peppard Road, Caversham,
Reading, Berkshire RG4 8JZ
Website:
www.chilterncollegeschool.co.uk
Age Range: 4–11

CLAIRES COURT SCHOOLS, RIDGEWAY

● ♠

Maidenhead Thicket,
Maidenhead, Berkshire
SL6 3QE
Website: www.clairescourt.com
Age Range: 4–11

CROSFIELDS SCHOOL

● ♠

Shinfield, Reading, Berkshire
RG2 9BL
Website: www.crosfields.com
Age Range: 4–13

DOLPHIN SCHOOL

● ♠

Waltham Road, Hurst, Reading,
Berkshire RG10 0FR
Website:
www.dolphinschool.com
Age Range: 3–13

EAGLE HOUSE*

● ♠

Crowthorne Road, Sandhurst,
Berkshire GU47 8PH
Website:
www.eaglehouseschool.com
Age Range: 3–13

ELSTREE SCHOOL

● ♠

Woolhampton, Reading,
Berkshire RG7 5TD
Website: www.elstreeschool.
org.uk
Age Range: 3–13 (Girls 3–7)

ETON END PNEU

● ♠

35 Eton Road, Datchet, Slough,
Berkshire SL3 9AX
Website: www.etonend.org
Age Range: 3–11 (Boys 3–7)

HERRIES SCHOOL

● ♠

Dean Lane, Cookham Dean,
Maidenhead, Berkshire
SL6 9BD
Website: www.herries.org.uk
Age Range: 3–11

HIGHFIELD SCHOOL

● ⌂

2 West Road, Maidenhead,
Berkshire SL6 1PD
Website:
www.highfield.berks.sch.uk
Age Range: 3–11

THE HIGHLANDS SCHOOL

● ⌂

Wardle Avenue, Tilehurst,
Reading, Berkshire RG31 6JR
Website:
www.highlandsschool.co.uk
Age Range: 2–11

HOLME GRANGE SCHOOL

● ⌂

Heathlands Road, Wokingham,
Berkshire RG40 3AL
Website: www.holmegrange.org
Age Range: 3–13

HORRIS HILL SCHOOL

● ⌂

Newtown, Newbury, Berkshire
RG20 9DJ
Website: www.horrishill.com
Age Range: 7–13

LAMBROOK*

● ⌂

Winkfield Row, Bracknell,
Berkshire RG42 6LU
Website:
www.lambrook.berks.sch.uk
Age Range: 3–13

LANGLEY MANOR SCHOOL

● ⌂

St Marys Road, Langley,
Berkshire SL3 6BZ
Website:
www.langleymanorschool.co.uk
Age Range: 3–11

LUDGROVE

● ⌂

Wokingham, Berkshire RG40
3AB
Website: www.ludgrove.net
Age Range: 8–13

**THE MARIST PREPARATORY
SCHOOL**

● ⌂ ▲

Kings Road, Sunninghill, Ascot,
Berkshire SL5 7PS
Website:
www.themaristschools.com
Age Range: 2–11

**MEADOWBROOK
MONTESSORI SCHOOL**

● ⌂

Malt Hill, Warfield, Bracknell,
Berkshire RG42 6JQ
Age Range: 3–11

NEWBOLD SCHOOL

● ⌂

Popeswood Road, Binfield,
Bracknell, Berkshire RG42 4AH
Website:
www.newboldschool.co.uk
Age Range: 3–11

**OUR LADY'S PREPARATORY
SCHOOL**

● ⌂

The Avenue, Crowthorne,
Berkshire RG45 6PB
Website:
www.ourladysprep.co.uk
Age Range: 1–11

PAPPLEWICK SCHOOL*

● ⌂

Windsor Road, Ascot, Berkshire
SL5 7LH
Website: www.papplewick.org.uk
Age Range: 6–13

ST ANDREW'S SCHOOL

● ⌂

Buckhold, Pangbourne,
Reading, Berkshire RG8 8QA
Website:
www.standrewspangbourne.
co.uk
Age Range: 3–13

**ST BERNARD'S
PREPARATORY SCHOOL**

● ⌂

Hawtrey Close, Slough,
Berkshire SL1 1TB
Website: www.st-bernards-prep.
slough.sch.uk
Age Range: 3–11

ST EDWARD'S SCHOOL

● ⌂

64 Tilehurst Road, Reading,
Berkshire RG30 2JH
Website: www.stedwards.org.uk
Age Range: 4–13

ST GEORGE'S SCHOOL

● ⌂

Windsor Castle, Windsor,
Berkshire SL4 1QF
Website: www.stgwindsor.co.uk
Age Range: 3–13

ST JOHN'S BEAUMONT

● ⌂

Priest Hill, Old Windsor,
Windsor, Berkshire SL4 2JN
Website:
www.stjohnsbeaumont.org.uk
Age Range: 4–13

**ST PIRAN'S PREPARATORY
SCHOOL***

● ⌂

Gringer Hill, Maidenhead,
Berkshire SL6 7LZ
Website: www.stpirans.co.uk
Age Range: 3–13

SUNNINGDALE SCHOOL

● ⌂

Dry Arch Road, Sunningdale,
Berkshire SL5 9PY
Website:
www.sunningdaleschool.co.uk
Age Range: 8–13

THORNGROVE SCHOOL

● ⌂

The Mount, Highclere, Newbury,
Berkshire RG20 9PS
Website:
www.thorngroveschool.co.uk
Age Range: 2–13

UPTON HOUSE SCHOOL*

● ⌂

115 St Leonard's Road,
Windsor, Berkshire SL4 3DF
Website:
www.uptonhouse.org.uk
Age Range: 2–11 (Boys 2–7)

WAVERLEY SCHOOL

Waverley Way, Finchampstead, Wokingham, Berkshire RG40 4YD
Website: www.waverley.wokingham.sch.uk
Age Range: 3–11

WHITE HOUSE PREPARATORY SCHOOL

Finchampstead Road, Wokingham, Berkshire RG40 3HD
Website: www.whitehouse.wokingham.sch.uk
Age Range: 2–11 (Boys 2–4)

WINBURY SCHOOL

Braywick Park, Hibbert Road, Bray, Maidenhead, Berkshire SL6 1UU
Website: www.winburyschool.co.uk
Age Range: 2–8

SENIOR

THE ABBEY SCHOOL*

17 Kendrick Road, Reading, Berkshire RG1 5DZ
Website: www.theabbey.co.uk
Age Range: 3–18

BEARWOOD COLLEGE

Bearwood Road, Wokingham, Berkshire RG41 5BG
Website: www.bearwoodcollege.co.uk
Age Range: 1–18 (Nursery 0–5 years, Pre-Prep 5–7 years, Prep 7–11 years, Senior (including Sixth Form) 11–18 years.)

BRADFIELD COLLEGE*

Bradfield, Reading, Berkshire RG7 6AU
Website: www.bradfieldcollege.org.uk
Age Range: 13–18

BRIGIDINE SCHOOL WINDSOR

Queensmead, Kings Road, Windsor, Berkshire SL4 2AX
Website: www.brigidine.org.uk
Age Range: 3–18 (Boys 3–7)

CLAIRES COURT SCHOOL

Ray Mill Road East, Maidenhead, Berkshire SL6 8TE
Website: www.clairescourt.com
Age Range: 11–16 (Co-ed VIth Form)

CLAIRES COURT SCHOOLS, THE COLLEGE

1 College Avenue, Maidenhead, Berkshire SL6 6AW
Website: www.clairescourt.com
Age Range: 3–16 (Boys 3–5, co-ed VIth Form)

DOWNE HOUSE

Cold Ash, Thatcham, Berkshire RG18 9JJ
Website: www.downehouse.net
Age Range: 11–18

ETON COLLEGE

Windsor, Berkshire SL4 6DW
Website: www.etoncollege.com
Age Range: 13–18

HEATHFIELD SCHOOL*

London Road, Ascot, Berkshire SL5 8BQ
Website: www.heathfieldschool.net
Age Range: 11–18

HEMDEAN HOUSE SCHOOL

Hemdean Road, Caversham, Reading, Berkshire RG4 7SD
Website: www.hemdeanhouse.co.uk
Age Range: 3–16

HURST LODGE SCHOOL

Bagshot Road, Ascot, Berkshire SL5 9JU
Website: www.hurstlodge.co.uk
Age Range: 3–18 (Boys and Girls 3–18)

LONG CLOSE SCHOOL

Upton Court Road, Slough, Berkshire SL3 7LU
Website: www.longcloseschool.co.uk
Age Range: 2–16

LUCKLEY-OAKFIELD SCHOOL

Luckley Road, Wokingham, Berkshire RG40 3EU
Website: www.luckley.wokingham.sch.uk
Age Range: 11–18

LVS ASCOT

London Road, Ascot, Berkshire SL5 8DR
Website: www.lvs.ascot.sch.uk
Age Range: 4–18

THE MARIST SENIOR SCHOOL

Kings Road, Sunninghill, Ascot, Berkshire SL5 7PS
Website: www.themaristschools.com
Age Range: 11–18

THE ORATORY SCHOOL

Woodcote, Reading, Berkshire RG8 0PJ
Website: www.oratory.co.uk
Age Range: 11–18

PANGBOURNE COLLEGE

Pangbourne, Berkshire RG8 8LA
Website: www.pangbournecollege.com
Age Range: 11–18

QUEEN ANNE'S SCHOOL
● 🏠 ▲

Henley Road, Caversham,
Berkshire RG4 6DX
Website: www.qas.org.uk
Age Range: 11–18

READING BLUE COAT SCHOOL
● 🏠 ▲

Holme Park, Sonning-on-
Thames, Reading, Berkshire
RG4 6SU
Website:
www.blue-coat.reading.sch.uk
Age Range: 11–18
(Co-ed VIth Form)

READING SCHOOL
● 🏠 ★ ▲

Erleigh Road, Reading,
Berkshire RG1 5LW
Website: www.readingschool.
reading.sch.uk
Age Range: 11–18

REDROOFS THEATRE SCHOOL
● 🏠

26 Bath Road, Maidenhead,
Berkshire SL6 34JT
Website: www.redroofs.co.uk
Age Range: 9–16

ST GABRIEL'S
● 🏠 ▲

Sandleford Priory, Newbury,
Berkshire RG20 9BD
Website: www.stgabriels.co.uk
Age Range: 3–18
(Girls 3–18 Boys 3–7)

ST GEORGE'S SCHOOL
● 🏠 ▲

Ascot, Berkshire SL5 7DZ
Website:
www.stgeorges-ascot.org.uk
Age Range: 11–18

ST JOSEPH'S COLLEGE
● 🏠 ▲

Upper Redlands Road,
Reading, Berkshire RG1 5JT
Website:
www.stjosephscollege.co.uk
Age Range: 3–18

ST MARY'S SCHOOL, ASCOT*
● 🏠 ▲

St Mary's Road, Ascot,
Berkshire SL5 9JF
Website:
www.st-marys-ascot.co.uk
Age Range: 11–18

ST MICHAELS SCHOOL
● 🏠 ▲

Harts Lane, Burghclere,
Newbury, Berkshire RG20 9JW
Age Range: 7–18 (Single-sex
ed 13–18)

WELLINGTON COLLEGE*
● 🏠 ★ ▲

Duke's Ride, Crowthorne,
Berkshire RG45 7PU
Website:
www.wellingtoncollege.org.uk
Age Range: 13–18

INDEPENDENT SIXTH FORM COLLEGE / TUTORIAL COLLEGE

PADWORTH INTERNATIONAL COLLEGE

Padworth, Reading, Berkshire
RG7 4NR

INTERNATIONAL SCHOOLS AND INTERNATIONAL STUDY CENTRES

ARDMORE LANGUAGE SCHOOLS

Berkshire College, Hall Place,
Burchetts Green, Maidenhead,
Berkshire SL6 6QR
Website: http://www.ardmore-
language-schools.com/

NEWBURY HALL INTERNATIONAL SCHOOL
● 🏠

Enborne Road, Newbury,
Berkshire RG14 6AD
Website: www.newburyhall.com
Age Range: 13–17 (We cater
for International students only.)

PADWORTH COLLEGE
● 🏠 ▲

Padworth, Reading, Berkshire
RG7 4NR
Website: www.padworth.com
Age Range: 13–19

BRISTOL

PREPARATORY

BRISTOL STEINER SCHOOL
Redland Hill House, Redland
Hill, Bristol BS6 6UX
Website:
www.steiner.bristol.sch.uk
Age Range: 3–14

CLEVE HOUSE SCHOOL
254 Wells Road, Bristol BS4
2PN
Website:
www.clevehouseschool.co.uk
Age Range: 3–11

CLIFTON COLLEGE PRE-
PREP – BUTCOMBE
Guthrie Road, Bristol BS8 3EZ
Website:
www.cliftoncollegeuk.com
Age Range: 3–8

CLIFTON COLLEGE
PREPARATORY SCHOOL
The Avenue, Clifton, Bristol BS8
3HE
Website:
www.cliftoncollegeuk.com
Age Range: 8–13

COLSTON'S LOWER SCHOOL
Park Road, Bristol BS16 1BA
Age Range: 3–11

THE DOWNS SCHOOL
Wraxall, Bristol BS48 1PF
Website:
www.thedownsschool.co.uk
Age Range: 4–13

FAIRFIELD SCHOOL
Fairfield Way, Backwell, Bristol
BS48 3PD
Website:
www.fairfieldschool.org.uk
Age Range: 3–11

GRACEFIELD PREPARATORY
SCHOOL
266 Overndale Road,
Fishponds, Bristol BS16 2RG
Website:
www.gracefieldschool.co.uk
Age Range: 4–11

OVERNDALE SCHOOL
Chapel Lane, Old Sodbury,
Bristol BS37 6NQ
Website:
www.overndaleschool.co.uk
Age Range: 1–11

TOCKINGTON MANOR
SCHOOL
Tockington, Bristol BS32 4NY
Website:
www.tockingtonmanorschool.
com
Age Range: 2–14

TORWOOD HOUSE SCHOOL
8 & 27–29 Durdham Park,
Redland, Bristol BS6 6XE
Website: www.
torwoodhousebristol.sch.uk

SENIOR

BADMINTON SCHOOL*
Westbury Road, Westbury-on-
Trym, Bristol BS9 3BA
Website: www.badminton.
bristol.sch.uk
Age Range: 3–18

BRISTOL CATHEDRAL
SCHOOL
College Square, Bristol BS1 5TS
Website: www.bristolcathedral.
bristol.sch.uk
Age Range: 10–18
(Co-ed VIth Form)

BRISTOL GRAMMAR
SCHOOL*
University Road, Bristol BS8
1SR
Website:
www.bristolgrammarschool.co.uk
Age Range: 5–18

CARMEL CHRISTIAN
SCHOOL
817A Bath Road, Brislington,
Bristol BS4 5NL
Website: www.carmelcentre.org
Age Range: 4–17

CLIFTON COLLEGE*
32 College Road, Clifton, Bristol
BS8 3JH
Website:
www.cliftoncollegeuk.com
Age Range: 3–18

CLIFTON HIGH SCHOOL
College Road, Clifton, Bristol
BS8 3JD
Website:
www.cliftonhigh.bristol.sch.uk
Age Range: 3–18

COLSTON'S COLLEGIATE
SCHOOL
Stapleton, Bristol BS16 1BJ
Website:
www.colstons.bristol.sch.uk
Age Range: 3–18

PROSPECT SCHOOL
1 Tramway Road, Brislington,
Bristol BS4 3DS
Age Range: 11–17

QUEEN ELIZABETH'S
HOSPITAL
Berkeley Place, Clifton, Bristol
BS8 1JX
Website: www.qehbristol.co.uk
Age Range: 7–18 (Sixth Form
International students are wel-
come on a Guardianship basis)

THE RED MAIDS' SCHOOL

Westbury-on-Trym, Bristol BS9 3AW
Website: www.redmaids.co.uk
Age Range: 11–18

REDLAND HIGH SCHOOL FOR GIRLS

Redland Court, Bristol BS6 7EF
Website: www.redlandhigh.com
Age Range: 3–18

ST URSULA'S HIGH SCHOOL

Brecon Road, Westbury-on-Trym, Bristol BS9 4DT
Website: www.st-ursulas.bristol.sch.uk
Age Range: 3–16

INDEPENDENT SIXTH FORM COLLEGE / TUTORIAL COLLEGE

ST BRENDAN'S VITH FORM COLLEGE
Broomhill Road, Brislington, Bristol BS4 5RQ
Website: www.stbrn.ac.uk

BUCKINGHAMSHIRE

NURSERY AND PRE-PREP

KINGSCOTE PRE-PREPARATORY SCHOOL

Oval Way, Gerrards Cross, Buckinghamshire SL9 8PZ
Website:
www.kingscoteschool.info
Age Range: 3–7

PREPARATORY

AKELEY WOOD LOWER SCHOOL

Lillingstone Dayrell, Buckingham, Buckinghamshire MK18 5AN
Website:
www.akeleywoodschool.co.uk
Age Range: 9–11

ASHFOLD SCHOOL
Dorton, Aylesbury, Buckinghamshire HP18 9NG
Website:
www.ashfoldschool.co.uk
Age Range: 3–13

THE BEACON SCHOOL
Amersham Road, Chesham Bois, Amersham, Buckinghamshire HP6 5PF
Website:
www.beaconschool.co.uk
Age Range: 3–13

BROUGHTON MANOR PREPARATORY SCHOOL
Newport Road, Broughton, Buckinghamshire MK10 9AA
Website: www.bmprep.co.uk

CALDICOTT SCHOOL

Crown Lane, Farnham Royal, Buckinghamshire SL2 3SL
Website: www.caldicott.com
Age Range: 7–13

CHESHAM PREPARATORY SCHOOL

Two Dells Lane, Orchard Leigh, Chesham, Buckinghamshire HP5 3QF
Website:
www.cheshamprep.co.uk
Age Range: 3–13

CROWN HOUSE SCHOOL

19 London Road, High Wycombe, Buckinghamshire HP11 1BJ
Website:
www.crownhouseschool.co.uk
Age Range: 4–11

DAIR HOUSE SCHOOL TRUST LTD

Bishops Blake, Beaconsfield Road, Farnham Royal, Buckinghamshire SL2 3BY
Website: www.dairhouse.co.uk
Age Range: 3–11

DAVENIES SCHOOL
● 🏠
73 Station Road, Beaconsfield,
Buckinghamshire HP9 1AA
Website: www.davenies.co.uk
Age Range: 4–13

FILGRAVE SCHOOL
● 🏠
Filgrave, Newport Pagnell,
Buckinghamshire MK16 9ET
Website:
www.filgraveschool.org.uk
Age Range: 3–9

GATEWAY SCHOOL
● 🏠
1 High Street, Great Missenden,
Buckinghamshire HP16 9AA
Age Range: 2–12

GAYHURST SCHOOL
● 🏠
Bull Lane, Gerrards Cross,
Buckinghamshire SL9 8RJ
Website:
www.gayhurstschool.eu
Age Range: 3–13

GODSTOWE PREPARATORY SCHOOL
● 🏠
Shrubbery Road, High
Wycombe, Buckinghamshire
HP13 6PR
Website: www.godstowe.org
Age Range: 3–13 (Boys 3–8)

GROVE INDEPENDENT SCHOOL
● 🏠
Redland Drive, Loughton, Milton
Keynes, Buckinghamshire MK5
8HD
Website:
www.groveindependentschool.
co.uk
Age Range: 2–13

HEATHERTON HOUSE SCHOOL
● 🏠
Copperkins Lane, Chesham
Bois, Amersham,
Buckinghamshire HP6 5QB
Website: www.heathertonhouse.
co.uk
Age Range: 3–11 (Girls can
start in Early Years from the age
of 2.5)

HIGH MARCH SCHOOL
● 🏠
23 Ledborough Lane,
Beaconsfield, Buckinghamshire
HP9 2PZ
Website: www.highmarch.co.uk
Age Range: 3–11 (Boys are
only admitted into our Upper
Nursery class)

LADYMEDE
● 🏠
Little Kimble, Aylesbury,
Buckinghamshire HP17 0XP
Website: www.ladymedeschool.
bucks.sch.uk
Age Range: 3–11

MALTMAN'S GREEN SCHOOL
● 🏠
Maltmans Lane, Gerrards Cross,
Buckinghamshire SL9 8RR
Website:
www.maltmansgreen.com
Age Range: 3–11

MILTON KEYNES PREPARATORY SCHOOL
● 🏠
Tattenhoe Lane, Milton Keynes,
Buckinghamshire MK3 7EG
Website: www.mkps.co.uk

ST TERESA'S CATHOLIC INDEPENDENT & NURSERY SCHOOL
● 🏠
Aylesbury Road, Princes
Risborough, Buckinghamshire
HP27 0JW
Website:
www.st-teresas.bucks.sch.uk
Age Range: 3–11

SWANBOURNE HOUSE SCHOOL*
● 🏠
Swanbourne, Milton Keynes,
Buckinghamshire MK17 0HZ
Website: www.swanbourne.org
Age Range: 3–13

SENIOR

AKELEY WOOD SCHOOL
● 🏠 ▲
Akeley Wood, Buckingham,
Buckinghamshire MK18 5AE
Website:
www.akeleywoodschool.co.uk
Age Range: 3–18

BURY LAWN SCHOOL
● 🏠 ▲
Soskin Drive, Stantonbury
Fields, Milton Keynes,
Buckinghamshire MK14 6DP
Website:
www.burylawnschool.co.uk
Age Range: 2–18

PIPERS CORNER SCHOOL*
● 🏠 ▲
Pipers Lane, Great Kingshill,
High Wycombe,
Buckinghamshire HP15 6LP
Website:
www.piperscorner.co.uk
Age Range: 3–18

ST MARY'S SCHOOL
● 🏠 ▲
94 Packhorse Road, Gerrards
Cross, Buckinghamshire SL9
8JQ
Website:
www.stmarysschool.co.uk
Age Range: 3–18

STOWE SCHOOL
● 🏠 ▲
Stowe, Buckingham,
Buckinghamshire MK18 5EH
Website: www.stowe.co.uk
Age Range: 13–18

SEFTON PARK SCHOOL
● 🏠 ▲
School Lane, Stoke Poges,
Buckinghamshire SL2 4QA
Age Range: 11–18

THORNTON COLLEGE CONVENT OF JESUS AND MARY
● 🏠
Thornton, Milton Keynes,
Buckinghamshire MK17 0HJ
Website:
www.thorntoncollege.com
Age Range: 2–16 (Boys 2–4)

THORPE HOUSE SCHOOL
● 🏠
Oval Way, Gerrards Cross,
Buckinghamshire SL9 8QA
Website:
www.thorpehouse.co.uk
Age Range: 3–16

WYCOMBE ABBEY SCHOOL
● 🏠 ▲
High Wycombe,
Buckinghamshire HP11 1PE
Website:
www.wycombeabbey.com
Age Range: 11–18

CAMBRIDGESHIRE

NURSERY AND PRE-PREP

MADINGLEY PRE-PREPARATORY SCHOOL
● 🏠
Cambridge Road, Madingley,
Cambridge, Cambridgeshire
CB23 8AH
Website:
www.madingleyschool.co.uk
Age Range: 3–8

PREPARATORY

ST FAITH'S
● 🏠
Trumpington Road, Cambridge,
Cambridgeshire CB2 8AG
Website: www.stfaiths.co.uk
Age Range: 4–13

ST JOHN'S COLLEGE SCHOOL
● 🏠
73 Grange Road, Cambridge,
Cambridgeshire CB3 9AB
Website: www.sjcs.co.uk
Age Range: 4–13

ST MARY'S JUNIOR SCHOOL
● 🏠
2 Brookside, Cambridge,
Cambridgeshire CB2 1JE
Website:
www.stmaryscambridge.co.uk
Age Range: 4–11

WHITEHALL SCHOOL
● 🏠
117 High Street, Somersham,
Huntingdon, Cambridgeshire
PE28 3EH
Website:
www.whitehallschool.com
Age Range: 3–11

SENIOR

CAMBRIDGE INTERNATIONAL SCHOOL
● 🏠
Cherry Hinton Hall, Cherry
Hinton Road, Cambridge,
Cambridgeshire CB1 8DW
Age Range: 4–16

KIMBOLTON SCHOOL
● 🏠 ▲
Kimbolton, Huntingdon,
Cambridgeshire PE28 0EA
Website:
www.kimbolton.cambs.sch.uk
Age Range: 4–18 (Boarders
from 11)

KING'S SCHOOL ELY
● 🏠 ▲
Ely, Cambridgeshire CB7 4DB
Website:
www.kingsschoolely.co.uk
Age Range: 2–18

THE LEYS SCHOOL*
● 🏠 ▲
Trumpington Road, Cambridge,
Cambridgeshire CB2 7AD
Website: www.theleys.net
Age Range: 11–18

THE PERSE SCHOOL
● 🏠 ▲
Hills Road, Cambridge,
Cambridgeshire CB2 8QF
Website: www.perse.co.uk
Age Range: 11–18

THE PERSE SCHOOL FOR GIRLS
● 🏠 ▲
Union Road, Cambridge,
Cambridgeshire CB2 1HF
Website:
www.perse.cambs.sch.uk
Age Range: 7–18

THE PETERBOROUGH SCHOOL
● 🏠 ▲
Thorpe Road, Peterborough,
Cambridgeshire PE3 6AP
Website:
www.thepeterboroughschool.
co.uk
Age Range: 4–18 (Boys 3–11)

ST MARY'S SCHOOL, CAMBRIDGE
● 🏠 ▲
Bateman Street, Cambridge,
Cambridgeshire CB2 1LY
Website:
www.stmaryscambridge.co.uk
Age Range: 4–18

SANCTON WOOD SCHOOL
● 🏠
2 St Paul's Road, Cambridge,
Cambridgeshire CB1 2EZ
Website:
www.sanctonwood.co.uk
Age Range: 1–16

WISBECH GRAMMAR SCHOOL

North Brink, Wisbech,
Cambridgeshire PE13 1JX
Website:
www.wgs.cambs.sch.uk
Age Range: 4–18

INDEPENDENT SIXTH FORM COLLEGE / TUTORIAL COLLEGE

BELLERBYS COLLEGE & EMBASSY CES CAMBRIDGE

Queens Campus, Bateman
Street, Cambridge,
Cambridgeshire CB2 1LU
Website: www.bellerbys.com
Age Range: 14–25

CAMBRIDGE CENTRE FOR SIXTH-FORM STUDIES

1 Salisbury Villas, Station Road,
Cambridge, Cambridgeshire
CB1 2JF
Website: www.ccss.co.uk
Age Range: 15–21

CATS COLLEGE CAMBRIDGE

13–14 Round Church Street,
Cambridge, Cambridgeshire
CB5 8AD
Website: www.catscollege.com
Age Range: 15–21

MPW (MANDER PORTMAN WOODWARD)

3/4 Brookside, Cambridge,
Cambridgeshire CB2 1JE
Website: www.mpw.co.uk
Age Range: 15–21

ST ANDREW'S

13 Station Road, Cambridge,
Cambridgeshire CB1 2JB
Website:
www.standrewscambridge.co.uk
Age Range: 14–18

INTERNATIONAL SCHOOLS AND INTERNATIONAL STUDY CENTRES

KING'S ELY INTERNATIONAL*

The King's School Ely,
Cambridge, Cambridgeshire
CB7 4DB
Website:
www.kingsschoolely.co.uk
Age Range: 14–16

CHANNEL ISLANDS

PREPARATORY

FCJ PRIMARY SCHOOL

Deloraine Road, St Saviour,
Jersey, Channel Islands JE2
7XB
Website: www.fcj.sch.je
Age Range: 4–11

ORMER HOUSE PREPARATORY SCHOOL

La Vallee, Alderney, Channel
Islands GY9 3XA
Website: www.ormerhouse.com
Age Range: 2–13

ST GEORGE'S PREPARATORY SCHOOL

La Hague Manor, Rue de la
Hague, St Peter, Jersey,
Channel Islands JE3 7DB
Website:
www.stgeorgesprep.co.uk
Age Range: 3–13

ST MICHAEL'S PREPARATORY SCHOOL

La Rue de la Houguette, St
Saviour, Jersey, Channel Islands
JE2 7UG
Website:
www.stmichaelsschool.je
Age Range: 3–13

VICTORIA COLLEGE PREPARATORY SCHOOL

Pleasant Street, St Helier,
Jersey, Channel Islands
Website: www.vcp.sch.je
Age Range: 7–11

SENIOR

BEAULIEU CONVENT SCHOOL

Wellington Road, Saint Helier,
Jersey, Channel Islands JE2 4RJ
Age Range: 4–18

ELIZABETH COLLEGE

Guernsey, Channel Islands GY1
2PY
Website: www.elizcoll.org
Age Range: 2–18 (Co-ed Pre-
prep and Prep School. Joint
Co-ed Sixth Form with local
girls' school)

THE LADIES' COLLEGE

Les Gravees, St Peter Port,
Guernsey, Channel Islands GY1
1RW
Website:
www.ladiescollege.sch.gg
Age Range: 4–18

VICTORIA COLLEGE

Jersey, Channel Islands JE1
4HT
Website: www.victoriacollege.je
Age Range: 11–19

CHESHIRE

PREPARATORY

ABBEY GATE SCHOOL

Clare Avenue, Hoole, Chester,
Cheshire CH2 3HR
Website:
www.abbeygateschool.org.uk
Age Range: 3–11

ALTRINCHAM PREPARATORY SCHOOL

Marlborough Road, Bowdon,
Altrincham, Cheshire WA14 2RR
Website: www.altprep.co.uk
Age Range: 3–11

BOWDON PREPARATORY SCHOOL FOR GIRLS

48 Stamford Road, Bowdon,
Altrincham, Cheshire WA14 2JP
Age Range: 2–12

BRABYNS SCHOOL

34–36 Arkwright Road, Marple,
Stockport, Cheshire SK6 7DB
Website:
www.brabynsprepschool.co.uk
Age Range: 2–11

THE FIRS SCHOOL

45 Newton Lane, Chester,
Cheshire CH2 2HJ
Website: www.firsschool.net
Age Range: 4–11

FOREST PARK SCHOOL

Lauriston House, 27 Oakfield,
Sale, Cheshire M33 6NB
Website:
www.forestparkschool.co.uk
Age Range: 3–11

FOREST SCHOOL

Moss Lane, Timperley,
Altrincham, Cheshire WA15 6LJ
Website:
www.forestschool.co.uk
Age Range: 2–11

GREENBANK PREPARATORY SCHOOL

Heathbank Road, Cheadle
Hulme, Cheadle, Cheshire SK8
6HU
Website:
www.greenbankschool.co.uk
Age Range: 3–11

HALE PREPARATORY SCHOOL

Broomfield Lane, Hale,
Altrincham, Cheshire WA15 9AS
Age Range: 4–11

HULME HALL SCHOOLS (JUNIOR SCHOOL)

75 Hulme Hall Road, Cheadle
Hulme, Cheadle, Cheshire SK8
6LA
Website:
www.hulmehallschool.org
Age Range: 3–11

LADY BARN HOUSE SCHOOL

Langlands, Schools Hill,
Cheadle Hulme, Cheadle,
Cheshire SK8 1JE
Website: www.ladybarnhouse.
stockport.sch.uk
Age Range: 3–11

LORETO PREPARATORY SCHOOL

Dunham Road, Altrincham,
Cheshire WA14 4GZ
Website: www.loretoprep.co.uk
Age Range: 3–11 (Boys 4–7)

MERTON HOUSE

Abbot's Park, Off Liverpool
Road, Chester, Cheshire CH1
4BD
Website:
mertonhousechester.co.uk
Age Range: 3–11

NORFOLK HOUSE PREPARATORY & KIDS CORNER NURSERY

Norfolk House, 120 Congleton
Road, Sandbach, Cheshire
CW11 1HF
Website: www.norfolkhouse.net

POWNALL HALL SCHOOL

Carrwood Road, Wilmslow,
Cheshire SK9 5DW
Website:
www.pownallhall.cheshire.sch.uk
Age Range: 2–11

RAMILLIES HALL SCHOOL

Ramillies Avenue, Cheadle
Hulme, Cheadle, Cheshire SK8
7AJ
Website: www.ramillieshall.co.uk

THE RYLEYS

Ryleys Lane, Alderley Edge,
Cheshire SK9 7UY
Website:
www.theryleys.cheshire.sch.uk
Age Range: 3–13

ST AMBROSE PREPARATORY SCHOOL

Hale Barns, Altrincham,
Cheshire WA15 0HE
Website: www.st-ambrose-prep.
trafford.sch.uk
Age Range: 3–11

ST CATHERINE'S PREPARATORY SCHOOL

Hollins Lane, Marple Bridge,
Stockport, Cheshire SK6 5BB
Website: www.stcatherinesprep.
stockport.sch.uk
Age Range: 3–11

STELLA MARIS JUNIOR SCHOOL

St John's Road, Heaton Mersey, Stockport, Cheshire SK4 3BR
Website:
www.stellamarisschool.co.uk
Age Range: 3–11

TERRA NOVA SCHOOL

Jodrell Bank, Holmes Chapel, Cheshire CW4 8BT
Website:
www.terranovaschool.co.uk
Age Range: 3–13

WILMSLOW PREPARATORY SCHOOL

Grove Avenue, Wilmslow, Cheshire SK9 5EG
Website:
www.wilmslowprep.co.uk
Age Range: 2–11

YORSTON LODGE SCHOOL

18 St John's Road, Knutsford, Cheshire WA16 0DP
Website:
www.yorstonlodge.com
Age Range: 3–11

SENIOR

ABBEY GATE COLLEGE

Saighton Grange, Saighton, Chester, Cheshire CH3 6EN
Website:
www.abbeygatecollege.org
Age Range: 4–18

ALDERLEY EDGE SCHOOL FOR GIRLS

Wilmslow Road, Alderley Edge, Cheshire SK9 7QE
Age Range: 3–18

BEECH HALL SCHOOL

Beech Hall Drive, Tytherington, Macclesfield, Cheshire SK10 2EG
Website:
www.beechallschool.org
Age Range: 4–16 (Kindergarten 1–5)

CHEADLE HULME SCHOOL

Claremont Road, Cheadle Hulme, Cheadle, Cheshire SK8 6EF
Website:
www.cheadlehulmeschool.co.uk
Age Range: 4–18

CRANSLEY SCHOOL

Belmont Hall, Great Budworth, Northwich, Cheshire CW9 6HN
Website:
www.cransleyschool.co.uk
Age Range: 3–16 (Boys 3–11)

THE GRANGE SCHOOL
Bradburns Lane, Hartford, Northwich, Cheshire CW8 1LU
Website: www.grange.org.uk
Age Range: 4–18

HAMMOND SCHOOL
Hoole Bank House, Mannings Lane, Chester, Cheshire CH2 4ES
Website:
www.thehammondschool.co.uk
Age Range: 11–18

HILLCREST GRAMMAR SCHOOL
Beech Avenue, Cale Green, Stockport, Cheshire SK3 8HB
Website:
www.hillcrest.stockport.sch.uk
Age Range: 3–16

HULME HALL SCHOOLS
75 Hulme Hall Road, Cheadle Hulme, Cheadle, Cheshire SK8 6LA
Website:
www.hulmehallschool.org
Age Range: 2–16

THE KING'S SCHOOL
Wrexham Road, Chester, Cheshire CH4 7QL
Website:
www.kingschester.co.uk
Age Range: 7–18

THE KING'S SCHOOL

Macclesfield, Cheshire SK10 1DA
Website: www.kingsmac.co.uk
Age Range: 3–18 (Single-sex ed 11–16)

NORTH CESTRIAN GRAMMAR SCHOOL

Dunham Road, Dunham Road, Altrincham, Cheshire WA14 4AJ
Website: www.ncgs.co.uk
Age Range: 11–18

THE QUEEN'S SCHOOL
City Walls Road, Chester, Cheshire CH1 2NN
Website:
www.queens.cheshire.sch.uk
Age Range: 4–18

STOCKPORT GRAMMAR SCHOOL
Buxton Road, Stockport, Cheshire SK2 7AF
Website:
www.stockportgrammar.co.uk
Age Range: 3–18

TRINITY SCHOOL
Birbeck Street, Stalybridge, Cheshire SK15 1SH
Website:
www.trinityschool.org.uk
Age Range: 4–18

CORNWALL

PREPARATORY

POLWHELE HOUSE SCHOOL
Newquay Road, Truro, Cornwall
TR4 9AE
Website:
www.polwhelehouse.co.uk
Age Range: 3–13

ROSELYON
St Blazey Road, Par, Cornwall
PL24 2HZ
Website:
www.roselyon.cornwall.sch.uk
Age Range: 2–11

ST IA SCHOOL
St Ives Road, Carbis Bay,
St Ives, Cornwall TR26 2SF
Website:
www.st-ia.cornwall.sch.uk
Age Range: 4–11

ST PETROC'S SCHOOL
Ocean View Road, Bude,
Cornwall EX23 8NJ
Website: www.stpetrocs.com
Age Range: 3–11 (Nursery from
3 mths)

TRURO SCHOOL PREPARATORY SCHOOL
Highertown, Truro, Cornwall TR1
3QN
Website: www.truroprep.com
Age Range: 3–11

SENIOR

GEMS BOLITHO SCHOOL
Polwithen Road, Penzance,
Cornwall TR18 4JR
Website:
www.bolithoschool.co.uk
Age Range: 4–18

HIGHFIELDS PRIVATE SCHOOL
Lower Cardrew Lane, Redruth,
Cornwall TR15 1SY
Website: highfields-school.com
Age Range: 4–16

ST JOSEPH'S SCHOOL
St Stephen's Hill, Launceston,
Cornwall PL15 8HN
Website:
www.st-josephs.cornwall.sch.uk
Age Range: 3–16 (Boys 3–11)

ST PIRAN'S SCHOOL
14 Trelissick Road, Hayle,
Cornwall TR27 4HY
Website: www.stpirans.net
Age Range: 3–16

TRURO HIGH SCHOOL
Falmouth Road, Truro, Cornwall
TR1 2HU
Website: www.trurohigh.co.uk
Age Range: 3–18 (Boys 3–5)

TRURO SCHOOL
Trennick Lane, Truro, Cornwall
TR1 1TH
Website: www.truroschool.com
Age Range: 11–18

CUMBRIA

PREPARATORY

HOLME PARK SCHOOL
Hill Top, New Hutton, Kendal,
Cumbria LA8 0AE
Website:
www.holme-park-school.com
Age Range: 2–12

HUNTER HALL SCHOOL
Frenchfield, Penrith, Cumbria
CA11 8UA
Age Range: 3–11

ST URSULAS CONVENT SCHOOL
Burnfoot, Wigton, Cumbria CA7
9HL
Website: www.stursulas.co.uk
Age Range: 2–11

SEDBERGH JUNIOR SCHOOL
Danson House, Loftus Hill,
Sedbergh, Cumbria LA10 5HG
Website:
www.sedberghjuniorschool.org
Age Range: 4–13

SENIOR

AUSTIN FRIARS ST MONICA'S SCHOOL

Etterby Scaur, Carlisle, Cumbria CA3 9PB
Website: www.austinfriars.cumbria.sch.uk
Age Range: 3–18

CASTERTON SCHOOL
Kirkby Lonsdale, Cumbria LA6 2SG
Website: www.castertonschool.co.uk
Age Range: 3–18
(Day boys 3–11)

CHETWYNDE SCHOOL*
Croslands, Rating Lane, Barrow-in-Furness, Cumbria LA13 0NY
Website: www.chetwynde.cumbria.sch.uk
Age Range: 3–18

DALLAM SCHOOL

Milnthorpe, Cumbria LA7 7DD
Website: www.dallam.eu
Age Range: 11–18

KESWICK SCHOOL
Vicarage Hill, Keswick, Cumbria CA12 5QE
Website: www.keswick.cumbria.sch.uk
Age Range: 11–18

LIME HOUSE SCHOOL

Holm Hill, Dalston, Carlisle, Cumbria CA5 7BX
Website: www.limehouseschool.co.uk
Age Range: 4–18

ST BEES SCHOOL

St Bees, Cumbria CA27 0DS
Website: www.st-bees-school.org
Age Range: 4–18

SEDBERGH SCHOOL

Sedbergh, Cumbria LA10 5HG
Website: www.sedberghschool.org
Age Range: 13–18

WINDERMERE SCHOOL

Patterdale Road, Windermere, Cumbria LA23 1NW
Website: www.windermereschool.co.uk
Age Range: 2–18

DERBYSHIRE

PREPARATORY

BARLBOROUGH HALL SCHOOL*
Barlborough, Chesterfield, Derbyshire S43 4TJ
Website: www.barlboroughhallschool.co.uk
Age Range: 3–11

EMMANUEL SCHOOL
Juniper Lodge, 43 Kedleston Road, Derby, Derbyshire DE22 1FP
Age Range: 3–14

FOREMARKE HALL

Milton, Derby, Derbyshire DE65 6EJ
Website: www.foremarke.org.uk
Age Range: 3–13

GATEWAY CHRISTIAN SCHOOL
Moor Lane, Dale Abbey, Ilkeston, Derbyshire DE7 4PP
Website: www.gatewayschool.org.uk
Age Range: 3–11

MORLEY HALL PREPARATORY SCHOOL

Hill House, Morley Road, Oakwood, Derby, Derbyshire DE21 4QZ
Website: www.morleyhallschool.co.uk
Age Range: 3–11

THE OLD VICARAGE SCHOOL

11 Church Lane, Darley Abbey, Derby, Derbyshire DE22 1EW
Website: www.oldvicarageschool.co.uk
Age Range: 3–11

S. ANSELM'S SCHOOL
Bakewell, Derbyshire DE45 1DP
Website: www.sanselms.co.uk
Age Range: 3–13

ST JOSEPH'S CONVENT
42 Newbold Road, Chesterfield, Derbyshire S41 7PL
Website: www.st-josephs-convent-sch.org.uk
Age Range: 2–11

ST PETER & ST PAUL SCHOOL
Brambling House, Hady Hill, Chesterfield, Derbyshire S41 0EF
Website: www.spsp.org.uk
Age Range: 4–11

ST WYSTAN'S SCHOOL

High Street, Repton, Derbyshire
DE65 6GE
Website: www.stwystans.org.uk
Age Range: 2–11

SENIOR

DERBY GRAMMAR SCHOOL

Rykneld Road, Littleover, Derby,
Derbyshire DE23 4BX
Website:
www.derbygrammar.co.uk
Age Range: 7–18

DERBY HIGH SCHOOL

Hillsway, Littleover, Derby,
Derbyshire DE23 3DT
Website:
www.derbyhigh.derby.sch.uk
Age Range: 3–18

MICHAEL HOUSE STEINER SCHOOL

The Field, Shipley, Heanor,
Derbyshire DE75 7JH
Website:
www.michaelhouseschool.co.uk
www.steinerwaldorf.org.uk
Age Range: 4–16

MOUNT ST MARY'S COLLEGE*

Spinkhill, Derbyshire S21 3YL
Website: www.msmcollege.com
Age Range: 11–18 (Boarders
are accepted into Barlborough
Hall at age 10.)

OCKBROOK SCHOOL

The Settlement, Ockbrook,
Derby, Derbyshire DE72 3RJ
Website:
www.ockbrook.derby.sch.uk
Age Range: 3–18

REPTON SCHOOL

Repton, Derby, Derbyshire
DE65 6FH
Website: www.repton.org.uk
Age Range: 13–18

DEVON

NURSERY AND PRE-PREP

ST MICHAEL'S

Tawstock Court, Tawstock,
Barnstaple, Devon EX31 3HY
Website:
www.stmichaels-nursery.org
Age Range: 0–5

PREPARATORY

THE ABBEY SCHOOL
Hampton Court, St Marychurch,
Torquay, Devon TQ1 4PR
Website:
www.abbeyschool.co.uk

ABBOTSBURY SCHOOL
90 Torquay Road, Newton
Abbot, Devon TQ12 2JD
Age Range: 2–7

BLUNDELL'S PREPARATORY SCHOOL
Milestones House, Blundell's
Road, Tiverton, Devon EX16
4NA
Website: www.blundells.org
Age Range: 3–11

THE DOLPHIN SCHOOL
Raddenstile Lane, Exmouth,
Devon EX8 2JH
Website:
www.dolphin-school.org.uk
Age Range: 3–11

EXETER CATHEDRAL SCHOOL
The Chantry, Palace Gate,
Exeter, Devon EX1 1HX
Website: www.exetercs.org
Age Range: 3–13

EXETER JUNIOR SCHOOL
Victoria Park Road, Exeter,
Devon EX2 4NS
Website:
www.exeterschool.org.uk
Age Range: 7–11

FLETEWOOD SCHOOL
88 North Road East, Plymouth,
Devon PL4 6AN
Website:
www.fletewoodschool.co.uk
Age Range: 3–11

KELLY COLLEGE PREPARATORY SCHOOL
Hazeldon House, Parkwood
Road, Tavistock, Devon PL19
0JS
Website:
www.kellycollegeprep.com
Age Range: 2–11

KING'S SCHOOL AND NURSERY
● 🏠

Hartley Road, Mannamead, Plymouth, Devon PL3 5LW
Website:
www.kingsschool-plymouth.co.uk

MARIA MONTESSORI SCHOOL
● 🏠

3 St Leonards Place, Exeter, Devon EX2 4LZ
Website:
www.exeter-montessori.com
Age Range: 3–7

MOUNT HOUSE SCHOOL
● 🏠

Mount Tavy Road, Tavistock, Devon PL19 9JL
Website:
www.mounthouse.devon.sch.uk
Age Range: 3–13

NEW SCHOOL
● 🏠

The Avenue, Exminster, Exeter, Devon EX6 8AT
Website: www.thenewschool.
supanet.com
Age Range: 3–8

PARK SCHOOL
● 🏠

Park Road, Dartington, Totnes, Devon TQ9 6EQ
Website:
www.park-school.org.uk
Age Range: 3–11

PLYMOUTH COLLEGE PREPRATORY SCHOOL
● 🏠

St Dunstan's Abbey, The Millfields, Plymouth, Devon PL1 3JL
Website:
www.plymouthcollege.com
Age Range: 3–11 (We have only just begun to offer boarding to Years 5 & 6. We do not have a Prep Boarding House but pupils reside in the Boarding House at our Senior School site)

ST CHRISTOPHERS SCHOOL
● 🏠

Mount Barton, Staverton, Totnes, Devon TQ9 6PF
Website: www.st-christophers.
devon.sch.uk
Age Range: 3–11

ST PETER'S SCHOOL
● 🏠

Harefield, Lympstone, Exmouth, Devon EX8 5AU
Website:
www.stpetersprep.co.uk
Age Range: 3–13

WEST BUCKLAND PREPARATORY SCHOOL
● 🏠

West Buckland, Barnstaple, Devon EX32 0SX
Website: www.westbuckland.
devon.sch.uk
Age Range: 3–11

SENIOR

BLUNDELL'S SCHOOL*
● 🏠 ▲

Blundell's Road, Tiverton, Devon EX16 4DN
Website: www.blundells.org
Age Range: 3–18

BRAMDEAN SCHOOL
● 🏠 ▲

Richmond Lodge, Homefield Road, Heavitree, Exeter, Devon EX1 2QR
Website:
www.bramdeanschool.co.uk
Age Range: 3–18

EDGEHILL COLLEGE
● 🏠 ▲

Northdown Road, Bideford, Devon EX39 3LY
Website:
www.edgehill.devon.sch.uk
Age Range: 2–18

EXETER SCHOOL
● 🏠 ▲

Victoria Park Road, Exeter, Devon EX2 4NS
Website:
www.exeterschool.org.uk
Age Range: 7–18

KELLY COLLEGE
● 🏠 ▲

Parkwood Road, Tavistock, Devon PL19 0HZ
Website: www.kellycollege.com
Age Range: 11–18

KINGSLEY SCHOOL
● 🏠 ◆ ▲

Kingsley School, Northdown Road, Bideford, Devon EX39 3LY
Website:
www.kingsleyschoolbideford.co.uk
Age Range: 11–18

MAGDALEN COURT SCHOOL
● 🏠 ▲

Mulberry House, Victoria Park Road, Exeter, Devon EX2 4NU
Website: www.
magdalencourtschool.co.uk
Age Range: 2–18

THE MAYNARD SCHOOL
● 🏠 ▲

Denmark Road, Exeter, Devon EX1 1SJ
Website: www.maynard.co.uk
Age Range: 7–18 (A selective independent day school for girls aged 7–17.)

PLYMOUTH COLLEGE
● 🏠 ★ ▲

Ford Park, Plymouth, Devon PL4 6RN
Website:
www.plymouthcollege.com
Age Range: 11–18

ST MARGARET'S SCHOOL
● 🏠 ▲

147 Magdalen Road, Exeter, Devon EX2 4TS
Website: www.stmargarets-school.co.uk
Age Range: 7–18

ST WILFRID'S SCHOOL
● 🏠

29 St David's Hill, Exeter, Devon EX4 4DA
Website:
www.stwilfrids.devon.sch.uk
Age Range: 5–16

SANDS SCHOOL

Greylands, 48 East Street,
Ashburton, Devon TQ13 7AX
Website:
www.sands-school.co.uk
Age Range: 11–17

STOODLEY KNOWLE SCHOOL

Ansteys Cove Road, Torquay,
Devon TQ1 2JB
Website: www.stoodleyknowle.
devon.sch.uk
Age Range: 2–18

STOVER SCHOOL*

Stover, Newton Abbot, Devon
TQ12 6QG
Website: www.stover.co.uk
Age Range: 3–18

SHEBBEAR COLLEGE

Shebbear, Beaworthy, Devon
EX21 5HJ
Website:
www.shebbearcollege.co.uk
Age Range: 5–18

THE SMALL SCHOOL

Fore Street, Hartland, Bideford,
Devon EX39 6AB
Website:
www.thesmallschool.org.uk
Age Range: 11–16

SOUTH DEVON STEINER SCHOOL

Hood Manor, Dartington, Devon
TQ9 6AB
Website:
steiner-south-devon.org
Age Range: 3–16

TOWER HOUSE SCHOOL

Fisher Street, Paignton, Devon
TQ4 5EW
Age Range: 2–16

TRINITY SCHOOL

Buckeridge Road, Teignmouth,
Devon TQ14 8LY
Website:
www.trinityschool.co.uk
Age Range: 4–20

WEST BUCKLAND SCHOOL

Barnstaple, Devon EX32 0SX
Website: www.westbuckland.
devon.sch.uk
Age Range: 3–18

INDEPENDENT SIXTH FORM COLLEGE / TUTORIAL COLLEGE

EXETER TUTORIAL COLLEGE

44/46 Magdalen Road, Exeter,
Devon EX2 4TE
Website:
www.tutorialcollege.com

INTERNATIONAL SCHOOLS AND INTERNATIONAL STUDY CENTRES

SIDMOUTH INTERNATIONAL SCHOOL

May Cottage, Sidmouth, Devon
EX10 8EN
Website: www.sidmouth.int.co.uk
Age Range: 8–13+

DORSET

PREPARATORY

BOURNEMOUTH COLLEGIATE PREP SCHOOL

40 St Osmund's Road,
Parkstone, Poole, Dorset
BH14 9JY
Website: www.bournemouth
collegiateschool.co.uk
Age Range: 3–11

BUCKHOLME TOWERS

18 Commercial Road,
Parkstone, Poole, Dorset BH14
0JW
Website:
www.buckholmetowers.com
Age Range: 3–12

CASTLE COURT PREPARATORY SCHOOL

The Knoll House, Knoll Lane,
Corfe Mullen, Wimborne, Dorset
BH21 3RF
Website: www.castlecourt.com
Age Range: 3–13

CLAYESMORE PREPARATORY SCHOOL

Iwerne Minster, Blandford
Forum, Dorset DT11 8PH
Website: www.clayesmore.com
Age Range: 3–13 (The age of
entry in to the Pre-Prep of the
school is 'rising 3'.)

DUMPTON SCHOOL

Deans Grove House, Wimborne,
Dorset BH21 7AF
Website: www.dumpton.com
Age Range: 2–13

KNIGHTON HOUSE
● 🏠
Durweston, Blandford Forum,
Dorset DT11 0PY
Website: www.knightonhouse.
dorset.sch.uk
Age Range: (Day boys 4–7)

THE PARK SCHOOL
● 🏠
Queen's Park South Drive,
Bournemouth, Dorset BH8 9BJ
Age Range: 4–11

PORT REGIS PREPARATORY SCHOOL
● 🏠
Motcombe Park, Shaftesbury,
Dorset SP7 9QA
Website: www.portregis.com
Age Range: 3–13

ST MARTIN'S SCHOOL
● 🏠
15 Stokewood Road,
Bournemouth, Dorset BH3 7NA
Website:
www.stmartinsschool.co.uk
Age Range: 4–12

ST THOMAS GARNET'S SCHOOL
● 🏠
Parkwood Road, Boscombe,
Bournemouth, Dorset BH5 2BH
Website: www.stg.web-page.net
Age Range: 5–11

SUNNINGHILL PREPARATORY SCHOOL
● 🏠
South Court, South Walks,
Dorchester, Dorset DT1 1EB
Website:
www.sunninghillprep.co.uk
Age Range: 3–13

TALBOT HOUSE PREPARATORY SCHOOL
● 🏠
8 Firs Glen Road, Bournemouth,
Dorset BH9 2LR
Age Range: 3–12

THORNLOW PREPARATORY SCHOOL
● 🏠
Connaught Road, Weymouth,
Dorset DT4 0SA
Website: www.thornlow.co.uk
Age Range: 3–13

YARRELLS SCHOOL
● 🏠
Yarrells House, Upton, Poole,
Dorset BH16 5EU
Website: www.yarrells.co.uk
Age Range: 2–13

SENIOR

BOURNEMOUTH COLLEGIATE SCHOOL
● 🏠 ▲
College Road, Bournemouth,
Dorset BH5 2DY
Website: www.bournemouth
collegiateschool.co.uk
Age Range: 11–18

BRYANSTON SCHOOL
● 🏠 ▲
Blandford Forum, Dorset DT11
0PX
Website: www.bryanston.co.uk
Age Range: 13–18

CANFORD SCHOOL
● 🏠 ▲
Wimborne, Dorset BH21 3AD
Website: www.canford.com
Age Range: 13–18

CLAYESMORE
 ● 🏠 ◆ ▲
Iwerne Minster, Blandford
Forum, Dorset DT11 8LL
Website: www.clayesmore.com
Age Range: 3–18 (Boys and
girls in the Pre-Prep join the
school as 'rising' 3 year olds.)

INTERNATIONAL COLLEGE, SHERBORNE SCHOOL
● 🏠
Newell Grange, Sherborne,
Dorset DT9 4EZ
Website: www.sherborne-ic.net
Age Range: 11–17

LEWESTON SCHOOL
● 🏠 ▲
Sherborne, Dorset DT9 6EN
Website: www.leweston.co.uk
Age Range: 2–18 (Boys 2–11)

MILTON ABBEY SCHOOL*
● 🏠 ◆ ▲
Milton Abbas, Blandford Forum,
Dorset DT11 0BZ
Website:
www.miltonabbey.co.uk
Age Range: 13–18

ST MARY'S SCHOOL, DORSET
● 🏠 ▲
Shaftesbury, Dorset SP7 9LP
Website:
www.st-marys-shaftesbury.co.uk
Age Range: 9–18

SHERBORNE GIRLS
● 🏠 ★ ▲
Bradford Road, Sherborne,
Dorset DT9 3QN
Website: www.sherborne.com
Age Range: 11–18

SHERBORNE SCHOOL
● 🏠 ★ ▲
Abbey Road, Sherborne, Dorset
DT9 3AP
Website: www.sherborne.org
Age Range: 13–18

TALBOT HEATH
● 🏠 ▲
Rothesay Road, Bournemouth,
Dorset BH4 9NJ
Website:
www.talbotheath.org.uk
Age Range: 3–18 (Boys 3–7)

COUNTY DURHAM

PREPARATORY

THE CHORISTER SCHOOL
● 🏠
The College, Durham, County Durham DH1 3EL
Website:
www.choristers.durham.sch.uk
Age Range: 4–13

HURWORTH HOUSE SCHOOL
● 🏠 ▲
The Green, Hurworth-on-Tees, Darlington, County Durham DL2 2AD
Website:
www.hurworthhouse.co.uk
Age Range: 3–18

YARM AT RAVENTHORPE SCHOOL
● 🏠
96 Carmel Road North, Darlington, County Durham DL3 8JB
Website: www.yarmschool.org
Age Range: 3–11

SENIOR

BARNARD CASTLE SCHOOL
● 🏠 ▲
Barnard Castle, County Durham DL12 8UN
Website: www.
barnardcastleschool.org.uk
Age Range: 4–18

DURHAM HIGH SCHOOL FOR GIRLS
● 🏠 ▲
Farewell Hall, Durham, County Durham DH1 3TB
Website: www.dhsfg.org.uk
Age Range: 3–18

DURHAM SCHOOL
● 🏠 ▲
Quarryheads Lane, Durham, County Durham DH1 4SZ
Website: www.durhamschool.
co.uk/prospectus.htm
Age Range: 3–18

POLAM HALL
● 🏠 ▲
Grange Road, Darlington, County Durham DL1 5PA
Website: www.polamhall.com
Age Range: 2–18
(Co-educational Junior School from age 2 to Year 4. Separate teaching Year 5 to Year 11. Co-educational Sixth Form)

ESSEX

PREPARATORY

ALLEYN COURT PREPARATORY SCHOOL
● 🏠
Wakering Road, Great Wakering, Southend-on-Sea, Essex SS3 0PW
Website: www.alleyn-court.co.uk
Age Range: 2–11

AVON HOUSE
● 🏠 ◆
490 High Road, Woodford Green, Essex IG8 0PN
Website:
www.avonhouse.org.uk
Age Range: 3–11

BEEHIVE PREPARATORY SCHOOL
● 🏠
233 Beehive Lane, Redbridge, Ilford, Essex IG4 5ED
Age Range: 4–11

COLLEGE SAINT-PIERRE
● 🏠
16 Leigh Road, Leigh-on-Sea, Essex SS9 1LE
Website:
www.saintpierreschool.com
Age Range: 2–11

COOPERSALE HALL SCHOOL
● 🏠
Flux's Lane, off Steward's Green Road, Epping, Essex CM16 7PE
Website:
www.coopersalehallschool.co.uk
Age Range: 3–11

CROWSTONE PREPARATORY SCHOOL
● 🏠
121–123 Crowstone Road, Westcliff-on-Sea, Essex SS0 8LH
Website:
crowstoneprepschool.com
Age Range: 2–11

THE DAIGLEN SCHOOL
● 🏠
68 Palmerston Road, Buckhurst Hill, Essex IG9 5LG
Website:
www.daiglenschool.co.uk
Age Range: 3–11

DAME BRADBURY'S SCHOOL

Ashdon Road, Saffron Walden,
Essex CB10 2AL
Website:
www.damebradburys.com
Age Range: 3–11

EASTCOURT INDEPENDENT SCHOOL

1 Eastwood Road, Goodmayes,
Ilford, Essex IG3 8UW
Age Range: 4–11

ELM GREEN PREPARATORY SCHOOL

Parsonage Lane, Little Baddow,
Chelmsford, Essex CM3 4SU
Website:
www.elmgreen.essex.sch.uk
Age Range: 4–11

GIDEA PARK COLLEGE

Balgores House, 2 Balgores
Lane, Romford, Essex RM2 5JR
Website:
www.gideaparkcollege.co.uk
Age Range: 2–11

GLENARM COLLEGE

20 Coventry Road, Ilford, Essex
IG1 4QR
Website:
www.glenarmcollege.com
Age Range: 3–11

GOODRINGTON SCHOOL

17 Walden Road, Emerson Park,
Hornchurch, Essex RM11 2JT
Website: www.goodrington.org
Age Range: 3–11

HEATHCOTE SCHOOL

Eves Corner, Danbury,
Chelmsford, Essex CM3 4QB
Website:
www.heathcoteschool.co.uk
Age Range: 2–11

HERINGTON HOUSE SCHOOL

Mount Avenue, Hutton,
Brentwood, Essex CM13 2NS
Website:
www.heringtonhouseschool.
co.uk
Age Range: 3–11

HOLMWOOD HOUSE

Chitts Hill, Lexden, Colchester,
Essex CO3 9ST
Website:
www.holmwood.essex.sch.uk
Age Range: 4–13

ILFORD PREPARATORY SCHOOL

Carnegie Buildings, 785 High
Road, Ilford, Essex IG3 8RW
Website: www.ilfordprep.co.uk
Age Range: 3–11

ILFORD URSULINE PREPARATORY SCHOOL

2–4 Coventry Road, Ilford,
Essex IG1 4QR
Website:
www.ilfordursuline-prep.org.uk
Age Range: 3–11

LITTLEGARTH SCHOOL

Horkesley Park, Nayland,
Colchester, Essex CO6 4JR
Website:
www.littlegarth.essex.sch.uk
Age Range: 2–11

LOYOLA PREPARATORY SCHOOL

103 Palmerston Road,
Buckhurst Hill, Essex IG9 5NH
Website:
www.loyola.essex.sch.uk
Age Range: 3–11

MALDON COURT PREPARATORY SCHOOL

Silver Street, Maldon, Essex
CM9 4QE
Website:
www.maldoncourtschool.org
Age Range: 3–11

OAKFIELDS MONTESSORI SCHOOLS LTD

Harwood Hall, Harwood Hall
Lane, Corbets Tey, Upminster,
Essex RM14 2YG
Website: www.oakfields
montessorischool.org.uk
Age Range: 2–11

OAKLANDS SCHOOL

8 Albion Hill, Loughton, Essex
IG10 4RA
Website:
www.oaklandsschool.co.uk
Age Range: 2–11

OXFORD HOUSE SCHOOL

2 Lexden Road, Colchester,
Essex CO3 3NE
Website:
www.oxfordhouseschool.net
Age Range: 2–11

ST ANNE'S PREPARATORY SCHOOL

154 New London Road,
Chelmsford, Essex CM2 0AW
Website: www.stannesprep.
essex.sch.uk
Age Range: 3–11

ST AUBYN'S SCHOOL

Bunces Lane, Woodford Green,
Essex IG8 9DU
Website: www.staubyns.com
Age Range: 3–13

ST CEDD'S SCHOOL

Maltese Road, Chelmsford,
Essex CM1 2PB
Website: www.stcedds.org.uk
Age Range: 4–11

ST MARGARET'S SCHOOL

Gosfield Hall Park, Gosfield,
Halstead, Essex CO9 1SE
Age Range: 2–11

ST MARY'S HARE PARK SCHOOL

● 🏠

South Drive, Gidea Park,
Romford, Essex RM2 6HH
Website: www.smhp.ik.org
Age Range: 2–11

ST MICHAEL'S SCHOOL

● 🏠

198 Hadleigh Road, Leigh-on-
Sea, Essex SS9 2LP
Website:
www.stmichaelsschool.com
Age Range: 3–11

ST PHILIP'S PRIORY SCHOOL

● 🏠

178 New London Road,
Chelmsford, Essex CM2 0AR
Age Range: 4–11

ST PHILOMENA'S PREPARATORY SCHOOL

● 🏠

Hadleigh Road, Frinton-on-Sea,
Essex CO13 9HQ
Website:
www.stphilomenas.com
Age Range: 3–11

URSULINE PREPARATORY SCHOOL

● 🏠

Old Great Ropers, Great Ropers
Lane, Warley, Brentwood, Essex
CM13 3HR
Website:
www.ursulineprepwarley.co.uk
Age Range: 3–11

WIDFORD LODGE

● 🏠

Widford Road, Chelmsford,
Essex CM2 9AN
Website:
www.widfordlodge.co.uk
Age Range: 2–11

WOODFORD GREEN PREPARATORY SCHOOL

● 🏠

Glengall Road, Woodford
Green, Essex IG8 0BZ
Website:
www.woodfordgreenprep.co.uk
Age Range: 3–11

WOODLANDS SCHOOLS

● 🏠

Warley Street, Great Warley,
Brentwood, Essex CM13 3LA
Website:
www.woodlandsschools.co.uk
Age Range: 3–11

SENIOR

BANCROFT'S SCHOOL

● 🏠 ▲

Woodford Green, Essex IG8
0RF
Website: www.bancrofts.org
Age Range: 7–18

BRAESIDE SCHOOL FOR GIRLS

● 🏠

130 High Road, Buckhurst Hill,
Essex IG9 5SD
Website:
www.braesideschool.co.uk
Age Range: 3–16 (Independent
day school for girls aged 3 to 16
years)

BRENTWOOD SCHOOL

● 🏠 ★ ▲

Ingrave Road, Brentwood,
Essex CM15 8AS
Website:
www.brentwoodschool.co.uk
Age Range: 3–18 (Single-sex
Education aged 11–16)

CHIGWELL SCHOOL

● 🏠 ▲

High Road, Chigwell, Essex IG7
6QF
Website:
www.chigwell-school.org
Age Range: 7–18

COLCHESTER HIGH SCHOOL

● 🏠

Wellesley Road, Colchester,
Essex CO3 3HD
Website:
www.colchesterhighschool.co.uk
Age Range: 3–16

CRANBROOK

● 🏠

34 Mansfield Road, Ilford,
Essex IG1 3BD
Website:
www.cranbrook-school.co.uk
Age Range: 3–16

FELSTED SCHOOL

● 🏠 ★ ▲

Felsted, Essex CM6 3LL
Website: www.felsted.org
Age Range: 13–18 (Felsted
Prep School accepts day and
boarding boys and girls from
ages 4–12. Pupils are able to
board from age 8.)

FRIENDS' SCHOOL

● 🏠 ▲

Mount Pleasant Road, Saffron
Walden, Essex CB11 3EB
Website: www.friends.org.uk
Age Range: 3–18

GOSFIELD SCHOOL

● 🏠 ▲

Halstead Road, Gosfield,
Halstead, Essex CO9 1PF
Website:
www.gosfieldschool.org.uk
Age Range: 4–18

IMMANUEL SCHOOL

● 🏠

Havering Grange Centre,
Havering Road, Romford, Essex
RM1 4HR
Website:
www.immanuelministries.org.uk
Age Range: 3–16

NEW HALL SCHOOL

● 🏠 ▲

The Avenue, Boreham,
Chelmsford, Essex CM3 3HS
Website:
www.newhallschool.co.uk
Age Range: 3–18 (Co-ed
Preparatory School (3–11)
Boys' Division (11–16)
Girls' Division (11–16)
Co-ed Sixth Form
Girls and boys between the
ages of 11–16 are educated in
a single-sex classes but with the
benefit of a mixed environment)

PARK SCHOOL FOR GIRLS
● 🏠

20–22 Park Avenue, Ilford,
Essex IG1 4RS
Website:
www.parkschool.org.uk
Age Range: 3–16

RAPHAEL INDEPENDENT SCHOOL
● 🏠

Park Lane, Hornchurch, Essex
RM11 1XY
Website:
www.raphaelschool.com
Age Range: 4–16

ST HILDA'S SCHOOL
● 🏠

15 Imperial Avenue, Westcliff-
on-Sea, Essex SS0 8NE
Website:
www.sthildasschool.co.uk
Age Range: 2–16 (Boys 2–7)

ST JOHN'S SCHOOL
● 🏠

Stock Road, Billericay, Essex
CM12 0AR
Website: www.stjohnsschool.net
Age Range: 3–16

ST MARY'S SCHOOL
● 🏠

91 Lexden Road, Colchester,
Essex CO3 3RB
Website:
www.stmarysschool.org.uk
Age Range: 4–16

ST NICHOLAS SCHOOL
● 🏠

Hillingdon House, Hobbs Cross
Road, Harlow, Essex CM17 0NJ
Website:
www.saintnicholasschool.net
Age Range: 4–16

THORPE HALL SCHOOL
● 🏠

Wakering Road, Southend-on-
Sea, Essex SS1 3RD
Website:
www.thorpehall.southend.sch.uk
Age Range: 2–16

GLOUCESTERSHIRE

PREPARATORY

AIRTHRIE SCHOOL
● 🏠

27–29 Christchurch Road,
Cheltenham, Gloucestershire
GL50 2NY
Website:
www.airthrie-school.co.uk
Age Range: 3–11

BEAUDESERT PARK SCHOOL
● 🏠

Minchinhampton, Stroud,
Gloucestershire GL6 9AF
Website:
www.beaudesert.gloucs.sch.uk
Age Range: 4–13

BERKHAMPSTEAD SCHOOL
● 🏠

Pittville Circus Road,
Cheltenham, Gloucestershire
GL52 2QA
Website:
www.berkhampsteadschool.
co.uk
Age Range: 3–11

CHELTENHAM COLLEGE JUNIOR SCHOOL
● 🏠

Thirlestaine Road, Cheltenham,
Gloucestershire GL53 7AB
Website:
www.cheltcoll.gloucs.sch.uk
Age Range: 3–13

DEAN CLOSE PREPARATORY SCHOOL
● 🏠

Lansdown Road, Cheltenham,
Gloucestershire GL51 6QS
Website: www.deanclose.org.uk
Age Range: 3–13

THE DORMER HOUSE PNEU SCHOOL
● 🏠

High Street, Moreton-in-Marsh,
Gloucestershire GL56 0AD
Website:
www.dormerhouse.co.uk
Age Range: 2–11

HATHEROP CASTLE SCHOOL
● 🏠

Hatherop, Cirencester,
Gloucestershire GL7 3NB
Website:
www.hatheropcastle.co.uk
Age Range: 2–13

HOPELANDS SCHOOL
● 🏠

38 Regent Street, Stonehouse,
Gloucestershire GL10 2AD
Website: www.hopelands.org.uk
Age Range: 3–11

KITEBROOK HOUSE
● 🏠

Moreton-in-Marsh,
Gloucestershire GL56 0RP
Website:
www.kitebrookhouse.com
Age Range: 4–13 (Boys 4–8)

THE RICHARD PATE SCHOOL
● 🏠

Southern Road, Leckhampton,
Cheltenham, Gloucestershire
GL53 9RP
Website: www.richardpate.co.uk
Age Range: 3–11

ROSE HILL SCHOOL

Alderley, Wotton-under-Edge, Gloucestershire GL12 7QT
Website:
www.rosehillschool.com
Age Range: 3–13

ROSE HILL WESTONBIRT SCHOOL

Tetbury, Gloucestershire GL8 8QG
Website:
www.querns.gloucs.sch.uk
Age Range: 3–13

ST ANTHONYS SCHOOL

93 Bellevue Road, Cinderford, Gloucestershire GL14 2AA
Website:
www.stanthonysconvent.gloucs.sch.uk
Age Range: 3–11

WYCLIFFE PREPARATORY SCHOOL

Ryeford Hall, Stonehouse, Gloucestershire GL10 2LD
Website: www.wycliffe.co.uk
Age Range: 2–13

SENIOR

THE ACORN SCHOOL

Church Street, Nailsworth, Gloucestershire GL6 0BP
Website:
www.theacornschool.com
Age Range: 6–19

BREDON SCHOOL*

Pull Court, Bushley, Tewkesbury, Gloucestershire GL20 6AH
Website: www.bredonschool.org
Age Range: 4–18

CHELTENHAM COLLEGE

Bath Road, Cheltenham, Gloucestershire GL53 7LD
Website:
www.cheltenhamcollege.org
Age Range: 13–18

CHELTENHAM LADIES' COLLEGE

Bayshill Road, Cheltenham, Gloucestershire GL50 3EP
Website:
www.cheltladiescollege.org
Age Range: 11–18

DEAN CLOSE SCHOOL

Shelburne Road, Cheltenham, Gloucestershire GL51 6HE
Website: www.deanclose.org.uk
Age Range: 13–18

GLOUCESTERSHIRE ISLAMIC SECONDARY SCHOOL FOR GIRLS

Sinope Street, off Widden Street, Gloucester, Gloucestershire GL1 4AW
Age Range: 11–16

THE KING'S SCHOOL

Gloucester, Gloucestershire GL1 2BG
Website: www.thekingsschool.co.uk
Age Range: 3–18

RENDCOMB COLLEGE*

Rendcomb, Cirencester, Gloucestershire GL7 7HA
Website:
www.rendcombcollege.org.uk
Age Range: 3–18

ST EDWARD'S SCHOOL CHELTENHAM

Cirencester Road, Cheltenham, Gloucestershire GL53 8EY
Website: www.stedwards.co.uk
Age Range: 11–18

THE SCHOOL OF THE LION

Beauchamp House, Churcham, Gloucester, Gloucestershire GL2 8AA
Website:
www.schoolofthelion.org.uk
Age Range: 4–18

WESTONBIRT SCHOOL

Tetbury, Gloucestershire GL8 8QG
Website: www.westonbirt.gloucs.sch.uk
Age Range: 11–18

WYCLIFFE COLLEGE

Bath Road, Stonehouse, Gloucestershire GL10 2JQ
Website: www.wycliffe.co.uk
Age Range: 2–18

WYNSTONES SCHOOL

Church Lane, Whaddon, Gloucester, Gloucestershire GL4 0UF
Website: www.wynstones.com
Age Range: 3–19

SOUTH GLOUCESTERSHIRE

PREPARATORY

SILVERHILL SCHOOL

Swan Lane, Winterbourne,
South Gloucestershire BS36
1RL
Website:
www.silverhillschool.co.uk
Age Range: 2–11

HAMPSHIRE

NURSERY AND PRE-PREP

CHERUBS PRE-SCHOOL

13 Milvil Road, Lee-on-the-
Solent, Hampshire PO13 9LU
Age Range: 2–8

STOCKTON HOUSE SCHOOL

Stockton Avenue, Fleet,
Hampshire GU51 4NS
Website:
www.stocktonhouseschool.co.uk
Age Range: 2–4

PREPARATORY

BALLARD SCHOOL

Fernhill Lane, New Milton,
Hampshire BH25 5SU
Website: www.ballardschool.
co.uk
Age Range: 2–16

BEDALES PREP SCHOOL, DUNHURST*

Alton Road, Steep, Petersfield,
Hampshire GU32 2DR
Website: www.bedales.org.uk
Age Range: 8–13

BOUNDARY OAK SCHOOL

Roche Court, Wickham Road,
Fareham, Hampshire PO17 5BL
Website:
www.boundaryoak.co.uk
Age Range: 3–13

CHURCHERS COLLEGE JUNIOR SCHOOL

Midhurst Road, Liphook,
Hampshire GU30 7HT
Website:
www.churcherscollege.com
Age Range: 4–11

DANESHILL SCHOOL

Stratfield Turgis, Basingstoke,
Hampshire RG27 0AR
Website:
www.daneshillprepschool.com
Age Range: 2–13

DURLSTON COURT

Becton Lane, Barton-on-Sea,
New Milton, Hampshire BH25
7AQ
Website:
www.durlstoncourt.co.uk
Age Range: 2–13

FARLEIGH SCHOOL

Red Rice, Andover, Hampshire
SP11 7PW
Website:
www.farleighschool.com
Age Range: 3–13

FORRES SANDLE MANOR

Station Road, Fordingbridge,
Hampshire SP6 1NS
Website: www.fsmschool.com
Age Range: 3–13

GLENHURST SCHOOL

16 Beechworth Road, Havant,
Hampshire PO9 1AX
Website:
www.glenhurstschool.co.uk
Age Range: 2–9

GREY HOUSE PREPARATORY SCHOOL

Mount Pleasant Road, Hartley
Wintney, Hook, Hampshire
RG27 8PW
Website:
www.greyhouseschool.com
Age Range: 4–11

HIGHFIELD SCHOOL

Highfield Lane, Liphook,
Hampshire GU30 7LQ
Website:
www.highfieldschool.org.uk
Age Range: 8–13

HORDLE WALHAMPTON SCHOOL

Lymington, Hampshire SO41
5ZG
Website:
www.hordlewalhampton.co.uk
Age Range: 2–13

KINGS PRIMARY SCHOOL

26 Quob Lane, West End,
Southampton, Hampshire SO30
3HN
Age Range: 5–11

KINGSCOURT SCHOOL

Catherington House,
Catherington Lane,
Catherington, Hampshire PO8
9NJ
Website: www.kingscourt.org.uk
Age Range: 2–11

MARYCOURT SCHOOL

27 Crescent Road, Alverstoke,
Gosport, Hampshire PO12 2DJ
Age Range: 2–9

THE PILGRIMS' SCHOOL
3 The Close, Winchester,
Hampshire SO23 9LT
Website:
www.pilgrims-school.co.uk
Age Range: 7–13

PRINCE'S MEAD SCHOOL
Worthy Park House,
Kingsworthy, Winchester,
Hampshire SO21 1AN
Website:
www.princesmeadschool.org.uk
Age Range: 3–11

ST NEOT'S PREPARATORY SCHOOL

St Neots Road, Eversley, Hook,
Hampshire RG27 0PN
Website:
www.st-neots-prep.co.uk
Age Range: 1–13

ST SWITHUN'S JUNIOR SCHOOL

Alresford Road, Winchester,
Hampshire S021 1HA
Website: www.stswithuns.com
Age Range: 3–11
(Accepts Boys 3–7)

ST WINIFRED'S SCHOOL

17–19 Winn Road,
Southampton, Hampshire S017
1EJ
Website:
www.stwinifreds.southampton.
sch.uk
Age Range: 2–11

THE STROUD SCHOOL

Highwood House, Highwood
Lane, Romsey, Hampshire SO51
9ZH
Website:
www.stroud-romsey.com
Age Range: 3–13

SHERBORNE HOUSE SCHOOL

Lakewood Road, Chandler's
Ford, Eastleigh, Hampshire
SO53 1EU
Website:
www.sherbornehouse.co.uk
Age Range: 3–11

TWYFORD SCHOOL
Twyford, Winchester, Hampshire
SO21 1NW
Website:
www.twyfordschool.com
Age Range: 3–13

WOODHILL PREPARATORY SCHOOL

Brook Lane, Botley,
Southampton, Hampshire SO30
2ER
Website:
www.woodhill.hants.sch.uk
Age Range: 3–11

WOODHILL SCHOOL

61 Brownhill Road, Chandler's
Ford, Hampshire SO53 2EH
Website:
www.woodhill.hants.sch.uk
Age Range: 3–11

YATELEY MANOR PREPARATORY SCHOOL

51 Reading Road, Yateley,
Hampshire GU46 7UQ
Website:
www.yateleymanor.com
Age Range: 3–13

SENIOR

ALTON CONVENT SCHOOL

Anstey Lane, Alton, Hampshire
GU34 2NG
Website:
www.alton-convent.hants.sch.uk
Age Range: 2–18 (Co-ed 2–11)

BEDALES SCHOOL*
Petersfield, Hampshire GU32
2DG
Website: www.bedales.org.uk
Age Range: 13–18

BROCKWOOD PARK SCHOOL
Bramdean, Hampshire SO24
0LQ
Website:
www.brockwood.org.uk
Age Range: 14–19

DITCHAM PARK SCHOOL
Ditcham Park, Petersfield,
Hampshire GU31 5RN
Website: www.ditchampark.com
Age Range: 4–16

FARNBOROUGH HILL
Farnborough Road,
Farnborough, Hampshire GU14
8AT
Website:
www.farnborough-hill.org.uk
Age Range: 11–18

THE GREGG SCHOOL
Townhill Park House, Cutbush
Lane, Southampton, Hampshire
SO18 2GF
Website:
www.gregg.southampton.sch.uk
Age Range: 11–16

HAMPSHIRE COLLEGIATE SCHOOL, UCST

Embley Park, Romsey,
Hampshire SO51 6ZE
Website:
www.hampshirecs.org.uk
Age Range: 3–18

KING EDWARD VI SCHOOL
Wilton Road, Southampton,
Hampshire SO15 5UQ
Website: www.kes.hants.sch.uk
Age Range: 11–18

THE KING'S SCHOOL
Basingstoke Community
Church, Sarum Hill,
Basingstoke, Hampshire RG21
8SR
Age Range: 7–16

THE KING'S SCHOOL SENIOR
Lakesmere House, Allington
Lane, Fair Oak, Eastleigh,
Hampshire SO50 7DB
Website:
www.kingssenior.hants.sch.uk
Age Range: 11–16

LORD WANDSWORTH COLLEGE

Long Sutton, Hook, Hampshire
RG29 1TB
Website:
www.lordwandsworth.org
Age Range: 11–18

MAYVILLE HIGH SCHOOL

35 St Simon's Road, Southsea,
Hampshire PO5 2PE
Website:
www.mayvilleschool.com

MEONCROSS SCHOOL
Burnt House Lane, Stubbington,
Fareham, Hampshire PO14 2EF
Website: www.meoncross.co.uk
Age Range: 3–16

MOYLES COURT SCHOOL

Moyles Court, Ringwood,
Hampshire BH24 3NF
Website:
www.moylescourt.co.uk
Age Range: 3–16

THE PORTSMOUTH GRAMMAR SCHOOL

High Street, Portsmouth,
Hampshire PO1 2LN
Website: www.pgs.org.uk
Age Range: 2–18

PORTSMOUTH HIGH SCHOOL GDST

Kent Road, Southsea,
Hampshire PO5 3EQ
Website:
www.portsmouthhigh.co.uk
Age Range: 3–18

RAMSHILL SCHOOL

Petersfield, Petersfield,
Hampshire GU31 4AS
Website:
www.churcherscollege.com
Age Range: 4–18

RINGWOOD WALDORF SCHOOL

Folly Farm Lane, Ashley,
Ringwood, Hampshire BH24
2NN
Website:
www.ringwoodwaldorfschool.
org.uk
Age Range: 3–17 (Ages 3–17)

ROOKWOOD SCHOOL
Weyhill Road, Andover,
Hampshire SP10 3AL
Website:
www.rookwood.hants.sch.uk
Age Range: 3–16
(Boy boarders from age 8)

ST JOHN'S COLLEGE

Grove Road South, Southsea,
Hampshire PO5 3QW
Website:
www.stjohnscollege.co.uk
Age Range: 2–18

ST MARY'S COLLEGE

57 Midanbury Lane, Bitterne
Park, Southampton, Hampshire
SO18 4DJ
Website: www.
stmaryscollegesoton.bizland.com
Age Range: 3–18

ST NICHOLAS' SCHOOL*
Redfields House, Redfields
Lane, Church Crookham, Fleet,
Hampshire GU52 0RF
Website:
www.st-nicholas.hants.sch.uk
Age Range: 3–16 (Boys 3–7)

ST SWITHUN'S SCHOOL

Alresford Road, Winchester,
Hampshire SO21 1HA
Website: www.stswithuns.com
Age Range: 11–18

SALESIAN COLLEGE
Reading Road, Farnborough,
Hampshire GU14 6PA
Website:
www.salesiancollege.com
Age Range: 11–18

SHERFIELD SCHOOL

Reading Road, Sherfield-on-Loddon, Hook, Hampshire RG27 0HT
Website:
www.sherfieldschool.co.uk
Age Range: 2–18 (Pupils enter baby Gems between ages 2 months and 2 years. The upper age of the school has recently increased to 18.)

WINCHESTER COLLEGE

College Street, Winchester, Hampshire SO23 9NA
Website:
www.winchestercollege.org
Age Range: 13–18

WYKEHAM HOUSE SCHOOL

East Street, Fareham, Hampshire PO16 0BW
Website:
www.wykehamhouse.com
Age Range: 2–16

INDEPENDENT SIXTH FORM COLLEGE / TUTORIAL COLLEGE

ALTON COLLEGE

Old Odiham Road, Alton, Hampshire GU34 2LX
Website:
www.altoncollege.ac.uk
Age Range: 16–19

HEREFORDSHIRE

PREPARATORY

THE HEREFORD CATHEDRAL JUNIOR SCHOOL

28 Castle Street, Hereford, Herefordshire HR1 2NW
Website: www.hcjs.org
Age Range: 3–11

ST RICHARD'S

Bredenbury Court, Bromyard, Herefordshire HR7 4TD
Website: www.st-richards.org.uk
Age Range: 3–13

SENIOR

HEREFORD CATHEDRAL SCHOOL

Old Deanery, The Cathedral Close, Hereford, Herefordshire HR1 2NG
Website: www.herefordcs.com
Age Range: 11–18

LUCTON SCHOOL

Lucton, Leominster, Herefordshire HR6 9PN
Website: www.luctonschool.org

HERTFORDSHIRE

NURSERY AND PRE-PREP

NORFOLK LODGE MONTESSORI NURSERY

Dancers Hill Road, Barnet, Hertfordshire EN5 4RP
Website:
www.norfolklodgeschool.co.uk
Age Range: 1–4

PREPARATORY

ALDWICKBURY SCHOOL

Wheathampstead Road, Harpenden, Hertfordshire AL5 1AD
Website:
www.aldwickbury.org.uk
Age Range: 4–13

BEECHWOOD PARK SCHOOL

Markyate, St Albans, Hertfordshire AL3 8AW
Website: www.beechwoodpark. herts.sch.uk
Age Range: 3–13

BERKHAMSTED SCHOOL

Kings Road, Berkhamsted,
Hertfordshire HP4 3YP
Website: www.
berkhamstedcollegiateschool.
org.uk
Age Range: 3–11

BISHOP'S STORTFORD COLLEGE JUNIOR SCHOOL

Maze Green Road, Bishop's
Stortford, Hertfordshire CM23
2PH
Website: www.bishops-stortford-
college.herts.sch.uk
Age Range: 4–13

DUNCOMBE SCHOOL

4 Warren Park Road, Bengeo,
Hertford, Hertfordshire SG14
3JA
Website:
www.duncombe-school.co.uk
Age Range: 2–11

EDGE GROVE

Aldenham Village, Hertfordshire
WD25 8NL
Website: www.edgegrove.com
Age Range: 3–13

FRANCIS HOUSE PREPARATORY SCHOOL

Aylesbury Road, Tring,
Hertfordshire HP23 4DL
Website:
www.francishouseschool.co.uk
Age Range: 2–11

HARESFOOT PREPARATORY SCHOOL

Chesham Road, Berkhamsted,
Hertfordshire HP4 2SZ
Website:
www.haresfoot.herts.sch.uk
Age Range: (Children may join
from 5 months of age into our
Day Nursery.)

HEATH MOUNT SCHOOL

Woodhall Park, Watton-at-Stone,
Hertford, Hertfordshire SG14
3NG
Website: www.heathmount.org
Age Range: 3–13

HIGH ELMS MANOR SCHOOL

High Elms Lane, Watford,
Hertfordshire WD25 0JX
Website: http://www.
highelmsmanorschool.com

HOMEWOOD PRE-PREPARATORY SCHOOL

Hazel Road, Park Street, St
Albans, Hertfordshire AL2 2AH
Age Range: 3–8

HOWE GREEN HOUSE SCHOOL

Great Hallingbury, Bishop's
Stortford, Hertfordshire CM22
7UF
Website: www.
howegreenhouseschool.co.uk
Age Range: 2–11

THE JUNIOR SCHOOL, BISHOP'S STORTFORD COLLEGE

Maze Green Road, Bishop's
Stortford, Hertfordshire CM23
2PH
Website: www.bishops-stortford-
college.herts.sch.uk
Age Range: 4–13

KINGSHOTT SCHOOL

St Ippolyts, Hitchin,
Hertfordshire SG4 7JX
Website:
www.kingshottschool.co.uk
Age Range: 4–13

LITTLE ACORNS MONTESSORI SCHOOL

Lincolnsfields Centre, Bushey
Hall Drive, Bushey, Hertfordshire
WD2 2ER
Website:
www.littleacorns-montessori.org
Age Range: 2–7

LOCKERS PARK

Lockers Park Lane, Hemel
Hempstead, Hertfordshire
HP1 1TL
Website: www.lockerspark.
herts.sch.uk
Age Range: 5–13

LONGWOOD SCHOOL

Bushey Hall Drive, Bushey,
Hertfordshire WD23 2QG
Website:
www.longwoodschool.co.uk
Age Range: (Day nursery
accepts children from 3 months
to 4 years.
School accepts children from
3 years to 11 year)

LYONSDOWN SCHOOL TRUST LTD

3 Richmond Road, New Barnet,
Barnet, Hertfordshire EN5 1SA
Website:
www.lyonsdownschool.co.uk
Age Range: 3–11

MANOR LODGE SCHOOL

Rectory Lane, Ridge Hill,
Shenley, Hertfordshire
WD7 9BG
Website:
www.manorlodgeschool.com
Age Range: 3–11

NORTHWOOD PREPARATORY SCHOOL

Moor Farm, Sandy Lodge Road,
Rickmansworth, Hertfordshire
WD3 1LW
Website:
www.northwoodprep.co.uk
Age Range: 3–13 (Girls 3–4)

RADLETT PREPARATORY SCHOOL

Kendal Hall, Watling Street,
Radlett, Hertfordshire WD7 7LY
Website:
www.radlett-prep.herts.sch.uk
Age Range: 4–11

RICKMANSWORTH PNEU SCHOOL

88 The Drive, Rickmansworth, Hertfordshire WD3 4DU
Website: www.rickmansworthpneu.co.uk
Age Range: 3–11

ST HILDA'S SCHOOL

High Street, Bushey, Hertfordshire WD23 3DA
Website: www.sthildas-school.co.uk
Age Range: 3–11 (Boys 3–5)

ST JOHN'S PREPARATORY SCHOOL

Brownlowes, The Ridgeway, Potters Bar, Hertfordshire EN6 5QT
Website: www.stjohnsprepschool.co.uk
Age Range: 4–11

ST JOSEPH'S IN THE PARK

St Mary's Lane, Hertingfordbury, Hertford, Hertfordshire SG14 2LX
Website: www.stjosephsinthepark.co.uk
Age Range: 3–11

ST HILDA'S SCHOOL

28 Douglas Road, Harpenden, Hertfordshire AL5 2ES
Website: www.sthildasharpenden.co.uk
Age Range: 2–11

STORMONT

The Causeway, Potters Bar, Hertfordshire EN6 5HA
Website: www.stormont.herts.sch.uk
Age Range: 4–11

WESTBROOK HAY PREPARATORY SCHOOL

London Road, Westbrook Hay, Hemel Hempstead, Hertfordshire HP1 2RF
Website: www.westbrookhay.co.uk
Age Range: 2–13

YORK HOUSE SCHOOL

Sarratt Road, Croxley Green, Rickmansworth, Hertfordshire WD3 4LW
Website: www.york-house.com
Age Range: 3–13 (Co-ed 2–5)

SENIOR

ABBOT'S HILL SCHOOL

Bunkers Lane, Hemel Hempstead, Hertfordshire HP3 8RP
Website: www.abbotshill.herts.sch.uk
Age Range: 3–16 (Boys 3–5)

ALDENHAM SCHOOL

Elstree, Hertfordshire WD6 3AJ
Website: www.aldenham.com
Age Range: 3–18

BERKHAMSTED SCHOOL

Castle Street, Berkhamsted, Hertfordshire HP4 2BB
Website: www. berkhamstedcollegiateschool. org.uk
Age Range: 11–18 (Single-sex ed 11–16)

BISHOP'S STORTFORD COLLEGE

Maze Green Road, Bishop's Stortford, Hertfordshire CM23 2PJ
Website: www.bishops-stortford-college.herts.sch.uk
Age Range: 13–18

HABERDASHERS' ASKE'S BOYS' SCHOOL

Butterfly Lane, Elstree, Hertfordshire WD6 3AF
Website: www.habsboys.org.uk
Age Range: 5–18

HABERDASHERS' ASKE'S SCHOOL FOR GIRLS

Aldenham Road, Elstree, Hertfordshire WD6 3BT
Website: www.habsgirls.org.uk
Age Range: 4–18

HAILEYBURY*

Hertford, Hertfordshire SG13 7NU
Website: www.haileybury.com
Age Range: 11–18

IMMANUEL COLLEGE

87/91 Elstree Road, Bushey, Hertfordshire WD23 4EB
Website: www.immanuelcollege.co.uk
Age Range: 4–18

THE KING'S SCHOOL

Elmfield, Ambrose Lane, Harpenden, Hertfordshire AL5 4DU
Website: www.thekingsschool.com
Age Range: 4–16

THE PURCELL SCHOOL

Aldenham Road, Bushey, Hertfordshire WD23 2TS
Website: www.purcell-school.org
Age Range: 8–18

QUEENSWOOD

Shepherds Way, Brookmans Park, Hatfield, Hertfordshire AL9 6NS
Website: www.queenswood.org
Age Range: 11–18

REDEMPTION ACADEMY
● ⌂ ▲
PO BOX 352, Stevenage,
Hertfordshire SG1 9AG
Website:
www.redemption-academy.org
Age Range: 3–18

THE ROYAL MASONIC SCHOOL FOR GIRLS*
● ⌂ ▲
Rickmansworth Park,
Rickmansworth, Hertfordshire
WD3 4HF
Website:
www.royalmasonic.herts.sch.uk
Age Range: 2–19 (Pre School
opened in January 2010 for
boys and girls aged 2–4.)

ST ALBANS HIGH SCHOOL FOR GIRLS
● ⌂ ▲
1–3 Townsend Avenue, St
Albans, Hertfordshire AL1 3SJ
Website: www.stahs.org.uk
Age Range: 4–18

ST ALBANS SCHOOL*
● ⌂ ▲
Abbey Gateway, St Albans,
Hertfordshire AL3 4HB
Website:
www.st-albans.herts.sch.uk
Age Range: 17–18
(Co-ed VIth Form)

ST CHRISTOPHER SCHOOL
● ⌂ ▲
Barrington Road, Letchworth
Garden City, Hertfordshire SG6
3JZ
Website: www.stchris.co.uk
Age Range: 2–18

ST COLUMBA'S COLLEGE
● ⌂ ▲
King Harry Lane, St Albans,
Hertfordshire AL3 4AW
Website:
www.stcolumbascollege.org
Age Range: 4–18

ST EDMUND'S COLLEGE & PREP SCHOOL*
● ⌂ ▲
Old Hall Green, Ware,
Hertfordshire SG11 1DS
Website:
www.stedmundscollege.org
Age Range: 3–18

ST FRANCIS' COLLEGE
● ⌂ ▲
The Broadway, Letchworth
Garden City, Hertfordshire SG6
3PJ
Website:
www.st-francis.herts.sch.uk
Age Range: 3–18

ST MARGARET'S SCHOOL
● ⌂ ▲
Merry Hill Road, Bushey,
Hertfordshire WD23 1DT
Website:
www.stmargaretsbushey.org.uk
Age Range: 4–18

ST MARTHA'S SENIOR SCHOOL
● ⌂ ▲
Camlet Way, Hadley, Barnet,
Hertfordshire EN4 0NJ
Website: www.st-marthas.org.uk
Age Range: 11–18

STANBOROUGH SCHOOL
● ⌂ ★
Stanborough Park, Garston,
Watford, Hertfordshire WD25
9JT
Website: www.stanboroughpark.
herts.sch.uk
Age Range: 3–16

SHERRARDSWOOD SCHOOL
● ⌂ ▲
Lockleys, Welwyn, Hertfordshire
AL6 0BJ
Website:
www.sherrardswood.co.uk
Age Range: 2–18

SUSI EARNSHAW THEATRE SCHOOL
● ⌂
The Bull Theatre, 68 High Street,
Barnet, Hertfordshire EN5 5SJ
Website:
www.susiearnshaw.co.uk
Age Range: 11–16

TRING PARK SCHOOL FOR THE PERFORMING ARTS*
● ⌂ ▲
Tring Park, Tring, Hertfordshire
HP23 5LX
Website: www.tringpark.com
Age Range: 8–19

WATFORD GRAMMAR SCHOOL FOR GIRLS
● ⌂ ▲
Lady's Close, Watford,
Hertfordshire WD1 8AE
Website: www.
watfordgrammarschoolforgirls.
org.uk
Age Range: 11–18

INDEPENDENT SIXTH FORM COLLEGE / TUTORIAL COLLEGE

JUSTIN CRAIG EDUCATION
● ⌂
Kinetic Centre, Theobald Street,
Borehamwood, Hertfordshire
WD6 4PJ
Website: www.justincraig.ac.uk
Age Range: 15–19

ST ALBANS TUTORS
69 London Road, St Albans,
Hertfordshire AL1 1LN
Website: www.stalbanstutors.
org.uk

ISLE OF MAN

PREPARATORY

THE BUCHAN SCHOOL
● ♠

Arbory Road, West Hill,
Castletown, Isle of Man IM9
1RD
Website: www.buchan.sch.im
Age Range: 4–11

SENIOR

KING WILLIAM'S COLLEGE
● ♠ ★ ▲

Castletown, Isle of Man IM9 1TP
Website: www.kwc.sch.im
Age Range: 11–18

ISLE OF WIGHT

SENIOR

PRIORY SCHOOL
● ♠ ▲

Alverstone Manor, Luccombe
Road, Shanklin, Isle of Wight
PO37 7JB
Website:
www.prioryschool.org.uk
Age Range: 2–18

RYDE SCHOOL
● ♠ ▲

Queen's Road, Ryde, Isle of
Wight PO33 3BE
Website:
www.rydeschool.org.uk
Age Range: 3–18

KENT

NURSERY AND
PRE-PREP

SOMERHILL PRE-PREPARATORY SCHOOL
● ♠

The Schools at Somerhill,
Tudeley Rd, Tonbridge, Kent
TN11 0NJ
Website:
www.schoolsatsomerhill.com
Age Range: 3–7

PREPARATORY

ASHGROVE SCHOOL
● ♠

116 Widmore Road, Bromley,
Kent BR1 3BE
Website: www.ashgrove.org.uk
Age Range: 3–11

BENEDICT HOUSE
PREPARATORY SCHOOL
● ♠

1-5 Victoria Road, Sidcup, Kent
DA15 7HD
Website: www.
BenedictHousePrepSchool.co.uk
Age Range: 3–11

BICKLEY PARK SCHOOL
● ♠

14/24 Page Heath Lane,
Bickley, Bromley, Kent BR1
2DS
Website:
www.bickleyparkschool.co.uk
Age Range: 3–13

BREASIDE PREPARATORY
SCHOOL
● ♠

41 Orchard Road, Bromley,
Kent BR1 2PR
Website:
www.breaside.co.uk
Age Range: 2–11

BRONTE SCHOOL

7 Pelham Road, Gravesend,
Kent DA11 0HN
Website:
www.bronteschool.co.uk
Age Range: 4–11

BRYONY SCHOOL

Marshall Road, Rainham,
Gillingham, Kent ME8 0AJ
Age Range: 2–11

CHARTFIELD SCHOOL

45 Minster Road, Westgate-on-
Sea, Kent CT8 8DA
Age Range: 4–11

CONVENT PREPARATORY SCHOOL

46 Old Road East, Gravesend,
Kent DA12 1NR
Website: www.sjcps.org
Age Range: 3–11

DERWENT LODGE SCHOOL FOR GIRLS

Somerhill, Tonbridge, Kent TN11
0NJ
Website:
www.schoolsatsomerhill.com
Age Range: 7–11

DULWICH PREPARATORY SCHOOL, CRANBROOK

Coursehorn, Cranbrook, Kent
TN17 3NP
Website: www.dcpskent.org
Age Range: 3–13

ELLIOTT PARK SCHOOL

18–20 Marina Drive, Minster,
Isle of Sheppey, Sheerness,
Kent ME12 2DP
Age Range: 4–11

FOSSE BANK SCHOOL

Mountains Country House,
Noble Tree Road,
Hildenborough, Tonbridge, Kent
TN11 8ND
Website:
www.fossebankschool.co.uk
Age Range: 3–11

THE GRANVILLE SCHOOL

2 Bradbourne Park Road,
Sevenoaks, Kent TN13 3LJ
Website:
www.granville-school.com
Age Range: 3–11 (Boys 3–5)

HADDON DENE SCHOOL

57 Gladstone Road,
Broadstairs, Kent CT10 2HY
Website:
www.haddondene.co.uk
Age Range: 3–11

HILDEN GRANGE SCHOOL

62 Dry Hill Park Road,
Tonbridge, Kent TN10 3BX
Website:
www.hildengrange.gdst.net
Age Range: 3–13

HILDEN OAKS SCHOOL

38 Dry Hill Park Road,
Tonbridge, Kent TN10 3BU
Website: www.hildenoaks.co.uk

HOLMEWOOD HOUSE*

Barrow Lane, Langton Green,
Tunbridge Wells, Kent TN3 0EB
Website:
www.holmewood.kent.sch.uk
Age Range: 3–13

JUNIOR KING'S CANTERBURY

Milner Court, Sturry, Canterbury,
Kent CT2 0AY
Website: www.junior-kings.co.uk
Age Range: 3–13

KENT COLLEGE INFANT & JUNIOR SCHOOL

Vernon Holme, Harbledown,
Canterbury, Kent CT2 9AQ
Website:
www.kentcollege.com/junior
Age Range: 3–11

KING'S PREPARATORY SCHOOL

King Edward Road, Rochester,
Kent ME1 1UB
Website: www.kings-school-
rochester.co.uk
Age Range: 8–13

LORENDEN PREPARATORY SCHOOL

Painter's Forstal, Faversham,
Kent ME13 0EN
Website: www.lorenden.org.uk
Age Range: 3–11

MARLBOROUGH HOUSE SCHOOL

High Street, Hawkhurst, Kent
TN18 4PY
Website: www.
marlboroughhouseschool.co.uk
Age Range: 3–13

THE MEAD SCHOOL

16 Frant Road, Tunbridge Wells,
Kent TN2 5SN
Website: www.meadschool.info
Age Range: 3–11

MERTON COURT PREPARATORY SCHOOL

38 Knoll Road, Sidcup, Kent
DA14 4QU
Website: www.mertoncourt.kent.
sch.uk
Age Range: 2–11

THE NEW BEACON

Brittains Lane, Sevenoaks, Kent
TN13 2PB
Website: www.newbeacon.kent.
org.uk
Age Range: 4–13

NORTHBOURNE PARK SCHOOL

● 🏠

Betteshanger, Deal, Kent CT14 0NW
Website:
www.northbournepark.com
Age Range: 3–13

RUSSELL HOUSE SCHOOL

● 🏠

Station Road, Otford, Sevenoaks, Kent TN14 5QU
Website:
www.russellhouseschool.co.uk
Age Range: 2–11

ST ANDREW'S SCHOOL

● 🏠

24–28 Watts Avenue, Rochester, Kent ME1 1SA
Website: www.st-andrews. rochester.sch.uk
Age Range: 3–11

ST CHRISTOPHER'S SCHOOL

● 🏠

New Dover Road, Canterbury, Kent CT1 3DT
Website:
www.stchristopherschool.co.uk
Age Range: 3–11

ST CHRISTOPHER'S SCHOOL

● 🏠

49 Bromley Road, Beckenham, Kent BR3 5PA
Website:
www.stchristophersthehall.co.uk
Age Range: 3–11

ST DAVID'S COLLEGE

● 🏠

Justin Hall, Beckenham Road, West Wickham, Kent BR4 0QS
Website:
www.stdavidscollege.com
Age Range: 4–11

ST EDMUNDS JUNIOR SCHOOL

● 🏠

St Thomas Hill, Canterbury, Kent CT2 8HU
Website: www.stedmunds.org.uk
Age Range: 7–13

ST FAITH'S AT ASH SCHOOL

● 🏠

5 The Street, Ash, Canterbury, Kent CT3 2HH
Age Range: 3–11

ST JOSEPH'S PREPARATORY SCHOOL

● 🏠

46 Old Road East, Gravesend, Kent DA12 1NR
Website: www.sjcps.org

ST LAWRENCE COLLEGE JUNIOR SCHOOL

● 🏠

College Road, Ramsgate, Kent CT11 7AF
Website: www.slcuk.com
Age Range: 3–11

ST MICHAEL'S SCHOOL

● 🏠

Otford Court, Otford, Sevenoaks, Kent TN14 5SA
Website:
www.stmichaels-otford.co.uk
Age Range: 2–13

STEEPHILL INDEPENDENT SCHOOL*

● 🏠

Castle Hill, Fawkham, Longfield, Kent DA3 7BG
Website: www.steephill.co.uk
Age Range: 3–11

SHERNOLD SCHOOL

🏠

Hill Place, Queens Avenue, Maidstone, Kent ME16 0ER
Website:
www.shernoldschool.co.uk
Age Range: 3–11

SOLEFIELD SCHOOL

● 🏠

Solefields Road, Sevenoaks, Kent TN13 1PH
Website:
www.solefieldschool.org
Age Range: 4–13

SPRING GROVE SCHOOL

● 🏠

Harville Road, Wye, Ashford, Kent TN25 5EZ
Website:
www.springgroveschool.co.uk
Age Range: 2–13

SUTTON VALENCE PREPARATORY SCHOOL

● 🏠

Church Road, Chart Sutton, Maidstone, Kent ME17 3RF
Website: www.svs.org.uk
Age Range: 3–11

WEST LODGE PREPARATORY SCHOOL

● 🏠

36 Station Road, Sidcup, Kent DA15 7DU
Website: www.westlodge.org.uk
Age Range: 3–11

YARDLEY COURT PREPARATORY SCHOOL

● 🏠

Somerhill, Tonbridge, Kent TN11 0NJ
Website:
www.schoolsatsomerhill.com
Age Range: 7–13

SENIOR

ASHFORD SCHOOL

● 🏠 ▲

East Hill, Ashford, Kent TN24 8PB
Website:
www.ashfordschool.co.uk
Age Range: 3–18 (Co-ed 3–11)

BABINGTON HOUSE SCHOOL

● 🏠

Grange Drive, Chislehurst, Kent BR7 5ES
Website:
www.babingtonhouse.com
Age Range: 3–16 (Boys 3–7)

BEECHWOOD SACRED HEART SCHOOL

● 🏠 ▲

Pembury Road, Tunbridge Wells, Kent TN2 3QD
Website:
www.beechwood.org.uk
Age Range: 3–18 (Boarding for Girls only
Boys may stay with host families.)

BENENDEN SCHOOL
● ♠ ▲
Cranbrook, Kent TN17 4AA
Website:
www.benenden.kent.sch.uk
Age Range: 11–18

BETHANY SCHOOL
● ♠ ◆ ▲
Curtisden Green, Goudhurst,
Cranbrook, Kent TN17 1LB
Website:
www.bethanyschool.org.uk
Age Range: 11–18

**BISHOP CHALLONER RC
SCHOOL***
● ♠ ▲
228 Bromley Road, Shortlands,
Bromley, Kent BR2 0BS
Website: www.
bishopchallonerschool.com
Age Range: 3–18

**BROMLEY HIGH SCHOOL
GDST**
● ♠ ▲
Blackbrook Lane, Bickley,
Bromley, Kent BR1 2TW
Website:
www.gdst.net/bromleyhigh
Age Range: 4–18

**CANTERBURY STEINER
SCHOOL**
● ♠
Garlinge Green, Chartham,
Canterbury, Kent CT4 5RU
Age Range: 4–17

COBHAM HALL*
● ♠ ★ ◆ ▲
Cobham, Gravesend, Kent
DA12 3BL
Website: www.cobhamhall.com
Age Range: 11–18

COMBE BANK SCHOOL
● ♠ ▲
Combe Bank Drive, Sundridge,
Sevenoaks, Kent TN14 6AE
Website:
www.combebank.kent.sch.uk
Age Range: 3–18

CRANBROOK SCHOOL*
● ♠ ▲
Cranbrook, Kent TN17 3JD
Website:
www.cranbrookschool.co.uk
Age Range: 13–18

DARUL ULOOM LONDON
● ♠ ▲
Foxbury Avenue, Perry Street,
Chislehurst, Kent BR7 6SD
Website:
www.darululoomlondon.co.uk
Age Range: 11–18

DOVER COLLEGE
● ♠ ▲
Effingham Crescent, Dover,
Kent CT17 9RH
Website:
www.dovercollege.org.uk
Age Range: 3–18

**DUKE OF YORK'S ROYAL
MILITARY SCHOOL**
● ♠ ▲
Dover, Kent CT15 5EQ
Website: www.doyrms.com
Age Range: 11–18

FARRINGTONS SCHOOL
● ♠ ▲
Perry Street, Chislehurst, Kent
BR7 6LR
Website: www.farringtons.org.uk
Age Range: 3–19

GAD'S HILL SCHOOL
● ♠
Higham, Rochester, Kent ME3
7PA
Website: www.gadshill.org
Age Range: 3–16

KENT COLLEGE
● ♠ ★ ▲
Whitstable Road, Canterbury,
Kent CT2 9DT
Website: www.kentcollege.com
Age Range: 3–18

KENT COLLEGE PEMBURY
● ♠ ▲
Old Church Road, Tunbridge
Wells, Kent TN2 4AX
Website:
www.kent-college.co.uk
Age Range: 3–18

KING'S ROCHESTER
● ♠ ◆ ▲
Satis House, Boley Hill,
Rochester, Kent ME1 1TE
Website:
www.kings-rochester.co.uk
Age Range: 3–18

THE KING'S SCHOOL
● ♠ ▲
Canterbury, Kent CT1 2ES
Website:
www.kings-school.co.uk
Age Range: 13–18

**ST EDMUND'S SCHOOL
CANTERBURY**
● ♠ ▲
St Thomas Hill, Canterbury, Kent
CT2 8HU
Website:
www.stedmunds.org.uk
Age Range: 3–18

ST LAWRENCE COLLEGE*
● ♠ ◆ ▲
College Road, Ramsgate, Kent
CT11 7AE
Website: www.slcuk.com
Age Range: 3–18

SACKVILLE SCHOOL
● ♠ ▲
Tonbridge Road,
Hildenborough, Tonbridge, Kent
TN11 9HN
Website:
www.sackvilleschool.co.uk
Age Range: 11–18

SEVENOAKS SCHOOL
● ♠ ★ ▲
High Street, Sevenoaks, Kent
TN13 1HU
Website:
www.sevenoaksschool.org
Age Range: 11–18

SUTTON VALENCE SCHOOL
● ♠ ▲
Sutton Valence, North Street,
Sutton Valence, Kent ME17 3HL
Website: www.svs.org.uk
Age Range: 3–18

TONBRIDGE SCHOOL*
● ♠ ▲

Tonbridge, Kent TN9 1JP
Website:
www.tonbridge-school.co.uk
Age Range: 13–18

WALTHAMSTOW HALL
● ♠ ▲

Hollybush Lane, Sevenoaks,
Kent TN13 3UL
Website:
www.walthamstow-hall.co.uk
Age Range: 2–18

WICKHAM COURT SCHOOL
● ♠

Layhams Road, West Wickham,
Kent BR4 9HW
Website:
www.wickhamcourt.org.uk
Age Range: 2–16

INDEPENDENT SIXTH FORM COLLEGE / TUTORIAL COLLEGE

CATS COLLEGE CANTERBURY
● ♠ ★

68 New Dover Road, Stafford
House, Canterbury, Kent CT1
3LQ
Website: www.catscollege.com/
canterbury
Age Range: 15–21

ROCHESTER INDEPENDENT COLLEGE
● ♠

Star Hill, Rochester, Kent ME1
1XF
Website:
www.rochester-college.org
Age Range: 11–18

WARNBOROUGH COLLEGE
● ♠

18, Lower Bridge Street,
Canterbury, Kent CT1 2LG
Website: www.warnborough.
ac.uk
Age Range: 16–20

INTERNATIONAL SCHOOLS AND INTERNATIONAL STUDY CENTRES

STAFFORD HOUSE SCHOOL OF ENGLISH
19 New Dover Road,
Canterbury, Kent CT1 3AH
Website:
www.staffordhouseelt.com

LANCASHIRE

PREPARATORY

ASHBRIDGE INDEPENDENT SCHOOL
● ♠

Lindle Lane, Hutton, Preston,
Lancashire PR4 4AQ
Age Range: 2–11

THE BENNETT HOUSE SCHOOL
● ♠

332 Eaves Lane, Chorley,
Lancashire PR6 0DX
Website: www.bennetthouse.
lancs.sch.uk

BURY CATHOLIC PREPARATORY SCHOOL
● ♠

Arden House, 172 Manchester
Road, Bury, Lancashire BL9 9BH
Website:
www.burycatholicprepschool.
co.uk
Age Range: 3–11

CLEVELANDS PREPARATORY SCHOOL
● ♠

Chorley New Road, Bolton,
Lancashire BL1 5DH
Website:
www.clevelandsprepschool.
co.uk
Age Range: 2–11

FARROWDALE HOUSE PREPARATORY SCHOOL
● ♠

Farrow Street, Shaw, Oldham,
Lancashire OL2 7AD
Website: www.farrowdale.co.uk
Age Range: 3–11

FIRWOOD MANOR PREP SCHOOL
● ♠

Broadway, Chadderton,
Oldham, Lancashire OL9 0AD
Website:
www.firwoodmanor.org.uk
Age Range: 2–11

GRASSCROFT INDEPENDENT SCHOOL
● ♠

Lydgate Parish Hall, Stockport
Road, Lydgate, Oldham,
Lancashire OL4 4JJ
Age Range: 2–7

HIGHFIELD PRIORY SCHOOL
● ♠

Fulwood Row, Fulwood, Preston,
Lancashire PR2 6SL
Website:
www.highfieldpriory.co.uk
Age Range: 2–11

LANCASTER STEINER SCHOOL
● ♠

Lune Road, Lancaster,
Lancashire LA1 5QU
Website:
www.lancastersteiner.org.uk
Age Range: 5–14

LANGDALE PREPARATORY SCHOOL

● 🏠

95 Warbreck Drive, Blackpool, Lancashire FY2 9RZ
Website:
www.langdaleprepschool.co.uk
Age Range: 3–11

OLDHAM HULME KINDERGARTEN

● 🏠

Plum Street, Oldham, Lancashire OL8 1TJ
Website:
www.hulmegrammar.oldham.sch.uk
Age Range: 3–7

THE POTTERS HOUSE SCHOOL

● 🏠

6 Arley Avenue, Bury, Lancashire BL9 5HD
Age Range: 5–10

ROSSALL SCHOOL

● 🏠

Fleetwood, Lancashire FY7 8JW
Website:
www.rossallschool.org.uk
Age Range: 2–11

ST JOSEPH'S SCHOOL, PARK HILL

● 🏠

Park Hill, Padiham Road, Burnley, Lancashire BB12 6TG
Website:
www.parkhillschool.co.uk
Age Range: 3–11

ST MARY'S HALL

● 🏠

Clitheroe, Lancashire BB7 9PU
Website: www.stonyhurst.ac.uk
Age Range: 3–13

ST PIUS X PREPARATORY SCHOOL

● 🏠

200 Garstang Road, Fulwood, Preston, Lancashire PR2 8RD
Website: www.stpiusx.co.uk
Age Range: 2–11

SADDLEWORTH PREPARATORY SCHOOL

● 🏠

Huddersfield Road, Scouthead, Oldham, Lancashire OL4 4AG
Website: www.
saddleworthpreparatoryschool.
org.uk
Age Range: 4–7

STONEHOUSE NURSERY SCHOOL

● 🏠

90 School Lane, Leyland, Lancashire PR25 2TU
Website: stonehousenursery
andprimaryschool.com

TASHBAR SCHOOL

● 🏠

20 Upper Park Road, Salford, Lancashire M7 4HL
Age Range: 2–11

SENIOR

AL-ISLAH SCHOOL

● 🏠

108 Audley Range, Blackburn, Lancashire BB1 1TF
Age Range: 5–16

ARNOLD SCHOOL

● 🏠 ▲

Lytham Road, Blackpool, Lancashire FY4 1JG
Website: www.arnoldschool.
com
Age Range: 2–18

BEECH HOUSE SCHOOL

● 🏠

184 Manchester Road, Rochdale, Lancashire OL11 4JQ
Website:
www.beechhouseschool.co.uk
Age Range: 2–16

BOLTON MUSLIM GIRLS SCHOOL

● 🏠

Swan Lane, Bolton, Lancashire BL3 6TQ
Age Range: 11–16

BOLTON SCHOOL (BOYS' DIVISION)

● 🏠 ▲

Chorley New Road, Bolton, Lancashire BL1 4PA
Website:
http://www.boltonschool.org
Age Range: 7–18

BOLTON SCHOOL (GIRLS' DIVISION)

● 🏠 ▲

Chorley New Road, Bolton, Lancashire BL1 4PB
Website: www.boltonschool.org/
seniorgirls
Age Range: 4–18 (Boys 4–7 before they move into Bolton School Boys' Division)

BURY GRAMMAR SCHOOL BOYS

● 🏠 ▲

Tenterden Street, Bury, Lancashire BL9 0HN
Website: www.bgsboys.co.uk
Age Range: 7–18

BURY GRAMMAR SCHOOL GIRLS

● 🏠 ▲

Bridge Road, Bury, Lancashire BL9 0HH
Website: www.bgsg.bury.sch.uk
Age Range: 3–18 (Boys 4–7)

HEATHLAND COLLEGE

● 🏠

Broadoak, Sandy Lane, Accrington, Lancashire BB5 2AN
Website:
www.heathlandschool.co.uk
Age Range: 1–16

THE HULME GRAMMAR SCHOOL FOR GIRLS

● 🏠 ▲

Chamber Road, Oldham, Lancashire OL8 4BX
Website: www.hulme-grammar.
oldham.sch.uk
Age Range: 3–18

ISLAMIYAH SCHOOL

● 🏠

Willow Street, Little Harwood, Blackburn, Lancashire BB1 5NQ
Age Range: 11–16

JAMEA AL KAUTHAR
● ♠ ▲

Ashton Road, Lancaster,
Lancashire LA1 5AJ
Website: www.jamea.co.uk
Age Range: 11–19

**KING EDWARD VII AND
QUEEN MARY SCHOOL**
● ♠ ▲

Clifton Drive South, Lytham St
Annes, Lancashire FY8 1DT
Website: www.keqms.co.uk
Age Range: 2–18

**KINGSWOOD COLLEGE
TRUST**
● ♠ ▲

Scarisbrick Hall, Southport
Road, Ormskirk, Lancashire L40
9RQ
Website:
www.kingswoodcollege.co.uk
Age Range: 2–19

**KIRKHAM GRAMMAR
SCHOOL**
● ♠ ▲

Ribby Road, Kirkham, Preston,
Lancashire PR4 2BH
Website:
www.kirkhamgrammar.co.uk
Age Range: 3–18

LORD'S COLLEGE
● ♠

53 Manchester Road, Bolton,
Lancashire BL2 1ES
Age Range: 10–17

MAHARISHI SCHOOL
●

Ashtons Farm, Cobbs Brow
Lane, Lathom, Ormskirk,
Lancashire L40 6JJ
Website:
www.maharishischool.com
Age Range: 4–16

MARKAZUL ULOOM
● ♠ ▲

Park Lee Road, Blackburn,
Lancashire BB2 3NY
Age Range: 11–19 (No
Boarding for girls)

MOORLAND SCHOOL
● ♠

Ribblesdale Avenue, Clitheroe,
Lancashire BB7 2JA
Website:
www.moorlandschool.co.uk
Age Range: 1–16

OAKHILL COLLEGE
● ♠

Wiswell Lane, Whalley,
Clitheroe, Lancashire BB7 9AF
Website:
www.oakhillcollege.co.uk
Age Range: 2–16

**THE OLDHAM HULME
GRAMMAR SCHOOLS**
● ♠ ▲

Chamber Road, Oldham,
Lancashire OL8 4BX
Website: www.hulme-grammar.
oldham.sch.uk
Age Range: 3–18

**QUEEN ELIZABETH'S
GRAMMAR SCHOOL**
● ♠ ▲

West Park Road, Blackburn,
Lancashire BB2 6DF
Website:
www.qegs.blackburn.sch.uk
Age Range: 3–18 (Girls and
boys admitted at all ages, 3 to
18.)

**RIVINGTON PARK
INDEPENDENT SCHOOL**
● ♠

Knowle House, Rivington Lane,
Rivington, Horwich, Lancashire
BL6 7RX
Website:
www.rivingtonparkschool.co.uk
Age Range: 1–16

ROCHDALE GIRLS SCHOOL
● ♠

36 Taylor Street, Rochdale,
Lancashire OL12 0HX
Age Range: 11–16

ROSSALL SCHOOL
● ♠ ★ ▲

Fleetwood, Lancashire FY7 8JW
Website:
www.rossallschool.org.uk
Age Range: 11–18

**ST ANNE'S COLLEGE
GRAMMAR SCHOOL**
● ♠ ▲

293 Clifton Drive South, St
Annes-on-Sea, Lytham St
Annes, Lancashire FY8 1HN
Website:
www.collgram.u-net.com
Age Range: 3–18

STONYHURST COLLEGE
● ♠ ▲

Clitheroe, Lancashire BB7 9PZ
Website: www.stonyhurst.ac.uk
Age Range: 13–18

**TAUHEEDUL ISLAM GIRLS
HIGH SCHOOL**
● ♠

31 Bicknell Street, Blackburn,
Lancashire BB1 7EY
Website:
www.tauheedulislam.com
Age Range: 11–16

WESTHOLME SCHOOL
● ♠ ▲

Wilmar Lodge, Meins Road,
Blackburn, Lancashire BB2
6QU
Website:
www.westholmeschool.com
Age Range: 3–18 (Boys 3–7)

INTERNATIONAL SCHOOLS AND INTERNATIONAL STUDY CENTRES

**ROSSALL SCHOOL
INTERNATIONAL STUDY
CENTRE**
● ♠ ▲

Rossall School, Broadway,
Fleetwood, Lancashire FY7 8JW
Website:
www.rossallschool.org.uk
Age Range: 11–16

LEICESTERSHIRE

PREPARATORY

AL-AQSA PRIMARY SCHOOL

The Wayne Way, Leicester,
Leicestershire LE5 4PP
Age Range: 3–11

FAIRFIELD PREPARATORY SCHOOL

Leicester Road, Loughborough,
Leicestershire LE11 2AE
Website: www.lesfairfield.org
Age Range: 4–11

GRACE DIEU MANOR SCHOOL

Grace Dieu, Thringstone,
Leicester, Leicestershire LE67 5UG
Website: www.gracedieu.com
Age Range: 3–13

LEICESTER GRAMMAR JUNIOR SCHOOL

Evington Hall, Spencefield Lane, Leicester, Leicestershire LE5 6HN
Website:
www.leicestergrammar.org
Age Range: 3–11

STONEYGATE COLLEGE

2 Albert Road, Stoneygate,
Leicester, Leicestershire LE2 2AA
Website:
www.stoneygate-college.co.uk
Age Range: 3–11

STONEYGATE SCHOOL

London Road, Great Glen,
Leicester, Leicestershire LE8 9DJ
Website:
www.stoneygateschool.co.uk
Age Range: 3–13

SENIOR

THE DIXIE GRAMMAR SCHOOL

Station Road, Market Bosworth,
Leicestershire CV13 0LE
Website: www.dixie.org.uk
Age Range: 3–18

LEICESTER GRAMMAR SCHOOL

London Road, Great Glen,
Leicester, Leicestershire LE8 9FL
Website:
www.leicestergrammar.org.uk
Age Range: 3–18

LEICESTER HIGH SCHOOL FOR GIRLS

454 London Road, Leicester,
Leicestershire LE2 2PP
Website:
www.leicesterhigh.co.uk
Age Range: 3–18

LEICESTER MONTESSORI GRAMMAR SCHOOL

58 Stoneygate Road, Leicester,
Leicestershire LE2 2BN
Age Range: 3–18

LEICESTER MONTESSORI SCHOOL

194 London Road, Leicester,
Leicestershire LE1 1ND
Website:
www.montessorigroup.com

LOUGHBOROUGH GRAMMAR SCHOOL

Burton Walks, Loughborough,
Leicestershire LE11 2DU
Website: www.lesgrammar.org
Age Range: 10–18

LOUGHBOROUGH HIGH SCHOOL

Burton Walks, Loughborough,
Leicestershire LE11 2DU
Website: www.leshigh.org
Age Range: 11–18

MANOR HOUSE SCHOOL

South Street, Ashby-de-la-Zouch, Leicestershire LE65 1BR
Website:
www.manorhouseashby.co.uk
Age Range: 4–16

OUR LADY'S CONVENT SCHOOL

Gray Street, Loughborough,
Leicestershire LE11 2DZ
Website: www.olcs.leics.sch.uk
Age Range: 3–18

RATCLIFFE COLLEGE

Fosse Way, Ratcliffe on the Wreake, Leicester,
Leicestershire LE7 4SG
Website:
www.ratcliffe-college.co.uk
Age Range: 3–18

ST CRISPIN'S SCHOOL

6 St Mary's Road, Leicester,
Leicestershire LE2 1XA
Website: members.aol.com/
bharrild/stcrispins
Age Range: 3–16

INDEPENDENT SIXTH FORM COLLEGE / TUTORIAL COLLEGE

BROOKE HOUSE COLLEGE*
● 🏠 ▲

12 Leicester Road, Market Harborough, Leicestershire LE16 7AU
Website:
www.brookehouse.com
Age Range: 14–20

LINCOLNSHIRE

PREPARATORY

AYSCOUGHFEE HALL SCHOOL
● 🏠

Welland Hall, London Road, Spalding, Lincolnshire PE11 2TE
Website: www.ahs.me.uk
Age Range: 3–11

BICKER PREPARATORY SCHOOL
● 🏠

School Lane, Bicker, Boston, Lincolnshire PE20 3DW
Website: www.bickerprep.co.uk
Age Range: 3–11

COPTHILL SCHOOL
● 🏠

Barnack Road, Uffington, Stamford, Lincolnshire PE9 4TD
Website: www.copthill.com
Age Range: 2–11

DUDLEY HOUSE SCHOOL
● 🏠

1 Dudley Road, Grantham, Lincolnshire NG31 9AA
Website:
www.dudleyhouseschool.co.uk
Age Range: 3–11
(All faiths welcome)

EXCELL INTERNATIONAL SCHOOL
● 🏠

Tunnard Street, Boston, Lincolnshire PE21 6PL
Website: www.xl1884.co.uk
Age Range: 2–11

THE GRANTHAM PREPARATORY SCHOOL
● 🏠

Gorse Lane, Grantham, Lincolnshire NG31 7UF
Website: www.tgps.co.uk
Age Range: 3–11

GREENWICH HOUSE INDEPENDENT SCHOOL
● 🏠

106 High Holme Road, Louth, Lincolnshire LN11 0HE

HANDEL HOUSE PREPARATORY SCHOOL
● 🏠

Northolme, Gainsborough, Lincolnshire DN21 2JB
Age Range: 2–11

ST HUGH'S SCHOOL
● 🏠

Cromwell Avenue, Woodhall Spa, Lincolnshire LN10 6TQ
Website:
www.st-hughs.lincs.sch.uk
Age Range: 2–13

ST MARY'S PREPARATORY SCHOOL
● 🏠

5 Pottergate, Lincoln, Lincolnshire LN2 1PH
Website:
www.stmarysprep.co.uk
Age Range: 2–11

STAMFORD JUNIOR SCHOOL
● 🏠

Stamford, Lincolnshire PE9 2LR
Website: www.ses.lincs.sch.uk
Age Range: 2–11

VIKING SCHOOL
● 🏠

140 Church Road North, Skegness, Lincolnshire PE25 2QJ
Age Range: 2–11

WITHAM HALL
● 🏠

Witham-on-the-Hill, Bourne, Lincolnshire PE10 0JJ
Website: www.withamhall.com
Age Range: 4–13

SENIOR

KING EDWARD VI SCHOOL

● ♠ ▲

Edwards Street, Louth,
Lincolnshire LN11 9LL
Website:
www.kevigs.lincs.sch.uk
Age Range: 14–18

KIRKSTONE HOUSE SCHOOL

● ♠

Main Street, Baston,
PETERBOROUGH, Bourne,
Lincolnshire PE6 9PA
Website:
www.kirkstonehouseschool.co.uk
Age Range: 4–16

LOCKSLEY CHRISTIAN SCHOOL

● ♠ ▲

Bilney Block, Manby Park,
Manby, Lincolnshire LN11 8UT
Website: www.locksley.org
Age Range: 3–19

MAYPOLE HOUSE SCHOOL

● ♠

Well Vale Hall, Alford,
Lincolnshire LN13 0ET
Website:
www.maypolehouseschool.co.uk
Age Range: 3–16

STAMFORD HIGH SCHOOL

● ♠ ▲

St Martin's, Stamford,
Lincolnshire PE9 2LL
Website: www.ses.lincs.sch.uk
Age Range: 11–18

STAMFORD SCHOOL

● ♠ ▲

Southfield's House, St Paul's
Street, Stamford, Lincolnshire
PE9 2BQ
Website: www.ses.lincs.sch.uk
Age Range: 11–18

NORTH EAST LINCOLNSHIRE

PREPARATORY

ST MARTIN'S PREPARATORY SCHOOL

● ♠

63 Bargate, Grimsby, North East
Lincolnshire DN34 5AA
Website:
www.stmartinsprep.com
Age Range: 3–11

SENIOR

ST JAMES' SCHOOL

● ♠ ▲

22 Bargate, Grimsby, North East
Lincolnshire DN34 4SY
Website:
www.saintjamesschool.co.uk
Age Range: 2–18

NORTH LINCOLNSHIRE

PREPARATORY

TRENTVALE PREPARATORY SCHOOL

● ♠

Trentside, Keadby, North
Lincolnshire DN17 3EF
Website:
www.trentvaleprep.co.uk
Age Range: 4–11

WEST LONDON

NURSERY AND PRE-PREP

CHEPSTOW HOUSE SCHOOL
19 Pembridge Villas, London
W11 3EP
Age Range: 3–7

FULHAM PREP SCHOOL (PRE-PREP)
● 🏠
47A Fulham High Street,
London SW6 3JJ
Website: www.fulhamprep.co.uk
Age Range: 4–7

GREAT BEGINNINGS MONTESSORI SCHOOL
● 🏠
39 Brendon Street, Marylebone,
Westminster, London W1H 5JE
Age Range: 2–6

HOLLAND PARK PRE-PREPARATORY SCHOOL
● 🏠
5 & 9 Holland Road, London
W14 8HJ
Website: www.hpps.co.uk

L'ECOLE DES PETITS
● 🏠
2 Hazlebury Road, London SW6
2NB
Website:
www.lecoledespetits.co.uk
Age Range: 2–6 (Bilingual)

LE HERISSON
● 🏠
c/o The Methodist Church,
Rivercourt Road, Hammersmith,
London W6 9JT
Website:
www.leherissonschool.co.uk
Age Range: 2–6

PAINT POTS MONTESSORI SCHOOL BAYSWATER
● 🏠
Bayswater United Reformed
Church, Newton Road, London
W2 5LS
Website: www.paint-pots.co.uk
Age Range: 2–5

PAINT POTS MONTESSORI SCHOOL CHELSEA
● 🏠
Chelsea Community Church,
Edith Grove, London SW10 0LB
Website: www.paint-pots.co.uk
Age Range: 2–5

PAINT POTS MONTESSORI SCHOOL HYDE PARK
● 🏠
St John's Parish Hall, Hyde Park
Crescent, London W2 2QD
Website: www.paint-pots.co.uk
Age Range: 2–5

PICASSO HOUSE MONTESSORI SCHOOL IN CHELSEA
● 🏠
Chelsea Community Church,
Edith Grove, London SW10 0LB
Website: www.paint-pots.co.uk
Age Range: 2–8

RAVENSTONE DAY NURSERY AND NURSERY SCHOOL
● 🏠
St George's Fields, The Long
Garden, Albion Street, London
W2 2AX
Website: www.
ravenstoneschoolslondon.com

THOMAS'S KINDERGARTEN
● 🏠
14 Ranelagh Grove, London
SW1W 8PD
Age Range: 2–4

PREPARATORY

AL-MUNTADA ISLAMIC SCHOOL
● 🏠
7 Bridges Place, Parsons
Green, London SW6 4HW
Age Range: 4–11

ASTON HOUSE SCHOOL
● 🏠
1 Aston Road, Ealing, London
W5 2RL
Website: www.happychild.co.uk
Age Range: 2–11

AVENUE HOUSE SCHOOL
● 🏠
70 The Avenue, Ealing, London
W13 8LS
Website: www.avenuehouse.org
Age Range: 3–11

BUTE HOUSE PREPARATORY SCHOOL FOR GIRLS
● 🏠
Luxemburg Gardens, London
W6 7EA
Website: www.butehouse.co.uk
Age Range: 4–11

CAMERON HOUSE SCHOOL*
● 🏠 ◆
4 The Vale, Chelsea, London
SW3 6AH
Website:
www.cameronhouseschool.org
Age Range: 4–11

CHISWICK AND BEDFORD PARK PREPARATORY SCHOOL
● 🏠
Priory House, Priory Avenue,
Bedford Park, London W4 1TX
Website:
www.cbppschool.co.uk
Age Range: 4–11

CLIFTON LODGE PREPARATORY SCHOOL

8 Mattock Lane, Ealing, London W5 5BG
Website:
www.cliftonlodgeschool.co.uk
Age Range: 4–13

CONNAUGHT HOUSE

47 Connaught Square, London W2 2HL
Website: www.
connaughthouseschool.co.uk
Age Range: 4–11

DURSTON HOUSE

12–14 & 26 Castlebar Road, Ealing, London W5 2DR
Website: www.durstonhouse.org
Age Range: 4–13

EATON HOUSE BELGRAVIA

3–5 Eaton Gate, London SW1W 9BA
Website:
www.eatonhouseschools.com
Age Range: 4–8

EATON HOUSE THE VALE

2 Elvaston Place, London SW7 5QH
Website:
www.eatonhouseschools.com
Age Range: 4–11

EATON SQUARE SCHOOL

79 Eccleston Square, London SW1V 1PP
Age Range: 2–13

ECOLE FRANCAISE JACQUES PREVERT

59 Brook Green, London W6 7BE
Website:
www.ecoleprevert.org.uk
Age Range: 4–11

ERIDGE HOUSE PREPARATORY

1 Fulham Park Road, Fulham, London SW6 4LJ
Website:
www.eridgehouse.co.uk
Age Range: 3–11

THE FALCONS SCHOOL FOR BOYS

2 Burnaby Gardens, Chiswick, London W4 3DT
Website: www.falconschool.com
Age Range: 3–8

THE FALCONS SCHOOL FOR GIRLS

15 Gunnersbury Avenue, Ealing, London W5 3XD
Website: www.falconschool.com
Age Range: 3–11

FALKNER HOUSE

19 Brechin Place, London SW7 4QB
Website:
www.falknerhouse.co.uk
Age Range: 3–11 (Co-ed 3–4)

FULHAM PREP SCHOOL (PREP DEPT)*

Prep Department, 200 Greyhound Road, London W14 9SD
Website: www.fulhamprep.co.uk
Age Range: 4–13

GARDEN HOUSE SCHOOL

Turks Row, London SW3 4TW
Website:
www.gardenhouseschool.co.uk
Age Range: 3–11
(Co-ed nursery)

GEMS HAMPSHIRE SCHOOL

Main School, 15 Manresa Road, London SW3 6NB
Website:
www.ths.westminster.sch.uk
Age Range: 3–13

GLENDOWER PREPARATORY SCHOOL*

86/87 Queen's Gate, South Kensington, London SW7 5JX
Website:
www.glendowerprep.org
Age Range: 4–11

HAWKESDOWN HOUSE SCHOOL*

27 Edge Street, Kensington, London W8 7PN
Website:
www.hawkesdown.co.uk
Age Range: 3–8

HEATHFIELD HOUSE SCHOOL

Turnham Green Church Hall, Chiswick, London W4 4JU
Website:
www.heathfieldhouse.co.uk
Age Range: 4–11

HILL HOUSE INTERNATIONAL JUNIOR SCHOOL

17 Hans Place, London SW1X 0EP
Website:
www.hillhouseschool.co.uk
Age Range: 4–13

KENSINGTON PREP SCHOOL

596 Fulham Road, London SW6 5PA
Website:
www.gdst.net/kensingtonprep
Age Range: 4–11

KNIGHTSBRIDGE SCHOOL

67 Pont Street, Knightsbridge, London SW1X 0BD
Website:
www.knightsbridgeschool.com
Age Range: 3–13 (Nursery Class for Siblings only – other entry from 4 (Reception class upwards))

LATYMER PREP SCHOOL

36 Upper Mall, Hammersmith,
London W6 9TA
Website: www.latymerprep.org
Age Range: 7–11

THE LLOYD WILLIAMSON SCHOOL

12 Telford Road, London W10
5SH
Website: www.
lloydwilliamsonschools.co.uk

NORLAND PLACE SCHOOL

162–166 Holland Park Avenue,
London W11 4UH
Website:
www.norlandplace.com
Age Range: 4–11

NOTTING HILL PREPARATORY SCHOOL

95 Lancaster Road, London
W11 1QQ
Website:
www.nottinghillprep.com
Age Range: 4–13

ORCHARD HOUSE SCHOOL

16 Newton Grove, Bedford Park,
London W4 1LB
Website: www.orchardhs.org.uk
Age Range: 3–11

PEMBRIDGE HALL

18 Pembridge Square, London
W2 4EH
Website:
www.pembridgehall.co.uk
Age Range: 4–11

QUEEN'S COLLEGE PREP SCHOOL

61 Portland Place, London W1B
1QP
Website: www.qcps.org.uk
Age Range: 4–11

RAVENSCOURT PARK PREPARATORY SCHOOL*

16 Ravenscourt Avenue,
Hammersmith, London W6 0SL
Website: www.rpps.co.uk
Age Range: 4–11

REDCLIFFE SCHOOL

47 Redcliffe Gardens, London
SW10 9JH
Website:
www.redcliffeschool.com
Age Range: 2–11

ST BENEDICT'S JUNIOR SCHOOL

5 Montpelier Avenue, Ealing,
London W5 2XP
Website:
www.stbenedictsealing.org.uk
Age Range: 3–11

ST JAMES JUNIOR SCHOOL

Earsby Street, near Kensington
Olympia, London W14 8SH
Website:
www.stjamesjuniors.co.uk
Age Range: 4–11

ST PHILIP'S SCHOOL

6 Wetherby Place, London SW7
4ND
Website:
www.stphilipschool.co.uk
Age Range: 7–13

SINCLAIR HOUSE SCHOOL

159 Munster Road, Fulham,
London SW6 6AD
Website:
www.sinclairhouseschool.co.uk
Age Range: 2–8

SUSSEX HOUSE SCHOOL

68 Cadogan Square, Chelsea,
London SW1X 0EA
Age Range: 8–13

THOMAS'S FULHAM

Hugon Road, London, Fulham,
London SW6 3ES
Website: www.thomas-s.co.uk
Age Range: 4–11

THOMAS'S PREPARATORY SCHOOL

17–19 Cottesmore Gardens,
London W8 5PR
Website: www.thomas-s.co.uk
Age Range: 4–11

WESTMINSTER ABBEY CHOIR SCHOOL

Dean's Yard, London SW1P 3NY
Website:
www.westminster-abbey.org
Age Range: 8–13

WESTMINSTER CATHEDRAL CHOIR SCHOOL

Ambrosden Avenue, London
SW1P 1QH
Website: www.choirschool.com
Age Range: 7–13

WESTMINSTER UNDER SCHOOL

Adrian House, 27 Vincent
Square, London SW1P 2NN
Website:
www.westminsterunder.org.uk
Age Range: 7–13

WETHERBY PREPARATORY SCHOOL

48 Bryanstan Square, London
W1H 2EA
Website:
www.wetherbyprep.co.uk
Age Range: 8–13

WETHERBY SCHOOL

11 Pembridge Square, London
W2 4ED
Website:
www.alphaplusgroup.co.uk
Age Range: 4–8

SENIOR

ARTS EDUCATIONAL SCHOOLS LONDON
● 🏠 ▲
Cone Ripman House, 14 Bath Road, Chiswick, London W4 1LY
Website: www.artsed.co.uk
Age Range: 11–16

ASHBOURNE MIDDLE SCHOOL
● 🏠
17 Old Court Place, Kensington, London W8 4PL
Website: www.ashbournecollege.co.uk
Age Range: 12–16

BARBARA SPEAKE STAGE SCHOOL
● 🏠
East Acton Lane, London W3 7EG
Website: www.barbaraspeake.com
Age Range: 3–16

EALING COLLEGE UPPER SCHOOL
🏠 ▲
83 The Avenue, Ealing, London W13 8JS
Age Range: 11–18
(Co-ed VIth Form)

FRANCIS HOLLAND SCHOOL, SLOANE SQUARE SW1*
● 🏠 ▲
39 Graham Terrace, London SW1W 8JF
Website: www.fhs-sw1.org.uk
Age Range: 4–18

THE GODOLPHIN AND LATYMER SCHOOL
● 🏠 ★ ▲
Iffley Road, Hammersmith, London W6 0PG
Website: www.godolphinandlatymer.com
Age Range: 11–18

HARVINGTON SCHOOL
● 🏠
20 Castlebar Road, Ealing, London W5 2DS
Website: harvingtonschool.com
Age Range: 3–16 (Boys 3–5)

INSTITUTO ESPANOL VICENTE CANADA BLANCH
● 🏠 ▲
317 Portobello Road, London W10 5SY
Age Range: 4–19

JAMAHIRIYA SCHOOL
● 🏠
Glebe Place, London SW3 5JP
Age Range: 5–17

THE JAPANESE SCHOOL
● 🏠
87 Creffield Road, Acton, London W3 9PU
Website: www.thejapaneseschool.ltd.uk
Age Range: 6–15

KING FAHAD ACADEMY
● 🏠 ★ ▲
Bromyard Avenue, East Acton, London W3 7HD
Website: www.thekfa.org.uk
Age Range: 5–18

LATYMER UPPER SCHOOL
● 🏠 ▲
King Street, Hammersmith, London W6 9LR
Website: www.latymer-upper.org
Age Range: 11–18

LYCEE FRANCAIS CHARLES DE GAULLE
● 🏠 ▲
35 Cromwell Road, London SW7 2DG
Website: www.lyceefrancais.org.uk
Age Range: 4–19

MANDER PORTMAN WOODWARD
● 🏠 ▲
90–92 Queen's Gate, London SW7 5AB
Website: www.mpw.co.uk
Age Range: 14–19

MORE HOUSE SCHOOL*
● 🏠 ▲
22–24 Pont Street, Knightsbridge, 22–24 Pont Street, London SW1X 0AA
Website: www.morehouse.org.uk
Age Range: 11–18

NOTTING HILL AND EALING HIGH SCHOOL GDST
● 🏠 ▲
2 Cleveland Road, Ealing, London W13 8AX
Website: www.gdst.net/nhehs
Age Range: 4–18

PORTLAND PLACE SCHOOL
● 🏠 ▲
56–58 Portland Place, London W1B 1NJ
Website: www.portland-place.co.uk
Age Range: 10–18

QUEEN'S GATE SCHOOL*
● 🏠 ▲
133 Queen's Gate, Kensington, London SW7 5LE
Website: www.queensgate.org.uk
Age Range: 4–18

ST AUGUSTINE'S PRIORY*
● 🏠 ▲
Hillcrest Road, Ealing, London W5 2JL
Website: www.saintaugustinespriory.org.uk
Age Range: 4–18

ST BENEDICT'S SCHOOL*
● 🏠 ▲
54 Eaton Rise, Ealing, London W5 2ES
Website: www.stbenedicts.org.uk
Age Range: 3–18

ST JAMES SENIOR GIRLS' SCHOOL
● 🏠 ▲
Earsby Street, London W14 8SH
Website: www.stjamesgirls.co.uk
Age Range: 10–18

ST PAUL'S GIRLS' SCHOOL
● 🏠 ▲
Brook Green, London W6 7BS
Website: www.spgs.org
Age Range: 11–18

SOUTHBANK INTERNATIONAL SCHOOL, WESTMINSTER
● ♠ ★ ▲
63–65 Portland Place, London
W1B 1QR
Website: www.southbank.org
Age Range: 11–18

TABERNACLE SCHOOL
● ♠ ▲
32 St Ann's Villas, London W11
4RS
Age Range: 3–16

THE WALMER ROAD SCHOOL
● ♠
221 Walmer Road, London W11
4EY
Website:
www.rugbyportobello.org.uk
Age Range: 14–16

WESTMINSTER SCHOOL*
● ♠ ▲
17 Dean's Yard, Westminster,
London SW1P 3PB
Website:
www.westminster.org.uk
Age Range: 13–18

INDEPENDENT SIXTH FORM COLLEGE / TUTORIAL COLLEGE

ABBEY COLLEGE
● ♠
22 Grosvenor Gardens, London
SW1W 0DH
Website:
www.abbeycolleges.co.uk

ALBEMARLE INDEPENDENT COLLEGE
● ♠
18 Dunraven Street, London
W1K 7FE
Website: www.albemarle.org.uk
Age Range: 14–21

ARTS EDUCATIONAL SCHOOLS LONDON – SIXTH FORM
● ♠
Cone Ripman House, 14 Bath
Road, Chiswick, London W4 1LY
Website: www.artsed.co.uk
Age Range: 16–18

BALES COLLEGE
● ♠
742 Harrow Road, London W10
4AA
Website:
www.balescollege.co.uk
Age Range: 11–19

CHELSEA INDEPENDENT COLLEGE*
● ♠ ▲
517–523 Fulham Road, London
SW6 1HD
Website: www.cic.ac
Age Range: 14–19

COLLINGHAM INDEPENDENT GCSE AND SIXTH FORM COLLEGE
● ♠
23 Collingham Gardens,
London SW5 0HL
Website: www.collingham.co.uk
Age Range: 14–20

DAVID GAME COLLEGE*
● ♠ ▲
69 Notting Hill Gate, London
W11 3JS
Website:
www.davidgame-group.com
Age Range: 15–19

DAVIES LAING AND DICK*
● ♠ ◆ ▲
100 Marylebone Lane, London
W1U 2QB
Website: www.dldcollege.org
Age Range: 14–24

DUFF MILLER
● ♠
59 Queen's Gate, London SW7
5JP
Website: www.duffmiller.com
Age Range: 14–19

EALING INDEPENDENT COLLEGE
● ♠
83 New Broadway, Ealing,
London W5 5AL
Website: www.
ealingindependentcollege.com
Age Range: 13–20 (College
assists students who did not
attain their desired results in a
previous school. This affects the
age range at the higher end.)

LANSDOWNE COLLEGE
● ♠
40–44 Bark Place, London W2
4AT
Website:
www.lansdownecollege.com
Age Range: 14–19 (Lansdowne
is an independent Sixth Form
College with a GCSE
Department from Year 10.)

MANDER PORTMAN WOODWARD
● ♠
90–92 Queen's Gate, London
SW7 5AB
Website: www.mpw.co.uk
Age Range: 14–19

WESTMINSTER TUTORS
● ♠
86 Old Brompton Road, London
SW7 3LQ
Website:
www.westminstertutors.co.uk
Age Range: 11–25

INTERNATIONAL SCHOOLS AND INTERNATIONAL STUDY CENTRES

FRANCES KING SCHOOL OF ENGLISH
77 Gloucester Road, London
SW7 4SS
Website: www.francesking.co.uk

INTERNATIONAL SCHOOL OF LONDON*

● 👥 ★ ▲

139 Gunnersbury Avenue,
London W3 8LG
Website: www.ISLlondon.org
Age Range: 3–19

SOUTHBANK INTERNATIONAL SCHOOL, KENSINGTON

● 👥

36–38 Kensington Park Road,
London W11 3BU
Website: www.southbank.org
Age Range: 3–11

NORTH WEST LONDON

NURSERY AND PRE-PREP

BROADHURST SCHOOL

● 👥

19 Greencroft Gardens, London
NW6 3LP
Website:
www.broadhurstschool.com
Age Range: 2–5

HAMPSTEAD HILL PRE-PREPARATORY & NURSERY SCHOOL

● 👥

St Stephen's Hall, Pond Street,
Hampstead, London NW3 2PP
Website:
www.hampsteadhillschool.co.uk
Age Range: 2–8

NORTH BRIDGE HOUSE NURSERY SCHOOL

● 👥

33 Fitzjohn's Avenue, London
NW3 5JY
Website:
www.northbridgehouse.com
Age Range: 3–6

ST JOHNS WOOD PRE-PREPARATORY SCHOOL

● 👥

St Johns Hall, Lords
Roundabout, London NW8 7NE
Website:
www.sjwpre-prep.org.uk
Age Range: 3–7

PREPARATORY

ABERCORN SCHOOL

● 👥

28 Abercorn Place, London
NW8 9XP
Website:
www.abercornschool.com
Age Range: 2–13

THE ACADEMY SCHOOL

● 👥

2 Pilgrims Place, Rosslyn Hill,
Hampstead, London NW3 1NG
Age Range: 6–12

ARNOLD HOUSE SCHOOL

● 👥

1, Loudoun Road, St John's
Wood, London NW8 0LH
Website:
www.arnoldhouse.co.uk
Age Range: 5–13

BELMONT (MILL HILL PREPARATORY SCHOOL)

● 👥

The Ridgeway, Mill Hill Village,
London NW7 4ED
Website:
www.belmontschool.com
Age Range: 7–13 (7–13)

THE CAVENDISH SCHOOL

● 👥

31 Inverness Street, London
NW1 7HB
Website:
www.cavendishschool.co.uk
Age Range: 3–11

DEVONSHIRE HOUSE PREPARATORY SCHOOL*

● 👥

2 Arkwright Road, Hampstead,
London NW3 6AE
Website: www.
devonshirehouseschool.co.uk
Age Range: 2–13

GOLDERS HILL SCHOOL

● 👥

666 Finchley Road, London
NW11 7NT
Age Range: 2–7

GOODWYN SCHOOL

● 👥

Hammers Lane, Mill Hill, London
NW7 4DB
Website:
www.goodwyn-school.co.uk
Age Range: 3–11

GOWER HOUSE SCHOOL

● 👥

Blackbird Hill, London NW9 8RR
Website:
www.gowerhouseschool.co.uk
Age Range: 2–11

THE HALL SCHOOL

● 👥

23 Crossfield Road,
Hampstead, London NW3 4NU
Website: www.hallschool.co.uk
Age Range: 4–13

HEATHSIDE PREPARATORY SCHOOL

● 👥

16 New End, Hampstead,
London NW3 1JA
Website: www.heathside.net
Age Range: 3–11

HENDON PREPARATORY SCHOOL

20 Tenterden Grove, Hendon, London NW4 1TD
Website:
www.hendonprep.co.uk
Age Range: 2–13

HEREWARD HOUSE SCHOOL

14 Strathray Gardens, Hampstead, London NW3 4NY
Website:
www.herewardhouse.co.uk
Age Range: 4–13

L'ILE AUX ENFANTS

22 Vicar's Road, London NW5 4NL
Website:
www.ileauxenfants.co.uk
Age Range: 3–11

LYNDHURST HOUSE PREPARATORY SCHOOL*

24 Lyndhurst Gardens, Hampstead, London NW3 5NW
Website:
www.lyndhursthouse.co.uk
Age Range: 4–13

MAPLE WALK SCHOOL

62A Crownhill Road, London NW10 4EB
Website:
www.newmodelschool.co.uk
Age Range: 4–11

MARIA MONTESSORI SCHOOL HAMPSTEAD

26 Lyndhurst Gardens, Hampstead, London NW3 5NW
Website: www.
mariamontessorischools.co.uk
Age Range: 2–11

THE MULBERRY HOUSE SCHOOL*

7 Minster Road, West Hampstead, London NW2 3SD
Website:
www.mulberryhouseschool.com
Age Range: 2–8

NAIMA JEWISH PREPARATORY SCHOOL

21 Andover Place, London NW6 5ED
Website: www.naimajps.co.uk
Age Range: 3–11

NORTH BRIDGE HOUSE JUNIOR SCHOOL

8 Netherhall Gardens, London NW3 5RR
Website:
www.northbridgehouse.com
Age Range: 6–8

NORTH BRIDGE HOUSE LOWER PREP SCHOOL

1 Gloucester Avenue, London NW1 7AB
Website:
www.northbridgehouse.com
Age Range: 8–11

NORTH BRIDGE HOUSE UPPER PREP SCHOOL

1 Gloucester Avenue, London NW1 7AB
Website:
www.northbridgehouse.com
Age Range: 10–13

OYH PRIMARY SCHOOL

Finchley Lane, Hendon, London NW4 1DJ
Age Range: 3–11

THE PHOENIX SCHOOL

36 College Crescent, London NW3 5LF
Website: www.ucs.org.uk
Age Range: 3–7

RAINBOW MONTESSORI JUNIOR SCHOOL

13 Woodchurch Road, West Hampstead, London NW6 3PL
Website:
www.rainbowmontessori.co.uk
Age Range: 5–12

ST ANTHONY'S PREPARATORY SCHOOL

90 Fitzjohns Avenue, Hampstead, London NW3 6NP
Website:
www.stanthonysprep.org.uk
Age Range: 5–13

ST CHRISTINA'S RC PREPARATORY SCHOOL

25 St Edmunds Terrace, Regents Park, London NW8 7PY
Website:
www.saintchristinas.org.uk
Age Range: 3–11 (Boys 3–7)

ST CHRISTOPHER'S SCHOOL

32 Belsize Lane, London NW3 5AE
Website: www.st-christophers.
hampstead.sch.uk
Age Range: 4–11

ST MARTIN'S SCHOOL

22 Goodwyn Avenue, Mill Hill, London NW7 3RG
Website:
www.stmartinsmillhill.co.uk
Age Range: 3–11

ST MARY'S SCHOOL HAMPSTEAD

47 Fitzjohn's Avenue, London NW3 6PG
Website: www.stmh.co.uk
Age Range: 2–11 (Boys 2–7)

ST NICHOLAS SCHOOL

22 Salmon Street, London NW9 8PN
Website: www.happychild.co.uk
Age Range: 2–11

SARUM HALL

15 Eton Avenue, London NW3 3EL
Website:
www.sarumhallschool.co.uk
Age Range: 3–11

SOUTHBANK INTERNATIONAL SCHOOL, HAMPSTEAD

16 Netherhall Gardens, Hampstead, London NW3 5TH
Website: www.southbank.org
Age Range: 3–11

TREVOR ROBERTS SCHOOL

57 Eton Avenue, London NW3 3ET
Age Range: 5–13

UNIVERSITY COLLEGE SCHOOL JUNIOR BRANCH
11 Holly Hill, Hampstead, London NW3 6QN
Website: www.ucs.org.uk
Age Range: 7–11

THE VILLAGE SCHOOL
2 Parkhill Road, Belsize Park, London NW3 2YN
Website: www.thevillageschool.co.uk
Age Range: 3–11

WELSH SCHOOL OF LONDON

Welsh School of London, c/o Stonebridge Primary School, Shakespeare Avenue, London NW10 8NG
Website: www.llundain.freeserve.co.uk
Age Range: 3–11

SENIOR

AL-SADIQ AND AL-ZAHRA SCHOOLS
134 Salusbury Road, London NW6 6PF
Website: www. al-sadiqal-zahraschools.co.uk
Age Range: 4–16

BEIS HAMEDRASH ELYON
211 Golders Green Rd, London NW11 9BY
Age Range: 11–14

BETH JACOB GRAMMAR FOR GIRLS
Stratford Road, Hendon, London NW4 2AT
Age Range: 10–16

BRONDESBURY COLLEGE FOR BOYS
8 Brondesbury Park, London NW6 7BT
Website: www.bcbcollege.com
Age Range: 11–16

FINE ARTS COLLEGE

24 Lambolle Place, Hampstead, London NW3 4PG
Website: www.hampsteadfinearts.com
Age Range: 14–19

FRANCIS HOLLAND SCHOOL, REGENT'S PARK NW1*

Clarence Gate, Ivor Place, London NW1 6XR
Website: www.francisholland.org.uk
Age Range: 11–18

ISLAMIA GIRLS' SCHOOL
129 Salusbury Road, London NW6 6PE
Website: www.islamiagirlsschool.com
Age Range: 11–16

THE KING ALFRED SCHOOL

149 North End Road, London NW11 7HY
Website: www.kingalfred.org.uk
Age Range: 4–18

LONDON JEWISH GIRLS' HIGH SCHOOL
18 Raleigh Close, Hendon, London NW4 2TA
Age Range: 11–16

MILL HILL SCHOOL

The Ridgeway, Mill Hill, London NW7 1QS
Website: www.millhill.org.uk
Age Range: 13–18

THE MOUNT SCHOOL

Milespit Hill, Mill Hill, London NW7 2RX
Website: www.mountschool.com
Age Range: 3–16

NORTH BRIDGE HOUSE SENIOR SCHOOL*
1 Gloucester Avenue, London NW1 7AB
Website: www.nbhseniorschool.co.uk
Age Range: 2–16

THE ROYAL SCHOOL, HAMPSTEAD

65 Rosslyn Hill, Hampstead, London NW3 5UD
Website: www.royalschoolhampstead.net
Age Range: 3–16

ST MARGARET'S SCHOOL
18 Kidderpore Gardens, London NW3 7SR
Website: www.st-margarets.co.uk
Age Range: 4–16

SOUTH HAMPSTEAD HIGH SCHOOL

3 Maresfield Gardens, London NW3 5SS
Website: www.shhs.gdst.net
Age Range: 4–18

SYLVIA YOUNG THEATRE SCHOOL
Rossmore Road, Marylebone, London NW1 6NJ
Website: www. sylviayoungtheatreschool.co.uk
Age Range: 10–16

UNIVERSITY COLLEGE SCHOOL

Frognal, Hampstead, London NW3 6XH
Website: www.ucs.org.uk
Age Range: 11–18 (Boys aged 11–18 Girls aged 16–18 (Co-educational Sixth Form only))

INDEPENDENT SIXTH FORM COLLEGE / TUTORIAL COLLEGE

BRAMPTON COLLEGE

● 🏠

Lodge House, Lodge Road, London NW4 4DQ
Website:
www.bramptoncollege.com
Age Range: 15–19

INTERNATIONAL SCHOOLS AND INTERNATIONAL STUDY CENTRES

THE AMERICAN SCHOOL IN LONDON*

● 🏠 ▲

1 Waverley Place, London NW8 0NP
Website: www.asl.org
Age Range: 4–18

INTERNATIONAL COMMUNITY SCHOOL*

● 🏠 ★ ▲

4 York Terrace East, Regents Park, London NW1 4PT
Website: www.icschool.co.uk
Age Range: 3–19

NORTH LONDON

NURSERY AND PRE-PREP

ANNEMOUNT SCHOOL

● 🏠

18 Holne Chase, Hampstead Garden Suburb, London N2 0QN
Website: www.annemount.co.uk
Age Range: 3–7 (Pupils are admitted from 2 years 9 months.)

THE MONTESSORI HOUSE

● 🏠

5 Princes Avenue, Muswell Hill, London N10 3LS
Website:
www.montessori-house.co.uk
Age Range: 1–5

PREPARATORY

CHANNING JUNIOR SCHOOL

● 🏠

Fairseat, 1 Highgate High Street, London N6 5JR
Website: www.channing.co.uk
Age Range: 4–11

EXCEL PREPARATORY SCHOOL

● 🏠

The Annex, Selby Centre, Off Whitehart Lane, Tottenham, London N17 8JL
Age Range: 2–12

EXCELSIOR COLLEGE

● 🏠

Selby Centre, Selby Road, Tottenham, London N17 8JN
Website:
www.excelsiorcollege.co.uk
Age Range: 3–11

GRANGE PARK PREPARATORY SCHOOL

● 🏠

13 The Chine, Grange Park, London N21 2EA
Website: www.gpps.org.uk
Age Range: 4–11

HOLLY PARK MONTESSORI SCHOOL

● 🏠

The Holly Park, Methodist Church, Crouch Hill, London N4 4BY
Website:
www.mariamontessorischools. co.uk
Age Range: 2–7

ISLAMIC SHAKHSIYAH FOUNDATION

● 🏠

1st Floor {Suffolk Road Entrance}, 277 St Ann's Road, London N15 5RG
Age Range: 5–11

KEBLE PREPARATORY SCHOOL

● 🏠

Wades Hill, Winchmore Hill, London N21 1BG
Website: www.kebleprep.co.uk
Age Range: 4–13

KEREM SCHOOL

● 🏠

Norrice Lea, London N2 0RE
Website: www.kerem.org.uk
Age Range: 4–11

NORFOLK HOUSE SCHOOL

● 🏠

10 Muswell Avenue, Muswell Hill, London N10 2EG
Website:
www.norfolkhouseschool.org
Age Range: 4–11

PARKSIDE PREPARATORY SCHOOL

● 🏠

Church Lane, Bruce Grove, Tottenham, London N17 7AA
Age Range: 3–11

PRIMROSE INDEPENDENT SCHOOL

● 🏠

Congregational Church, Highbury Quadrant, Highbury, London N5 2TE
Age Range: 2–11

SALCOMBE PREPARATORY SCHOOL

● 🏠

224–226 Chase Side, Southgate, London N14 4PL
Website:
www.salcombeprep.co.uk
Age Range: 4–11

TALMUD TORAH BOBOV PRIMARY SCHOOL

● 🏠

87 Egerton Road, London N16 6UE
Age Range: 2–13

VITA ET PAX PREPARATORY SCHOOL

● 🏠

6A Priory Close, Green Road, Southgate, London N14 4AT
Website: www.vitaetpax.co.uk
Age Range: 3–11

YETEV LEV DAY SCHOOL FOR BOYS

● 🏠

111–115 Cazenove Road, London N16 6AX
Age Range: 3–11

SENIOR

BEIS CHINUCH LEBANOS GIRLS SCHOOL

● 🏠

Woodberry Down Centre, Woodberry Down, London N4 2SH
Age Range: 2–16

BEIS ROCHEL D'SATMAR GIRLS SCHOOL

● 🏠

51–57 Amhurst Park, London N16 5DL
Age Range: 2–17

CHANNING SCHOOL

● 🏠 ▲

Highgate, London N6 5HF
Website: www.channing.co.uk
Age Range: 4–18

HIGHGATE SCHOOL

● 🏠 ▲

North Road, London N6 4AY
Website:
www.highgateschool.org.uk
Age Range: 3–18

LUBAVITCH HOUSE SENIOR SCHOOL FOR GIRLS

● 🏠 ▲

107–115 Stamford Hill, Hackney, London N16 5RP
Website:
lubavitchseniorgirls.com
Age Range: 11–18

MECHINAH LIYESHIVAH ZICHRON MOSHE

● 🏠

86 Amhurst Park, London N16 5AR
Age Range: 11–16

PALMERS GREEN HIGH SCHOOL

● 🏠

104 Hoppers Road, Winchmore Hill, London N21 3LJ
Website: www.pghs.co.uk
Age Range: 3–16

PARDES GRAMMAR BOYS' SCHOOL

● 🏠

Hendon Lane, London N3 1SA
Age Range: 11–17

TAWHID BOYS SCHOOL, TAWHID EDUCATIONAL TRUST

● 🏠

21 Cazenove Road, London N16 6PA
Age Range: 9–16

TAYYIBAH GIRLS SCHOOL

● 🏠 ▲

88 Filey Avenue, Stamford Hill, London N16 6JJ
Age Range: 5–18

YESODEY HATORAH JEWISH SCHOOL

● 🏠

2–4 Amhurst Park, London N16 5AE
Age Range: 3–16

INTERNATIONAL SCHOOLS AND INTERNATIONAL STUDY CENTRES

THE NORTH LONDON INTERNATIONAL SCHOOL

● 🏠 ★ ▲

6 Friern Barnet Lane, London N11 3LX
Website: www.nlis.org
Age Range: 2–19

LONDON CITY

PREPARATORY

CHARTERHOUSE SQUARE SCHOOL

40 Charterhouse Square, London EC1M 6EA
Website: www. charterhousesquareschool.co.uk
Age Range: 3–11

DALLINGTON SCHOOL

8 Dallington Street, London EC1V 0BW
Website: www.dallingtonschool.co.uk
Age Range: 3–11

THE LYCEUM

6 Paul Street, London EC2A 4JH
Website: www.lyceumschool.org
Age Range: 3–11

ST PAUL'S CATHEDRAL SCHOOL*

2 New Change, London EC4M 9AD
Website: www.spcs.london.sch.uk
Age Range: 4–13

SENIOR

CITY OF LONDON SCHOOL*

Queen Victoria Street, London EC4V 3AL
Website: www.clsb.org.uk
Age Range: 10–18

CITY OF LONDON SCHOOL FOR GIRLS

St Giles' Terrace, Barbican, London EC2Y 8BB
Website: www.clsg.org.uk
Age Range: 7–18

THE ITALIA CONTI ACADEMY OF THEATRE ARTS

23 Goswell Road, London EC1M 7AJ
Website: www.italiaconti-acting.co.uk
Age Range: 9–21

ROYAL BALLET SCHOOL

46 Floral Street, London WC2E 9DA
Website: www.royal-ballet-school.org.uk
Age Range: 11–18

THE URDANG ACADEMY OF BALLET

The Old Finsbury Town Hall, Roseberry Avenue, London EC1R 4RP
Website: www.theurdangacademy.com
Age Range: 16–23

INDEPENDENT SIXTH FORM COLLEGE / TUTORIAL COLLEGE

CATS COLLEGE LONDON

43–45 Bloomsbury Square, London WC1A 2RA
Website: www.catscollege.com/london
Age Range: 15–21

EAST LONDON

PREPARATORY

FARADAY SCHOOL

Trinity Buoy Wharf, 64 Orchard Place, London E14 0JW
Website: www.newmodelschool.co.uk
Age Range: 4–11

GATEHOUSE SCHOOL

Sewardstone Road, Victoria Park, London E2 9JG
Website: www.gatehouseschool.co.uk
Age Range: 3–11

GRANGEWOOD INDEPENDENT SCHOOL

Chester Road, Forest Gate, London E7 8QT
Website: www.grangewoodschool.com
Age Range: 3–11

GREEN GABLES MONTESSORI PRIMARY SCHOOL
● ✿

The Institute, 302 The Highway, Wapping, London E1W 3DH
Website:
www.greengables.org.uk

HYLAND HOUSE
● ✿

896 Forest Road, Walthamstow, London E17 4AE
Age Range: 3–11

JAMIAH MADANIYAH PRIMARY SCHOOL
● ✿

80–82 Stafford Road, Forest Gate, London E7 8NN
Age Range: 3–8

LUBAVITCH HOUSE SCHOOL (JUNIOR BOYS)
● ✿

135 Clapton Common, London E5 9AE
Website: www.lubavitchuk.com
Age Range: 5–13

NOOR UL ISLAM PRIMARY SCHOOL
● ✿

135 Dawlish Road, Leyton, London E10 6QW
Website: www.noorulislam.co.uk
Age Range: 4–11

PARAGON CHRISTIAN ACADEMY
● ✿

233–241 Glyn Road, London E5 0JP
Age Range: 3–11

QUWWATT UL ISLAM GIRLS SCHOOL
● ✿

16 Chaucer Road, Forest Gate, London E7 9NB
Website:
www.quwwatulislam.com
Age Range: 4–13

RIVER HOUSE MONTESSORI SCHOOL
● ✿

Unit C Great Eastern Enterprise, 3 Millharbour, London E14 9XP
Website: www.river-house.co.uk
Age Range: 3–11

ST JOSEPH'S CONVENT SCHOOL
● ✿

59 Cambridge Park, London E11 2PR
Age Range: 3–11

SNARESBROOK COLLEGE PREPARATORY SCHOOL
● ✿

75 Woodford Road, South Woodford, London E18 2EA
Age Range: 3–11

WALTHAMSTOW MONTESSORI SCHOOL
● ✿

Penryhn Hall, Penryhn Avenue, Walthamstow, London E17 5DA
Website:
www.walthamstowmontessori.com
Age Range: 3–11

SENIOR

AL-MIZAN PRIMARY & LONDON EAST ACADEMY SECONDARY & SIXTH FORM
● ✿ ▲

82–92 Whitechapel Road, London E1 1JX
Website: www.leacademy.com
Age Range: 7–18

DARUL HADIS LATIFIAH
● ✿ ▲

1 Cornwall Avenue, London E2 0HW
Age Range: 11–19

EAST LONDON CHRISTIAN CHOIR SCHOOL
● ✿

St. Mark's Community Halls, Colvestone Crescent, Dalston, London E8 2NL
Website: www.elccs.org.uk
Age Range: 3–16

FOREST SCHOOL*
● ✿ ▲

College Place, Snaresbrook, London E17 3PY
Website: www.forest.org.uk
Age Range: 4–18
(Single-sex ed 7–16)

LONDON ISLAMIC SCHOOL
● ✿

18–22 Damien Street, London E1 2HX
Age Range: 11–16

MADNI GIRLS SCHOOL
● ✿ ▲

Myrdle Street, London E1 1HL
Age Range: 12–18

NORMANHURST SCHOOL
● ✿

68/74 Station Road, Chingford, London E4 7BA
Website:
www.normanhurstschool.co.uk
Age Range: 3–16

SOUTH EAST LONDON

NURSERY AND PRE-PREP

THE VILLA PRE-PREPARATORY SCHOOL

54 Lyndhurst Grove, London SE15 5AH
Website:
www.thevillaschoolandnursery.com
Age Range: 4–7

PREPARATORY

BLACKHEATH PREPARATORY SCHOOL

4 St Germans Place, Blackheath, London SE3 0NJ
Website:
www.blakcheathprepschool.com
Age Range: 3–11

DULWICH COLLEGE PREPARATORY SCHOOL

42 Alleyn Park, Dulwich, London SE21 7AA
Website: www.dcpslondon.org
Age Range: 3–13 (Girls 3–5)

HEATH HOUSE PREPARATORY SCHOOL

37 Wemyss Road, Blackheath, London SE3 0TG
Website: www.
heathhouseprepschool.com
Age Range: 4–11

HERNE HILL SCHOOL

The Old Vicarage, 127 Herne Hill, London SE24 9LY
Website:
www.hernehillschool.co.uk
Age Range: 3–7

JAMES ALLEN'S PREPARATORY SCHOOL

East Dulwich Grove, London SE22 8TE
Website: www.jags.org.uk/japs
Age Range: 4–11

OAKFIELD PREPARATORY SCHOOL

125–128 Thurlow Park Road, Dulwich, London SE21 8HP
Website: www.oakfield.dulwich.sch.uk
Age Range: 2–11

THE POINTER SCHOOL

19 Stratheden Road, Blackheath, London SE3 7TH
Website: www.pointers-school.co.uk
Age Range: 3–11

ROSEMEAD PREPARATORY SCHOOL

70 Thurlow Park Road, London SE21 8HZ
Website: www.
rosemeadprepschool.org.uk
Age Range: 3–11

ST OLAVE'S PREPARATORY SCHOOL

106–110 Southwood Road, New Eltham, London SE9 3QS
Website: www.stolaves.org.uk
Age Range: 3–11

SPRINGFIELD CHRISTIAN SCHOOL

145 Perry Hill, Catford, London SE6 4LP
Website:
www.springfieldsch.co.uk

THEODORE MCLEARY PRIMARY SCHOOL

31 East Dulwich Grove, Clapham, London SE22 8PW
Age Range: 5–10

VIRGO FIDELIS

147 Central Hill, Upper Norwood, London SE19 1RS
Age Range: 3–11

SENIOR

ALLEYN'S SCHOOL

Townley Road, Dulwich, London SE22 8SU
Website: www.alleyns.org.uk
Age Range: 4–18

BLACKHEATH HIGH SCHOOL GDST

Vanbrugh Park, Blackheath, London SE3 7AG
Website:
www.blackheathhighschool.gdst.net
Age Range: 3–18

COLFE'S SCHOOL

Horn Park Lane, London SE12 8AW
Website: www.colfes.com
Age Range: 3–18

DULWICH COLLEGE

Dulwich Common, London SE21 7LD
Website: www.dulwich.org.uk
Age Range: 7–18

ELTHAM COLLEGE

Grove Park Road, Mottingham, London SE9 4QF
Website:
www.eltham-college.org.uk
Age Range: 7–18

JAMES ALLEN'S GIRLS' SCHOOL

East Dulwich Grove, London SE22 8TE
Website: www.jags.org.uk
Age Range: 4–18

RIVERSTON SCHOOL

63–69 Eltham Road, London SE12 8UF
Website: www.riverston.greenwich.sch.uk
Age Range: 1–16

ST DUNSTAN'S COLLEGE

Stanstead Road, London SE6 4TY
Website: www.stdunstans.org.uk
Age Range: 3–18

SYDENHAM HIGH SCHOOL GDST

19 Westwood Hill, London SE26 6BL
Website: www.gdst.net/sydenhamhigh/
Age Range: 4–18

INDEPENDENT SIXTH FORM COLLEGE / TUTORIAL COLLEGE

HOLBORN COLLEGE
Woolwich Road, London SE7 8LN
Website: www.holborncollege.ac.uk

SOUTH WEST LONDON

NURSERY AND PRE-PREP

EATON HOUSE THE MANOR PRE-PREPARATORY

58 Clapham Common Northside, London SW4 9RU
Website: www.eatonhouseschools.com
Age Range: 4–8

THOMAS'S KINDERGARTEN, BATTERSEA
The Crypt, Saint Mary's Church, Battersea Church Road, London SW11 3NA
Website: www.thomas-s.co.uk
Age Range: 2–5

PREPARATORY

BALHAM PREPARATORY SCHOOL
47a Balham High Road, London SW12 9AW
Age Range: 3–16

BROOMWOOD HALL SCHOOL
68–74 Nightingale Lane, London SW12 8NR
Website: www.broomwood.co.uk
Age Range: 4–13

COLET COURT
St Paul's Preparatory School, Lonsdale Road, London SW13 9JT
Website: www.coletcourt.org.uk
Age Range: 7–13

DOLPHIN SCHOOL (INCLUDING NOAH'S ARK NURSERY SCHOOL)*
106 Northcote Road, Battersea, London SW11 6QW
Website: www.dolphinschool.org.uk
Age Range: 2–11

THE DOMINIE
55 Warriner Gardens, Battersea, London SW11 4DX
Website: www.thedominie.co.uk
Age Range: 6–12

DONHEAD PREP SCHOOL
33 Edge Hill, Wimbledon, London SW19 4NP
Website: www.donhead.org.uk
Age Range: 4–11

EATON HOUSE THE MANOR PREPARATORY
58 Clapham Common Northside, London SW4 9RU
Website: www.eatonhouseschools.com
Age Range: 3–13

EVELINE DAY SCHOOL
14 Trinity Crescent, Upper Tooting, London SW17 7AE
Website: www.evelinedayschool.com
Age Range: 3–11

FINTON HOUSE SCHOOL
171 Trinity Road, London SW17 7HL
Website: www.fintonhouse.org.uk
Age Range: 4–11

HALL SCHOOL WIMBLEDON (JUNIOR SCHOOL)

Stroud Crescent, Putney Vale, London SW15 3EQ
Website: www.hsw.co.uk
Age Range: 4–11

HORNSBY HOUSE SCHOOL

Hearnville Road, London SW12 8RS
Website:
www.hornsby-house.co.uk
Age Range: 4–11

THE HURLINGHAM SCHOOL

122 Putney Bridge Road, Putney, London SW15 2NQ
Website:
www.hurlinghamschool.co.uk
Age Range: 4–11

KING'S COLLEGE JUNIOR SCHOOL

Southside, Wimbledon Common, London SW19 4TT
Website: www.kcs.org.uk
Age Range: 7–13

LION HOUSE SCHOOL

The Old Methodist Hall, Gwendolen Avenue, London SW15 6EH
Website:
www.lionhouseschool.co.uk
Age Range: 3–8

THE MERLIN SCHOOL

4 Carlton Drive, Putney, London SW15 2BZ
Age Range: 4–8

NEWTON PREP

149 Battersea Park Road, London SW8 4BX
Website:
www.newtonprepschool.co.uk
Age Range: 3–13

NORTHCOTE LODGE SCHOOL

26 Bolingbroke Grove, London SW11 6EL
Website:
www.northcotelodge.co.uk
Age Range: 8–13

PARKGATE HOUSE SCHOOL*

80 Clapham Common North Side, London SW4 9SD
Website:
www.parkgate-school.co.uk
Age Range: 2–11

PROSPECT HOUSE SCHOOL

75 Putney Hill, London SW15 3NT
Website:
www.prospecths.org.uk
Age Range: 3–11

THE ROCHE SCHOOL

11 Frogmore, Wandsworth, London SW18 1HW
Website:
www.therocheschool.co.uk
Age Range: 2–11

THE ROWANS SCHOOL

19 Drax Avenue, Wimbledon, London SW20 0EG
Website: www.kcs.org.uk
Age Range: 3–8

THE STUDY PREPARATORY SCHOOL

Wilberforce House, Camp Road, Wimbledon Common, London SW19 4UN
Website:
www.thestudyprep.co.uk
Age Range: 4–11

THOMAS'S PREPARATORY SCHOOL

28–40 Battersea High Street, London SW11 3JB
Website: www.thomas-s.co.uk
Age Range: 4–13

THOMAS'S PREPARATORY SCHOOL CLAPHAM

Broomwood Road, London SW11 6JZ
Website: www.thomas-s.co.uk
Age Range: 4–13

TOWER HOUSE SCHOOL

188 Sheen Lane, East Sheen, London SW14 8LF
Website:
http://www.thsboys.org.uk/
Age Range: 4–13

URSULINE PREPARATORY SCHOOL

18 The Downs, London SW20 8HR
Website: www.ursuline-prep.
merton.sch.uk
Age Range: 3–11 (Boys 3–7)

WALDORF SCHOOL OF SOUTH WEST LONDON

Woodfields, Abbotswood Road, London SW16 1AP
Website:
www.waldorf-swlondon.org
Age Range: 4–14

THE WHITE HOUSE PREP & WOODENTOPS KINDERGARTEN

24 Thornton Road, Clapham Park, London SW12 0LF
Website:
www.whitehouseschool.com
Age Range: 2–11

WILLINGTON SCHOOL

Worcester Road, Wimbledon, London SW19 7QQ
Website:
www.willingtonschool.co.uk
Age Range: 4–13

England – Greater Manchester

WIMBLEDON COMMON PREPARATORY SCHOOL
●🏠
113 Ridgway, Wimbledon, London SW19 4TA
Website: www.wimbledoncommonprep.co.uk
Age Range: 4–8

SENIOR

EMANUEL SCHOOL
●🏠▲
Battersea Rise, London SW11 1HS
Website: www.emanuel.org.uk
Age Range: 10–18

HALL SCHOOL WIMBLEDON (SENIOR SCHOOL)
●🏠
17 The Downs, Wimbledon, London SW20 8HF
Website: www.hsw.co.uk
Age Range: 11–16

THE HARRODIAN
●🏠▲
Lonsdale Road, London SW13 9QN
Website: www.harrodian.com
Age Range: 5–18

IBSTOCK PLACE SCHOOL
●🏠▲
Clarence Lane, London SW15 5PY
Website: www.ibstockplaceschool.co.uk
Age Range: 3–18

KING'S COLLEGE SCHOOL
●🏠★▲
Wimbledon Common, London SW19 4TT
Website: www.kcs.org.uk
Age Range: 13–18

THE NORWEGIAN SCHOOL
●🏠
28 Arterberry Road, Wimbledon, London SW20 8AH
Age Range: 3–16

PUTNEY HIGH SCHOOL GDST
●🏠▲
35 Putney Hill, London SW15 6BH
Website: www.gdst.net/putneyhigh
Age Range: 4–18

PUTNEY PARK SCHOOL*
●🏠◆
11 Woodborough Road, Putney, London SW15 6PY
Website: www.putneypark.london.sch.uk
Age Range: 4–16

ST PAUL'S SCHOOL
●🏠▲
Lonsdale Road, Barnes, London SW13 9JT
Website: www.stpaulsschool.org.uk
Age Range: 13–18

STREATHAM & CLAPHAM HIGH SCHOOL
●🏠▲
42 Abbotswood Road, London SW16 1AW
Website: www.gdst.net/streathamhigh
Age Range: 3–18 (Boys 3–5)

THAMES CHRISTIAN COLLEGE
●🏠◆
Wye Street, Battersea, London SW11 2HB
Website: www.thameschristiancollege.org.uk
Age Range: 11–16

WiMBLEDON HIGH SCHOOL GDST
●🏠▲
Mansel Road, London SW19 4AB
Website: www.wimbledonhigh.gdst.net
Age Range: 4–18

GREATER MANCHESTER

PREPARATORY

ABBOTSFORD PREPARATORY SCHOOL
●🏠
211 Flixton Road, Urmston, Manchester, Greater Manchester M41 5PR
Website: www.abbotsfordprepschool.co.uk
Age Range: 3–11

BRANWOOD PREPARATORY SCHOOL
●🏠
Stafford Road, Monton, Eccles, Greater Manchester M30 9HN
Age Range: 3–11

CLARENDON COTTAGE SCHOOL
●🏠
Ivy Bank House, Half Edge Lane, Eccles, Greater Manchester M30 9BJ
Website: www.clarendoncottage.com
Age Range: 1–11

LIGHTHOUSE CHRISTIAN SCHOOL
●🏠
193 Ashley Lane, Moston, Manchester, Greater Manchester M9 4NQ
Website: www.lighthousechristianschool.co.uk
Age Range: 2–14

MANCHESTER MUSLIM PREPARATORY SCHOOL

551 Wilmslow Road, Withington, Manchester, Greater Manchester M20 4BA
Age Range: 3–11

MONTON PREP SCHOOL WITH MONTESSORI NURSERIES

The School House, Francis Street, Monton, Eccles, Greater Manchester M30 9PR
Website: www.montonvillageschool.com
Age Range: 2–13

MOOR ALLERTON SCHOOL

131 Barlow Moor Road, Manchester, Greater Manchester M20 2PW
Website: www.moorallertonschool.com
Age Range: 3–11

PRESTWICH PREPARATORY SCHOOL

400 Bury Old Road, Prestwich, Greater Manchester M25 1PZ
Age Range: 2–11

SENIOR

AL JAMIAH AL ISLAMIYYAH

Hospital Road, Bromley Cross, Bolton, Greater Manchester BL7 9PY
Website: www.al-jamiah-al-islamiyyah. org.uk
Age Range: 13–16

BRIDGEWATER SCHOOL

Drywood Hall, Worsley Road, Worsley, Manchester, Greater Manchester M28 2WQ
Website: www.bridgewater-school.co.uk
Age Range: 3–18

CHETHAM'S SCHOOL OF MUSIC

Long Millgate, Manchester, Greater Manchester M3 1SB
Website: www.chethams.com
Age Range: 8–18

KASSIM DARWISH GRAMMAR SCHOOL FOR BOYS

Hartley Hall, Alexandra Road South, Chorlton-cum-Hardy, Manchester, Greater Manchester M16 8NH
Age Range: 11–16

KING OF KINGS SCHOOL

142 Dantzic Street, Manchester, Greater Manchester M4 4DN
Age Range: 3–16

THE MANCHESTER GRAMMAR SCHOOL

Old Hall Lane, Manchester, Greater Manchester M13 0XT
Website: www.mgs.org
Age Range: 9–18

MANCHESTER HIGH SCHOOL FOR GIRLS

Grangethorpe Road, Manchester, Greater Manchester M14 6HS
Website: www.manchesterhigh.co.uk
Age Range: 4–18

MANCHESTER ISLAMIC HIGH SCHOOL

55 High Lane, Chorlton, Manchester, Greater Manchester M21 9FA
Age Range: 11–16

ST BEDE'S COLLEGE

Alexandra Park, Manchester, Greater Manchester M16 8HX
Website: www.stbedescollege.co.uk
Age Range: 4–18

WITHINGTON GIRLS' SCHOOL

100, Wellington Road, Fallowfield, Manchester, Greater Manchester M14 6BL
Website: www.withington.manchester. sch.uk
Age Range: 7–18

INDEPENDENT SIXTH FORM COLLEGE / TUTORIAL COLLEGE

ABBEY COLLEGE

Cheapside, King Street, Manchester, Greater Manchester M2 4WG
Website: www.abbeymanchester.co.uk
Age Range: 14–19

MERSEYSIDE

PREPARATORY

ATHERTON HOUSE SCHOOL
6 Alexandra Road, Crosby,
Liverpool, Merseyside L23 7TF
Website:
www.athertonhouse.ndo.co.uk
Age Range: 2–11

AVALON PREPARATORY SCHOOL
Caldy Road, West Kirby, Wirral,
Merseyside CH48 2HE
Website:
www.avalon-school.co.uk
Age Range: 2–11

BEECHENHURST PREPARATORY SCHOOL
145 Menlove Avenue, Liverpool,
Merseyside L18 3EE
Website:
www.beechenhurst-school.
org.uk
Age Range: 3–11

CARLETON HOUSE PREPARATORY SCHOOL
Lyndhurst Road, Mossley Hill,
Liverpool, Merseyside L18 8AQ
Website:
www.carletonhouse.co.uk
Age Range: 4–11

NEWTON BANK SCHOOL
34 High Street, Newton-Le-
Willows, Merseyside WA12 9SN
Age Range: 2–10

PRENTON PREPARATORY SCHOOL
Mount Pleasant, Oxton, Wirral,
Merseyside
Website:
www.prentonprep.co.uk
Age Range: 2–11

REDCOURT- ST ANSELMS
7 Devonshire Place, Prenton,
Merseyside CH43 1TX
Website:
www.redcourtstanselms.com
Age Range: 3–11

RUNNYMEDE ST EDWARD'S SCHOOL
North Drive, Sandfield Park,
Liverpool, Merseyside L12 1LE
Website:
www.runnymede-school.org.uk
Age Range: 3–11

SUNNYMEDE SCHOOL
4 Westcliffe Road, Birkdale,
Southport, Merseyside PR8 2BN
Website:
www.sunnymedeschool.org
Age Range: 3–11

SENIOR

ARDEN COLLEGE
40 Derby Road, Southport,
Merseyside PR9 0TZ
Website: www.ardencollege.
ac.uk
Age Range: 16–25

AUCKLAND COLLEGE
65–67 Parkfield Road,
Liverpool, Merseyside L17 4LE
Website:
www.aucklandcollege.com
Age Range: 7–18

BIRKENHEAD SCHOOL
58 Beresford Road, Oxton,
Wirral, Merseyside CH43 2JD
Website:
www.birkenheadschool.co.uk
Age Range: 3–18

HIGHFIELD SCHOOL
96 Bidston Road, Oxton,
Birkenhead, Merseyside CH43
6TW
Website: www.btinternet.com/
highfield.school
Age Range: 2–16

KINGSMEAD SCHOOL
Bertram Drive, Hoylake, Wirral,
Merseyside CH47 0LL
Website:
www.kingsmeadschool.com
Age Range: 2–16

LIVERPOOL COLLEGE
Queens's Drive, Mossley Hill,
Liverpool, Merseyside L18 8BG
Website:
www.liverpoolcollege.org.uk
Age Range: 3–18

MERCHANT TAYLORS' BOYS' SCHOOLS
Liverpool Road, Crosby,
Liverpool, Merseyside L23 0QP
Website:
www.merchanttaylors.com
Age Range: 4–18

MERCHANT TAYLORS' GIRLS' SCHOOL
Liverpool Road, Crosby,
Liverpool, Merseyside L23 5SP
Website:
www.merchanttaylors.com
Age Range: 4–18
(Infant Boys 4–7)

ST MARY'S COLLEGE
Crosby, Liverpool, Merseyside
L23 5TW
Website: www.stmarys.ac

STREATHAM HOUSE SCHOOL

Victoria Road West,
Blundellsands, Liverpool,
Merseyside L23 8UQ
Website:
www.streathamhouse.co.uk
Age Range: 2–16 (Boys 2–11)

TOWER COLLEGE

Mill Lane, Rainhill, Prescot,
Merseyside L35 6NE
Website: www.towercollege.com
Age Range: 3–16

MIDDLESEX

NURSERY AND PRE-PREP

JACK AND JILL SCHOOL

30 Nightingale Road, Hampton,
Middlesex TW12 3HX
Website:
www.jackandjillschool.co.uk
Age Range: 2–7 (Boys 3–5)

PREPARATORY

ALPHA PREPARATORY SCHOOL

21 Hindes Road, Harrow,
Middlesex HA1 1SH
Website:
www.alpha.harrow.sch.uk
Age Range: 4–11

ASHTON HOUSE SCHOOL

50/52 Eversley Crescent,
Isleworth, Middlesex TW7 4LW
Website: www.ashtonhouse.com
Age Range: 3–11

ATHELSTAN HOUSE SCHOOL

36 Percy Road, Hampton,
Middlesex TW12 2LA
Website: www.
athelstanhouseschool.co.uk
Age Range: 3–7

BUCKINGHAM COLLEGE PREPARATORY SCHOOL

458 Rayners Lane, Pinner,
Middlesex HA5 5DT
Website: www.buckprep.org
Age Range: 4–11

BUXLOW PREPARATORY SCHOOL

5/6 Castleton Gardens,
Wembley, Middlesex HA9 7QJ
Website:
www.buxlowschool.com
Age Range: 4–11

DENMEAD SCHOOL

41–43 Wensleydale Road,
Hampton, Middlesex TW12 2LP
Website:
www.denmead.richmond.sch.uk
Age Range: 3–11 (Girls 3–7)

HOLLAND HOUSE

1 Broadhurst Avenue, Edgware,
Middlesex HA8 8TP
Website:
www.hollandhouse.org.uk
Age Range: 4–11

INNELLAN HOUSE SCHOOL

44 Love Lane, Pinner, Middlesex
HA5 3EX
Age Range: 3–7

THE MALL SCHOOL

185 Hampton Road, 185
Hampton Road, Twickenham,
Middlesex TW2 5NQ
Website:
www.mall.richmond.sch.uk
Age Range: 4–13

NEWLAND HOUSE SCHOOL

Waldegrave Park, Twickenham,
Middlesex TW1 4TQ
Website:
www.newlandhouse.co.uk
Age Range: 4–13

ORLEY FARM SCHOOL

South Hill Avenue, Harrow,
Middlesex HA1 3NU
Age Range: 4–13

QUAINTON HALL SCHOOL

91 Hindes Road, Harrow,
Middlesex HA1 1RX
Website:
www.quaintonhall.org.uk
Age Range: 4–13

REDDIFORD

36–38 Cecil Park, Pinner,
Middlesex HA5 5HH
Website: www.reddiford.org.uk
Age Range: 2–11

ROXETH MEAD SCHOOL

Buckholt House, 25 Middle Road, Harrow on the Hill, Middlesex HA2 0HW
Website: www.roxethmead.com
Age Range: 3–7

ST CHRISTOPHER'S SCHOOL

71 Wembley Park Drive, Wembley, Middlesex HA9 8HE
Website:
www.happychildschools.co.uk
Age Range: 4–11

ST HELEN'S COLLEGE

Parkway, Hillingdon, Middlesex UB10 9JX
Website: sthelenscollege.com
Age Range: 3–11

ST JOHN'S NORTHWOOD

Potter Street Hill, Northwood, Middlesex HA6 3QY
Website: www.st-johns.org.uk
Age Range: 3–13

ST MARTIN'S SCHOOL

40 Moor Park Road, Northwood, Middlesex HA6 2DJ
Website: www.stmartins.org.uk
Age Range: 3–13

STAINES PREPARATORY SCHOOL

3 Gresham Road, Staines, Middlesex TW18 2BT
Website:
www.stainesprep.co.uk
Age Range: 3–11 (The earliest we can accept pupils is in the term they are rising three years of age.)

TWICKENHAM PREPARATORY SCHOOL

Beveree, 43 High Street, Hampton, Middlesex TW12 2SA
Website:
www.twickenhamprep.co.uk
Age Range: 4–13

SENIOR

BUCKINGHAM COLLEGE SCHOOL

11–17 Hindes Road, Harrow, Middlesex HA1 1SH
Website: www.buckcoll.org
Age Range: 11–18 (Co-ed VIth Form, but currently boys only.)

HALLIFORD SCHOOL

Russell Road, Shepperton, Middlesex TW17 9HX
Website:
www.hallifordschool.co.uk
Age Range: 11–18
(Co-ed VIth Form)

HAMPTON SCHOOL

Hanworth Road, Hampton, Middlesex TW12 3HD
Website: www.hamptonschool. org.uk
Age Range: 11–18

HARROW SCHOOL

1 High Street, Harrow on the Hill, Middlesex HA1 3HT
Website:
www.harrowschool.org.uk
Age Range: 13–18

HEATHFIELD SCHOOL

Beaulieu Drive, Pinner, Middlesex HA5 1NB
Website:
www.heathfield.gdst.net
Age Range: 3–18

THE JOHN LYON SCHOOL

Middle Road, Harrow, Middlesex HA2 0HN
Website: www.johnlyon.org
Age Range: 11–18

THE LADY ELEANOR HOLLES SCHOOL

102 Hanworth Road, Hampton, Middlesex TW12 3HF
Website: www.lehs.org.uk
Age Range: 7–18

LITTLE EDEN & EDEN HIGH SDA

St George's Hall, Green Dragaon Lane, Brentford, Middlesex TW8 0EN
Website:
www.theedenschool.com
Age Range: 3–16

MERCHANT TAYLORS' SCHOOL

Sandy Lodge, Northwood, Middlesex HA6 2HT
Website: www.mtsn.org.uk
Age Range: 11–18

NORTH LONDON COLLEGIATE

Canons Drive, Edgware, Middlesex HA8 7RJ
Website: www.nlcs.org.uk
Age Range: 4–18

NORTHWOOD COLLEGE*

Maxwell Road, Northwood, Middlesex HA6 2YE
Website:
www.northwoodcollege.co.uk
Age Range: 3–18

PETERBOROUGH & ST MARGARET'S SCHOOL

Common Road, Stanmore, Middlesex HA7 3JB
Website: www.psmschool.org
Age Range: 4–16

RAVENSCOURT THEATRE SCHOOL

3 Thameside Centre, Kew Bridge Road, Middlesex TW8 0HF
Website: www.ravenscourt.net
Age Range: 8–16

ST CATHERINE'S SCHOOL*

Cross Deep, Twickenham, Middlesex TW1 4QJ
Website:
www.stcatherineschool.co.uk
Age Range: 3–18 (Girls 3–18)

ST HELEN'S SCHOOL*

● ♔ ★ ▲

Eastbury Road, Northwood,
Middlesex HA6 3AS
Website: www.sthn.co.uk
Age Range: 3–18

ST JOHN'S SENIOR SCHOOL

● ♔ ▲

North Lodge, The Ridgeway,
Enfield, Middlesex EN2 8BE
Website: www.
stjohnsseniorschool.com
Age Range: 10–18

INDEPENDENT SIXTH FORM COLLEGE / TUTORIAL COLLEGE

ACORN INDEPENDENT COLLEGE

● ♔

39–47 High Street, Southall,
Middlesex UB1 3HF
Website:
www.acorn-college.co.uk
Age Range: 13–20

INTERNATIONAL SCHOOLS AND INTERNATIONAL STUDY CENTRES

ACS HILLINGDON INTERNATIONAL SCHOOL*

● ♔ ★ ▲

Hillingdon Court, 108 Vine Lane,
Hillingdon, Middlesex UB10 0BE
Website: www.acs-schools.com
Age Range: 4–18

NORFOLK

NURSERY AND PRE-PREP

STRETTON SCHOOL

● ♔

1 Albemarle Road, Norwich,
Norfolk NR2 2DF
Website:
www.stretton-school.co.uk
Age Range: 1–8

PREPARATORY

BEESTON HALL SCHOOL

● ♔

West Runton, Cromer, Norfolk
NR27 9NQ
Website: www.beestonhall.co.uk
Age Range: 7–13

DOWNHAM PREP SCHOOL AND MONTESSORI NURSERY

● ♔

The Old Rectory, Stow
Bardolph, Kings Lynn, Norfolk
PE34 3HT
Website:
www.dpsmn.norfolk.sch.uk
Age Range: 2–11

GLEBE HOUSE SCHOOL

● ♔

2 Cromer Road, Hunstanton,
Norfolk PE36 6HW
Website:
www.glebehouseschool.co.uk
Age Range: 4–13

LANGLEY PREPARATORY SCHOOL & NURSERY

● ♔

Beech Hill, 11 Yarmouth Road,
Thorpe St Andrew, Norwich,
Norfolk NR7 0EA
Website:
www.langleyprep.norfolk.sch.uk
Age Range: 2–11

NOTRE DAME PREPARATORY SCHOOL

● ♔

147 Dereham Road, Norwich,
Norfolk NR2 3TA
Website:
www.notredameprepschool.
co.uk
Age Range: 3–11

RIDDLESWORTH HALL

● ♔ ◆

Diss, Norfolk IP22 2TA
Website:
www.riddlesworthhall.com
Age Range: 2–13
(Coeducational boarding)

ST CHRISTOPHER'S SCHOOL

● ♔

George Hill, Old Catton,
Norwich, Norfolk NR6 7DE
Website:
www.stchristophersnorwich.
co.uk
Age Range: 2–8

ST NICHOLAS HOUSE KINDERGARTEN & PREP SCHOOL

● ♔

Yarmouth Road, North Walsham,
Norfolk NR28 9AT
Website:
www.stnicholashouse.com
Age Range: 3–11

TAVERHAM HALL PREPARATORY SCHOOL

● ♔

Taverham Park, Taverham,
Norwich, Norfolk NR8 6HU
Website:
www.taverhamhall.co.uk
Age Range: 1–13

TOWN CLOSE HOUSE PREPARATORY SCHOOL

● ♔

14 Ipswich Road, Norwich,
Norfolk NR2 2LR
Website: www.townclose.com
Age Range: 3–13

SENIOR

ALL SAINTS SCHOOL

School Road, Lessingham,
Norwich, Norfolk NR12 0DJ
Website:
www.allsaintslessingham.co.uk
Age Range: 2–16

GRESHAM'S SCHOOL

Cromer Road, Holt, Norfolk
NR25 6EA
Website: www.greshams.com
Age Range: 13–18

HETHERSETT OLD HALL SCHOOL

Norwich Road, Hethersett,
Norwich, Norfolk NR9 3DW
Website: www.hohs.co.uk
Age Range: 4–18 (Day boys
admitted aged 4–11 Day girls
admitted aged 4–18 Boarding
girls admitted aged 9–18 No
boys boarding)

LANGLEY SCHOOL

Langley Park, Loddon, Norwich,
Norfolk NR14 6BJ
Website:
www.langleyschool.co.uk
Age Range: 10–18

THE NEW ECCLES HALL SCHOOL

Quidenham, Norwich, Norfolk
NR16 2NZ
Website:
www.neweccleshall.com
Age Range: 4–16

NORWICH HIGH SCHOOL FOR GIRLS GDST

Eaton Grove, 95 Newmarket
Road, Norwich, Norfolk NR2
2HU
Website: www.gdst.net/norwich
Age Range: 3–18

NORWICH SCHOOL

70 The Close, Norwich, Norfolk
NR1 4DD
Website:
www.norwich-school.org.uk
Age Range: 7–18
(Co-ed VIth Form)

SACRED HEART SCHOOL

17 Mangate Street, Swaffham,
Norfolk PE37 7QW
Website:
www.sacredheart.norfolk.sch.uk
Age Range: 3–16

THETFORD GRAMMAR SCHOOL

Bridge Street, Thetford, Norfolk
IP24 3AF
Website:
www.thetgram.norfolk.sch.uk
Age Range: 3–18

THORPE HOUSE SCHOOL

7 Yarmouth Road, Norwich,
Norfolk NR7 0EA
Website:
www.thorpehouseschool.com
Age Range: 3–16

WOOD DENE SCHOOL

Aylmerton Hall, Holt Road,
Aylmerton, Norwich, Norfolk
NR11 8QA
Website: www.wood-dene.co.uk
Age Range: 2–16

NORTHAMPTONSHIRE

NURSERY AND PRE-PREP

SLAPTON PRE-PREPARATORY SCHOOL

Chapel Lane, Slapton,
Towcester, Northamptonshire
NN12 8PE
Website:
www.slaptonpreprep.org
Age Range: 4–8

PREPARATORY

BEACHBOROUGH SCHOOL

Westbury, Brackley,
Northamptonshire NN13 5LB
Website:
www.beachborough.com
Age Range: 2–13

GREAT HOUGHTON SCHOOL*

Great Houghton Hall,
Northampton, Northamptonshire
NN4 7AG
Website: www.ghschool.net
Age Range: 3 months–13

LAXTON JUNIOR SCHOOL*

East Road, Oundle, Nr
Peterborough,
Northamptonshire PE8 4BX
Website:
www.laxtonjunior.org.uk
Age Range: 4–11

MAIDWELL HALL SCHOOL

Maidwell, Northamptonshire
NN6 9JG
Website:
www.maidwellhall.co.uk
Age Range: 7–13 (The school is
accepting girls for the first time
in September 2010.)

ST MATTHEWS SCHOOL

100 Park Avenue North,
Northampton, Northamptonshire
NN3 2JB
Age Range: 2–9

ST PETER'S SCHOOL

52 Headlands, Kettering,
Northamptonshire NN15 6DJ
Website: www.st-peters.org.uk
Age Range: 2–11

SPRATTON HALL

Smith Street, Spratton,
Northampton, Northamptonshire
NN6 8HP
Website: www.sprattonhall.com
Age Range: 4–13

WINCHESTER HOUSE SCHOOL

High Street, Brackley,
Northamptonshire NN13 7AZ
Website:
www.winchester-house.org
Age Range: 3–13

SENIOR

NORTHAMPTON HIGH SCHOOL

Newport Pagnell Road,
Hardingstone, Northampton,
Northamptonshire NN4 6UU
Website:
www.gdst.net/northamptonhigh
Age Range: 3–18

OUNDLE SCHOOL

The Great Hall, New Street,
Oundle, Nr Peterborough,
Northamptonshire PE8 4GH
Website:
www.oundleschool.org.uk
Age Range: 11–19

PITSFORD SCHOOL

Pitsford Hall, Moulton Lane,
Pitsford, Northamptonshire NN6
9AX
Website:
www.pitsfordschool.com
Age Range: 3–18

QUINTON HOUSE SCHOOL

Upton Hall, Upton,
Northampton, Northamptonshire
NN5 4UX
Website:
www.quintonhouseschool.co.uk
Age Range: 2–18

ST PETER'S INDEPENDENT SCHOOL

Lingswood Park, Blackthorn,
Northamptonshire NN3 8TA
Website: www.
stpetersindependentschool.co.uk
Age Range: 4–18

WELLINGBOROUGH SCHOOL

Wellingborough,
Northamptonshire NN8 2BX
Website:
www.wellingboroughschool.org
Age Range: 3–18

INDEPENDENT SIXTH FORM COLLEGE / TUTORIAL COLLEGE

BOSWORTH INDEPENDENT COLLEGE

Nazareth House, Barrack Road,
Northampton, Northamptonshire
NN2 6AF
Website:
www.bosworthcollege.com
Age Range: 14–21

NORTHUMBERLAND

PREPARATORY

MOWDEN HALL SCHOOL

Newton, Stocksfield,
Northumberland NE43 7TP
Website:
www.mowdenhall.co.uk
Age Range: 3–13

ROCK HALL SCHOOL

Rock, Alnwick, Northumberland
NE66 3SB
Website:
www.rockhallschool.com
Age Range: 3–13

SENIOR

LONGRIDGE TOWERS SCHOOL

Berwick-upon-Tweed,
Northumberland TD15 2XQ
Website: www.lts.org.uk
Age Range: 4–18

ST OSWALD'S SCHOOL

Spring Gardens, South Road,
Alnwick, Northumberland
NE66 2NU
Website: www.st-oswalds.
northumberland.sch.uk
Age Range: 3–16

NOTTINGHAMSHIRE

PREPARATORY

ARLEY HOUSE SCHOOL

8 Station Road, East Leake,
Nottinghamshire LE12 6LQ
Website:
www.arley-pneu.eastleake.sch.uk
Age Range: 3–11

COTESWOOD HOUSE SCHOOL

19 Thackeray's Lane,
Woodthorpe, Nottingham,
Nottinghamshire NG5 4HT
Age Range: 3–11

GREENHOLME SCHOOL

392 Derby Road, Nottingham,
Nottinghamshire NG7 2DX
Website:
www.greenholmeschool.co.uk
Age Range: 3–11

GROSVENOR SCHOOL

Edwalton Grange, 218 Melton
Road, Edwalton, Nottingham,
Nottinghamshire NG12 4BS
Website:
www.grosvenorschool.co.uk
Age Range: 1–13

HAZEL HURST SCHOOL

400 Westdale Lane, Mapperley,
Nottingham, Nottinghamshire
NG3 6DG
Website:
www.hazelhurstschool.co.uk
Age Range: 2–8

HIGHFIELDS SCHOOL

London Road, Newark,
Nottinghamshire NG24 3AL
Website:
www.highfieldsschool.co.uk
Age Range: 3–11

MOUNTFORD HOUSE SCHOOL

373 Mansfield Road,
Nottingham, Nottinghamshire
NG5 2DA
Age Range: 3–11

NOTTINGHAM HIGH JUNIOR SCHOOL

Waverley Mount, Nottingham,
Nottinghamshire NG7 4ED
Website: www.nottinghamhigh.
co.uk
Age Range: 7–11

PLUMTREE SCHOOL

Church Hill, Plumtree,
Nottingham, Nottinghamshire
NG12 5ND
Website:
www.plumtreeschool.co.uk
Age Range: 3–11

RANBY HOUSE SCHOOL

Retford, Nottinghamshire DN22
8HX
Website:
www.ranbyhouseschool.co.uk
Age Range: 3–13

ST JOSEPH'S SCHOOL

33 Derby Road, Nottingham,
Nottinghamshire NG1 5AW
Website:
www.st-josephs.nottingham.
sch.uk
Age Range: 1–11

SALTERFORD HOUSE SCHOOL

Salterford Lane, Calverton,
Nottingham, Nottinghamshire
NG14 6NZ
Website:
www.salterfordhouseschool.
co.uk
Age Range: 2–11

SAVILLE HOUSE SCHOOL

11 Church Street, Mansfield
Woodhouse, Mansfield,
Nottinghamshire NG19 8AH
Website:
www.savillehouse.co.uk
Age Range: 3–11

WELLOW HOUSE SCHOOL

Wellow, Newark,
Nottinghamshire NG22 0EA
Website:
www.wellowhouse.notts.sch.uk
Age Range: 3–13

SENIOR

AL KARAM SECONDARY SCHOOL

Eaton Hall, Retford, Nottinghamshire DN22 0PR
Website: www.alkaram.org
Age Range: 11–16

DAGFA HOUSE SCHOOL

57 Broadgate, Beeston, Nottingham, Nottinghamshire NG9 2FU
Website: www.dagfahouse.notts.sch.uk
Age Range: 2–16

THE KING'S SCHOOL
Green Street, The Meadows, Nottingham, Nottinghamshire NG2 2LA
Website: www.thekingsschool.info
Age Range: 3–16

LAMMAS SCHOOL
Lammas Road, Sutton in Ashfield, Nottinghamshire NG17 2AD
Website: www.lammas-school.co.uk.
Age Range: 4–16

NOTTINGHAM HIGH SCHOOL FOR GIRLS GDST

9 Arboretum Street, Nottingham, Nottinghamshire NG1 4JB
Website: www.gdst.net/nottinghamgirlshigh
Age Range: 4–18

TRENT COLLEGE & THE ELMS

Long Eaton, Nottingham, Nottinghamshire NG10 4AD
Website: www.trentcollege.net
Age Range: 3–18

WORKSOP COLLEGE
Worksop, Nottinghamshire S80 3AP
Website: www.worksopcollege.notts.sch.uk
Age Range: 13–18

INDEPENDENT SIXTH FORM COLLEGE / TUTORIAL COLLEGE

WELBECK COLLEGE
Worksop, Nottinghamshire S80 3LN
Website: www.dsfc.ac.uk

OXFORDSHIRE

PREPARATORY

ABINGDON PREPARATORY SCHOOL
Josca's House, Kingston Road, Frilford, Abingdon, Oxfordshire OX13 5NX
Website: www.abingdon.org.uk/prep
Age Range: 4–13 (Girls 4–7)

THE CARRDUS SCHOOL

Overthorpe Hall, Banbury, Oxfordshire OX17 2BS
Website: www.carrdusschool.co.uk
Age Range: 3–11 (Boys 3–8)

CHANDLINGS MANOR SCHOOL
Bagley Wood, Kennington, Oxford, Oxfordshire OX1 5ND
Website: www.chandlings.com
Age Range: 4–11

CHRIST CHURCH CATHEDRAL SCHOOL

3 Brewer Street, Oxford, Oxfordshire OX1 1QW
Website: www.cccs.org.uk
Age Range: 3–13 (Girls 2–4)

COTHILL HOUSE PREPARATORY SCHOOL

Cothill, Abingdon, Oxfordshire OX13 6JL
Website: www.cothill.net
Age Range: 8–13

DRAGON SCHOOL
Bardwell Road, Oxford, Oxfordshire OX2 6SS
Website: www.dragonschool.org
Age Range: 4–13

EMMANUEL CHRISTIAN SCHOOL

Sandford Road, Littlemore, Oxford, Oxfordshire OX4 4PU
Website: www.ecschool.co.uk
Age Range: 3–11

FERNDALE PREPARATORY SCHOOL
5–7 Bromsgrove, Faringdon, Oxfordshire SN7 7JF
Website: www.ferndaleschool.co.uk
Age Range: 3–11

THE KING'S SCHOOL, PRIMARY
● 🏠

New Yatt Road, Witney,
Oxfordshire OX29 6TA
Website: www.occ.org.uk/tks/
Age Range: 5–11

THE MANOR PREPARATORY SCHOOL
● 🏠

Faringdon Road, Abingdon,
Oxfordshire OX13 6LN
Website: www.manorprep.org
Age Range: 2–11

MOULSFORD PREPARATORY SCHOOL
● 🏠

Moulsford, Wallingford,
Oxfordshire OX10 9HR
Website: www.moulsford.com
Age Range: 4–13

NEW COLLEGE SCHOOL
● 🏠

2 Savile Road, Oxford,
Oxfordshire OX1 3UA
Website:
www.newcollegeschool.org
Age Range: 4–13

THE ORATORY PREPARATORY SCHOOL
● 🏠

Goring Heath, Reading,
Oxfordshire RG8 7SF
Website:
www.oratoryprep.org.uk
Age Range: 3–13

OUR LADY'S ABINGDON JUNIOR SCHOOL
● 🏠

St John's Road, Abingdon,
Oxfordshire OX14 2HB
Website: www.olab.org.uk
Age Range: 3–11

OXFORD MONTESSORI SCHOOLS
● 🏠

Forest Farm, Elsfield, Oxford,
Oxfordshire OX3 9UW
Website:
www.oxfordmontessori.co.uk
Age Range: 2–12

RUPERT HOUSE
● 🏠

90 Bell Street, Henley-on-
Thames, Oxfordshire RG9 2BN
Website: www.ruperthouse.org
Age Range: 4–11

ST ANDREW'S
● 🏠

Wallingford Street, Wantage,
Oxfordshire OX12 8AZ
Website:
www.standrewswantage.org.uk
Age Range: 3–11

ST HUGH'S SCHOOL
● 🏠

Carswell Manor, Faringdon,
Oxfordshire SN7 8PT
Website: www.st-hughs.co.uk
Age Range: 3–13

ST JOHN'S PRIORY SCHOOL
● 🏠

St John's Road, Banbury,
Oxfordshire OX16 5HX
Website: www.stjohnspriory.com
Age Range: 2–11

ST MARY'S SCHOOL
● 🏠

13 St Andrew's Road,
Henley-on-Thames,
Oxfordshire RG9 1HS
Website:
www.cognitaschools.co.uk
Age Range: 3–11

SUMMER FIELDS
● 🏠

Mayfield Road, Oxford,
Oxfordshire OX2 7EN
Website:
www.summerfields.oxon.sch.uk
Age Range: 7–13

WINDRUSH VALLEY SCHOOL
● 🏠

The Green, London Lane,
Ascott-U-Wychwood, Chipping
Norton, Oxfordshire OX7 6AN
Website:
www.windrushvalley@aol.com
Age Range: 3–11

SENIOR

ABINGDON SCHOOL
● 🏠 ▲

Park Road, Abingdon,
Oxfordshire OX14 IDE
Website: www.abingdon.org.uk
Age Range: 11–18

ASH-SHIFA SCHOOL
● 🏠

Merton Street, Banbury,
Oxfordshire OX16 8RU
Website: www.ash-shifa.org.uk
Age Range: 11–16

COKETHORPE SCHOOL
● 🏠 ▲

Witney, Oxfordshire OX29 7PU
Website:
www.cokethorpe.org.uk
Age Range: 4–18

CRANFORD HOUSE SCHOOL
● 🏠

Moulsford, Wallingford,
Oxfordshire OX10 9HT
Website:
www.cranford-house.org
Age Range: 3–16 (Boys 3–7)

HEADINGTON SCHOOL
● 🏠 ▲

Oxford, Oxfordshire OX3 7TD
Website: www.headington.org
Age Range: 3–18 (Co-ed 3–4)

IQRA SCHOOL
● 🏠

Lawn Upton House, David
Nicholls Close, Littlemore,
Oxford, Oxfordshire OX4 4PU
Website: www.iqraschool.org.uk
Age Range: 10–16

KINGHAM HILL SCHOOL
● 🏠 ◆ ▲

Kingham, Chipping Norton,
Oxfordshire OX7 6TH
Website:
www.kingham-hill.oxon.sch.uk
Age Range: 11–18

LECKFORD PLACE SCHOOL
● 🏠

Leckford Road, Oxford,
Oxfordshire OX2 6HX
Website: www.leckfordplace.
com
Age Range: 11–16

MAGDALEN COLLEGE SCHOOL

Cowley Place, Oxford, Oxfordshire OX4 1DZ
Website: www.mcsoxford.org
Age Range: 7–18

OUR LADY'S ABINGDON SCHOOL

Radley Road, Abingdon, Oxfordshire OX14 3PS
Website: www.olab.org.uk
Age Range: 3–18 (Coed Junior school. Boys admitted to Senior school in Yr 7 & 6th form. Fully co-ed in 2013.)

OXFORD HIGH SCHOOL GDST

Belbroughton Road, Oxford, Oxfordshire OX2 6XA
Website: www.oxfordhigh.gdst.net
Age Range: 3–18 (Boys 4–6)

RADLEY COLLEGE
Abingdon, Oxfordshire OX14 2HR
Website: www.radley.org.uk
Age Range: 13–18

ST EDWARD'S SCHOOL
Woodstock Road, Oxford, Oxfordshire OX2 7NN
Website: www.stedwards.oxon.sch.uk
Age Range: 13–18

ST HELEN & ST KATHARINE
Faringdon Road, Abingdon, Oxfordshire OX14 1BE
Website: www.shsk.org.uk
Age Range: 9–18

ST. CLARE'S, OXFORD
139 Banbury Road, Oxford, Oxfordshire OX2 7AL
Website: www.stclares.ac.uk/ib
Age Range: 15–19

SHIPLAKE COLLEGE

Henley-on-Thames, Oxfordshire RG9 4BW
Website: www.shiplake.org.uk
Age Range: 11–18
(Day girls 16–18)

SIBFORD SCHOOL

Sibford Ferris, Banbury, Oxfordshire OX15 5QL
Website: www.sibford.oxon.sch.uk
Age Range: 4–18

TUDOR HALL SCHOOL*
Wykham Park, Banbury, Oxfordshire OX16 9UR
Website: www.tudorhallschool.com
Age Range: 11–18

WYCHWOOD SCHOOL

74 Banbury Road, Oxford, Oxfordshire OX2 6JR
Website: www.wychwood-school.org.uk
Age Range: 11–18

INDEPENDENT SIXTH FORM COLLEGE / TUTORIAL COLLEGE

ABACUS COLLEGE

Threeways House, Gloucester Green, Oxford, Oxfordshire OX1 2BT
Website: www.abacuscollege.co.uk
Age Range: 16–21

CHERWELL COLLEGE
Greyfriars, Paradise Street, Oxford, Oxfordshire OX1 1LD
Website: www.cherwell-college.co.uk
Age Range: (Focus on A-levels with the addition of A-level retake and final year GCSE, 16–19)

GREENE'S TUTORIAL COLLEGE

45 Pembroke Street, Oxford, Oxfordshire OX1 1BP
Website: www.greenes.org.uk
Age Range: 6–75 (Boarding (host families))

THE HENLEY COLLEGE
Deanfield Avenue, Henley-On-Thames, Oxfordshire RG9 1UH
Website: www.henleycol.ac.uk

OXFORD TUTORIAL COLLEGE
12 King Edward Street, Oxford, Oxfordshire OX1 4HT
Website: www.otc.ac.uk
Age Range: (16+)

INTERNATIONAL SCHOOLS AND INTERNATIONAL STUDY CENTRES

D'OVERBROECK'S COLLEGE OXFORD
The Swan Building, 111 Banbury Road, Oxford, Oxfordshire OX2 6JX
Website: www.doverbroecks.com
Age Range: 11–19 (Many students join our Sixth Form from other schools.)

RUTLAND

PREPARATORY

BROOKE PRIORY SCHOOL
● ♠

Station Approach, Oakham,
Rutland LE15 6QW
Website:
www.brooke.rutland.sch.uk
Age Range: 2–11

SENIOR

OAKHAM SCHOOL
● ♠ ★ ▲

Chapel Close, Oakham, Rutland
LE15 6DT
Website:
www.oakham.rutland.sch.uk
Age Range: 10–18

UPPINGHAM SCHOOL
● ♠ ▲

Uppingham, Rutland LE15 9QE
Website: www.uppingham.co.uk
Age Range: 13–18 (Year 9 –
Fourth Form
Year 10 – Lower Fifth
Year 11 – Upper Fifth
Year 12 – Lower VI
Year 13 – Upper VI)

SHROPSHIRE

PREPARATORY

CASTLE HOUSE SCHOOL
● ♠

Chetwynd End, Newport,
Shropshire TF10 7JE
Website:
www.castlehouseschool.co.uk
Age Range: 2–11

DOWER HOUSE SCHOOL
● ♠

Quatt, Bridgnorth, Shropshire
WV15 6QW
Website:
www.dowerhouseschool.co.uk
Age Range: 2–11

KINGSLAND GRANGE
● ♠

Old Roman Road, Shrewsbury,
Shropshire SY3 9AH
Website:
www.kingslandgrange.com
Age Range: 4–13

MOOR PARK SCHOOL
● ♠

Moor Park, Ludlow, Shropshire
SY8 4DZ
Website: www.moorpark.org.uk
Age Range: 3–13

THE OLD HALL SCHOOL
● ♠

Stanley Road, Wellington,
Telford, Shropshire TF1 3LB
Website: www.oldhall.co.uk
Age Range: 4–11

OSWESTRY SCHOOL
BELLAN HOUSE
● ♠

Bellan House, Church Street,
Oswestry, Shropshire SY11 2ST
Website:
www.oswestryschool.org.uk
Age Range: 2–9

PACKWOOD HAUGH SCHOOL
● ♠

Ruyton XI Towns, Shrewsbury,
Shropshire SY4 1HX
Website:
www.packwood-haugh.co.uk
Age Range: 4–13

PRESTFELDE PREPARATORY
SCHOOL
● ♠

London Road, Shrewsbury,
Shropshire SY2 6NZ
Website: www.prestfelde.co.uk
Age Range: 3–13

ST WINEFRIDE'S CONVENT
SCHOOL
● ♠

Belmont, Shrewsbury,
Shropshire SY1 1TE
Age Range: 3–11

WHITE HOUSE SCHOOL
● ♠

Heath Road, Whitchurch,
Shropshire SY13 2AA
Age Range: 3–11

SENIOR

ADCOTE SCHOOL FOR GIRLS
● ♠ ▲

Little Ness, Shrewsbury,
Shropshire SY4 2JY
Website:
www.adcoteschool.co.uk
Age Range: 4–18

BEDSTONE COLLEGE
● ♠ ▲

Bedstone, Bucknell, Shropshire
SY7 0BG
Website: www.bedstone.org
Age Range: 3–18

ELLESMERE COLLEGE
● ♠ ★ ◆ ▲

Ellesmere, Shropshire SY12 9AB
Website: www.ellesmere.com
Age Range: 7–18

MORETON HALL SCHOOL
● ♠ ▲

Weston Rhyn, Oswestry,
Shropshire SY11 3EW
Website: www.moretonhall.org
Age Range: 3–18 (Boys 3–11)

OSWESTRY SCHOOL
● ♠ ▲

Upper Brook Street, Oswestry,
Shropshire SY11 2TL
Website:
www.oswestryschool.org.uk
Age Range: 4–18

SHREWSBURY HIGH SCHOOL GDST
● 🏠 ▲

32 Town Walls, Shrewsbury, Shropshire SY1 1TN
Website:
www.shrewsburyhigh.gdst.net
Age Range: 3–18

SHREWSBURY SCHOOL
● 🏠 ▲

The Schools, Shrewsbury, Shropshire SY3 7BA
Website:
www.shrewsbury.org.uk
Age Range: 13–18 (Boys are admitted at 13+ and 14+, and boys and girls at 16+ into the Sixth Form.)

WREKIN COLLEGE
● 🏠 ▲

Wellington, Shropshire TF1 3BH
Website:
www.wrekincollege.ac.uk
Age Range: 11–19

INDEPENDENT SIXTH FORM COLLEGE / TUTORIAL COLLEGE

CONCORD COLLEGE
● 🏠

Acton Burnell Hall, Shrewsbury, Shropshire SY5 7PF
Website:
www.concordcollegeuk.com
Age Range: 13–19

SOMERSET

PREPARATORY

ALL HALLOWS*
● 🏠

Cranmore Hall, East Cranmore, Shepton Mallet, Somerset BA4 4SF
Website:
www.allhallowsschool.co.uk
Age Range: 4–13

CHARD SCHOOL
● 🏠

Fore Street, Chard, Somerset TA20 1QA
Website:
www.chardschool.ik.org
Age Range: 2–11

HAZLEGROVE
● 🏠 ◆

Hazlegrove, Sparkford, Yeovil, Somerset BA22 7JA
Website: www.hazlegrove.co.uk
Age Range: 2–13

KING'S HALL
● 🏠

Kingston Road, Taunton, Somerset TA2 8AA
Website:
www.kingshalltaunton.co.uk
Age Range: 3–13

MILLFIELD PREPARATORY SCHOOL
● 🏠 ◆

Glastonbury, Somerset BA6 8LD
Website: www.millfieldprep.com
Age Range: 2–13

PERROTT HILL SCHOOL
● 🏠

North Perrott, Crewkerne, Somerset TA18 7SL
Website: www.perrotthill.com
Age Range: 3–13

QUEEN'S COLLEGE JUNIOR, PRE-PREP & NURSERY SCHOOLS
● 🏠

Trull Road, Taunton, Somerset TA1 4QP
Website:
www.queenscollege.org.uk
Age Range: 3–11

SOUTHLEIGH KINDERGARTEN
● 🏠

11 Rectory Road, Burnham-on-Sea, Somerset TA8 2BY
Website: www.southleigh.org.uk
Age Range: 2–7

TAUNTON PREPARATORY SCHOOL
● 🏠

Staplegrove Road, Taunton, Somerset TA2 6AE
Website:
www.tauntonschool.co.uk
Age Range: 2–13

WELLS CATHEDRAL JUNIOR SCHOOL
● 🏠

8 New Street, Wells, Somerset BA5 2LQ
Website: marketing@wellscs.somerset.sch.uk
Age Range: 3–11

SENIOR

BRUTON SCHOOL FOR GIRLS
● 🏠 ▲

Sunny Hill, Bruton, Somerset BA10 0NT
Website:
www.brutonschool.co.uk
Age Range: 2–18
(Boys aged 2–7)

CHILTON CANTELO SCHOOL
● 🏠

Chilton Cantelo, Yeovil, Somerset BA22 8BG
Age Range: 7–16

DOWNSIDE SCHOOL
● 🏠 ▲

Stratton-on-the-Fosse, Radstock, Bath, Somerset BA3 4RJ
Website: www.downside.co.uk
Age Range: 11–18

KING'S BRUTON AND HAZLEGROVE
● 🏠 ◆ ▲

Bruton, Somerset BA10 0ED
Website: www.kingsbruton.com and hazlegrove.co.uk
Age Range: 2–18

KING'S COLLEGE
● 🏠 ▲

South Road, Taunton, Somerset TA1 3LA
Website: www.kings-taunton.co.uk
Age Range: 13–18

MILLFIELD SCHOOL
● 🏠 ◆ ▲

Butleigh Road, Street, Somerset BA16 0YD
Website: www.millfieldschool.com
Age Range: 13–18

THE PARK SCHOOL
● 🏠 ▲

The Park, Yeovil, Somerset BA20 1DH
Website: www.parkschool.com
Age Range: 3–19

QUEEN'S COLLEGE
● 🏠 ▲

Trull Road, Taunton, Somerset TA1 4QS
Website: www.queenscollege.org.uk
Age Range: 3–18

TAUNTON SCHOOL SENIOR
● 🏠 ★ ▲

Staplegrove Road, Taunton, Somerset TA2 6AD
Website: www.tauntonschool.co.uk
Age Range: 13–18

WELLINGTON SCHOOL
● 🏠 ▲

South Street, Wellington, Somerset TA21 8NT
Website: www.wellington-school.org.uk
Age Range: 10–18

WELLS CATHEDRAL SCHOOL
● 🏠 ★ ▲

The Liberty, Wells, Somerset BA5 2ST
Website: www.wells-cathedral-school.com
Age Range: 3–18

INDEPENDENT SIXTH FORM COLLEGE / TUTORIAL COLLEGE

BATH ACADEMY
● 🏠

27 Queen Square, Bath, Somerset BA1 2HX
Website: www.bathacademy.co.uk
Age Range: 16–20

BRIDGWATER COLLEGE
★

Bath Road, Bridgwater, Somerset TA6 4PZ
Website: www.bridgwater.ac.uk

INTERNATIONAL SCHOOLS AND INTERNATIONAL STUDY CENTRES

TAUNTON SCHOOL INTERNATIONAL
● 🏠

Taunton School, Staplegrove Road, Taunton, Somerset TA2 6AD
Website: www.tauntoninternational.co.uk
Age Range: 14–17

BATH & NORTH EAST SOMERSET

PREPARATORY

KING EDWARD'S JUNIOR SCHOOL
● 🏠

North Road, Bath, Bath & North East Somerset BA2 6JA
Website: www.kesbath.com
Age Range: 7–11

KING EDWARD'S PRE-PREP SCHOOL
● 🏠

Weston Lane, Bath, Bath & North East Somerset BA1 4AQ
Age Range: 3–7

KINGSWOOD PREPARATORY SCHOOL
● 🏠

College Road, Lansdown, Bath, Bath & North East Somerset BA1 5SD
Website: www.kingswood.bath.sch.uk
Age Range: 3–11

PARAGON SCHOOL, PRIOR PARK COLLEGE JUNIOR
● ♠

Lyncombe House, Lyncombe Vale, Bath, Bath & North East Somerset BA2 4LT
Website:
www.paragonschool.co.uk
Age Range: 3–11

SENIOR

BEECHEN CLIFF SCHOOL
● ♠ ★ ▲

Alexandra Park, Bath, Bath & North East Somerset BA2 4RE
Website:
www.beechencliff.org.uk
Age Range: 11–18

KING EDWARD'S SCHOOL, BATH*
● ♠ ▲

North Road, Bath, Bath & North East Somerset BA2 6HU
Website: www.kesbath.com.uk
Age Range: 3–18

KINGSWOOD SCHOOL
● ♠ ▲

Lansdown, Bath, Bath & North East Somerset BA1 5RG
Website:
www.kingswood.bath.sch.uk
Age Range: 3–18

PRIOR PARK COLLEGE*
● ♠ ▲

Ralph Allen Drive, Bath, Bath & North East Somerset BA2 5AH
Website:
www.thepriorfoundation.com
Age Range: 11–18
(Boarding from 13)

THE ROYAL HIGH SCHOOL, BATH*
● ♠ ★ ▲

Lansdown Road, Bath, Bath & North East Somerset BA1 5SZ
Website:
www.royalhighbath.gdst.net
Age Range: 3–18
(Boarding from Year 5)

NORTH SOMERSET

PREPARATORY

ASHBROOKE HOUSE
● ♠

9 Ellenborough Park North, Weston-Super-Mare, North Somerset BS23 1XH
Age Range: 3–11

LANCASTER HOUSE SCHOOL
● ♠

38 Hill Road, Weston-Super-Mare, North Somerset BS23 2RY
Website: www.lhslhs.co.uk
Age Range: 4–11

SENIOR

SIDCOT SCHOOL*
● ♠ ★ ♦ ▲

Oakridge Lane, Winscombe, North Somerset BS25 1PD
Website: www.sidcot.org.uk
Age Range: 3–18

STAFFORDSHIRE

PREPARATORY

BROOKLANDS SCHOOL & LITTLE BROOKLANDS NURSERY
● ♠

167 Eccleshall Road, Stafford, Staffordshire ST16 1PD
Website:
www.brooklandsschool.com
Age Range: (0–3 year old children in Day Nursery total 63 in addition to main School total of 110.)

EDENHURST SCHOOL
● ♠

Westlands Avenue, Newcastle-under-Lyme, Staffordshire ST5 2PU
Website: www.edenhurst.co.uk
Age Range: 3–14

ST DOMINIC'S INDEPENDENT JUNIOR SCHOOL
● ♠

Hartshill Road, Stoke-on-Trent, Staffordshire ST4 7LY
Website:
www.stdominicsstoke.co.uk
Age Range: 3–11

ST JOSEPH'S PREPARATORY SCHOOL
● ♠

Rookery Lane, Trent Vale, Stoke-on-Trent, Staffordshire ST4 5RF
Website:
www.stjosephsprepschool.co.uk
Age Range: 3–11

SMALLWOOD MANOR PREPARATORY SCHOOL
● ♠

Uttoxeter, Staffordshire ST14 8NS
Website:
www.smallwoodmanor.co.uk
Age Range: 2–11

VERNON LODGE PREPARATORY SCHOOL
● 🏠
School Lane, Stretton, Brewood, Staffordshire ST19 9LJ
Website: www.vernonlodge.co.uk
Age Range: 2–11

YARLET SCHOOL
● 🏠
Yarlet, Near Stafford, Stafford, Staffordshire ST18 9SU
Website: www.yarletschool.co.uk
Age Range: 2–13

THE YARLET SCHOOLS
● 🏠
Yarlet, Stafford, Staffordshire ST18 9SU
Website: www.yarletschool.org
Age Range: 3–13

SENIOR

ABBOTS BROMLEY SCHOOL*
● 🏠 ▲
Abbots Bromley, Staffordshire WS15 3BW
Website: www.abbotsbromley.net
Age Range: 3–18

ABBOTSHOLME SCHOOL
● 🏠 ▲
Rocester, Uttoxeter, Staffordshire ST14 5BS
Website: www.abbotsholme.co.uk
Age Range: 5–18

CHASE ACADEMY
● 🏠 ▲
Lyncroft House, St John's Road, Cannock, Staffordshire WS11 0UR
Website: www.chaseacademy.com
Age Range: 3–18 (3–18 years Boys and Girls)

DENSTONE COLLEGE
● 🏠 ▲
Uttoxeter, Staffordshire ST14 5HN
Website: www.denstonecollege.org
Age Range: 11–18

LICHFIELD CATHEDRAL SCHOOL
● 🏠
The Close, Lichfield, Staffordshire WS13 7LH
Website: www.lichfieldcathedralschool.com
Age Range: 3–16

NEWCASTLE-UNDER-LYME SCHOOL
● 🏠 ▲
Mount Pleasant, Newcastle-under-Lyme, Staffordshire ST5 1DB
Website: www.nuls.org.uk
Age Range: 3–18

ST DOMINIC'S PRIORY SCHOOL
● 🏠 ▲
21 Station Road, Stone, Staffordshire ST15 8EN
Website: www.stdominicspriory.co.uk
Age Range: 2–18 (Boys 2–11)

ST DOMINIC'S SCHOOL
● 🏠 ▲
32 Bargate Street, Brewood, Stafford, Staffordshire ST19 9BA
Website: www.stdominicsschool.co.uk
Age Range: 2–18 (Co-ed 2–7)

STAFFORD GRAMMAR SCHOOL
● 🏠 ▲
Burton Manor, Stafford, Staffordshire ST18 9AT
Website: www.staffordgrammar.staffs.sch.uk
Age Range: 11–18

STOCKTON-ON-TEES

SENIOR

RED HOUSE SCHOOL
● 🏠
36 The Green, Norton, Stockton-on-Tees TS20 1DX
Website: www.redhouseschool.co.uk
Age Range: 3–16

TEESSIDE HIGH SCHOOL
● 🏠 ▲
The Avenue, Eaglescliffe, Stockton-on-Tees TS16 9AT
Website: www.teessidehigh.co.uk
Age Range: 3–18

YARM SCHOOL
● 🏠 ▲
The Friarage, Yarm, Stockton-on-Tees TS15 9EJ
Website: www.yarmschool.org
Age Range: 3–18

SUFFOLK

PREPARATORY

THE ABBEY

The Prep School for Woodbridge School, Church Street, WOODBRIDGE, Suffolk IP12 1DS
Website: www.woodbridge.suffolk.sch.uk/the_abbey
Age Range: 4–11

ARBOR PREPARATORY

Flempton Road, Risby, Bury St Edmunds, Suffolk IP28 6QJ
Website: www.arborschool.co.uk

BARNARDISTON HALL PREPARATORY SCHOOL

Barnardiston, Haverhill, Suffolk CB9 7TG
Website: www.barnardiston-hall.co.uk
Age Range: 2–13

BRANDESTON HALL, THE PREPARATORY SCHOOL FOR FRAMLINGHAM COLLEGE

Brandeston Hall, Brandeston, Suffolk IP13 7AH
Website: www.framlinghamcollege.co.uk
Age Range: 3–13

FAIRSTEAD HOUSE SCHOOL

Fordham Road, Newmarket, Suffolk CB8 7AA
Website: www.fairsteadhouse.co.uk
Age Range: 3–11

IPSWICH PREPARATORY SCHOOL

3 Ivry Street, Ipswich, Suffolk IP1 3QW
Website: www.ipswich.suffolk.sch.uk
Age Range: 3–11

MORETON HALL PREPARATORY SCHOOL

Mount Road, Bury St Edmunds, Suffolk IP32 7BJ
Website: www.moretonhall.net
Age Range: 2–13

OLD BUCKENHAM HALL SCHOOL

Brettenham Park, Brettenham, Ipswich, Suffolk IP7 7PH
Website: www.obh.co.uk
Age Range: 2–13

THE OLD SCHOOL

Henstead, Beccles, Suffolk NR34 7LG
Age Range: 4–11

ORWELL PARK

Nacton, Ipswich, Suffolk IP10 0ER
Website: www.orwellpark.co.uk
Age Range: 3–13

ST GEORGE'S SCHOOL

Southwold, Suffolk IP18 6SD
Age Range: 2–11

SOUTH LEE PREPARATORY SCHOOL

Nowton Road, Bury St Edmunds, Suffolk IP33 2BT
Website: www.southlee.co.uk
Age Range: 2–13

SENIOR

AMBERFIELD SCHOOL

Nacton, Ipswich, Suffolk IP10 0HL
Website: www.amberfield.suffolk.sch.uk
Age Range: 2–16 (Boys 2–7)

CULFORD SCHOOL*

Bury St Edmunds, Suffolk IP28 6TX
Website: www.culford.co.uk
Age Range: 3–18

FINBOROUGH SCHOOL

The Hall, Great Finborough, Stowmarket, Suffolk IP14 3EF
Website: www.finborough.suffolk.sch.uk
Age Range: 2–18

FRAMLINGHAM COLLEGE*

Framlingham, Woodbridge, Suffolk IP13 9EY
Website: www.framcollege.co.uk
Age Range: 13–18

IPSWICH HIGH SCHOOL GDST

Woolverstone, Ipswich, Suffolk IP9 1AZ
Website: www.ipswichhigh.gdst.net
Age Range: 3–18

IPSWICH SCHOOL

Henley Road, Ipswich, Suffolk IP1 3SG
Website: www.ipswich.suffolk.sch.uk
Age Range: 11–18

THE ROYAL HOSPITAL SCHOOL

Holbrook, Ipswich, Suffolk IP9 2RX
Website: www.royalhospitalschool.org
Age Range: 11–18

ST JOSEPH'S COLLEGE

Belstead Road, Birkfield, Ipswich, Suffolk IP2 9DR
Website: www.stjos.co.uk
Age Range: 2–18

SAINT FELIX SCHOOL

Halesworth Road, Reydon,
Southwold, Suffolk IP18 6SD
Website: www.stfelix.co.uk
Age Range: 1–18 (Boarding
(girls only) 11+)

STOKE COLLEGE
Stoke by Clare, Sudbury, Suffolk
CO10 8JE
Website:
www.stokecollege.co.uk
Age Range: 3–16

WOODBRIDGE SCHOOL

Burkitt Road, Woodbridge,
Suffolk IP12 4JH
Website:
www.woodbridge.suffolk.sch.uk
Age Range: 11–18

INTERNATIONAL SCHOOLS AND INTERNATIONAL STUDY CENTRES

ALEXANDERS INTERNATIONAL SCHOOL
Bawdsey Manor, Bawdsey,
Woodbridge, Suffolk IP12 3AZ
Website:
www.alexandersschool.com
Age Range: 11–17

FELIXSTOWE INTERNATIONAL COLLEGE
Maybush House, Maybush
Lane, Felixstowe, Suffolk IP11
7NA
Age Range: 9–17

SUMMERHILL SCHOOL

Westward Ho, Leiston, Suffolk
IP16 4HY
Website:
www.summerhillschool.co.uk
Age Range: 5–17

SURREY

NURSERY AND PRE-PREP

DOWNSEND SCHOOL – ASHTEAD LODGE
22 Oakfield Road, Ashtead,
Surrey KT21 2RE
Website: www.downsend.co.uk
Age Range: 2–6

DOWNSEND SCHOOL – EPSOM LODGE
6 Norman Avenue, Epsom,
Surrey KT17 3AB
Website: www.downsend.co.uk
Age Range: 2–6

PARK HILL SCHOOL
8 Queens Road, Kingston-upon-
Thames, Surrey KT2 7SH
Website:
www.parkhillschool.com
Age Range: 3–8 (Children may
join Park Hill at the beginning of
the term in which they celebrate
their 3rd birthday, or at another,
later, date to suit the family.)

PREPARATORY

ABERDOUR
Brighton Road, Burgh Heath,
Tadworth, Surrey KT20 6AJ
Website:
www.aberdourschool.co.uk
Age Range: 2–13

ABERDOUR SCHOOL
Brighton Road, Burgh Heath,
Tadworth, Surrey KT20 6AJ
Website:
www.aberdourschool.co.uk
Age Range: 3–13

ALDRO SCHOOL

Lombard Street, Shackleford,
Godalming, Surrey GU8 6AS
Website: www.aldro.org
Age Range: 7–13

AMESBURY
Hazel Grove, Hindhead, Surrey
GU26 6BL
Website:
www.amesburyschool.co.uk
Age Range: 3–13

BARFIELD SCHOOL AND NURSERY

Guildford Road, Runfold,
Farnham, Surrey GU10 1PB
Website:
www.barfieldschool.com
Age Range: 3–13

BARROW HILLS SCHOOL
Roke Lane, Witley, Godalming,
Surrey GU8 5NY
Website: www.barrowhills.org.uk
Age Range: 3–13

BISHOPSGATE SCHOOL
Englefield Green, Egham,
Surrey TW20 0YJ
Website:
www.bishopsgate.surrey.sch.uk
Age Range: 2–13

BRAMLEY SCHOOL
● 🏠

Chequers Lane, Walton-on-the-Hill, Tadworth, Surrey KT20 7ST
Website:
www.bramleyschool.co.uk
Age Range: 3–11

BROOMFIELD HOUSE SCHOOL
● 🏠

10 Broomfield Road, Kew Gardens, Richmond, Surrey TW9 3HS
Website:
www.broomfieldhouse.com
Age Range: 3–11

CATERHAM PREPARATORY SCHOOL
● 🏠

Harestone Valley Road, Caterham, Surrey CR3 6YB
Website:
www.caterhamschool.co.uk
Age Range: 3–11

CHINTHURST SCHOOL
● 🏠

Tadworth Street, Tadworth, Surrey KT20 5QZ
Website:
www.chinthurstschool.co.uk
Age Range: 3–13

COLLINGWOOD SCHOOL
● 🏠

3 Springfield Road, Wallington, Surrey SM6 0BD
Website:
www.collingwood.sutton.sch.uk
Age Range: 2–11

COWORTH-FLEXLANDS SCHOOL
● 🏠

Valley End, Chobham, Woking, Surrey GU24 8TE
Website:
www.coworthflexlands.co.uk
Age Range: 3–11

CRANLEIGH PREPARATORY SCHOOL
● 🏠

Horseshoe Lane, Cranleigh, Surrey GU68 8QH
Website: www.cranleigh.org
Age Range: 7–13

CRANMORE SCHOOL
● 🏠

West Horsley, Leatherhead, Surrey KT24 6AT
Website:
www.cranmoreprep.co.uk
Age Range: 3–13

CUMNOR HOUSE SCHOOL
● 🏠

168 Pampisford Road, South Croydon, Surrey CR2 6DA
Website:
www.cumnorhouse.com
Age Range: 4–13

CUMNOR HOUSE SCHOOL
● 🏠

1 Woodcote Lane, Purley, Surrey CR8 3HB
Website:
www.cumnorhouse.com.
Age Range: 4–13

DANES HILL SCHOOL
● 🏠 ◆

Leatherhead Road, Oxshott, Leatherhead, Surrey KT22 0JG
Website:
www.daneshillschool.co.uk
Age Range: 3–13

DANESFIELD MANOR SCHOOL
● 🏠

Rydens Avenue, Walton-on-Thames, Surrey KT12 3JB
Website:
www.danesfieldmanorschool. co.uk
Age Range: 1–11

DATE VALLEY SCHOOL
● 🏠

9 – 11 Commonside East, Mitcham, Surrey CR4 2QA
Website: www.datevalley.com
Age Range: 2–11

DOWNSEND SCHOOL
● 🏠

1 Leatherhead Road, Leatherhead, Surrey KT22 8TJ
Website: www.downsend.co.uk
Age Range: 2–13 (Children age 2 – 6 attend one of our three Nursery & Pre-Preparatory Departments or Lodges, based in Ashtead, Epsom & Leatherhead.)

DRAYTON HOUSE SCHOOL
● 🏠

35 Austen Road, Guildford, Surrey GU1 3NP
Website:
www.draytonhouse.co.uk
Age Range: 3–8 (Nursery 1–3)

EDGEBOROUGH
● 🏠

Frensham, Farnham, Surrey GU10 3AH
Website:
www.edgeborough.co.uk
Age Range: 2–13

EDUCARE SMALL SCHOOL
● 🏠

12 Cowleaze Road, Kingston-upon-Thames, Surrey KT2 6DZ
Website:
educaresmallschool.org.uk
Age Range: 3–11

ELMHURST SCHOOL
● 🏠

44–48 South Park Hill Road, South Croydon, Surrey CR2 7DW
Website:
www.elmhurstschool.net
Age Range: 4–11

EMBERHURST
● 🏠

94 Ember Lane, Esher, Surrey KT10 8EN
Website:
www.emberhurst-school.com
Age Range: 2–8

ESSENDENE LODGE SCHOOL
● 🏠

Essendene Road, Caterham, Surrey CR3 5PB
Website: www.essendenelodge. surrey.sch.uk
Age Range: 2–11

FELTONFLEET SCHOOL
● 🏠

Cobham, Surrey KT11 1DR
Website: www.feltonfleet.co.uk
Age Range: 3–13

GLENESK SCHOOL

Ockham Road North, East Horsley, Leatherhead, Surrey KT24 6NS
Website: www.glenesk.co.uk
Age Range: 2–7

GRANTCHESTER HOUSE
5 Hinchley Way, Hinchley Wood, Esher, Surrey KT10 0BD
Website:
www.grantchesterhouseschool.com
Age Range: 3–7

GREENFIELD SCHOOL
Brooklyn Road, Woking, Surrey GU22 7TP
Website:
www.greenfield.surrey.sch.uk
Age Range: 3–11

HALL GROVE SCHOOL

London Road, Bagshot, Surrey GU19 5HZ
Website: www.hallgrove.co.uk
Age Range: 4–13

HALSTEAD PREPARATORY SCHOOL
Woodham Rise, Woking, Surrey GU21 4EE
Website:
www.halstead-school.org.uk
Age Range: 2–11

HASLEMERE PREPARATORY SCHOOL
The Heights, Hill Road, Haslemere, Surrey GU27 2JP
Website:
www.haslemere-prep.co.uk
Age Range: 2–14

THE HAWTHORNS SCHOOL
Pendell Court, Bletchingley, Redhill, Surrey RH1 4QJ
Website: www.hawthorns.com
Age Range: 2–13

HOE BRIDGE SCHOOL*

Hoe Place, Old Woking Road, Woking, Surrey GU22 8JE
Website:
www.hoebridgeschool.co.uk
Age Range: 2–13

HOLY CROSS PREPARATORY SCHOOL

George Road, Kingston upon Thames, Surrey KT2 7NU
Website:
www.holycrossprepschool.co.uk
Age Range: 4–11

HOMEFIELD SCHOOL*

Western Road, Sutton, Surrey SM1 2TE
Website:
www.homefield.sutton.sch.uk
Age Range: 3–13

KEW COLLEGE

24/26 Cumberland Road, Kew, Richmond, Surrey TW9 3HQ
Website: www.kewcollege.com
Age Range: 3–11

KEW GREEN PREPARATORY SCHOOL*
Layton House, Ferry Lane, Richmond, Surrey TW9 3AF
Website: www.kgps.co.uk
Age Range: 4–11

KING'S HOUSE SCHOOL

68 Kings Road, Richmond, Surrey TW10 6ES
Website: www.
kingshouse.richmond.sch.uk
Age Range: 4–13

KINGSWOOD HOUSE SCHOOL
56 West Hill, Epsom, Surrey KT19 8LG
Website:
www.kingswoodhouse.org
Age Range: 3–13

LALEHAM LEA SCHOOL

29 Peaks Hill, Purley, Surrey CR8 3JJ
Website: www.lalehamlea.co.uk
Age Range: 3–11

LANESBOROUGH*

Maori Road, Guildford, Surrey GU1 2EL
Website: www.lanesborough.surrey.sch.uk
Age Range: 3–13

LINLEY HOUSE
6 Berrylands Road, Surbiton, Surrey KT5 8RA
Website:
www.linleyhouseschool.com
Age Range: 3–7

LONGACRE SCHOOL
Hullbrook Lane, Shamley Green, Guildford, Surrey GU5 0NQ
Website:
www.longacre.surrey.sch.uk
Age Range: 2–11

LYNDHURST SCHOOL

36 The Avenue, Camberley, Surrey GU15 3NE
Website:
www.lyndhurstschool.co.uk
Age Range: 2–12

MICKLEFIELD SCHOOL
10 Somers Road, Reigate, Surrey RH2 9DU
Website:
www.micklefieldschool.co.uk
Age Range: 3–11

MILBOURNE LODGE SCHOOL
43 Arbrook Lane, Esher, Surrey KT10 9EG
Website:
www.milbournelodge.co.uk
Age Range: 4–13

NEW LIFE CHRISTIAN SCHOOL

Cairo New Road, Croydon, Surrey CR0 1XP
Website: www.newlifecroydon/
nlcs.co.uk
Age Range: 4–11

NOTRE DAME PREPARATORY SCHOOL

Burwood House, Cobham, Surrey KT11 1HA
Website: www.notredame.co.uk
Age Range: 2–11 (Boys 2–5)

OAKHYRST GRANGE SCHOOL

160 Stanstead Road, Caterham, Surrey CR3 6AF
Website:
www.oakhyrstgrangeschool.
co.uk
Age Range: 4–11

OAKWOOD SCHOOL & NURSERY

Godstone Road, Purley, Surrey CR8 2AN
Website: www.oakwoodschool.
org.uk
Age Range: 2–11

OLD VICARAGE SCHOOL

48 Richmond Hill, Richmond, Surrey TW10 6QX
Age Range: 4–11

PARKSIDE SCHOOL

The Manor, Stoke D'Abernon, Cobham, Surrey KT11 3PX
Website:
www.parkside-school.co.uk
Age Range: 2–13 (Co-ed 2–4)

PEASLAKE SCHOOL

Colmans Hill, Peaslake, Guildford, Surrey GU5 9ST
Website: peaslake.surrey.sch.uk
Age Range: 3–7

PRIORY PREPARATORY SCHOOL

Bolters Lane, Banstead, Surrey SM7 2AJ
Website: www.prioryprep.co.uk
Age Range: 2–13

REDEHALL PREPARATORY SCHOOL

Redehall Road, Smallfield, Horley, Surrey RH6 9QA
Website:
www.redehallschool.com
Age Range: 3–11

REIGATE ST MARY'S PREPARATORY AND CHOIR SCHOOL

Chart Lane, Reigate, Surrey RH2 7RN
Website:
www.reigatestmarys.org
Age Range: 3–11 (Rising 3 year olds to 11 year olds)

RIPLEY COURT SCHOOL

Rose Lane, Ripley, Woking, Surrey GU23 6NE
Website: www.ripleycourt.co.uk
Age Range: 3–13

ROKEBY SCHOOL

George Road, Kingston-upon-Thames, Surrey KT2 7PB
Website:
www.rokebyschool.co.uk
Age Range: 4–13

ROWAN PREPARATORY SCHOOL

6 Fitzalan Road, Claygate, Esher, Surrey KT10 0LX
Website:
www.rowan.surrey.sch.uk
Age Range: 2–11

RYDES HILL PREPARATORY SCHOOL

Aldershot Road, Guildford, Surrey GU2 8BP
Website: www.rydeshill.com
Age Range: 3–11

ST CHRISTOPHER'S SCHOOL

6 Downs Road, Epsom, Surrey KT18 5HE
Website: www.st-christophers.
surrey.sch.uk
Age Range: 3–7

ST DAVID'S SCHOOL

23 Woodcote Valley Road, Purley, Surrey CR8 3AL
Website:
www.st-davidsschool.co.uk
Age Range: 3–11

ST EDMUND'S SCHOOL

Portsmouth Road, Hindhead, Surrey GU26 6BH
Website:
www.saintedmunds.co.uk
Age Range: 2–13

ST GEORGE'S COLLEGE JUNIOR SCHOOL

Thames Street, Weybridge, Surrey KT13 8NL
Website:
www.st-georges-college.co.uk
Age Range: 3–11

ST HILARY'S SCHOOL

Holloway Hill, Godalming, Surrey GU7 1RZ
Website:
www.sthilarysschool.com
Age Range: 1–11

ST IVES SCHOOL

Three Gates Lane, Haslemere, Surrey GU27 2ES
Website:
www.stiveshaslemere.com
Age Range: 3–11 (Boys 3–5)

ST TERESA'S PREPARATORY SCHOOL

Grove House, Guildford Road, Effingham, Surrey KT24 5QA
Website:
www.stteresasschool.com
Age Range: 2–11

ST ANDREW'S (WOKING) SCHOOL TRUST

Church Hill House, Wilson Way, Horsell, Woking, Surrey GU21 4QW
Website:
www.st-andrews.woking.sch.uk
Age Range: 3–13

THE STUDY SCHOOL

57 Thetford Road, New Malden, Surrey KT3 5DP
Website:
www.thestudyschool.co.uk
Age Range: 3–11

SEATON HOUSE SCHOOL

67 Banstead Road South, Sutton, Surrey SM2 5LH
Website:
www.seatonhouse.sutton.sch.uk
Age Range: 3–11 (Boys 3–5 Girls 3–11)

SHREWSBURY HOUSE SCHOOL

107 Ditton Road, Surbiton, Surrey KT6 6RL
Website:
www.shrewburyhouse.net
Age Range: 7–13

SURBITON PREPARATORY SCHOOL

3 Avenue Elmers, Surbiton, Surrey KT6 4SP
Website: www.surbitonhigh.com
Age Range: 4–11

UNICORN SCHOOL

238 Kew Road, Kew, Richmond, Surrey TW9 3JX
Website:
www.unicornschool.org.uk
Age Range: 3–11

WARLINGHAM PARK SCHOOL

Chelsham Common, Warlingham, Croydon, Surrey CR6 9PB
Website:
www.warlinghamparkschool.com
Age Range: 2–11

WEST DENE SCHOOL

167 Brighton Road, Purley, Surrey CR8 4HE
Age Range: 2–11

WESTBURY HOUSE SCHOOL

80 Westbury Road, New Malden, Surrey KT3 5AS
Website:
westburyhouse.surrey.sch.uk
Age Range: 3–11

WESTON GREEN SCHOOL

Weston Green Road, Thames Ditton, Surrey KT7 0JN
Website:
www.westongreenschool.org.uk
Age Range: 2–8

WESTWARD PREPARATORY SCHOOL

47 Hersham Road, Walton-on-Thames, Surrey KT12 1LE
Age Range: 3–11

WOODCOTE HOUSE SCHOOL

Snow's Ride, Windlesham, Surrey GU20 6PF
Website:
www.woodcotehouseschool.co.uk
Age Range: 7–14

SENIOR

BOX HILL SCHOOL*

Old London Road, Mickleham, Dorking, Surrey RH5 6EA
Website: www.boxhillschool.com
Age Range: 11–18

CANBURY SCHOOL

Kingston Hill, Kingston-upon-Thames, Surrey KT2 7LN
Website:
www.canburyschool.org.uk
Age Range: 10–16

CHARTERHOUSE

Godalming, Surrey GU7 2DX
Website:
www.charterhouse.org.uk
Age Range: 13–18
(Co-ed Sixth Form)

CITY OF LONDON FREEMEN'S SCHOOL

Ashtead Park, Ashtead, Surrey KT21 1ET
Website: www.clfs.surrey.sch.uk
Age Range: 7–18

CLAREMONT FAN COURT SCHOOL*

Claremont Drive, Esher, Surrey KT10 9LY
Website:
www.claremont-school.co.uk
Age Range: 3–18

CRANLEIGH SCHOOL

Horseshoe Lane, Cranleigh, Surrey GU6 8QQ
Website: www.cranleigh.org
Age Range: 13–18

CROYDON HIGH SCHOOL GDST

Old Farleigh Road, Selsdon, South Croydon, Surrey CR2 8YB
Website:
www.croydonhigh.gdst.net
Age Range: 3–18

DUKE OF KENT SCHOOL

Peaslake Road, Ewhurst, Guildford, Surrey GU6 7NS
Website:
www.dukeofkentschool.org.uk
Age Range: 3–16

DUNOTTAR SCHOOL

High Trees Road, Reigate,
Surrey RH2 7EL
Website:
www.dunottarschool.com
Age Range: 3–18

**EAGLE HOUSE SCHOOL –
SUTTON**

95 Brighton Road, Sutton,
Surrey SM2 5SJ
Website:
www.eaglehousesutton.co.uk
Age Range: 11–19

EPSOM COLLEGE

College Road, Epsom, Surrey
KT17 4JQ
Website:
www.epsomcollege.org.uk
Age Range: 13–18

EWELL CASTLE SCHOOL

Church Street, Ewell, Epsom,
Surrey KT17 2AW
Website: www.ewellcastle.co.uk
Age Range: 3–18
(Girls 3–11)

**FRENSHAM HEIGHTS
SCHOOL**

Rowledge, Farnham, Surrey
GU10 4EA
Website:
www.frensham-heights.org.uk
Age Range: 3–18

THE GERMAN SCHOOL

Douglas House, Petersham
Road, Richmond, Surrey
TW10 7AH
Website: www.dslondon.org.uk
Age Range: 5–19

**GREENACRE SCHOOL FOR
GIRLS**

Sutton Lane, Banstead, Surrey
SM7 3RA
Website:
www.greenacre.surrey.sch.uk
Age Range: 3–18

GUILDFORD HIGH SCHOOL

London Road, Guildford, Surrey
GU1 1SJ
Website:
www.guildfordhigh.surrey.sch.uk
Age Range: 4–18

HAMPTON COURT HOUSE

Hampton Court Road, East
Molesey, Surrey KT8 9BS
Website:
www.hamptoncourthouse.co.uk
Age Range: 3–17

HAWLEY PLACE SCHOOL

Fernhill Road, Blackwater,
Camberley, Surrey GU17 9HU
Website: www.hawleyplace.com
Age Range: 2–16

HURTWOOD HOUSE*

Holmbury St Mary, Dorking,
Surrey RH5 6NU
Website:
www.hurtwoodhouse.com
Age Range: 16–18

**KING EDWARD'S SCHOOL
WITLEY**

Petworth Road, Witley,
Godalming, Surrey GU8 5SG
Website: www.kesw.org
Age Range: 11–18

**KINGSTON GRAMMAR
SCHOOL**

London Road, Kingston-upon-
Thames, Surrey KT2 6PY
Website: www.kgs.org.uk
Age Range: 10–18

**LINGFIELD NOTRE DAME
SCHOOL**

St Piers Lane, Lingfield, Surrey
RH7 6PH
Website:
www.lingfieldnotredame.co.uk
Age Range: 2–18

MANOR HOUSE SCHOOL

Manor House Lane, Little
Bookham, Leatherhead, Surrey
KT23 4EN
Website:
www.manorhouseschool.org
Age Range: 2–16

**MARYMOUNT
INTERNATIONAL SCHOOL***

George Road, Kingston-upon-
Thames, Surrey KT2 7PE
Website:
www.marymountlondon.com
Age Range: 11–18

**NOTRE DAME SENIOR
SCHOOL**

Burwood House, Cobham,
Surrey KT11 1HA
Website: www.notredame.co.uk
Age Range: 11–18

OAKFIELD SCHOOL

Coldharbour Road, Pyrford,
Woking, Surrey GU22 8SJ
Website:
www.oakfieldschool.co.uk
Age Range: 3–16

**OLD PALACE OF JOHN
WHITGIFT SCHOOL***

Old Palace Road, Croydon,
Surrey CR0 1AX
Website:
www.oldpalaceofjohnwhitgift.org
Age Range: 1–19

PRIOR'S FIELD SCHOOL

Priorsfield Road, Godalming,
Surrey GU7 2RH
Website:
www.priorsfieldschool.com
Age Range: 11–18

REED'S SCHOOL

Sandy Lane, Cobham, Surrey
KT11 2ES
Website:
www.reeds.surrey.sch.uk
Age Range: 11–18
(Co-ed VIth Form)

REIGATE GRAMMAR SCHOOL
● ♠ ▲
Reigate Road, Reigate, Surrey
RH2 0QS
Website:
www.reigategrammar.org
Age Range: 11–18

ROYAL ALEXANDRA AND ALBERT SCHOOL*
● ♠ ▲
Gatton Park, Reigate, Surrey
RH2 0TD
Website: www.raa-school.co.uk
Age Range: 7–18

ROYAL BALLET SCHOOL
● ♠
White Lodge, Richmond Park,
Richmond, Surrey TW10 5HR
Age Range: 11–16

ROYAL GRAMMAR SCHOOL
● ♠ ▲
High Street, Guildford, Surrey
GU1 3BB
Website:
www.rgs-guildford.co.uk
Age Range: 11–18

ROYAL RUSSELL SCHOOL
● ♠ ▲
Coombe Lane, Croydon, Surrey
CR9 5BX
Website: www.royalrussell.co.uk
Age Range: 3–18

THE ROYAL SCHOOL
● ♠ ▲
Farnham Lane, Haslemere,
Surrey GU27 1HQ
Website: www.royal-school.org
Age Range: 6–18 (Boys 2–4)

THE ROYAL SCHOOL FOR GIRLS
● ♠ ▲
Farnham Lane, Haslemere,
Surrey GU27 1HQ
Website:
www.royal.surrey.sch.uk
Age Range: 11–18

ST CATHERINE'S SCHOOL
● ♠ ▲
Station Road, Bramley,
Guildford, Surrey GU5 0DF
Website: www.stcatherines.info
Age Range: 4–18

ST GEORGE'S COLLEGE
● ♠ ▲
Weybridge Road, Addlestone,
Weybridge, Surrey KT15 2QS
Website:
www.st-georges-college.co.uk
Age Range: 11–18

ST JAMES INDEPENDENT SCHOOL FOR BOYS (SENIOR)
● ♠ ▲
Church Road, Ashford, Surrey
TW15 3DZ
Website:
www.stjamesboys.co.uk
Age Range: 10–18

ST JOHN'S SCHOOL
● ♠ ▲
Epsom Road, Leatherhead,
Surrey KT22 8SP
Website:
www.stjohnsleatherhead.co.uk
Age Range: 13–18
(Co-ed VIth Form)

ST TERESA'S SCHOOL
● ♠ ▲
Effingham Hill, Dorking, Surrey
RH5 6ST
Website:
www.stteresasschool.com
Age Range: 11–18

SIR WILLIAM PERKINS'S SCHOOL
● ♠ ▲
Guildford Road, Chertsey,
Surrey KT16 9BN
Website: www.swps.org.uk
Age Range: 11–18

SURBITON HIGH SCHOOL
● ♠ ▲
Surbiton Crescent, Kingston-
upon-Thames, Surrey KT1 2JT
Website: www.surbitonhigh.com
Age Range: 4–18 (Boys 4–11)

SUTTON HIGH SCHOOL GDST
● ♠ ▲
55 Cheam Road, Sutton, Surrey
SM1 2AX
Website:
www.gdst.net/suttonhigh
Age Range: 3–18

TORMEAD SCHOOL
● ♠ ▲
27 Cranley Road, Guildford,
Surrey GUI 2JD
Website:
www.tormeadschool.org.uk
Age Range: 4–18

TRINITY SCHOOL*
● ♠ ▲
Shirley Park, Croydon, Surrey
CR9 7AT
Website: www.trinity-school.org
Age Range: 10–18 (Boys 10–18
Girls 16–18)

WHITGIFT SCHOOL
● ♠ ★ ▲
Haling Park, South Croydon,
Surrey CR2 6YT
Website: www.whitgift.co.uk
Age Range: 10–18

YEHUDI MENUHIN SCHOOL
● ♠ ▲
Stoke D'Abernon, Cobham,
Surrey KT11 3QQ
Website:
www.yehudimenuhinschool.
co.uk
Age Range: 8–18

INDEPENDENT SIXTH FORM COLLEGE / TUTORIAL COLLEGE

CAMBRIDGE TUTORS COLLEGE
● ♠
Water Tower Hill, Croydon,
Surrey CR0 5SX
Website: www.ctc.ac.uk
Age Range: 15–22

INTERNATIONAL SCHOOLS AND INTERNATIONAL STUDY CENTRES

ACS COBHAM INTERNATIONAL SCHOOL*
● ♠ ★ ▲
Heywood, Portsmouth Road, Cobham, Surrey KT11 1BL
Website: www.acs-schools.com
Age Range: 2–18

ACS EGHAM INTERNATIONAL SCHOOL*
● ♠ ★ ▲
Woodlee, London Road (A30), Egham, Surrey TW20 0HS
Website: www.acs-schools.com
Age Range: 2–18

TASIS THE AMERICAN SCHOOL IN ENGLAND
● ♠ ★ ▲
Coldharbour Lane, Thorpe, Surrey TW20 8TE
Website: www.tasisengland.org
Age Range: 3–18

EAST SUSSEX

PREPARATORY

ASHDOWN HOUSE SCHOOL
● ♠
Forest Row, East Sussex RH18 5JY
Website: www.ashdownhouse.co.uk
Age Range: 8–13

BRICKLEHURST MANOR PREPARATORY
● ♠
Bardown Road, Stonegate, Wadhurst, East Sussex TN5 7EL
Website: www.bricklehurst.co.uk
Age Range: 3–11

BRIGHTON COLLEGE PRE-PREPARATORY SCHOOL
● ♠
Sutherland Road, Brighton, East Sussex BN2 0EQ
Website: www.brightoncollege.org.uk
Age Range: 3–8

BRIGHTON COLLEGE PREP SCHOOL
● ♠
Walpole Lodge, Walpole Road, Brighton, East Sussex BN2 0EU
Website: www.brightoncollege.org.uk
Age Range: 8–13

CLAREMONT SCHOOL
● ♠
Baldslow, St Leonards-on-Sea, East Sussex TN37 7PW
Website: www.Claremontschool.co.uk
Age Range: 1–14

DEEPDENE SCHOOL
● ♠
Hove, East Sussex BN3 4ED
Website: www.deepdeneschool.com
Age Range: 1–8

DHARMA SCHOOL
● ♠
White House, Ladies Mile Road, Patcham, Brighton, East Sussex BN1 8TB
Website: www.dharmaschool.co.uk
Age Range: 3–11

THE FOLD SCHOOL
● ♠
201 New Church Road, Hove, East Sussex BN3 4ED
Age Range: 3–11

LANCING COLLEGE PREPARATORY SCHOOL AT MOWDEN
● ♠
The Droveway, Hove, East Sussex BN3 6LU
Website: www.lancingprep.co.uk
Age Range: 3–13

MOIRA HOUSE SCHOOL
● ♠
Upper Carlisle Road, Eastbourne, East Sussex BN20 7TE
Website: www.moirahouse.e-sussex.sch.uk/moirahouse
Age Range: 2–11

ST ANDREW'S SCHOOL
● ♠
Meads, Eastbourne, East Sussex BN20 7RP
Website: www.androvian.co.uk
Age Range: 2–13

ST AUBYN'S

High Street, Rottingdean, Brighton, East Sussex BNZ 7JN
Website: staubynsschoolbrighton.co.uk
Age Range: 4–13

ST AUBYNS SCHOOL

76 High Street, Rottingdean,
Brighton, East Sussex BN2 7JN
Website:
www.staubynsschoolbrighton.
co.uk
Age Range: 3–13

ST BEDE'S PREP SCHOOL

Duke's Drive, Eastbourne,
East Sussex BN20 7XL
Website: www.stbedesschool.org
Age Range: 2–13

SACRED HEART R.C. PRIMARY SCHOOL

Mayfield Lane, Durgates,
Wadhurst, East Sussex TN5
6DQ
Website: www.
sacredheartwadhurst.org.uk
Age Range: 3–11

SKIPPERS HILL MANOR PREPARATORY SCHOOL

Five Ashes, Mayfield, East
Sussex TN20 6HR
Website: www.skippershill.com
Age Range: 3–13

VINEHALL SCHOOL

Robertsbridge, East Sussex
TN32 5JL
Website:
www.vinehallschool.com
Age Range: 2–13

SENIOR

BATTLE ABBEY SCHOOL

High Street, Battle, East Sussex
TN33 0AD
Website:
www.battleabbeyschool.com
Age Range: 2–18

BRIGHTON AND HOVE HIGH SCHOOL GDST

Montpelier Road, Brighton,
East Sussex BN1 3AT
Age Range: 3–18

BRIGHTON COLLEGE

Eastern Road, Brighton,
East Sussex BN2 0AL
Website: www.brightoncollege.
net
Age Range: 11–18

BRIGHTON STEINER SCHOOL LIMITED

Roedean Road, Brighton,
East Sussex BN2 5RA
Website: www.
brightonsteinerschool.org.uk
Age Range: 2–16

DARVELL SCHOOL

Darvell Bruderhof,
Robertsbridge, East Sussex
TN32 5DR
Age Range: 4–16

THE DRIVE PREP SCHOOL

101 The Drive, Hove, East
Sussex BN3 6GE
Website: www.driveprep.co.uk
Age Range: 3–16

EASTBOURNE COLLEGE*

Old Wish Road, Eastbourne,
East Sussex BN21 4JY
Website: www.eastbourne-
college.co.uk
Age Range: 13–18
(50% boarding / 50% day
60% boys / 40% girls)

GREENFIELDS INDEPENDENT DAY AND BOARDING SCHOOL

Priory Road, Forest Row,
East Sussex RH18 5JD
Website:
www.greenfieldsschool.com
Age Range: 2–19 (3 to 19)

LEWES OLD GRAMMAR SCHOOL

140 High Street, Lewes,
East Sussex BN7 1XS
Website: www.
oldgrammar.e-sussex.sch.uk
Age Range: 3–18

MICHAEL HALL (STEINER WALDORF SCHOOL)

Kidbrooke Park, Forest Row,
East Sussex RH18 5JA
Website: www.michaelhall.co.uk

MOIRA HOUSE GIRLS SCHOOL

42–44 Upper Carlisle Road,
Eastbourne, East Sussex BN20
7TE
Website: www.moirahouse.co.uk
Age Range: 2–19

NEWLANDS SCHOOL

Eastbourne Road, Sutton
Avenue, Seaford, East Sussex
BN25 4NP
Website:
www.newlands-school.com
Age Range: 2–18 (nursery &
pre-prep)

ROEDEAN SCHOOL

Roedean Way, Brighton, East
Sussex BN2 5RQ
Website: www.roedean.co.uk
Age Range: 11–18

ST BEDE'S SCHOOL

Upper Dicker, Hailsham, East
Sussex BN27 3QH
Website:
www.stbedesschool.org
Age Range: 13–19

ST LEONARDS-MAYFIELD SCHOOL

The Old Palace, Mayfield, East
Sussex TN20 6PH
Website: www.mayfieldgirls.org
Age Range: 11–19

STONELANDS SCHOOL OF BALLET & THEATRE ARTS

170A Church Road, Hove, East
Sussex BN3 2DJ
Website:
www.stonelandsschool.co.uk
Age Range: 5–16

INDEPENDENT SIXTH FORM COLLEGE / TUTORIAL COLLEGE

BARTHOLOMEWS TUTORIAL COLLEGE

22–23 Prince Albert Street, Brighton, East Sussex BN1 1HF
Website: www.bartscollege.co.uk

BELLERBYS COLLEGE

● 🏠

1 Billinton Way, Brighton, East Sussex BN1 4LF
Website: www.bellerbys.com

INTERNATIONAL SCHOOLS AND INTERNATIONAL STUDY CENTRES

BUCKSWOOD SCHOOL*

● 🏠 ★ ▲

Rye Road, Guestling, Hastings, East Sussex TN35 4LT
Website: www.buckswood.co.uk
Age Range: 10–19

WEST SUSSEX

PREPARATORY

ARDINGLY COLLEGE JUNIOR SCHOOL

● 🏠

Haywards Heath, West Sussex RH17 6SQ
Website: www.ardingly.com
Age Range: 7–13 (and pre-prep)

BROADWATER MANOR SCHOOL

● 🏠

Broadwater Road, Worthing, West Sussex BN14 8HU
Website: www.broadwatermanor.com
Age Range: 2–13

CONIFERS SCHOOL

● 🏠

Egmont Road, Midhurst, West Sussex GU29 9BG
Website: www.conifersschool.com
Age Range: 3–11

COPTHORNE PREP SCHOOL

● 🏠

Effingham Lane, Copthorne, West Sussex RH10 3HR
Website: www.copthorneprep.co.uk
Age Range: 2–13

COTTESMORE SCHOOL

● 🏠

Buchan Hill, Pease Pottage, West Sussex RH11 9AU
Website: www.cottesmoreschool.com
Age Range: 7–13

DORSET HOUSE SCHOOL

● 🏠

The Manor, Church Lane, Bury, Pulborough, West Sussex RH20 1PB
Website: www.dorsethouseschool.com
Age Range: 3–13

FONTHILL LODGE

● 🏠

Coombe Hill Road, East Grinstead, West Sussex RH19 4LY
Website: www.fonthill-lodge.co.uk
Age Range: 2–11
(Single-sex ed 8–11)

GREAT BALLARD SCHOOL

● 🏠

Eartham, Chichester, West Sussex PO18 0LR
Website: www.greatballard.co.uk
Age Range: 2–13

GREAT WALSTEAD

● 🏠

East Mascalls Lane, Lindfield, Haywards Heath, West Sussex RH16 2QL
Website: www.greatwalstead.co.uk
Age Range: 3–13

HANDCROSS PARK SCHOOL

● 🏠

Handcross, Haywards Heath, West Sussex RH17 6HF
Website: www.handcrossparkschool.co.uk
Age Range: 2–13

OAKWOOD SCHOOL

● 🏠

Oakwood, Chichester, West Sussex PO18 9AN
Website: www.oakwoodschool.co.uk
Age Range: 2–11

PENNTHORPE SCHOOL

● 🏠

Church Street, Rudgwick, Horsham, West Sussex RH12 3HJ
Website: www.pennthorpe.com
Age Range: 2–14

THE PREBENDAL SCHOOL
● 🏠
54 West Street, Chichester,
West Sussex PO19 1RT
Website:
www.prebendalschool.org.uk
Age Range: 3–14

**PREBENDAL SCHOOL
(NORTHGATE HOUSE)**
● 🏠
38 North Street, Chichester,
West Sussex PO19 1LX
Age Range: 3–7

ST MARGARET'S SCHOOL
● 🏠
Petersfield Road, Midhurst,
West Sussex GU29 9JN
Website:
www.conventofmercy.org
Age Range: 2–11

**SOMPTING ABBOTTS
SCHOOL**
● 🏠
Church Lane, Sompting,
West Sussex BN15 0AZ
Website:
www.somptingabbotts.com
Age Range: 3–13

**TAVISTOCK & SUMMERHILL
SCHOOL**
● 🏠
Summerhill Lane, Haywards
Heath, West Sussex RH16 1RP
Website:
www.tavistockandsummerhill.
co.uk
Age Range: 3–13

**WESTBOURNE HOUSE
SCHOOL**
● 🏠
Coach Road, Shopwyke,
Chichester, West Sussex
PO20 2BH
Website:
www.westbournehouse.org
Age Range: 2–13

**WILLOW TREE MONTESSORI
SCHOOL**
● 🏠
Charlwood House, Charlwood
Road, Lowfield Heath, Crawley,
West Sussex RH11 0QA
Website:
www.wt-montessori-school.co.uk
Age Range: 1–8

**WINDLESHAM HOUSE
SCHOOL***
● 🏠
Washington, Pulborough,
West Sussex RH20 4AY
Website: www.windlesham.com
Age Range: 4–13

SENIOR

ARDINGLY COLLEGE
● 🏠 ★ ▲
Haywards Heath, West Sussex
RH17 6SQ
Website: www.ardingly.com
Age Range: 3–17

**BURGESS HILL SCHOOL
FOR GIRLS***
● 🏠 ▲
Keymer Road, Burgess Hill,
West Sussex RH15 0EG
Website:
www.burgesshill-school.com
Age Range: 2–18

CHRIST'S HOSPITAL
● 🏠 ★ ▲
Horsham, West Sussex RH13
0YP
Website:
www.christs-hospital.org.uk
Age Range: 11–18

FARLINGTON SCHOOL
● 🏠 ▲
Strood Park, Horsham, West
Sussex RH12 3PN
Website:
www.farlingtonschool.net
Age Range: 3–18

HURSTPIERPOINT COLLEGE
● 🏠 ▲
College Lane, Hurstpierpoint,
West Sussex BN6 9JS
Website: www.hppc.co.uk
Age Range: 7–18

OUR LADY OF SION SCHOOL
● 🏠 ▲
Gratwicke Road, Worthing,
West Sussex BN11 4BL
Website: www.sionschool.org.uk
Age Range: 2–18

SEAFORD COLLEGE*
● 🏠 ▲
Lavington Park, Petworth,
West Sussex GU28 0NB
Website: www.seaford.org
Age Range: 7–18

SHOREHAM COLLEGE
● 🏠
St Julian's Lane, Shoreham-by-
Sea, West Sussex BN43 6YW
Website:
www.shorehamcollege.co.uk
Age Range: 3–16

SLINDON COLLEGE
● 🏠 ◆
Slindon, Arundel, West Sussex
BN18 0RH
Website:
www.slindoncollege.co.uk
Age Range: 8–16

**THE TOWERS CONVENT
SCHOOL**
● 🏠
Henfield Road, Upper Beeding,
Steyning, West Sussex BN44
3TF
Website:
www.towers.w-sussex.sch.uk
Age Range: 3–16 (Boys 3–11)

WORTH SCHOOL
● 🏠 ★ ▲
Paddockhurst Road, Turners
Hill, West Sussex RH10 4SD
Website:
www.worthschool.co.uk
Age Range: 11–18 (Co-ed Sixth
Form at present, welcoming day
girls into Year 7 (age 11) and
day and boarding girls into
Year 9 (age 13) from September
2010)

INDEPENDENT SIXTH FORM COLLEGE / TUTORIAL COLLEGE

CHICHESTER COLLEGE
★
Westgate Fields, Chichester,
West Sussex PO19 1SB
Website: www.chichester.ac.uk

TYNE AND WEAR

PREPARATORY

DAME ALLAN'S JUNIOR SCHOOL

● ⌂

72 Station Road, Forest Hall, Newcastle upon Tyne, Tyne and Wear NE12 9BQ
Website: www.dameallans.co.uk
Age Range: 3–11

NEWCASTLE PREPARATORY SCHOOL

● ⌂

6 Eslington Road, Jesmond, Newcastle upon Tyne, Tyne and Wear NE2 4RH
Website: www.
newcastleprepschool.org.uk
Age Range: 3–11

SENIOR

ARGYLE HOUSE SCHOOL

● ⌂

19/20 Thornhill Park, Sunderland, Tyne and Wear SR2 7LA
Website:
www.argylehouseschool.co.uk
Age Range: 3–16

CENTRAL NEWCASTLE HIGH SCHOOL GDST

● ⌂ ▲

Eskdale Terrace, Newcastle upon Tyne, Tyne and Wear NE2 4DS
Website:
newcastlehigh.gdst.net
Age Range: 3–18

CHURCH HIGH SCHOOL, NEWCASTLE UPON TYNE

● ⌂ ▲

Tankerville Terrace, Jesmond, Newcastle upon Tyne, Tyne and Wear NE2 3BA
Website: www.churchhigh.com
Age Range: 3–18 (We have a Pre School Nursery on site and Sixth Form.)

DAME ALLAN'S BOYS SCHOOL

● ⌂ ▲

Fowberry Crescent, Fenham, Newcastle upon Tyne, Tyne and Wear NE4 9YJ
Website: www.dameallans.co.uk
Age Range: 8–18
(Co-ed VIth Form)

DAME ALLAN'S GIRLS SCHOOL

● ⌂ ▲

Fowberry Crescent, Fenham, Newcastle upon Tyne, Tyne and Wear NE4 9YJ
Website: www.dameallans.co.uk
Age Range: 8–18
(Co-ed VIth Form)

GRINDON HALL CHRISTIAN SCHOOL

● ⌂ ▲

Nookside, Sunderland, Tyne and Wear SR4 8PG
Website: www.grindonhall.com
Age Range: 3–18

THE KING'S SCHOOL

● ⌂ ▲

Huntington Place, Tynemouth, Tyne and Wear NE30 4RF
Website:
www.kings-tynemouth.org
Age Range: 4–18

NEWCASTLE SCHOOL FOR BOYS

● ⌂ ▲

34 The Grove, Gosforth, Newcastle upon Tyne, Tyne and Wear NE3 1NH
Website:
www.newcastleschool.co.uk
Age Range: 3–18

ROYAL GRAMMAR SCHOOL

● ⌂ ▲

Eskdale Terrace, Newcastle upon Tyne, Tyne and Wear NE2 4DX
Website:
www.rgs.newcastle.sch.uk
Age Range: 8–18
(Co-ed VIth form)

SUNDERLAND HIGH SCHOOL

● ⌂ ▲

Mowbray Road, Sunderland, Tyne and Wear SR2 8HY
Website:
www.sunderlandhigh.co.uk
Age Range: 2–18

WESTFIELD SCHOOL

● ⌂ ▲

Oakfield Road, Gosforth, Newcastle upon Tyne, Tyne and Wear NE3 4HS
Website:
www.westfield.newcastle.sch.uk
Age Range: 3–18

WARWICKSHIRE

PREPARATORY

ARNOLD LODGE SCHOOL

Kenilworth Road, Leamington
Spa, Warwickshire CV32 5TW
Age Range: 3–13

BILTON GRANGE

Rugby Road, Dunchurch,
Rugby, Warwickshire CV22 6QU
Website:
www.biltongrange.co.uk
Age Range: 4–13

CRACKLEY HALL SCHOOL

St Joseph's Park, Kenilworth,
Warwickshire CV8 2FT
Website:
www.crackleyhall.co.uk
Age Range: 2–11

THE CRESCENT SCHOOL

Bawnmore Road, Bilton, Rugby,
Warwickshire CV22 7QH
Website:
www.crescentschool.co.uk
Age Range: 3–11

THE CROFT PREPARATORY SCHOOL

Alveston Hill, Loxley Road,
Stratford-upon-Avon,
Warwickshire CV37 7RL
Website: www.croftschool.co.uk
Age Range: 2–11

THE DIXIE GRAMMAR JUNIOR SCHOOL

Temple Hall, Wellsborough,
Nuneaton, Warwickshire
CV13 6PA
Website:
www.pipemedia.net/dixie
Age Range: 3–10

EMSCOTE HOUSE SCHOOL AND NURSERY

46 Warwick Place, Leamington
Spa, Warwickshire CV32 5DE
Website:
www.emscotehouseschool.co.uk
Age Range: 2–8

MILVERTON HOUSE SCHOOL

Holman Way, Park Street,
Attleborough, Nuneaton,
Warwickshire CV11 4NS
Website:
www.milvertonschool.com

STRATFORD PREPARATORY SCHOOL

Church House, Old Town,
Stratford-upon-Avon,
Warwickshire CV37 6BG
Website:
www.stratfordprep.co.uk
Age Range: 2–11

THE TERRACE SCHOOL

54 High Street, Leamington
Spa, Warwickshire CV31 1LW
Age Range: 2–13

WARWICK PREPARATORY SCHOOL

Bridge Field, Banbury Road,
Warwick, Warwickshire
CV34 6PL
Website: www.warwickprep.com
Age Range: 3–11

SENIOR

KING'S HIGH SCHOOL, WARWICK

Smith Street, Warwick,
Warwickshire CV34 4HJ
Website:
kingshighwarwick.co.uk
Age Range: 10–18

THE KINGSLEY SCHOOL

Beauchamp Avenue,
Leamington Spa, Warwickshire
CV32 5RD
Website:
www.thekingsleyschool.com
Age Range: 3–18 (Boys 2–7)

PRINCETHORPE COLLEGE

Leamington Road, Princethorpe,
Rugby, Warwickshire CV23 9PX
Website:
www.princethorpe.co.uk
Age Range: 11–18

RUGBY SCHOOL

School House, Rugby,
Warwickshire CV22 5EH
Website: www.rugbyschool.net
Age Range: 11–18

TWYCROSS HOUSE SCHOOL

Twycross, Atherstone,
Warwickshire CV9 3PL
Website:
www.twycrosshouseschool.org.
uk
Age Range: 8–19

WARWICK SCHOOL

Myton Road, Warwick,
Warwickshire CV34 6PP
Website:
www.warwickschool.org
Age Range: 7–18

WEST MIDLANDS

PREPARATORY

AL HIJRAH SCHOOL

Cherrywood Centre, Burbidge Road, Bordesley Green, Birmingham, West Midlands B9 4US
Website:
www.alhijrahschool.co.uk
Age Range: 4–11

BABLAKE JUNIOR SCHOOL

Coundon Road, Coundon, Coventry, West Midlands CV1 4AU
Website: www.bablakejs.co.uk
Age Range: 7–11

BIRCHFIELD SCHOOL

Albrighton, Wolverhampton, West Midlands WV7 3AF
Website:
www.birchfieldschool.co.uk
Age Range: 4–13

THE BLUE COAT SCHOOL

Somerset Road, Edgbaston, Birmingham, West Midlands B17 0HR
Website:
www.bluecoat.bham.sch.uk
Age Range: 2–11

CHESHUNT PRE-PREPARATORY SCHOOL

8 Park Road, Coventry, West Midlands CV1 2LH
Website:
www.bablakeschools.com
Age Range: 3–8

COVENTRY PREP SCHOOL

Kenilworth Road, Coventry, West Midlands CV3 6PT
Website:
www.coventryprep.co.uk
Age Range: 3–11

DAVENPORT LODGE SCHOOL

21 Davenport Road, Earlsdon, Coventry, West Midlands CV5 6QA
Website: www.davenportlodge.
coventry.sch.uk

THE DRIVE PREPARATORY SCHOOL

Wood Road, Tettenhall, Wolverhampton, West Midlands WV6 8RX
Website: www.tettcoll.co.uk
Age Range: 2–7

EVERSFIELD PREPARATORY SCHOOL

Warwick Road, Solihull, West Midlands B91 1AT
Website: www.eversfield.co.uk
Age Range: 3–11

HALLFIELD SCHOOL

48 Church Road, Edgbaston, Birmingham, West Midlands B15 3SJ
Website:
www.hallfieldschool.co.uk
Age Range: 2–11

HARPER BELL SCHOOL

29 Ravenhurst Street, Birmingham, West Midlands B2 0EP
Age Range: 2–11

KINGSWOOD SCHOOL

St James Place, Shirley, Solihull, West Midlands B90 2BA
Website:
www.kingswoodschool.co.uk
Age Range: 2–11

LAMBS CHRISTIAN SCHOOL

86–95 Bacchus Road, Winson Green, Birmingham, West Midlands B18 4QY
Website:
www.christian-education.org
Age Range: 4–11

MAYFIELD PREPARATORY SCHOOL

Sutton Road, Walsall, West Midlands WS1 2PD
Website:
www.mayfieldprep.co.uk
Age Range: 3–11

NEWBRIDGE PREPARATORY SCHOOL

51 Newbridge Crescent, Tettenhall, Wolverhampton, West Midlands WV6 0LH
Age Range: 3–11

NORFOLK HOUSE SCHOOL

4 Norfolk Road, Edgbaston, Birmingham, West Midlands B15 3PS
Age Range: 3–11

RATHVILLY SCHOOL

119 Bunbury Road, Birmingham, West Midlands B31 2NB
Age Range: 3–11

ROSSLYN SCHOOL

1597 Stratford Road, Hall Green, Birmingham, West Midlands B28 9JB
Website:
www.rosslynschool.co.uk
Age Range: 2–11

THE ROYAL WOLVERHAMPTON JUNIOR SCHOOL

Penn Road, Wolverhampton, West Midlands WV3 0EF
Website: www.theroyalschool.co.uk
Age Range: 2–11

RUCKLEIGH SCHOOL

17 Lode Lane, Solihull, West Midlands B91 2AB
Website: www.ruckleigh.co.uk
Age Range: 3–11

THE SHRUBBERY SCHOOL

Walmley Ash Road, Walmley, Sutton Coldfield, West Midlands B76 1HY
Website: www.shrubberyschool.co.uk
Age Range: 3–11

WEST HOUSE SCHOOL

24 St James's Road, Edgbaston, Birmingham, West Midlands B15 2NX
Website: www.westhouse.bham.sch.uk
Age Range: 1–11 (Girls 1–4)

WOODSTOCK GIRLS' SCHOOL
11–15 Woodstock Road, Moseley, Birmingham, West Midlands B13 9BB
Age Range: 11–15

SENIOR

ABU BAKR INDEPENDENT SCHOOL
154–160 Wednesbury Road, Palfrey, Walsall, West Midlands WS1 4JJ
Website: www.abubakrtrust.org
Age Range: 11–16

AL-BURHAN GRAMMAR SCHOOL

28A George Street, Balsall Heath, Birmingham, West Midlands B12 9RG
Website: www.alburhan.org.uk
Age Range: 11–16

BABLAKE SCHOOL

Coundon Road, Coventry, West Midlands CV1 4AU
Website: www.bablake.com
Age Range: 11–19

BIRCHFIELD INDEPENDENT GIRLS SCHOOL

Beacon House, 30 Beacon Hill, Aston, Birmingham, West Midlands B6 6JU
Website: www.bigs.org.uk
Age Range: 11–16

COVENTRY MUSLIM SCHOOL

643 Foleshill Road, Coventry, West Midlands CV6 5JQ
Website: www.coventrymuslimschool.com
Age Range: 4–16

EDGBASTON HIGH SCHOOL FOR GIRLS

Westbourne Road, Edgbaston, Birmingham, West Midlands B15 3TS
Website: www.edgbastonhigh.co.uk
Age Range: 3–18

ELMHURST SCHOOL FOR DANCE
247–249 Bristol Road, Edgbaston, Birmingham, West Midlands B5 7UH
Website: www.elmhurstdance.co.uk
Age Range: 11–19

EMMANUEL SCHOOL

Bath Street Centre, Bath Street, Walsall, West Midlands WS1 3DB
Website: www.emmanuel.walsall.sch.uk
Age Range: 3–16

HIGHCLARE SCHOOL

10 Sutton Road, Erdington, Birmingham, West Midlands B23 6QL
Website: www.highclareschool.co.uk
Age Range: 1–18 (Boys 1–12 & 16–18
(Boys are being accepted into Senior School from September 2011 from Year 7))

HYDESVILLE TOWER SCHOOL
25 Broadway North, Walsall, West Midlands WS1 2QG
Website: www.hydesville.com
Age Range: 3–16

KING EDWARD VI HIGH SCHOOL FOR GIRLS

Edgbaston Park Road, Birmingham, West Midlands B15 2UB
Website: www.kehs.org.uk
Age Range: 11–18

KING EDWARD'S SCHOOL

Edgbaston Park Road, Birmingham, West Midlands B15 2UA
Website: www.kes.org.uk
Age Range: 11–18

KING HENRY VIII SCHOOL

Warwick Road, Coventry, West Midlands CV3 6AQ
Website: www.khviii.com
Age Range: 7–18

PATTISON COLLEGE

90 Binley Road, Coventry, West Midlands CV3 1FQ
Website: www.pattisons.co.uk
Age Range: 3–16

PRIORY SCHOOL

39 Sir Harry's Road, Edgbaston,
Birmingham, West Midlands
B15 2UR
Website: www.prioryschool.net
Age Range: (Co-ed 1–11)

ST GEORGE'S SCHOOL, EDGBASTON

31 Calthorpe Road, Edgbaston,
Birmingham, West Midlands
B15 1RX
Website: www.sgse.co.uk
Age Range: 3–18

SAINT MARTIN'S SCHOOL

Malvern Hall, Brueton Avenue,
Solihull, West Midlands B91
3EN
Website:
www.saintmartins-school.com
Age Range: 3–18 (Girls may
join the school from 2 years
9 months.)

SOLIHULL SCHOOL

Warwick Road, Solihull,
West Midlands B91 3DJ
Website: www.solsch.org.uk
Age Range: 7–18

TETTENHALL COLLEGE

Wood Road, Tettenhall,
Wolverhampton, West Midlands
WV6 8QX
Website:
www.tettenhallcollege.co.uk
Age Range: 2–18

WOLVERHAMPTON GRAMMAR SCHOOL

Compton Road,
Wolverhampton, West Midlands
WV3 9RB
Website: www.wgs.org.uk
Age Range: 10–18

INDEPENDENT SIXTH FORM COLLEGE / TUTORIAL COLLEGE

ABBEY COLLEGE

10 St Pauls Square,
Birmingham, West Midlands
B3 1QU
Website:
www.abbeybirmingham.co.uk

MANDER PORTMAN WOODWARD

17–18 Greenfield Crescent,
Edgbaston, Birmingham,
West Midlands B15 3AU
Website: www.mpw.co.uk

WILTSHIRE

NURSERY AND PRE-PREP

STEPPING STONES NURSERY AND PRE-PREPARATORY SCHOOL

Oakhill Farm, Froxfield,
Marlborough, Wiltshire SN8 3JT
Website: www.
steppingstonesschool.org.uk
Age Range: 2–8 (Ratio 1:4
2 year olds
Ratio 1:8 3–4 year olds
Normal school ratios age 4–8
years (Recept - Yr 3))

PREPARATORY

AVONDALE SCHOOL

High Street, Bulford, Salisbury,
Wiltshire SP4 9DR
Age Range: 3–11

CHAFYN GROVE SCHOOL*

33 Bourne Avenue, Salisbury,
Wiltshire SP1 1LR
Website:
www.chafyngrove.co.uk
Age Range: 3–13

GODOLPHIN PREPARATORY SCHOOL

Laverstock Road, Salisbury,
Wiltshire SP1 2RB
Website:
www.godolphinprep.org
Age Range: 3–11

HEYWOOD PREPARATORY SCHOOL

The Priory, Priory Street,
Corsham, Wiltshire SN13 0AP
Website:
www.heywoodprep.com
Age Range: 2–11

LEADEN HALL SCHOOL

70 The Close, Salisbury,
Wiltshire SP1 2EP
Website: www.leaden-hall.com
Age Range: 3–11 (Boys 3–4)

MEADOWPARK SCHOOL AND NURSERY

Calcutt Street, Cricklade,
Wiltshire SN6 6BA
Website:
www.meadowparkschool.co.uk

THE MILL SCHOOL

Whistley Road, Potterne,
Devizes, Wiltshire SN10 5TE
Website: www.mill.wilts.sch.uk
Age Range: 3–11

NORMAN COURT PREPARATORY SCHOOL

West Tytherley, Salisbury, Wiltshire SP5 1NH
Website: www.normancourt.co.uk.
Age Range: 3–13

PINEWOOD SCHOOL

Bourton, Shrivenham, Wiltshire SN6 8HZ
Website: www.pinewoodschool.co.uk
Age Range: 3–13

PRIOR PARK PREPARATORY SCHOOL*

Calcutt Street, Cricklade, Wiltshire SN6 6BB
Website: www.priorparkprep.com
Age Range: 3–13

ROUNDSTONE PREPARATORY SCHOOL

Courtfield House, Polebarn Road, Trowbridge, Wiltshire BA14 7EG
Website: www.roundstone.ik.org
Age Range: 4–11

ST FRANCIS SCHOOL

Marlborough Road, Pewsey, Wiltshire SN9 5NT
Website: www.st-francis.wilts.sch.uk
Age Range: 2–13

ST MARGARET'S PREPARATORY SCHOOL

Curzon Street, Calne, Wiltshire SN11 0DF
Website: www.stmargaretsprep.org.uk
Age Range: 3–11

SALISBURY CATHEDRAL SCHOOL

1 The Close, Salisbury, Wiltshire SP1 2EQ
Website: www. salisburycathedralschool.com
Age Range: 3–13

SANDROYD SCHOOL

Rushmore, Tollard Royal, Salisbury, Wiltshire SP5 5QD
Website: www.sandroyd.org
Age Range: 7–13 (The Walled Garden pre prep ages 2 1/2–7 years
Sandroyd 7–13 years)

SOUTH HILLS SCHOOL

Home Farm Road, Wilton, Salisbury, Wiltshire SP2 8PJ
Website: www.southhillsschool.com

SENIOR

DAUNTSEY'S SCHOOL*

High Street, West Lavington, Devizes, Wiltshire SN10 4HE
Website: www.dauntseys.org
Age Range: 11–18

EMMAUS SCHOOL

School Lane, Staverton, Trowbridge, Wiltshire BA14 6NZ
Website: www.emmaus-school.org.uk
Age Range: 5–16

THE GODOLPHIN SCHOOL

Milford Hill, Salisbury, Wiltshire SP1 2RA
Website: www.godolphin.org
Age Range: 11–18

GRITTLETON HOUSE SCHOOL

Grittleton, Chippenham, Wiltshire SN14 6AP
Website: www.grittletonhouseschool.org
Age Range: 2–16

LEEHURST SWAN

Campbell Road, Salisbury, Wiltshire SP1 3BQ
Website: www.leehurstswan.org.uk
Age Range: 2–16

MARANATHA CHRISTIAN SCHOOL

Queenlaines Farm, Sevenhampton, Swindon, Wiltshire SN6 7SQ
Website: www.christian-education.org
Age Range: 3–18

MARLBOROUGH COLLEGE

Marlborough, Wiltshire SN8 1PA
Website: www.marlboroughcollege.org
Age Range: 13–18

ST MARY'S CALNE*

63 Curzon Street, Calne, Wiltshire SN11 0DF
Website: www.stmaryscalne.org
Age Range: 11–18

STONAR SCHOOL

Cottles Park, Atworth, Wiltshire SN12 8NT
Website: www.stonarschool.com
Age Range: 2–18

WARMINSTER SCHOOL

Church Street, Warminster, Wiltshire BA12 8PJ
Website: www.warminsterschool.org.uk
Age Range: 3–19

INTERNATIONAL SCHOOLS AND INTERNATIONAL STUDY CENTRES

BISHOPSTROW COLLEGE

Bishopstrow, Warminster, Wiltshire BA12 9HU
Website: www.bishopstrow.com
Age Range: 8–17

WORCESTERSHIRE

NURSERY AND PRE-PREP

BROMSGROVE PRE-PREPARATORY AND NURSERY SCHOOL
● 🏠
Avoncroft House, Hanbury Road, Bromsgrove, Worcestershire B60 4JS
Website:
www.bromsgrove-school.co.uk
Age Range: 2–7

PREPARATORY

ABBERLEY HALL
● 🏠
Abberley Hall, Worcester, Worcestershire WR6 6DD
Website:
www.abberleyhall.co.uk
Age Range: 2–13

BROMSGROVE PREPARATORY SCHOOL
● 🏠
Old Station Road, Bromsgrove, Worcestershire B60 2BU
Website:
www.bromsgrove-school.co.uk
Age Range: 7–13

THE DOWNS, MALVERN
● 🏠
Brockhill Road, Colwall, Malvern, Worcestershire WR13 6EY
Website:
www.thedowns.malcol.org
Age Range: 3–13

THE ELMS
● 🏠
Colwall, Malvern, Worcestershire WR13 6EF
Website: www.elmsschool.co.uk
Age Range: 3–13

KING'S HAWFORD
● 🏠
Hawford Lock Lane, Claines, Worcester, Worcestershire WR3 7SD
Website: www.ksw.org.uk
Age Range: 2–11

THE KNOLL SCHOOL
● 🏠
33 Manor Avenue, Kidderminster, Worcestershire DY11 6EA
Website:
www.knoll.worcs.sch.uk
Age Range: 2–11

MADRESFIELD EARLY YEARS CENTRE
● 🏠
Hayswood Farm, Madresfield, Malvern, Worcestershire WR13 5AA
Age Range: 1–8

MOFFATS SCHOOL
● 🏠
Kinlet Hall, Kinlet, Bewdley, Worcestershire DY12 3AY
Website: www.moffats.co.uk
Age Range: 3–13

RGS THE GRANGE
● 🏠
Grange Lane, Claines, Worcester, Worcestershire WR3 7RR
Website: www.rgsao.org
Age Range: 2–11

WINTERFOLD HOUSE
● 🏠
Chaddesley Corbett, Kidderminster, Worcestershire DY10 4PW
Website:
www.winterfoldhouse.co.uk
Age Range: 2–13

SENIOR

BOWBROOK HOUSE SCHOOL
● 🏠
Peopleton, Pershore, Worcestershire WR10 2EE
Website:
www.bowbrookhouseschool.co.uk
Age Range: 3–16

BROMSGROVE SCHOOL*
● 🏠 ▲
Worcester Road, Bromsgrove, Worcestershire B61 7DU
Website:
www.bromsgrove-school.co.uk
Age Range: 13–18

DODDERHILL SCHOOL
● 🏠
Droitwich Spa, Worcestershire WR9 0BE
Website: www.dodderhill.co.uk
Age Range: 3–16 (Boys 3–9)

GREEN HILL SCHOOL
● 🏠
Evesham, Worcestershire WR11 4NG
Website:
www.greenhillschool.co.uk
Age Range: 3–13

HEATHFIELD SCHOOL
● 🏠
Wolverley, Kidderminster, Worcestershire DY10 3QE
Website:
www.heathfieldschool.co.uk
Age Range: 3–16

HOLY TRINITY SCHOOL
● 🏠 ▲
Birmingham Road, Kidderminster, Worcestershire DY10 2BY
Website: www.holytrinity.co.uk

THE KING'S SCHOOL
● 🏠 ▲
5 College Green, Worcester, Worcestershire WR1 2LL
Website: www.ksw.org.uk
Age Range: 3–18

MALVERN ST JAMES*

15 Avenue Road, Great
Malvern, Worcestershire
WR14 3BA
Website:
www.malvernstjames.co.uk
Age Range: 4–18

RGS WORCESTER & THE ALICE OTTLEY SCHOOL

Upper Tything, Worcester,
Worcestershire WR1 1HP
Website: www.rgsao.org
Age Range: 11–18

RIVER SCHOOL

Oakfield House, Droitwich
Road, Worcester,
Worcestershire WR3 7ST
Website: www.riverschool.co.uk
Age Range: 5–16

ST MARY'S

Mount Battenhall, Worcester,
Worcestershire WR5 2HP
Website: www.stmarys.org.uk
Age Range: 2–18 (Boys 2–8)

SAINT MICHAEL'S COLLEGE

Oldwood Road, St Michaels,
Tenbury Wells, Worcestershire
WR15 8PH
Website:
www.st-michaels.uk.com
Age Range: 14–19

SPRINGFIELD SCHOOL

Britannia Square, Worcester,
Worcestershire WR1 3DL
Website: www.rgso.org
Age Range: 2–11

INDEPENDENT SIXTH FORM COLLEGE / TUTORIAL COLLEGE

THE ABBEY COLLEGE

253 Wells Road, Malvern Wells,
Worcestershire WR14 4JF
Website:
www.abbeycollege.co.uk
Age Range: 14–23
(English Courses (12+)
Vacation Courses (8+)
Academic Courses (14+))

EAST RIDING OF YORKSHIRE

PREPARATORY

FROEBEL HOUSE SCHOOL

5 Marlborough Avenue, Princes
Avenue, Hull, East Riding of
Yorkshire HU5 3JP
Website: www.the-village.co.uk/
froebelhouse
Age Range: 4–11

HESSLE MOUNT SCHOOL

Jenny Brough Lane, Hessle,
East Riding of Yorkshire
HU13 0JX
Website:
www.hesslemountschool.org.uk
Age Range: 3–8

POCKLINGTON MONTESSORI SCHOOL

Carr Lane, Pocklington, East
Riding of Yorkshire YO42 1NT
Website:
www.pocklingtonmontessori.com

SENIOR

HULL COLLEGIATE SCHOOL

Tranby Croft, Anlaby, East
Riding of Yorkshire HU10 7EH
Website:
www.hullcollegiateschool.co.uk
Age Range: 3–18

HYMERS COLLEGE

Hymers Avenue, Hull, East
Riding of Yorkshire HU3 1LW
Website:
www.hymerscollege.co.uk
Age Range: 8–18

POCKLINGTON SCHOOL

West Green, Pocklington, East
Riding of Yorkshire YO42 2NJ
Website:
www.pocklingtonschool.com
Age Range: 7–18

NORTH YORKSHIRE

PREPARATORY

AYSGARTH PREPARATORY SCHOOL*
Newton-Le-Willows, Bedale,
North Yorkshire DL8 1TF
Website:
www.aysgarthschool.com
Age Range: 3–13 (Co-ed day 3–8)

BELMONT GROSVENOR SCHOOL
Swarcliffe Hall, Birstwith,
Harrogate, North Yorkshire
HG3 2JG
Website:
www.belmontgrosvenor.co.uk
Age Range: 2–11

BOOTHAM JUNIOR SCHOOL
Rawcliffe Lane, York,
North Yorkshire YO30 6NP
Website:
www.boothamschool.com
Age Range: 3–11

BOTTON VILLAGE SCHOOL
Danby, Whitby, North Yorkshire
YO21 2NJ
Age Range: 4–14

BRACKENFIELD SCHOOL
128 Duchy Road, Harrogate,
North Yorkshire HG1 2HE
Website:
www.brackenfieldschool.co.uk
Age Range: 2–11

BRAMCOTE SCHOOL
Filey Road, Scarborough,
North Yorkshire YO11 2TT
Website:
www.bramcoteschool.com
Age Range: 3–13

CUNDALL MANOR SCHOOL
Helperby, York, North Yorkshire
YO61 2RW
Website:
www.cundallmanor.n-yorks.sch.uk
Age Range: 2–13

GIGGLESWICK JUNIOR SCHOOL
Giggleswick, Settle, North
Yorkshire BD24 0DG
Website:
www.giggleswick.org.uk
Age Range: 3–11

HIGHFIELD PREPARATORY SCHOOL
Clarence Drive, Harrogate,
North Yorkshire HG1 2QG
Website:
www.highfieldprep.org.uk
Age Range: 4–11

LISVANE, SCARBOROUGH COLLEGE JUNIOR SCHOOL

Filey Road, Scarborough,
North Yorkshire YO11 3BA
Website:
www.scarboroughcollege.co.uk
Age Range: 3–11

MALSIS SCHOOL
Cross Hills, Near Skipton,
North Yorkshire BD20 8DT
Website: www.malsis.com
Age Range: 4–13

THE MINSTER SCHOOL
Deangate, York, North Yorkshire
YO1 7JA
Website:
www.minster.york.sch.uk
Age Range: 3–13

RIPON CATHEDRAL CHOIR SCHOOL

Whitcliffe Lane, Ripon,
North Yorkshire HG4 2LA
Website:
www.cathedralchoirschool.co.uk
Age Range: 3–13

ST MARTIN'S AMPLEFORTH
Gilling Castle, Gilling East, York,
North Yorkshire YO62 4HP
Website:
www.stmartins.ampleforth.org.uk
Age Range: 3–13

TERRINGTON HALL
Terrington, York, North Yorkshire
YO60 6PR
Website:
www.terringtonhall.com
Age Range: 3–13

TREGELLES
The Mount Junior School, Dalton
Terrace, York, North Yorkshire
YO24 4DD
Website:
www.mount.n-yorks.sch.uk
Age Range: 3–11

WOODLEIGH SCHOOL
Langton, Malton, North
Yorkshire YO17 9QN
Website:
www.woodleighschool.com
Age Range: 3–13

SENIOR

AMPLEFORTH COLLEGE
● 🏠 ▲

York, North Yorkshire YO62 4ER
Website:
www.college.ampleforth.org.uk
Age Range: 13–18

ASHVILLE COLLEGE
● 🏠 ▲

Green Lane, Harrogate,
North Yorkshire HG2 9JP
Website: www.ashville.co.uk
Age Range: 4–18

BOOTHAM SCHOOL
● 🏠 ▲

Bootham, York, North Yorkshire
YO30 7BU
Website:
www.boothamschool.com
Age Range: 11–18

FYLING HALL SCHOOL
● 🏠 ▲

Robin Hood's Bay, Whitby,
North Yorkshire YO22 4QD
Website: www.fylinghall.org
Age Range: 4–19

GIGGLESWICK SCHOOL
● 🏠 ▲

Giggleswick, Settle,
North Yorkshire BD24 0DE
Website:
www.giggleswick.org.uk
Age Range: 4–18

HARROGATE LADIES' COLLEGE
● 🏠 ▲

Clarence Drive, Harrogate,
North Yorkshire HG1 2QG
Website: www.hlc.org.uk
Age Range: 11–18 (Highfield
Prep School, part of the HLC
Group of Schools is co-ed from
age 4–11.)

THE MOUNT SCHOOL
● 🏠 ▲

Dalton Terrace, York, North
Yorkshire YO24 4DD
Website:
www.mountschoolyork.co.uk
Age Range: 3–18

QUEEN ETHELBURGA'S COLLEGE
● 🏠 ★ ▲

Thorpe Underwood Hall,
Ouseburn, York, North Yorkshire
YO26 9SS
Website:
www.queenethelburgas.edu
Age Range: 3–20

QUEEN MARY'S SCHOOL
● 🏠

Baldersby Park, Topcliffe,
Thirsk, North Yorkshire YO7 3BZ
Website: www.queenmarys.org
Age Range: 2–16 (Boys 3–7)

READ SCHOOL
● 🏠 ▲

Drax, Selby, North Yorkshire
YO8 8NL
Website: www.readschool.co.uk
Age Range: 4–18

ST PETER'S SCHOOL
● 🏠 ▲

York, North Yorkshire YO30 6AB
Website:
www.st-peters.york.sch.uk
Age Range: 3–18

SCARBOROUGH COLLEGE & LISVANE SCHOOL
● 🏠 ★ ▲

Filey Road, Scarborough,
North Yorkshire YO11 3BA
Website:
www.scarboroughcollege.co.uk
Age Range: 3–18

INDEPENDENT SIXTH FORM COLLEGE / TUTORIAL COLLEGE

HARROGATE TUTORIAL COLLEGE
● 🏠

2 The Oval, Harrogate,
North Yorkshire HG2 9BA
Website: www.htcuk.org
Age Range: 15–20

INTERNATIONAL SCHOOLS AND INTERNATIONAL STUDY CENTRES

HARROGATE LANGUAGE ACADEMY
● 🏠

8a Royal Parade, Harrogate,
North Yorkshire HG1 2SZ
Website: www.hla.co.uk

SOUTH YORKSHIRE

PREPARATORY

ASHDELL PREPARATORY SCHOOL
● ⛪

266 Fulwood Road, Sheffield,
South Yorkshire S10 3BL
Website:
www.ashdellprep.co.uk
Age Range: 3–11
(Co-educational Pre-School for
rising threes in association with
Birkdale School)

MYLNHURST PREPARATORY SCHOOL & NURSERY
● ⛪

Button Hill, Ecclesall, Sheffield,
South Yorkshire S11 9HJ
Website: www.mylnhurst.co.uk
Age Range: 3–11

RUDSTON PREPARATORY SCHOOL
● ⛪

59–63 Broom Road, Rotherham,
South Yorkshire S60 2SW
Website:
www.rudstonschool.com
Age Range: 2–11

SYCAMORE HALL PREPARATORY SCHOOL
● ⛪

1 Hall Flat Lane, Balby,
Doncaster, South Yorkshire DN4
8PT
Age Range: 3–11

SENIOR

BARNSLEY CHRISTIAN SCHOOL
● ⛪

Hope House, 2 Blucher Street,
Barnsley, South Yorkshire S70
1AP
Website:
www.barnsleychristianschool.
org.uk
Age Range: 5–16

BIRKDALE SCHOOL
● ⛪ ▲

Oakholme Road, Sheffield,
South Yorkshire S10 3DH
Website: www.birkdaleschool.
org.uk
Age Range: 4–18
(Co-ed VIth Form)

HANDSWORTH CHRISTIAN SCHOOL
● ⛪

231 Handsworth Road,
Handsworth, Sheffield, South
Yorkshire S13 9BJ
Website: www.
handsworthchristianschool.co.uk
Age Range: 4–16

HILL HOUSE SCHOOL
● ⛪

Sixth Avenue, Auckley,
Doncaster, South Yorkshire
DN9 3GG
Website:
www.hillhousestmarys.co.uk
Age Range: 2–16

SHEFFIELD HIGH SCHOOL GDST
● ⛪ ▲

10 Rutland Park, Broomhill,
Sheffield, South Yorkshire S10
2PE
Website:
www.sheffieldhighschool.org.uk
Age Range: 4–18

WESTBOURNE SCHOOL
● ⛪

60 Westbourne Road, Sheffield,
South Yorkshire S10 2QT
Website:
www.westbourneschool.co.uk
Age Range: 4–16

WEST YORKSHIRE

PREPARATORY

BRONTE HOUSE SCHOOL

Apperley Bridge, Bradford,
West Yorkshire BD10 0PQ
Website:
www.woodhousegrove.co.uk
Age Range: 3–11

DALE HOUSE SCHOOL

Ruby Street, Carlinghow, Batley,
West Yorkshire WF17 8HL
Website: www.dhschool.co.uk
Age Range: 2–11

THE FROEBELIAN SCHOOL

Clarence Road, Horsforth,
Leeds, West Yorkshire LS18 4LB
Website: www.froebelian.co.uk
Age Range: 3–11

GHYLL ROYD SCHOOL

Greystone Manor, Ilkley Road,
Burley in Wharfedale, Ilkley,
West Yorkshire LS29 7HW
Website:
www.ghyllroydschool.co.uk
Age Range: 3–11

THE GLEDDINGS PREPARATORY SCHOOL

Birdcage Lane, Savile Park,
Halifax, West Yorkshire HX3 0JB
Website:
www.thegleddings.co.uk
Age Range: 3–11

GLEN HOUSE MONTESSORI SCHOOL

Cragg Vale, Hebden Bridge,
West Yorkshire HX7 5SQ
Website:
www.glenhousemontessori.
calderdale.sch.uk
Age Range: 3–15

INGLEBROOK SCHOOL

Northgate Close, Pontefract,
West Yorkshire WF8 1HJ
Age Range: 2–11

LADY LANE PARK SCHOOL

Lady Lane, Bingley,
West Yorkshire BD16 4AP
Website: www.ladylanepark.
bradford.sch.uk
Age Range: 2–11

MOORFIELD SCHOOL

Wharfedale Lodge, Ben
Rhydding Road, Ilkley,
West Yorkshire LS29 8RL
Website: www.moorfieldschool.
co.uk
Age Range: 2–11

MOORLANDS SCHOOL

Foxhill Drive, Weetwood Lane,
Leeds, West Yorkshire LS16 5PF
Website:
www.moorlands-school.co.uk
Age Range: 2–13

MOUNT SCHOOL

3 Binham Road, Edgerton,
Huddersfield, West Yorkshire
HD2 2AP
Website: www.themount.org.uk
Age Range: 3–11

MOUNTJOY HOUSE SCHOOL

63 New North Road,
Huddersfield, West Yorkshire
HD1 5ND
Age Range: 3–11

NETHERLEIGH AND ROSSEFIELD SCHOOL

Parsons Road, Heaton,
Bradford, West Yorkshire BD9
4AY
Age Range: 3–11

THE PREPARATORY SCHOOL LIGHTCLIFFE

Wakefield Road, Halifax,
West Yorkshire HX3 8AQ
Website: www.hgsf.org.uk
Age Range: 2–11

THE RASTRICK INDEPENDENT SCHOOL

Ogden Lane, Rastrick,
Brighouse, West Yorkshire
HD6 3HF
Website:
www.rastrickschool.co.uk
Age Range: (Day Pupils from
Birth to Sixteen years of age.)

RICHMOND HOUSE SCHOOL

170 Otley Road, Leeds,
West Yorkshire LS16 5LG
Website: www.rhschool.org
Age Range: 3–11

ST AGNES PNEU SCHOOL

25 Burton Crescent, Leeds,
West Yorkshire LS6 4DN
Website:
www.st-agnes.demon.co.uk
Age Range: 2–7

ST HILDA'S SCHOOL

Dovecote Lane, Horbury,
Wakefield, West Yorkshire WF4
6BB
Website:
www.silcoates.wakefield.sch.uk
Age Range: 3–11

SUNNY HILL HOUSE SCHOOL

Wrenthorpe Lane, Wrenthorpe,
Wakefield, West Yorkshire WF2
0QB
Website: www.silcoates.
wakefield.sch.uk/
sunnyhillhouse.html
Age Range: 2–7

WAKEFIELD TUTORIAL PREPARATORY SCHOOL
● 🏠

Commercial Street, Morley, Leeds, West Yorkshire LS27 8HY
Website: www.wtschool.co.uk
Age Range: 4–11

WESTVILLE HOUSE PREPARATORY SCHOOL
● 🏠

Carter's Lane, Middleton, Ilkley, West Yorkshire LS29 0DQ
Website:
www.westvilleschool.co.uk
Age Range: 3–11

SENIOR

ACKWORTH SCHOOL
● 🏠 ▲

Ackworth, Pontefract, West Yorkshire WF7 7LT
Website:
www.ackworthschool.com
Age Range: 2–18

BATLEY GRAMMAR SCHOOL
● 🏠 ▲

Carlinghow Hill, Batley, West Yorkshire WF17 0AD
Website:
www.batleygrammar.co.uk
Age Range: 2–18

BRADFORD CHRISTIAN SCHOOL
● 🏠

Livingstone Road, Bolton Woods, Bradford, West Yorkshire BD2 1BT
Website:
www.bradfordchristianschool.com
Age Range: 4–16

BRADFORD GIRLS' GRAMMAR SCHOOL
● 🏠 ▲

Squire Lane, Bradford, West Yorkshire BD9 6RB
Website: www.bggs.com
Age Range: 2–18

BRADFORD GRAMMAR SCHOOL
● 🏠 ▲

Keighley Road, Bradford, West Yorkshire BD9 4JP
Website:
www.bradfordgrammar.com
Age Range: 6–18

THE BRANCH CHRISTIAN SCHOOL
● 🏠

8–10 Thomas Street, Heckmondwike, West Yorkshire WF16 0NW
Age Range: 3–17

BROWNBERRIE SCHOOL
● 🏠

173–179 New Road Side, Horsforth, Leeds, West Yorkshire LS18 4DR
Age Range: 11–17

FULNECK SCHOOL
● 🏠 ◆ ▲

Fulneck, Leeds, West Yorkshire LS28 8DS
Website:
www.fulneckschool.co.uk
Age Range: 3–18

GATEWAYS SCHOOL
● 🏠 ▲

Harewood, Leeds, West Yorkshire LS17 9LE
Website:
www.gatewaysschool.co.uk
Age Range: 3–18 (Boys 3–7)

THE GRAMMAR SCHOOL AT LEEDS
● 🏠 ★ ▲

Alwoodley Gates, Harrogate Road, Leeds, West Yorkshire LS17 8GS
Website: www.gsal.org.uk
Age Range: 3–18

HIPPERHOLME GRAMMAR SCHOOL
● 🏠 ▲

Bramley Lane, Hipperholme, Halifax, West Yorkshire HX3 8JE
Website: www.hipperholme grammar.calderdale.co.uk
Age Range: 11–18

HUDDERSFIELD GRAMMAR SCHOOL
● 🏠

Royds Mount, Luck Lane, Marsh, Huddersfield, West Yorkshire HD1 4QX
Website: www.huddersfield-grammar.co.uk
Age Range: 3–16

ISLAMIA GIRLS HIGH SCHOOL
● 🏠

Thornton Lodge Road, Thornton Lodge, Huddersfield, West Yorkshire HD1 3JQ
Age Range: 11–16

NEW HORIZON COMMUNITY SCHOOL
● 🏠

Newton Hill House, Newton Hill Road, Leeds, West Yorkshire LS7 4JE
Website: nhss.org.uk
Age Range: 11–16

OLIVE SECONDARY
● 🏠 ▲

8 Cunliffe Villas, Bradford, West Yorkshire BD8 7AN
Website:
www.olivesecondary.org.uk
Age Range: 11–18

QUEEN ELIZABETH GRAMMAR SCHOOL
● 🏠 ▲

154 Northgate, Wakefield, West Yorkshire WF1 3QX
Website: www.wgsf.org.uk
Age Range: 7–18

RATHBONE CHOICES
● 🏠

8–10 Highfields Road, Huddersfield, West Yorkshire HD1 5LP
Website: www.rathboneuk.org
Age Range: 14–16

RISHWORTH SCHOOL
● 🏠 ▲

Rishworth, West Yorkshire HX6 4QA
Website:
www.rishworth-school.co.uk
Age Range: 3–18

SILCOATES SCHOOL

Wrenthorpe, Wakefield,
West Yorkshire WF2 0PD
Website: www.silcoates.co.uk
Age Range: 7–18

WAKEFIELD GIRLS' HIGH SCHOOL

Wentworth Street, Wakefield,
West Yorkshire WF1 2QS
Website: www.wgsf.org.uk
Age Range: 11–18

WAKEFIELD INDEPENDENT SCHOOL

The Nostell Centre, Doncaster
Road, Nostell, Wakefield, West
Yorkshire WF4 1QG
Website: www.
wakefieldindependentschool.
org.uk
Age Range: 3–16

WOODHOUSE GROVE SCHOOL

Apperley Bridge, West Yorkshire
BD10 0NR
Website:
www.woodhousegrove.co.uk
Age Range: 11–18

2.3

Northern Ireland

COUNTY ANTRIM

PREPARATORY

CABIN HILL SCHOOL
● ⌂

562–594 Upper Newtownards
Road, Knock, Belfast,
County Antrim BT4 3HJ
Website: www.cabinhill.org.uk
Age Range: 3–13
(Co-ed kindergarten)

SENIOR

BELFAST ROYAL ACADEMY
● ⌂ ▲

Belfast, County Antrim BT14 6JL
Website:
www.belfastroyalacademy.com
Age Range: 4–19

CAMPBELL COLLEGE
● ⌂ ▲

Belmont Road, Belfast,
County Antrim BT4 2ND
Website:
www.campbellcollege.co.uk
Age Range: 11–18

HUNTERHOUSE COLLEGE
● ⌂

Finaghy, Belfast, County Antrim
BT10 0LE
Website:
www.hunterhousecollege.net
Age Range: 5–19

METHODIST COLLEGE
● ⌂ ▲

1 Malone Road, Belfast,
County Antrim BT9 6BY
Website: www.rmplc.co.uk/
eduweb/sites/mcb
Age Range: 4–19

ROYAL BELFAST
ACADEMICAL INSTITUTION
● ⌂ ▲

College Square East, Belfast,
County Antrim BT1 6DL
Website: www.rbai.org.uk
Age Range: 4–18

VICTORIA COLLEGE
BELFAST
● ⌂ ▲

Cranmore Park, Belfast,
County Antrim BT9 6JA
Website:
www.victoriacollege.org.uk
Age Range: 4–18

COUNTY ARMAGH

SENIOR

**THE ROYAL SCHOOL
ARMAGH**
● ♠ ▲
College Hill, Armagh,
County Armagh BT61 9DH
Website:
www.royalschoolarmagh.com
Age Range: 4–19

COUNTY DOWN

SENIOR

**BANGOR GRAMMAR
SCHOOL**
● ♠ ▲
13 College Avenue, Bangor,
County Down BT20 5HJ
Website: www.
bangorgrammarschool.org.uk
Age Range: 11–18

**BANGOR INDEPENDENT
CHRISTIAN SCHOOL**
● ♠
277A Clandeboye Road, Bangor,
County Down BT19 1AA
Website:
www.freepres.org/schools
Age Range: 4–16

**THE HOLYWOOD RUDOLF
STEINER SCHOOL**
● ♠
The Highlands, 34 Croft Road,
Holywood, County Down
BT18 0PR
Website:
www.holywood-steiner.co.uk
Age Range: 4–17

ROCKPORT SCHOOL
● ♠
15 Rockport Road, Craigavad,
Holywood, County Down
BT18 0DD
Website:
www.rockportschool.com
Age Range: 3–16
(Boarding 7–13)

COUNTY FERMANAGH

SENIOR

PORTORA ROYAL SCHOOL
● ♠ ▲
Enniskillen, County Fermanagh
BT74 7HA
Website: www.portoraroyal.co.uk
Age Range: 11–19

COUNTY TYRONE

SENIOR

**THE ROYAL SCHOOL
DUNGANNON**
● ⌂ ▲
1 Ranfurly Road, Dungannon,
County Tyrone BT71 6EG
Website:
www.royaldungannon.com
Age Range: 11–19

2.4

Scotland

ABERDEENSHIRE

PREPARATORY

THE HAMILTON SCHOOL

55–57 Queens Road,
Aberdeen, Aberdeenshire
AB15 4YP
Website: www.
thehamilton.aberdeen.sch.uk
Age Range: 2–12

SENIOR

ABERDEEN WALDORF SCHOOL

Craigton Road, Cults,
Aberdeen, Aberdeenshire
AB15 9QD
Website:
www.aberdeen waldorf.co.uk
Age Range: 3–16

ALBYN SCHOOL

17–23 Queen's Road,
Aberdeen, Aberdeenshire
AB15 4PB
Website:
www.albynschool.co.uk
Age Range: 1–18

ROBERT GORDON'S COLLEGE

Schoolhill, Aberdeen,
Aberdeenshire AB10 1FE
Website:
www.rgc.aberdeen.sch.uk
Age Range: 4–18

ST MARGARET'S SCHOOL FOR GIRLS

17 Albyn Place, Aberdeen,
Aberdeenshire AB10 1RU
Website: www.
stmargaret.aberdeen.sch.uk
Age Range: 3–18 (Boys 3–5)

INTERNATIONAL SCHOOLS AND INTERNATIONAL STUDY CENTRES

INTERNATIONAL SCHOOL OF ABERDEEN

'Fairgirth', 296 North Deeside
Road, Milltimber, Aberdeen,
Aberdeenshire AB13 OAB
Website:
www.isa.aberdeen.sch.uk
Age Range: 3–18

ANGUS

SENIOR

HIGH SCHOOL OF DUNDEE

Euclid Crescent, Dundee,
Angus DD1 1HU
Website:
www.highschoolofdundee.org.uk
Age Range: 5–18

LATHALLAN SCHOOL
Brotherton Castle, Johnshaven,
Montrose, Angus DD10 0HN
Website: www.lathallan.org.uk
Age Range: 5–19

ARGYLL AND BUTE

SENIOR

LOMOND SCHOOL

10 Stafford Street, Helensburgh,
Argyll and Bute G84 9JX
Website:
www.lomond-school.org
Age Range: 3–18

SOUTH AYRSHIRE

SENIOR

WELLINGTON SCHOOL
Carleton Turrets, Craigweil
Road, Ayr, South Ayrshire
KA7 2XH
Website:
www.wellingtonschool.org
Age Range: 3–18

CLACKMANNANSHIRE

SENIOR

DOLLAR ACADEMY*

Dollar, Clackmannanshire
FK14 7DU
Website:
www.dollaracademy.org
Age Range: 10–18

FIFE

SENIOR

ST LEONARDS SCHOOL

South Street, St Andrews,
Fife KY16 9QJ
Website:
www.stleonards-fife.org
Age Range: 4–19

GLASGOW

PREPARATORY

THE GLASGOW ACADEMY DAIRSIE
54 Newlands Road,
Glasgow G43 2JG
Website:
www.theglasgowacademy.org.uk
Age Range: 3–9

GLASGOW STEINER SCHOOL
52 Lumsden Street, Glasgow
G3 8RH
Website: www.
glasgowsteinerschool.org.uk
Age Range: 3–14

ST ALOYSIUS JUNIOR SCHOOL
56–58 Hill Street,
Glasgow G3 6RH
Website: www.staloysius.org
Age Range: 5–12

SENIOR

CRAIGHOLME SCHOOL

72 St Andrew's Drive,
Pollokshields, Glasgow G41
4HS
Website: www.craigholme.co.uk
Age Range: 3–18 (Boys 3–5 in
Nursery only)

THE GLASGOW ACADEMY
Colebrooke Street, Glasgow
G12 8HE
Website:
www.theglasgowacademy.org.uk
Age Range: 3–18

THE HIGH SCHOOL OF GLASGOW
637 Crow Road,
Glasgow G13 1PL
Website: www.glasgowhigh.com
Age Range: 3–18

HUTCHESONS' GRAMMAR SCHOOL

21 Beaton Road,
Glasgow G41 4NW
Website: www.hutchesons.org
Age Range: 5–18

KELVINSIDE ACADEMY
33 Kirklee Road,
Glasgow G12 0SW
Website:
www.kelvinsideacademy.org.uk
Age Range: 3–18

ST ALOYSIUS' COLLEGE
45 Hill Street, Glasgow G3 6RJ
Website: www.staloysius.org
Age Range: 3–18

INVERCLYDE

PREPARATORY

CEDARS SCHOOL OF EXCELLENCE

31 Ardgowan Square,
Greenock, Inverclyde PA16 8NJ
Website:
www.cedars.inverclyde.sch.uk
Age Range: 5–14

SENIOR

ST COLUMBA'S SCHOOL
Duchal Road, Kilmacolm,
Inverclyde PA13 4AU
Website: www.st-columbas.org
Age Range: 3–18

LANARKSHIRE

SENIOR

HAMILTON COLLEGE
Bothwell Road, Hamilton,
Lanarkshire ML3 0AY
Website:
www.hamiltoncollege.co.uk
Age Range: 3–18

SOUTH LANARKSHIRE

SENIOR

FERNHILL SCHOOL

Fernbrae Avenue, Burnside,
Rutherglen, Glasgow, South
Lanarkshire G73 4SG
Website:
www.fernhillschool.co.uk
Age Range: 3–18 (Boys 4–11)

LOTHIAN

PREPARATORY

BELHAVEN HILL
● ♠
Dunbar, Lothian EH42 1NN
Website: www.belhavenhill.com
Age Range: 7–13

CARGILFIELD
● ♠
Barnton Avenue West,
Edinburgh, Lothian EH4 6HU
Website: www.cargilfield.com
Age Range: 3–13

THE COMPASS SCHOOL
● ♠
West Road, Haddington,
Lothian EH41 3RD
Website:
www.thecompassschool.co.uk
Age Range: 4–12

LORETTO JUNIOR SCHOOL
● ♠
North Esk Lodge, 1 North High
Street, Musselburgh, Lothian
EH21 6JA
Website: www.loretto.com
Age Range: 3–12

MANNAFIELDS CHRISTIAN SCHOOL
● ♠
170 Easter Road, Edinburgh,
Lothian EH7 5QE
Website:
www.mannafields.og.uk
Age Range: 5–14

REGIUS CHRISTIAN SCHOOL
● ♠
41a South Clerk Street,
Edinburgh, Lothian EH8 8NZ
Website: www.regius.edin.sch.uk

SENIOR

CLIFTON HALL SCHOOL
● ♠ ▲
Newbridge, Edinburgh,
Lothian EH28 8LQ
Website: www.cliftonhall.org.uk
Age Range: 3–18

DUNEDIN SCHOOL
● ♠
Liberton Bank House,
5 Nether Liberton Lane,
Edinburgh, Lothian EH16 5TY
Website:
www.dunedin.edin.sch.uk
Age Range: 10–17

THE EDINBURGH ACADEMY
● ♠ ▲
42 Henderson Row, Edinburgh,
Lothian EH3 5BL
Website:
www.edinburghacademy.org.uk
Age Range: 5–18
(Co-ed VIth Form)

THE EDINBURGH RUDOLF STEINER SCHOOL
● ♠ ▲
60 Spylaw Road, Edinburgh,
Lothian EH10 5BR
Website: www.members.aol.com/
ERSschool/
Age Range: 3–18

FETTES COLLEGE
● ♠ ★ ▲
Carrington Road, Edinburgh,
Lothian EH4 1QX
Website: www.fettes.com
Age Range: 7–18

GEORGE HERIOT'S SCHOOL
● ♠ ▲
Lauriston Place, Edinburgh,
Lothian EH3 9EQ
Website:
www.george-heriots.com
Age Range: 3–18

GEORGE WATSON'S COLLEGE
● ♠ ▲
67–71 Colinton Road,
Edinburgh, Lothian EH10 5EG
Website: www.gwc.org.uk
Age Range: 3–18

LORETTO SCHOOL
● ♠ ▲
Linkfield Road, Musselburgh,
Lothian EH21 7RE
Website: www.lorettoschool.co.uk
Age Range: 3–18

THE MARY ERSKINE SCHOOL
● ♠ ▲
Ravelston, Edinburgh,
Lothian EH4 3NT
Website: www.esms.edin.sch.uk
Age Range: 12–18
(Co-ed VIth Form)

MERCHISTON CASTLE SCHOOL*
● ♠ ▲
Colinton, Edinburgh,
Lothian EH13 0PU
Website: www.merchiston.co.uk
Age Range: 8–18

ST GEORGE'S SCHOOL FOR GIRLS*
● ♠ ▲
Garscube Terrace, Edinburgh,
Lothian EH12 6BG
Website:
www.st-georges.edin.sch.uk
Age Range: 1–18 (Boys 2–4)

ST MARY'S MUSIC SCHOOL
● ♠ ▲
Coates Hall, 25 Grosvenor
Crescent, Edinburgh, Lothian
EH12 5EL
Website: www.st-marys-music-
school.co.uk
Age Range: 9–19

ST SERF'S SCHOOL
● ♠ ▲
5 Wester Coates Gardens,
Edinburgh, Lothian EH12 5LT
Website:
www.st-serfs.edin.sch.uk
Age Range: 5–18

STEWART'S MELVILLE COLLEGE
● ♠ ▲
Queensferry Road, Edinburgh,
Lothian EH4 3EZ
Website: www.esms.edin.sch.uk
Age Range: 12–18
(Co-ed VIth Form)

INDEPENDENT SIXTH FORM COLLEGE / TUTORIAL COLLEGE

BASIL PATERSON TUTORIAL COLLEGE
● 🏠

66 Queen Street, Edinburgh,
Lothian EH2 4NA
Website:
www.basilpaterson.co.uk
Age Range: 16–20 (Most of our
students are aged between
16–20 but we accept any
student over the age of 16.)

WALLACE COLLEGE
● 🏠

12 George IV Bridge,
Edinburgh, Lothian EH1 1EE
Website:
www.wallacecollege.co.uk
Age Range: 15–21

MORAYSHIRE

PREPARATORY

ROSEBRAE SCHOOL
● 🏠

Spynie, Elgin,
Morayshire IV30 8XT
Website:
www.rosebrae.moray.sch.uk
Age Range: 2–8

SENIOR

GORDONSTOUN SCHOOL*
● 🏠 ▲

Elgin, Morayshire IV30 5RF
Website:
www.gordonstoun.org.uk
Age Range: 8–18

PERTH AND KINROSS

PREPARATORY

ARDVRECK SCHOOL
● 🏠

Gwydyr Road, Crieff,
Perth and Kinross PH7 4EX
Website:
www.ardvreckschool.co.uk
Age Range: 3–13

CRAIGCLOWAN PREPARATORY SCHOOL
● 🏠

Edinburgh Road, Perth,
Perth and Kinross PH2 8PS
Website:
www.craigclowan-school.co.uk
Age Range: 3–13

SENIOR

GLENALMOND COLLEGE*
● 🏠 ▲

Perth, Perth and Kinross
PH1 3RY
Website:
www.glenalmondcollege.co.uk
Age Range: 12–18

KILGRASTON
● 🏠 ◆ ▲
Bridge of Earn, Perth, Perth and
Kinross PH2 9BQ
Website: www.kilgraston.com
Age Range: 2–18
(Boys day 2–9)

MORRISON'S ACADEMY
● 🏠 ▲
Ferntower Road, Crieff,
Perth and Kinross PH7 3AN
Website:
www.morrisonsacademy.org
Age Range: 3–18

QUEEN VICTORIA SCHOOL
● 🏠 ▲
Dunblane, Perth and Kinross
FK15 0JY
Website: www.qvs.org.uk
Age Range: 11–18

STRATHALLAN SCHOOL*
● 🏠 ▲
Forgandenny, Perth,
Perth and Kinross PH2 9EG
Website: www.strathallan.co.uk
Age Range: 9–18 (Junior House
for Boys and Girls aged 9 to 13
Senior School for Boys and Girls
aged 13 to 18)

RENFREWSHIRE

SENIOR

BELMONT HOUSE
● 🏠 ▲
Sandringham Avenue, Newton
Mearns, Renfrewshire G77 5DU
Website:
www.belmontschool.co.uk
Age Range: 3–18

ROXBURGHSHIRE

PREPARATORY

ST MARY'S PREPARATORY SCHOOL
● 🏠
Abbey Park, Melrose,
Roxburghshire TD6 9LN
Website:
www.stmarysmelrose.org.uk
Age Range: 2–13

STIRLING

PREPARATORY

BEACONHURST SCHOOL
● ⌂ ▲
52 Kenilworth Road, Bridge of
Allan, Stirling FK9 4RR
Website: www.beaconhurst.com
Age Range: 3–18

2.5

Wales

ANGLESEY

PREPARATORY

TREFFOS SCHOOL
● ♟
Llansadwrn, Menai Bridge,
Anglesey LL59 5SD
Website: www.treffos.org.uk

BRIDGEND

SENIOR

ST CLARE'S SCHOOL
● ♟ ▲
Newton, Porthcawl,
Bridgend CF36 5NR
Website:
www.stclares-school.co.uk
Age Range: 3–18

ST JOHN'S SCHOOL
● ♟
Church Street, Newton,
Porthcawl, Bridgend CF36 5NP
Website: www.stjohnsschool-
porthcawl.com
Age Range: 3–16

CAERPHILLY

PREPARATORY

**WYCLIF INDEPENDENT
CHRISTIAN SCHOOL**

● 🏠

Ebenezer Baptist Chapel,
Wyndham Street, Machen,
Caerphilly CF83 8PU
Website:
www.wyclifchristianschool.org
Age Range: 4–16

CARDIFF

PREPARATORY

THE CATHEDRAL SCHOOL

● 🏠

Cardiff Road, Llandaff,
Cardiff CF5 2YH
Website:
www.cathedral-school.co.uk
Age Range: 3–16

ST JOHN'S COLLEGE

● 🏠 ▲

College Green, Newport Road,
Old St Mellons, Cardiff CF3 5YX
Website:
www.stjohnscollegecardiff.co.uk
Age Range: 3–18

SENIOR

**HOWELL'S SCHOOL,
LLANDAFF GDST**

● 🏠 ▲

Cardiff Road, Llandaff,
Cardiff CF5 2YD
Website:
www.howells-cardiff.gdst.net
Age Range: 3–18

KINGS MONKTON SCHOOL

● 🏠 ▲

6 West Grove, Cardiff CF24 3XL
Website:
www.kingsmonkton.org.uk
Age Range: 2–18

UWC ATLANTIC COLLEGE

● 🏠 ▲

St Donat's Castle, Llantwit Major,
Cardiff CF61 1WF
Website:
www.atlanticcollege.org
Age Range: 16–19

WESTBOURNE SCHOOL

● 🏠 ▲

Hickman Road, Penarth,
Cardiff CF64 2AJ
Website:
www.westbourneschool.com
Age Range: 3–18

INDEPENDENT SIXTH FORM COLLEGE / TUTORIAL COLLEGE

THE CARDIFF ACADEMY

● 🏠

40–41 The Parade, Roath,
Cardiff CF24 3AB
Website:
www.cardiffacademy.co.uk
Age Range: 14–18

**UNITED WORLD COLLEGE OF
THE ATLANTIC**

St Donat's Castle, Llantwit Major,
Cardiff CF6 9WF
Website:
www.atlanticcollege.org

CARMARTHENSHIRE

SENIOR

LLANDOVERY COLLEGE

Llandovery, Carmarthenshire
SA20 0EE
Website:
www.llandoverycollege.com
Age Range: 3–18

ST MICHAEL'S SCHOOL

Bryn, Llanelli, Carmarthenshire
SA14 9TU
Website: www.stmikes.co.uk
Age Range: 3–18

CONWY

SENIOR

ST DAVID'S COLLEGE

Llandudno, Conwy LL30 1RD
Website:
www.stdavidscollege.co.uk
Age Range: 11–18

DENBIGHSHIRE

PREPARATORY

FAIRHOLME PREPARATORY SCHOOL

Mount Road, St Asaph,
Denbighshire LL17 0DH
Website:
www.fairholmeschool.com
Age Range: 3–11

SENIOR

HOWELL'S SCHOOL

Park Street, Denbigh,
Denbighshire LL16 3EN
Website: www.howells.org
Age Range: 2–18

RUTHIN SCHOOL

Mold Road, Ruthin,
Denbighshire LL15 1EE
Website:
www.ruthinschool.co.uk
Age Range: 11–20

GWYNEDD

SENIOR

HILLGROVE SCHOOL

Ffriddoedd Road, Bangor,
Gwynedd LL57 2TW
Website:
hillgrove.gwynedd.sch.uk
Age Range: 3–16

ST GERARD'S SCHOOL

Ffriddoedd Road, Bangor,
Gwynedd LL57 2EL
Age Range: 3–18

MONMOUTHSHIRE

PREPARATORY

LLANGATTOCK SCHOOL

Llangattock-Vibon-Avel,
Monmouth, Monmouthshire
NP25 5NG
Website:
llangattockschool.co.uk
Age Range: 2–12

ST JOHN'S-ON-THE-HILL
Castleford Hill, Tutshill,
Chepstow, Monmouthshire
NP16 7LE
Website:
www.stjohnsonthehill.co.uk
Age Range: (Nursery from
3 months)

SENIOR

HABERDASHERS' MONMOUTH SCHOOL FOR GIRLS
Hereford Road, Monmouth,
Monmouthshire NP25 5XT
Website:
www.habs-monmouth.org
Age Range: 7–18

MONMOUTH SCHOOL
Almshouse Street, Monmouth,
Monmouthshire NP25 3XP
Website:
www.habs-monmouth.org
Age Range: 7–18
(Boarding 11–18)

NEWPORT

SENIOR

ROUGEMONT SCHOOL

Llantarnam Hall, Malpas Road,
Newport NP20 6QB
Website:
www.rougemontschool.co.uk
Age Range: 3–18

POWYS

SENIOR

CHRIST COLLEGE

Brecon, Powys LD3 8AF
Website:
www.christcollegebrecon.com
Age Range: 11–18

SWANSEA

PREPARATORY

CRAIG-Y-NOS SCHOOL
Clyne Common, Bishoptston,
Swansea SA3 3JB
Website: www.craigynos.com
Age Range: 2–11

OAKLEIGH HOUSE SCHOOL
38 Penlan Crescent, Uplands,
Swansea SA2 0RL
Website:
www.oakleighhouseschool.co.uk
Age Range: 3–11

SENIOR

FFYNONE HOUSE SCHOOL

36 St James' Crescent,
Swansea SA1 6DR
Website:
www.ffynonehouseschool.co.uk
Age Range: 9–18

Overseas Schools

FRANCE

SENIOR

MOUGINS SCHOOL*
615 Avenue Dr Maurice Donat,
Font de l'Orme, BP 1218, 06524
Mougins CEDEX
Website:
www.mougins-school.com
Age Range: 3–18

SWITZERLAND

SENIOR

AIGLON COLLEGE*
1885 Chesieres-Villars,
Switzerland,
Website: www.aiglon.ch
Age Range: 9–18

PART THREE

SCHOOL PROFILES

COUNTIES OF ENGLAND, SCOTLAND AND WALES

SCOTLAND

Highland

Moray

Aberdeenshire

Aberdeen City

Perth and Kinross

Angus

Argyll and Bute

Stirling

Fife

1. Inverclyde
2. North Ayrshire
3. Renfrewshire
4. West Dunbartonshire
5. East Dunbartonshire
6. North Lanarkshire

7. Falkirk
8. Clackmannanshire
9. West Lothian
10. City of Edinburgh
11. Midlothian
12. East Lothian

South Lanarkshire

South Ayrshire

East Ayrshire

Borders

Dumfries and Galloway

NORTHERN ENGLAND

Northumberland

Newcastle upon Tyne

Hartlepool

Stockton-on-Tees

Middlesbrough

Cumbria

Durham

North Yorkshire

York

Isle of Man

Lancashire

West Yorkshire

East Riding of Yorkshire

North Lincolnshire

North East Lincolnshire

Merseyside

G. M.

South Yorkshire

EASTERN ENGLAND

Cheshire

Derbyshire

Nottinghamshire

Lincolnshire

Rutland

WALES

Denbighshire

Flintshire

Conwy

Wrexham

Stafford-shire

Leicester-shire

Norfolk

1. Monmouthshire
2. Torfaen
3. Newport
4. Blaenau Gwent
5. Caerphilly
6. Cardiff
7. Merthyr Tydfil
8. Cynon Taff
9. Vale of Glamorgan
10. Bridgend
11. Neath Port Talbot
12. Swansea

Gwynedd

Ceredigion

Powys

Shropshire

W.M.

Worcester-shire

Warwick-shire

Northampton-shire

Cambridge-shire

Suffolk

Hereford-shire

Bedford-shire

Carmarthenshire

Gloucester-shire

Oxford-shire

Buckingham-shire

Hertford-shire

Essex

HOME COUNTIES (North)

Pembrokeshire

Berkshire

CENTRAL ENGLAND

13. South Gloucestershire
14. Bath and North East Somerset
15. City of Bristol
16. North Somerset

Greater London

LONDON

Wiltshire

Surrey

Kent

Somerset

Hampshire

West Sussex

East Sussex

Devon

Dorset

Cornwall

Isle of Wight

HOME COUNTIES (South)

SOUTH WEST ENGLAND

3.1

England

MAP OF NORTHERN ENGLAND

ISLE
OF
MAN

PROFILED SCHOOLS IN NORTHERN ENGLAND

(Incorporating the counties of Cheshire, Cumbria, Derbyshire, Durham, Hartlepool, Lancashire, North East Lincolnshire, North Lincolnshire, Greater Manchester, Merseyside, Middlesbrough, Northumberland, Nottinghamshire, Staffordshire, Stockton-on-Tees, East Riding of Yorkshire, North Yorkshire, South Yorkshire, West Yorkshire)

SYMBOL KEY

Gender

● Girls
● Boys
● Coed

Accommodation

🏠 Boarding only
🏠 Boarding and Day
🏠 Day and Boarding
🏠 Day only

International Bacc.

★ Offers IB

CReSTeD

◆ Crested Registered

Has 6th Form

▲ Has 6th Form

Chetwynde School ● ♠ ▲

Croslands, Rating Lane, Barrow-in-Furness, Cumbria LA13 0NY
T: (01229) 824210
F: (01229) 871440
E: info@chetwynde.cumbria.sch.uk
W: www.chetwynde.cumbria.sch.uk

Head of School Mrs I Nixon
Founded 1938
School status Co-ed Independent Day Only
Religious denomination Inter-denominational

Member of ISA, SHMIS
Accredited by ISC
Age range 3–18
Fees per annum *(day)* £6,600–£7,800

Chetwynde School occupies an attractive site situated near the Lake District. It has grown into a substantial and successful school with an excellent academic and outstanding sporting reputation. The school prides itself on high academic standards based on good teaching and individual attention. The GCSE pass rate has been at or above 97 per cent five Grades A–C for over three years and the A level pass rate stands at or above 99 per cent over the same period. All our Sixth Form pupils go on to higher education. The curriculum is broad and challenging, but there is also an emphasis on music, sport and outdoor pursuits including a vibrant Duke of Edinburgh Award Scheme.

Barlborough Hall School ● ♠

Barlborough, Chesterfield, Derbyshire S43 4TJ
T: (01246) 810511
F: (01246) 570605
E: barlborough.hall@virgin.net
W: www.barlboroughhallschool.co.uk

Headteacher Mrs W E Parkinson B Ed
Founded 1939
School status Co-ed Day Only
Religious denomination Roman Catholic
Member of HMC, IAPS
Accredited by HMC, ISC

Age range 3–11
No of pupils *Nursery* 30;
   Nursery to pre-prep 85; *Prep* 141
Teacher:pupil ratio 1:7
Average class size 15
Fees per annum *(day)* £5,985–£7,985

Barlborough Hall School, preparatory school to Mount St Mary's College, is seen as one of the premier independent Catholic schools in the South Yorkshire/Derbyshire area, welcoming pupils of all denominations. Set in 300 acres of beautiful surroundings, small classes, well-motivated teachers and exceptional specialist facilities, including a technology centre, science laboratory, art studio, IT suite, theatre and indoor heated pool, ensure that our pupils receive the very best educational opportunities. The school has an excellent nursery provision (from 3 years) in a secure and safe environment with facilities second to none. A regular minibus service and an 'out of school club', with a full range of activities and run by qualified staff until 6 pm, ensure the flexibility and peace of mind required by many working parents.

Mount St Mary's College

Spinkhill, Derbyshire S21 3YL
T: (01246) 433388 **F:** (01246) 435511
E: info@msmcollege.com **W:** www.msmcollege.com
Admissions secretary: Mrs Sarah Birks 01246 432872

Headmaster Mr L McKell MA, MEd
Founded 1842
School status Co-ed Independent Boarding
and Day
Religious denomination Roman Catholic
Member of BSA, CIS, HMC
Accredited by HMC, ISC
Age range 11–18; *Boarders from* 10 (Boarders
are accepted into Barlborough Hall at age 10.)

No of pupils 410; *(boarding)* 69; *(full
boarding)* 51; *(weekly boarding)* 18; *Senior*
410; *Sixth Form* 88; *Girls* 161; *Boys* 249
Teacher:pupil ratio 1:8
Average class size 20
Fees per annum *(full boarding)* £15,222–
£20,000; *(weekly)* £13,031–£17,108;
(day) £9,021–£10,367

Mount St Mary's College welcomes children of all denominations. In beautiful surroundings close to junction 30 of the M1, with minibus services to local areas, the school is also popular with local, national and international boarders. Proudly non-academically selective, the school achieves success for pupils at all levels; with many pupils going onto chosen universities. Emphasis is placed on developing the whole person, with a wide range of extra-curricular activities rated outstanding by a recent Independent Schools Inspection. Sport, drama and music are particularly strong. The new international-standard athletics facility has attracted much interest. The jazz band, several choirs, ensembles and orchestra provide many opportunities for music-making.

Aysgarth Preparatory School ● ♠

Newton-Le-Willows, Bedale, North Yorkshire DL8 1TF
T: (01677) 450240 **F:** (01677) 450736
E: lfoster@aysgarthschool.co.uk **W:** www.aysgarthschool.com

Head Mr Anthony Goddard MA (Cantab)
Founded 1877
School status Boys' Independent Day and
Boarding
Religious denomination Church of England
Member of AGBIS, BSA, IAPS, ISBA, NAHT,
SATIPS
Accredited by ISC, IAPS
Age range 3–13; *Boarders from* 8 (Co-ed day
3–8)

No of pupils 218; *(boarding)* 180;
(full boarding) 130; *(weekly boarding)* 50;
Nursery 28; *Nursery to pre-prep* 48;
Prep 150; *Girls* 38; *Boys* 180
Teacher:pupil ratio 1:7
Average class size 12
Fees per annum *(full boarding)* £19,470;
(weekly) £19,470; *(day)* £14,970

Where boys can be boys! Aysgarth School, set in the foothills of the Yorkshire Dales, is the only all-boys boarding and day prep school in the North of England. It is one of the leading preparatory schools in the country and in the North has an unmatched record of sending boys to Eton, Harrow, Radley, Shrewsbury, Stowe, Uppingham and Winchester as well as Ampleforth and Sedbergh closer by. Staff at Aysgarth are passionate about the benefits that boarding provides. Boys are introduced to a wide range of opportunities and become happy, confident, courteous and independent.

Abbots Bromley School ● ♠ ▲

Abbots Bromley, Staffordshire WS15 3BW
T: (+44 (0)1283 840232 **F:** (+44 (0)1283 840988
E: enquiries@abbotsbromley.net
W: www.abbotsbromley.net

The Headmistress Mrs Julie Dowling MA, PGCE, NPQH
Founded 1874
School status Girls' Independent Boarding and Day
Religious denomination Church of England
Member of AGBIS, BSA, GSA, ISA, ISBA, WOODWARD

Accredited by BRITISH, GSA, ISC, ISA, IAPS
Age range 3–18; *Boarders from* 8
No of pupils 251; *(boarding)* 73; *(full boarding)* 59; *(weekly boarding)* 14; *Sixth Form* 54; *Girls* 247; *Boys* 4
Fees per annum *(full boarding)* £20,295–£24,975; *(weekly)* £16,545–£20,925; *(day)* £4,386–£14,910

At Abbots Bromley School, there is so much on offer to suit a wide variety of individuals. As a day and boarding school, we welcome everyone to our family friendly community.

In Roch House Preparatory School, we educate boys and girls from Kindergarten to Year 6. This co-educational school sits within the main site and offers its own dedicated facilities.

In the Senior School, we offer a girls-only programme from the age of 11. Whilst our pupils are expected to work hard and focus carefully on their academic studies, we also offer numerous extra-curricular opportunities including riding, dance, sports, music and speech & drama.

Our homely boarding community caters for weekly, flexi, full or occasional boarding for girls aged 8–18.

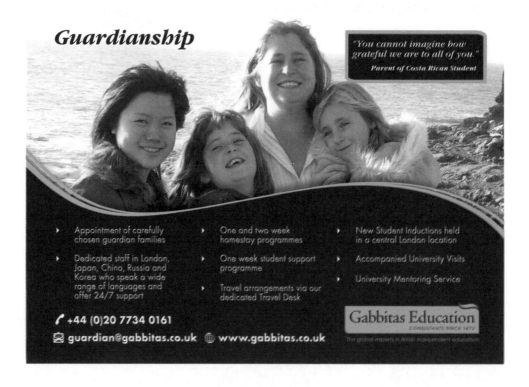

SYMBOL KEY

Gender

● Girls
● Boys
● Coed

Accommodation

🏠 Boarding only
🏠 Boarding and Day
🏠 Day and Boarding
🏠 Day only

International Bacc.

★ Offers IB

CReSTeD

◆ Crested Registered

Has 6th Form

▲ Has 6th Form

MAP OF EASTERN ENGLAND

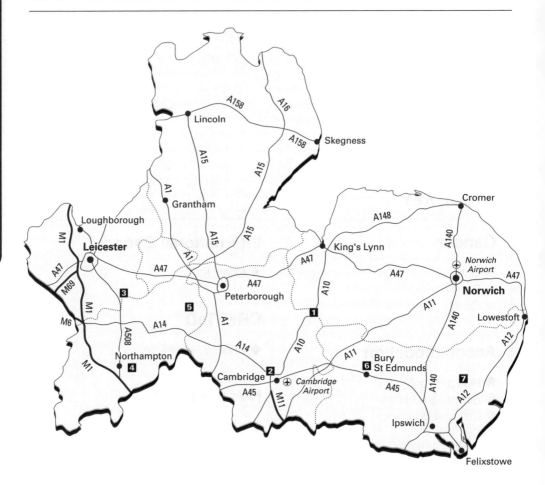

PROFILED SCHOOLS IN EASTERN ENGLAND

(Incorporating the counties of Cambridgeshire, Leicestershire, Lincolnshire, Norfolk, Northamptonshire, Suffolk)

King's Ely International   ● ♠

King's Ely, Barton Road, Ely, Cambridgeshire CB7 4DB
T: (01353) 653900 **F:** (01353) 653947
E: kei@kingsely.org
W: www.kingsely.org

Director Mrs Sarah Bellotti
School status Co-ed Boarding Only
Religious denomination Inter-denominational

Age range 14–16
Fees per annum *(full boarding)* £31,857

King's Ely International is part of King's Ely, an independent British Boarding School, founded in 973AD and located in Ely, a small market town, just north of Cambridge in East England. International students from all over the world come to study in our vibrant community and to experience the rich life of an established British boarding school. King's Ely International offers 2 types of courses for 14–16 year olds. The first is the 'Pre-GCSE' which offers academic study for students aged between 14 and 16 years of age. Students study the full British curriculum: English, maths, all the sciences, geography, history and ICT. Students usually study for one year but, subject to availability, they can also study for 1 or 2 terms. The second course is the 1 year GCSE course which is an intensive year programme where the students choose a minimum of 5 GCSE subjects in preparation for further study (A levels/IB programme). We also have a thriving Summer School where students can study for 2 or 4 weeks in July. This has an academic programme and the students study traditional subjects such as science, maths, history as well as English. There is also a rich programme of activities and excursions.Both King's Ely International and King's Ely Summer School offer full boarding and students are accommodated in historic Boarding Houses next to the school.

The Leys School   ● ♠ ▲

Trumpington Road, Cambridge, Cambridgeshire CB2 7AD
T: (01223) 508904 **F:** (01223) 505303
E: admissions@theleys.net
W: www.theleys.net

Headmaster Mr Mark Slater MA
Founded 1875
School status Co-ed Boarding and Day
Religious denomination Methodist
(all faiths welcome)
Member of HMC
Accredited by ISG, ISI, HMC
Age range 11–18

No of pupils 558; *(boarding)* 271;
(full boarding) 271; *Girls* 228; *Boys* 330
Teacher:pupil ratio 1:7
Average class size 12/20
Fees per annum *(full boarding)*
£19,635–£26,970; *(day)* £12,795–£17,940

The Leys is one of East Anglia's finest co-educational boarding and day schools for 11– to 18-year-olds, situated in the thriving hub that is Cambridge, in a 50-acre campus. Made famous by the novel *Goodbye Mr Chips*, the author James Hilton was an old boy of the school, which has kept true to its original ethos and values with pastoral care a major selling point. Current-day Leys' pupils enjoy a myriad of extra-curricular activities, the finest sports facilities and coaches, music in the state-of-the-art music school and drama that is the envy of most – life at the school is full. The Leys is primarily a boarding school and headmaster Mark Slater places great importance on providing a caring, friendly and secure environment for all its pupils.

Brooke House College

12 Leicester Road, Market Harborough, Leicestershire LE16 7AU
T: (01858) 462452
F: (01858) 462487
E: enquiries@brookehouse.com
W: www.brookehouse.com

Principal Mr G E I Williams MA (Oxon)
Founded 1967
School status Co-ed Independent Boarding
  and Day
Religious denomination Non-denominational
Member of CIFE
Accredited by BAC
Age range 14–20; *Boarders from* 14

No of pupils 240; *(boarding)* 210;
  (full boarding) 210; *Senior* 50;
  Sixth Form 190; *Girls* 120; *Boys* 120
Teacher:pupil ratio 1:6
Average class size 8
Fees per annum *(full boarding)* £24,450;
  (day) £13,950

Situated in the heart of rural England in the historic town of Market Harborough, Brooke House is a fully residential, international college, offering GCSE, A level and pre-university foundation courses in intensive, small classes. The college possesses excellent academic facilities, including science laboratories, an art and design studio and two recently developed IT suites. The academic and social welfare of pupils is paramount and is safeguarded by a system of personal tutors and by a secure and friendly learning environment. The college's full-time universities admissions adviser gives advice and guidance, and Brooke House has an enviable tradition of assisting international and UK pupils to gain places at the most prestigious of universities in the UK and the United States.

Great Houghton School

Great Houghton Hall, Northampton, Northamptonshire NN4 7AG
T: (01604) 761907
F: (01604) 761251
E: office@ghschool.net
W: www.ghschool.net

Heads Mrs Jane Lancaster-Adlam BEd, MEd,
  NPQH and Mr Craig Gibbs BA, HDipEd
School status Co-ed Independent Day Only

Religious denomination Non-denominational
Age range 3 months–16 years
No of pupils 330; *Girls* 130; *Boys* 200

The school consists of a Nursery department from 3 months of age and a two form entry from Reception to Year 10 (GCSE) where we maintain an adult:pupil ratio of 1:8 within the Early Years. Class sizes within the school are small ensuring that all pupils are able to reach their maximum potential.

  The school offers a very broad, inclusive approach to education with specialist expertise. Our emphasis is on the development of the whole child and we therefore offer a creative and stimulating curriculum. When pupils move on to their next independent school or college they are confident of their own abilities and have a thirst for knowledge. We believe that it is our role to work with children and parents to develop this knowledge and understanding whilst emphasizing the importance or nurturing other talents outside of the curriculum.

Laxton Junior School

East Road, Oundle, Nr Peterborough, Northamptonshire
PE8 4BX
T: (01832) 277159
F: (01832) 277271
E: admissions@laxtonjunior.org.uk
W: www.laxtonjunior.org.uk

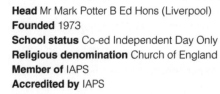

Head Mr Mark Potter B Ed Hons (Liverpool)	**Age range** 4–11
Founded 1973	**No of pupils** 271; *Nursery to pre-prep* 120;
School status Co-ed Independent Day Only	*Prep* 151; *Girls* 137; *Boys* 134
Religious denomination Church of England	**Teacher:pupil ratio** 1:12
Member of IAPS	**Average class size** 19
Accredited by IAPS	**Fees per annum** *(day)* £8,370–£9,180

Founded in September 1973 and moved to new purpose-built premises in 2002, Laxton Junior acts as a preparatory school for Oundle School but also prepares children for many other schools.

The aim of the School is to provide the best possible preparatory education in the area, where our pupils' strengths and areas for improvement are identified and nurtured, in order for them to become life-long learners. We also seek to find the right senior school to suit your child. We can take 280 boys and girls from 4–11 years.

Your child will receive personal attention in classes containing no more than 20 pupils and our staff members make every effort to help each individual realize their full potential. There are 25 fully qualified teachers plus 7 specialist teachers who all work as a team in a concerted effort to help your child become a happy, self-confident individual with an academic foundation that will prepare them for the future. We do our utmost to combine the best of both traditional and modern methods of education using National Curriculum guidelines as a foundation and your child learns to acquire excellent skills in reading, English, maths and science supplemented by art and design, computer studies, French, geography, history, performing arts, religious education and sport.

Through the caring pastoral system and broad academic curriculum, the school lays solid foundations in the development of well-motivated, confident and happy children who are willing to give of their best on the road to high achievement. At Laxton Junior, it is recognized that children bring to the school a wide and colourful variety of experience and talent. We believe that, through building happy working relationships, each child is enabled to thrive both inside and outside the classroom.

Laxton Junior offers a wide variety of extra-curricular activities, where pupils are encouraged to express themselves through sports and hobbies. It is acknowledged that the importance of play cannot be stressed enough and we view it as a vital component to a rounded education, complementing the teaching and learning that occurs within the classroom.

Why not visit on a school day, as you will have many questions relating to your child's education and the only way to have them satisfied is by talking to us and seeing the school in action.

Culford School

Bury St Edmunds, Suffolk IP28 6TX
T: (01284) 385308 **F:** (01284) 385513
E: admissions@culford.co.uk **W:** www.culford.co.uk

Headmaster Mr J F Johnson-Munday MA, MBA
Founded 1881
School status Co-ed Independent Boarding and Day
Religious denomination Methodist
Member of AGBIS, BSA, HMC, IAPS
Accredited by HMC, IAPS
Age range 3–18; *Boarders from* 7

No of pupils 695; *(boarding)* 250; *(full boarding)* 250; *Nursery* 15; *Nursery to pre-prep* 65; *Prep* 225; *Senior* 225; *Sixth Form* 165; *Girls* 320; *Boys* 375
Teacher:pupil ratio 1:9
Average class size 18
Fees per annum *(full boarding)* £18,780–£26,460; *(weekly)* £18,780–£26,460; *(day)* £7,965–£16,500

Culford is set in 480 acres of beautiful Suffolk parkland, located 40 minutes from Cambridge and 90 minutes from London. Culford is a friendly, caring school with superb sporting and academic facilities and aims to educate the whole person. We offer a rich after-school and weekend activities programme, from art, music and drama through to the Combined Cadet Force and the Duke of Edinburgh's Award Scheme. Academic facilities include ICT suites; a dedicated centre for art and design technology; and superb facilities in the William Miller Science Centre. Music and drama are well catered for in the new studio theatre and redeveloped Music School in Culford Hall. The sports centre boasts impressive facilities, including an indoor climbing wall, 25-metre pool and a championship-standard indoor tennis centre.

Framlingham College

Framlingham, Woodbridge, Suffolk IP13 9EY
T: (01728) 723789 **F:** (01728) 724546
E: admissions@framcollege.co.uk **W:** www.framcollege.co.uk

Headmaster Mr P B Taylor BA (Hons)
School status Co-ed Independent Day and Boarding
Religious denomination Church of England
Member of HMC, IAPS
Accredited by HMC, ISC, IAPS
Age range 13–18; *Boarders from* 13
No of pupils 680; *(boarding)* 265;

(full boarding) 200; *(weekly boarding)* 65; *Girls* 290; *Boys* 390
Teacher:pupil ratio 1:8
Average class size 18
Fees per annum *(full boarding)* £18,693–£23,706; *(weekly)* £18,693–£23,706; *(day)* £11,625–£15,237

Situated close to the Suffolk Heritage coast and within easy reach of London, Cambridge and Norwich, Framlingham College is a centre of all-round excellence and enjoys a magnificent site with unparalleled views over the Mere to the famous 12th-century castle. The college has a fine record in stretching the most able, with an excellent reputation in sport, music and drama. Our 'value-added' rating for those pupils who are not automatically destined to achieve A grades at GCSE and A level stands alongside the very best in the country. The school has superb facilities on campus, including a state-of-the-art specialist theatre and music facility, an indoor swimming pool, a modern library and a dedicated centre for art and design technology.

MAP OF CENTRAL ENGLAND

PROFILED SCHOOLS IN CENTRAL ENGLAND

(Incorporating the counties of Gloucestershire, Herefordshire, Oxfordshire, West Midlands, Shropshire, Warwickshire, Worcestershire)

Bredon School ● ♠ ◆ ▲

Pull Court, Bushley, Tewkesbury, Gloucestershire GL20 6AH
T: (01684) 293156 **F:** (01684) 298008
E: enquiries@bredonschool.co.uk **W:** www.bredonschool.org
If using a sat nav, the School's postcode is inaccurate by a
couple of miles.

Headmaster Mr J Hewitt MBA BA
Founded 1962
School status Co-ed Independent Boarding and Day
Religious denomination Church of England
Member of BSA, CRESTED, ISA, ISBA, SHA, SHMIS
Accredited by ISC, ISA, SHMIS
Age range 4–18; *Boarders from* 7

No of pupils 240; *(boarding)* 78; *(full boarding)* 47; *(weekly boarding)* 31; *Prep* 30; *Senior* 180; *Sixth Form* 30; *Girls* 80; *Boys* 160
Teacher:pupil ratio 1:7
Average class size 7
Fees per annum *(full boarding)* £18,180–£25,740; *(weekly)* £17,715–£25,260; *(day)* £6,045–£16,410

Bredon is a co-educational day and boarding school for children aged 4–18. The school stands in attractive rural surroundings near the River Severn, on the Worcestershire and Gloucestershire border in an estate of 84 acres. We have a range of unusual facilities including a working farm and forest school. Bredon follows the National Curriculum at all Key Stages through to GCSE and A level. In addition Bredon offers extensive vocational programmes at Foundation, Intermediate and Advanced levels. Pupils are able to benefit from the experience of the Access Centre and its team of highly qualified learning support staff. The school is CReSTeD registered. Excellent facilities exist in sport, art, design and technology, and computer studies. We have about 240 pupils with the average class size being 1:7.

Rendcomb College ● ♠ ▲

Rendcomb, Cirencester, Gloucestershire
GL7 7HA
T: (01285) 831213
F: (01285) 831121
E: info@Rendcomb.gloucs.sch.uk
W: www.rendcombcollege.org.uk

Headmaster Mr Roland J Martin	**Age range** 3–18
Headmaster Juniors' School Mr Martin	**No of pupils** 416; *(boarding)* 117;
Watson MA, BEd Hons	*Juniors* 159; *Seniors* 257; *Sixth Form* 71;
Founded 1920	*Girls* 183; *Boys* 232
School status Co-ed Day and Boarding	**Teacher:pupil ratio** 1:7
Religious denomination Church of England	**Average class size** 14
Member of AGBIS, BSA, SOH	**Fees per annum** *(full boarding)*
Accredited by SOH	£19,350–£26,625; *(day)* £6,150–£9,840

Rendcomb College, Cirencester was founded in 1920, by Noel Wills. In an act of generosity and vision; he established a school which was inclusive and offered a broad-ranging education for its pupils. The Rendcomb of 2012 is a thriving co-educational, day and boarding school for 3–18 year olds. The Founder believed in adding educational value and the School has been delivering on that belief for almost a century.

Ninety years on, the School enjoys a beautiful 230 acre Cotswold estate as the backdrop to daily education. Rendcombians benefit from this wonderful setting from an early age. The School was quick to embrace the Forest School movement, and our Juniors' enjoy outdoor classrooms, dens and a purpose built woodland classroom. Rendcomb Seniors' has just developed programmes with an Outdoor Education specialist which also make use of the woodland areas and help them to develop beyond the classroom.

But it is not just about enjoying the great outdoors.

Each and every day, in and out of lessons, there are things to do and people with whom to do them. All our boys and girls, boarding and day, benefit from this culture. The academic, sport and music co-curricular activities and drama opportunities open to our students at Rendcomb are central to our idea of curriculum. The Activities programme is growing all the time, with new Activities being offered by staff in line with their own enthusiasms and interests. The School places great value on mutual respect for the individual, promotes collaboration and offers support within the strength of a family-centred environment.

Rencombians work hard at their studies. This year, 74 per cent of our A level leavers went on to their first choice University. They had experienced a pastoral framework that engenders physical, emotional and spiritual wellbeing. Rendcombians enjoy a Sixth Form which takes in a Cultural Enrichment Programme and a two-week stint of independent living within a fixed budget, in a house in the village. Many useful lessons are learnt in those two weeks!

Rendcomb's Headmaster believes that adding value is imperative in the demanding market that young people enter. "The generation for whom we are responsible need to learn skills as well as learning how to pass examinations. Some of the value that can be added in a small School is developing individuals to have a range of interests, transferable team and leadership qualities and nurturing confidence in order that these strengths can be presented to future employers. At Rendcomb, young people start to learn these qualities in the Juniors' and develop them throughout their time in the Seniors'."

England

Tudor Hall School ● ♠ ▲

Wykham Park, Banbury, Oxfordshire OX16 9UR
T: (01295) 263434
F: (01295) 253264
E: admissions@tudorhallschool.com
W: www.tudorhallschool.com

Headmistress Miss W Griffiths BSc PGCE
School status Girls' Independent Boarding and Day
Religious denomination Church of England
Member of BSA, GSA, ISA
Accredited by GSA, ISC
Age range 11–18; *Boarders from* 11

No of pupils 333; *(boarding)* 243; *(full boarding)* 243; *Senior* 115; *Sixth Form* 100; *Girls* 333
Teacher:pupil ratio 1:16
Fees per annum *(full boarding)* £28,035; *(day)* £17,862

Tudor Hall is a boarding and day school, set in 48 acres of rolling parkland just south of Banbury. Girls enter the school at 11 and 13 through interview and Common Entrance, and at 16 through interview, GCSE results and school references. We pride ourselves on encouraging girls to meet a wide range of challenges; physical, intellectual and social, while preparing them for a future of possibilities. All girls are involved in a broad spectrum of extra-curricular activities, including ACF, Duke of Edinburgh Awards and Mock United Nations. We encourage and develop cooperation, social skills and the sense of responsibility to a wider community, as featured in the school motto Habeo ut Dem, 'I have that I may give'. Academic results speak for themselves: in 2012, 95 per cent of A level pupils achieved grades A* to C and 100 per cent of GCSE grades were A* to C.

Bromsgrove School ● ♠ ▲

Worcester Road, Bromsgrove, Worcestershire B61 7DU
T: (01527) 579679 **F:** (01527) 576177
E: admissions@bromsgrove-school.co.uk
W: www.bromsgrove-school.co.uk

Headmaster Mr C Edwards MA Oxon
Founded 1553
School status Co-ed Independent Boarding and Day
Religious denomination Church of England
Member of BSA, HMC, IAPS
Accredited by HMC, ISC, IAPS

Age range 13–18; *Boarders from* 7
No of pupils 683; *(boarding)* 407; *(full boarding)* 407; *Girls* 399; *Boys* 284
Teacher:pupil ratio 1:9
Average class size 20
Fees per annum *(full boarding)* £25,185– £28,155; *(day)* £12,855

Bromsgrove School, a self-contained campus near the town of Bromsgrove, is easily accessible from the national motorway network; Birmingham International airport is 35 minutes away and London Heathrow just two hours by car. The school is opportunity oriented and provides a very wide range of academic, extra-curricular and sporting activities. Bromsgrove School, though unashamedly academic, is not as selective at 13 as its very high league table position suggests. Entry between ages 7 and 11 is based on assessment tests and at 13 on interview and tests, or Common Entrance. Entry into the sixth form is dependent on results at GCSE.

Malvern St James ● ⌂ ▲

15 Avenue Road, Great Malvern, Worcestershire WR14 3BA
T: (01684) 584624
F: (01684) 566204
E: registrar@malvernstjames.co.uk
W: www.malvernstjames.co.uk

Headmistress Mrs P Woodhouse BMus (Hons)
Founded 1890
School status Girls' Independent Boarding
and Day
Religious denomination Church of England
Member of BSA, GSA, ISBA, NAHT, SHA
Accredited by GSA
Age range 4–18; *Boarders from* 7
No of pupils 400; *(boarding)* 197;
(full boarding) 184; *(weekly boarding)* 13;
Nursery to pre-prep 18; *Prep* 34; *Senior* 200;
Sixth Form 148; *Girls* 400

Teacher:pupil ratio 1:7
Average class size 15
Fees per annum
(full boarding) £16,935–£29,955;
(weekly) £15,240–£27,030;
(day) £7,095–£15,645

Malvern St James is a leading boarding and day school which presents an imaginative vision of education for girls from the age of 4 through to 18, taught within a positive, purposeful atmosphere. MSJ fosters creativity and bold thinking, and every girl is challenged and encouraged to extend her personal horizons and realize her full potential. The school is home to a warm and welcoming community with a buoyant atmosphere of shared celebration, extolling personal success in every field of endeavour.

Small classes, led by dedicated and dynamic teachers provide a first class education tailored to the individual. Our teaching facilities include a state-of-the-art science centre, multimedia language centre and new sports centre with fitness suite, all of which provide the best in 21st-century teaching facilities.

Our academic results are first class. Last summer, over 50 per cent of all GCSE grades were A* or A. At A level, 91 per cent of girls achieved all grades A* to C.

Girls take full advantage of the enviable setting and superb facilities, which inspire a wonderfully rich and imaginative extra-curricular life. Boarding is possible on a full, weekly or flexi-basis allowing parents and daughters to choose the option that's right for them. We offer a busy and varied weekend programme of activities to suit all interests, including watersports, rock climbing, abseiling, music, drama, Model United Nations and expeditions leading to the Duke of Edinburgh's Award. Girls leave Malvern St James as poised, self-assured and articulate young women who are able to meet and greet, with integrity, the challenges and risks of our modern world.

The school was the subject of an ISI inspection in October 2011 and was found to be compliant with all of the DfE Regulatory Requirements. The Inspectors were very complimentary about all that they saw and heard throughout the school and their Report highlights our pupils' excellent attitude to their work and activities, alongside their impeccable behaviour.

Malvern St James is situated at the foot of the beautiful Malvern Hills in the heart of Worcestershire. InterCity trains run from Great Malvern, the M5 and M50 are nearby and London, Birmingham and Manchester airports are within easy reach.

Admission is through the school's own examination, or through Common Entrance examination. The school offers academic entrance scholarships and exhibitions, as well as scholarships in art, music, drama, riding and physical education.

MAP OF THE HOME COUNTIES (NORTH)

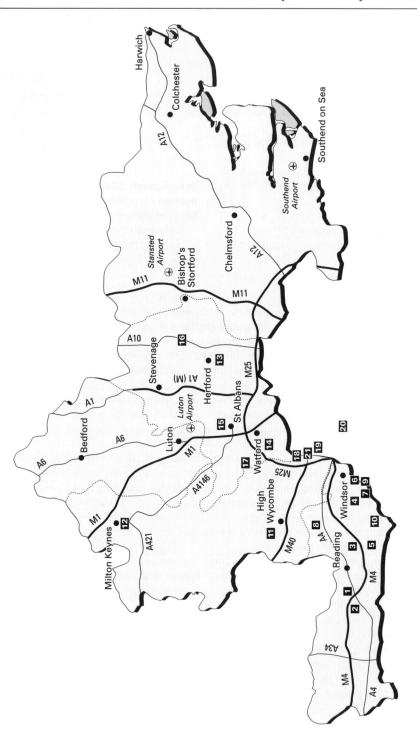

PROFILED SCHOOLS IN THE HOME COUNTIES (NORTH)

(Incorporating the counties of Bedfordshire, Berkshire, Buckinghamshire, Essex, Hertfordshire, Middlesex)

The Abbey School ● ♠ ★ ▲

17 Kendrick Road, Reading, Berkshire RG1 5DZ
T: (0118) 987 2256 **F:** (0118) 987 1478
E: schooloffice@theabbey.co.uk
W: www.theabbey.co.uk

Head Mistress Mrs B E Stanley BA (Hons),
   PGCE, FRGS
Founded 1887
School status Girls' Independent Day Only
Religious denomination Church of England
Member of CASE, GSA, IB, ISA, ISBA

Accredited by GSA, ISC, ISA
Age range 3–18
No of pupils 1098; *Nursery* 32; *Nursery to pre-prep* 126; *Prep* 228; *Senior* 522; *Sixth Form* 190; *Girls* 1098
Fees per annum *(day)* £8,355–£13,290

The Abbey School in Reading, Berkshire is one of the leading academic schools in the country, offering an outstanding education for 1,098 girls between the ages of 3 and 18. The junior school provides a first-class foundation with many enrichment workshops and trips. Girls become confident, independent learners in a caring, friendly environment. In the Senior School girls enjoy a wide extra-curricular programme and strong pastoral care, supporting excellent adacemic performance. In the VIth form, pupils choose between the IB and A levels. They gain entry to the universities of their choice. Many go to top destinations such as Oxbridge, University College and Bristol.

Enquiries to Admissions Secretary, Mrs Theresa Sexon, tel: 0118 987 2256 e-mail: admissions@theabbey. co.uk, or visit www.theabbey.co.uk.

Bradfield College ● ♠ ★ ▲

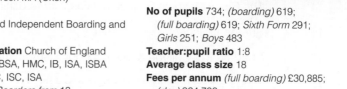

Bradfield, Reading, Berkshire RG7 6AU
T: (0118) 964 4500 **F:** (0118) 964 4513
E: admissions@bradfieldcollege.org.uk
W: www.bradfieldcollege.org.uk

Head Mr S C Henderson MA (Oxon)
Founded 1850
School status Co-ed Independent Boarding and
   Day
Religious denomination Church of England
Member of AGBIS, BSA, HMC, IB, ISA, ISBA
Accredited by HMC, ISC, ISA
Age range 13–18; *Boarders from* 13

No of pupils 734; *(boarding)* 619;
   (full boarding) 619; *Sixth Form* 291;
   Girls 251; *Boys* 483
Teacher:pupil ratio 1:8
Average class size 18
Fees per annum *(full boarding)* £30,885;
   (day) £24,708

Bradfield College offers a wide selection of subjects in both the Junior and Senior schools, including the IB Diploma at Sixth Form, providing challenge and choice for all through personalized programmes of study inspired by passionate and engaging teaching. Learning extends beyond the classroom through the Athena General Studies lectures and tutorial programme including Minerva seminars for scholars. Academic and Dr Gray all-rounder scholarships are available at 13+ and 16+. Awards are available at 13+ with entrance by the Common Academic Scholarship, the Bradfield College Scholarship, Common Entrance or the Bradfield College Entrance Examinations. Academic and Dr Gray all-rounder Exhibitions, are available at 16+ with entrance on attainment of a minimum of 6 B grades at GCSE (minimum C grades in English and maths), assessment at Bradfield and Headteacher's reference if transferring from elsewhere into the large and vibrant Sixth Form. The College delivers an outstanding academic education for all, unparalleled pastoral care and a diverse range of co-curricular activities, enabling every individual to find his or her niche.

Eagle House ● ♠

Crowthorne Road, Sandhurst, Berkshire GU47 8PH
T: (01344) 772134 **F:** (01344) 779039
E: info@eaglehouseschool.com **W:** www.eaglehouseschool.com

SUBLIMIORA PETAMUS

Headmaster Mr Andrew Barnard BA Hons PGCE
Founded 1820
School status Co-ed Independent Day and
   Boarding
Religious denomination Church of England
Member of BSA, IAPS, NAHT, SATIPS
Accredited by ISC, IAPS
Age range 3–13; *Boarders from* 8

No of pupils 318; *(boarding)*
   49; *(full boarding)* 21;
   (weekly boarding) 28; *Nursery* 26; *Nursery to*
   pre-prep 114; *Prep* 178; *Girls* 120; *Boys* 198
Teacher:pupil ratio 1:8
Average class size 14
Fees per annum *(full boarding)* £17,850;
   (weekly) £17,850; *(day)* £8,295–£13,290

At Eagle House every child is unique. From 3 to 13, girls and boys develop in a friendly, creative and expressive environment. Working closely with parents, Eagle House nurtures the individual talents of every child, so that they grow in self-esteem and confidence through their success in academic subjects, sports, art, music and drama. The school believes in rewards and praise for good work and exemplary behaviour to encourage high standards and good citizenship. Eagle House benefits from superb facilities and small class sizes, and dedicated staff ensure that all children have the best academic start possible. The high sporting achievements of the pupils are testament to the opportunities and coaching offered by the school. A diverse activities programme, called Golden Eagle, is enjoyed by all pupils, helping to give them an all-round education. With boarding opportunities from Year 3 and late-stay facilities for all children, Eagle House caters for the busy lives families lead.

Heathfield School ● ♠ ▲

London Road, Ascot, Berkshire SL5 8BQ
T: (01344) 898343
F: (01344) 890689
E: registrar@heathfieldschool.net
W: www.heathfieldschool.net

Headmistress Mrs Jo Heywood BSc Hons
   (Kingston), PGCE (Kingston)
Founded 1899
School status Girls' Independent Boarding
   Only
Religious denomination Christian
Member of BSA, GSA, IAPS, SHA
Accredited by GSA, ISC, IAPS

Age range 11–18; *Boarders from* 11
No of pupils 200; *(boarding)* 200;
   (full boarding) 200; *Senior* 200;
   Sixth Form 70; *Girls* 200
Teacher:pupil ratio 1:6
Average class size 12
Fees per annum *(full boarding)* £28,887–
   £29,991

Heathfield encourages academic success but also prepares girls for the realities of the outside world. Our philosophy is to focus on the needs of individuals, nurturing both academic and personal development to help every girl achieve her potential. Modern teaching, sporting and leisure facilities make education a positive, exciting experience. Boarding accommodation is excellent, two-thirds of the pupils having single bedrooms. We have a new performing arts centre and plans for future refurbishments. Set in spacious surroundings on the outskirts of Ascot, the school is 45 minutes from London and 30 minutes from London Heathrow. A series of Open Mornings are run throughout the year; please contact Rebecca Farha, Registrar, for more details, registrar@heathfieldschool.net, 01344 898 342.

Lambrook ● ♠

Winkfield Row, Bracknell, Berkshire RG42 6LU
T: (01344) 882717
F: (01344) 891114
E: info@lambrook.berks.sch.uk
W: www.lambrook.berks.sch.uk

Headmaster Mr Jonathan Perry BA PGCE
School status Co-ed Boarding and Day
Religious denomination Church of England
Member of AGBIS, BSA, IAPS, ISA, ISBA
Age range 3–13

No of pupils 450; *(boarding)* 18;
(weekly boarding) 18; *Girls* 155; *Boys* 295
Fees per annum *(full boarding)* £18,219–
£19,479; *(weekly)* £17,559–£18,819;
(day) £9,486–£15,864

The school was established in 1860. It has an impressive history of academic success and is proud of the excellent education it provides. The strength of the school is to be found in the enthusiasm and commitment of its accomplished staff and the support of the parents and children, underpinned by the strong leadership of the governors and headmaster. The 40 acres of grounds provide a tranquil setting conducive to learning and a wonderful space to enjoy the rewards of teamwork, the thrill of competing and the delight of success. Lambrook provides a high-quality education which is enduring and will serve a lifetime.

Papplewick School ● ♠

Windsor Road, Ascot, Berkshire SL5 7LH
T: (01344) 621488 **F:** (01344) 874639
E: hm@papplewick.org.uk **W:** www.papplewick.org.uk
Enquiries to Registrar, Mrs Sarah Tysoe
at registrar@papplewick.org.uk

Head Mr T W Bunbury BA (Hons) PGCE
Founded 1947
School status Boys' Independent Boarding
    and Day
Religious denomination Church of England
Member of BSA, IAPS, SATIPS
Accredited by ISC, IAPS
Age range 6–13; *Boarders from 7*

No of pupils 190; *(boarding)* 126;
(full boarding) 55; *(weekly boarding)* 71;
Boys 190
Teacher:pupil ratio 1:8
Average class size 13
Fees per annum *(full boarding)* £24,120;
(day) £13,350–£18,510

Papplewick provides an atmosphere where boys can be boys and individuality is celebrated. Academic achievement is at the highest level and feeds UK top senior schools-13 scholarships in 2012 to Eton, Harrow, Winchester, Radley, Uppingham. Day, weekly and full boarding are offered in a family-friendly atmosphere. Situated in 15 acres of land opposite Ascot racecourse in Berkshire, Papplewick enjoys easy access to the M4, M3, M25, Heathrow and Gatwick. Two daily London runs to and from Chiswick and Brook Green. The broad range of academic and extra-curricular activities includes the popular snake club and rocket-making. Strong traditions of art and music. Facilities include a sports hall, music school, IT department and covered swimming pool. Entry is by interview, followed by a placement test.

St Mary's School, Ascot ● ♠ ▲

St Mary's Road, Ascot, Berkshire SL5 9JF
T: (01344) 296600 **F:** (01344) 873281
E: admissions@st-marys-ascot.co.uk
W: www.st-marys-ascot.co.uk

Headmistress Mrs Mary Breen MSc BSc
Founded 1885
School status Girls' Independent Boarding
and Day
Religious denomination Roman Catholic
Member of BSA, GSA
Accredited by GSA
Age range 11–18; *Boarders from* 11

No of pupils 382; *(boarding)* 370;
(full boarding) 370; *Senior* 295;
Sixth Form 121; *Girls* 382
Teacher:pupil ratio 1:10
Average class size 16
Fees per annum *(full boarding)* £30,240;
(day) £21,510

St Mary's School Ascot is a Roman Catholic boarding school for girls aged 11–18 years. Entry at 11+, 13+ and 16+ is subject to the school's own entry procedure. Facilities are excellent, as is our record in public examinations. We are a friendly, stable and caring community, proud of our academic, sporting and musical achievements and dedicated to bringing out the full potential of each of our pupils. We are committed to full boarding, with spaces for a few day pupils living nearby. We offer a stimulating range of extra-curricular activities which take place in the evenings and throughout the weekend.

St Piran's Preparatory School ● ♠

Gringer Hill, Maidenhead, Berkshire SL6 7LZ
T: (01628) 594302 **F:** (01628) 594301
E: registrar@stpirans.co.uk
W: www.stpirans.co.uk

Head Master Mr J Carroll BA Hons BPhilEd
PGCE
Founded 1805
School status Co-ed Independent Day Only
Religious denomination Christian
Member of IAPS, ISBA, NAHT, SATIPS
Accredited by IAPS

Age range 3–13
No of pupils 344; *Nursery* 54; *Nursery to
pre-prep* 112; *Prep* 159; *Senior* 19; *Girls* 129;
Boys 215
Teacher:pupil ratio 1:8
Average class size 18
Fees per annum *(day)* £2,970–£11,040

Curriculum: National Curriculum subjects up to Year 8. French is offered from Reception to Year 8. Latin and Spanish are options for seniors. Sport: A comprehensive range for all pupils. Facilities are excellent and include a sports hall, indoor swimming pool, all-weather pitch, dance studio, music room, ICT suite and a learning resource centre. Fully networked ICT department, PCs and interactive whiteboards in classrooms. We have specialist teachers for those who need additional support. Trampolining, drama, games and crafts, among others, are activities for Year 5 to Year 8 at the end of the day. Entry requirements: Entry is by interview, school report and, where necessary, a short assessment if entry is higher up in the school.

Upton House School ● ♠

115 St Leonard's Road, Windsor, Berkshire SL4 3DF
T: (01753) 862610 **F:** (01753) 621950
E: info@uptonhouse.org.uk
W: www.uptonhouse.org.uk

Headmistress Mrs Madeleine Collins BA
 (Hons) PGCE
Founded 1936
School status Co-ed Independent Day Only
Religious denomination Church of England
Member of AGBIS IAPS, ISA, SATIPS
Accredited by ISC, ISA, IAPS

Age range 2–11 (Boys 2–7)
No of pupils 250; *Nursery* 60; *Nursery to*
 pre-prep 110; *Prep* 80; *Girls* 170; *Boys* 80
Teacher:pupil ratio 1:10
Average class size 19
Fees per annum *(day)* £4,875–£12,585

Upton House, set in the heart of Windsor, is a happy and successful school with 250 children and 45 members of staff. It combines a dynamic learning environment with a caring ethos dedicated to allowing each child to develop his or her individual talents and, at the same time, to learn the importance of generosity to others in the wider world. A very full syllabus is offered and we take particular pride in making the whole learning process fun – with a range of extra-curricular activities, off-site visits, after-school clubs, dramatic productions, summer camps, etc. For further information or a copy of our prospectus, please contact the registrar, Mrs Jill Gilmour, on (01753) 862610 or at registrar@uptonhouse.org.uk or www.uptonhouse.org.uk.

Wellington College ● ♠ ★ ▲

Duke's Ride, Crowthorne, Berkshire RG45 7PU
T: (01344) 444013 **F:** (01344) 444115
E: admissions@wellingtoncollege.org.uk
W: www.wellingtoncollege.org.uk

Master Dr A F Seldon MA PhD FRSA MBA
 FRHisS
Founded 1853
School status Co-ed Independent Boarding
 and Day
Religious denomination Church of England
Member of AGBIS, BSA, HMC, IB, ISBA,
 Round Square
Accredited by HMC

Age range 13–18; *Boarders from* 13
No of pupils 1050; *(full boarding)* 821;
 Senior 566; *Sixth Form* 484; *Girls* 404;
 Boys 646
Teacher:pupil ratio 1:8
Average class size 16
Fees per annum *(full boarding)* £31,500;
 (day) £23,610–£26,760

Wellington College is one of the country's leading independent schools. It stands in an attractive 400-acre woodland estate, 40 minutes from London and Heathrow. A sensible priority is given to academic study (98 per cent of leavers go on to degree courses), but the highest standards are also achieved in other aspects of school life, including sport, art, technology, writing, music and drama. Extra-curricular activities are important, as they develop self-confidence and provide experience in teamwork, initiative and leadership. Wellington provides a well-disciplined framework within which pupils have a wide range of opportunities to fulfil their personal potential.

Pipers Corner School ● 🏠 ▲

Pipers Lane, Great Kingshill, High Wycombe, Buckinghamshire
HP15 6LP
T: (01494) 718255 **F:** (01494) 719806
E: theschool@piperscorner.co.uk **W:** www.piperscorner.co.uk
When using Sat Nav and our postcode HP15 6LP please
ensure that you select the Pipers Lane option in order to obtain
the correct directions.

Headmistress Mrs H J Ness-Gifford BA
(Hons), PGCE
Founded 1930
School status Girls' Independent Day and
Boarding
Religious denomination Church of England
Member of AGBIS, AHIS, BSA, GSA, ISBA
Accredited by GSA, ISC
Age range 3–18; *Boarders from* 8

No of pupils 527; *(boarding)* 28;
(full boarding) 17; *(weekly boarding)* 11;
Nursery to pre-prep 42; *Prep* 93; *Senior* 330;
Sixth Form 62; *Girls* 527
Teacher:pupil ratio 1:12
Average class size 20
Fees per annum *(full boarding)* £18,990–
£23,085; *(weekly)* £18,750–£22,845;
(day) £7,230–£14,010

At Pipers Corner all girls are supported and challenged to achieve their full potential. Our nurturing and encouraging environment enables them to grow into mature, confident and independent individuals. Academically successful, our girls progress to further study at Oxbridge and other top universities or specialist arts and music colleges.

All girls benefit from the use of the excellent facilities offered on our 36 acre site and are encouraged to cultivate any sporting or creative talents they have through a wide range of extra-curricular clubs and activities.

Our friendly boarding community offers flexibility, freedom and peace of mind to both girls and their parents. Our range of boarding options means that we can provide practical solutions to the often demanding needs of modern family life.

Swanbourne House School ● 🏠

Swanbourne, Milton Keynes, Buckinghamshire MK17 0HZ
T: (01296) 720264 **F:** (01296) 728089
E: office@swanbourne.org **W:** www.swanbourne.org

Joint Head Mr S D Goodhart BEd (Hons)
Joint Head Mrs J S Goodhart BEd Cert Ed
Founded 1920
School status Co-ed Independent Boarding
and Day
Religious denomination Church of England
Member of BSA, IAPS, ISBA, SATIPS
Accredited by IAPS
Age range 3–13; *Boarders from* 7

No of pupils 403; *(boarding)* 39;
(full boarding) 27; *(weekly boarding)* 12;
Nursery 52; *Nursery to pre-prep* 100;
Prep 251; *Girls* 185; *Boys* 218
Average class size 16
Fees per annum *(full boarding)* £18,750;
(weekly) £18,750; *(day)* £4,020–£15,255

Swanbourne House is a successful IAPS preparatory school from which academic scholarships and awards in arts, sport and music are won every year. There are many opportunities for personal development through activities, sport, the arts, holiday clubs and trips abroad. Pastoral care is our beacon and our leadership training is renowned. We have excellent facilities. London parents say we have the 'wow' factor. Come and visit, you can be assured of a warm welcome. Entry is by a familiarization day and short assessment test. Our latest inspections describe the school, boarding, spirituality, pastoral care, organization and management as outstanding.

Haileybury ● ♠ ▲

Hertford, Hertfordshire SG13 7NU
T: (01992) 706353 **F:** (01992) 470663
E: registrar@haileybury.com **W:** www.haileybury.com

The Master Mr J S Davies MA (Cantab)
Founded 1862
School status Co-ed Independent Boarding and
  Day
Religious denomination Church of England
Member of BSA, HMC
Accredited by HMC, ISC, IBO
Age range 11–18; *Boarders from* 11

No of pupils 763; *(boarding)* 482;
  (full boarding) 763; *Senior* 654;
  Sixth Form 298; *Girls* 332; *Boys* 441
Teacher:pupil ratio 1:7
Average class size 16
Fees per annum *(full boarding)* £17,976–£28,341;
  (day) £14,145–£21,285

Boys and girls, mostly boarding, admitted at 11 into the lower school, at 13 into the main school, and also at 16 into the sixth form. Magnificent classical buildings are complemented by modern, state-of-the-art developments. Set in 500 rural acres and situated 20 miles north of central London, Haileybury combines high academic standards with broad-ranging excellence in art, music, drama and sport. The school is pleased to offer the International Baccalaureate Diploma Programme alongside A levels. Please contact the Registrar for further details.

The Royal Masonic School for Girls ● ♠ ▲

Rickmansworth Park, Rickmansworth, Hertfordshire WD3 4HF
T: (01923) 773168 **F:** (01923) 896729
E: admissions@royalmasonic.herts.sch.uk
W: www.royalmasonic.herts.sch.uk
For further details about the School, please contact Mrs G Braiden, Admissions Manager.

The Headmistress Mrs D Rose MA (Cantab)
Founded 1788
School status Girls' Independent Day and
  Boarding
Religious denomination Non-denominational
Member of BSA, GSA, ISBA, SHA
Accredited by GSA, ISC
Age range 2–19; *Boarders from* 7 (Pre School
  opened in January 2010 for boys and girls
  aged 2–4.)

No of pupils 942; *(boarding)* 137;
  (full boarding) 95; *(weekly boarding)* 37;
  Nursery 80; *Pre-Prep to Prep* 221; *Senior* 466;
  Sixth Form 175; *Girls* 916; *Boys* 26
Teacher:pupil ratio 1:10
Average class size 20
Fees per annum *(full boarding)* £15,105–
  £24,120; *(weekly)* £14,850–£23,535;
  (day) £8,490–£14,550

RMS offers an exceptionally wide-ranging curriculum in a supportive and friendly environment, where the highest standards prevail. The school has outstanding facilities and occupies a stunning 200-acre site, only 30 minutes from central London by Underground. An impressive sports hall, indoor swimming pool, squash, tennis and netball courts, and hockey pitches maintain sporting excellence. Rickmansworth is close to the M25, with easy access to London and its airports. Boarding pupils are cared for in well-appointed and spacious houses, with experienced, caring residential staff. Our boarding community is made up of British and overseas boarders and is well balanced. Admission is by the school's own entrance examination and interview. A number of generous scholarships and bursaries are available.

St Albans School ● 🏠 ▲

Abbey Gateway, St Albans, Hertfordshire AL3 4HB
T: (01727) 855521
F: (01727) 843447
E: hm@st-albans-school.org.uk
W: www.st-albans.herts.sch.uk

The Headmaster Mr Andrew Grant MA, PGCE, FRSA
Founded 948
School status Boys' Independent Day Only
Religious denomination Inter-denominational
Member of AGBIS, HMC

Accredited by HMC
Age range 17–18 (Co-ed VIth Form)
No of pupils 828; *Senior* 534; *Sixth Form* 294;
Girls 70; *Boys* 758
Teacher:pupil ratio 1:10
Fees per annum *(day)* £14,733

The school is able to offer some assistance with fees, in certain circumstances of proven need, from its own endowed bursary fund. All bursaries are means-tested. A variable number of academic scholarships worth up to 50 per cent of the annual fees are awarded on academic merit at 11+, 13+ and 16+. Choral scholarships are offered at 11+ and scholarships for music and art at 13+. A music scholarship is awarded on the basis of an annual competition for Year 8 pupils already in the school. Further details of all awards are available from the head. The school is a registered charity and aims to provide an excellent education, enabling pupils to achieve the highest standard of academic success according to ability, and to develop their character and personality so as to become caring and self-disciplined adults.

St Edmund's College & Prep School ● 🏠 ▲

Old Hall Green, Ware, Hertfordshire SG11 1DS
T: (01920) 821504 **F:** (01920) 823011
E: admissions@stedmundscollege.org
W: www.stedmundscollege.org

Headmaster Mr C P Long BA
Founded 1568
School status Co-ed Independent Day and Boarding
Religious denomination Roman Catholic
Member of BSA, EUK, HMC
Accredited by BRITISH, HMC, ISC
Age range 3–18; *Boarders from* 11
No of pupils 801; *(boarding)* 112;
(full boarding) 96; *(weekly boarding)* 16;

Nursery 61; *Nursery to pre-prep* 61; *Prep* 99;
Senior 641; *Sixth Form* 148; *Girls* 333;
Boys 468
Teacher:pupil ratio 1:9
Average class size 20
Fees per annum *(full boarding)* £21,015–
£24,030; *(weekly)* £19,065–£21,705;
(day) £13,380–£14,580

St Edmund's College is England's oldest Catholic school, founded in 1568. One of the key aspects of St Edmund's is its unique style and atmosphere, which values academic excellence and the achievement of a personal best, right through from St Edmund's, the prep school, to sixth form and beyond. In addition, all pupils are supported by a high level of pastoral care, based on a successful house system. Facilities include state-of-the-art IT suites, art and design technology workshops, tennis courts and an indoor swimming pool.

Tring Park School for the Performing Arts ● ♠ ▲

Tring Park, Tring, Hertfordshire HP23 5LX
T: (01442) 824255
F: (01442) 891069
E: info@tringpark.com
W: www.tringpark.com

The Principal Mr S Anderson MA (Cantab) BMus, ARCM
Founded 1919
School status Co-ed Independent Boarding and Day
Religious denomination Inter-denominational
Member of BSA, HMC, ISA, SHA, SHMIS
Accredited by ISA, SHMIS

Age range 8–19; *Boarders from* 9
No of pupils 300; *Prep* 13; *Senior* 153; *Sixth Form* 109; *Girls* 222; *Boys* 78
Teacher:pupil ratio 1:15
Average class size 15
Fees per annum *(full boarding)* £21,285–£30,090; *(day)* £12,870–£20,100

Tring Park offers exciting educational opportunities for pupils who show talent in one or more of the performing arts and we are committed to ensuring that all pupils fulfil their potential.

The school is set in 17 acres parkland and the main house was formerly a Rothschild mansion. The school accommodates 208 boarders and 92 day pupils and aims to provide an environment ideally suited to the teaching of the performing arts, combined with academic study to GCSE, A level and BTEC.

Tring Park is part of the Music and Dance Scheme, funded and administered by the DfE, and places are awarded annually under this scheme for talented classical dancers. A number of dance and drama awards are available for the sixth form dance course.

Up to age 14 all pupils study dance, music and drama combined with a full and vigorous academic curriculum. The pupils all study eight or nine GCSE subjects combined with the Dance or Performance foundation course. In the sixth form pupils may study up to three or four A levels or the BTEC in Performing Arts combined with the Dance, Musical Theatre or Drama Course. Academic study receives equal emphasis and the department provides a broad and balanced curriculum for all pupils.

Following success in their sixth form examinations, many of our pupils proceed to higher vocational or academic studies at universities and colleges. For others, the opportunity to perform becomes a reality immediately.

For those entering the dance course, we believe in training the whole dancer in body, mind and in artistic understanding. Dancers are encouraged to fulfil their own individual potential and each pupil's progress is monitored carefully.

Sixth form pupils joining the drama course will undertake a wide-ranging preparation for either direct entry into the theatre, further training at drama school or, with appropriate A levels, higher education on a relevant degree course. The Musical Theatre course for sixth form pupils is designed to extend the skills of the all-round performer and to focus them in this popular entertainment area.

Throughout the school, pupils have frequent opportunities to present work in the Markova Theatre and there are regular public shows given by junior and senior pupils. The range of work undertaken provides pupils with the opportunity to become versatile and able to communicate skilfully, whatever the chosen field.

Individual appointments are made to visit the school and auditions are held on a regular basis.

ACS Hillingdon International School

Hillingdon Court, 108 Vine Lane, Hillingdon, Middlesex UB10 0BE
T: (01895) 818402 **F:** (01895) 818404
E: hillingdonadmissions@acs-schools.com
W: www.acs-schools.com

Head of School Linda LaPine	**Age range** 4–18
Founded 1967	**No of pupils** 640
School status Co-ed Independent Day Only	**Teacher:pupil ratio** 1:15
Religious denomination Non-denominational	**Average class size** 15
Member of CIS, IB, IBSCA, ISA, LISA, NEASC	**Fees per annum** *(day)* £9,490–£20,370

ACS Hillingdon International School offers both the IB Middle Years programme and IB Diploma. Its students have consistently achieved results well above international results, which have led to placements in top universities in America and around the world. Occupying an 11-acre site, ACS Hillingdon is situated in a Grade II listed stately mansion with a modern wing accommodating classrooms, computer labs, an integrated IT network, libraries, cafeteria, a gymnasium and an auditorium. The school also has separate early-childhood pavilions and a music technology centre with a digital recording studio, rehearsal rooms, practice studios and a computer lab. The school is approximately 30 minutes' drive from central London and has an extensive busing service (door-to-door and shuttle) including central London.

Northwood College ● 🏠 ▲

Maxwell Road, Northwood, Middlesex HA6 2YE
T: (01923) 825446 **F:** (01923) 836526
E: admissions@northwoodcollege.co.uk
W: www.northwoodcollege.co.uk

Head Mistress Miss Jacqualyn Pain MA, MA, MBA	
Founded 1878	**Age range** 3–18
School status Girls' Independent Day Only	**No of pupils** 800; *Nursery* 30; *Nursery to pre-prep* 125; *Prep* 168; *Senior* 372; *Sixth Form* 125; *Girls* 800
Religious denomination Non-denominational	
Member of AGBIS, GSA, IAPS, ISBA	**Average class size** 22
Accredited by GSA, ISC, IAPS	**Fees per annum** *(day)* £8,400–£13,800

Northwood College is an Independent Day School for girls aged 3 to 18 years with two very special features at its heart. Our unique 'Thinking Skills' programme enables girls to develop independent and creative thinking that takes them far beyond an exam curriculum. Our emphasis on pastoral care meanwhile rests on the premise that a happy girl will always achieve her best. Put the two together and you have a school that buzzes with life, where pupils achieve outstanding results.

Our Thinking Skills programme is integrated into the curriculum and runs from Nursery through to Sixth Form. Over the years the girls build up their reasoning skills, improve their creativity and acquire strategies for tackling complex problems and decisions. They become self-sufficient learners – autonomous, inquisitive and brave. It gives the girls a life skill that will be as useful at university and in the workplace as it is now.

St Catherine's School ● ♠ ▲

Cross Deep, Twickenham, Middlesex TW1 4QJ
T: (020) 8891 2898
F: (020) 8744 9629
E: info@st-catherines-twickenham.org.uk
W: www.stcatherineschool.co.uk

Headmistress Sister P Thomas BEd (Hons)
   MA
Founded 1914
School status Girls' Independent Day Only
Religious denomination Roman Catholic
Member of GSA, ISA

Accredited by GSA, ISC
Age range 3–18
No of pupils 390; *Prep* 100; *Senior* 290;
   Sixth Form 5; *Girls* 390
Average class size 18
Fees per annum *(day)* £7,950–£11,115

St Catherine's, Twickenham: Focus on the individual. St Catherine's combines nearly 100 years' experience of Catholic independent education with a modern curriculum that prepares all pupils for success in the 21st century. We are a Catholic school in the ecumenical tradition, where every pupil is a valued member of a happy community. Emphasis is placed on providing a broad education and on responsibility and the importance of respect for others. We are a school with a strong community spirit and as such are able to focus on the individual and help every child achieve high value added scores and her personal academic best.

St Helen's School ● ♠ ★ ▲

Eastbury Road, Northwood, Middlesex HA6 3AS
T: (01923) 843210
F: (01923) 843211
E: enquiries@sthn.co.uk
W: www.sthn.co.uk

Headmistress Dr M Short BA (London)
   PhD (Cantab)
Founded 1899
School status Girls' Independent Day Only
Religious denomination Christian
Member of GSA
Accredited by GSA, ISC

Age range 3–18
No of pupils 1116; *Nursery* 41; *Nursery to
   pre-prep* 174; *Prep* 257; *Senior* 492;
   Sixth Form 152; *Girls* 1116
Average class size 20
Fees per annum *(day)* £9,516–£13,830

St Helen's is a highly academic school and pupils consistently achieve outstanding results, going on to prestigious universities of their first choice. Staff are subject specialists who inspire and encourage pupils to learn independently in a friendly, secure and disciplined environment. In senior school, girls study two modern foreign languages together with Latin, and science is taught throughout as three separate subjects. We offer excellent facilities, including our new state-of-the-art sports centre; specialist facilities for science, design and technology, art, drama, music and ICT; a digital, multi-media language laboratory; an excellent library housing an extensive collection of books, ICT facilities, newspapers and periodicals; and well-equipped teaching rooms.

SYMBOL KEY

Gender

● Girls
● Boys
● Coed

Accommodation

🏠 Boarding only
🏠 Boarding and Day
🏠 Day and Boarding
🏠 Day only

International Bacc.

★ Offers IB

CReSTeD

◆ Crested Registered

Has 6th Form

▲ Has 6th Form

MAP OF THE HOME COUNTIES (SOUTH)

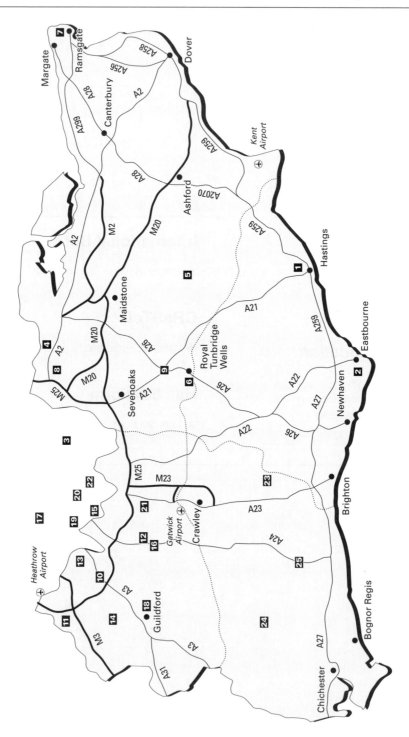

PROFILED SCHOOLS IN THE HOME COUNTIES (SOUTH)

(Incorporating the counties of Kent, Surrey, East Sussex, West Sussex)

Buckswood School ● ♠ ★ ▲

Rye Road, Guestling, Hastings, East Sussex TN35 4LT
T: (+44 (0)142) 813813 **F:** (+44 (0)142) 812100
E: achieve@buckswood.co.uk **W:** www.buckswood.co.uk
For overseas admissions please contact Mr David Whitehill
admissions@buckswood.co.uk We also have speakers of Spanish,
Russian, Slovakian and Chinese in the Admissions office.

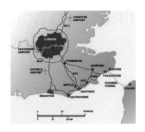

Director Mr Giles Sutton
Head Teacher Mr Mark Redsell CTEFLA (Notts);
  BA Hons Archaeology (Notts)
Founded 1933
School status Co-ed Independent Day and
  Boarding
Religious denomination Non-denominational
Member of BHS, CIS, COBIS
Accredited by BRITISH, COBIS, CIS

Age range 10–19; *Boarders from* 10
No of pupils 380; *(boarding)* 212;
  (full boarding) 210; *(weekly boarding)* 2;
  Senior 270; *Sixth Form* 90; *Girls* 140;
  Boys 240
Teacher:pupil ratio 1:14
Average class size 14
Fees per annum *(full boarding)* £18,480–
  £23,700; *(weekly)* £17,355; *(day)* £10,740

A truly international educational environment awaits your child at Buckswood. Parents select Buckswood because they know it is a school that contributes something special to their children's education. Its size allows the school to preserve a more home-like atmosphere, where the care and welfare of pupils are a priority. Buckswood follows the British curriculum, and small classes for GCSE, IB and A levels ensure pupils receive more individual attention. We have a large campus near the seaside town of Hastings, just 90 minutes from central London by direct train. On-campus facilities include: indoor heated swimming pool, stables and riding school, football academy with all-weather synthetic pitch, tennis courts, basketball courts, indoor sports hall and extensive sports grounds.

Eastbourne College ● ♠ ▲

Old Wish Road, Eastbourne, East Sussex BN21 4JY
T: (01323) 452323 **F:** (01323) 452327
E: admissions@eastbourne-college.co.uk
W: www.eastbourne-college.co.uk
50% boarding / 50% day   60% boys / 40% girls

Headmaster Mr S P Davies MA
Founded 1867
School status Co-ed Independent Boarding
  and Day
Religious denomination Church of England
Member of BSA, HMC, ISA, ISBA
Accredited by HMC

Age range 13–18 (50% boarding / 50% day
  60% boys / 40% girls)
No of pupils 622; *(boarding)* 310;
  (full boarding) 310; *Senior* 622;
  Sixth Form 271; *Girls* 261; *Boys* 361
Average class size 15
Fees per annum *(full boarding)*
  £28,605–£28,875; *(day)* £18,750–£19,020

'All schools go to great lengths to celebrate their pupils' achievements. At Eastbourne College we also work hard to develop in every pupil values that we deem to be fundamental to success at every level' says the Headmaster, Simon Davies. With over 620 pupils in the school, it is a community in which every child is extremely well known. Boys and girls, day pupils and boarders are totally involved in a school that believes wholeheartedly in full co-education and full boarding and prides itself in giving its pupils the best possible grounding for a successful life at school and beyond.

Bishop Challoner RC School ● ♠ ▲

228 Bromley Road, Shortlands, Bromley, Kent BR2 0BS
T: (020) 8460 3546 **F:** (020) 8466 8885
E: admissions@bishopchallonerschool.com
W: www.bishopchallonerschool.com

Headteacher Ms Karen Barry
School status Co-ed Independent Day Only
Religious denomination Roman Catholic
Member of ISA, ISBA, NAHT
Accredited by ISC, ISA
Age range 3–18

No of pupils 413; *Nursery* 47; *Nursery to*
pre-prep 52; *Prep* 73; *Senior* 212;
Sixth Form 33; *Girls* 126; *Boys* 287
Teacher:pupil ratio 1:9
Average class size 22
Fees per annum *(day)* £6,519–£9,036

At Bishop Challoner your child will learn within a caring, happy and secure environment. We are committed to 'outstanding pastoral care' and the highest level of academic achievement. As a Catholic, independent, co-educational day school, all our pupils from 3 to 18 are able to grow to their full potential so that they may become confident, responsible and caring members of society. Our ethos is one that nurtures individual talent, respects all faiths and creates a learning partnership for all. We are proud of our pupils, who flourish in a community where individual support and attention are second to none. We achieve excellent results at GCSE and A level, representing a lot of hard work and dedication. Our motto challenges each and every pupil to 'dare to do their very best'. We are recognized for outstanding success in fencing at local and national level. We look forward to extending a very warm welcome to you and your child at Bishop Challoner School.

Cobham Hall ● ♠ ★ ◆ ▲

Cobham, Gravesend, Kent DA12 3BL
T: (01474) 823371 **F:** (01474) 825906
E: enquiries@cobhamhall.com **W:** www.cobhamhall.com

Headmaster Mr Paul A Mitchell BSc
Founded 1962
School status Girls' Independent Boarding
and Day
Religious denomination Inter-denominational
Member of BSA, CRESTED, GSA, IB, ISA,
ISBA, Round Square
Accredited by GSA, ISC
Age range 11–18; *Boarders from* 11

No of pupils 200; *(boarding)* 110;
(full boarding) 90; *(weekly boarding)* 20;
Senior 200; *Sixth Form* 60; *Girls* 200
Teacher:pupil ratio 1:6
Average class size 15
Fees per annum *(full boarding)* £22,047–
£27,789; *(weekly)* £22,047–£27,789;
(day) £14,595–£18,474

One of Britain's leading girls' schools, Cobham Hall promotes excellence in all subjects. Pre-IB and IB offered in sixth form. The majority of pupils proceed to higher education. Specialist help is provided for dyslexic pupils and our EFL department offers English language support. The school is housed in an outstanding 16th-century mansion set in 150 acres with purpose-built classroom block, modern boarding houses, an indoor swimming pool and sports centre. Membership of Round Square provides the opportunity for international exchanges and education outside the classroom. Cobham Hall is situated 25 miles from central London (17 minutes by fast train from Ebbsfleet International Station), with easy access to international airports and the Continent.

Cranbrook School   ● ♠ ▲

Cranbrook, Kent TN17 3JD
T: (01580) 711800 **F:** (01580) 711828
E: registrar@cranbrook.kent.sch.uk
W: www.cranbrookschool.co.uk

Headteacher Mr John Weeds MA
Founded 1518
School status Co-ed State (Voluntary-aided)
  Day and Boarding
Religious denomination Non-denominational
Member of BSA, ISBA

Age range 13–18; *Boarders from 13*
No of pupils 756; *Sixth Form 320; Girls 354;*
  Boys 402
Average class size 30
Fees per annum *(full boarding)*
  £10,665–£12,795

Cranbrook is a selective co-educational state boarding and day school offering a superb all-round education at a very reasonable cost. It has a wide range of extra-curricular activities and high academic standards of 100 per cent A–C grades at GCSE and 100 per cent pass rate (74 per cent A/B grades) at A level. Music, art and drama thrive. Cranbrook has fine facilities for the creative arts, including a performing arts centre, a sixth form centre and a design/technology centre. The School has a strong sporting tradition with 55 acres of playing fields, a swimming pool, a sports hall and astro-turf pitches. Teams play at the highest levels locally and nationally. Entry at 13+ is competitive and by examination. Entry at 16+ is competitive and based on school reference and 7 B GCSE grades. Boarding candidates at both 13+ and 16+ are interviewed to ensure suitability for boarding.

Holmewood House   ● ♠

Barrow Lane, Langton Green, Tunbridge Wells, Kent TN3 0EB
T: (01892) 860006 **F:** (01892) 863970
E: registrar@holmewood.kent.sch.uk
W: www.holmewood.kent.sch.uk

Headmaster Mr J D B Marjoribanks BEd
  (Hons)
Founded 1945
School status Co-ed Independent Day and
  Boarding
Religious denomination Inter-denominational
Member of BSA, IAPS, ISBA
Accredited by ISC, IAPS

Age range 3–13; *Boarders from 9*
No of pupils 450; *(boarding) 5; (weekly*
  boarding) 5; Nursery 28; Nursery to pre-prep
  125; Prep 297; Girls 195; Boys 255
Teacher:pupil ratio 1:8
Average class size 15
Fees per annum *(weekly)* £18,975–£18,975;
  (day) £5,550–£15,975

Set in 30 acres of beautiful grounds, Holmewood House School is a happy, busy place, where every child is considered unique and will be inspired to learn. The breadth of curriculum, specialist teaching in all subjects resulting in excellent academic results, superb facilities, a vast range of afternoon activities, in an 'outstanding family atmosphere'* all combine to make Holmewood one of the leading prep schools in the country. Holmewood is 'a happy community where pupils are confident and articulate, enthusiastic and motivated, friendly and courteous'*. Holmewood pupils 'clearly enjoy coming to school and revel in the opportunities the school provides'*. Visit us in Tunbridge Wells to see what an inspiring place for children Holmewood truly is.

* *ISI Inspection Report*

St Lawrence College ● ♠ ♦ ▲

College Road, Ramsgate, Kent CT11 7AE
T: (01843) 572931 **F:** (01843) 572901
E: ah@slcuk.com **W:** www.slcuk.com

Headmaster Rev C W M Aitken BA (Durham)
Cert Theol FRSA
Founded 1879
School status Co-ed Independent Boarding
and Day
Religious denomination Christian
Member of AGBIS, BSA, CRESTED, HMC,
IAPS, ISA, ISBA
Accredited by HMC, ISC, IAPS
Age range 3–18; *Boarders from 7*

No of pupils 509;
(boarding) 200; *(full boarding)* 200; *Nursery*
23; *Nursery to pre-prep* 60; *Prep* 96; *Senior*
328; *Sixth Form* 107; *Girls* 198; *Boys* 311
Teacher:pupil ratio 1:7
Average class size 15
Fees per annum *(full boarding)* £20,715–
£27,564; *(weekly)* £20,715–£27,564;
(day) £6,297–£15,882

Walk through the historic arch at St Lawrence College in Kent and you will immediately feel at home. The newly opened Kirby House accommodates pupils aged 11 and 12 in modern five-bedded dormitories with en-suite facilities. Senior pupils are accommodated in double and single rooms. Outstanding results are achieved by the most academic pupils who progress to many of the top universities. The school is also highly regarded as a centre of excellence for 'value added'. The school has excellent transport links to London and Europe.

Steephill Independent School ● ♠

Castle Hill, Fawkham, Longfield, Kent DA3 7BG
T: (01474) 702107 **F:** (01474) 706011
E: secretary@steephill.co.uk **W:** www.steephill.co.uk

Headteacher Mrs C Birtwell BSc MBA PGCE
Founded 1935
School status Co-ed Independent Day Only
Religious denomination Church of England
Member of ISA
Accredited by ISA

Age range 3–11
No of pupils 125; *Nursery* 20; *Nursery to*
pre-prep 67; *Prep* 58; *Girls* 63; *Boys* 62
Teacher:pupil ratio 1:12
Average class size 14
Fees per annum *(day)* £6,735

Steephill is situated in the beautiful Fawkham Valley countryside in a quiet lane overlooking the 13th-century village church. Our small classes bring out the best in young children, who receive all the help and encouragement they need from Steephill's qualified, dedicated teachers. The high standards of care and teaching are reflected in the excellent academic results. Although a mixed ability school, all the children attain a very high standard, with typically 80 per cent of a year group gaining a grammar school place. With just a maximum of 16 pupils in a class, each child benefits from the individual attention necessary to achieve his or her full potential. Non-academic pursuits such as sport, drama and the arts also have a very high level of importance. The school has a silver Artsmark award and its choir has won the Gravesham festival two years running. As a small school the staff, parents and children all know each other and this contributes to our happy, family atmosphere.

Tonbridge School ● 🏠 ▲

Tonbridge, Kent TN9 1JP
T: (01732) 304297 **F:** (01732) 363424
E: admissions@tonbridge-school.org
W: www.tonbridge-school.co.uk
Visitors to the school are always welcome.
Please contact us to arrange an appointment.

Headmaster Mr T H P Haynes BA
Founded 1553
School status Boys' Independent Boarding
and Day
Religious denomination Church of England
Member of BSA, HMC
Accredited by ISC

Age range 13–18; *Boarders from* 13
No of pupils 780; *(boarding)* 461; *(full boarding)* 461; *Sixth Form* 330; *Boys* 780
Teacher:pupil ratio 1:7
Average class size 12
Fees per annum *(full boarding)* £31,263; *(day)* £23,340

Tonbridge School is one of the leading boys' boarding schools in the country and highly respected internationally. Boarders and day boys of varying backgrounds are offered an education remarkable both for its breadth of opportunity and the exceptional standards routinely achieved in all areas of school life. We welcome you to visit Tonbridge to meet us and see the school. For further information or for an appointment, please contact the admissions office on 01732 304297 or e-mail admissions@tonbridge-school.org.

ACS Cobham International School ● 🏠 ★ ▲

Heywood, Portsmouth Road, Cobham, Surrey KT11 1BL
T: (01932) 867251 **F:** (01932) 869789
E: cobhamadmissions@acs-schools.com **W:** www.acs-schools.com

Head of School Mr Tony Eysele
Founded 1967
School status Co-ed Independent Boarding
and Day
Religious denomination Non-denominational
Member of BSA, CIS, IBSCA, ISA, LISA,
NEASC
Age range 2–18; *Boarders from* 12
No of pupils 1349; *(boarding)* 90;
(full boarding) 60; *(weekly boarding)* 30;

Nursery 103; *Nursery to pre-prep* 377;
Prep 371; *Senior* 498; *Girls* 585; *Boys* 764
Teacher:pupil ratio 1:9
Average class size 15
Fees per annum *(full boarding)* £36,220–
£38,260; *(weekly)* £31,800–£33,840;
(day) £9,610–£21,860

Offering an international curriculum including both the IB Diploma and American Advanced Placement (AP) courses, ACS Cobham graduates attend leading universities throughout the world. Situated on a 128-acre site, the ACS Cobham campus has excellent indoor and outdoor sports facilities, with soccer and rugby fields, softball and baseball diamonds, an Olympic-sized track, tennis courts, a six-hole golf course and a sports centre with a basketball show court, swimming pool, dance studio, fitness suite and cafeteria. Students and teachers can interact with the world of learning through a state-of-the-art Interactive Learning Centre, with audio and video conferencing, delegate voting, and online streaming media. A co-ed boarding house provides separate-wing accommodation for 110 pupils aged between 12 and 18.

ACS Egham International School ● 🏠 ★ ▲

Woodlee, London Road (A30), Egham, Surrey TW20 0HS
T: (01784) 430800 **F:** (01784) 430626
E: eghamadmissions@acs-england.co.uk **W:** www.acs-schoools.com

Head of School Mr Jeremy Lewis
Founded 1967
School status Co-ed Independent Day Only
Religious denomination Non-denominational
Member of CIS, IB, IBSCA, ISA, LISA, NEASC
Accredited by CIS, ISA
Age range 2–18

No of pupils 640;
  Nursery 81; *Nursery to pre-prep* 183;
  Prep 127; *Senior* 179; *Girls* 282; *Boys* 321
Teacher:pupil ratio 1:9
Average class size 15
Fees per annum *(day)* £9,580–£20,890

ACS Egham International School is the UK's most successful young International Baccalaureate (IB) school. Its pupils have regularly achieved 100 per cent pass rates and Diploma score averages well above international results. This has led to placements in top universities worldwide. Additionally, the school is one of only four schools in the UK offering the IB Primary Years Programme (PYP), the Middle Years Programme (MYP) and the IB Diploma programme. Situated on a 20-acre site, ACS Egham has pupils from 29 nationalities speaking 19 languages, all seeking a world-class education. A new IB Diploma Centre opened in 2011, and a new sports centre opened in August 2012.

Box Hill School ● 🏠 ★ ▲

Old London Road, Mickleham, Dorking, Surrey RH5 6EA
T: (01372) 373382 **F:** (01372) 363942
E: enquiries@boxhillschool.org.uk **W:** www.boxhillschool.com
Twitter @boxhillschool
Facebook http://www.facebook.com/BoxHillSchool

Headmaster Mr Mark Eagers MA (Cantab),
  MA (Bath)
Founded 1959
School status Co-ed Independent Boarding
  and Day
Religious denomination Non-denominational
Member of AGBIS, BSA, IBO, IBSCA, ISBA,
  NAGC, Round Square, The Society of Heads
Accredited by BAISC, ISC, IBO

Age range 11–18; *Boarders from* 11
No of pupils 422; *(boarding)* 155; *(full boarding)* 129; *(weekly boarding)* 26; *Senior* 315; *Sixth Form* 107; *Girls* 132; *Boys* 290
Teacher:pupil ratio 1:9
Average class size 18
Fees per annum *(full boarding)* £26,775–£32,400; *(weekly)* £22,080–£23,160; *(day)* £14,520–£16,050

Box Hill School is based around the ideals of pupil responsibility, service to others, outdoor adventure and international understanding. Whilst placing academic achievement at the heart of the school at GCSE and IB level, we stress the importance of education as an all-round preparation for life. We pride ourselves on small classes, good tutoring and a flexible curriculum. All pupils are allocated to a house with a supportive family ethos, as well as a personal tutor to support their academic and pastoral development. Parents can monitor their child's progress via our 'Parents in Touch' website. Numerous activities and opportunities to represent the school are available, and our Round Square membership gives unique opportunities for international exchanges and projects in adventurous parts of the world.

Claremont Fan Court School ● ♠ ▲

Claremont Drive, Esher, Surrey KT10 9LY
T: (01372) 467841 **F:** (01372) 471109
E: seniorschoolenquiries@claremont.surrey.sch.uk
W: www.claremont-school.co.uk
prepschool@claremont.surrey.sch.uk
preprepschool@claremont.surrey.sch.uk

Head of Senior School Mr Jonathan
  Insall-Reid BSc, DipT, BArch Hons
Head of Preparatory School Mr Duncan
  Murphy BA (Hons), MEd, FRSA, FCMI,
  FCollT
Head of Pre-Preparatory Mrs Louise Fox BEd
  Hons

Founded 1922
School status Co-ed Independent Day Only
Religious denomination Christian
Member of The Society of Heads
Age range 2½–18
No of pupils 700; *Girls* 340; *Boys* 360
Fees per annum *(day)* £4,245–£14,190

Claremont Fan Court School is a co-educational school for pupils aged 2½–18 years situated just outside Esher, Surrey. The School is set in the historic landscaped grounds of the Claremont Estate. The School is founded on Christian values and welcomes children from all faiths and none. The ethos recognizes, cares for and values the potential of every child. With this recognition comes the expectation of high academic achievement and participation in sporting and cultural activities.

The School consists of the Pre-Preparatory and Nursery School for pupils aged 2½–7 years, the Preparatory School for pupils aged 7–11 years and the Senior School for pupils aged 11–18 years.

Hoe Bridge School ● ♠

Hoe Place, Old Woking Road, Woking, Surrey
GU22 8JE
T: (01483) 760018 **F:** (01483) 757560
E: enquiriesprep@hoebridgeschool.co.uk
W: www.hoebridgeschool.co.uk

Headmaster Mr N M H Arkell BSc
Founded 1987
School status Co-ed Independent Day Only
Religious denomination Non-denominational
Member of AGBIS, IAPS, ISBA
Accredited by IAPS

Age range 2–13
No of pupils 460; *Nursery* 45; *Nursery to
  pre-prep* 176; *Prep* 238; *Girls* 131; *Boys* 329
Teacher:pupil ratio 1:10
Average class size 19
Fees per annum *(day)* £1,800–£12,840

Hoe Bridge School is an academic, co-educational Preparatory and Pre-Preparatory school for children aged 2½ to 13. It is set in twenty beautiful acres on the outskirts of Woking and the facilities are both modern and outstanding. A major recent development has added three Science Laboratories and both new classrooms and changing rooms. The School has an outstanding Pre-Prep Department dedicated to children between the ages of 2½ and 7.

A broad curriculum is followed with children gaining scholarships to all local and national senior schools. Sport is important and is played every day with successes enjoyed both locally and nationally. A very happy atmosphere exists within the school, allowing pupils to develop into confident and successful children.

Homefield School ● ♠

Western Road, Sutton, Surrey SM1 2TE
T: (020) 8642 0965
F: (020) 8661 8039
E: administration@homefield.sutton.sch.uk
W: www.homefield.sutton.sch.uk

Head Master Mr P R Mowbray MA Cant
Deputy Head Mr M Till BA PGCE
Founded 1870
School status Boys' Independent Day Only
Religious denomination Non-denominational
Member of IAPS
Accredited by AGBIS, IAPS, ISC, ISBA

Age range 3–13
No of pupils 400; *Nursery* 40; Early years Unit
(Nursery and Reception) 70; *Prep* 330;
Boys 400
Teacher:pupil ratio 1:9
Average class size 17
Fees per annum *(day)* £4,500–£10,470

Homefield is a leading preparatory school housed in an extensive purpose-built complex complemented by a two-acre adjoining playing field. A new £1.8 million development comprising two science laboratories, a music suite, an art and DT suite and a learning resources centre was opened in September 2008. Rated by *The Sunday Times* Parent Power as 'Amongst the best performing schools in Greater London', Homefield is renowned for its family atmosphere, small class sizes, the fulfilment of individual potential, the openness of communication, and the provision of specialist teaching at the earliest opportunity. 83 scholarships have been won to senior independent schools for academic, musical, sporting, artistic and all round accomplishment in the last three years. Minibus service from Wimbledon and other areas available, as well as breakfast and after-school clubs.

Hurtwood House ● ♠ ▲

Holmbury St Mary, Dorking, Surrey RH5 6NU
T: (01483) 279000 **F:** (01483) 267586
E: ted.jackson@hurtwood.net **W:** www.hurtwoodhouse.com

The Headmaster Mr CM Jackson BEd
Founded 1970
School status Co-ed Independent Sixth Form
College Boarding and Day
Religious denomination Non-denominational
Member of BSA, ISA
Accredited by BAC, BRITISH, ISC, ISA
Age range 16–18; *Boarders from* 16
No of pupils 300; *(boarding)* 600;

(full boarding) 300; *(weekly
boarding)* 300; *Sixth Form*
295; *Girls* 155; *Boys* 145
Teacher:pupil ratio 1:6
Average class size 10
Fees per annum *(full boarding)*
£30,600–£32,767; *(weekly)* £30,600–
£32,767; *(day)* £20,400

Hurtwood House has the biggest and best

drama and media departments in England, with superb professional facilities. It is also hugely successful academically and has been top of the league tables two out of the last four years as the best co-educational predominantly boarding school in the UK. Uniquely, our 300 boarding pupils join us after GCSE, when they are ready for the fresh challenge of a sixth form where life is as exciting and stimulating as it is at university. Structured and secure, innovative and dynamic, Hurtwood House is one of England's most successful and exciting schools.

England

Kew Green Preparatory School ● ♠

Layton House, Ferry Lane, Richmond, Surrey TW9 3AF
T: (020) 8948 5999
F: (020) 8948 4774
E: secretary@kgps.co.uk
W: www.kgps.co.uk

Head Mrs M Gardener PGCE
Founded 2004
School status Co-ed Independent Day Only
Religious denomination Non-denominational
Member of IAPS, ISA, ISBA
Accredited by ISC, IAPS

Age range 4–11
No of pupils 260; *Prep* 260; *Girls* 130;
 Boys 130
Teacher:pupil ratio 1:7
Average class size 20
Fees per annum *(day)* £13,305

Kew Green Preparatory School provides an education of the highest quality. Unlike many private schools, LPS Ltd is owned by fully qualified and experienced teachers who understand that effective learning is achieved without pressure in a warm and nurturing environment. We are committed to co-education, opposed to 'cramming', and work on the basis of keeping pupils from age 4 to secondary transfer at 11 years. Within this timescale we are able to allow children to develop at their own pace whilst providing a rich curriculum. We strive to inculcate in our pupils a proper self-esteem and respect for others. Above all, we want our children to be clamouring at our gates every morning and to show a marked reluctance to leave at the end of the day!

Lanesborough ● ♠

Maori Road, Guildford, Surrey GU1 2EL
T: (01483) 880650
F: (01483) 880651
E: secretary@lanesborough.surrey.sch.uk
W: www.lanesborough.surrey.sch.uk

Head Mrs C Turnbull BA (Hons)
School status Boys' Independent Day Only
Religious denomination Church of England

Age range 3–13
No of pupils 358; *Boys* 358
Fees per annum *(day)* £7,185–£9,687

Lanesborough's academic reputation is justly well known but what sets us apart is the warm and purposeful atmosphere. We offer our pupils a happy, well-ordered and stimulating environment where they can progress to their fullest potential. An excellent all-round education based on skilled teaching in small classes is at the heart of our approach.

The school has occupied the same site in a quiet, leafy residential area of Guildford since 1930 and is the choir school for Guildford Cathedral.

The three original late nineteenth century houses which the school occupies have been updated and greatly extended with new buildings to provide extensive facilities for the boys.

The school is easily accessible by car and is close to Guildford's London Road railway station and bus routes.

Marymount International School

George Road, Kingston-upon-Thames, Surrey KT2 7PE
T: (020) 8949 0571
F: (020) 8336 2485
E: admissions@marymountlondon.com
W: www.marymountlondon.com

Headmistress Ms Sarah Gallagher BA (hons), HDipEd, MA (hons)
Founded 1955
School status Girls' Independent Day and Boarding
Religious denomination Roman Catholic
Member of CIS, GSA, IB, IBSCA, ISA, LISA, SHA
Accredited by CIS, GSA, ISC, MSAUSA

Age range 11–18; *Boarders from* 11
No of pupils 252; *(boarding)* 103;
(full boarding) 92; *(weekly boarding)* 11;
Sixth Form 99; *Girls* 252
Teacher:pupil ratio 1:6
Average class size 12
Fees per annum *(full boarding)* £30,340–£32,770; *(weekly)* £28,950–£31,380;
(day) £17,050–£19,480

Curriculum: Marymount has taught International Baccalaureate for over 30 years and has consistently been ranked within the top five per cent globally. Students go on to top universities worldwide. Marymount offers the pre-IB Middle Years Programmes: stretching students without the need for incessant testing. The school has a strong community spirit and achieves a shared purpose for girls of over 40 nationalities.

Old Palace of John Whitgift School

Old Palace Road, Croydon, Surrey CR0 1AX
T: (020) 8688 2027
F: (020) 8680 5877
E: schooloffice@oldpalace.croydon.sch.uk
W: www.oldpalaceofjohnwhitgift.org

Head Dr Judy Harris
School status Girls' Day Only
Religious denomination Church of England

Age range 1–19
No of pupils 823
Fees per annum *(day)* £7,914–£10,584

Old Palace offers an exciting world of exploration and discovery, building upon every child's natural curiosity. We are renowned as a vibrant community of individuals, celebrating diversity with a passion for excellence and achievement. Our team of dedicated and talented staff prioritize our pupils' well-being and happiness whilst inspiring a love of learning and creativity. We are proud of the outstanding academic, cultural and sporting successes attained in our friendly and stimulating environment as identified in our Inspection reports. An extensive, stimulating and challenging programme of learning together with an enhanced co-curricular programme of activities and sport is available at every stage of Old Palace.

Royal Alexandra and
Albert School ● ♠ ▲

Gatton Park, Reigate, Surrey RH2 0TD
T: (01737) 649001 **F:** (01737) 649002
E: admissions@gatton-park.org.uk
W: www.raa-school.co.uk

Headmaster Mr Paul D Spencer Ellis BA
  M.Phil NPQH
Founded 1758
School status Co-ed State (Voluntary-aided)
  Boarding and Day
Religious denomination Church of England
Member of BHS, BSA, HMC, SHA
Accredited by HMC

Age range 7–18; *Boarders from 7*
No of pupils 910; *(boarding)* 420; *(full
  boarding)* 420; *Prep* 150; *Senior* 610;
  Sixth Form 150; *Girls* 440; *Boys* 470
Average class size 26
Fees per annum *(full boarding)* £13,020;
  (day) £3,555–£4,875

This is a true boarding school in the sense that the majority of pupils are boarders. We have Saturday morning lessons and longer holidays, and run a vast range of sporting and other activities in the afternoons, evenings and at weekends. Admission is by confidential reference from the current school and interview but is restricted to citizens of the UK and other EU countries and those with the right of residence in the UK. Set in 260 acres of parkland yet close to London, we have an excellent range of facilities, including a sports hall, riding school, indoor swimming pool, drama studio, chapel, new music centre and nine boarding houses.

Trinity School ● ♠ ▲

Shirley Park, Croydon, Surrey CR9 7AT
T: (020) 8656 9541 **F:** (020) 8655 0522
E: admissions@trinity.croydon.sch.uk
W: www.trinity-school.org

Headmaster Mr MJ Bishop MA MBA
Founded 1592
School status Boys' Independent Day Only
Religious denomination Christian
Member of HMC
Age range 10–18 (Boys 10–18 Girls 16–18)

No of pupils 1000; *Senior* 940; *Sixth Form* 200;
  Girls 60; *Boys* 940
Teacher:pupil ratio 1:9
Average class size 22
Fees per annum *(day)* £13,056

Trinity School is part of the Whitgift Foundation which allows more than half of parents to benefit from some form of financial assistance with fees. Boys are drawn from a wide catchment area, with entry at 10, 11, 13 and boys and girls at 16. Academic results are consistently strong at GCSE and A level, with many boys gaining places at Oxbridge and other leading universities. There is a broad and balanced curriculum offering a wide choice of subjects. Trinity's choirs and orchestras enjoy an international reputation, with regular performances around the UK as well as professional engagements overseas. Outstanding sports facilities and top-level coaches, current and ex-professionals have enabled an impressive number of pupils to be selected to compete at national and international level. The extra-curricular provision is one of Trinity's distinctive strengths, with around 100 clubs and activities on offer.

Burgess Hill School for Girls ● ⌂ ▲

Keymer Road, Burgess Hill, West Sussex RH15 0EG
T: (01444) 241050 **F:** (01444) 870314
E: registrar@burgesshill-school.com
W: www.burgesshill-school.com
For the Junior School, please telephone 01444 233167.

Headmistress Mrs Ann Aughwane BSc (Hons)
CertEd NPQH
Founded 1906
School status Girls' Independent Boarding
and Day
Religious denomination Inter-denominational
Member of BSA, GSA, IAPS, ISA
Accredited by GSA, ISC, ISA, IAPS
Age range 2–18; *Boarders from* 11

No of pupils 688; *(boarding)* 54;
(full boarding) 54; *Nursery* 100; *Prep* 187;
Senior 300; *Sixth Form* 73; *Girls* 638;
Boys 50
Teacher:pupil ratio 1:1
Average class size 20
Fees per term *(full boarding)* £8,400;
(day) £4,750

A day and boarding school for girls aged 2½ to 18. Burgess Hill School for Girls has a happy, challenging, supportive atmosphere, which encourages young people to use their initiative, be inquisitive and creative, and develop responsibility and independence.

The school stands in 14 acres of beautiful grounds within a conservation area close to the centre of the town.

Our pastoral system is designed to encourage and support the development of each individual from the moment she arrives in school until the time she leaves. We want to provide your daughter with the skills and confidence which will help her to make the most of her time with us, at university and thereafter.

A recent ISI inspection found that 'The quality of pastoral care is outstanding. The support for and nurturing of individuals are key elements in shaping the outstanding personal development of pupils'.

Comments from the 2012 Parent Satisfaction survey illustrate the quality of education at Burgess Hill.

'Hard to sum up simply, but the main enthusiasm I have for Burgess Hill School for Girls is that my daughter is being stretched but not overstretched, challenged but not made anxious, is understood fully by staff members. There are some very gifted teachers at the school who explain clearly and all staff seem completely dedicated to seeking every opportunity to provide extra challenges for my daughter. She is also receiving clear guidance on university and careers choices. This means that at the end of her stay she will have amassed an extraordinary number of extra qualifications which will allow her to fulfil her ambitions. Perhaps more importantly, she will have grown so much as a person that she will be fully equipped to shoulder the responsibilities which her high demands on herself will create for her.'

'This is a school that is rightly proud of its pupils and what they achieve as individuals. Things like academic success naturally follow but the school does not chase statistics.'

'One of the many reasons we chose Burgess Hill School for Girls was the impeccable conduct of the girls on the train in the morning. I regularly commuted to Brighton and was impressed by their intelligent conversations and obvious support of each other in an environment outside of the school gates. Although my daughter has only been at the school for just under a year, the impact of the school's values and pride is already starting to show.'

It is a five minute walk from the railway station, which is on the Brighton to London line and so easily accessible from around the UK.

Seaford College ● ♠ ▲

Lavington Park, Petworth, West Sussex GU28 0NB
T: (01798) 867392 **F:** (01798) 867606
E: seaford@clara.co.uk **W:** www.seaford.org

The Headmaster Mr T J Mullins BA, MBA
Founded 1884
School status Co-ed Independent Boarding
and Day
Religious denomination Church of England
Member of HMC, SHMIS
Accredited by HMC, SHMIS
Age range 7–18; *Boarders from* 10
No of pupils 602; *(boarding)* 226;

(full boarding) 123; *(weekly boarding)* 103;
Prep 173; *Senior* 429; *Sixth Form* 128;
Girls 203; *Boys* 399
Teacher:pupil ratio 1:9
Average class size 15
Fees per annum *(full boarding)* £18,030–
£24,075; *(weekly)* £15,900–£20,400;
(day) £6,858–£15,600

Seaford is situated within 400 acres at the foot of the South Downs, the college is close to historic Petworth and seven miles from the closest railway station. Heathrow and Gatwick airports are within an hour's drive.

Pupils may board flexi, 4-day (Mon–Fri), weekly or full-time and a bus service collects day pupils from a wide area.

Curriculum
A wide range of subjects is offered at GCSE and A level. Ninety-six per cent of leavers go on to university.

Entry requirements and procedures
Entrance to the junior house at 10+ and 11+ is based on a trial day and ability test. Entrance to the senior school at 13+ is based on similar lines, along with Common Entrance examination results. Sixth form entry is dependent on GCSE results (minimum requirement is 45 points, A* = 8, A = 7, B = 6 etc) and an interview. Overseas pupils must pass an English exam set by the college and past academic achievements will also be taken into account.

Academic and leisure facilities
The college boasts an impressive art, design and technology centre. Outstanding sports facilities, including six rugby pitches, an all-weather hockey pitch and a new golf course and driving range, along with staff who have coached at international level. The hockey and rugby teams have toured Argentina, Barbados, South Africa, Australia, Canada and New Zealand and our pupils have played at county and national level. Music and drama feature strongly in the life of the college and the chapel choir enjoys an international reputation.

Scholarships
Scholarships are offered for academic, design and technology, music (instrumental or choral), sport or art but must be accompanied by a good all-round academic standard. Value: £500. Parents who require further discount from the fees may apply for a bursary.

Bursaries
Bursaries are available to Forces' families and siblings.

Boarding facilities
Boys aged 13–18 are divided between two houses with separate boarding and day accommodation. The older boys have individual studies and the younger boys sleep in rooms of two or three. Second-year A level pupils are accommodated in a separate house, offering more privileges and responsibility and helping with the transition from the protection of school life to the relative freedom of university. The girls' boarding house, comprising dormitories for pre-GCSE girls and single and twin rooms for lower sixth, is located in the mansion house. Dormitory facilities are provided in the junior house for girls and boys aged 10–13.

For further info please contact admissions on 01798 867456 or e-mail jmackay@seaford.org.

Windlesham House School ● ⌂

Washington, Pulborough, West Sussex RH20 4AY
T: (01903) 874700
F: (01903) 874702
E: office@windlesham.com
W: www.windlesham.com

Headmaster Mr R Foster BEd (Hons)
Founded 1837
School status Co-ed Independent Boarding and Day
Religious denomination Church of England
Member of BSA, IAPS, ISBA, SATIPS
Accredited by IAPS
Age range 4–13; *Boarders from 7*

No of pupils 324; *(boarding)* 191; *(full boarding)* 191; *Nursery to pre-prep* 46; *Prep* 278; *Girls* 137; *Boys* 187
Teacher:pupil ratio 1:7
Average class size 16
Fees per annum *(full boarding)* £19,950–£20,280; *(day)* £7,350–£17,280

Windlesham is one of the country's leading (and oldest) IAPS co-educational prep boarding and day schools, with a history of being in the forefront of educational development. Whilst academic excellence and success is a high priority Windlesham provides a warm, secure, caring and very happy family atmosphere. The Headmaster, Richard Foster – and his wife Rachel – put every effort into getting to know each and every child well, and derive enormous pleasure in seeing children flourish in what is a wonderful environment and an unrivalled setting.

Windlesham has had amazing recent successes including an 'Outstanding' Ofsted report and a glowing ISI Inspection, not to mention the strong public examination results.

MAP OF LONDON

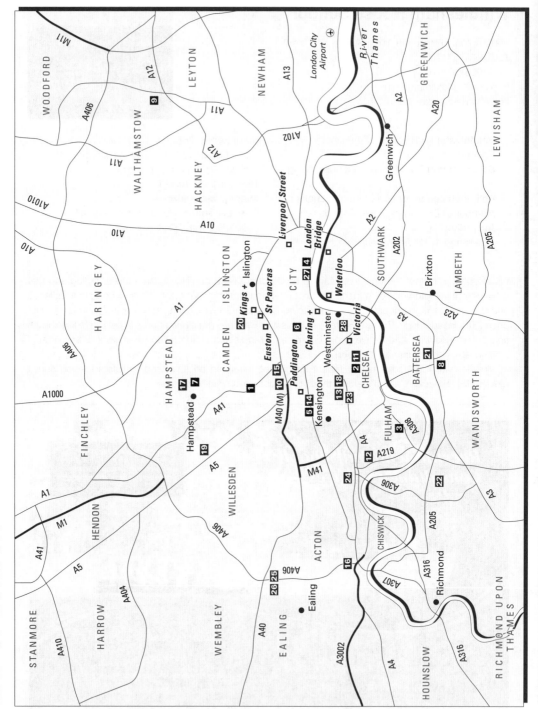

PROFILED SCHOOLS IN LONDON

The American School in London

● ♟ ▲

1 Waverley Place, London NW8 0NP
T: (020) 7449 1200 **F:** (020) 7449 1350
E: admissions@asl.org **W:** www.asl.org

Head of School Mrs C R Hester
Founded 1951
School status Co-ed Independent Day Only
Religious denomination Non-denominational
Member of CASE, CIS, NAIS

Accredited by CIS, MSAUSA
Age range 4–18
No of pupils 1350; *Girls* 670; *Boys* 680
Teacher:pupil ratio 1:9
Fees per annum *(day)* £18,600–£21,700

The American School in London is a co-educational, non-profit institution which offers an outstanding American education. The curriculum leads to an American High School Diploma, and a strong Advanced Placement programme enables pupils to enter the top universities in the United States, the UK and other countries. The core curriculum of English, maths, science and social studies is enriched with courses in modern languages, computing, fine arts and physical education. Small classes allow teachers to focus on individuals; pupils are encouraged to take an active role in learning to develop the skills necessary for independent critical thinking and expression. Many extra-curricular activities, including sports, music, drama and community service, are available for pupils of all ages. The American School in London welcomes pupils of all nationalities, including non-English speakers below the age of 10, who meet the scholastic standards. Entry is at any time throughout the year.

Cameron House School ● 🏠 ◆

4 The Vale, Chelsea, London SW3 6AH
T: (020) 7352 4040
F: (020) 7352 2349
E: info@cameronhouseschool.org
W: www.cameronhouseschool.org

The Headmistress Mrs Lucie Moore BEd
  (Hons)
Founded 1980
School status Co-ed Independent Day Only
Religious denomination Non-denominational
Member of CRESTED, IAPS, NAHT, SATIPS
Accredited by ISC, IAPS

Age range 4–11
No of pupils 118; *Nursery to pre-prep* 60;
  Prep 58; *Girls* 69; *Boys* 49
Teacher:pupil ratio 1:11
Average class size 18
Fees per annum *(day)* £15,285

The Curriculum

'The school fully meets its aim of maintaining high academic standards and helping each pupil to do their best.' (ISI Inspection)

Our academic curriculum prepares all our children for Common Entrance exams. All study a comprehensive range of subjects. High staff:pupil ratios allow the dedicated, highly-qualified teachers to create a stimulating, tailored learning environment. While emphasis is placed on the core curriculum, the school's teaching goes far beyond. French is taught from Reception, music, singing, speech and drama are popular, as is debating. The IT room, Interactive Whiteboards in every classroom and bank of laptops, provide access to online learning, and each class has its own library. A varied sports program gives the children opportunities to take part in lessons, matches and tournaments several times a week. Numerous after school clubs foster interests including: fencing, drama, karate, ballet, orchestra, chess, choir and Latin to name just a few.

Both boys and girls are thoroughly prepared for entrance exams and scholarships at 11 for prestigious London day and boarding schools.

Setup and Atmosphere

Cameron House has a nurturing environment that gives children a strong sense of belonging and purpose. With the guidance of the highly qualified staff, children of all abilities achieve excellent standards.

Pastoral Care

We encourage all our children to consider and care for others. 'Exemplary pastoral care is a strong feature of the school and staff are united in their approach to the promotion of pupils' well-being and development.' (ISI Inspection)

Outstanding Characteristics

Cameron House is a vibrant school well-known for maintaining high academic standards while encouraging individual creativity. Children leave Cameron House as independent thinkers, brimming with intellectual curiosity. 'The headteacher is highly skilled at moulding the staff into a unified team who work with a shared goal of a positive and caring approach towards each individual pupil, that has produced the outstanding response in the attitudes of pupils towards learning and to school.' (ISI Report)

Chelsea Independent College ● 🏠 ▲

517–523 Fulham Road, London SW6 1HD
T: (020) 7610 1114
F: (020) 7610 3404
E: admissions@cic.ac
W: www.cic.ac

Principal Mr Paul Fear
Founded 1952
School status Co-ed Independent Day Only
Religious denomination Non-denominational
Member of CIFE
Accredited by BAC

Age range 14–19
No of pupils 170
Teacher:pupil ratio 1:6
Average class size 6
Fees per annum *(day)* £13,950–£16,520

Chelsea Independent College benefits from modern, well-resourced buildings in the heart of London. It has developed an enviable reputation for excellent teaching in a supportive, caring environment. Many of the staff are graduates of Oxford, Cambridge and colleges of the University of London, and are chosen for their ability to relate to young people. Our small size encourages a warm and supportive atmosphere in which pupils can benefit from a high standard of pastoral care coupled with a strong sense of academic discipline. The college curriculum encompasses traditional GCSE and A levels, in addition to a number of courses aimed specifically at international pupils, with every effort being made to teach according to pupils' abilities and to stretch the ablest well beyond the demands of the syllabus.

City of London School ● 🏠 ▲

Queen Victoria Street, London EC4V 3AL
T: (020) 7489 0291
F: (020) 7329 6887
E: headmaster@clsb.org.uk
W: www.clsb.org.uk

Headmaster Mr David Levin B Econ MA FRSA
Founded 1442
School status Boys' Independent Day Only
Religious denomination Non-denominational
Member of HMC

Age range 10–18
No of pupils 920; *Sixth Form* 250; *Boys* 920
Teacher:pupil ratio 1:10
Average class size 22
Fees per annum *(day)* £13,401

The ethos of the school fosters good relationships between members of the staff and the pupils. Bullying, harassment, victimization and discrimination will not be tolerated. The school and its staff will act fairly in relation to the pupils and parents and we expect the same of pupils and parents in relation to the school. The City of London School aims to welcome talented boys from a diversity of backgrounds into a tolerant, harmonious community in which they achieve the highest academic standards, make full use of their potential and develop towards responsible adulthood. Academic achievement is very high. In 2011, 85.2 per cent of GCSE entries were passed at A* or A grade. At A level, 90.1 per cent of entries were passed at A* to B, with 23 per cent at A*. For a central London school, this is a sporty place and the school plays 12 sports competitively. There is an on-site swimming pool, sports hall and fitness suite, and a beautiful 20-acre sports ground 30 minutes' coach drive away.

David Game College ● ♠ ▲

69 Notting Hill Gate, London W11 3JS
T: (020) 7221 6665
F: (020) 7243 1730
E: nhg@davidgamecollege.com
W: www.davidgamecollege.com

Principal Mr David Game MA MPhil
Founded 1974
School status Co-ed Independent Day Only
Religious denomination Inter-denominational
Accredited by BAC, BRITISH
Age range 15–19; *Boarders from* 16

No of pupils 150; *Sixth Form* 160; *Girls* 75; *Boys* 75
Teacher:pupil ratio 1:10
Average class size 8
Fees per annum *(day)* £12,000

David Game College is one of London's leading independent colleges. The college specializes in one-year intensive courses in GCSE and A level, and has an outstanding record in preparing students for entry to the best UK universities. David Game College also runs one of the UK's most successful University Foundation Programmes, which specializes in preparing international students for university entry. The college has excellent relations with the top universities in the UK, in particular Imperial, LSE, UCL, Warwick and Bath, all of which regularly take David Game students for some of the most competitive degree courses. Extensive support is provided for our students during their studies, with small classes, close academic monitoring and support.

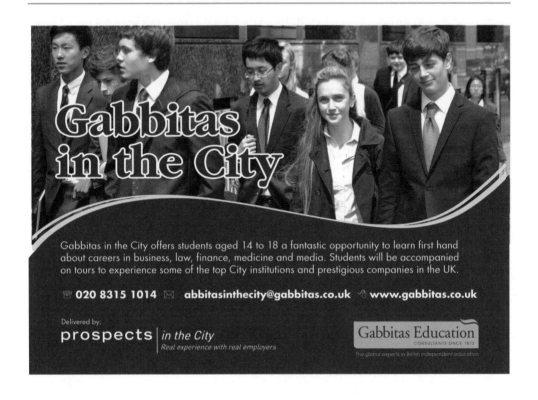

Davies Laing and Dick ● ♠ ◆ ▲

100 Marylebone Lane, London W1U 2QB
T: (020) 7935 8411
F: (020) 7935 0755
E: dld@dld.org
W: www.dldcollege.org
Visitors' entrance: 9 Bulstrode Street, London W1U 2JD

Principal Mr D Lowe MA (Cantab) FRSA
Founded 1931
School status Co-ed Independent Day Only
Religious denomination Non-denominational
Member of CIFE, CRESTED, ISA
Age range 14–24; *Boarders from* 16

No of pupils 312; *Girls* 148; *Boys* 164
Teacher:pupil ratio 1:5
Average class size 7
Fees per annum *(day)* £2,226–£7,200

Davies Laing and Dick (DLD) College was founded in 1931 to provide tutoring for Oxbridge and Colonial Service entrance exams. Over the years the College's reputation has grown and today DLD is a leading independent fifth and sixth form college with 330 students.

Our aims are:

- To help our students to achieve high academic standards;
- To offer an environment where the individual is valued and respected and where confidence is built;
- To prepare young people for university and their future career.

The College offers superb learning accommodation and facilities in a prestigious and safe central London location. There are three laboratories, two IT classrooms, a library for private study with an IT annexe, a GCSE study area, and an eighty-seat theatre, which is also used to screen films. There is a recording studio and a film edit suite. All classrooms are equipped with interactive white boards. Students are taught in small highly-focused groups enabling clear evaluation of progress. Parents receive five reports a year with regular interim test results emailed fortnightly.

The student day is a stimulating mix of traditional classes, study periods and breaks, with room for a variety of extra-curricular activities; sporting, social and cultural. A new enrichment programme encourages all students to participate in one or more of our range of extra-curricular activities, drawn from the creative arts, sport, debating and the Extended Project Qualification. This participation is important for students both as an opportunity for recreation and as an effective way to improve the quality of their UCAS personal statement and CV in the future.

Our e-learning platform allows remote access to a range of online resources, providing an exciting new dimension to the learning process. Above all, DLD is a learning community where the right attitudes to study are encouraged.

DLD offers international students accommodation in Urbanest student boarding and in homestays across London. Urbanest boarding provides students with a studio en-suite bedroom on one of DLD's three secure floors. All rooms are equipped with a study space with internet access and telephone, a sofa and TV, an en-suite shower room, and a kitchen. Each floor has a live-in houseparent who offers 24-hour support to our students. Breakfast is provided daily and students have a private kitchen to prepare their evening meals. Students can choose additional services such as laundry, cleaning, and school buses, and can take part in our social calendar which includes weekend events and activities, cooking lessons and sports teams.

Devonshire House Preparatory School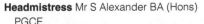

2 Arkwright Road, Hampstead, London NW3 6AE
T: (020) 7435 1916
F: (020) 7431 4787
E: enquiries@devonshirehouseprepschool.co.uk
W: www.devonshirehouseschool.co.uk

Headmistress Mr S Alexander BA (Hons) PGCE
Founded 1989
School status Co-ed Independent Day Only
Religious denomination Non-denominational
Member of IAPS, SATIPS

Accredited by ISC, IAPS
Age range 2–13
No of pupils 580; *Girls* 261; *Boys* 319
Teacher:pupil ratio 1:9
Average class size 18
Fees per annum *(day)* £7,365–£14,010

The school, situated in fine premises in the heart of Hampstead, aims to achieve high academic standards whilst developing enthusiasm and initiative throughout a wide range of interests.

Early literacy and numeracy are very important and traditional academic subjects form the core curriculum. Computers are used from an early age and sciences form an important part of the timetable as children grow older. Lessons are also taken in art, music, drama, French and PE.

The Oak Tree Nursery takes children from 2½ years of age. For children entering the junior school from age three to five, places are offered following an assessment. From six, places are usually subject to a written test.

Entry to the upper school is principally from the junior school. For pupils seeking to join the school from elsewhere, places are normally subject to a written entrance test.

Dolphin School (Including Noah's Ark Nursery School)

106 Northcote Road, Battersea, London SW11 6QW
T: (020) 7924 3472 **F:** (020) 8265 8700
E: admissions@dolphinschool.org.uk
W: www.dolphinschool.org.uk

Principal Mrs J Glen B A Hons
Head of Noah's Ark Nursery Schools
  Miss Annette Miller Teaching Degree
Founded 1986
School status Co-ed Independent Day Only
Religious denomination Christian

Age range 2–11
No of pupils 279; *Nursery* 112; *Nursery to pre-prep* 89; *Prep* 78; *Girls* 119; *Boys* 160
Teacher:pupil ratio 1:10
Average class size 14
Fees per annum *(day)* £5,250–£9,750

Our aim at Dolphin School is to help your child become the best they can possibly be. School is a training ground and our small classes enable us to focus on each individual. We train children academically, giving priority to English and maths and adding hands-on science, colourful geography, history and whole-school Spanish. We train pupils in the arts with fantastic specialist teaching and in a wide range of sports through dynamic coaching and a superb fixture list. Our Christian foundation gives us the impetus to develop children's character, teaching them the priority of good relationships throughout life.

Forest School

College Place, Snaresbrook, London E17 3PY
T: (020) 8520 1744 **F:** (020) 8520 3656
E: info@forest.org.uk **W:** www.forest.org.uk

Head Mrs S J Kerr-Dineen MA
School status Co-ed Independent Day Only
Religious denomination Church of England   **No of pupils** 1280; *Girls* 640; *Boys* 640
Age range 4–18 (Single-sex ed 7–16)   **Fees per annum** *(day)* £2,825–£4,298

Forest School is a large, vibrant and happy school with more than 1,250 pupils from the ages of 4 to 18.

The unique diamond structure means that Pre-Prep students are taught in small mixed classes, moving onto single-sex classes in the Prep School from 7. Single-sex teaching continues when pupils join either the Boys' or Girls' School. In the Sixth Form classes are once again mixed.

Co-curricular activities are mixed throughout, so the pupils have the best of all worlds. Pupils can join the school at most stages between 4 and 18, but almost all stay at Forest from Pre Prep until Sixth Form.

Pupils are treated as individuals, of whom staff have the highest expectations. The size of the school enables it to offer breadth and depth of opportunity through art, drama and varied sporting activities including use of the Sylvestrian Centre's leisure facilities.

A humane, open minded school, where pupils' personal development is outstanding and academic attainment high.

Francis Holland School, Regent's Park NW1

Clarence Gate, Ivor Place, London NW1 6XR
T: (020) 7723 0176 **F:** (020) 7706 1522
E: registrar@fhs-nw1.org.uk **W:** www.francisholland.org.uk
To enquire about admissions please contact the Registrar,
   Mrs Sandy Bailey

Headmistress Mrs V M Durham   **Accredited by** GSA, ISA, IAPS
Founded 1878   **Age range** 11–18
School status Girls' Independent Day Only   **No of pupils** 450; *Girls* 450
Religious denomination Church of England   **Average class size** 20
Member of GSA, IAPS, ISA, SHA   **Fees per annum** *(day)* £15,000

Francis Holland, Regent's Park, is a happy, academic day school for girls aged 11 to 18. Within a friendly and supportive atmosphere, pupils achieve excellent examination results. All pupils transfer to universities, including Oxford and Cambridge. Sixth formers attend weekly lectures from visiting guest speakers. Sport, art, drama and music contribute strongly to the school's lively extra-curricular schedule. The school has its own swimming pool and uses Regent's Park for tennis, hockey, rounders and netball. The Gloucester Wing provides additional classrooms, a fourth art studio and a performance area. There are two school orchestras, several choirs and a jazz band. The school runs more than 70 clubs and societies, such as history and politics, ju jitsu, cookery, water polo, Mandarin Chinese, gymnastics and yoga. Charitable initiatives include funding of a summer activity camp for local children.

Francis Holland School, Sloane Square SW1 ● 🏠 ▲

39 Graham Terrace, London SW1W 8JF
T: (020) 7730 2971 **F:** (020) 7823 4066
E: education@fhs-sw1.org.uk **W:** www.fhs-sw1.org.uk
To enquire about admissions, please contact the registrar,
Mrs Jane Ruthven

Headmistress Mrs L Elphinstone MA (Cantab)
School status Girls' Day Only
Religious denomination Church of England
Member of GSA

Age range 4–18
No of pupils 460; *Girls* 460
Teacher:pupil ratio 1:9
Fees per annum *(day)* £13,350–£15,300

A 460-strong day school for girls aged 4 to 18, with high academic standards and excellent pastoral care. There is a happy and purposeful atmosphere and pupils are respected as individuals. With a challenging curriculum, the school generates an enthusiasm for learning, intellectual curiosity and creativity. This approach leads pupils to consistently high levels of academic achievement. The constant upgrading of facilities enables the school to offer an extensive extra-curricular programme, including music, art, drama and sport. Recently acquired premises next door, provide a new Performing Arts Centre including specialist music and drama facilities opened in Autumn 2010. Charity fundraising is strong, as are links with the local community. Conveniently located near Sloane Square, the school takes full advantage of its location with frequent trips to museums, galleries and theatres.

Fulham Prep School (Prep Dept) ● 🏠

Prep Department, 200 Greyhound Road, London W14 9SD
T: (020) 7386 2444 **F:** (020) 7386 2449
E: prepadmin@fulhamprep.co.uk **W:** www.fulhamprep.co.uk
Pre-Prep (4–7+) based at 47A Fulham High Street,
London SW6 3JJ

Principal & Head of Prep School
Mrs J Emmett
Founded 1996
School status Co-ed Independent Day Only
Religious denomination Non-denominational
Member of SATIPS

Age range 4–13
No of pupils 585; *Pre-prep* 252; *Prep* 333;
Girls 242; *Boys* 243
Teacher:pupil ratio 1:9
Average class size 16
Fees per annum *(day)* £13,425–£14,925

Curriculum: In the pre-prep school, the curriculum, though broadly based, lays particular emphasis on the early acquisition of the traditional basic skills of reading, writing and numeracy. We do not prepare children for 7+ and 8+ exams. The curriculum in the prep school is based on the demands of the 11+ and 13+ Common Entrance exams. Entry requirements: The school is non-selective at the Reception stage, while entry into other years is by assessment in maths and English. Siblings of current pupils are given priority. Academic and extra curricula: Academic achievement is strong but we also put a lot of emphasis on all-round development, providing an extensive range of activities featuring sport, music, art and drama. The school has two choirs and an orchestra. A wide range of lunchtime and after-school clubs is offered each term.

England

Glendower Preparatory School ● ⌂

86/87 Queen's Gate, South Kensington, London SW7 5JX
T: (020) 7370 1927 **F:** (020) 78352849
E: admissions@glendowerprep.org **W:** www.glendowerprep.org

Head Mistress Mrs Sarah Knollys
Founded 1895
School status Girls' Independent Day Only
Religious denomination Non-denominational
Age range 4–11

No of pupils 210;
 Girls 210
Average class size 16
Fees per annum (day) £14,280

Why choose Glendower for your daughter? Our school is small in numbers; 210 pupils, aged between 4 and 11, but high in expectation and achievement. We aim to provide a stimulating environment in which each girl is valued and can enjoy developing her particular talents to the full, whether in art, music, sport, drama or other social activities. In the family atmosphere of Glendower, girls acquire the confidence to develop their talents to the utmost of their ability and gain the solid academic foundations necessary for competitive entry into a leading London day school or boarding school. We are a happy school! For further details please contact the school office.

Hawkesdown House School ● ⌂

27 Edge Street, Kensington, London W8 7PN
T: (020) 7727 9090 **F:** (020) 7727 9988
E: admin@hawkesdown.co.uk **W:** www.hawkesdown.co.uk

Head Mrs C Bourne
Founded 2001
School status Boys' Independent Day Only
Religious denomination Inter-denominational
Member of IAPS
Accredited by ISC, IAPS
Age range 3–8

No of pupils 146; Nursery 16;
 Nursery to pre-prep 130; Boys 146
Teacher:pupil ratio 1:9
Average class size 18
Fees per annum (day) £12,825–£14,685

Hawkesdown House is an independent school for boys from the ages of 3 to 8. Early literacy and numeracy are of prime importance and the traditional academic subjects form the core curriculum. A balanced education helps all aspects of learning and a wide range of interests is encouraged. The school finds and fosters individual talents in each pupil. Boys are prepared for entry at 8 to the main London and other preparatory schools. The Headmistress places the greatest importance on matching boys happily and successfully to potential schools and spends time with parents ensuring that the transition is smooth and free of stress. Sound and thorough early education is important for success, and also for self-confidence. The thoughtful and thorough teaching and care at Hawkesdown House ensures high academic standards and promotes initiative, kindness and courtesy. Hawkesdown is a school with fun and laughter, where boys develop their own personalities together with a sense of personal responsibility. The school provides an excellent traditional education, with the benefits of modern technology, in a safe, happy and caring atmosphere. Many of the boys coming to the school live within walking distance and the school is an important part of the Kensington community. There are clear expectations and the boys are encouraged by positive motivation and by the recognition and praise of their achievements, progress and effort. Individual attention and pastoral care for each of the boys is of great importance. Hawkesdown House has a fine building in Edge Street, off Kensington Church Street. Parents who would like further information or to visit the school and meet the Headmistress, should contact the School Office for a prospectus or an appointment.

International Community School

4 York Terrace East, Regents Park, London NW1 4PT
T: (+44 (0) 20) 7935 1206
E: admissions@ics.uk.net
W: www.icschool.co.uk
ICS Secondary School 21 Star Street London W2 1QB
Contact – Matthew Cook 020 7402 0416 matthew.cook@ics.uk.net

Head of School Mr P Hurd BSc PGCE
Founded 1979
School status Co-ed Independent Day and
Boarding
Religious denomination Non-denominational
Member of CIS, EUK, IB, ISA, LISA
Accredited by BRITISH

Age range 3–19; *Boarders from* 11
No of pupils 230; *(boarding)* 4;
(full boarding) 4; *Girls* 100; *Boys* 130
Teacher:pupil ratio 1:10
Average class size 17
Fees per annum *(day)* £13,500–£18,450

ICS is a friendly central London school for pupils aged 3 to 18 years. We are a co-educational, inclusive school, specializing in teaching to different ability groups. We offer the International Baccalaureate Curriculum at all levels – IB Primary Years, IB Middle Years and IB Diploma. We also provide year-round English language courses. ICS has a strong pastoral care/welfare reputation and classes are kept to a maximum of 18 pupils. A large team of assistants and specialists support class teachers. Children and faculty are from 45 countries and form a dynamic learning community. We have an extensive Travel and Learn Programme giving students the opportunity to visit many different parts of the world and our own outdoor education centre in Suffolk. The admissions team welcomes year-round applications.

International School of London

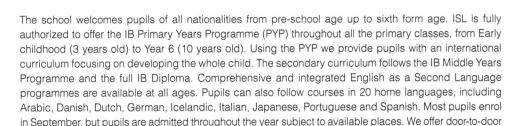

139 Gunnersbury Avenue, London W3 8LG
T: (020) 8992 5823 **F:** (020) 8993 7012
E: mail@isllondon.org **W:** www.ISLlondon.org

Head of School Mr Huw Davies
Founded 1972
School status Co-ed Independent Day Only
Religious denomination Non-denominational
Member of CIS, IBSCA, LISA

Accredited by CIS
Age range 3–19
No of pupils 337; *Girls* 151; *Boys* 186
Average class size 12
Fees per annum *(day)* £16,000–£21,500

The school welcomes pupils of all nationalities from pre-school age up to sixth form age. ISL is fully authorized to offer the IB Primary Years Programme (PYP) throughout all the primary classes, from Early childhood (3 years old) to Year 6 (10 years old). Using the PYP we provide pupils with an international curriculum focusing on developing the whole child. The secondary curriculum follows the IB Middle Years Programme and the full IB Diploma. Comprehensive and integrated English as a Second Language programmes are available at all ages. Pupils can also follow courses in 20 home languages, including Arabic, Danish, Dutch, German, Icelandic, Italian, Japanese, Portuguese and Spanish. Most pupils enrol in September, but pupils are admitted throughout the year subject to available places. We offer door-to-door transport covering west, central and south London.

England

Lyndhurst House Preparatory School ● ⌂

24 Lyndhurst Gardens, Hampstead, London NW3 5NW
T: (020) 7435 4936
E: pmg@lyndhursthouse.co.uk
W: www.lyndhursthouse.co.uk
A large detached Victorian red-brick building with its own playground in a quiet leafy side street.

Headmaster Mr Andrew Reid MA (Oxon)
   PGCE
Founded 1952
School status Boys' Independent Day Only
Religious denomination Non-denominational
Member of IAPS, NAHT, SATIPS
Accredited by ISC, IAPS

Age range 4–13
No of pupils 160; *Nursery to pre-prep* 54;
   Prep 106; *Boys* 160
Teacher:pupil ratio 1:7
Average class size 18
Fees per annum *(day)* £14,460–£16,110

Lyndhurst is a friendly and lively traditional boys' school, with its own special atmosphere and character. The environment is warm and friendly, small and familiar in feel, yet full of bustle, activity and purpose, in which every boy can find opportunities for engagement and fulfilment. Limited bursary support is available to boys already attending the school.

The Mulberry House School ● ⌂

The **M** Mulberry House School

7 Minster Road, West Hampstead, London NW2 3SD
T: (020) 8452 7340
F: (020) 8830 7015
E: info@mulberryhouseschool.com
W: www.mulberryhouseschool.com

Headteacher Ms J Kirwan
School status Co-ed Independent Day Only
Religious denomination Non-denominational
Member of ISA, ISBA

Accredited by ISA
Age range 2–8
Fees per annum *(day)* £9,071–£16,779

The Mulberry House School is an established independent school for two-to eight-year-olds, offering a stimulating and caring environment that meets the needs of individuals, while preparing them for the next stage of their schooling at 4+ or 7+. Extended day, full-time and part-time places available. For brochures and details of open evenings, please visit the Registration section of our website www.mulberryhouseschool.com.

More House School ● 🏠 ▲

22–24 Pont Street, Knightsbridge, London SW1X 0AA
T: (020) 7235 2855
F: (020) 7259 6782
E: publications@morehouse.org.uk
W: www.morehouse.org.uk

Head Master Mr R Carlysle BA MBA PGCE
  CertDys&Lit AKC MCoIP
Founded 1953
School status Girls' Independent Day Only
Religious denomination Roman Catholic
Member of GSA, HMC

Accredited by GSA, HMC
Age range 11–18
No of pupils 200; *Girls* 200
Teacher:pupil ratio 1:15
Average class size 15
Fees per annum *(day)* £13,710

More House was founded in 1953 at the request of parents wanting a central London Catholic day school for their daughters. The school is a Catholic Foundation, which accepts pupils of all faiths. It is an educational trust with a board of governors drawn partly from present and past parents. Despite our smaller size, we offer a full range of academic subjects up to GCSE and A level. Girls go on to a range of prestigious universities to follow courses including medicine, law, history, art, modern languages, drama, mathematics, classics, economics and biochemistry. Extra-curricular activities include running, swimming, fencing, choirs, orchestra, art, drama, photography, mathematics competition, public speaking and dance. Girls are encouraged to become involved in a range of activities, although the younger girls also benefit from supervised homework after school. Two full scholarships and smaller awards are made on entry to Year 7 and sixth form for academic and musical excellence. Occasional scholarships may be awarded at other levels of entry on academic grounds.

North Bridge House Senior School

1 Gloucester Avenue, London NW1 7AB
T: (020) 7267 6266
F: (020) 7284 2508
E: seniorschool@northbridgehouse.com
W: www.nbhseniorschool.co.uk

Head of Senior School Ms A Ayre	**Age range** 2–16
School status Co-ed Day Only	**No of pupils** 170; *Girls* 85; *Boys* 85
Religious denomination Non-denominational	**Fees per annum** *(day)* £4,355

North Bridge House School provides a complete education for children aged 2½ to 16 years. The school comprises two Victorian villas in Hampstead and one large site on Gloucester Avenue by Regent's Park. All buildings benefit from close proximity to local amenities, public transport links and road access.

At North Bridge House we aim to ensure that every child realizes their full potential. Alongside successful academic, sporting, artistic and pastoral achievement, we emphasize an environment that encourages good manners, tolerance, consideration for others and a strong sense of social responsibility.

Nursery:
The nursery is accommodated in a spacious Victorian villa containing bright, attractive classrooms and a large modern gym. It backs onto two large, safely enclosed playgrounds which offer plenty of opportunities for play and exercise.

Junior school:
Most children attend the junior school for three years before moving up to the prep school. The children participate enthusiastically in a wide range of activities both inside and outside the classroom. They continue to develop academic skills, as well as their creative and sporting abilities, in a nurturing environment which prepares them for their further education.

Prep school:
Children enter the lower prep at Year 4. All classes are taught by form teachers with specialists for music, French, PE and IT. At age 10, girls are prepared for the 11+ examination, while boys move to the upper prep for Years 6–8 to prepare for the Common Entrance. North Bridge House prep school has an outstanding record of success with many children annually entering senior schools such as St Paul's, Westminster, UCS, Highgate, City of London, South Hampstead and North London Collegiate.

Senior school:
The senior school has long been achieving excellent results at GCSE, with 97 per cent of of all GCSE grades awarded being between A* and C. Our pupils graduate to sixth forms in many schools in London, including Westminster, UCS, Highgate, City of London, South Hampstead, North London Collegiate, Channing and Francis Holland.

Parkgate House School ● ♠

80 Clapham Common North Side, London SW4 9SD
T: (020) 7350 2461
F: (020) 7738 1633
E: admissions@parkgate-school.co.uk
W: www.parkgate-school.co.uk

Principal Ms C Shanley
Founded 1987
School status Co-ed Day Only
Religious denomination Non-denominational
Member of SATIPS

Age range 2–11
No of pupils 230; *Girls* 120; *Boys* 110
Teacher:pupil ratio 1:5
Average class size 18
Fees per annum *(day)* £4,080–£11,250

Parkgate House School is an independent school educating over 200 children aged from 2 to 11 years. Residing in an historic Georgian Grade II listed building overlooking Clapham Common, the school is supported by an impressive staff of over 40 teaching professionals. Children receive focused attention in one of three specialized areas: the Montessori nursery for two- to four-year-olds; the pre-preparatory department for those aged four to seven and the preparatory department for the 7 to 11 age range. At any age, children enjoy an expansive, high-quality curriculum, which is further enhanced by an established after-school programme including choir, IT, drama, French, sport and horse-riding. A recent Ofsted report praised Parkgate House as 'a very good school with a friendly and welcoming atmosphere and an attractive learning environment'.

Putney Park School ● ♠ ◆

11 Woodborough Road, Putney, London SW15 6PY
T: (020) 8788 8316
F: (020) 8780 2376
E: office@putneypark.london.sch.uk
W: www.putneypark.london.sch.uk

Headmistress Miss Sarah Mostyn Bsc (Hons)
  PGCE NPQH MA
Founded 1953
School status Co-ed Independent Day Only
Religious denomination Church of England
Member of CRESTED, ISA
Accredited by ISC, ISA

Age range 4–16
No of pupils 220; *Prep* 120; *Senior* 100;
  Girls 180; *Boys* 40
Teacher:pupil ratio 1:10
Average class size 12
Fees per annum *(day)* £10,695–£12,216

Putney Park School established in 1953 is situated in a quiet conservation area and consists of four delightful Edwardian houses with a welcoming, family atmosphere. The aim of the school is personal success and academic achievement in a happy and secure environment. Pupils are offered a varied curriculum enabling them to develop their creativity and individual talents to their full potential. Pupils thrive in the caring and supportive environment. The school prepares boys for entry to their future schools at 7+, 8+ and 11+ and these include Kings College, Wimbledon and Colet Court.

Queen's Gate School ● ♠ ▲

133 Queen's Gate, Kensington, London SW7 5LE
T: (020) 7589 3587 **F:** (020) 7584 7691
E: registrar@queensgate.org.uk **W:** www.queensgate.org.uk
The Registrar, Miss Micklewright, can be contacted on her direct line
   0207 594 4982.

Principal Mrs R M Kamaryc BA MSc PGCE
Founded 1891
School status Girls' Independent Day Only
Religious denomination Non-denominational
Member of AGBIS, GSA
Accredited by GSA, ISC

Age range 4–18; *Nursery to pre-prep* 24;
   Prep 147; *Senior* 247; *Sixth Form* 55
Teacher:pupil ratio 1:6
Average class size 24
Fees per annum *(day)* £13,275–£15,300

The curriculum is rich, varied, well balanced and as wide as possible during the years leading to GCSE and is frequently reviewed to take into account new approaches. All girls sit GCSEs in English language and English literature, mathematics, a modern language, a science, as well as options in a wide range of subjects. Junior School: At 4, girls enter the Preliminary Form after assessment. Candidates entering the Junior School sit papers in maths, English, and non-verbal reasoning. Year 6 pupils sit the North London Independent Girls' Day Schools' Consortium 11+ examination for entry to Year 7 of the Senior School and elsewhere. From Year 8 candidates sit the Senior School's entry examinations. Girls entering the Sixth Form are expected to achieve six GCSE passes at grade A, with an A grade required for subjects to be studied at AS and A2. They are expected to study 4–5 A/S levels and to continue 3 of those subjects to A2. Scholarships are offered to internal pupils at 7 and 16 with 11+ Scholarships offered to internal and external candidates. Means tested bursaries are also available.

Ravenscourt Park Preparatory School ● ♠

16 Ravenscourt Avenue, Hammersmith, London W6 0SL
T: (020) 8846 9153 **F:** (020) 8846 9413
E: secretary@rpps.co.uk **W:** www.rpps.co.uk

Headmaster Mr R Relton
Founded 1991
School status Co-ed Independent Day Only
Religious denomination Non-denominational
Member of IAPS
Accredited by ISC, IAPS

Age range 4–11
No of pupils 340; *Girls* 170; *Boys* 170
Teacher:pupil ratio 1:7
Average class size 18
Fees per annum *(day)* £13,305

The School provides an education of the highest quality, preparing children for transfer to the best and most selective independent schools. Parents seeking places in state or independent secondary schools can be confident that their child will develop a range of skills and knowledge on which further specialized learning can be based. The school ethos is quite simply to ensure that each child is happy while at school – children who are content learn well. In order to achieve this we have developed a relaxed and attractive environment where a structured programme meets the needs of each individual. We have a dedicated and talented teaching staff that is prepared to go that 'extra mile'. Finally, we understand that this is a partnership and we work closely with parents to create a trusting relationship based on mutual respect.

St Augustine's Priory ● 🏠 ▲

Hillcrest Road, Ealing, London W5 2JL
T: (020) 8997 2022
F: (020) 8810 6501
E: registrar@staugustinespriory.org.uk
W: www.saintaugustinespriory.org.uk

Headteacher Mrs Sarah Raffray MA
Founded 1634
School status Girls' Independent Day Only
Religious denomination Roman Catholic

Age range 3–18
No of pupils 494; *Girls* 490; *Boys* 4
Average class size 20
Fees per annum *(day)* £8250–£11760

'A school out of the ordinary.'

Founded in 1634 St Augustine's Priory is both one of the oldest established girls' schools in the country, and also a truly vibrant, dynamic and modern community.

A rare luxury for a London School, St Augustine's Priory is set in 13 acres of beautiful grounds. High on a hill, our windows afford impressive views across London, and both literally and figuratively keep us outward-looking.

St Augustine's Priory offers an exciting range of activities which complement study and add colour and fulfilment to lives. Academic achievement is one part of our success, but we are committed to developing every individual's all-round potential.

Our purpose built Nursery is open to both girls and boys. The Early Years Department believe that the child is at the centre of the learning process. Their interests and experiences are valued and acknowledged as a starting point for learning.

Our Prep and Junior Departments offer girls a stimulating, varied and challenging curriculum, and teachers invest considerable time in knowing their pupils well and discovering the unique talents of each individual.

We offer a wide range of GCSE courses, and girls can study almost any combination of the 23 subjects available at A level. Sixth-form tutors work closely with them to assist with university and course selection, Oxbridge applications, and prepare them to be successful in whatever they choose to do.

We are proud of our record of academic success across the whole curriculum and are committed to high standards. The GCSE pass rate with 5 grades A* to C and the A level pass rate are both currently 100 per cent. Our experience is that if the bar is set high our girls rise to the challenge. We teach girls that there are no limitations, save those which we impose upon ourselves.

England

St Benedict's School   ● ♠ ▲

54 Eaton Rise, Ealing, London W5 2ES
T: (020) 8862 2254 **F:** (020) 8862 2199
E: enquiries@stbenedicts.org.uk **W:** www.stbenedicts.org.uk
Junior School contact: 5, Montpelier Avenue, Ealing,
  London W5 2XP Tel: 020 8862 2054

Headmaster Mr Chris Cleugh MSc BSc
Founded 1902
School status Co-ed Independent Day Only
Religious denomination Roman Catholic
Member of HMC, IAPS
Age range 3–18

No of pupils 1086; *Nursery* 34; *Nursery to pre-prep* 106; *Prep* 174; *Senior* 559; *Sixth Form* 213; *Girls* 292; *Boys* 794
Teacher:pupil ratio 1:9
Average class size 18
Fees per annum *(day)* £10,560–£12,360

St Benedict's is proud of its uniqueness. Our mission, 'Teaching a way of living', defines us as a Benedictine school. Come and join us and experience our dynamic educational environment. We will have high expectations of you in everything that you do. We will equip you to deal with the challenges that life in the 21st century presents, teaching you the joys of learning while enabling you to retain a moral and spiritual sensibility. The £6.2 million Cloisters complex demonstrates the school's commitment to providing the best possible facilities for pupils and staff. We invite you to come to visit our school. You can be sure of a warm Benedictine welcome.

St Paul's Cathedral School   ● ♠

2 New Change, London EC4M 9AD
T: (020) 7248 5156 **F:** (020) 7329 6568
E: admissions@spcs.london.sch.uk **W:** www.spcs.london.sch.uk

Head Master Mr N R Chippington MA, FRCO
Founded 1123
School status Coed Independent Boarding and Day
Religious denomination Church of England
Member of IAPS, ISBA, NAHT
Accredited by ISC, ISA, IAPS
Age range 4–13; *Boarders from* 7

No of pupils 249; *(boarding)* 32; *(full boarding)* 29; *Nursery to pre-prep* 62; *Prep* 185; *Girls* 87; *Boys* 162
Average class size 18
Fees per annum *(full boarding)* £7,194; *(day)* £11,550–£12,435

Governed by the Dean and Chapter, the original residential choir school now includes non-chorister day boys and girls aged 4–13. Curriculum: A broad curriculum leads to scholarship and Common Entrance examinations at 13 and the school has an excellent record in placing pupils in senior schools of their choice, many with scholarships. A wide variety of sport and musical instrument tuition is offered. Choristers receive an outstanding choral training as members of the renowned St Paul's Cathedral Choir. Facilities: The refurbishment of the school's facilities has provided a separate Pre-preparatory department, improved classrooms and new boarding facilities for the choristers. Admission: Children are interviewed and tested before September entry at 4+ or 7+ years old. Voice trials and tests for choristers are held three times a year for boys of nearly 7 years and upwards.

Westminster School ● 🏠 ▲

17 Dean's Yard, Westminster, London SW1P 3PB
T: (020) 7963 1003
F: (020) 7963 1002
E: registrar@westminster.org.uk
W: www.westminster.org.uk

Head Master Dr Stephen Spurr
School status Co-ed Boarding and Day
Religious denomination Church of England
Age range 13–18; *Boarders from* 13
No of pupils 747; *(boarding)* 161;
   (weekly boarding) 161; *Girls* 132; *Boys* 615

Teacher:pupil ratio 1:7
Fees per annum
   (full boarding)
   £19,626–£21,282;
   (weekly) £27,516;
   (day) £19,056–£20,664

Situated in the heart of London next to Westminster Abbey and the Houses of Parliament, Westminster is one of the country's leading academic schools. Most A level passes are grades A or B and many leavers go on to Oxford or Cambridge. Approximately 25 per cent of pupils board and day pupils also benefit from the school's boarding ethos. For more information or to arrange a tour call 020 7963 1003.

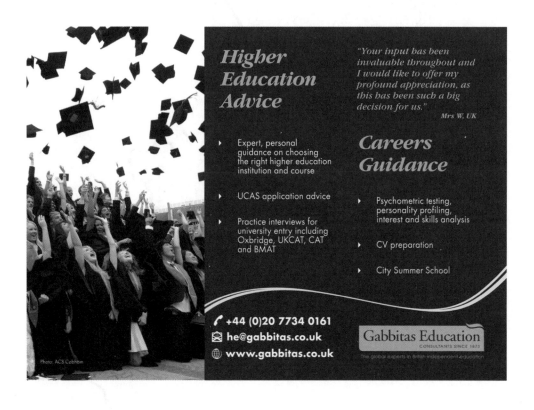

MAP OF SOUTH WEST ENGLAND

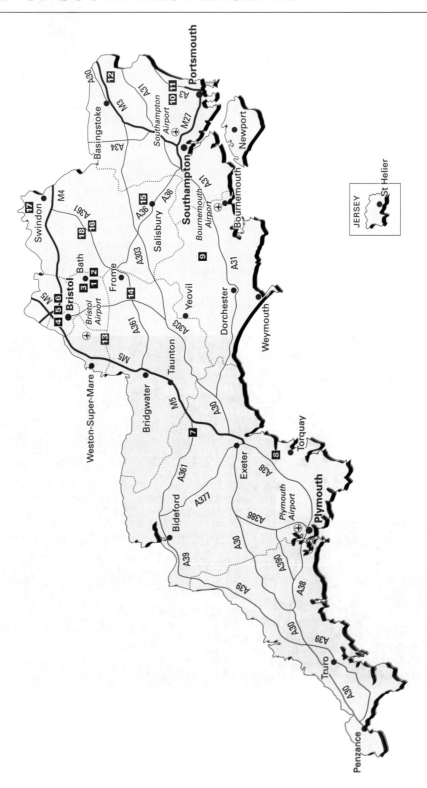

PROFILED SCHOOLS IN SOUTH WEST ENGLAND

(Incorporating the counties of Bath and North East Somerset, City of Bristol, Cornwall, Devon, Dorset, South Gloucestershire, Hampshire, Isle of Wight, Somerset, North Somerset, Wiltshire)

King Edward's School, Bath ● ♦ ▲

North Road, Bath, Bath & North East Somerset BA2 6HU
T: (01225) 464313
F: (01225) 481363
E: headmaster@kesbath.com
W: www.kesbath.com.uk

Head Mr Martin Boden
School status Co-ed Independent Day Only
Religious denomination Non-denominational
Member of HMC, IAPS, ISA, ISBA, NAHT, NAIS
Accredited by HMC, ISC, ISA, IAPS
Age range 3–18

No of pupils 970; *Nursery* 30; *Nursery to pre-prep* 60; *Prep* 180; *Senior* 250; *Sixth Form* 180; *Girls* 380; *Boys* 590
Average class size 25
Fees per annum *(day)* £6,435–£11,091

King Edward's School, Bath is an independent co-educational day school for children aged from 3 to 18 years. Founded in 1552 by King Edward VI; King Edward's School is one of the country's leading independent schools.

Academic performance is one of the School's many strengths; with results at A level, AS level and GCSE placing the School in the premier tier of schools in the country. Pupils go on to the top universities and successful careers. A recent ISI report judged the School's pastoral care to be 'outstanding'. King Edward's has a strong reputation for sporting excellence, as well as being strong in the creative arts; music, drama and art. The School offers an extensive extra-curricular programme. The facilities are first rate and the School continues to invest in new developments to enhance the already excellent provision.

Prior Park College ● ♦ ▲

Ralph Allen Drive, Bath, Bath & North East Somerset BA2 5AH
T: (01225) 831000 **F:** (01225) 835753
E: admissions@priorpark.co.uk **W:** www.thepriorfoundation.com

Headmaster Mr J Murphy-O'Connor MA
Founded 1831
School status Co-ed Independent Boarding and Day
Religious denomination Roman Catholic
Member of CIS, HMC
Accredited by CIS, HMC
Age range 11–18; *Boarders from* 13

No of pupils 587; *(boarding)* 126; *(full boarding)* 126; *Senior* 587; *Sixth Form* 189; *Girls* 276; *Boys* 311
Teacher:pupil ratio 1:9
Average class size 20
Fees per annum *(full boarding)* £25,434; *(weekly)* £20,154; *(day)* £12,657–£14,103

Prior Park College is a high-achieving, co-educational, Catholic, day and boarding senior school. Its encouraging ethos nurtures pupils to become confident, capable, compassionate and independent-minded young people. Led by James Murphy-O'Connor, the College achieved an outstanding report in its November 2011 ISI Inspection. To quote from the report: 'Prior Park College is outstandingly successful in achieving its aims. The College's ethos is rooted in the best traditions of Catholic education and redolent of aspiration for the highest standards in academic endeavour and in every area of young people's skills and talents.'

The Royal High School, Bath ● ♠ ★ ▲

Lansdown Road, Bath, Bath & North East Somerset BA1 5SZ
T: (01225) 313877 **F:** (01225) 465446
E: l.bevan@bat.gdst.net **W:** www.royalhighbath.gdst.net

Headmistress Mrs Rebecca Dougall BA MA
Founded 1864
School status Girls' Independent Boarding
and Day
Religious denomination Non-denominational
Member of GSA, GDST, IB
Accredited by GSA
Age range 3–18; *Boarders from* Year 5

No of pupils 770; *(boarding)* 140;
(full boarding) 130; *(weekly boarding)* 10;
Nursery 24; *Nursery to pre-prep* 52; *Prep*
152; *Senior* 375; *Sixth Form* 160; *Girls* 770
Teacher:pupil ratio 1:10
Average class size 22
Fees per annum *(full boarding)*
£19,326–£22,530; *(weekly)*
£17,394–£20,175; *(day)* £8,025–£11,130

In our inspirational school we celebrate individuality hand-in-hand with a spirit of community. We ask every girl to give the best that she can give, helping her to develop the confidence, capabilities and character needed to transform her future and achieve her aspirations in every aspect of life.

Academic rigour and a strong work ethic underpin ambition and achievement in an environment which champions tolerance, responsibility, commitment and respect for the individual and for society. Our girls discover what they can do well and learn to do it better than they ever thought possible. Talents are nurtured by dedicated teaching staff and celebrated by their friends, their peers and the school community as a whole.

For admissions, scholarship, and bursary details, HM Forces discounts or to arrange a private visit, please contact our Registrar, Lynda Bevan l.bevan@bat.gdst.net

---

Badminton School ● ♠ ▲

Westbury Road, Westbury-on-Trym, Bristol BS9 3BA
T: (0117) 905 5271 **F:** (0117) 962 3049
E: admissions@badminton.bristol.sch.uk
W: www.badminton.bristol.sch.uk

The Headmistress Mrs R Tear BSc
Founded 1858
School status Girls' Independent Boarding
and Day
Religious denomination Non-denominational
Member of BSA, GSA, IAPS, ISBA
Accredited by BRITISH, GSA, ISC, IAPS
Age range 3–18; *Boarders from* 9
No of pupils 445; *(boarding)* 195;
(full boarding) 180; *(weekly boarding)* 15;

Nursery 15; *Prep* 110; *Senior* 210;
Sixth Form 110; *Girls* 445
Teacher:pupil ratio 1:7
Average class size 16
Fees per annum
(full boarding) £19,590–£30,840;
(weekly) £19,590–£29,550;
(day) £7,320–£16,440

Badminton School is an independent boarding, weekly boarding and day school, located on a 15-acre campus in the heart of the attractive university city of Bristol. The school is ranked highly in the national league table and around 15 per cent of girls go on to Oxford and Cambridge. The community spirit of the school encourages girls to develop as individuals and enables them to realize their potential. By the time they leave school, the girls are confident and caring team players.

Bristol Grammar School

University Road, Bristol BS8 1SR
T: (0117) 973 6006
F: (0117) 946 7485
E: headmaster@bgs.bristol.sch.uk
W: www.bristolgrammarschool.co.uk

Head Master Mr R I MacKinnon BSc
Founded 1532
School status Co-ed Independent Day Only
Religious denomination Inter-denominational
Member of AGBIS, HMC, IAPS, ISBA

Age range 5–18
No of pupils 1210; *Nursery to pre-prep* 80;
Prep 180; *Senior* 650; *Sixth Form* 300;
Girls 475; *Boys* 735
Fees per annum *(day)* £5,993–£11,135

Bristol Grammar School aims high and is proud to do so, inspiring a love of learning, self-confidence and a sense of adventure among its pupils. Founded almost 500 years ago, BGS is an independent, co-educational day school for pupils aged 4 to 18 and considered one of the leading academic schools in the Southwest. BGS provides an excellent education, developing independence of thought through high-quality teaching of a broad curriculum and wide-ranging intellectual, physical and cultural pursuits. An exceptional pastoral care system, based around six houses, gives every pupil a sense of belonging and the security and confidence to make the most of the many opportunities offered. Prospective pupils and their families are most welcome to visit, with tours available throughout the year.

Clifton College

32 College Road, Clifton, Bristol BS8 3JH
T: (0117) 315 7000 **F:** (0117) 315 7101
E: admissions@clifton-college.avon.sch.uk
W: www.cliftoncollegeuk.com

Head Master Mr Mark Moore MA
Founded 1862
School status Co-ed Independent Boarding
and Day
Religious denomination Church of England
Member of HMC, IAPS
Accredited by HMC, IAPS
Age range 3–18

No of pupils *Upper School* 710;
Preparatory 380; *pre-preparatory* 230
Teacher:pupil ratio 1:8
Average class size 15
Fees per annum *(Upper School)* £20,700–
£31,500; *Preparatory* £13,470–£23,175;
Pre-preparatory £5,100–£10,740

Clifton College is one of England's most famous boarding schools. Clifton has always enjoyed the reputation of being at the forefront of education and the vast range of activities and opportunities reflect this.

The three schools that form Clifton College are bound by a common purpose and a shared ethos but are separate and distinct schools each with its own character. Located in what the poet Betjeman described as 'the handsomest suburb in Europe' each of the three schools share the same splendid surroundings, and have the advantage of being close to the resources of a thriving modern city and also spectacular countryside too.

Clifton offers a broad and flexible curriculum with an unusually large number of subjects on offer. Scholarships, Bursaries and Awards are available at 11+, 13+ and 16+.

Blundell's School

Blundell's Road, Tiverton, Devon EX16 4DN
T: (01884) 252543 **F:** (01884) 243232
E: registrars@blundells.org **W:** www.blundells.org
For prep school admissions ring 01884 252393

Head Mrs Nicola Huggett MA PGCE
Headmaster of Prep School
  Mr Andy Southgate BA Ed(Hons)
Founded 1604
School status Co-ed Independent Boarding and
  Day
Religious denomination Church of England
Member of AGBIS, BSA, HMC, ISBA
Accredited by HMC, ISC
Age range 3–18; *Boarders from* 11

No of pupils 584; *(boarding)* 362; *(full boarding)*
  117; *(weekly boarding)* 245; *Nursery* 28;
  Nursery to pre-prep 57; *Prep* 144; *Senior* 452;
  Sixth Form 178; *Girls* 232; *Boys* 352
Teacher:pupil ratio 1:9
Average class size 15
Fees per annum *(full boarding)*
  £19,260–£28,200; *(weekly)* £17,430–£24,810;
  (day) £11,490–£18,195

Blundell's, a key West Country School, combines the traditional values on which it was founded with the best of modern teaching methods and facilities. Academic excellence lies at the school's heart and its strength is in the diversity of options which gives every pupil a chance to shine. Blundell's also has a richly deserved reputation in sport, drama and music.

Equal importance is placed on pastoral care and developing the whole person: courtesy and good manners are deeply rooted in Blundellians and strong, supportive friendships ensure that community life at the school is richly rewarding. These qualities, together with the intellectual, physical and cultural interests they develop at Blundell's, provide pupils with skills for life.

Stover School

Stover, Newton Abbot, Devon TQ12 6QG
T: (01626) 354505 **F:** (01626) 361475
E: registrar@stover.co.uk **W:** www.stover.co.uk

Principal Mrs Sue Bradley BSc (Hons) CBiol MSB
Founded 1932
School status Co-ed Independent Day and
  Boarding
Religious denomination Christian
Member of AGBIS, BSA, SHMIS
Accredited by BRITISH, SHMIS
Age range 3–18; *Boarders from* 8
No of pupils 424; *(boarding)* 92;
  (full boarding) 84; *(weekly boarding)* 8;

Nursery 33; *Nursery to pre-prep* 41;
Prep 100; *Senior* 187; *Sixth Form* 67;
Girls 235; *Boys* 189
Teacher:pupil ratio 1:12
Average class size 15
Fees per annum *(full boarding)*
  £18,015–£22,659; *(weekly)*
  £15,714–£19,221; *(day)* £6,882–£11,070

Stover is one of the South West's leading independent day and boarding schools for girls and boys aged 3 to 18.

Set in 60 acres of beautiful grounds close to Dartmoor, Stover enjoys a rural location with an excellent transportation network including rail, road and airport links.

Stover provides a supportive, hardworking and purposeful atmosphere in which pupils live and learn. Creativity and independent thought are encouraged through good working and learning habits.

A non-selective school, Stover welcomes girls and boys of mixed abilities and supports them to achieve excellent results in all aspects of school life.

The house system encourages a sense of 'togetherness' for all pupils and an extensive extra-curricular programme provides opportunity to participate in activities including horse riding, the DOE Award and outdoor pursuits.

Milton Abbey School

Milton Abbas, Blandford Forum, Dorset DT11 0BZ
T: (01258) 880484 **F:** (01258) 881194
E: info@miltonabbey.co.uk **W:** www.miltonabbey.co.uk

The Headmaster Mr G E Doodes MA
Founded 1954
School status Co-ed Independent Boarding
and Day
Religious denomination Church of England
Member of BSA, CRESTED, Round Square,
SHMIS
Accredited by SHMIS
Age range 13–18; *Boarders from 13*

No of pupils 212; *(boarding)* 200;
(full boarding) 200; *Senior* 212;
Sixth Form 98; *Girls* 25; *Boys* 187
Teacher:pupil ratio 1:6
Average class size 10
Fees per annum *(full boarding)* £10,075;
(day) £7,575

Milton Abbey is a very personal place – a school in which everybody genuinely knows everybody. We have achieved what other schools strive in vain to achieve: an intimate community in which achievement in any area of life is never rated more highly than quality of character. No one is overlooked. Everyone is famous.

Bedales Prep School, Dunhurst

Alton Road, Steep, Petersfield, Hampshire GU32 2DR
T: (01730) 711733
F: (01730) 711820
E: jjarman@bedales.org.uk
W: www.bedales.org.uk
General enquiries: 01730 300200 or
email dunhurst@bedales.org.uk

Head Mrs Jane Grubb MA Brighton, BA
Newcastle, PGCE Leeds
Founded 1902
School status Co-ed Independent Boarding
and Day
Religious denomination Non-denominational
Member of BSA, HMC, IAPS, ISBA, SHMIS
Accredited by IAPS, SHMIS

Age range 8–13; *Boarders from 8*
No of pupils 204; *(boarding)* 86;
(full boarding) 43; *(weekly boarding)* 43;
Prep 204; *Girls* 108; *Boys* 96
Teacher:pupil ratio 1:7
Average class size 20
Fees per annum *(full boarding)* £21,255;
(day) £16,635

Bedales Prep School, Dunhurst School follows J H Badley's vision of focusing on all aspects of a child's life: head, hand and heart. We believe education should empower children through opportunity and experience. Much learning takes place through making and doing. Children are encouraged to find their own voice. Confidence grows as the children grow and with it their desire to question and discuss. Our distinctive approach to learning helps children excel academically. We are not bound by the Common Entrance syllabus; although guided by the National Curriculum, we are not locked into it. As children move up the school they learn to take responsibility for themselves. Pupils are expected to work hard on the academic curriculum, creative and performing arts, sport, and the wealth of activities on offer.

Bedales School

Petersfield, Hampshire GU32 2DG
T: (01730) 300100 **F:** (01730) 300500
E: admissions@bedales.org.uk **W:** www.bedales.org.uk
Contact for admissions: Janie Jarman, Registrar
(direct line 01730 711733; jjarman@bedales.org.uk)

Headmaster Mr Keith Budge MA, PGCE Oxford
Managing Head of the Senior School Mr Dominic
   Oliver BA Sheffield, MPhil Oxford (St Peter's)
Founded 1893
School status Co-ed Independent Boarding and Day
Religious denomination Non-denominational
Member of BSA, HMC, ISBA, SHMIS
Accredited by HMC, ISC, SHMIS

Age range 13–18; *Boarders from* 13
No of pupils 448; *(boarding)* 310; *(full boarding)* 310;
   Senior 448; *Sixth Form* 172; *Girls* 238; *Boys* 210
Teacher:pupil ratio 1:7
Average class size 20
Fees per annum *(full boarding)* £30,930;
   (day) £24,315

In 1893, Bedales founder, John Badley, created a school profoundly different from the public schools of his day – a school that focused on what was best for the individual child's educational welfare and happiness. Two strands predominated: breadth ('head, hand and heart') and the cultivation of the individual's intellectual and personal qualities ('intelligence, initiative and individuality').

Today, the contrast between Bedales and other schools remains strong. We believe that our informality engenders a genuine sense of partnership between teacher and student – a shared excitement about ideas and educational discovery. Educational innovation continues with our Bedales Assessed Courses (BACs), a unique curriculum to counter-act the dissatisfaction with GCSEs. BACs are recognized by UCAS and are well regarded by universities as they combine rigour with flexibility and allow scope for individual exploration within a clear syllabus framework.

Our top higher education destinations are a diverse mix of Oxbridge, red brick and art college, with 10 per cent of students progressing to Oxbridge. Bedales students therefore arrive at a similar place to those in more formal education settings. They have just taken a different route.

St Nicholas' School

Redfields House, Redfields Lane, Church Crookham, Fleet, Hampshire
GU52 0RF
T: (01252) 850121 **F:** (01252) 850718
E: registrar@st-nicholas.hants.sch.uk
W: www.st-nicholas.hants.sch.uk

Headmistress Mrs A V Whatmough BA(Hons) Cert
   Ed
Founded 1935
School status Girls' Independent Day Only
Religious denomination Church of England
Member of GSA
Accredited by GSA, ISC

Age range 3–16 (Boys 3–7)
No of pupils 367; *Nursery to pre-prep* 73;
   Junior 92; *Senior* 202
Teacher:pupil ratio 1:12
Average class size 15
Fees per annum *(day)* £8,499–£11,745

At St Nicholas' School we believe that the best education is a partnership between teachers, pupils and parents. By creating a supportive environment, the personal and academic potential of each pupil can be developed. Classes are small and facilities are excellent. The personal and academic progress of each individual is monitored carefully and should any help be needed, it is available. The secure base laid at St Nicholas' gives pupils a wide range of choice for the next stage of their education.

England

Sidcot School ● ♠ ★ ◆ ▲

Oakridge Lane, Winscombe, North Somerset BS25 1PD
T: (01934) 843102 **F:** (01934) 844181
E: admissions@sidcot.org.uk **W:** www.sidcot.org.uk

The Headmaster Mr I Kilpatrick
Founded 1699
School status Co-ed Independent Boarding
and Day
Religious denomination Quaker
Member of BSA, CRESTED, IAPS, IB, ISBA,
SHMIS
Accredited by ISC, SHMIS
Age range 3–18
No of pupils 520; *(boarding)* 173;
(full boarding) 163; *(weekly boarding)* 10;

Nursery 10; *Nursery to pre-prep* 62;
Prep 115; *Senior* 188; *Sixth Form* 145;
Girls 245; *Boys* 275
Teacher:pupil ratio 1:15
Average class size 15
Fees per annum
(full boarding) £22,050–£28,650;
(weekly) £21,750–£23,100;
(day) £6,300–£14,700

Sidcot School is a thriving independent co-educational day and boarding school situated in 160 acres. Sidcot offers a blend of excellent traditional and state-of-the-art facilities. It is well equipped, with academic facilities, a new performing and creative arts centre, learning resource and sixth form centre, sports hall complex with heated swimming pool, extensive playing fields and a riding centre. Our Quaker philosophy means that we value all children whatever their abilities. Pupils gain excellent exam results but also develop as caring and confident individuals. Happy children learn, and small classes and good working relationships make for a positive and inclusive atmosphere. Scholarships are available. Quaker bursaries are available for members of the Society of Friends. We welcome pupils of all faiths or none.

All Hallows ● ♠

Cranmore Hall, East Cranmore, Shepton Mallet, Somerset BA4 4SF
T: (01749) 881600 **F:** (01749) 880709
E: info@allhallwsschool.co.uk
W: www.allhallowsschool.co.uk

Headmaster Mr Ian Murphy BA Hons PGCE
School status Co-ed Boarding and Day
Religious denomination Roman Catholic

Age range 4–13
No of pupils 293; *(boarding)* 65;
(full boarding) 65; *Girls* 125; *Boys* 168

All Hallows is a Christian School in the Roman Catholic tradition. The school welcomes children from all Christian families and from other faiths. Our guiding stars, experienced throughout our daily school life are the two great commandments to love God and our neighbour.

We embrace the fact that happiness, safety and wellbeing of body, mind and spirit are of paramount importance in a child's development. Our boarding houses are carefully structured to nurture and support boarders to succeed in all aspects of their lives.

Pupils are challenged to increase their ability and through well-developed skills and attitudes achieve well in both their academic and broader education. The school is highly successful in enabling pupils to access places at the senior schools of their parents' choice.

Chafyn Grove School

33 Bourne Avenue, Salisbury, Wiltshire SP1 1LR
T: (01722) 333423 **F:** (01722) 323114
E: office@chafyngrove.co.uk **W:** www.chafyngrove.co.uk

Headmaster Mr Eddy Newton BA (Hons)
PGCE MA (Cantab)
Founded 1916
School status Co-ed Independent Boarding
and Day
Religious denomination Church of England
Member of BSA, IAPS, ISBA
Accredited by IAPS
Age range 3–13; *Boarders from 7*

No of pupils 301; *(boarding)* 48;
(full boarding) 48; *Nursery* 15; *Nursery to
pre-prep* 75; *Prep* 226; *Girls* 91; *Boys* 210
Teacher:pupil ratio 1:9
Average class size 15
Fees per annum *(full boarding)*
£15,330–£18,675; *(day)* £6,930–£13,755

High standards in a relaxed environment is our goal! At Chafyn Grove we offer a warm and welcoming setting where your child's learning experience can be nurtured in small class sizes. We aim to help each child to have high academic expectations of themselves relative to their own ability, and to take advantage of the many opportunities on offer outside the classroom. Our aim is to enable your child to thrive in the happy atmosphere that is created by a mixture of caring pastoral support, good discipline, clear traditional values and a team of talented and committed teachers. The most recent ISI inspection indicates our success: 'Pupils' excellent personal development enables them to grow into confident and friendly young people who enjoy responsibility. Relationships are excellent....'

Dauntsey's School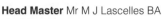

High Street, West Lavington, Devizes, Wiltshire SN10 4HE
T: (01380) 814500 **F:** (01380) 814501
E: sagersjh@dauntseys.wilts.sch.uk
W: www.dauntseys.org

Head Master Mr M J Lascelles BA
Founded 1542
School status Co-ed Independent Boarding
and Day
Religious denomination Inter-denominational
Member of BSA, HMC
Accredited by HMC, ISC
Age range 11–18; *Boarders from 11*

No of pupils 775; *(boarding)* 311;
(full boarding) 311; *Senior* 775;
Sixth Form 271; *Girls* 343; *Boys* 432
Teacher:pupil ratio 1:9
Average class size 14
Fees per annum *(full boarding)*
£27,060–£30,675; *(day)* £16,050

Dauntsey's is a leading co-educational boarding and day school for 11–18-year-olds set in an estate of 150 acres of idyllic countryside on the northern edge of Salisbury Plain. The school ranks very high in the league tables for both GCSE and A levels. However, all pupils discover a breadth and depth of education that takes them beyond academic achievement. Drama, music, art and sport all flourish and the rural surroundings provide an ideal setting for many outdoor activities, which include sailing on the school's very own Tall Ship, the famous 56ft gaff cutter, the Jolie Brise. All information about Dauntsey's can be found on the school's regularly updated and informative website.

Prior Park Preparatory School ● ♠ ◆

Calcutt Street, Cricklade, Wiltshire SN6 6BB
T: (01793) 750275 **F:** (01793) 750910
E: schoolsecretary@priorpark.co.uk **W:** www.priorparkprep.com

Headmaster Mr M A Pearse
Founded 1946
School status Co-ed Independent Boarding
and Day
Religious denomination Roman Catholic
Member of BSA, CRESTED, IAPS
Accredited by ISC, IAPS
Age range 3–13

No of pupils 187; *(boarding)* 44; *(full boarding)*
40; *(weekly boarding)* 4; *Nursery to pre-prep*
54; *Prep* 280; *Girls* 87; *Boys* 100
Teacher:pupil ratio 1:10
Average class size 15
Fees per annum *(full boarding)*
£14,643–£17,211; *(day)* £5,942–£12,312

Prior Park Preparatory School is a leading independent school based in Cricklade. With a reputation built on excellence, it provides a nurturing yet challenging school environment and ably prepares children for life's journey.

We are small enough to care for the individual but large enough to offer the best opportunities. As a non-selective Catholic Christian school for children aged 3 to 13, we carefully nurture and encourage our children to flourish, and to identify their gifts and talents. We develop lively and enquiring young minds through a broad and balanced curriculum.

Our ethos is based upon ensuring we provide not only a first class academic education but also an education for life. Our quality education produces major results.

St Mary's Calne ● ♠ ▲

63 Curzon Street, Calne, Wiltshire SN11 0DF
T: (01249) 857200 **F:** (01249) 857207
E: office@stmaryscalne.org
W: www.stmaryscalne.org

ST MARY'S CALNE

Headmistress Dr Helen M Wright MA (Oxon)
MA (Leics), EdD (Exeter), PGCE (Oxon)
FRSA, MIoD
Founded 1873
School status Girls' Independent Boarding
and Day
Religious denomination Church of England
Member of AGBIS, BSA, GSA, ISA
Accredited by BRITISH, GSA, ISC, ISA

Age range 11–18; *Boarders from* 11
No of pupils 325; *(boarding)* 257;
(full boarding) 257; *Senior* 325;
Sixth Form 104; *Girls* 325
Teacher:pupil ratio 1:6
Average class size 15
Fees per annum *(full boarding)*
£29,694–£30,300; *(day)* £21,609–£22,050

St Mary's has a cutting-edge curriculum that is continually developing in order to provide girls with an education that motivates, challenges and inspires them. Girls consistently perform well in public examinations and all go on to higher education. We look for girls who have potential and an eagerness to learn, whatever their education before joining us. Extra-curricular activity enhances and is a key part of the curriculum. Eighty per cent of the girls play musical instruments and the Chamber Choir has recently performed in London, Paris and New York. Drama productions have transferred to both the London stage, owing to our unique relationship with RADA, and the Edinburgh Festival Fringe. The school is represented nationally and at county level in sport, and the girls benefit from being in a rural location which is nonetheless only just over an hour from London by train.

3.2

Scotland

MAP OF SCOTLAND

THE
WESTERN
ISLES

Inverness

ISLE
OF
SKYE

Aberdeen
Airport

Aberdeen

Fort
William

Montrose

ISLE
OF
MULL

5 Perth   A85

6   Dundee

Stirling

1

Edinburgh
Airport

Dumbarton

Edinburgh

Glasgow
Airport

Glasgow

2 **3**

Prestwick
Airport

ISLE
OF
ARRAN

Dumfries   A75

4

PROFILED SCHOOLS IN SCOTLAND

(Incorporating the counties of Aberdeen City, Aberdeenshire, Angus, Argyll and Bute, East Ayrshire, North Ayrshire, South Ayrshire, Borders, City of Edinburgh, Dumfries and Galloway, East Dunbartonshire, West Dunbartonshire, Falkirk, Fife, Highland, Inverclyde, East Lothian, Midlothian, Moray, Perth and Kinross, Renfrewshire, Stirling, South Lanarkshire, West Lothian)

Dollar Academy   ● ♠ ▲

Dollar, Clackmannanshire FK14 7DU
T: (01259) 742511 **F:** (01259) 742867
E: rector@dollaracademy.org.uk **W:** www.dollaracademy.org

Rector Mr David Knapman M Phil BSc BA
Founded 1818
School status Co-ed Independent Day and
  Boarding
Religious denomination Non-denominational
Member of BSA, HMC, ISA, ISBA, SCIS
Accredited by BRITISH, HMC, ISC
Age range 10–18; *Boarders from* 10

No of pupils 1200; *(boarding)* 94;
  (full boarding) 90; *(weekly boarding)* 4;
  Prep 348; *Senior* 852; *Sixth Form* 146;
  Girls 579; *Boys* 621
Teacher:pupil ratio 1:9
Average class size 18
Fees per annum *(full boarding)*
  £20,916–£23,517; *(weekly)*
  £19,647–£22,248; *(day)* £7,704–£10,305

Dollar Academy is a beautiful school with an outstanding reputation, offering a full boarding experience for boys and girls aged 10–18 years.

Traditional values of courtesy, endeavour and respect are promoted alongside academic achievement as well as sporting and cultural participation and excellence.

Dollar supports each child, academically, socially and personally, treating them with respect, building their confidence, celebrating their success and encouraging their ambition.

This school encourages a sense of belonging and trust and helps its students develop skills for learning, life and work, and a clear sense of moral purpose.

Academic: High quality teaching produces outstanding academic achievement. Each year Dollar delivers top examination results and Dollar students are highly successful in winning places at leading universities. The art and music departments are of national renown.

Extra-Curricular: With over 70 sports, art, music, drama and social activities on offer, there is no shortage of options at Dollar and a full itinerary available to boarders.

Musically, there is a variety of large- and small-scale productions and concerts, and a choice of twelve choirs and orchestras. A large number of sports are offered, with a particular focus on rugby, cricket, hockey and tennis. There is also a full CCF programme with a very well supported Duke of Edinburgh Award scheme.

Dollar teams are always among the strongest in the country and this school has Internationalists across a range of activities. However, it is perhaps more important to note that the school places great emphasis on taking part; every student has the opportunity to perform and compete, often achieving success in activities that they have never tried before.

Boarding: The boarding facilities at Dollar Academy are excellent. They are spacious, beautifully designed, and very well equipped. Boarding pupils also benefit from an on-site gymnasium, swimming pool, extensive playing fields and all weather courts.

Location: Dollar Academy occupies a 70-acre open campus in the centre of a picturesque Scottish town; edged on one side by a golf course, with breathtaking views of Scottish scenery.

Dollar Academy is just 30 minutes' drive from Edinburgh Airport with dozens of direct flights each day to London and the continent.

Applications: For further information entry requirements and the application process, please contact rector@dollaracademy.org.uk

Merchiston Castle School ● ♠ ▲

Colinton, Edinburgh, Lothian EH13 0PU
T: (0131) 312 2200 **F:** (0131) 441 6060
E: admissions@merchiston.co.uk **W:** www.merchiston.co.uk

Head Mr A R Hunter BA
Founded 1833
School status Boys' Independent Boarding
  and Day
Religious denomination Inter-denominational
Member of BSA, HMC, IBSCA, ISBA, SCIS
Accredited by HMC, ISC
Age range 8–18; *Boarders from* 8

No of pupils 470; *(boarding)* 330;
  (full boarding) 330; *Prep* 108; *Senior* 200;
  Sixth Form 173; *Boys* 470
Teacher:pupil ratio 1:9
Fees per annum *(full boarding)*
  £16,485–£25,755; *(day)* £11,625–£18,750

Set in 100 acres of parkland, Merchiston is a school renowned for academic and sporting excellence. A full range of GCSEs and A levels are offered with selected Highers and results are very strong.

Merchiston pupils are regular winners of national engineering, electronic and mathematics prizes. Sporting achievements include pupils participating at international level. Strongly featured music department with prestigious school choir and pipe band. Integral junior department (8–12 years). Strong links with two girls' schools. Junior teaching centre, refurbished science labs, modern IT suite, music school and library. Indoor pool, sports hall and new sixth form boarding house with 126 en-suite bedrooms. Extensive co-curricular activities. Entry is by the school's own entrance exam; Scholarship exams or Common Entrance. Scholarships and means-tested financial assistance are available.

St George's School for Girls ● ♠ ▲

Garscube Terrace, Edinburgh, Lothian EH12 6BG
T: (0131) 311 8000 **F:** (0131) 311 8120
E: admissions@st-georges.edin.sch.uk **W:** www.st-georges.edin.sch.uk

Headmistress Mrs Helen Mackie BA (Hons)
  PGCE
Founded 1888
School status Girls' Independent Day and
  Boarding
Religious denomination Non-denominational
Age range 1–18; Boys 2–4

No of pupils 858; *(boarding)* 60;
  (full boarding) 54;
  (weekly boarding) 6; *Girls* 850; *Boys* 8
Teacher:pupil ratio 1:1
Average class size 16
Fees per annum *(full boarding)* £22,573;
  (day) £6,765–£11,113

St George's School for Girls was founded in 1888 by a group of women who had been denied access to university education. Today the ethos of our founders remains; we put girls first by design and aim to give each one the confidence and competence to fulfil her potential. St George's provides a caring, stimulating and challenging environment in which girls learn and develop. Emphasis is placed on personal achievement, responsibility, diversity and on partnerships. Girls, staff and parents work cooperatively throughout. In partnership, we aim to ensure that the education of St George's girls meets the needs of the outside world as well as the individual. Academic excellence is valued and our examination results are outstanding, with over 98 per cent of our girls going on to university or college. Law, science, medicine, international relations, modern languages, the arts and social sciences are favoured degree courses. We welcome enquiries throughout the year and assessments are held to suit parental needs.

Gordonstoun School ● ♠ ▲

Elgin, Morayshire IV30 5RF
T: (01343) 837837
F: (01343) 837808
E: admissions@gordonstoun.org.uk
W: www.gordonstoun.org.uk

Principal Mr Simon Reid
Founded 1934
School status Co-ed Independent Boarding
and Day
Religious denomination Non-denominational
Member of BSA, ISBA, Round Square, SCIS
Accredited by BRITISH
Age range 8–18; *Boarders from* 8

No of pupils 600; *(boarding)* 490;
(full boarding) 474; *(weekly boarding)* 16;
Prep 103; *Senior* 497; *Sixth Form* 252;
Girls 248; *Boys* 352
Teacher:pupil ratio 1:7
Average class size 12
Fees per annum *(full boarding)* £18,720–
£30,657; *(weekly)* £18,720–£18,720;
(day) £11,508–£22,884

Set in a magnificent estate, Gordonstoun (and its junior school, Aberlour House) lies between the sea and mountains in beautiful countryside. It is well located for easy access to international airports as well as mainline railway stations. The school's distinctive, holistic ethos is based on internationalism, challenge, responsibility and service and aims to prepare pupils to make a positive contribution to society. Offering a broad, integrated curriculum, Gordonstoun combines study for GCSE and AS/A level with sporting, creative and outdoor education, including the school's unique sail training programme, to help pupils encompass the school motto, Plus est en Vous (There is more in you).

Glenalmond College ● ⌂ ▲

Perth, Perth and Kinross PH1 3RY
T: (01738) 842000
F: (01738) 842063
E: registrar@glenalmondcollege.co.uk
W: www.glenalmondcollege.co.uk

The Warden Mr G Woods MA Oxon, PGCE
Founded 1847
School status Co-ed Independent Boarding
and Day
Religious denomination Episcopalian
Member of AGBIS, BSA, HMC, ISBA, SCIS
Accredited by HMC, ISC
Age range 12–18; *Boarders from* 12

No of pupils 395; *(boarding)* 355;
(full boarding) 355; *Senior* 395;
Sixth Form 175; *Girls* 157; *Boys* 238
Teacher:pupil ratio 1:7
Average class size 10
Fees per annum
(full boarding) £21,075–£38,110;
(day) £14,370–£19,170

Glenalmond College stretches its pupils – academically, physically, creatively, spiritually and emotionally. The strong and supportive community helps them to develop self-belief, generosity of spirit and independence of mind, enabling them to mature into successful, confident adults.

The school is located in 300 acres of stunning countryside just outside Perth, and is an inspirational environment for the 400 boys and girls aged 12 to 18 to grow and learn.

The school offers unique outdoor opportunities for pupils to develop. It is away from the distractions of the city, but only one hour from Edinburgh or Glasgow with easy transport links from the rest of the UK and overseas. Boarders and day pupils are welcomed and all benefit from the outstanding pastoral care and individual attention that are central to the school's ethos.

The full seven-days-a-week boarding environment provides the time and commitment to develop each child's potential – making the most of every pupil's talents and nurturing academic excellence. The recent HMI inspection identified the high levels of attainment and achievement, the outstanding pastoral care and the relationships among all the members of the schools as being among Glenalmond's particular strengths.

This pursuit of excellence is fundamental to the school's commitment to its pupils and is demonstrated by the results achieved. All Glenalmond pupils study for A levels, most students pass, and many at A* or A grade; the GCSE pass rate is also very high. However, education at Glenalmond extends far beyond the classroom and encompasses all aspects of the individual.

Academic work is balanced with an extensive range of creative, sporting, social and adventure activities, and each child is encouraged to find areas in which they can shine. Two pipe bands, a fantastic choir, acclaimed dramatic productions, lively debating and outstanding art and design shows offer opportunities for all. Rugby, hockey, lacrosse, cross-country, sailing and horse riding are just a few of the sports on offer. The school also has its own golf course – one of the best in the United Kingdom. Many pupils gain their Duke of Edinburgh's Award, there is a thriving Combined Cadet Force and Glenalmond is the most significant contributor to officer training of any Scottish school. In addition, all pupils work with local charities and in the community.

The atmosphere at the school is happy and friendly; the pupils work hard and bring out the best in each other, both in work and play. Pupils go on to achieve great things in life; most go to their first choice of university.

Strathallan School

Forgandenny, Perth, Perth and Kinross PH2 9EG
T: (+44 (0) 17) 812546 **F:** (+44 (0) 173) 812549
E: marketing@strathallan.co.uk **W:** www.strathallan.co.uk
Strathallan offers a very safe and secure environment yet accessible to all
parts of the world. Edinburgh and Glasgow are both international airports
and have direct flights. Perth has a mainline train station with direct trains to all parts of the UK.

Headmaster Mr B K Thompson MA
Founded 1913
School status Co-ed Independent Boarding and
Day
Religious denomination Non-denominational
Member of AGBIS, BSA, CASE, HMC, ISA, ISBA,
SCIS, SHA
Accredited by BRITISH, HMC, ISC, ISA
Age range 9–18; *Boarders from* 9 (Junior House for

Boys and Girls aged 9 to 13; Senior School for
Boys and Girls aged 13 to 18)
No of pupils 563; *(full boarding)* 367; *Prep* 90;
Senior 473; *Sixth Form* 197; *Girls* 249; *Boys* 314
Teacher:pupil ratio 1:7
Average class size 13
Fees per annum *(full boarding)*
£19,437–£27,249; *(day)* £12,132–£18,489

> **"Life is wonderful at Strathallan, and I have made so many friends. Most of the pupils
> board so it makes a huge difference to the atmosphere of the School and there is never
> a dull moment as we have so much to do academically as well as sport, music and activities."**

Holding an international reputation within its own portfolio of achievements, we need little introduction to those
seeking a high-quality boarding establishment for their children. With a nurturing environment and support from
teachers passionate about their subjects we achieved 82 per cent A*/B at A level. Set in glorious countryside
with 153 acres we offer a safe and secure environment for children to grow and develop and within 35 minutes
from international airports.

3.3

Schools in Continental Europe

MAP OF SCHOOLS IN CONTINENTAL EUROPE

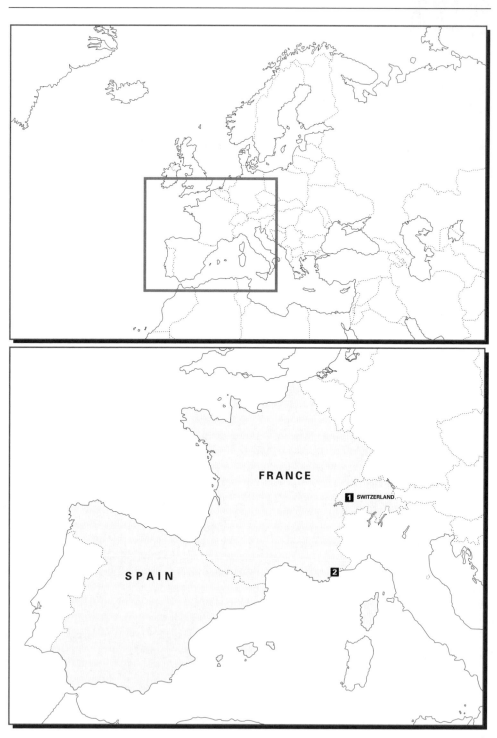

PROFILED SCHOOLS IN CONTINENTAL EUROPE

Aiglon College

1885 Chesieres-Villars, Switzerland
T: (+41) (0) 24 496 6126 **F:** (+41) (0) 24 469 6162
E: info@aiglon.ch **W:** www.aiglon.ch

Head Master Mr R McDonald
Founded 1949
School status Co-ed Independent Day and
   Boarding
Religious denomination Non-denominational
Member of CASE, CIS, COBIS, HMC, IAPS,
   IB, NEASC, ROUND
Accredited by CIS, HMC, IAPS
Age range 9–18; *Boarders from* 9

No of pupils 350; *Nursery to pre-prep* 25;
   Prep 50; *Senior* 275; *Sixth Form* 120;
   Girls 175; *Boys* 175
Teacher:pupil ratio 1:6
Average class size 12
Fees per annum *(full boarding)* £40,350–
   £56,470; *(weekly)* £35,925–£38,710;
   (day) £26,182–£39,940

Aiglon College is an international boarding school with an enrolment of over 55 nationalities. Offering a holistic education in a secure and friendly international community, the college is located on a 25-acre campus within an Alpine ski village.

There are eight boarding houses, each with its own houseparents and tutors offering a high degree of pastoral care. Aiglon has developed an international curriculum built around the English National Curriculum and the IB Diploma Programme.

The Junior School offers a balanced programme for 9 to 13 year olds in the first two years and an ESL programme for all non-English speakers aged 10–14. In the Middle School, students prepare for I/GCSEs and, in the final two years, for the IB Diploma and SATs. Aiglon's graduates are enrolled in leading international universities. Personal responsibility is fostered through social service projects around the globe, while Sports and expeditions form an essential component of a well-rounded approach to development.

Mougins School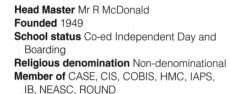

615 Avenue Dr Maurice Donat, CS 12180,
06524 Mougins CEDEX, France
T: (33) (0) 4 93 90 15 47 **F:** (33) (0) 4 93 75 31 40
E: information@mougins-school.com **W:** www.mougins-school.com

Headmaster Mr B G Hickmore
Deputy Head Ms Jane Hart
Founded 1964
School status Co-ed Independent Day Only
Religious denomination Non-denominational
Member of COBIS

Age range 3–18
No of pupils 512; *Nursery* 18; *Nursery to
   pre-prep* 22; *Prep* 158; *Senior* 241;
   Sixth Form 73; *Girls* 242; *Boys* 270
Teacher:pupil ratio 1:14
Average class size 22

Mougins School is situated on the Côte d'Azur, north of Cannes and west of Nice, on a purpose-built campus. Facilities include a library, three science laboratories, IT centre, two art studios, music room, performing arts centre, gymnasium, all-weather football pitch and dining room. The school accepts pupils aged 3 to 18, representing over 30 nationalities. The school follows the British curriculum, modified to meet the needs of an international market with examinations in IGCSE, AS and A level. The caring family atmosphere complements the high quality of the teaching and helps to enhance the academic, cultural and physical development of our pupils. We offer a comprehensive education that produces excellent results, not only academically but also in the sporting and artistic domains, leading to entry to the world's leading universities.

PART FOUR

SCHOOLS BY CATEGORY

4.1

Classified listings

This section comprises schools listed alphabetically by category heading. Categories include *Boys Day School, Co-educational Day and Boarding School, Horse Riding and Mountain Biking Provision*, amongst others.

Each entry contains details, including website address and a brief description of the school's particular characteristics.

BOYS DAY & BOARDING SCHOOL

ALDWICKBURY SCHOOL
Wheathampstead Road,
Harpenden, Hertfordshire AL5 1AD
Tel: (01582) 713022
Fax: (01582) 767696
Email:
registrar@aldwickbury.org.uk
Web: www.aldwickbury.org.uk
A day and boarding school for boys ages 4–13 in Harpenden. Aldwickbury is renowned for polite, friendly pupils who move on to a wide range of senior schools.

CO-EDUCATIONAL DAY AND BOARDING SCHOOL

ABBERLEY HALL
Abberley Hall, Worcester,
Worcestershire WR6 6DD
Tel: (01299) 896275
Fax: (01299) 896875
Email:
john.walker@abberleyhall.co.uk
Web: www.abberleyhall.co.uk
Abberley Hall is a co-educational full boarding school for 8–13 year olds preparing pupils for all major public schools, providing academic, sporting and social grounding required for sustained success.

BATH ACADEMY
27 Queen Square, Bath,
Somerset BA1 2HX
Tel: (01225) 334577
Fax: (01225) 482414
Email:
admissions@bathacademy.co.uk
Web: www.bathacademy.co.uk
Bath Academy is an International College Offering the University Foundation Programme, GCSE, A level and International GCSE and A level (CIE). Accommodation is available in hostels or homestay.

LICHFIELD CATHEDRAL SCHOOL

The Close, Lichfield,
Staffordshire WS13 7LH
Tel: (01543) 306170
Fax: (01543) 306176
Email: reception@
lichfieldcathedralschool.com
Web: www.
lichfieldcathedralschool.com
We aim to provide all children
from Nursery to Secondary with
a thorough academic foundation
together with a range of
opportunities to develop
individual interests and talents.
There is strong emphasis on
pastoral care, providing a
secure and ordered framework
through which all children can
develop their self-esteem and
find success. In September
2010, the School will launch
a Sixth Form.

CO-EDUCATIONAL DAY SCHOOL

ALBEMARLE INDEPENDENT COLLEGE

18 Dunraven Street, London
W1K 7FE
Tel: (020) 7409 7273
Fax: (020) 7629 9146
Email: james@eytle.com
Web: www.albemarle.org.uk
Based in heart of central
London Albemarle is an
independent sixth form college
offering a wide range of GCSE
and A-level subjects, with
emphasis on producing
excellent exam results.

AUSTIN FRIARS ST MONICA'S SCHOOL

Etterby Scaur, Carlisle,
Cumbria CA3 9PB
Tel: (01228) 528042
Fax: (01228) 810327
Email: office@austinfriars.
cumbria.sch.uk
Web:
www.austinfriars.cumbria.sch.uk
Academic achievement
underpins all that we do, and
the outstanding results of boys
and girls from 3–18 speak for
themselves. Music, drama,
creative and physical activity
contribute a vital part in
educating the whole student.
All are welcome in the
supportive school community,
underpinned by Christian
values, and are encouraged to
share their talents with and for
others.

CHEADLE HULME SCHOOL

Claremont Road, Cheadle,
Cheshire SK8 6EF
Tel: (0161) 488 3330
Fax: (0161) 488 3344
Email: registrar@chschool.co.uk
Web: www.cheadlehulmeschool.
co.uk
With high academic standards,
exceptional extra-curricular
opportunities and extensive
facilities, Cheadle Hulme School
provides an outstanding
education for boys and girls
aged 4 to 18.

KINGSTON GRAMMAR SCHOOL

London Road, Kingston-upon-
Thames, Surrey KT2 6PY
Tel: (020) 8546 5875
Fax: (020) 8547 1499
Email: registar@kgs.org.uk
Web: www.kgs.org.uk
Kingston Grammar School is
proud of the outstanding
achievements of its pupils
academically and in sport,
music, drama and a wide range
of other co-curricular activities.

LONGWOOD SCHOOL

Bushey Hall Drive, Bushey,
Hertfordshire WD23 2QG
Tel: (01923) 253715
Fax: (01923) 222760
Email:
info@longwoodschool.co.uk
Web:
www.longwoodschool.co.uk
Day Nursery and Primary
School offering continual
education for children from
three months to eleven years
in a truly family atmosphere.
Our aim is to provide a happy,
stimulating, healthy and safe
environment where all children
can attain high standards and
develop into well-balanced
citizens. Open weekdays
between 7am and 7pm
throughout the year, except
Bank Holidays.

ST MARTIN'S SCHOOL

22 Goodwyn Avenue,
London NW7 3RG
Tel: (020) 8959 1965
Fax: (020) 8959 9065
Email:
info@stmartinsmillhill.co.uk
Web: www.stmartinsmillhill.co.uk
"If children are happy and feel
safe and secure in their
environment they will learn."
St. Martin's coed prep school
established, in its own right,
for many years has provided
generations of pupils a happy
and successful start to their
school life. We look forward to
welcoming you to our school.

CO-EDUCATIONAL PREPARATORY SCHOOL

ELM GREEN PREPARATORY SCHOOL
Parsonage Lane, Chelmsford, Essex CM3 4SU
Tel: (01245) 225230
Fax: (01245) 226008
Email:
admin@elmgreen.essex.sch.uk
Web:
www.elmgreen.essex.sch.uk
Elm Green Preparatory School is a thriving educational community in an idyllic woodland setting, offering excellent academic, sporting and musical opportunities with outstanding pastoral care.

DAY & NURSERY SCHOOL

QUAINTON HALL SCHOOL
91 Hindes Road, Harrow, Middlesex HA1 1RX
Tel: (020) 8427 1304
Fax: (020) 8861 8861
Email:
admin@quaintonhall.org.uk
Web: www.quaintonhall.org.uk
Quainton Hall School is an IAPS day preparatory school & nursery for children aged 2½ to 13 years offering a very wide range of academic, sporting and extra-curricular opportunities.

GIRLS DAY SCHOOL

THE STUDY PREPARATORY SCHOOL
Wilberforce House, London SW19 4UN
Tel: (020) 8947 6969
Fax: (020) 8944 5975
Email:
wilberforce@thestudyprep.co.uk
Web: www.thestudyprep.co.uk
The Study is a long established, prep school for girls aged four to eleven, situated on the borders of leafy Wimbledon Common.
A specialist in educating young girls, the study feeds some of the best senior schools in the country. Pupils are attracted from Wimbledon and across South West London and Surrey. 'A very special community that the girls and their teachers create together.'

HORSE RIDING AND MOUNTAIN BIKING PROVISION

BEDSTONE COLLEGE
Bucknell, Shropshire SY7 0BG
Tel: (01547) 530303
Fax: (01547) 530740
Email:
admissions@bedstone.org
Web: www.bedstone.org
Bedstone College is South Shropshire's leading independent, co-educational, boarding and day school catering for children 3 to 18 years. It enjoys a warm and supportive family atmosphere, where each child is encouraged to fulfil their potential.

OUTSTANDING ACADEMIC ACHIEVEMENTS

LEIGHTON PARK SCHOOL
Shinfield Road, Reading, Berkshire RG2 7ED
Tel: (0118) 987 9600
Fax: (0118) 987 9625
Email:
admissions@leightonpark.com
Web: www.leightonpark.com
Founded in 1890, the school offers outstanding academic teaching and facilities, first class pastoral care, and a wealth of cultural, sporting and extra-curricular opportunities, all set in 60 acres of beautiful parkland, near Reading.

PART FIVE

REFERENCE
SECTION

www.independentschoolsguide.com

Scholarships

The following is based on information provided by schools. The entry age, where given, is the age at which scholarships are available to pupils. Please note that for each school, not every scholarship listed is offered at all the stated entry ages. Further details of scholarships available at individual schools may be found in Part Three: School Profiles. The abbreviations are as follows:

A	Art		I	Instrumental music/Choral
AA	Academic ability		O	All-round ability
D	Drama		S	Science
G	Games		6	Sixth Form entry

ENGLAND

BEDFORDSHIRE

Bedford High School for Girls, Bedford	6 AA I O
Bedford Modern School, Bedford	
Entry age: 11+	A D G
Bedford Preparatory School, Bedford	AA
Bedford School, Bedford Entry age:	
11, 13 and 16	6 AA G I
Moorlands School, Luton	
Entry age: 7+	A AA I O

BERKSHIRE

The Abbey School, Reading	
Entry age: 11+,13+,16+	6 A AA D G I O
The Ark School, Reading	
Entry age: 7	A AA I
Bearwood College, Wokingham	
Entry age: 11/13	6 A AA D G I O S
Bradfield College, Reading	
Entry age: 13+, 16+	6 A AA D G I O

Brigidine School Windsor,	
Windsor Entry age: 11, 16	6 A AA D G I
Brockhurst and Marlston	
House Schools, Newbury	A AA D G I O S
Cheam School, Newbury Entry age:	
Bursary from 8 years old	AA
Claires Court School,	
Maidenhead	6 A AA D G I O
Claires Court Schools, The College,	
Maidenhead	6 A AA D G I O
Claires Court Schools, Ridgeway,	
Maidenhead	A AA D G I O
Dolphin School, Reading	A AA D G I O
Downe House, Thatcham Entry age:	
11+, 12+, 13+ and 16+	6 A AA G I
Eagle House, Sandhurst Entry age: 11	AA I
Elstree School, Reading Entry age: 7	AA
Eton College, Windsor	6 AA I
Heathfield School, Ascot	6 A AA G I O
Hemdean House School, Reading	AA I O
Holme Grange School, Wokingham	
Entry age: 11+	AA O
Horris Hill School, Newbury	AA O

Hurst Lodge School, Ascot Entry
age: various 6 A AA D I O
Langley Manor School AA G I O
Long Close School, Slough Entry
age: 7yrs AA G I O
Luckley-Oakfield School, Wokingham
Entry age: 11+ 6 A AA G I
LVS Ascot, Ascot Entry age: Scholarship Year 7
(11+) and 6th Form. Bursary – HM Forces
bursaries available to boarders from Year 3
(7+). Hardship bursaries available Licensed
Trade Charity members. 6 A AA D G I
The Marist Senior School, Ascot
Entry age: 11 6 A AA D G I O
The Oratory School, Reading
Entry age: 11+, 13+ 6 A AA D G I O
Padworth College, Reading
Entry age: 14, 16 6 A AA
Pangbourne College, Pangbourne
Entry age: 11+, 13+, 16+ 6 A AA D G I O S
Papplewick School, Ascot
Entry age: 6–11 A AA G I O
Queen Anne's School,
Entry age: 11+, 13+, 16+ 6 A AA D G I O
Reading Blue Coat School, Reading A AA I
St Edward's School, Reading AA O
St Gabriel's, Entry age:
11+, 13+, 16+ 6 A AA D G I
St George's School, Ascot
Entry age: 11+, 16+ A AA D I
St George's School, Windsor
Entry age: 7+, 9+ AA I
St Joseph's College, Reading 6 AA D G I O
St Mary's School, Ascot, Ascot
Entry age: 11+, 13+ & 16+ A AA G I O S
St Piran's Preparatory School, Maidenhead
Entry age: Scholarship – Year 3.
Bursary any age A AA G I O
Sunningdale School, Sunningdale A AA D G I O
Thorngrove School, Newbury AA G I O
Upton House School, Windsor A AA O
Wellington College, Crowthorne 6 A AA D G I O

BRISTOL

Badminton School, Westbury-on-Trym Entry age:
Scholarships 11+, 13+ and 16+ for academic,
music, art and all round ability. Bursaries are
available in the senior school. 6 A AA I O
Bristol Cathedral School,
Entry age: 11+, 13+, 16+ 6 AA G I
Bristol Grammar School,
Entry age: 7, 11, 13, 16 6 A AA D G I
Clifton College, Entry age:
13+, 16+ 6 A AA G I O
Clifton College Pre-Prep – Butcombe O
Clifton College Preparatory School,
Entry age: 11+ AA G I O

Clifton High School, Entry age:
11+, 13+, 16+ 6 AA G I
Colston's Collegiate School 6 A AA D G I O
The Downs School, Wraxall
Entry age: 8+ A AA G I O
Fairfield School, Backwell AA
Queen Elizabeth's Hospital,
Entry age: 11, 13, 16 6 AA I S
The Red Maids' School,
Entry age: 11+, 13+, 16+ 6 AA G I O
Redland High School for Girls,
Entry age: 9, 11, 16 6 A AA G I
St Ursula's High School, Westbury-on-Trym AA
Tockington Manor School,
Tockington A AA G I O
Torwood House School, Redland O

BUCKINGHAMSHIRE

Bury Lawn School, Milton Keynes 6
Davenies School, Beaconsfield A AA G I O
Gateway School, Great Missenden O
Godstowe Preparatory School,
High Wycombe Entry age: 8, 11 AA
High March School, Beaconsfield
Entry age: 8 and 10 AA
Ladymede, Aylesbury Entry age: 7+ AA O
Milton Keynes Preparatory School,
Milton Keynes A AA G I
Pipers Corner School, High Wycombe
Entry age: 11+, 16+ 6 A AA D G I O
St Mary's School, Gerrards Cross
Entry age: 7+/11+/16+ for
scholarships, any age for bursaries 6 AA I
Stowe School, Buckingham
Entry age: 13, 16 6 A AA G I O
Swanbourne House School,
Milton Keynes Entry age: 11+ AA G I
Thornton College Convent of Jesus and
Mary, Milton Keynes Entry age: 11 AA
Thorpe House School, Gerrards Cross AA
Wycombe Abbey School, High Wycombe Entry
age: 11+, 13+ and sixth form entry 6 AA I

CAMBRIDGESHIRE

Bellerbys College & Embassy CES
Cambridge, Cambridge AA O
Cambridge Centre for Sixth-form Studies,
Cambridge 6 AA O
CATS College Cambridge,
Cambridge Entry age:
6th Form entry (16+) 6 AA S
Kimbolton School, Huntingdon Entry
age: 11+, 13+, 16+ 6 A AA G I O
King's School Ely, Ely
Entry age: 11+ 6 A AA D G I

The Leys School, Cambridge
Entry age: 11, 13, 16   6 A AA D G I O
MPW (Mander Portman Woodward),
Cambridge   6 AA O
The Perse School, Cambridge Entry
age: Year 7 and Year 9 – Academic
Scholarship, Music Scholarship.
Sixth Form – Academic Scholarship,
Art Scholarship, General Award,
Music Scholarship. Bursaries – all
entry points.   6 A AA I
The Perse School for Girls, Cambridge   6 I
The Peterborough School, Peterborough
Entry age: 11, 16   6 A AA G I O
St Faith's, Cambridge Entry age: 7+, 11+   AA
St John's College School, Cambridge   I
St Mary's School, Cambridge, Cambridge   6 AA I
Sancton Wood School, Cambridge   AA O

CHANNEL ISLANDS

Elizabeth College, Guernsey   I O
Ormer House Preparatory School,
Alderney   AA
St George's Preparatory School,
Jersey Entry age: 7+   A AA G I O S
St Michael's Preparatory School, Jersey   AA
Victoria College, Jersey   AA I S

CHESHIRE

Abbey Gate College, Chester
Entry age: 11+, 16+   6 AA I
Abbey Gate School, Chester
Entry age: 5 and 7   AA
Alderley Edge School for Girls,
Alderley Edge   6 A AA G I
Beech Hall School, Macclesfield   O
Brabyns School, Stockport   AA
Cransley School, Northwich
Entry age: 11+   A AA G I O S
The Grange School, Northwich   6 AA I
Hammond School, Chester   AA D I
Hulme Hall Schools, Cheadle   AA
The King's School, Macclesfield   AA I
Merton House, Chester   AA G
The Ryleys, Alderley Edge   AA O
Stockport Grammar School,
Stockport Entry age: 11+   I
Terra Nova School, Holmes
Chapel   A AA D G I O S

CORNWALL

Gems Bolitho School, Penzance
Entry age: 7+   6 A AA G I O

Polwhele House School, Truro   AA I
Roselyon, Par   AA I O
St Joseph's School, Launceston
Entry age: 7+, 11+   AA G I O
St Petroc's School, Bude
Entry age: 7+   A AA D G I O S
St Piran's School, Hayle   O
Truro High School, Truro
Entry age: 11+, 16+   6 A AA G I
Truro School, Truro   6 A AA G I

CUMBRIA

Austin Friars St Monica's School,
Carlisle Entry age: 11+   AA G I
Casterton School, Kirkby
Lonsdale Entry age:
Scholarships 11+, 13+
and 16+   6 A AA D G I O
Chetwynde School, Barrow-in-Furness   6 AA G O
Holme Park School, Kendal
Entry age: 7+   AA D G O S
Lime House School, Carlisle   AA G O
St Bees School, St Bees Entry age:
Scholarships 11+/12+
Bursaries also available   6 A AA G I
Sedbergh Junior School,
Sedbergh Entry age: 11   A AA D G I O
Sedbergh School, Sedbergh
Entry age: 13+, 16+, 17+   6 A AA D G I O
Windermere School, Windermere
Entry age: 11+, 13+, 16+   6 A AA D G I O

DERBYSHIRE

Derby Grammar School, Derby   6 AA G I
Derby High School, Derby
Entry age: 11/16   6 AA G I O
Foremarke Hall, Derby Entry
age: 7+ and 11+ Scholarships   A AA D G I
Mount St Mary's College, Spinkhill
Entry age: 11+, 13+, 15+   6 AA G I O
Ockbrook School, Derby   A AA D G I
Repton School, Derby
Entry age: 13+, 16+   6 A AA D G I O
St Wystan's School,
Repton Entry age: 7+   AA

DEVON

The Abbey School, Torquay   AA O
Blundell's School, Tiverton
Entry age: 11, 13, 16   6 A AA D G I O
Bramdean School, Exeter
Entry age: 7/11   AA D G I
Edgehill College, Bideford   6 A AA D G I O

Exeter Cathedral School,
   Exeter Entry age: 7/12+   AA I O
Exeter Junior School, Exeter
   Entry age: 7+, 8+   AA
Exeter School, Exeter
   Entry age: 7, 11, 12, 13   6 A AA I S
Kelly College, Tavistock
   Entry age: 11, 13, 16   6 A AA G I O
KINGSLEY SCHOOL, Bideford
   Entry age: 11, 12, 13, 16+   6 A AA D G I O
The Maynard School, Exeter
   Entry age: 7+, 9+, 16+   6 A AA G I O S
Mount House School, Tavistock
   Entry age: Generally in the latter
   years of the School eg Year 7,
   but all will be considered.   AA G I
Plymouth College, Plymouth
   Entry age: 11, 13, 16   6 A AA G I
Plymouth College Prepratory School,
   Plymouth Entry age:
   Scholarships 11+, Bursaries are
   means tested   A AA D G I O
St Christophers School, Totnes   O
St Margaret's School, Exeter   6 A AA D I
St Michael's, Barnstaple   A AA D G I O
St Peter's School, Exmouth   A AA G I O
St Wilfrid's School, Exeter Entry age: 7   O
Stoodley Knowle School,
   Torquay   6 O
Stover School, Newton Abbot Entry age:
   Scholarships 7+, 11+, 13+ & Sixth Form.
   Bursaries usually only in the Senior School.
   Means-tested Scholarships at
   Sixth Form entry.   6 A AA D G I O S
Shebbear College, Beaworthy
   Entry age: 11+, 13+, 16+   6 A AA D G I O
Tower House School, Paignton
   Entry age: 11   A AA D G I O S
Trinity School, Teignmouth Entry age:
   Entry is considered at all times
   to allow young people to get
   the best education   6 A AA D G I O S
West Buckland Preparatory School,
   Barnstaple   AA O
West Buckland School,
   Barnstaple   6 AA G I O

DORSET

Bournemouth Collegiate School,
   Bournemouth Entry age:
   Means tested bursary at 11+.
   Scholarships at 11+, 12+,
   13+, 16+   6 A AA D G I O
Bryanston School, Blandford Forum
   Entry age: 13, 16   6 A AA G I O S
Canford School, Wimborne
   Entry age: 13+ and 16+   6 A AA D G I

Castle Court Preparatory School,
   Wimborne   AA I
Claysmore, Blandford Forum
   Entry age: Prep School:
   8 years of age Senior School
   13 years and 16 years of age   6 A AA G I O
Claysmore Preparatory School,
   Blandford Forum Entry age:
   Scholarships from
   Year 3 and Bursaries are
   offered from reception   A AA G I O
Dumpton School, Wimborne   AA O
Knighton House, Blandford Forum A AA D G I O
Leweston School, Sherborne
   Entry age: 7–13,16   6 A AA D G I O S
Milton Abbey School, Blandford
   Forum Entry age: 13 and 16 6 A AA D G I O
The Park School, Bournemouth   AA I O
Port Regis Preparatory School,
   Shaftesbury Entry age:
   From ages 7 to 12   A AA G I O
St Martin's School, Bournemouth   AA G O
St Mary's School, Dorset, Shaftesbury
   Entry age: 11+, 13+, 16+   6 A AA G I
Sherborne Girls, Sherborne   6 A AA I O
Sherborne School, Sherborne
   Entry age: 13+, 16+   6 A AA D G I
Talbot Heath, Bournemouth 6 A AA D G I O
Thornlow Preparatory School, Weymouth AA G
Yarrells School, Poole Entry age:
   Scholarships at 8+   AA G I O

COUNTY DURHAM

Barnard Castle School, Barnard
   Castle Entry age: 11+, 13+ and
   Sixth Form   6 A AA D G I O
The Chorister School, Durham   I
Durham High School For Girls,
   Durham Entry age: 11, 16   6 A AA D G I
Durham School, Durham
   Entry age: 7, 11, 13, 16   6 A AA D G I
Hurworth House School, Darlington AA G O
Polam Hall, Darlington
   Entry age: 7, 11, 14, 16   6 AA G I O
Yarm at Raventhorpe School, Darlington O

ESSEX

Alleyn Court Preparatory School,
   Southend-on-Sea Entry age: 7   AA I O
Bancroft's School, Woodford Green
   Entry age: 7, 11, 13, 16   6 AA I
Brentwood School, Brentwood
   Entry age: 11, 16   6 A AA D G I O
Chigwell School, Chigwell   A AA D I O
Colchester High School, Colchester   AA

College Saint-Pierre, Leigh-on-Sea O
Cranbrook, Ilford A AA I O
Crowstone Preparatory School,
 Westcliff-on-Sea O
The Daiglen School, Buckhurst Hill AA
Dame Bradbury's School, Saffron
 Walden Entry age: Bursary from
 Year 3 for children with a specific
 aptitude (ie Art, Sport, Drama) I
Felsted School, Felsted Entry age:
 Ages 11, 13 and 16 6 A AA D G I O
Friends' School, Entry age:
 11, 13, 16 6 A AA G I
Gosfield School, Halstead
 Entry age: All 6 AA G O
Herington House School,
 Brentwood D G I O
Holmwood House, Colchester A AA G I O
Loyola Preparatory School,
 Buckhurst Hill AA
New Hall School, Chelmsford
 Entry age: 3–18 6 AA D G I O
St Aubyn's School, Woodford Green AA
St Hilda's School, Westcliff-on-Sea O
St John's School, Billericay O
St Margaret's School, Halstead
 Entry age: 8+ A AA G I
St Mary's School, Colchester
 Entry age: 11+ O

GLOUCESTERSHIRE

Berkhampstead School, Cheltenham AA G I
Bredon School, Tewkesbury
 Entry age: 5–15 years A AA G I O
Cheltenham College, Cheltenham
 Entry age: 13, 16 6 A AA D G I O S
Cheltenham College Junior School,
 Cheltenham Entry age: 11+ A AA G I
Cheltenham Ladies' College,
 Cheltenham Entry age: 11+,
 12+, 13+ and 16+ 6 A AA G I
Dean Close Preparatory School,
 Cheltenham Entry age: 7+
 scholarship for Year 3 entry; 11+
 scholarship for Year 7 entry; chorister
 awards offered ages 7–11 A AA G I O
Dean Close School, Cheltenham
 Entry age: 11+, 13+, 16+ 6 A AA D G I O
Hatherop Castle School, Cirencester
 Entry age: 7+ AA D G I O
The King's School, Gloucester
 Entry age: Scholarships and
 Bursaries at 11+, 13+, 16+ 6 A AA D G I O
Rendcomb College, Cirencester
 Entry age: 11, 13, 16 6 A AA D G I O
The Richard Pate School, Cheltenham
 Entry age: 7+ AA

Rose Hill School,
 Wotton-under-Edge A AA D G I O
St Edward's School Cheltenham,
 Cheltenham Entry age:
 At Year 7 entry: Means-tested
 Bursary Scholarships, Academic,
 Music and Sport Scholarships.
 At Sixth Form entry: Academic,
 All-rounder, Art, Sport,
 Drama & Music Scholarships 6 A AA D G I O
Westonbirt School, Tetbury 6 A AA D G I O S
Wycliffe College, Stonehouse
 Entry age: 11+, 13+ and
 Sixth Form 6 A AA D G I O
Wycliffe Preparatory School,
 Stonehouse Entry age: 11 A AA D G I

HAMPSHIRE

Alton College, Alton O
Alton Convent School, Alton
 Entry age: 11/16 6 AA I
Ballard School, New Milton Entry age:
 Year 3 and Year 6 A AA G I O
Bedales Prep School, Dunhurst,
 Petersfield AA I
Bedales School, Petersfield 6 A AA I
Boundary Oak School, Fareham AA G I
Brockwood Park School, Bramdean O
Daneshill School, Basingstoke
 Entry age: Scholarship entries
 are available at
 Year 4 (8 years old) and
 Year 7 (11 years old) A AA D G I O S
Ditcham Park School, Petersfield
 Entry age: 11 AA I
Durlston Court, New Milton Entry age:
 Over 7 in September of year of entry A AA G I
Farnborough Hill, Farnborough
 Entry age: Scholarships 11+,16+.
 Bursaries all Year Groups 6 A AA G I
The Gregg School, Southampton A AA I
Hampshire Collegiate School,
 UCST, Romsey 6 A AA D G I O S
Highfield School, Liphook AA
Hordle Walhampton School,
 Lymington AA I O
King Edward VI School, Southampton
 Entry age: 11+, 13+, 16+ 6 A AA D I S
Lord Wandsworth College, Hook
 Entry age: 11+, 13+, 16+ 6 A AA D G I O
Marycourt School, Gosport
 Entry age: 7 O
Mayville High School,
 Southsea A AA D G I
Meoncross School, Fareham
 Entry age: 11 AA
The Pilgrims' School, Winchester I

The Portsmouth Grammar School,
Portsmouth   6 A AA D G I O S
Portsmouth High School GDST, Southsea Entry
age: 11+, 13+, 16+   6 A AA D G I
Prince's Mead School, Winchester   A AA G I
Ramshill School, Petersfield   6 AA I
Rookwood School, Andover   AA G I
St John's College, Southsea   6 AA G I O
St Mary's College, Southampton   AA
St Neot's Preparatory School, Hook   O
St Nicholas' School, Fleet
Entry age: 11, 13   AA I O
St Swithun's School, Winchester
Entry age: 11+, 13+, 16+   6 AA G I
The Stroud School, Romsey   A AA D G I O
Sherborne House School, Eastleigh   A AA G I O
Sherfield School, Hook   6 A AA D G I O S
Winchester College, Winchester
Entry age: 13, 16   6 AA I
Wykeham House School, Fareham   AA
Yateley Manor Preparatory School,
Yateley Entry age: 7+   AA G I O

HEREFORDSHIRE

Hereford Cathedral School, Hereford
Entry age: Scholarships available for entry into
Years 7, 9 and Sixth Form.   6 A AA G I O
Lucton School, Leominster
Entry age: 11, 13, 16   6 A AA D G I O S
St Richard's, Bromyard   AA

HERTFORDSHIRE

Abbot's Hill School, Hemel Hempstead
Entry age: 11   A AA G I O
Aldenham School, Elstree
Entry age: 11, 13, 16   A AA G I O
Berkhamsted School, Berkhamsted   6 A AA G I
Berkhamsted School, Berkhamsted   AA
Bishop's Stortford College,
Bishop's Stortford Entry age:
11+, 13+, 16+   6 A AA G I
Bishop's Stortford College Junior
School, Bishop's Stortford
Entry age: 10+ and 11+ years   A AA I
Edge Grove, Entry age: 7–13 yrs   AA G I O
Haberdashers' Aske's Boys' School,
Elstree Entry age: 11, 13   AA I
Haberdashers' Aske's School for Girls,
Elstree   AA I
Haileybury, Hertford Entry age:
11, 13, 16   6 A AA G I O
Haresfoot Preparatory School,
Berkhamsted Entry age:
Scholarships Year 3 Bursaries from
Reception   A AA D I O

Heath Mount School, Hertford
Entry age: 7+, 11+   A AA I
High Elms Manor School, Watford   AA O
Immanuel College, Bushey
Entry age: 4/11/16   6 A AA I
The Junior School, Bishop's Stortford
College, Bishop's Stortford
Entry age: Academic and Music
scholarships (under 11 and 12),
Art scholarship (under 12)   A AA I O
Lockers Park, Hemel Hempstead
Entry age: From Year 3
(7 years)   A AA D G I O S
The Purcell School, Bushey   I
Queenswood, Hatfield   6 AA D G I
The Royal Masonic School for
Girls, Rickmansworth
Entry age: 7, 11, 16   6 A AA D G I O
St Albans High School for Girls,
St Albans Entry age: Scholarships:
11+ and 16+ Fees Assistance
from 4+ (Reception)   6 AA I O
St Albans School, St Albans
Entry age: 11+, 13+, 16+   6 A AA I
St Christopher School, Letchworth
Garden City Entry age: ages from 11.
Specific Sixth Form bursaries also
available.   6 AA
St Columba's College, St Albans
Entry age: 11+/13+   6 AA I O
St Edmund's College, Ware   6 AA I O
St Edmund's College & Prep
School, Ware Entry age: 7+,
11+ and 16+   6 A AA G I O
St Francis' College, Letchworth
Garden City   6 AA D G I
St Margaret's School, Bushey   6 A AA I O
Stanborough School, Watford   AA G I
Tring Park School for the Performing
Arts, Tring Entry age: From 8–16   6 D
Westbrook Hay Preparatory School, Hemel
Hempstead Entry age: 8+   AA G O

ISLE OF MAN

King William's College, Castletown
Entry age: 11 and 16   6 AA D G I O

ISLE OF WIGHT

Ryde School, Ryde   6 AA I

KENT

Ashford School, Ashford   6 A AA D G I O
Babington House School, Chislehurst AA D G I O

Beechwood Sacred Heart School,
Tunbridge Wells Entry age:
11+, 13+, 16+   6 A AA D G I
Benenden School, Cranbrook
Entry age: 11, 13, 16   6 A AA G I
Bethany School, Cranbrook
Entry age: 11+, 13+, 16+   6 A AA D G I
Bishop Challoner RC School,
Bromley Entry age: 11+   AA I
Bromley High School GDST,
Bromley Entry age: 11/16+   6 A AA G I
CATS College Canterbury,
Canterbury Entry age:
At 6th Form (16+)   6 AA S
Cobham Hall, Gravesend
Entry age: 11+, 13+, 6th Form   6 A AA D G I O
Cranbrook School, Cranbrook   AA I
Darul Uloom London,
Chislehurst   AA G O S
Derwent Lodge School for Girls,
Tonbridge   AA
Dover College, Dover Entry
age: 11, 13, 16   6 A AA G I O
Duke of York's Royal Military School,
Dover   6 A AA G I
Elliott Park School, Sheerness   O
Farringtons School, Chislehurst   6 A AA D G I
Fosse Bank School, Tonbridge   G
Gad's Hill School, Rochester
Entry age: 11   A AA D G I O
Haddon Dene School, Broadstairs   O
Hilden Grange School, Tonbridge   AA I
Holmewood House, Tunbridge Wells
Entry age: Scholarships and
Bursaries available for entry to
Year 3 and above   A AA G I
Kent College, Canterbury Entry
age: 8, 11, 13, 16+   6 A AA D G I O
Kent College Pembury, Tunbridge
Wells Entry age: 11, 13, 16   6 A AA D G I O
King's Preparatory School, Rochester   AA I
King's Rochester, Rochester   6 AA I
The King's School, Canterbury   6 A AA I
Merton Court Preparatory School,
Sidcup   AA D G I O
Northbourne Park School, Deal   AA G I O
Rochester Independent College,
Rochester   6 A AA D I O S
St Christopher's School, Canterbury   O
St Edmund's School Canterbury,
Canterbury Entry age:
11+, 13+, 16+   6 A AA D G I O
St Edmunds Junior School,
Canterbury Entry age: 11   AA G I
St Lawrence College, Ramsgate
Entry age: 8, 11, 13, 16   6 A AA G I O
St Lawrence College Junior School,
Ramsgate Entry age: Scholarships
from age 7.   AA G

St Michael's School, Sevenoaks
Entry age: 7   AA G I O
Sackville School, Tonbridge   6 A AA D G I
Sevenoaks School, Sevenoaks
Entry age: 11+, 13+, 16+   6 A AA G I
Solefield School, Sevenoaks   I
Spring Grove School, Ashford
Entry age: 7+   A AA D G I O S
Sutton Valence School,
Sutton Valence Entry age:
11+, 13+, 16+   6 A AA D G I
Tonbridge School, Tonbridge
Entry age: 13+, 16+   6 A AA D G I O
Walthamstow Hall, Sevenoaks
Entry age: 11+, 13+, 16+   6 A AA D G I
Yardley Court Preparatory School,
Tonbridge   AA O

LANCASHIRE

Arnold School, Blackpool
Entry age: 11+, 16+   6 A AA D G I O
Bury Grammar School Boys, Bury   6 AA
Bury Grammar School Girls,
Bury Entry age: 11   6 AA
Clevelands Preparatory School, Bolton   AA O
Firwood Manor Prep School, Oldham   AA O
Heathland College, Accrington   AA I
The Hulme Grammar School for Girls,
Oldham   AA
King Edward VII and Queen Mary
School, Lytham St Annes
Entry age: 11, 16   6 AA G I
Kingswood College Trust, Ormskirk   AA G I
Kirkham Grammar School,
Preston Entry age:
11 years 16 years   6 AA G I
Queen Elizabeth's Grammar School,
Blackburn Entry age: 11+, 16+   6 AA S
Rossall School, Fleetwood   6 A AA G I O
Rossall School, Fleetwood
Entry age: 11, 13, 16   6 A AA G I O S
Rossall School International Study
Centre, Fleetwood Entry age:
11+, 16+   6 AA G I
St Anne's College Grammar School,
Lytham St Annes   6 AA
St Joseph's School, Park Hill, Burnley   I
St Mary's Hall, Clitheroe   A AA I O
Stonyhurst College, Clitheroe
Entry age: 13, 16   6 A AA I O
Westholme School, Blackburn   6 A AA I

LEICESTERSHIRE

Brooke House College, Market
Harborough   6 A AA G O S

The Dixie Grammar School, Market
    Bosworth Entry age: 10, 11, 14, 16 6 A AA G I
Leicester Grammar School,
    Leicester   6 A AA G I O
Leicester High School For Girls,
    Leicester   6 AA I
Loughborough Grammar School,
    Loughborough Entry age:
    10+, 11+, 13+, 16+   6 AA I
Loughborough High School,
    Loughborough   AA I
Ratcliffe College, Leicester
    Entry age: 11+, 13+, 16+   6 A AA D G I
St Crispin's School, Leicester
    Entry age: 7+, 11+, 13+   AA G
Stoneygate School, Leicester   AA

LINCOLNSHIRE

Copthill School, Stamford Entry age: 11   AA
The Grantham Preparatory School,
    Grantham   I
Kirkstone House School, Bourne
    Entry age: Various   A AA G I O
Maypole House School, Alford   AA O
Stamford High School, Stamford   6 A AA I O
Stamford School, Stamford
    Entry age: 11, 13 and 16   6 A AA I
Witham Hall, Bourne   AA O

NORTH EAST LINCOLNSHIRE

St James' School, Grimsby   6 AA G I O

LONDON

Abercorn School   O
Albemarle Independent College,
    Entry age: 14+, 19+   AA
Alleyn's School, Entry
    age: 11+, 16+   6 A AA D G I O S
Arts Educational Schools London –
    Sixth Form   6 A AA D O
Ashbourne Middle School,
    Entry age: 13/16   6 A AA D O S
Barbara Speake Stage School   O
Belmont (Mill Hill Preparatory School),
    Entry age: Academic and Music 11
    Bursary 10   AA I
Blackheath High School GDST,
    Entry age: 11+/16+   6 A AA G I
Blackheath Preparatory School   AA
Cameron House School, Chelsea   AA
CATS College London, Entry age:
    At Sixth Form (16+); also at 1 yr
    GCSE (15+)   6 AA S

Channing School, Entry age: 11, 16   6 AA I
Chelsea Independent College   AA
City of London School, Entry
    age: 10+, 11+, 13+, 16+   6 AA G I
City of London School for Girls,
    Entry age: 11, 16   6 A AA D I
Colet Court, Entry age: 7+, 8+ and 11+   AA I
Colfe's School, Entry age:
    11+, 13+ and 16+   6 A AA D G I
Connaught House, Entry age: 6, 8   A AA I O
David Game College   AA
Davies Laing and Dick   6 AA O
Devonshire House Preparatory School   AA I
Duff Miller   6 AA D O S
Dulwich College, Entry age: 11, 13, 16 6 A AA G I
Ealing College Upper School   6 AA
Ealing Independent College, Ealing   AA
Eaton House Belgravia, London
    Entry age: 4   O
Eaton House The Manor Pre-Preparatory,
    London   AA O
Eaton House The Manor Preparatory,
    Entry age: 8+   A AA G I O
Eaton House The Vale, London   AA O
Eaton Square School   O
Eltham College, Entry age: 11+, 16+ 6 A AA D G I
Emanuel School, Entry age:
    10+, 11+, 13+, 16+   6 A AA D G I O
Eridge House Preparatory   A AA D
Excelsior College   AA
Fine Arts College, London   6
Forest School   6 A AA D G I S
Francis Holland School, Regent's
    Park NW1   6 AA I
Francis Holland School, Sloane
    Square SW1, Entry age: 11+, 16+   6 AA I
GEMS Hampshire School   AA I O
The Godolphin and Latymer School   I
Hall School Wimbledon
    (Senior School)   A AA D G I O
Hampstead Hill Pre-Preparatory & Nursery
    School   O
Harvington School   D I
Hendon Preparatory School, Hendon   AA O
Highgate School   6 AA I
Hill House International Junior School,
    Entry age: 11   A I
The Hurlingham School, Entry age: 7+   O
Ibstock Place School,
    Entry age: 7+, 11+, 16+   6 A AA D G I O
International Community School   O
The Italia Conti Academy of Theatre Arts   D
James Allen's Girls' School,
    Entry age: 11+, 16+   6 A AA G I
Keble Preparatory School, Entry age: 11 AA G O
King's College Junior School, Entry age:
    Scholarship at 11+ entry
    Bursary at all entry stages   AA
King's College School   6 A AA I

Lansdowne College, Entry age:
14+, 16+   6 AA O
Latymer Prep School   AA
Latymer Upper School   6 A AA D G I
The Lloyd Williamson School   O
Lycee Francais Charles de Gaulle   6 AA
The Lyceum   I
Mander Portman Woodward   6 AA
Mill Hill School   6 A AA D G I O S
More House School, London Entry age:
bursaries from year 7, scholarships
13+ & 6th Form   6 A AA D G I
The Mount School   AA I
Newton Prep, Entry age: from years 3 and 7   AA
Normanhurst School, Entry age: 11   AA
North Bridge House Lower Prep School   AA I
North Bridge House Senior School   I
The North London International School,
London   6 A AA D G I O
Notting Hill and Ealing High School GDST,
Entry age: 11+, 16+   6 AA I
Orchard House School, Entry age: 8+   AA
Palmers Green High School, Entry age: 11+   AA I
Parkgate House School   AA I O
The Pointer School, Entry age: age
7+ for scholarship   AA D G O
Portland Place School   6 A AA D G I
Prospect House School, Entry age:
Academic bursaries available from
Year 3 (aged 7+).   AA O
Putney High School GDST,
Entry age: 11+, 16+   6 A AA D G I S
Queen's Gate School, Entry age:
Bursaries and Scholarships available to
Pupils entering the Senior
School from 11+.   6 A AA G O
Riverston School   AA G I O
The Roche School, Entry age: 7   AA
The Royal School, Hampstead,
Entry age: 7, 16   A AA I
St Augustine's Priory, Ealing   6 I O
St Benedict's School, Ealing
Entry age: 11+, 16+   6 AA G I O
St Christopher's School, Entry age: 4+/5+   O
St Dunstan's College, Entry age:
11+ and Sixth Form   6 A AA D G I
St Margaret's School, Entry age:
Bursary for any age group   AA
St Mary's School Hampstead   A AA G I
St Paul's Cathedral School   I
St Paul's Girls' School   6 A AA I
St Paul's School   6 AA I
Streatham & Clapham High School,
Entry age: 11, 16   6 A AA D G I S
Sinclair House School   O
South Hampstead High School,
Entry age: 11+ and 16+   6 AA I
Southbank International School, Westminster   6
Sussex House School   I

Sydenham High School GDST,
Entry age: 11/16+   6 AA I
Sylvia Young Theatre School,
Entry age: 10–14   D I
Thomas's Preparatory School   O
University College School   AA I
Virgo Fidelis, Entry age: 7–11   AA
Welsh School of London   O
Westminster Abbey Choir School   I
Westminster Cathedral Choir School   I
Westminster School, Westminster   AA I
Westminster Tutors   6 AA O
Westminster Under School, Entry age: 11+   I
The White House Prep & Woodentops
Kindergarten   AA G
Willington School   AA
Wimbledon High School GDST   6 AA I S

GREATER MANCHESTER

Abbey College, Manchester   6 AA
Branwood Preparatory School, Eccles   O
Bridgewater School, Manchester
Entry age: 11/16+   6 AA
Chetham's School of Music, Manchester   I
Manchester High School for Girls,
Manchester Entry age:
Scholarships and Bursaries at 11.
Bursaries at 16.   AA G I
St Bede's College, Manchester   6 AA I

MERSEYSIDE

Avalon Preparatory School, Wirral
Entry age: 7   AA
Birkenhead School, Wirral   6 AA G I O
Kingsmead School, Wirral
Entry age: 7/11+   AA G I
Liverpool College, Liverpool   6 A AA D G I O
Merchant Taylors' Boys' Schools,
Liverpool Entry age: 11   6 AA G
Merchant Taylors' Girls' School,
Liverpool Entry age: 11+ and 16+   6 AA O
Runnymede St Edward's School, Liverpool   I
St Mary's College, Liverpool
Entry age: 11/16+   6 A AA G I
Streatham House School, Liverpool   AA
Tower College, Prescot Entry age: 7, 11   AA I

MIDDLESEX

Buckingham College Preparatory
School, Pinner   AA
Buckingham College School, Harrow   6 AA
Halliford School, Shepperton
Entry age: 11+, 13+ Sixth Form   6 A AA D G I

Hampton School, Hampton
  Entry age: 11, 13, 16   6 A AA G I O
Harrow School, Harrow on the Hill
  Entry age: 13, 16   6 A AA G I
Heathfield School, Pinner   6 AA I
The John Lyon School, Harrow
  Entry age: 11+ and 13+   A AA D G I O
The Lady Eleanor Holles School,
  Hampton   6 AA I
Merchant Taylors' School, Northwood   6 AA I
North London Collegiate, Edgware   6 AA I
Northwood College, Northwood
  Entry age: 11+, 16+   6 A AA G I
St Catherine's School, Twickenham
  Entry age: 11   6 A AA G I
St Helen's School, Northwood Entry age:
  Academic, art, music and sport
  scholarships available at 11+;
  academic, art, drama,
  music and sport scholarship
  available at 16+.   6 A AA D G I
Twickenham Preparatory School, Hampton
  Entry age: Bursaries together with
  Academic, All-Rounder, Sport and
  Music Awards are available for
  boys entering Year 7.   AA G I O

NORFOLK

All Saints School, Norwich   AA I
Glebe House School, Hunstanton   A AA G I O
Gresham's School, Holt Entry age:
  Scholarships – Third Form and
  Sixth Form at the Senior School,
  Bursary also available from
  Year 7 onwards   6 A D G I O
Hethersett Old Hall School, Norwich
  Entry age: Bursaries available
  age 7–18. Scholarships
  available in Years 7–10 and
  Year 12.   6 A AA D G I
Langley Preparatory School & Nursery,
  Norwich   AA I
Langley School, Norwich Entry
  age: 11, 13, 16   6 A AA D G I O
The New Eccles Hall School, Norwich
  Entry age: 8   AA I O
Norwich High School for Girls GDST,
  Norwich   6 AA I
Norwich School, Norwich Entry
  age: 11+, 13+, 16+   6 A AA D G I
Sacred Heart School, Swaffham
  Entry age: 11+   AA
Taverham Hall Preparatory School,
  Norwich Entry age: Age 5–13   AA G I
Town Close House Preparatory School,
  Norwich Entry age: 7+   AA G I
Wood Dene School, Norwich   A AA D

NORTHAMPTONSHIRE

Beachborough School, Brackley
  Entry age: 8–11   AA I O
Bosworth Independent College,
  Northampton   AA O S
Great Houghton School, Northampton   A AA I
Maidwell Hall School   AA G I
Northampton High School, Northampton
  Entry age: 11, 13, 16   6 A AA D G I
Oundle School, Nr Peterborough   6 A AA D I O
Pitsford School, Pitsford   6 A AA D G I
Quinton House School, Northampton   6 AA O
Winchester House School, Brackley   A AA G I O

NORTHUMBERLAND

Longridge Towers School, Berwick-upon-Tweed
  Entry age: 9, 11, 13, 16   6 AA G I
Mowden Hall School, Stocksfield   AA
St Oswald's School, Alnwick   AA O

NOTTINGHAMSHIRE

Coteswood House School,
  Nottingham   A AA D G I O
Grosvenor School, Nottingham
  Entry age: Bursaries age 4 – 13
  Scholarships Yr 4 and Yr 7   AA G I O
Nottingham High School for Girls GDST,
  Nottingham   O
Ranby House School, Retford
  Entry age: 7+, 11+   A AA D G I O
Trent College & The Elms,
  Nottingham   A AA D G I O
Wellow House School, Newark   A AA G I O
Worksop College, Worksop   6 A AA G I O

OXFORDSHIRE

Abingdon Preparatory School, Abingdon   AA
Abingdon School, Abingdon   6 A AA D G I
Christ Church Cathedral School, Oxford   I
Cokethorpe School, Witney Entry age:
  Means-tested scholarships Year 7,
  Year 9 and Sixth Form. Modern
  Languages scholarships are available.
  Means-tested bursaries,
  from 11 to 18   6 A AA D G I O
Cranford House School,
  Wallingford   A AA D G I O
d'Overbroeck's College Oxford,
  Oxford Entry age: 16   A AA D S
Dragon School, Oxford Entry age:
  Bursaries – Yr 4
  Scholarships – Yrs 4, 5, 6, 7   AA

Ferndale Preparatory School, Faringdon AA
Headington School, Oxford
    Entry age: 11, 13, 16   6 A AA D G I
Kingham Hill School, Chipping Norton
    Entry age: 11+, 13+, 6th form   6 A D G I O
Leckford Place School, Oxford   A AA D I
Magdalen College School, Oxford
    Entry age: 11+, 13+, 16+   6 A AA G I O
New College School, Oxford Entry age: 7   I
Our Lady's Abingdon School, Abingdon
    Entry age: 5–17   6 AA I
Oxford High School GDST, Oxford
    Entry age: Year 7, Academic & Music,
    Year 12, Academic, All-Rounder, Art,
    Drama, Music, Sports Year 7 &
    Year 12 entry, Bursaries   6 A AA D G I O
Oxford Tutorial College, Oxford   AA O
Radley College, Abingdon
    Entry age: 13+   6 A AA D I O
St Edward's School, Oxford Entry age: 13+ 16+
    Bursaries for university dons   6 A AA D G I O
St Helen & St Katharine, Abingdon   6 AA I
St Hugh's School, Faringdon   AA
St. Clare's, Oxford, Oxford Entry age: 16+ 6 AA O
Shiplake College, Henley-on-Thames
    Entry age: 13+, 16+   6 A AA D G I
Sibford School, Banbury   6 A AA I
Tudor Hall School, Banbury
    Entry age: 11, 13, 16   A AA D G I
Wychwood School, Oxford   6 A AA I S

RUTLAND

Oakham School, Oakham
    Entry age: 11+, 13+ 16+   6 A AA D G I O S
Uppingham School, Uppingham   6 A AA I O

SHROPSHIRE

Adcote School for Girls, Shrewsbury
    Entry age: Bursaries and
    Scholarships are available
    Junior and Senior Schools.   6 A AA D G I O S
Bedstone College, Bucknell   6 A AA G I O
Concord College, Shrewsbury   6 AA O S
Dower House School, Bridgnorth
    Entry age: 7, 8, 9   AA O
Ellesmere College, Ellesmere   6 A AA D G I O S
Kingsland Grange, Shrewsbury
    Entry age: 7–11   AA G I
Moor Park School, Ludlow   AA O
Moreton Hall School, Oswestry Entry age: Junior
    Scholarships, 11+, 13+, 16+   6 A AA D G I O
The Old Hall School, Telford   AA I
Oswestry School, Oswestry Entry age: 9+, 11+,
    13+, 16+   6 A AA G I O S
Oswestry School Bellan House, Oswestry   AA I O

Packwood Haugh School, Shrewsbury A AA G I
Prestfelde Preparatory School,
    Shrewsbury Entry age: 7+, 11+   A AA G I
Shrewsbury High School GDST,
    Shrewsbury   6 AA I
Shrewsbury School, Shrewsbury 6 A AA D G I O S
Wrekin College, Entry age:
    11, 13, 16   6 A AA G I O

SOMERSET

All Hallows, Shepton Mallet Entry age: 11+   A I O
Bath Academy, Bath Entry age: 16+   6
Bruton School for Girls, Bruton
    Entry age: 11+, 13+, 16+   6 A AA D G I O S
Chilton Cantelo School, Yeovil   O
Downside School, Bath   6 A AA G I O
Hazlegrove, Yeovil Entry age: 7 & 11   AA G I
King's Bruton and Hazlegrove,
    Bruton   6 A AA D G I O
King's College, Taunton   6 A AA D G I O S
King's Hall, Taunton   AA G I
Millfield Preparatory School,
    Glastonbury Entry age: 7–13   A AA G I O
Millfield School, Street
    Entry age: 13, 14, 16   6 A AA G I O
The Park School, Yeovil
    Entry age: 8–18+   6 A AA D I
Perrott Hill School, Crewkerne   A AA D G I O
Queen's College, Taunton Entry age:
    Scholarships available at
    11+, 13+ and Sixth Form entry.
    Music also available at 10+
    and 12+ entry   6 A AA D G I O
Queen's College Junior, Pre-Prep
    & Nursery Schools, Taunton Entry age:
    10+ music scholarship   A AA D G I O
Taunton Preparatory School, Taunton
    Entry age: 11+   AA G I
Taunton School International, Taunton   AA
Taunton School Senior, Taunton   6 AA G I O
Wellington School, Wellington
    Entry age: 10+, 11+, 13+, 16+   6 AA I O
Wells Cathedral Junior School, Wells
    Entry age: 8–11   AA I
Wells Cathedral School, Wells
    Entry age: 11, 13, 16   6 AA I S

BATH & NORTH EAST SOMERSET

King Edward's School, Bath,
    Bath Entry age: 11–18   6 A AA D G I
Kingswood School, Bath   6 A AA D G I O
Paragon School, Prior Park College
    Junior, Bath   AA G I O

Prior Park College, Bath   6 A AA D G I O
The Royal High School, Bath, Bath
    Entry age: 11/16+   6 A AA D G I

NORTH SOMERSET

Sidcot School, Winscombe Entry age:
    Bursary all ages Scholarships at
    Year 7, 9 and Sixth Form   6 A AA D G I O S

STAFFORDSHIRE

Abbots Bromley School, Abbots Bromley
    Entry age: 11/16+   6 A AA D G I O
Chase Academy, Cannock
    Entry age: 3+   6 A AA G I O
Denstone College, Uttoxeter
    Entry age: 11, 13, 16   6 A AA D G I O
Edenhurst School, Newcastle-under-Lyme   O
Lichfield Cathedral School, Lichfield
    Entry age: 7, 9, 11   A AA D G I O
Newcastle-under-Lyme School,
    Newcastle-under-Lyme   6 AA G
St Dominic's Independent Junior School,
    Stoke-on-Trent Entry age: 8+   AA
St Dominic's Priory School, Stone 6 A AA D G I O
St Dominic's School, Stafford
    Entry age: 11, 12   6 A AA D G I
Stafford Grammar School, Stafford 6 A AA D G I O
Vernon Lodge Preparatory School,
    Brewood   AA O
Yarlet School, Stafford
    Entry age: 11+   A AA D G I O

STOCKTON-ON-TEES

Teesside High School, Eaglescliffe   6 AA I
Yarm School, Yarm
    Entry age: 7+, 11+, 16+   6 AA I S

SUFFOLK

Amberfield School, Ipswich
    Entry age: 11/13+   A AA G I
Arbor Preparatory, Bury St Edmunds   AA
Brandeston Hall, The Preparatory
    School for Framlingham College,
    Brandeston Entry age: 11+   A AA D G I
Culford School, Bury St Edmunds Entry age:
    Scholarships 11, 13 and 16.
    Bursaries are also available 6 A AA D G I O S
Fairstead House School, Newmarket Entry age:
    Scholarships offered at the beginning
    of Years 4, 5 & 6   AA G I
Felixstowe International College, Felixstowe AA O

Finborough School, Stowmarket   6 A AA G I O
Framlingham College, Woodbridge
    Entry age: 11+, 13+, 16+   6 A AA D G I O S
Ipswich High School GDST, Ipswich
    Entry age: 11+   6 AA I
Ipswich School, Ipswich
    Entry age: 11, 13, 16   6 A AA G I O
Moreton Hall Preparatory School,
    Bury St Edmunds   AA I
Orwell Park, Ipswich Entry age: 7+   A AA I O
The Royal Hospital School, Ipswich
    Entry age: 11+, 13+ and 16+   6 A AA G I O
St George's School, Southwold   AA I O
St Joseph's College, Ipswich   6 A AA D G I O
Saint Felix School, Southwold
    Entry age: 11, 13, 16   6 A AA D G I
Stoke College, Sudbury   AA I
South Lee Preparatory School,
    Bury St Edmunds Entry age: 8+, 11+   AA O
Woodbridge School, Woodbridge
    Entry age: scholarships and
    bursaries at 11+, 13+ and 16+ 6 A AA D G I O

SURREY

Aberdour, Tadworth   AA
Aberdour School, Tadworth   AA
Amesbury, Hindhead   AA G I
Barfield School and Nursery, Farnham   AA G I O
Box Hill School, Dorking
    Entry age: 11, 13, 16   6 A AA D G I O
Cambridge Tutors College, Croydon   6 AA
Charterhouse, Godalming Entry age: 13+
    Academic, Music, Art, All-rounder,
    Sport.16+ Academic, Music, Art 6 A AA G I O
City of London Freemen's School, Ashtead Entry
    age: Scholarships at 11+, 13+, 16+   6 AA I O
Claremont Fan Court School, Esher
    Entry age: Scholarships Year 3
    Academic, Year 7 Academic and Music;
    Year 9 Academic, Sport (internal only) and
    Music; Sixth Form Academic,
    Sport, Drama, Music and Art 6 A AA D G I
Cranleigh Preparatory School, Cranleigh   AA I
Cranleigh School, Cranleigh
    Entry age: 13+, 16+   6 A AA I O
Croydon High School GDST, South Croydon
    Entry age: Year 7 and 12 only 6 A AA D G I
Cumnor House School, South Croydon   AA G I
Danes Hill School, Leatherhead   AA
Danesfield Manor School, Walton-on-Thames
    Entry age: Year 2 and above.   AA I S
Downsend School, Leatherhead Entry age: 7+
    Scholarships for entry into Year 3.   AA
Duke of Kent School, Guildford
    Entry age: 7+, 10+, 11+   AA G I
Dunottar School, Reigate
    Entry age: 11, 13, 16   6 A AA G I

Edgeborough, Farnham O
Epsom College, Epsom Entry age:
  13+, 16+ 6 A AA D G I O
Essendene Lodge School, Caterham AA O
Ewell Castle School, Epsom
  Entry age: 11+, 13+, 16+ 6 A AA D G I O
Feltonfleet School, Cobham A AA I O
Frensham Heights School, Farnham 6 A AA D G I
Greenacre School for Girls,
  Banstead 6 A AA D G I O
Guildford High School, Guildford 6 AA I
Hampton Court House, East Molesey AA I
Haslemere Preparatory School,
  Haslemere Entry age:
  Entry from Year 2 to Year 7 A AA D G I O
Hawley Place School, Camberley
  Entry age: 7, 11 A AA D G I O
Hoe Bridge School, Woking
  Entry age: 7+ AA O
Homefield School, Sutton A AA G I O
Hurtwood House, Dorking Entry age: 16 6 D O S
King Edward's School Witley, Godalming
  Entry age: 11, 13, 16 6 A AA D G I O S
Kingston Grammar School, Kingston-upon-
  Thames Entry age: 11+, 13+, 16+ 6 A AA G I
Kingswood House School, Epsom AA G
Laleham Lea School, Purley Entry age:
  Entry to Year 1 and Year 2 classes. O
Lanesborough, Guildford Entry age: 7+ I
Lingfield Notre Dame School, Lingfield
  Entry age: 11+ 6 AA I O
Lyndhurst School, Camberley AA
Manor House School, Leatherhead
  Entry age: Scholarships at 11+
  Bursaries at any age A AA D G I
Marymount International School, Kingston-upon-
  Thames Entry age: 11, 16 AA O
Notre Dame Preparatory School, Cobham O
Notre Dame Senior School, Cobham 6 AA
Oakfield School, Woking
  Entry age: 7+, 11+ AA I O
Old Palace of John Whitgift School,
  Croydon AA I
Prior's Field School, Godalming
  Entry age: 11+, 13+ and 16+ 6 A AA D G I O
Reed's School, Cobham 6 A AA D G I O
Reigate Grammar School, Reigate 6 AA I O
Reigate St Mary's Preparatory and
  Choir School, Reigate Entry age: 7+ I
Ripley Court School, Woking A AA D G I O
Rokeby School, Kingston-upon-Thames A AA G I
Royal Grammar School, Guildford
  Entry age: 11+/13+ A AA I
Royal Russell School, Croydon
  Entry age: 11+/16 6 AA D I
The Royal School, Haslemere
  Entry age: 11+, 13+, 16+ 6 A AA D G I O
The Royal School For Girls,
  Haslemere 6 AA D I O S

St Catherine's School, Guildford
  Entry age: 11/16+ 6 A AA G I O
St Edmund's School, Hindhead
  Entry age: 7/8 A AA D G I O
St George's College, Weybridge 6 A AA I O
St Hilary's School, Godalming
  Entry age: Scholarships
  Years 3–6 Bursary Year 3 A AA D I
St Ives School, Haslemere A AA D G I O
St James Independent School for
  Boys (Senior), Ashford I
St John's School, Leatherhead
  Entry age: 13+, 16+ 6 A AA G I O
St Teresa's School, Dorking 6 A AA D G I O
St Andrew's (Woking) School Trust,
  Woking Entry age: 7+ A AA G I O
Seaton House School, Sutton Entry age:
  Form II Founder's Scholarship for entry into
  Form III AA
Sir William Perkins's School, Chertsey
  Entry age: Year 7 Academic,
  Music and Art Scholarship. Sixth Form
  Academic Scholarships. Yr 7 Perkins
  Foundation Bursaries available 6 A AA I
Surbiton High School,
  Kingston-upon-Thames 6 A AA G I
Sutton High School GDST, Sutton
  Entry age: 11+, 16+ 6 A AA D G I O
Tormead School, Guildford 6 A AA I
Trinity School, Croydon
  Entry age: 10+, 11+, 13+, 16+ 6 A AA D G I O
West Dene School, Purley Entry age: 7 I
Whitgift School, South Croydon
  Entry age: 10–13, 16 6 A AA D G I O
Woodcote House School, Windlesham A AA G I O
Yehudi Menuhin School, Cobham I

EAST SUSSEX

Battle Abbey School, Battle
  Entry age: 13/16+ 6 A AA D G I O
Bellerbys College, Brighton 6 AA
Bricklehurst Manor Preparatory, Wadhurst AA
Brighton and Hove High School GDST,
  Brighton 6 AA
Brighton College, Brighton
  Entry age: 13+, 16+ 6 A AA D G I O
Brighton College Prep School,
  Brighton Entry age: 11+ A AA D G I O
Buckswood School, Hastings AA G I
Claremont School,
  St Leonards-on-Sea A AA D G I O
Eastbourne College, Eastbourne
  Entry age: Scholarships for entry into
  Yr 9 and Yr 12 6 A AA D G I
The Fold School, Hove Entry age: 3+ AA I
Lancing College Preparatory School
  at Mowden, Hove Entry age: 7+, 11+ AA

Lewes Old Grammar School, Lewes   6 AA I O
Moira House School, Eastbourne   O
Newlands School, Seaford   6 A AA D G I O
Roedean School, Brighton
    Entry age: 11+, 12+, 13+, 16+   6 A AA D G I S
St Andrew's School, Eastbourne   A AA D G I O
St Aubyn's, Brighton   AA G O
St Aubyns School, Brighton   A AA D G I O
St Bede's Prep School, Eastbourne   A AA D G I
St Bede's School, Hailsham   6 A AA D G I
St Leonards-Mayfield School, Mayfield
    Entry age: 11+, 13+, 16+   6 A AA D G I
Stonelands School of Ballet & Theatre Arts,
    Hove   D O
Vinehall School, Robertsbridge
    Entry age: 8+   A AA D G I O

WEST SUSSEX

Ardingly College, Haywards Heath
    Entry age: 7+, 11+, 13+, 16+   6 A AA D G I O
Ardingly College Junior School,
    Haywards Heath Entry age: 11+   A AA G I
Burgess Hill School for Girls,
    Burgess Hill   6 A AA D G I
Conifers School, Midhurst   A AA G I O
Copthorne Prep School,
    Copthorne   A AA D G I
Dorset House School, Pulborough   AA I
Farlington School, Horsham   6 A AA D G I O
Great Ballard School, Chichester
    Entry age: 7   A AA D G I O
Great Walstead, Haywards Heath
    Entry age: 7–11   A AA D G I
Handcross Park School, Haywards
    Heath Entry age: 7–11   A AA G I O
Hurstpierpoint College,
    Hurstpierpoint   6 A AA D G I O
Oakwood School, Chichester   AA O
Our Lady of Sion School, Worthing
    Entry age: 11 & 16   6 AA
The Prebendal School, Chichester
    Entry age: 7   AA I
Shoreham College, Shoreham-by-Sea   AA G I O
Slindon College, Arundel Entry age: 10   AA O
Tavistock & Summerhill School,
    Haywards Heath   AA
The Towers Convent School, Steyning   AA D I O
Westbourne House School, Chichester   I
Windlesham House School   AA G I O
Worth School, Turners Hill
    Entry age: 11, 13, 16   6 A AA G I O

TYNE AND WEAR

Central Newcastle High School GDST, Newcastle
    upon Tyne Entry age: 11+, 16+   6 AA

Church High School, Newcastle upon Tyne,
    Newcastle upon Tyne Entry age: Bursaries are
    available to pupils from Year 3 to Year 13.
    Bursaries are subject to means testing and
    academic ability.   6 AA I
Dame Allan's Boys School,
    Newcastle upon Tyne   6 AA
Dame Allan's Girls School, Newcastle
    upon Tyne Entry age: 11   6 AA I
The King's School, Tynemouth
    Entry age: 11+   6 A AA I O
Newcastle School for Boys,
    Newcastle upon Tyne   AA
Sunderland High School, Sunderland   6 AA I
Westfield School,
    Newcastle upon Tyne   6 A AA G I O

WARWICKSHIRE

Bilton Grange, Rugby Entry age: Bursary: 4+
    Scholarship: 8+   AA
The Croft Preparatory School,
    Stratford-upon-Avon Entry age: 8   AA
King's High School, Warwick, Warwick   6 AA I
The Kingsley School, Leamington
    Spa   6 A AA D I
Princethorpe College, Rugby
    Entry age: 11/18+   6 A AA G I O
Rugby School, Rugby   6 A AA G I
Warwick School, Warwick   6 A AA I

WEST MIDLANDS

Abbey College, Birmingham   6 AA O
Al Hijrah School, Birmingham   AA
Al-Burhan Grammar School,
    Birmingham Entry age: 11 years old   AA
Bablake Junior School, Coventry   AA
Bablake School, Coventry   6 A AA I O
Birchfield School, Wolverhampton
    Entry age: 4   A AA G I O
The Blue Coat School, Birmingham
    Entry age: 7+   AA I O
Coventry Prep School, Coventry
    Entry age: 7+   A AA I O
Edgbaston High School for Girls,
    Birmingham Entry age: 11+, 16+   6 A AA D G I
Elmhurst School for Dance, Birmingham   6
Highclare School, Birmingham
    Entry age: 11/16+   6 A AA G I O
Hydesville Tower School, Walsall   AA G I O
King Edward VI High School for Girls,
    Birmingham   AA
King Edward's School, Birmingham
    Entry age: Academic and Music
    Scholarships available at 11+, 13+ and 16+.
    Bursaries at 11+ and 16+   6 AA I

King Henry VIII School, Coventry   6 A AA I O
Norfolk House School, Birmingham   AA
Priory School, Birmingham
   Entry age: 11, 16   6 A AA D G I
St George's School, Edgbaston,
   Birmingham Entry age: 11+   6 AA I O
Saint Martin's School, Solihull
   Entry age: 7+, 11+, 16+   6 AA G I
Solihull School, Solihull   6 A AA I S
Tettenhall College, Wolverhampton
   Entry age: 11   6 A AA D G I O
Wolverhampton Grammar School,
   Wolverhampton
   Entry age: 11+, 13+, 16+   6 AA I O S

WILTSHIRE

Chafyn Grove School, Salisbury
   Entry age: Bursary – all ages
   Scholarship – for entry in
   Years 3, 5 and 7   A AA D G I O
Dauntsey's School, Devizes
   Entry age: 11+, 13+, 16+   6 A AA D G I O S
Godolphin Preparatory School,
   Salisbury   AA
The Godolphin School, Salisbury   6 A AA D G I
Grittleton House School, Chippenham Entry age:
   Junior and Senior School   A AA D G I S
Leaden Hall School, Salisbury   AA
Leehurst Swan, Salisbury
   Entry age: 7, 11, 14   A AA G I
Marlborough College, Marlborough
   Entry age: 13+, 16+   6 A AA G I O
Norman Court Preparatory School,
   Salisbury Entry age: 7, 8, 11   A AA D G I O
Prior Park Preparatory School, Cricklade   AA
St Francis School, Pewsey Entry age:
   Scholarships – Age 7+
   Bursaries – Age 9+   A AA G I O
St Mary's Calne, Calne
   Entry age: 11+, 13+, 16+   6 A AA D G I O
Salisbury Cathedral School,
   Salisbury Entry age: 7, 10   A AA D G I
Stonar School, Entry age: Scholarships from
   Year 7 to Sixth Form. Bursaries from Pre-prep.
   Riding Scholarships available.   6 A AA D G I O
Warminster School, Warminster
   Entry age: 7, 9, 11, 13, 16   6 A AA D G I O

WORCESTERSHIRE

The Abbey College, Malvern Wells   6 AA O S
Bromsgrove Preparatory School,
   Bromsgrove Entry age: 11+   AA I O
Bromsgrove School, Bromsgrove   6 A AA D G I O
Dodderhill School, Droitwich Spa
   Entry age: 11+   AA I

The Downs, Malvern, Malvern Entry age:
   Scholarships 11+,
   Bursaries from age 5   A AA D G I O
The Elms, Malvern   AA G I O
Holy Trinity School, Kidderminster   6 AA I O S
King's Hawford, Worcester
   Entry age: 7+, 8+   AA
The King's School, Worcester   6 AA I
The Knoll School, Kidderminster   AA
Malvern St James, Great Malvern
   Entry age: 11+, 12+, 13+, 16+   6 A AA D G I
Moffats School, Bewdley   A AA D G I O S
RGS The Grange, Worcester   AA
RGS Worcester & The Alice Ottley School,
   Worcester   A AA I
St Mary's , Worcester Entry age:
   11+, 16+   6 A AA G I
Saint Michael's College, Tenbury Wells   6 AA O S
Winterfold House, Kidderminster   A AA G I O

EAST RIDING OF YORKSHIRE

Hull Collegiate School, Anlaby
   Entry age: 11   6 A AA G I
Pocklington School, Pocklington   6 AA I O

NORTH YORKSHIRE

Ampleforth College, York
   Entry age: 13, 16   6 A AA D G I O
Ashville College, Harrogate
   Entry age: 11–18   6 A AA D G I
Aysgarth Preparatory School, Bedale
   Entry age: Normally between
   8 and 11 years old   AA G I
Belmont Grosvenor School, Harrogate   AA
Bootham School, York Entry age: Scholarships at
   11+, 13+ Bursaries 11+, 13+   AA I O
Bramcote School, Scarborough   AA G I O
Cundall Manor School, York   AA G I
Fyling Hall School, Whitby   6 AA G I O
Giggleswick Junior School, Settle
   Entry age: 10, 11   AA G I O
Giggleswick School, Settle
   Entry age: 13, 16   6 A AA D G I O
Harrogate Ladies' College, Harrogate
   Entry age: 11+, 16+   6 AA I O
Harrogate Tutorial College, Harrogate
   Entry age: 15+   6 AA O
Lisvane, Scarborough College Junior School,
   Scarborough Entry age: 7–9   AA
Malsis School, Near Skipton Entry age:
   Year 3 and above   A AA D G I O
The Minster School, York   I
The Mount School, York   6 A AA D G I O S
Queen Ethelburga's College, York
   Entry age: 11   6 A AA D G I O S

Queen Mary's School, Thirsk
Entry age: 11+, 12+, 13+ — A AA I
Read School, Selby
Entry age: 11+, 13+, 16+ — 6 AA O
Ripon Cathedral Choir School, Ripon — AA I
St Martin's Ampleforth, York
Entry age: 7/12+ — AA G I O
St Peter's School, York Entry age: 13/16+ — 6 AA I O
Scarborough College & Lisvane School,
Scarborough — 6 A AA I
Terrington Hall, York — A AA D G I O
Woodleigh School, Malton — A AA D G I

SOUTH YORKSHIRE

Birkdale School, Sheffield
Entry age: 11, 16 — 6 AA I S
Hill House School, Doncaster — A AA G I
Rudston Preparatory School, Rotherham — AA
Sheffield High School GDST, Sheffield
Entry age: 11, 16 — 6 AA I O
Westbourne School, Sheffield — AA G I O

WEST YORKSHIRE

Ackworth School, Pontefract — 6 A AA I
Batley Grammar School, Batley — 6
Bradford Girls' Grammar School, Bradford — I

Bradford Grammar School, Bradford
Entry age: 11+ — I
Bronte House School, Bradford
Entry age: 9 — AA
Fulneck School, Leeds — 6 A AA G I O
Gateways School, Leeds
Entry age: 11 — 6 A AA D G I
Ghyll Royd School, Ilkley Entry age: 7 — AA
The Grammar School at Leeds, Leeds
Entry age: 11+, 16+ — 6 AA I
Hipperholme Grammar School, Halifax
Entry age: 16+ — 6 AA
Huddersfield Grammar School,
Huddersfield — AA G I
Moorfield School, Ilkley Entry age:
Bursary from Reception — AA I
Queen Elizabeth Grammar School,
Wakefield — 6 AA I
The Rastrick Independent School, Brighouse
Entry age: 11+ — AA O
Richmond House School, Leeds
Entry age: 7/8 — AA
Rishworth School, Rishworth
Entry age: 11, 16 — 6 AA D G I O
Silcoates School, Wakefield Entry age: 11 — AA I
Wakefield Girls' High School, Wakefield — 6 AA
Wakefield Independent School, Wakefield — AA
Wakefield Tutorial Preparatory School, Leeds — O
Woodhouse Grove School, Apperley
Bridge — AA D G I O

NORTHERN IRELAND

COUNTY ANTRIM

Campbell College, Belfast Entry age: Scholarships
years 8, 9, 10, 11, 12, 13 and 14 — 6 A AA G I
Hunterhouse College, Belfast — AA
Methodist College, Belfast — 6 I

COUNTY TYRONE

The Royal School Dungannon, Dungannon
Entry age: 11–16 — AA G I

SCOTLAND

ABERDEENSHIRE

Albyn School, Aberdeen — A AA G I
International School of Aberdeen,
Aberdeen — 6
Robert Gordon's College,
Aberdeen — 6 AA G I O

ANGUS

High School of Dundee, Dundee
Entry age: 12 — AA
Lathallan School, Montrose Entry age:
Primary 7 and S5 — A AA D G I O

ARGYLL AND BUTE

Lomond School, Helensburgh
    Entry age: 11, 16   6 I

CLACKMANNANSHIRE

Dollar Academy, Dollar Entry age:
    Senior School. Age 12+   6 A AA D G I O S

FIFE

St Leonards School, St Andrews   6 A AA D G I

GLASGOW

Craigholme School, Entry age: 11   AA
The Glasgow Academy, Entry age: 11+   6 AA
The High School of Glasgow   AA
Kelvinside Academy   6 AA

LANARKSHIRE

Hamilton College, Hamilton   AA I

LOTHIAN

Cargilfield, Edinburgh   AA I O
The Edinburgh Academy,
    Edinburgh   6 A AA I
Fettes College, Edinburgh
    Entry age: 11+, 13+, 16+   6 A AA G I O
George Heriot's School, Edinburgh
    Entry age: 11+   6 A AA D I
George Watson's College,
    Edinburgh   6 AA G I S

Loretto Junior School, Musselburgh
    Entry age: 10/11   A AA D G I O
Loretto School, Musselburgh
    Entry age: all age groups
    from 12 years   6 A AA D G I O
The Mary Erskine School, Edinburgh   6 AA I
Merchiston Castle School,
    Edinburgh   6 A AA G I O
St Mary's Music School, Edinburgh
    Entry age: 9+   I
Stewart's Melville College, Edinburgh   6 AA I

MORAYSHIRE

Gordonstoun School, Elgin
    Entry age: 8+ at Junior School
    Entry 13+ at Lower School
    Entry 16+ at Sixth Form Entry   6 A AA D G I O

PERTH AND KINROSS

Ardvreck School, Crieff   AA
Glenalmond College, Perth
    Entry age: 12, 13, 16   6 A AA G I O
Kilgraston, Perth   6 A AA D G I O S
Morrison's Academy, Crieff   6 AA
Strathallan School, Perth Entry age:
    9,10,11,12,13&16   6 A AA D G I O S

ROXBURGHSHIRE

St Mary's Preparatory School, Melrose   G I O

STIRLING

Beaconhurst School   AA

WALES

BRIDGEND

St John's School, Porthcawl   AA G O

CARDIFF

The Cardiff Academy   AA
The Cathedral School, Entry age: 11   AA G I
Howell's School, Llandaff GDST,
    Entry age: 11, 16   6 AA I
Kings Monkton School   6 A AA G I S

CARMARTHENSHIRE

Llandovery College, Llandovery
    Entry age: Year 7 to 12   6 AA D G I O
St Michael's School, Llanelli   6 AA D G I O

CONWY

St David's College, Llandudno
    Entry age: 11   6 A AA D G I O S

DENBIGHSHIRE

Howell's School, Denbigh   6 A AA D G I
Ruthin School, Ruthin
    Entry age: 11 and 16   6 A AA D G I O S

MONMOUTHSHIRE

Haberdashers' Monmouth School For Girls,
    Monmouth   6 AA I
Llangattock School, Monmouth   O
Monmouth School, Monmouth
    Entry age: 11, 13, 16   6 AA G I
St John's-on-the-Hill, Chepstow Entry age:
    External scholarships and bursaries
    available from Year 2   A AA D G I O

NEWPORT

Rougemont School   AA

POWYS

Christ College, Brecon
    Entry age: 11, 13, 16   6 A AA G I O S

SWANSEA

Ffynone House School,
    Entry age: 11   6 A AA D G I

CONTINENTAL EUROPE

Aiglon College, Switzerland   6
Chavagnes International College,
    Chavagnes-en-Paillers, France   6 AA I O

King's College Madrid, Madrid   6
St Columba's College,
    Entry age: 11, 13, 16   AA O

Bursaries and Reserved Entrance Awards

The following is compiled from information provided by schools. For further information please contact the school directly. The abbreviations used are as follows:

E	Christian Missionary or full-time worker	FO	Foreign Office
		H	Financial or domestic hardship
F1	The Royal Navy	M	Medical profession
F2	The Royal Marines	T	Teaching profession
F3	The Army	+	The Clergy
F4	The Royal Air Force		

ENGLAND

BEDFORDSHIRE

Bedford High School for Girls, Bedford	H
Bedford Modern School, Bedford Entry age: 11+	H
Bedford Preparatory School, Bedford	F1 F2 F4 F3 H
Dame Alice Harpur School, Bedford	H
Moorlands School, Luton Entry age: 7+	H T

BERKSHIRE

The Abbey School, Reading Entry age: 11+,13+,16+	H
The Ark School, Reading Entry age: 7	H T
Bearwood College, Wokingham Entry age: 11/13	F1 F4 F3 H +
Brigidine School Windsor, Windsor Entry age: 11, 16	H
Brockhurst and Marlston House Schools, Newbury	E F1 F2 F4 F3 FO H M T +
Cheam School, Newbury Entry age: Bursary from 8 years old	H
Dolphin School, Reading	H T
Downe House, Thatcham Entry age: 11+, 12+, 13+ and 16+	H
Elstree School, Reading Entry age: 7	E H T +
Eton College, Windsor	H
Heathfield School, Ascot	F1 F2 F4 F3 FO H +
Hemdean House School, Reading	H
Highfield School, Maidenhead	H
Horris Hill School, Newbury	F1 F2 F4 F3
Hurst Lodge School, Ascot Entry age: various	F1 F2 F4 F3 H
Lambrook, Bracknell	T
Luckley-Oakfield School, Wokingham Entry age: 11+	F1 F2 F4 F3 H

LVS Ascot, Ascot Entry age: Scholarship Year 7
(11+) and 6th Form. Bursary – HM Forces
bursaries available to boarders from Year 3
(7+). Hardship bursaries available Licensed
Trade Charity members.   F1 F2 F4 F3 H
The Oratory School, Reading
Entry age: 11+, 13+   F1 F2 F4 F3 FO H T
Padworth College, Reading Entry age: 14, 16   H
Pangbourne College, Pangbourne
Entry age: 11+, 13+, 16+   F1 F2 F4 F3 H
Papplewick School, Ascot
Entry age: 6–11   F1 F2 F4 F3 H T
Queen Anne's School,
Entry age: 11+, 13+, 16+   F1 F2 F4 F3 H T +
Reading Blue Coat School, Reading   H T
St Andrew's School, Reading   +
St Gabriel's, Entry age: 11+, 13+, 16+   H
St George's School, Ascot Entry age: 11+, 16+   H
St John's Beaumont, Windsor Entry age: Selected
bursaries are available in every year group on
a means tested basis and granted at the
Headmaster's discretion.   H
St Joseph's College, Reading   H
St Mary's School, Ascot, Ascot
Entry age: 11+, 13+ & 16+   H
St Michaels School, Newbury   H
St Piran's Preparatory School,
Maidenhead Entry age:
Scholarship – Year 3. Bursary any age   H T
Sunningdale School,
Sunningdale   F1 F2 F4 F3 FO T
Upton House School, Windsor   H
Wellington College, Crowthorne   F1 F2 F4 F3 H
White House Preparatory School, Wokingham
Entry age: White House will consider children
for bursaries at all levels of entry.   E H +

BRISTOL

Badminton School, Westbury-on-Trym
Entry age: Scholarships 11+, 13+
and 16+ for academic, music, art and all
round ability. Bursaries are available in
the senior school.   F1 F2 F4 F3 H
Bristol Cathedral School, Entry age: 11+, 13+,
16+   H
Bristol Grammar School,
Entry age: 7, 11, 13, 16   H
Clifton College,
Entry age: 13+, 16+   F1 F2 F4 F3 H T +
Clifton College Preparatory School,
Entry age: 11+   F1 F2 F4 F3 +
Clifton High School, Entry age: 11+, 13+, 16+   H
Colston's Collegiate School,   F1 F2 F3
The Downs School, Wraxall
Entry age: 8+   F1 F2 F3 H +
Fairfield School, Backwell   H
Overndale School, Old Sodbury   H

Queen Elizabeth's Hospital,
Entry age: 11, 13, 16   H
The Red Maids' School,
Entry age: 11+, 13+, 16+   H
Redland High School for Girls,
Entry age: 9, 11, 16   F1 F2 F4 F3 H

BUCKINGHAMSHIRE

Akeley Wood School, Buckingham   H
Ashfold School, Aylesbury   E F1 F2 F4 F3 +
The Beacon School, Amersham Entry age:
Means tested bursary from Year 3   H
Bury Lawn School, Milton Keynes   H
Caldicott School, Farnham Royal   H T
Davenies School, Beaconsfield   H
Gayhurst School, Gerrards Cross   H +
Godstowe Preparatory School, High Wycombe
Entry age: 8, 11   F1 F2 F4 F3 H +
High March School, Beaconsfield
Entry age: 8 and 10   H T
Ladymede, Aylesbury Entry age: 7+   F4 H
Maltman's Green School, Gerrards
Cross Entry age: From Year 1   H
Milton Keynes Preparatory School,
Milton Keynes   H
Pipers Corner School, High Wycombe
Entry age: 11+, 16+   F1 F2 F4 F3 H
St Mary's School, Gerrards Cross
Entry age: 7+/11+/16+ for scholarships,
any age for bursaries   H +
St Teresa's Catholic Independent & Nursery
School, Princes Risborough   H
Stowe School, Buckingham Entry age: 13, 16   H
Swanbourne House School, Milton Keynes
Entry age: 11+   F1 F2 F4 F3 FO H +
Thornton College Convent of Jesus and Mary,
Milton Keynes Entry age: 11   F1 F2 F4 F3 H
Thorpe House School, Gerrards Cross   H T
Wycombe Abbey School, High Wycombe
Entry age: 11+, 13+ and sixth form entry   H

CAMBRIDGESHIRE

Bellerbys College & Embassy CES Cambridge,
Cambridge   H
Cambridge Centre for Sixth-form Studies,
Cambridge   F1 F2 F4 F3 H
CATS College Cambridge,
Cambridge Entry age:
6th Form entry (16+)   F1 F2 F4 F3 H
Kimbolton School, Huntingdon
Entry age: 11+, 13+, 16+   H
King's School Ely, Ely
Entry age: 11+   F1 F2 F4 F3 H +
The Leys School, Cambridge
Entry age: 11, 13, 16   F1 F2 F4 F3 H +

Madingley Pre-Preparatory School, Cambridge   H
MPW (Mander Portman Woodward), Cambridge   H
The Perse School, Cambridge Entry age:
   Year 7 and Year 9 – Academic Scholarship,
   Music Scholarship. Sixth Form – Academic
   Scholarship, Art Scholarship,
   General Award, Music Scholarship.
   Bursaries – all entry points.   H
The Perse School for Girls, Cambridge   H
The Peterborough School, Peterborough
   Entry age: 11, 16   H
St John's College School, Cambridge   H
St Mary's School, Cambridge, Cambridge   H
Sancton Wood School, Cambridge   H T
Wisbech Grammar School, Wisbech   H

CHANNEL ISLANDS

Ormer House Preparatory School, Alderney   H
St George's Preparatory School, Jersey
   Entry age: 7+   H T
St Michael's Preparatory School, Jersey   H +
Victoria College, Jersey   H

CHESHIRE

Abbey Gate College, Chester
   Entry age: 11+, 16+   H
Abbey Gate School, Chester Entry age: 5 and 7   H
Alderley Edge School for Girls, Alderley Edge   H
Beech Hall School, Macclesfield   E H T +
Cheadle Hulme School, Cheadle   H
The Grange School, Northwich   H
Greenbank Preparatory School, Cheadle
   Entry age: Juniors Y3–Y6   H
Hillcrest Grammar School, Stockport   H
Hulme Hall Schools, Cheadle   H T
The King's School, Chester Entry age: 11/16+   H
The King's School, Macclesfield   H
North Cestrian Grammar School,
   Altrincham Entry age: 11–13 & 16   H
Pownall Hall School, Wilmslow   T
The Queen's School, Chester   H
Ramillies Hall School, Cheadle   F1 F2 F4 F3
The Ryleys, Alderley Edge   H
Stockport Grammar School,
   Stockport Entry age: 11+   H
Terra Nova School, Holmes
   Chapel   E F1 F2 F4 F3 H +
Wilmslow Preparatory School,
   Wilmslow Entry age: from 2.5 yrs   H T

CORNWALL

Gems Bolitho School, Penzance
   Entry age: 7+   F1 F2 F4 F3 H T +

Polwhele House School, Truro   H T +
Roselyon, Par   H
St Joseph's School, Launceston
   Entry age: 7+, 11+   H
St Petroc's School, Bude
   Entry age: 7+   F1 F2 F4 F3 H T +
Truro High School, Truro
   Entry age: 11+, 16+   E H +
Truro School, Truro   H +
Truro School Preparatory School, Truro   H

CUMBRIA

Austin Friars St Monica's School, Carlisle
   Entry age: 11+   H
Casterton School, Kirkby Lonsdale
   Entry age: Scholarships 11+, 13+
   and 16+   F1 F2 F4 F3 H T +
Chetwynde School, Barrow-in-Furness   H +
Hunter Hall School, Penrith   H
Lime House School, Carlisle   E F1 F2 F4 F3 FO H T
St Bees School, St Bees Entry age:
   Scholarships 11+/12+ Bursaries
   also available   F1 F2 F4 F3 H +
St Ursulas Convent School, Wigton   H
Sedbergh Junior School, Sedbergh
   Entry age: 11   F1 F2 F4 F3 H
Sedbergh School, Sedbergh Entry age: 13+, 16+,
   17+   E F1 F2 F4 F3 FO H T +
Windermere School, Windermere
   Entry age: 11+, 13+, 16+   H

DERBYSHIRE

Barlborough Hall School, Chesterfield   H
Derby Grammar School, Derby   H
Derby High School, Derby Entry age: 11/16   H +
Foremarke Hall, Derby Entry age:
   7+ and 11+ Scholarships   F1 F2 F4 F3 H T
Michael House Steiner School, Heanor   H
Mount St Mary's College, Spinkhill
   Entry age: 11+, 13+, 15+   F2 F4 F3 FO H
Repton School, Derby
   Entry age: 13+, 16+   F1 F2 F4 F3 H +
S. Anselm's School, Bakewell
   Entry age: 7+   F1 F2 F4 F3 FO +
St Peter & St Paul School, Chesterfield   H
St Wystan's School, Repton Entry age: 7+   H

DEVON

Blundell's School, Tiverton
   Entry age: 11, 13, 16   F1 F2 F4 F3 FO H T
Bramdean School, Exeter
   Entry age: 7/11   FO H
Edgehill College, Bideford   E F1 F2 F4 F3 H +

Exeter Cathedral School, Exeter
  Entry age: 7/12+   H +
Exeter Junior School, Exeter
  Entry age: 7+, 8+   H
Exeter School, Exeter Entry age: 7, 11, 12, 13   H
Exeter Tutorial College, Exeter   H
Kelly College, Tavistock
  Entry age: 11, 13, 16   E F1 F2 F4 F3 H T
Kelly College Preparatory School,
  Tavistock   F1 F2 F4 F3
Kingsley School, Bideford
  Entry age: 11, 12, 13, 16+   F1 F2 F4 F3 H T +
The Maynard School, Exeter
  Entry age: 7+, 9+, 16+   H
Mount House School, Tavistock Entry age:
  Generally in the latter years of the School
  eg Year 7, but all will be considered.   H T
Park School, Totnes   H
Plymouth College, Plymouth
  Entry age: 11, 13, 16   H
Plymouth College Prepratory School, Plymouth
  Entry age: Scholarships 11+, Bursaries are
  means tested   F1 F2 F4 F3 H
St Christophers School, Totnes   H
St Margaret's School, Exeter   E H
St Michael's, Barnstaple   F1 F2 F4 F3 H T +
St Wilfrid's School, Exeter Entry age: 7   H
Sands School, Ashburton   H
Stover School, Newton Abbot Entry age:
  Scholarships 7+, 11+, 13+ & Sixth Form.
  Bursaries usually only in the Senior School.
  Means-tested Scholarships at
  Sixth Form entry   F1 F2 F4 F3 FO H +
Shebbear College, Beaworthy
  Entry age: 11+, 13+, 16+   F1 F2 F4 F3 H +
Tower House School, Paignton Entry age: 11   H
Trinity School, Teignmouth Entry age:
  Entry is considered at all times to
  allow young people to get the
  best education   F1 F2 F4 F3 H
West Buckland Preparatory School,
  Barnstaple   H
West Buckland School, Barnstaple   H

DORSET

Bournemouth Collegiate Prep School,
  Poole Entry age: H
Bournemouth Collegiate School,
  Bournemouth Entry age: Means tested
  bursary at 11+. Scholarships at
  11+, 12+, 13+, 16+   F1 F2 F4 F3 H +
Bryanston School, Blandford Forum
  Entry age: 13, 16   H
Canford School, Wimborne Entry age:
  13+ and 16+   H
Castle Court Preparatory School,
  Wimborne   E H +

Claysemore, Blandford Forum Entry age:
  Prep School: 8 years of age Senior School 13
  years and 16 years of age   F1 F2 F4 F3
Claysmore Preparatory School,
  Blandford Forum Entry age:
  Scholarships from Year 3 and Bursaries are
  offered from reception   F1 F2 F4 F3 H
Dumpton School, Wimborne   H
Knighton House, Blandford
  Forum   F1 F2 F4 F3 H T
Leweston School, Sherborne
  Entry age: 7–13, 16   F1 F2 F4 F3 H
Milton Abbey School, Blandford Forum
  Entry age: 13 and 16   F1 F2 F4 F3 H
The Park School, Bournemouth   H
Port Regis Preparatory School, Shaftesbury
  Entry age: From ages 7 to 12   F1 F2 F4 F3 T
St Martin's School,
  Bournemouth   E F1 F2 F4 F3 H T +
Sherborne Girls, Sherborne   H
Sherborne School, Sherborne
  Entry age: 13+, 16+   F1 F2 F4 F3 H T +
Talbot Heath, Bournemouth   H

COUNTY DURHAM

Barnard Castle School, Barnard Castle Entry age:
  11+ 13+ and Sixth Form   F1 F2 F4 F3 FO H
The Chorister School, Durham   H +
Durham High School For Girls, Durham
  Entry age: 11, 16   H +
Durham School, Durham
  Entry age: 7, 11, 13, 16   F1 F2 F4 F3 H +
Hurworth House School, Darlington   H
Polam Hall, Darlington
  Entry age: 7, 11, 14, 16   F1 F2 F4 F3 H T

ESSEX

Alleyn Court Preparatory School,
  Southend-on-Sea Entry age: 7   H T +
Bancroft's School, Woodford Green
  Entry age: 7, 11, 13, 16   H
Brentwood School, Brentwood
  Entry age: 11, 16   H T
Chigwell School, Chigwell   H T
Dame Bradbury's School, Saffron Walden Entry
  age: Bursary from Year 3 for children with a
  specific aptitude (ie Art, Sport, Drama)   H
Felsted School, Felsted Entry age:
  Ages 11, 13 and 16   F1 F2 F4 F3 H
Friends' School, Entry age: 11, 13, 16   F1 F4 F3
Gosfield School, Halstead Entry age: All   F3 H T
Holmwood House, Colchester   H
Littlegarth School, Colchester   H
New Hall School, Chelmsford
  Entry age: 3–18   F1 F2 F4 F3 H

Park School for Girls, Ilford Entry age:
   20% bursary offered in Year 3 and
   Year 7 only. Means tested.   H
St Hilda's School, Westcliff-on-Sea   H
St Michael's School, Leigh-on-Sea   E T +
St Nicholas School, Harlow   H T
Thorpe Hall School, Southend-on-Sea
   Entry age: 7/11   H
Woodford Green Preparatory School,
   Woodford Green Entry age: 7+   H

GLOUCESTERSHIRE

Berkhampstead School, Cheltenham   H
Bredon School, Tewkesbury
   Entry age: 5–15 years   F1 F2 F4 F3 H
Cheltenham College, Cheltenham
   Entry age: 13, 16   F1 F2 F4 F3 H
Cheltenham College Junior School,
   Cheltenham Entry age: 11+   F1 F2 F4 F3
Cheltenham Ladies' College, Cheltenham
   Entry age: 11+, 12+, 13+ and 16+   H
Dean Close Preparatory School, Cheltenham
   Entry age: 7+ scholarship for Year 3 entry; 11+
   scholarship for Year 7 entry; chorister awards
   offered ages 7–11   E F1 F2 F4 F3 H +
Dean Close School, Cheltenham
   Entry age: 11+, 13+, 16+   E F1 F2 F4 F3 H +
Hatherop Castle School, Cirencester
   Entry age: 7+   F1 F2 F4 F3 H
The King's School, Gloucester
   Entry age: Scholarships and
   Bursaries at 11+, 13+, 16+   H
Rendcomb College, Cirencester
   Entry age: 11, 13, 16   F1 F2 F4 F3 H
Rose Hill School,
   Wotton-under-Edge   F1 F2 F4 F3 H T
St Edward's School Cheltenham, Cheltenham
   Entry age: At Year 7 entry: Means-tested
   Bursary Scholarships, Academic, Music and
   Sport Scholarships. At Sixth Form entry:
   Academic, All-rounder, Art, Sport, Drama &
   Music Scholarships   H
The School of the Lion, Gloucester   E H
Westonbirt School, Tetbury   F1 F2 F4 F3 FO H T +
Wycliffe College, Stonehouse Entry age: 11+, 13+
   and Sixth Form   F1 F2 F4 F3 H T
Wycliffe Preparatory School, Stonehouse
   Entry age: 11   F1 F2 F4 F3 FO H T
Wynstones School, Gloucester   H

HAMPSHIRE

Ballard School, New Milton Entry age:
   Year 3 and Year 6   H
Bedales Prep School, Dunhurst, Petersfield   H
Bedales School, Petersfield   H

Boundary Oak School, Fareham   F1 F2 F4 F3 H
Daneshill School, Basingstoke Entry age:
   Scholarship entries are available at Year 4
   (8 years old) and Year 7 (11 years old)   T
Durlston Court, New Milton Entry age:
   Over 7 in September of year of entry   H
Farleigh School, Andover   F1 F2 F4 F3 H
Farnborough Hill, Farnborough Entry age:
   Scholarships 11+, 16+.
   Bursaries all Year Groups   H
Forres Sandle Manor,
   Fordingbridge   F1 F2 F4 F3
The Gregg School, Southampton   H
Hampshire Collegiate School, UCST,
   Romsey   F1 F2 F4 F3 FO H T +
Highfield School, Liphook   E F1 F2 F4 F3 +
Hordle Walhampton School, Lymington   H
King Edward VI School, Southampton
   Entry age: 11+, 13+, 16+   H
Mayville High School, Southsea   H T
The Pilgrims' School, Winchester   H
The Portsmouth Grammar School,
   Portsmouth   H T
Portsmouth High School GDST,
   Southsea Entry age: 11+, 13+, 16+   H
Prince's Mead School, Winchester   H
Ramshill School, Petersfield   H
Rookwood School, Andover   H
St Neot's Preparatory School,
   Hook   F1 F2 F4 F3 H
St Nicholas' School, Fleet
   Entry age: 11, 13   H
St Swithun's School, Winchester
   Entry age: 11+, 13+, 16+   H
Salesian College, Farnborough   H
Stockton House School, Fleet
   Entry age: 2 years   H
Sherborne House School, Eastleigh   H
Winchester College, Winchester
   Entry age: 13, 16   H
Wykeham House School, Fareham   H

HEREFORDSHIRE

Hereford Cathedral School, Hereford Entry age:
   Scholarships available for entry into
   Years 7, 9 and Sixth Form   H
Lucton School, Leominster
   Entry age: 11, 13, 16   E H
St Richard's, Bromyard   F1 F2 F4 F3

HERTFORDSHIRE

Abbot's Hill School, Hemel Hempstead
   Entry age: 11   H T
Berkhamsted School, Berkhamsted   H
Berkhamsted School, Berkhamsted   H

Bishop's Stortford College, Bishop's Stortford
  Entry age: 11+, 13+, 16+   H
Bishop's Stortford College Junior School,
  Bishop's Stortford Entry age:
  10+ and 11+ years   F1 F2 F4 F3 H
Edge Grove, Entry age:
  7–13 yrs   F1 F2 F4 F3 H T +
Haberdashers' Aske's Boys' School,
  Elstree Entry age: 11, 13   H
Haberdashers' Aske's School for Girls,
  Elstree   H +
Haileybury, Hertford Entry age: 11, 13, 16   H
Haresfoot Preparatory School, Berkhamsted
  Entry age: Scholarships Year 3
  Bursaries from Reception   H
High Elms Manor School,
  Watford   F4 H T
Immanuel College, Bushey
  Entry age: 4/11/16   H
The Junior School, Bishop's Stortford College,
  Bishop's Stortford Entry age: Academic
  and Music scholarships(under 11 and 12),
  Art scholarship (under 12)   H
Lockers Park, Hemel Hempstead Entry age:
  From Year 3 (7 years)   F1 F2 F4 F3 H T
Manor Lodge School, Shenley   H
The Purcell School, Bushey   H
Queenswood, Hatfield   H
Redemption Academy, Stevenage   E H +
Rickmansworth PNEU School,
  Rickmansworth   H
The Royal Masonic School for Girls,
  Rickmansworth Entry age:
  7, 11, 16   F1 F2 F4 F3 H
St Albans High School for Girls, St Albans
  Entry age: Scholarships: 11+ and
  16+ Fees Assistance from 4+
  (Reception)   H
St Albans School, St Albans
  Entry age: 11+, 13+, 16+   H
St Christopher School, Letchworth Garden City
  Entry age: ages from 11. Specific Sixth Form
  bursaries also available.   H
St Columba's College, St Albans
  Entry age: 11+/13+   H
St Edmund's College, Ware   F1 F2 F4 F3 H
St Edmund's College & Prep School,
  Ware Entry age: 7+, 11+ and 16+   H
St Francis' College, Letchworth
  Garden City   H
St Hilda's School, Bushey   H
St Margaret's School, Bushey   F1 F2 F4 F3 H +
Stormont, Potters Bar   H
Tring Park School for the Performing Arts,
  Tring Entry age: From 8–16   F1 F2 F4 F3 H
Westbrook Hay Preparatory School, Hemel
  Hempstead Entry age: 8+   H
York House School, Entry age:
  Pre Prep onwards   H T

ISLE OF MAN

King William's College, Castletown
  Entry age: 11 and 16   F1 F2 F4 F3 H +

ISLE OF WIGHT

Ryde School, Ryde   H

KENT

Ashford School, Ashford   F1 F2 F4 F3 H +
Beechwood Sacred Heart School,
  Tunbridge Wells Entry age:
  11+, 13+, 16+   E F1 F2 F4 F3 FO H M T +
Benenden School, Cranbrook
  Entry age: 11, 13, 16   H
Bethany School, Cranbrook
  Entry age: 11+, 13+, 16+   E F1 F2 F4 F3 H +
Bromley High School GDST, Bromley
  Entry age: 11/16+   H
CATS College Canterbury, Canterbury
  Entry age: At 6th Form (16+)   F1 F2 F4 F3
Derwent Lodge School for Girls, Tonbridge   H
Dover College, Dover
  Entry age: 11, 13, 16   F1 F2 F4 F3
Dulwich Preparatory School,
  Cranbrook, Cranbrook   H
Elliott Park School, Sheerness   H
Farringtons School, Chislehurst   E F1 F2 F4 F3 +
Fosse Bank School, Tonbridge   H
Gad's Hill School, Rochester
  Entry age: 11   H
The Granville School, Sevenoaks   H
Hilden Grange School, Tonbridge   H
Hilden Oaks School, Tonbridge   H
Holmewood House, Tunbridge Wells Entry age:
  Scholarships and Bursaries available for
  entry to Year 3 and above   H
Kent College, Canterbury Entry
  age: 8, 11, 13, 16+   F1 F2 F4 F3 H +
Kent College Pembury, Tunbridge Wells
  Entry age: 11, 13, 16   F1 F2 F4 F3 H +
King's Preparatory School, Rochester   E F1 F2 F4
  F3 H +
King's Rochester, Rochester   F1 F2 F4 F3 H +
Lorenden Preparatory School,
  Faversham   H
Marlborough House School,
  Hawkhurst   H T
The Mead School, Tunbridge Wells   E H +
Merton Court Preparatory School,
  Sidcup   H T
Northbourne Park School,
  Deal   F1 F2 F4 F3 H T +
Rochester Independent College, Rochester   H

St Christopher's School, Canterbury   H
St Edmund's School Canterbury, Canterbury
   Entry age: 11+, 13+, 16+   F1 F2 F4 F3 FO H +
St Edmunds Junior School, Canterbury
   Entry age: 11   F1 F2 F4 F3 FO +
St Joseph's Preparatory School, Gravesend   H
St Lawrence College, Ramsgate
   Entry age: 8, 11, 13, 16   F1 F2 F4 F3 H
St Lawrence College Junior School,
   Ramsgate Entry age:
   Scholarships from age 7.   F1 F2 F4 F3 H
St Michael's School, Sevenoaks
   Entry age: 7   H
Sackville School, Tonbridge   H
Sevenoaks School, Sevenoaks
   Entry age: 11+, 13+, 16+   H
Solefield School, Sevenoaks   H T
Sutton Valence School, Sutton Valence
   Entry age: 11+, 13+, 16+   F1 F2 F4 F3 FO H
Tonbridge School, Tonbridge
   Entry age: 13+, 16+   F1 F2 F4 F3 H
Walthamstow Hall, Sevenoaks
   Entry age: 11+, 13+, 16+   E H +
Yardley Court Preparatory School, Tonbridge   H

LANCASHIRE

Arnold School, Blackpool Entry age: 11+, 16+ H +
Beech House School, Rochdale   H
Bolton School (Boys' Division), Bolton   H
Bolton School (Girls' Division), Bolton
   Entry age: 11+, 16+   H
Bury Grammar School Boys, Bury   H
Bury Grammar School Girls, Bury
   Entry age: 11   H
Heathland College, Accrington   H
The Hulme Grammar School for Girls,
   Oldham   H
King Edward VII and Queen Mary School,
   Lytham St Annes Entry age: 11, 16   H
Kingswood College Trust, Ormskirk   H T
Kirkham Grammar School, Preston
   Entry age: 11 years 16 years   H
Moorland School, Clitheroe   F1 F2 F4 F3
The Oldham Hulme Grammar Schools,
   Oldham   H
Queen Elizabeth's Grammar School,
   Blackburn Entry age: 11+, 16+   H
Rossall School, Fleetwood   F3 +
Rossall School, Fleetwood
   Entry age: 11, 13, 16   F1 F2 F3 +
Rossall School International Study Centre,
   Fleetwood Entry age: 11+, 16+ E F1 F4 F3 H +
St Anne's College Grammar School,
   Lytham St Annes   F1 F2 F4 F3 FO
St Mary's Hall, Clitheroe   H
Stonyhurst College, Clitheroe
   Entry age: 13, 16   F1 F2 F4 F3 FO H M T +

LEICESTERSHIRE

Leicester Grammar School, Leicester   H
Leicester High School For Girls, Leicester   H
Loughborough Grammar School,
   Loughborough Entry age:
   10+, 11+, 13+, 16+   F1 F2 F4 F3 H +
Loughborough High School,
   Loughborough   H
Manor House School, Ashby-de-la-Zouch   H
Ratcliffe College, Leicester Entry
   age: 11+, 13+, 16+   F1 F2 F4 F3 H
St Crispin's School, Leicester
   Entry age: 7+, 11+, 13+   H
Stoneygate School, Leicester   E H +

LINCOLNSHIRE

The Grantham Preparatory School,
   Grantham   H
Kirkstone House School, Bourne
   Entry age: Various   H
Maypole House School, Alford   H
St Hugh's School, Woodhall Spa   F1 F2 F4 F3 T
St Mary's Preparatory School, Lincoln F1 F2 F4 F3
Stamford High School, Stamford   H
Stamford School, Stamford
   Entry age: 11, 13 and 16   H
Witham Hall, Bourne   H T

NORTH EAST LINCOLNSHIRE

St James' School, Grimsby   F1 F2 F4 FO H T +

LONDON

Albemarle Independent College,
   Entry age: 14+, 19+   H
Alleyn's School, Entry age: 11+, 16+   H
The American School in London,   H
Arnold House School,   H
Arts Educational Schools London,   H
Ashbourne Middle School, Entry age:
   13/16 F4 FO H M T + Bales College,   H
Barbara Speake Stage School,   H
Belmont (Mill Hill Preparatory School), Entry age:
   Academic and Music 11 Bursary 10   H
Blackheath High School GDST,
   Entry age: 11+/16+   H
CATS College London, Entry age:
   At Sixth Form (16+); also at 1 yr
   GCSE (15+)   F1 F2 F4 F3 FO
The Cavendish School,   H
Channing School, Entry age: 11 16   H
City of London School,
   Entry age: 10+, 11+, 13+, 16+   H T

City of London School for Girls,
    Entry age: 11, 16   H
Colet Court, Entry age: 7+, 8+ and 11+   H
Colfe's School, Entry age: 11+, 13+ and 16+   H
Collingham Independent GCSE and
    Sixth Form College,   FO H T
Dallington School,   H
Davies Laing and Dick,   H
Dolphin School (Including Noah's Ark Nursery
    School),   H
Duff Miller,   H M
Dulwich College, Entry age: 11, 13, 16   H
Dulwich College Preparatory School,
    Entry age: 7 or 8 years old   H
Durston House, London Entry age:
    7–12 years old   H
Ealing College Upper School,   H
Eaton House Belgravia, London
    Entry age: 4   H T
Eaton House The Manor Preparatory,
    Entry age: 8+   H T
Eltham College, Entry age: 11+, 16+   E H
Emanuel School, Entry age: 10+, 11+, 13+, 16+ H
Fine Arts College, London   H
Forest School,   H +
Francis Holland School, Regent's Park NW1,   E
Francis Holland School, Sloane Square SW1,
    Entry age: 11+, 16+   E FO H +
Garden House School,   H
The Godolphin and Latymer School,   H
The Hall School,   H
Hampstead Hill Pre-Preparatory & Nursery
    School,   H
Hereward House School,   +
Highgate School,   H
Hill House International Junior School,
    Entry age: 11   T
The Hurlingham School, Entry age: 7+   H
Ibstock Place School, Entry age: 7+, 11+, 16+   H
James Allen's Girls' School,
    Entry age: 11+, 16+   H
Kerem School,   H
King Fahad Academy,   H
King's College Junior School, Entry age:
    Scholarship at 11+ entry Bursary at all entry
    stages   H
King's College School,   H
Knightsbridge School, Entry age: 11   H
Lansdowne College, Entry age: 14+, 16+   H
Latymer Upper School,   H
Mander Portman Woodward,   FO T
Mander Portman Woodward, London   H T
Mill Hill School,   H
More House School, London Entry age: bursaries
    from year 7, scholarships 13+ & 6th Form   H
Naima Jewish Preparatory School,   H
Newton Prep, Entry age: from years 3 and 7   H
The North London International School, London H
The Norwegian School,   F1 F2 F4 F3 FO

Notting Hill and Ealing High School GDST,
    Entry age: 11+, 16+   H
Palmers Green High School, Entry age: 11+   H
The Pointer School, Entry age:
    age 7+ for scholarship   E F1 F2 F4 F3 H +
Putney High School GDST, Entry age: 11+, 16+ H
Queen's Gate School, Entry age: Bursaries and
    Scholarships available to Pupils entering the
    Senior School from 11+   H
Redcliffe School,   H
Riverston School,   H +
The Roche School, Entry age: 7   H
Royal Ballet School,   H
The Royal School, Hampstead,
    Entry age: 7, 16   F1 F4 F3 H
St Augustine's Priory, Ealing   H
St Benedict's School, Ealing
    Entry age: 11+ 16+   H
St Dunstan's College, Entry age:
    11+ and Sixth Form   H
St James Junior School, Entry age:
    From Reception Class where applicable   H
St James Senior Girls' School,   H
St Johns Wood Pre-Preparatory School,   H
St Margaret's School, Entry age:
    Bursary for any age group   H
St Mary's School Hampstead,   H
St Paul's Cathedral School,   H
St Paul's Girls' School,   H
St Paul's School,   H
Streatham & Clapham High School,
    Entry age: 11, 16   H
Sarum Hall,   H
Sinclair House School,   H
South Hampstead High School,
    Entry age: 11+ and 16+   H
Sussex House School,   E T +
Sydenham High School GDST,
    Entry age: 11/16+   H
Sylvia Young Theatre School,
    Entry age: 10–14   H
Thames Christian College,   E +
University College School,   H
Westminster Cathedral Choir School,   H
Westminster School, Westminster   H
Westminster Tutors,   H
Westminster Under School, Entry age: 11+   H
The White House Prep & Woodentops
    Kindergarten,   H
Willington School,   H

GREATER MANCHESTER

Abbey College, Manchester   M
Bridgewater School, Manchester Entry age:
    11/16+   H
The Manchester Grammar School,
    Manchester   H

Manchester High School for Girls, Manchester
   Entry age: Scholarships and Bursaries at 11.
   Bursaries at 16.   H
Monton Prep School with Montessori Nurseries,
   Eccles   H T
St Bede's College, Manchester   H
Withington Girls' School, Manchester
   Entry age: 11–18   H

MERSEYSIDE

Avalon Preparatory School, Wirral Entry age: 7   H
Birkenhead School, Wirral   H
Highfield School, Birkenhead   H
Kingsmead School, Wirral
   Entry age: 7/11+   E F1 F2 F4 F3 H +
Liverpool College,
   Liverpool   E F1 F2 F4 F3 H M +
Merchant Taylors' Boys' Schools, Liverpool
   Entry age: 11   H
Merchant Taylors' Girls' School, Liverpool
   Entry age: 11+ and 16+   H
St Mary's College, Liverpool Entry age: 11/16+   H
Streatham House School, Liverpool   H
Sunnymede School, Southport   H T
Tower College, Prescot Entry age: 7, 11   E

MIDDLESEX

Alpha Preparatory School, Harrow   T
Halliford School, Shepperton Entry age:
   11+ 13+ Sixth Form   H
Hampton School, Hampton
   Entry age: 11, 13, 16   H
Harrow School, Harrow on the Hill
   Entry age: 13, 16   H +
Heathfield School, Pinner   H
The John Lyon School, Harrow
   Entry age: 11+ and 13+   H
The Lady Eleanor Holles School, Hampton   H
The Mall School, Twickenham
   Entry age: 7+/8+   H
Merchant Taylors' School, Northwood   H
Newland House School, Twickenham   H
North London Collegiate, Edgware   H
Northwood College, Northwood
   Entry age: 11+, 16+   H
Quainton Hall School, Harrow   H T +
St Helen's School, Northwood
   Entry age: Academic, art, music and sport
   scholarships available at 11+; academic, art,
   drama, music and sport scholarship available
   at 16+.   F1 F2 F4 F3 H
St John's Northwood, Northwood   H
Staines Preparatory School, Staines
   Entry age: Reception through to
   Year 6 only.   H

Twickenham Preparatory School, Hampton
   Entry age: Bursaries together with Academic,
   All-Rounder, Sport and Music Awards are
   available for boys entering Year 7.   H

NORFOLK

Beeston Hall School, Cromer Entry age:
   All ages considered   F1 F2 F4 F3 H
Glebe House School, Hunstanton   T +
Gresham's School, Holt Entry age:
   Scholarships – Third Form and
   Sixth Form at the Senior School,
   Bursary also available from
   Year 7 onwards   F1 F2 F4 F3
Hethersett Old Hall School, Norwich
   Entry age: Bursaries available age 7–18.
   Scholarships available in
   Years 7–10 and Year 12.   F1 F4 F3 H +
Langley Preparatory School & Nursery,
   Norwich   F1 F2 F4 F3 H
Langley School, Norwich
   Entry age: 11, 13, 16   E F1 F2 F4 F3 FO H
The New Eccles Hall School, Norwich
   Entry age: 8   F1 F2 F4 F3 H +
Norwich High School for Girls GDST,
   Norwich   H
Norwich School, Norwich
   Entry age: 11+, 13+, 16+   H
Riddlesworth Hall, Diss   F1 F2 F4 F3 H
Sacred Heart School, Swaffham
   Entry age: 11+   E H T
Taverham Hall Preparatory School,
   Norwich Entry age:
   Age 5–13   F1 F2 F4 F3 H +
Thetford Grammar School,
   Thetford Entry age: 16+   H
Town Close House Preparatory School, Norwich
   Entry age: 7+   H
Wood Dene School, Norwich   H

NORTHAMPTONSHIRE

Beachborough School, Brackley
   Entry age: 8–11   H
Bosworth Independent College,
   Northampton   F1 F2 F4 F3 H
Great Houghton School, Northampton   H
Maidwell Hall School,   F1 F2 F4 F3 H
Northampton High School, Northampton
   Entry age: 11, 13, 16   H
Oundle School, Nr Peterborough   H T
Pitsford School, Pitsford   H +
Quinton House School, Northampton   H
St Peter's School, Kettering   H
Spratton Hall, Northampton
   Entry age: 7/8   H T +

NORTHUMBERLAND

Longridge Towers School, Berwick-upon-Tweed
    Entry age: 9, 11, 13, 16   F1 F2 F4 F3 H
Mowden Hall School, Stocksfield F1 F2 F4 F3 H T
St Oswald's School, Alnwick   E H T

NOTTINGHAMSHIRE

Greenholme School, Nottingham   F1 F2 F4 F3 +
Grosvenor School, Nottingham Entry age:
    Bursaries age 4–13 Scholarships
    Yr 4 and Yr 7   F1 F2 F4 F3 H +
The King's School, Nottingham   H
Nottingham High School for Girls GDST,
    Nottingham   H
Ranby House School, Retford
    Entry age: 7+, 11+   F1 F2 F4 F3 H
Trent College & The Elms,
    Nottingham   F1 F2 F4 F3 H
Wellow House School, Newark   H
Worksop College, Worksop   F1 F2 F4 F3 H +

OXFORDSHIRE

Abingdon Preparatory School, Abingdon   H
Abingdon School, Abingdon   H
The Carrdus School, Banbury
    Entry age: 3/11   H T
Cherwell College, Oxford   F1 F2 F3 H
Cokethorpe School, Witney Entry age:
    Means-tested scholarships Year 7,
    Year 9 and Sixth Form. Modern
    Languages scholarships are available.
    Means-tested bursaries, from 11 to 18   H
Cranford House School, Wallingford   H T
Dragon School, Oxford Entry age:
    Bursaries – Yr 4 Scholarships – Yrs 4, 5, 6, 7 H
Emmanuel Christian School, Oxford
    Entry age: 5   H
Headington School, Oxford
    Entry age: 11, 13, 16   F1 F2 F4 F3 H +
Kingham Hill School, Chipping Norton Entry age:
    11+, 13+, 6th form   E F1 F2 F4 F3 FO H +
Magdalen College School,
    Oxford Entry age: 11+, 13+, 16+   H
The Manor Preparatory School,
    Abingdon Entry age: All age groups   H
The Oratory Preparatory School,
    Reading   F1 F2 F4 F3 H
Our Lady's Abingdon School, Abingdon
    Entry age: 5–17   H
Oxford High School GDST, Oxford Entry age:
    Year 7, Academic & Music, Year 12,
    Academic, All-Rounder, Art, Drama, Music,
    Sports Year 7 & Year 12 entry, Bursaries   H

Oxford Tutorial College, Oxford   H
Radley College, Abingdon Entry age: 13+ H +
St Andrew's, Wantage   H
St Edward's School, Oxford
    Entry age: 13+ 16+ Bursaries for university
    dons   +
St Helen & St Katharine, Abingdon   H
St Hugh's School, Faringdon   F1 F2 F4 F3 H
St. Clare's, Oxford, Oxford Entry age: 16+   H
Shiplake College, Henley-on-Thames
    Entry age: 13+, 16+   H
Sibford School, Banbury   H
Tudor Hall School, Banbury
    Entry age: 11, 13, 16   H
Wychwood School, Oxford   H

RUTLAND

Oakham School, Oakham Entry age: 11+, 13+
    16+   H
Uppingham School, Uppingham   H

SHROPSHIRE

Adcote School for Girls, Shrewsbury
    Entry age: Bursaries and
    Scholarships are available Junior and Senior
    Schools.   E F1 F2 F4 F3 FO H M T +
Bedstone College, Bucknell   F1 F2 F3 H
Castle House School, Newport Entry age:
    Kindergarten (Reception) year or any age
    up to Year 6. Means tested bursaries
    available on application.   H
Concord College, Shrewsbury   H
Dower House School, Bridgnorth
    Entry age: 7, 8, 9   H
Ellesmere College,
    Ellesmere   F1 F2 F4 F3 FO H T +
Kingsland Grange, Shrewsbury
    Entry age: 7–11   H T
Moor Park School, Ludlow   F1 F2 F4 F3 H
Moreton Hall School, Oswestry
    Entry age: Junior Scholarships,
    11+, 13+, 16+   E F1 F2 F4 F3 FO H T
Oswestry School, Oswestry
    Entry age: 9+, 11+, 13+, 16+ F1 F2 F4 F3 H T
Oswestry School Bellan House,
    Oswestry   F1 F2 F4 F3 T +
Packwood Haugh School,
    Shrewsbury   F1 F2 F4 F3 H T +
Prestfelde Preparatory School, Shrewsbury
    Entry age: 7+, 11+   H T +
Shrewsbury High School GDST,
    Shrewsbury   H
Shrewsbury School, Shrewsbury   H
Wrekin College,
    Entry age: 11, 13, 16   F1 F2 F4 F3 FO H T

SOMERSET

All Hallows, Shepton Mallet
    Entry age: 11+   F1 F2 F4 F3 FO H
Bruton School for Girls, Bruton
    Entry age: 11+, 13+, 16+   F1 F2 F4 F3 H
Chard School, Chard   H
Downside School, Bath   F3 H
Hazlegrove, Yeovil
    Entry age: 7 & 11   F1 F2 F4 F3 H
King's Bruton and Hazlegrove,
    Bruton   F1 F2 F4 F3 H +
King's College, Taunton   E F1 F2 F3 H +
King's Hall, Taunton   F1 F2 F4 F3 +
Millfield Preparatory School, Glastonbury
    Entry age: 7–13   F1 F4 H
Millfield School, Street
    Entry age: 13, 14, 16   F1 F2 F4 F3 H
The Park School, Yeovil
    Entry age: 8–18+   E F1 F2 F4 F3 +
Perrott Hill School,
    Crewkerne   F1 F2 F4 F3 FO H T +
Queen's College, Taunton Entry age:
    Scholarships available at
    11+, 13+ and Sixth Form entry.
    Music also available at
    10+ and 12+ entry   F1 F2 F4 F3 H
Queen's College Junior, Pre-Prep & Nursery
    Schools, Taunton Entry age: 10+ music
    scholarship   H
Taunton Preparatory School, Taunton
    Entry age: 11+   F1 F2 F4 F3 H +
Taunton School Senior,
    Taunton   E F1 F2 F4 F3
Wellington School,
    Wellington Entry age:
    10+, 11+, 13+, 16+   F1 F2 F4 F3 H T
Wells Cathedral Junior School, Wells
    Entry age: 8–11   H +
Wells Cathedral School, Wells
    Entry age: 11, 13, 16   F1 F2 F4 F3 H

BATH & NORTH EAST SOMERSET

King Edward's School, Bath, Bath
    Entry age: 11–18   H
Kingswood Preparatory School, Bath
    Entry age: 7+   F1 F2 F4 F3 +
Kingswood School,
    Bath   E F1 F2 F4 F3 FO H +
Paragon School, Prior Park College
    Junior, Bath   H
Prior Park College, Bath   F1 F2 F4 F3 H
The Royal High School, Bath, Bath
    Entry age: 11/16+   F1 F2 F4 F3 H

NORTH SOMERSET

Sidcot School, Winscombe Entry age:
    Bursary all ages Scholarships at
    Year 7, 9 and Sixth Form   H

STAFFORDSHIRE

Abbots Bromley School, Abbots Bromley
    Entry age: 11/16+   F1 F4 F3 H +
Abbotsholme School, Uttoxeter   F1 F2 F4 F3 FO
Brooklands School & Little Brooklands Nursery,
    Stafford Entry age: Any   H
Chase Academy, Cannock
    Entry age: 3+   F1 F2 F4 F3 H
Denstone College, Uttoxeter
    Entry age: 11, 13, 16   F1 F2 F4 F3 H T +
Edenhurst School, Newcastle-under-Lyme T +
Lichfield Cathedral School, Lichfield
    Entry age: 7, 9, 11   F1 F2 F4 F3 H +
Newcastle-under-Lyme School,
    Newcastle-under-Lyme   H
St Dominic's Priory School, Stone   H
St Dominic's School, Stafford
    Entry age: 11, 12   H
St Joseph's Preparatory School, Stoke-on-Trent
    Entry age: 3   H
Stafford Grammar School, Stafford   H
Yarlet School, Stafford Entry age: 11+   H T
The Yarlet Schools, Stafford   F1 F4 F3 T +

STOCKTON-ON-TEES

Teesside High School, Eaglescliffe   H
Yarm School, Yarm Entry age: 7+, 11+, 16+ H

SUFFOLK

Amberfield School, Ipswich Entry age: 11/13+ H
Barnardiston Hall Preparatory School,
    Haverhill   F1 F2 F4 F3 +
Brandeston Hall, The Preparatory School for
    Framlingham College, Brandeston
    Entry age: 11+   F1 F2 F4 F3 H
Culford School, Bury St Edmunds
    Entry age: Scholarships
    11, 13 and 16. Bursaries
    are also available   E F1 F2 F4 F3 H T +
Fairstead House School, Newmarket
    Entry age: Scholarships offered at
    the beginning of Years 4, 5 & 6   H
Framlingham College, Woodbridge
    Entry age: 11+ 13+ 16+   F1 F2 F4 F3 H
Ipswich High School GDST, Ipswich
    Entry age: 11+   H

Ipswich School, Ipswich
  Entry age: 11, 13, 16   F1 F4 F3 H
Moreton Hall Preparatory School,
  Bury St Edmunds   F1 F2 F4 F3 H T
Old Buckenham Hall School,
  Ipswich   E F1 F2 F4 F3 +
Orwell Park, Ipswich
  Entry age: 7+   F1 F2 F4 F3 H T
The Royal Hospital School, Ipswich
  Entry age: 11+, 13+ and 16+   F1 F2 F4 F3
St George's School, Southwold   H T
St Joseph's College, Ipswich   F1 F2 F4 F3 H
Saint Felix School, Southwold
  Entry age: 11, 13, 16   F1 F4 F3 FO H T
Stoke College, Sudbury   H
Woodbridge School, Woodbridge
  Entry age: scholarships and bursaries
  at 11+, 13+ and 16+   H

SURREY

Aberdour, Tadworth   H
Aberdour School, Tadworth   T +
Aldro School, Godalming   E F1 F2 F4 F3 H +
Amesbury, Hindhead   T
Barfield School and Nursery,
  Farnham   F1 F2 F4 F3 H
Barrow Hills School, Godalming   H
Bishopsgate School, Egham   H
Box Hill School, Dorking
  Entry age: 11, 13, 16   F1 F2 F4 F3 H
Bramley School, Tadworth Entry age: 7+   H
Cambridge Tutors College, Croydon   H
Caterham Preparatory School, Caterham   +
Charterhouse, Godalming Entry age: 13+
  Academic, Music, Art, All-rounder,
  Sport.16+ Academic, Music, Art   H
Cranleigh School, Cranleigh
  Entry age: 13+, 16+   F1 F2 F4 F3 H T +
Croydon High School GDST, South Croydon
  Entry age: Year 7 and 12 only   H
Drayton House School, Guildford   H
Duke of Kent School, Guildford
  Entry age: 7+, 10+, 11+   F1 F2 F4 F3
Dunottar School, Reigate Entry age: 11, 13, 16 H
Edgeborough, Farnham   F1 F2 F4 F3 H
Epsom College, Epsom Entry age: 13+, 16+   M
Essendene Lodge School, Caterham   H
Ewell Castle School, Epsom
  Entry age: 11+, 13+, 16+   H
Feltonfleet School, Cobham   H
Frensham Heights School, Farnham   H
Glenesk School, Leatherhead   H
Greenacre School for Girls, Banstead   H
Guildford High School, Guildford   H +
Halstead Preparatory School, Woking   H
Haslemere Preparatory School, Haslemere
  Entry age: Entry from Year 2 to Year 7   T

Hawley Place School, Camberley
  Entry age: 7, 11   H
The Hawthorns School, Redhill   H +
Hoe Bridge School, Woking Entry age: 7+   H
Homefield School, Sutton   H
King Edward's School Witley, Godalming
  Entry age: 11, 13, 16   E F1 F2 F4 F3 H T +
King's House School, Richmond   H
Kingston Grammar School, Kingston-upon-
  Thames Entry age: 11+, 13+, 16+   H
Kingswood House School, Epsom   H T +
Laleham Lea School, Purley Entry age:
  Entry to Year 1 and Year 2 classes.   H
Lingfield Notre Dame School, Lingfield
  Entry age: 11+   H
Lyndhurst School, Camberley   H
Manor House School, Leatherhead
  Entry age: Scholarships at 11+
  Bursaries at any age   H
Marymount International School,
  Kingston-upon-Thames Entry age: 11, 16   H
Notre Dame Preparatory School, Cobham   H
Oakfield School, Woking
  Entry age: 7+, 11+   H T
Oakwood School & Nursery, Purley   H
Parkside School, Cobham   H
Prior's Field School, Godalming
  Entry age: 11+, 13+ and 16+   F1 F2 F4 F3 H T
Priory Preparatory School, Banstead   T
Redehall Preparatory School, Horley
  Entry age: Charity Bursary   H
Reed's School, Cobham   H
Reigate Grammar School, Reigate   H
Reigate St Mary's Preparatory and
  Choir School, Reigate Entry age: 7+   H
Ripley Court School, Woking   H T
Royal Alexandra and Albert School, Reigate   H +
Royal Grammar School, Guildford
  Entry age: 11+/13+   H
Royal Russell School, Croydon
  Entry age: 11+/16   F1 F2 F4 F3 H
The Royal School, Haslemere
  Entry age: 11+, 13+, 16+   F1 F2 F4 F3 H T
The Royal School For Girls, Haslemere   F1 F2 H
St Catherine's School, Guildford
  Entry age: 11/16+   H
St David's School, Purley   H
St Edmund's School, Hindhead
  Entry age: 7/8   F1 F2 F4 F3 H T
St Hilary's School, Godalming Entry age:
  Scholarships Years 3–6 Bursary Year 3   H
St Ives School, Haslemere   H
St James Independent School for
  Boys (Senior), Ashford   H
St John's School, Leatherhead
  Entry age: 13+, 16+   +
St Teresa's School, Dorking   F1 F2 F4 F3 H T
St. Andrew's (Woking) School Trust,
  Woking Entry age: 7+   H

Shrewsbury House School, Surbiton   T
Sir William Perkins's School, Chertsey
   Entry age: Year 7 Academic,
   Music and Art Scholarship. Sixth Form
   Academic Scholarships. Yr 7 Perkins
   Foundation Bursaries available   H
Surbiton High School, Kingston-upon-Thames   H +
Sutton High School GDST, Sutton
   Entry age: 11+, 16+   H
TASIS The American School in England,
   Thorpe   H
Trinity School, Croydon Entry age:
   10+, 11+, 13+, 16+   H
Warlingham Park School, Croydon   H
Whitgift School, South Croydon
   Entry age: 10–13, 16   H
Woodcote House School, Windlesham   H T
Yehudi Menuhin School, Cobham   H

EAST SUSSEX

Ashdown House School, Forest Row   T +
Battle Abbey School, Battle
   Entry age: 13/16+   F1 F2 F4 F3 H T
Bricklehurst Manor Preparatory,
   Wadhurst   H
Brighton and Hove High School GDST,
   Brighton   H
Brighton College, Brighton
   Entry age: 13+, 16+   F3 H T +
Buckswood School, Hastings   F1 F2 F4 F3 FO H
Eastbourne College, Eastbourne
   Entry age: Scholarships for entry into
   Yr 9 and Yr 12   F1 F4 F3 FO H
The Fold School, Hove Entry age: 3+   H
Greenfields Independent Day and Boarding
   School, Forest Row   H
Lancing College Preparatory School at
   Mowden, Hove Entry age: 7+, 11+   H +
Michael Hall (Steiner Waldorf School),
   Forest Row Entry age: On entry to
   Kindergarten (age 3/4)   H
Moira House School, Eastbourne   H T
Newlands School, Seaford   F1 F2 F4 F3
Roedean School, Brighton Entry age:
   11+, 12+, 13+, 16+   F1 F2 F4 F3 FO H +
St Andrew's School, Eastbourne   F1 F2 F4 F3
St Aubyn's, Brighton   T +
St Aubyns School, Brighton   H T +
St Bede's Prep School,
   Eastbourne   F1 F2 F4 F3 H
St Bede's School, Hailsham   F1 F2 F4 F3 H +
St Leonards-Mayfield School, Mayfield
   Entry age: 11+, 13+, 16+   F1 F2 F4 F3 FO H
Sacred Heart R.C. Primary School,
   Wadhurst   H
Vinehall School, Robertsbridge
   Entry age: 8+   F1 F2 F4 F3 H

WEST SUSSEX

Ardingly College, Haywards Heath
   Entry age: 7+, 11+, 13+, 16+   H +
Ardingly College Junior School,
   Haywards Heath Entry age: 11+   H
Burgess Hill School for Girls, Burgess Hill   H
Christ's Hospital, Horsham   F1 F2 F4 H +
Conifers School, Midhurst   H T
Copthorne Prep School, Copthorne   H T
Cottesmore School, Pease Pottage   H
Dorset House School, Pulborough   H T +
Farlington School, Horsham   F1 F2 F3 H +
Fonthill Lodge, East Grinstead   H
Great Ballard School, Chichester
   Entry age: 7   F1 F2 F4 F3
Great Walstead, Haywards Heath
   Entry age: 7–11   E H T +
Handcross Park School, Haywards Heath
   Entry age: 7–11   H T
Pennthorpe School, Horsham   H
The Prebendal School, Chichester
   Entry age: 7   H +
Shoreham College, Shoreham-by-Sea   H +
Slindon College, Arundel
   Entry age: 10   F1 F2 F4 F3 H
Sompting Abbotts School, Sompting   T
Tavistock & Summerhill School,
   Haywards Heath   H
The Towers Convent School, Steyning   H T
Windlesham House School   F1 F2 F4 F3 FO H

TYNE AND WEAR

Central Newcastle High School GDST, Newcastle
   upon Tyne Entry age: 11+, 16+   H
Dame Allan's Boys School, Newcastle upon
   Tyne   H
Dame Allan's Girls School, Newcastle upon
   Tyne Entry age: 11   H
Grindon Hall Christian School, Sunderland   E T +
The King's School, Tynemouth
   Entry age: 11+   E H +
Newcastle Preparatory School,
   Newcastle upon Tyne   H
Sunderland High School, Sunderland   E H
Westfield School, Newcastle upon Tyne   H

WARWICKSHIRE

Bilton Grange, Rugby Entry age: Bursary: 4+
   Scholarship: 8+   F1 F2 F4 F3 H
King's High School, Warwick, Warwick   H
The Kingsley School, Leamington Spa   H
Princethorpe College, Rugby
   Entry age: 11/18+   H

Rugby School, Rugby   H
Warwick School, Warwick   H

WEST MIDLANDS

Abbey College, Birmingham   H
Al-Burhan Grammar School, Birmingham
    Entry age: 11 years old   H
Bablake Junior School, Coventry   H
Bablake School, Coventry   H
Birchfield School, Wolverhampton
    Entry age: 4   F4 H T
The Blue Coat School, Birmingham
    Entry age: 7+   H
Edgbaston High School for Girls,
    Birmingham Entry age: 11+, 16+   H
Elmhurst School for Dance,
    Birmingham   F1 F4 F3 H
Eversfield Preparatory School, Solihull Entry age:
    Bursaries are available for 7+ entry.   H
Highclare School, Birmingham
    Entry age: 11/16+   H
King Edward VI High School for Girls,
    Birmingham   H
King Edward's School, Birmingham
    Entry age: Academic and Music
    Scholarships available at 11+, 13+ and 16+.
    Bursaries at 11+ and 16+   H
King Henry VIII School, Coventry   H
Newbridge Preparatory School,
    Wolverhampton   +
Pattison College, Coventry   H
Priory School, Birmingham Entry age: 11, 16   H
The Royal Wolverhampton Junior School,
    Wolverhampton   F1 F3 H
St George's School, Edgbaston, Birmingham
    Entry age: 11+   H +
Saint Martin's School, Solihull
    Entry age: 7+, 11+, 16+   H
Solihull School, Solihull   +
Tettenhall College, Wolverhampton
    Entry age: 11   F1 F2 F4 F3 H +
West House School, Birmingham   H T
Wolverhampton Grammar School, Wolverhampton
    Entry age: 11+, 13+, 16+   H

WILTSHIRE

Chafyn Grove School, Salisbury Entry age:
    Bursary – all ages Scholarship – for entry in
    Years 3, 5 and 7   F1 F2 F4 F3 H T
Dauntsey's School, Devizes
    Entry age: 11+, 13+, 16+   H
Godolphin Preparatory School,
    Salisbury   F1 F2 F4 F3 H
The Godolphin School, Salisbury   F1 F2 F4 F3 H
Leaden Hall School, Salisbury   +

Marlborough College, Marlborough
    Entry age: 13+, 16+   +
Norman Court Preparatory School,
    Salisbury Entry age: 7, 8, 11   F1 F2 F4 F3 H
Pinewood School, Shrivenham   H
Prior Park Preparatory School,
    Cricklade   F1 F2 F4 F3
St Francis School, Pewsey Entry age:
    Scholarships – Age 7+
    Bursaries – Age 9+   H T
St Mary's Calne, Calne
    Entry age: 11+, 13+, 16+   F1 F2 F4 F3 H
Stonar School, Entry age: Scholarships from
    Year 7 to Sixth Form. Bursaries from Pre-prep.
    Riding Scholarships available.   F1 F2 F4 F3 H
South Hills School, Salisbury   H
Warminster School, Warminster
    Entry age: 7, 9, 11, 13, 16   F1 F2 F4 F3 H

WORCESTERSHIRE

Abberley Hall, Worcester   F1 F2 F4 F3
The Abbey College, Malvern Wells   H
Bromsgrove Preparatory School,
    Bromsgrove Entry age: 11+   F1 F2 F4 F3 H
Bromsgrove School,
    Bromsgrove   F1 F2 F4 F3 H T
The Downs, Malvern, Malvern
    Entry age: Scholarships 11+,
    Bursaries from age 5   F1 F2 F4 F3 FO H T
The Elms, Malvern   F1 F2 F4 F3 H T
King's Hawford, Worcester
    Entry age: 7+, 8+   +
The King's School, Worcester   H
Malvern St James, Great Malvern
    Entry age: 11+, 12+, 13+, 16+   H
Moffats School,
    Bewdley   E F1 F2 F4 F3 FO H M T +
RGS Worcester & The Alice Ottley School,
    Worcester   H
River School, Worcester   H
St Mary's, Worcester Entry age: 11+, 16+   H
Winterfold House, Kidderminster   H

EAST RIDING OF YORKSHIRE

Hull Collegiate School, Anlaby
    Entry age: 11   H
Hymers College, Hull   H
Pocklington School, Pocklington   F1 F2 F4 F3 H

NORTH YORKSHIRE

Ampleforth College, York Entry age: 13, 16   H
Ashville College, Harrogate
    Entry age: 11–18   E F1 F2 F4 F3 H T +

Aysgarth Preparatory School, Bedale
   Entry age: Normally between 8 and 11 years
   old   E F1 F2 F4 F3 H T +
Belmont Grosvenor School,
   Harrogate   F1 F2 F4 F3 +
Bootham School, York Entry age:
   Scholarships at 11+,13+ Bursaries
   11+, 13+   H
Bramcote School, Scarborough   F1 F2 F4 F3 H T
Cundall Manor School, York   F1 F2 F4 F3 FO
Fyling Hall School, Whitby   H
Giggleswick Junior School, Settle
   Entry age: 10, 11   F1 F2 F4 F3 T
Giggleswick School, Settle
   Entry age: 13, 16   F1 F2 F4 F3 H T
Harrogate Ladies' College, Harrogate
   Entry age: 11+, 16+   E F1 F2 F4 F3 H T +
Harrogate Tutorial College, Harrogate
   Entry age: 15+   F1 F2 F4 F3 FO H T
Highfield Preparatory School,
   Harrogate   E F1 F2 F4 F3 T +
Malsis School, Near Skipton Entry age:
   Year 3 and above   F1 F2 F4 F3 H T +
The Mount School, York   H
Queen Ethelburga's College, York
   Entry age: 11   F1 F2 F4 F3 FO M T +
Queen Mary's School, Thirsk
   Entry age: 11+, 12+, 13+ F1 F2 F4 F3 H T +
Read School, Selby
   Entry age: 11+, 13+, 16+   H
Ripon Cathedral Choir School,
   Ripon   F1 F2 F4 F3 H
St Martin's Ampleforth, York
   Entry age: 7/12+   F1 F2 F4 F3
St Peter's School, York
   Entry age: 13/16+   F1 F2 F4 F3 H +
Scarborough College & Lisvane School,
   Scarborough   F2 F4 F3 H
Terrington Hall, York   F1 F2 F4 F3 H T +
Woodleigh School, Malton   F1 F2 F3

SOUTH YORKSHIRE

Ashdell Preparatory School, Sheffield
   Entry age: 4+   H
Birkdale School, Sheffield Entry age: 11, 16   H +
Handsworth Christian School, Sheffield   H
Rudston Preparatory School, Rotherham   H T
Sheffield High School GDST, Sheffield
   Entry age: 11, 16   H
Westbourne School, Sheffield   H

WEST YORKSHIRE

Ackworth School, Pontefract   H
Batley Grammar School, Batley   H
Bradford Girls' Grammar School, Bradford   H
Bradford Grammar School, Bradford
   Entry age: 11+   H
Bronte House School, Bradford
   Entry age: 9   F1 F2 F3 H
The Froebelian School, Leeds   H
Fulneck School, Leeds   E F1 F2 F4 F3 H +
Gateways School, Leeds Entry age: 11   H
The Grammar School at Leeds, Leeds
   Entry age: 11+, 16+   H
Hipperholme Grammar School, Halifax
   Entry age: 16+   H
Huddersfield Grammar School, Huddersfield   H
Moorfield School, Ilkley Entry age: Bursary from
   Reception   H
Moorlands School, Leeds   H
Queen Elizabeth Grammar School, Wakefield   H
Richmond House School, Leeds
   Entry age: 7/8   H T
Rishworth School, Rishworth Entry age: 11, 16   H
Silcoates School, Wakefield Entry age: 11   +
Wakefield Girls' High School, Wakefield   H
Woodhouse Grove School, Apperley
   Bridge   F1 F2 F4 F3 H +

NORTHERN IRELAND

COUNTY ANTRIM

Cabin Hill School, Belfast   F3
Methodist College, Belfast   +
Royal Belfast Academical Institution, Belfast   H

COUNTY ARMAGH

The Royal School ARMAGH, Armagh   +

COUNTY DOWN

The Holywood Rudolf Steiner School,
   Holywood   H

COUNTY TYRONE

The Royal School Dungannon, Dungannon
   Entry age: 11–16   E F1 F2 F4 F3 +

SCOTLAND

ABERDEENSHIRE

Aberdeen Waldorf School, Aberdeen	H
International School of Aberdeen, Aberdeen	H
Robert Gordon's College, Aberdeen	H
St Margaret's School for Girls, Aberdeen	H

ANGUS

High School of Dundee, Dundee Entry age: 12	H
Lathallan School, Montrose Entry age: Primary 7 and S5	F1 F2 F4 F3 H

SOUTH AYRSHIRE

Wellington School, Ayr	H

CLACKMANNANSHIRE

Dollar Academy, Dollar Entry age: Senior School. Age 12+	F1 F2 F4 F3 H

FIFE

St Leonards School, St Andrews	F1 F2 F4 F3 H

GLASGOW

Craigholme School, Entry age: 11	F1 F2 F4 F3 H +
The Glasgow Academy, Entry age: 11+	H +
The High School of Glasgow	H
Hutchesons' Grammar School, Entry age: S1 (age 11/12)	H
St Aloysius' College, Entry age: Senior School only	H

INVERCLYDE

St Columba's School, Kilmacolm	H

SOUTH LANARKSHIRE

Fernhill School, Glasgow	H

LOTHIAN

Belhaven Hill, Dunbar Entry age: 8+	H T
Cargilfield, Edinburgh	F1 F2 F4 F3 T
Clifton Hall School, Edinburgh	F1 F2 F4 F3 H
The Compass School, Haddington Entry age: 9/11	H
The Edinburgh Academy, Edinburgh	H
Fettes College, Edinburgh Entry age: 11+, 13+, 16+	F1 F2 F4 F3 H T
George Heriot's School, Edinburgh Entry age: 11+	H
George Watson's College, Edinburgh	H
Loretto Junior School, Musselburgh Entry age: 10/11	F1 F2 F4 F3 H
Loretto School, Musselburgh Entry age: all age groups from 12 years	F1 F2 F4 F3 H
The Mary Erskine School, Edinburgh	H
Merchiston Castle School, Edinburgh	F1 F2 F4 F3 H
St George's School for Girls, Edinburgh Entry age: 12, 13, 16–18	H
Stewart's Melville College, Edinburgh	H

MORAYSHIRE

Gordonstoun School, Elgin Entry age: 8+ at Junior School Entry 13+ at Lower School Entry 16+ at Sixth Form Entry	H
Rosebrae School, Elgin	H

PERTH AND KINROSS

Ardvreck School, Crieff	F1 F2 F4 F3
Craigclowan Preparatory School, Perth	H T
Glenalmond College, Perth Entry age: 12, 13, 16	E F1 F2 F4 F3 H T +
Kilgraston, Perth	F1 F2 F4 F3 H T
Morrison's Academy, Crieff	H
Queen Victoria School, Dunblane	F1 F2 F4 F3
Strathallan School, Perth Entry age: 9, 10, 11, 12, 13 & 16	E F1 F2 F4 F3 FO H M T +

STIRLING

Beaconhurst School	H

WALES

ANGLESEY

Treffos School, Menai Bridge   F4

BRIDGEND

St John's School, Porthcawl   H

CARDIFF

The Cathedral School, Entry age: 11   H
Howell's School, Llandaff GDST,
    Entry age: 11, 16   H

CARMARTHENSHIRE

Llandovery College, Llandovery
    Entry age: Year 7 to 12   E F1 F2 F4 F3 H +
St Michael's School, Llanelli   H

CONWY

St David's College, Llandudno
    Entry age: 11   E F1 F2 F4 F3 FO H +

DENBIGHSHIRE

Howell's School, Denbigh   F1 F2 F4 F3 H T +
Ruthin School, Ruthin
    Entry age: 11 and 16   F1 F2 F4 F3 H

GWYNEDD

Hillgrove School, Bangor   E

MONMOUTHSHIRE

Haberdashers' Monmouth School For Girls,
    Monmouth   F1 F2 F4 F3 H
Llangattock School, Monmouth   H
Monmouth School, Monmouth
    Entry age: 11, 13, 16   F1 F2 F4 F3 H T
St John's-on-the-Hill, Chepstow Entry age:
    External scholarships and bursaries
    available from Year 2   F1 F2 F4 F3 H

NEWPORT

Rougemont School   H

POWYS

Christ College, Brecon
    Entry age: 11, 13, 16   F1 F4 F3 H T +

SWANSEA

Ffynone House School, Entry age: 11   H
Oakleigh House School   H

CONTINENTAL EUROPE

Aiglon College, Switzerland   H
Chavagnes International College,
    CHAVAGNES-EN-PAILLERS, France   H
St Columba's College, Entry age: 11, 13, 16.   +

Specialist Schools

Schools in the directory which specialize in the theatre, dance or music are listed below. For full details about entrance requirements and the curriculum, parents are advised to contact schools directly.

ARTS SCHOOLS

Arts Educational Schools, London W4
Barbara Speake Stage School, London W3
The Italia Conti Academy of Theatre Arts, London EC1
Pattison College, Coventry
Ravenscourt Theatre School, London W6
Sylvia Young Theatre School, London NW1
Tring Park School for the Performing Arts, Tring

DANCE SCHOOLS

Elmhurst School for Dance, Birmingham
Hammond School, Chester
Royal Ballet School, London WC2E
Stonelands School of Ballet & Theatre Arts, Hove
The Urdang Academy of Ballet, London WC2

MUSIC SCHOOLS

Chetham's School of Music, Manchester
The Purcell School, Bushey
St Mary's Music School, Edinburgh
Yehudi Menuhin School, Cobham

Single-Sex Schools

For details consult the school listings in Part 2.

BOYS: ENGLAND

BEDFORDSHIRE

Bedford Preparatory School, Bedford	7–13
Bedford School, Bedford	7–18

BERKSHIRE

Claires Court School, Maidenhead	11–16 (Co-ed VIth Form)
Claires Court Schools, Ridgeway, Maidenhead	4–11
Elstree School, Reading	3–13 (Girls 3–7)
Eton College, Windsor	13–18
Horris Hill School, Newbury	7–13
Ludgrove, Wokingham	8–13
The Oratory School, Reading	11–18
Papplewick School, Ascot	6–13
Reading Blue Coat School, Reading	11–18 (Co-ed VIth Form)
Reading School, Reading	11–18
St Edward's School, Reading	4–13
St John's Beaumont, Windsor	4–13
Sunningdale School, Sunningdale	8–13

BRISTOL

Queen Elizabeth's Hospital, Bristol	7–18 (Sixth Form International students are welcome on a Guardianship basis)

BUCKINGHAMSHIRE

The Beacon School, Amersham	3–13
Caldicott School, Farnham Royal	7–13
Davenies School, Beaconsfield	4–13
Kingscote Pre-Preparatory School, Gerrards Cross	3–7
Thorpe House School, Gerrards Cross	3–16

CHANNEL ISLANDS

Victoria College, Jersey	11–19
Victoria College Preparatory School, Jersey	7–11

CHESHIRE

Altrincham Preparatory School, Altrincham	3–11
The Ryleys, Alderley Edge	3–13
St Ambrose Preparatory School, Altrincham	3–11

DORSET

Sherborne School, Sherborne	13–18

COUNTY DURHAM

Hurworth House School, Darlington	3–18

ESSEX

Loyola Preparatory School, Buckhurst Hill	3–11

HAMPSHIRE

The Pilgrims' School, Winchester	7–13
Salesian College, Farnborough	11–18
Winchester College, Winchester	13–18

HERTFORDSHIRE

Aldwickbury School, Harpenden	4–13
Haberdashers' Aske's Boys' School, Elstree	5–18
Lockers Park, Hemel Hempstead	5–13
Northwood Preparatory School, Rickmansworth	4–13 (Girls 3–4)
St Albans School, St Albans	17–18 (Co-ed VIth Form)
St Columba's College, St Albans	4–18

KENT

Bickley Park School, Bromley	3–13
Darul Uloom London, Chislehurst	11–18
The New Beacon, Sevenoaks	4–13
Solefield School, Sevenoaks	4–13
Tonbridge School, Tonbridge	13–18
Yardley Court Preparatory School, Tonbridge	7–13

LANCASHIRE

Bolton School (Boys' Division), Bolton	7–18
Bury Grammar School Boys, Bury	7–18
Tashbar School, Salford	2–11

LEICESTERSHIRE

Loughborough Grammar School, Loughborough	10–18

LINCOLNSHIRE

Stamford School, Stamford	11–18

LONDON

Al-Mizan Primary & London East Academy Secondary & Sixth Form	7–18
Arnold House School	5–13
Beis Hamedrash Elyon	11–14
Brondesbury College For Boys	11–16
City of London School	10–18
Clifton Lodge Preparatory School	4–13
Colet Court	7–13
Darul Hadis Latifiah	11–19
Donhead Prep School	4–11
Dulwich College	7–18
Dulwich College Preparatory School	3–13 (Girls 3–5)
Durston House	4–13
Eaton House Belgravia	4–8
Eaton House The Manor Pre-Preparatory	4–8
Eaton House The Manor Preparatory	3–13
The Falcons School for Boys	3–8
The Hall School	4–13
Hawkesdown House School	3–8
Hereward House School	4–13
Keble Preparatory School	4–13
King's College Junior School	7–13
King's College School	13–18
London Islamic School	11–16
Lubavitch House School (Junior Boys)	5–13
Lyndhurst House Preparatory School	4–13
Mechinah Liyeshivah Zichron Moshe	11–16
North Bridge House Upper Prep School	10–13
Northcote Lodge School	8–13
Pardes Grammar Boys' School	11–17
St Anthony's Preparatory School	5–13
St Paul's School	13–18
St Philip's School	7–13
Sussex House School	8–13
Talmud Torah Bobov Primary School	2–13
Tawhid Boys School, Tawhid Educational Trust	9–16
Tower House School	4–13
University College School Junior Branch	7–11
Westminster Abbey Choir School	8–13
Westminster Cathedral Choir School	7–13
Westminster Under School	7–13
Wetherby Preparatory School	8–13
Wetherby School	4–8
Willington School	4–13
Wimbledon Common Preparatory School	4–8
Yetev Lev Day School for Boys	3–11

GREATER MANCHESTER

Al Jamiah Al Islamiyyah, Bolton	13–16
Kassim Darwish Grammar School for Boys, Manchester	11–16
The Manchester Grammar School, Manchester	9–18

MERSEYSIDE

Merchant Taylors' Boys' Schools, Liverpool	4–18

MIDDLESEX

Buckingham College Preparatory
    School, Pinner   4–11
Buckingham College School,
    Harrow 11–18 (Co-ed VIth Form, but currently
        boys only.)
Denmead School, Hampton   3–11 (Girls 3–7)
Halliford School,
    Shepperton   11–18 (Co-ed VIth Form)
Hampton School, Hampton   11–18
Harrow School, Harrow on the Hill   13–18
The John Lyon School, Harrow   11–18
The Mall School, Twickenham   4–13
Merchant Taylors' School, Northwood   11–18
St John's Northwood, Northwood   3–13
St Martin's School, Northwood   3–13

NOTTINGHAMSHIRE

Al Karam Secondary School, Retford   11–16
Nottingham High Junior School, Nottingham 7–11

OXFORDSHIRE

Abingdon School, Abingdon   11–18
Christ Church Cathedral School,
    Oxford   3–13 (Girls 2–4)
Cothill House Preparatory School, Abingdon 8–13
Moulsford Preparatory School, Wallingford 4–13
New College School, Oxford   4–13
Radley College, Abingdon   13–18
Summer Fields, Oxford   7–13

SHROPSHIRE

Kingsland Grange, Shrewsbury   4–13

BATH & NORTH EAST SOMERSET

Beechen Cliff School, Bath   11–18

SURREY

Aldro School, Godalming   7–13
Charterhouse,
    Godalming   13–18 (Co-ed Sixth Form)
Chinthurst School, Tadworth   3–13
Cranmore School, Leatherhead   3–13
Cumnor House School, South Croydon   4–13
Elmhurst School, South Croydon   4–11
Haslemere Preparatory School, Haslemere 2–14
Homefield School, Sutton   2–13

King's House School, Richmond   4–13
Kingswood House School, Epsom   3–13
Lanesborough, Guildford   3–13
Parkside School, Cobham   2–13 (Co-ed 2–4)
Priory Preparatory School, Banstead   2–13
Reed's School, Cobham 11–18 (Co-ed VIth Form)
Rokeby School, Kingston-upon-Thames   4–13
Royal Grammar School, Guildford   11–18
St James Independent School for
    Boys (Senior), Ashford   10–18
Shrewsbury House School, Surbiton   7–13
Surbiton Preparatory School, Surbiton   4–11
Trinity School,
    Croydon   10–18 (Boys 10–18 Girls 16–18)
Whitgift School, South Croydon   10–18
Woodcote House School, Windlesham   7–14

WEST SUSSEX

Slindon College, Arundel   8–16

TYNE AND WEAR

Dame Allan's Boys School, Newcastle upon
    Tyne   8–18 (Co-ed VIth Form)
Newcastle School for Boys, Newcastle upon
    Tyne   3–18
Royal Grammar School, Newcastle upon
    Tyne   8–18 (Co-ed VIth form)

WARWICKSHIRE

Warwick School, Warwick   7–18

WEST MIDLANDS

King Edward's School, Birmingham   11–18
West House School, Birmingham 1–11 (Girls 1–4)

NORTH YORKSHIRE

Aysgarth Preparatory School,
    Bedale   3–13 (Co-ed day 3–8)

SOUTH YORKSHIRE

Birkdale School, Sheffield 4–18 (Co-ed VIth Form)

WEST YORKSHIRE

Olive Secondary, Bradford   11–18
Queen Elizabeth Grammar School,
    Wakefield   7–18

NORTHERN IRELAND

COUNTY ANTRIM

Cabin Hill School,
　Belfast　　　3–13 (Co-ed kindergarten)
Campbell College, Belfast　　　　　11–18
Royal Belfast Academical Institution, Belfast　4–18

COUNTY DOWN

Bangor Grammar School, Bangor　　11–18

COUNTY FERMANAGH

Portora Royal School, Enniskillen　　11–19

SCOTLAND

LOTHIAN

The Edinburgh Academy,
　Edinburgh　　　5–18 (Co-ed VIth Form)

Merchiston Castle School, Edinburgh　　8–18
Stewart's Melville College,
　Edinburgh　　　12–18 (Co-ed VIth Form)

WALES

MONMOUTHSHIRE

Monmouth School,
　Monmouth　　　7–18 (Boarding 11–18)

GIRLS: ENGLAND

BEDFORDSHIRE

Bedford High School for Girls, Bedford　7–18
Dame Alice Harpur School, Bedford　　7–18
St Andrew's School, Bedford　　3–9 (Boys 3–7)

BERKSHIRE

The Abbey School, Reading　　　　　3–18
Brigidine School Windsor,
　Windsor　　　　　3–7 (Boys 3–7)
Claires Court Schools, The College,
　Maidenhead　3–5 (Boys 3–5, co-ed VIth Form)
Downe House, Thatcham　　　　　11–18
Heathfield School, Ascot　　　　　11–18
Highfield School, Maidenhead　　　　3–5
Luckley-Oakfield School, Wokingham　11–18
The Marist preparatory school,
　Ascot　　　　　　2–11
The Marist Senior School, Ascot　　11–18
Queen Anne's School　　　　　11–18

St Gabriel's　　　　3–7 (Girls 3–18 Boys 3–7)
St George's School, Ascot　　　　11–18
St Mary's School, Ascot, Ascot　　11–18

BRISTOL

Badminton School, Westbury-on-Trym　3–18
The Red Maids' School　　　　　11–18
Redland High School for Girls　　　3–18

BUCKINGHAMSHIRE

Godstowe Preparatory School,
　High Wycombe　　　3–8 (Boys 3–8)
Heatherton House School,
　Amersham　3–11 (Girls can start in Early Years
　　　　　from the age of 2.5)
High March School,
　Beaconsfield　3–4 (Boys are only admitted into
　　　　　our Upper Nursery class)

Maltman's Green School, Gerrards Cross 3–11
Pipers Corner School, High Wycombe 3–18
St Mary's School, Gerrards Cross 3–18
Thornton College Convent of Jesus and Mary,
    Milton Keynes 2–4 (Boys 2–4)
Wycombe Abbey School,
    High Wycombe 11–18

CAMBRIDGESHIRE

The Perse School for Girls, Cambridge 7–18
St Mary's Junior School, Cambridge 4–11
St Mary's School, Cambridge,
    Cambridge 4–18

CHANNEL ISLANDS

Beaulieu Convent School, Jersey 4–18
The Ladies' College, Guernsey 4–18

CHESHIRE

Alderley Edge School for Girls,
    Alderley Edge 3–18
Bowdon Preparatory School For Girls,
    Altrincham 2–12
The Queen's School, Chester 4–18
Wilmslow Preparatory School,
    Wilmslow 2–11

CORNWALL

Truro High School, Truro 3–5 (Boys 3–5)

DERBYSHIRE

Ockbrook School, Derby 3–11

DEVON

The Maynard School,
    Exeter 7–18 (A selective independent day
        school for girls aged 7–17.)
St Margaret's School, Exeter 7–18
Stoodley Knowle School,
    Torquay 2–18

DORSET

Knighton House, Blandford
    Forum 2–13 (Day boys 4–7)
Leweston School, Sherborne 2–8 (Boys 2–11)

St Mary's School, Dorset,
    Shaftesbury 9–18
Sherborne Girls, Sherborne 11–18
Talbot Heath, Bournemouth 3–7 (Boys 3–7)

COUNTY DURHAM

Durham High School For Girls, Durham 3–18

ESSEX

Braeside School for Girls,
    Buckhurst Hill 3–16 (Independent day school
        for girls aged 3 to 16 years)
Ilford Ursuline Preparatory School,
    Ilford 3–4
Park School for Girls, Ilford 3–16
St Hilda's School,
    Westcliff-on-Sea 2–7 (Boys 2–7)
St Mary's School, Colchester 4–16

GLOUCESTERSHIRE

Cheltenham Ladies' College, Cheltenham 11–18
Gloucestershire Islamic Secondary School For
    Girls, Gloucester 11–16
Kitebrook House,
    Moreton-in-Marsh 4–8 (Boys 4–8)
Westonbirt School, Tetbury 11–18

HAMPSHIRE

Alton Convent School, Alton 2–11 (Co-ed 2–11)
Farnborough Hill, Farnborough 11–18
Portsmouth High School GDST,
    Southsea 3–18
St Nicholas' School, Fleet 3–7 (Boys 3–7)
St Swithun's School, Winchester 11–18
Wykeham House School, Fareham 2–16

HERTFORDSHIRE

Abbot's Hill School, Hemel
    Hempstead 3–5 (Boys 3–5)
Haberdashers' Aske's School for Girls,
    Elstree 4–18
Queenswood, Hatfield 11–18
Rickmansworth PNEU School,
    Rickmansworth 3–11
The Royal Masonic School for Girls,
    Rickmansworth 2–4 (Pre School opened in
        January 2010 for boys and
        girls aged 2–4.)
St Albans High School for Girls, St Albans 4–18

St Francis' College, Letchworth
  Garden City   3–18
St Hilda's School, Bushey   3–5 (Boys 3–5)
St Margaret's School, Bushey   4–18
St Martha's Senior School, Barnet   11–18
St. Hilda's School, Harpenden   2–11
Stormont, Potters Bar   4–11
Watford Grammar School For Girls,
  Watford   11–18

KENT

Babington House School,
  Chislehurst   3–7 (Boys 3–7)
Benenden School, Cranbrook   11–18
Bromley High School GDST, Bromley   4–18
Cobham Hall, Gravesend   11–18
Combe Bank School, Sevenoaks   3–5
Derwent Lodge School for Girls, Tonbridge   7–11
The Granville School, Sevenoaks   3–5 (Boys 3–5)
Kent College Pembury, Tunbridge Wells   3–18
Walthamstow Hall, Sevenoaks   2–18

LANCASHIRE

Bolton Muslim Girls School, Bolton   11–16
Bolton School (Girls' Division),
  Bolton   4–7 (Boys 4–7 before they move into
             Bolton School Boys' Division)
Bury Grammar School Girls,
  Bury   3–7 (Boys 4–7)
The Hulme Grammar School for Girls,
  Oldham   3–18
Islamiyah School, Blackburn   11–16
Jamea Al Kauthar, Lancaster   11–19
Rochdale Girls School, Rochdale   11–16
Tauheedul Islam Girls High School,
  Blackburn   11–16
Westholme School, Blackburn   3–11 (Boys 3–7)

LEICESTERSHIRE

Leicester High School For Girls, Leicester   3–18
Loughborough High School,
  Loughborough   11–18

LINCOLNSHIRE

Stamford High School, Stamford   11–18

LONDON

Beis Chinuch Lebanos Girls School   2–16
Beis Rochel D'Satmar Girls School   2–17

Beth Jacob Grammar for Girls   10–16
Blackheath High School GDST   3–18
Bute House Preparatory School for Girls   4–11
The Cavendish School   3–11
Channing Junior School   4–11
Channing School   4–18
City of London School for Girls   7–18
The Falcons School for Girls   3–11
Falkner House   3–4 (Co-ed 3–4)
Francis Holland School, Regent's
  Park NW1   11–18
Francis Holland School, Sloane Square
  SW1   4–18
Glendower Preparatory School   4–11
The Godolphin and Latymer School   11–18
Grange Park Preparatory School   4–11
Harvington School   3–5 (Boys 3–5)
Islamia Girls' School   11–16
James Allen's Girls' School   4–18
Kensington Prep School   4–11
London Jewish Girls' High School   11–16
Lubavitch House Senior School for
  Girls   11–18
Madni Girls School   12–18
More House School, London   11–18
The Mount School   3–16
Notting Hill and Ealing High School GDST   4–18
Palmers Green High School   3–16
Pembridge Hall   4–11
Putney High School GDST   4–18
Queen's College Prep School   4–11
Queen's Gate School   4–18
Quwwatt Ul Islam Girls School   4–13
The Royal School, Hampstead   3–16
St Augustine's Priory, Ealing   4–18
St Christopher's School   4–11
St James Senior Girls' School   10–18
St Joseph's Convent School   3–11
St Margaret's School   4–16
St Paul's Girls' School   11–18
Streatham & Clapham High
  School   3–5 (Boys 3–5)
Sarum Hall   3–11
The Study Preparatory School   4–11
South Hampstead High School   4–18
Sydenham High School GDST   4–18
Tayyibah Girls School   5–18
Ursuline Preparatory School   3–7 (Boys 3–7)
The Village School   3–11
Wimbledon High School GDST   4–18

GREATER MANCHESTER

Manchester High School for Girls,
  Manchester   4–18
Manchester Islamic High School,
  Manchester   11–16
Withington Girls' School, Manchester   7–18

MERSEYSIDE

Merchant Taylors' Girls' School,
Liverpool   4–18 (Infant Boys 4–7)

MIDDLESEX

Heathfield School, Pinner   3–18
Jack and Jill School, Hampton   2–5 (Boys 3–5)
The Lady Eleanor Holles School,
Hampton   7–18
North London Collegiate,
Edgware   4–18
Northwood College, Northwood   3–18
Peterborough & St Margaret's School,
Stanmore   4–16
St Catherine's School,
Twickenham   3–18 (Girls 3–18)
St Helen's School, Northwood   3–18

NORFOLK

Norwich High School for Girls GDST,
Norwich   3–18
Thorpe House School, Norwich   3–16

NORTHAMPTONSHIRE

Northampton High School,
Northampton   3–18

NOTTINGHAMSHIRE

Nottingham High School for Girls
GDST, Nottingham   4–18

OXFORDSHIRE

Ash-Shifa School, Banbury   11–16
The Carrdus School, Banbury   3–8 (Boys 3–8)
Headington School, Oxford   3–18 (Co-ed 3–4)
IQRA School, Oxford   10–16
Oxford High School GDST,
Oxford   4–6 (Boys 4 -6)
St Helen & St Katharine, Abingdon   9–18
Tudor Hall School, Banbury   11–18
Wychwood School, Oxford   11–18

SHROPSHIRE

Adcote School for Girls, Shrewsbury   4–18
Moreton Hall School,
Oswestry   3–11 (Boys 3–11)

SOMERSET

Bruton School for Girls,
Bruton   2–7 (Boys aged 2–7)

BATH & NORTH EAST SOMERSET

The Royal High School,
Bath, Bath   3–18 (Boys admitted (day only) into Sixth Form)

STAFFORDSHIRE

Abbots Bromley School, Abbots Bromley   3–11
St Dominic's School, Stafford   2–7 (Co-ed 2–7)

SUFFOLK

Ipswich High School GDST, Ipswich   3–18

SURREY

Bramley School, Tadworth   3–11
Croydon High School GDST,
South Croydon   3–18
Cumnor House School, Purley   4–13
Dunottar School, Reigate   3–18
Greenacre School for Girls, Banstead   3–18
Guildford High School, Guildford   4–18
Halstead Preparatory School, Woking   2–11
Holy Cross Preparatory School,
Kingston upon Thames   4–11
Manor House School, Leatherhead   2–16
Marymount International School,
Kingston-upon-Thames   11–18
Notre Dame Preparatory School, Cobham
2–5 (Boys 2–5)
Notre Dame Senior School, Cobham   11–18
Old Palace of John Whitgift School,
Croydon   1–4
Old Vicarage School, Richmond   4–11
Prior's Field School, Godalming   11–18
Rowan Preparatory School, Esher   2–11
The Royal School, Haslemere   6–4 (Boys 2–4)
The Royal School For Girls, Haslemere   11–18
St Catherine's School, Guildford   4–18
St Ives School, Haslemere   3–5 (Boys 3–5)
St Teresa's Preparatory School,
Effingham   2–11
St Teresa's School, Dorking   11–18
Seaton House School,
Sutton   3–5 (Boys 3–5 Girls 3–11)
Sir William Perkins's School, Chertsey   11–18

Surbiton High School,
   Kingston-upon-Thames   4–11 (Boys 4–11)
Sutton High School GDST, Sutton   3–18
Tormead School, Guildford   4–18

EAST SUSSEX

Brighton and Hove High School GDST,
   Brighton   3–18
Moira House Girls School, Eastbourne   2–4
Moira House School, Eastbourne   2–11
Roedean School, Brighton   11–18
St Leonards-Mayfield School, Mayfield   11–19

WEST SUSSEX

Burgess Hill School for Girls,
   Burgess Hill   2–4
Farlington School, Horsham   3–18
The Towers Convent School,
   Steyning   3–11 (Boys 3–11)

TYNE AND WEAR

Central Newcastle High School GDST,
   Newcastle upon Tyne   3–18
Church High School, Newcastle upon Tyne,
   Newcastle upon Tyne   3–18 (We have a Pre
                  School Nursery on
                  site and Sixth Form.)
Dame Allan's Girls School, Newcastle upon
   Tyne   8–18 (Co-ed VIth Form)
Westfield School, Newcastle upon Tyne   3–18

WARWICKSHIRE

King's High School, Warwick,
   Warwick   10–18
The Kingsley School,
   Leamington Spa   3–7 (Boys 2–7)

WEST MIDLANDS

Al-Burhan Grammar School,
   Birmingham   11–16
Birchfield Independent Girls School,
   Birmingham   11–16
Coventry Muslim School, Coventry   4–16
Edgbaston High School for Girls,
   Birmingham   3–18

King Edward VI High School for Girls,
   Birmingham   11–18
Newbridge Preparatory School,
   Wolverhampton   3–4
Saint Martin's School,
   Solihull   3–18 (Girls may join the school
                  from 2 years 9 months.)
Woodstock Girls' School,
   Birmingham   11–15

WILTSHIRE

Godolphin Preparatory School,
   Salisbury   3–11
The Godolphin School, Salisbury   11–18
Leaden Hall School, Salisbury   3–4 (Boys 3–4)
St Mary's Calne, Calne   11–18
Stonar School   2–11

WORCESTERSHIRE

Dodderhill School,
   Droitwich Spa   3–7 (Boys 3–9)
Malvern St James, Great Malvern   4–18
St Mary's, Worcester   2–8 (Boys 2–8)

NORTH YORKSHIRE

Harrogate Ladies' College,
   Harrogate   11–18 (Highfield Prep School, part
                  of the HLC Group of Schools is
                  co-ed from age 4–11.)
Queen Mary's School, Thirsk   2–7 (Boys 3–7)

SOUTH YORKSHIRE

Ashdell Preparatory School,
   Sheffield   3–5 (Co-educational Pre-School for
                  rising threes in association with
                  Birkdale School)
Sheffield High School GDST, Sheffield   4–18

WEST YORKSHIRE

Bradford Girls' Grammar School,
   Bradford   2–7
Gateways School, Leeds   3–7 (Boys 3–7)
Islamia Girls High School, Huddersfield   11–16
New Horizon Community School, Leeds   11–16
Wakefield Girls' High School, Wakefield   11–18

NORTHERN IRELAND

COUNTY ANTRIM

Hunterhouse College, Belfast	5–19
Victoria College Belfast, Belfast	4–18

SCOTLAND

ABERDEENSHIRE

St Margaret's School for Girls, Aberdeen	3–5 (Boys 3–5)

GLASGOW

Craigholme School	3–5 (Boys 3–5 in Nursery only)

LOTHIAN

The Mary Erskine School, Edinburgh	16–18 (Co-ed VIth Form)
St George's School for Girls, Edinburgh	1–4 (Boys 2–4)

PERTH AND KINROSS

Kilgraston, Perth	2–9 (Boys day 2–9)

WALES

DENBIGHSHIRE

Howell's School, Denbigh	2–18

MONMOUTHSHIRE

Haberdashers' Monmouth School For Girls, Monmouth	7–18

COED BUT EDUCATED SEPARATELY: ENGLAND

BERKSHIRE

Brockhurst & Marlston House Pre-Preparatory School, Thatcham	3–6
Brockhurst and Marlston House Schools, Newbury	3–13
St Michaels School, Newbury	7–18 (Single-sex ed 13–18)

CHESHIRE

The King's School, Macclesfield	3–18 (Single-sex ed 11–16)

COUNTY DURHAM

Polam Hall, Darlington	2–18 (Co-educational Junior School from age 2 to Year 4. Separate teaching Year 5 to Year 11. Co-educational Sixth Form)

ESSEX

Brentwood School, Brentwood	3–18 (Single-sex Education aged 11–16)

New Hall School,
  Chelmsford   3–18 (Co-ed Preparatory School
                (3–11), Boys' Division (11–16),
                Girls' Division (11–16), Co-ed
                Sixth Form, Girls and boys
                between the ages of 11–16 are
                educated in a single-sex
                classes but with the benefit of a
                mixed environment)

GLOUCESTERSHIRE

Berkhampstead School, Cheltenham   3–11

HERTFORDSHIRE

Berkhamsted School,
  Berkhamsted   11–18 (Single-sex ed 11–16)
Immanuel College, Bushey   4–18

LANCASHIRE

Markazul Uloom,
  Blackburn   11–19 (No Boarding for girls)

LONDON

Al-Sadiq and Al-Zahra
  Schools   4–16
Forest School   4–18 (Single-sex ed 7–16)
Garden House School   3–11 (Co-ed nursery)
Yesodey Hatorah Jewish School   3–16

MIDDLESEX

St John's Senior School,
  Enfield   11–18

WEST SUSSEX

Fonthill Lodge,
  East Grinstead   2–11 (Single-sex ed 8–11)

WEST MIDLANDS

Al Hijrah School, Birmingham   4–11

5.5

Boarding Provision (Full, Weekly and Flexi-Boarding, Host Families)

The schools and colleges listed below offer boarding/residential accommodation. Full boarding is indicated by 'F', weekly boarding by 'W'. Many schools now offer flexi-boarding (FI), ie pupils may board for part of the week or on an occasional basis. Please note that in some cases independent Sixth Form colleges may offer accommodation with host families (H) or in hostels. For further details please contact schools directly.

ENGLAND

BEDFORDSHIRE

Bedford High School for Girls, Bedford	F
Bedford Preparatory School, Bedford	F W FI
Bedford School, Bedford	F W FI
Bedford School Study Centre, Bedford	F

BERKSHIRE

Bearwood College, Wokingham	F W FI
Bradfield College, Reading	F W
Brockhurst and Marlston House Schools, Newbury	W FI
Cheam School, Newbury	W FI
Downe House, Thatcham	F
Eagle House, Sandhurst	F W FI
Elstree School, Reading	F W FI
Eton College, Windsor	F
Heathfield School, Ascot	F
Horris Hill School, Newbury	F
Hurst Lodge School, Ascot	W FI
Lambrook, Bracknell	W FI
Luckley-Oakfield School, Wokingham	F W FI
Ludgrove, Wokingham	F
LVS Ascot, Ascot	F W
Newbury Hall International School, Newbury	F H
The Oratory School, Reading	F
Padworth College, Reading	F W FI
Pangbourne College, Pangbourne	F W FI
Papplewick School, Ascot	F W
Queen Anne's School	F W FI
St Andrew's School, Reading	W FI
St George's School, Ascot	F
St George's School, Windsor	F W FI
St John's Beaumont, Windsor	F W

St Mary's School, Ascot, Ascot	F
St Michaels School, Newbury	F W Fl
Sunningdale School, Sunningdale	F
Wellington College, Crowthorne	F

BRISTOL

Badminton School, Westbury-on-Trym	F W Fl
Clifton College	F Fl
Clifton College Preparatory School	F W Fl
Clifton High School	H
Colston's Collegiate School	F Fl
The Downs School, Wraxall	F W Fl
Queen Elizabeth's Hospital	H
Tockington Manor School, Tockington	F W Fl

BUCKINGHAMSHIRE

Ashfold School, Aylesbury	W Fl
Caldicott School, Farnham Royal	F
Godstowe Preparatory School, High Wycombe	F W Fl
Pipers Corner School, High Wycombe	F W Fl
Stowe School, Buckingham	F
Swanbourne House School, Milton Keynes	F W Fl
Thornton College Convent of Jesus and Mary, Milton Keynes	F W Fl
Wycombe Abbey School, High Wycombe	F

CAMBRIDGESHIRE

Bellerbys College & Embassy CES Cambridge, Cambridge	F
Cambridge Centre for Sixth-form Studies, Cambridge	F W Fl
CATS College Cambridge, Cambridge	F W Fl H
Kimbolton School, Huntingdon	F Fl
King's School Ely, Ely	F W Fl
The Leys School, Cambridge	F
MPW (Mander Portman Woodward), Cambridge	Fl
The Peterborough School, Peterborough	F W Fl
St Andrew's, Cambridge	Fl
St John's College School, Cambridge	F W Fl
St Mary's School, Cambridge, Cambridge	F W H

CHESHIRE

Hammond School, Chester	F W
Terra Nova School, Holmes Chapel	W Fl

CORNWALL

Gems Bolitho School, Penzance	F W Fl
Polwhele House School, Truro	W Fl
Truro High School, Truro	F W Fl
Truro School, Truro	F Fl

CUMBRIA

Casterton School, Kirkby Lonsdale	F Fl
Holme Park School, Kendal	Fl
Lime House School, Carlisle	F W
St Bees School, St Bees	F W Fl
Sedbergh Junior School, Sedbergh	F W Fl
Sedbergh School, Sedbergh	F
Windermere School, Windermere	F W Fl

DERBYSHIRE

Foremarke Hall, Derby	F W Fl
Mount St Mary's College, Spinkhill	F W Fl
Ockbrook School, Derby	F W Fl
Repton School, Derby	F
S. Anselm's School, Bakewell	F

DEVON

Blundell's School, Tiverton	F W Fl
Edgehill College, Bideford	F W Fl
Exeter Cathedral School, Exeter	F W Fl
Exeter Tutorial College, Exeter	Fl H
Kelly College, Tavistock	F W Fl
Kelly College Preparatory School, Tavistock	F W Fl
Kingsley School, Bideford	F W
The Maynard School, Exeter	H
Mount House School, Tavistock	F Fl
Plymouth College, Plymouth	F W
St Peter's School, Exmouth	W Fl
Stover School, Newton Abbot	F W Fl H
Shebbear College, Beaworthy	F W Fl
Trinity School, Teignmouth	F W Fl
West Buckland Preparatory School, Barnstaple	F Fl
West Buckland School, Barnstaple	F W Fl

DORSET

Bournemouth Collegiate School, Bournemouth	F W Fl
Bryanston School, Blandford Forum	F
Canford School, Wimborne	F
Clayesmore, Blandford Forum	F W
Clayesmore Preparatory School, Blandford Forum	F W Fl
International College, Sherborne School, Sherborne	F
Knighton House, Blandford Forum	F W Fl
Leweston School, Sherborne	F W Fl
Milton Abbey School, Blandford Forum	F

Port Regis Preparatory School, Shaftesbury	F W
St Mary's School, Dorset, Shaftesbury	F
Sherborne Girls, Sherborne	F
Sherborne School, Sherborne	F
Talbot Heath, Bournemouth	F W Fl
Thornlow Preparatory School, Weymouth	Fl

COUNTY DURHAM

Barnard Castle School, Barnard Castle	F Fl
The Chorister School, Durham	F W Fl
Durham School, Durham	F W Fl
Polam Hall, Darlington	F W Fl

ESSEX

Brentwood School, Brentwood	F W
Chigwell School, Chigwell	F W Fl
Felsted School, Felsted	F Fl
Friends' School	F W Fl
Gosfield School, Halstead	F W Fl
Holmwood House, Colchester	W Fl
New Hall School, Chelmsford	F W Fl

GLOUCESTERSHIRE

Beaudesert Park School, Stroud	W Fl
Bredon School, Tewkesbury	F W Fl
Cheltenham College, Cheltenham	F Fl
Cheltenham College Junior School, Cheltenham	F W Fl
Cheltenham Ladies' College, Cheltenham	F
Dean Close Preparatory School, Cheltenham	F Fl
Dean Close School, Cheltenham	F Fl
Hatherop Castle School, Cirencester	F W Fl
Kitebrook House, Moreton-in-Marsh	W
Rendcomb College, Cirencester	F W Fl
Westonbirt School, Tetbury	F W Fl
Wycliffe College, Stonehouse	F Fl H
Wycliffe Preparatory School, Stonehouse	F W
Wynstones School, Gloucester	F W Fl H

HAMPSHIRE

Bedales Prep School, Dunhurst, Petersfield	F W Fl
Bedales School, Petersfield	F
Boundary Oak School, Fareham	F W Fl H
Brockwood Park School, Bramdean	F
Farleigh School, Andover	F W Fl
Forres Sandle Manor, Fordingbridge	F W
Hampshire Collegiate School, UCST, Romsey	F W Fl
Highfield School, Liphook	F
Hordle Walhampton School, Lymington	F W
Lord Wandsworth College, Hook	F W Fl

Moyles Court School, Ringwood	F
The Pilgrims' School, Winchester	F W
Rookwood School, Andover	F W Fl
St John's College, Southsea	F Fl
St Neot's Preparatory School, Hook	W Fl
St Swithun's School, Winchester	F W
Twyford School, Winchester	W Fl H
Winchester College, Winchester	F

HEREFORDSHIRE

Lucton School, Leominster	F W Fl
St Richard's, Bromyard	F W Fl

HERTFORDSHIRE

Aldenham School, Elstree	F W Fl
Aldwickbury School, Harpenden	W Fl
Beechwood Park School, St Albans	W Fl
Berkhamsted School, Berkhamsted	F W Fl
Bishop's Stortford College, Bishop's Stortford	F W Fl
Bishop's Stortford College Junior School, Bishop's Stortford	F W Fl
Edge Grove	F W Fl
Haileybury, Hertford	F Fl
Heath Mount School, Hertford	W Fl
Lockers Park, Hemel Hempstead	F W Fl
The Purcell School, Bushey	F
Queenswood, Hatfield	F Fl
The Royal Masonic School for Girls, Rickmansworth	F W Fl
St Christopher School, Letchworth Garden City	F W Fl
St Edmund's College & Prep School, Ware	F W Fl
St Francis' College, Letchworth Garden City	F W Fl
St Margaret's School, Bushey	F W Fl
Stanborough School, Watford	F W Fl
Tring Park School for the Performing Arts, Tring	F
Westbrook Hay Preparatory School, Hemel Hempstead	Fl

ISLE OF MAN

King William's College, Castletown	F W

ISLE OF WIGHT

Ryde School, Ryde	F W Fl

KENT

Ashford School, Ashford	F W Fl

Beechwood Sacred Heart School,	
Tunbridge Wells	F W Fl
Benenden School, Cranbrook	F
Bethany School, Cranbrook	F W
CATS College Canterbury, Canterbury	F W Fl H
Cobham Hall, Gravesend	F W Fl
Cranbrook School, Cranbrook	F
Darul Uloom London, Chislehurst	F
Dover College, Dover	F W Fl
Duke of York's Royal Military School, Dover	F
Dulwich Preparatory School, Cranbrook,	
Cranbrook	W Fl
Farringtons School, Chislehurst	F W Fl
Holmewood House, Tunbridge Wells	W Fl
Junior King's Canterbury, Canterbury	F W Fl
Kent College, Canterbury	F W Fl
Kent College Infant & Junior School,	
Canterbury	F W Fl
Kent College Pembury, Tunbridge Wells	F W Fl
King's Preparatory School, Rochester	F W Fl
King's Rochester, Rochester	F W
The King's School, Canterbury	F
Marlborough House School, Hawkhurst	Fl
The New Beacon, Sevenoaks	Fl
Northbourne Park School, Deal	F W Fl
Rochester Independent College,	
Rochester	F W Fl
St Edmund's School Canterbury,	
Canterbury	F W Fl
St Edmunds Junior School,	
Canterbury	F Fl
St Lawrence College, Ramsgate	F
St Lawrence College Junior School,	
Ramsgate	F W Fl
Sevenoaks School, Sevenoaks	F
Sutton Valence School, Sutton Valence	F W Fl
Tonbridge School, Tonbridge	F W
Warnborough College, Canterbury	F W Fl H

LANCASHIRE

Jamea Al Kauthar, Lancaster	F
Kirkham Grammar School, Preston	F W Fl
Markazul Uloom, Blackburn	F
Moorland School, Clitheroe	F W Fl
Rossall School, Fleetwood	F Fl
Rossall School, Fleetwood	F Fl
Rossall School International Study Centre,	
Fleetwood	F
St Anne's College Grammar School,	
Lytham St Annes	F W Fl H
St Mary's Hall, Clitheroe	F W Fl
Stonyhurst College, Clitheroe	F W

LEICESTERSHIRE

Brooke House College, Market Harborough	F H

Loughborough Grammar School,	
Loughborough	F W Fl
Ratcliffe College, Leicester	F W Fl

LINCOLNSHIRE

St Hugh's School, Woodhall Spa	F W
Stamford High School,	
Stamford	F W Fl
Stamford Junior School,	
Stamford	F W Fl
Stamford School,	
Stamford	F W Fl
Witham Hall, Bourne	F W Fl

NORTH EAST LINCOLNSHIRE

St James' School, Grimsby	F W Fl

LONDON

Albemarle Independent College	Fl
CATS College London	F W Fl
Chelsea Independent College	H
David Game College	Fl H
Davies Laing and Dick	H
Dulwich College	F W
Dulwich College Preparatory School	W
International Community School	F W H
Mill Hill School	F
The North London International School	H
Royal Ballet School	F
The Royal School, Hampstead	F W Fl
St Paul's Cathedral School	F
St Paul's School	F W Fl
Sylvia Young Theatre School	F W H
Walthamstow Montessori School	Fl
Westminster Abbey Choir School	F Fl
Westminster Cathedral Choir School	F
Westminster School, Westminster	F W
Westminster Tutors	Fl H

GREATER MANCHESTER

Abbey College, Manchester	Fl
Chetham's School of Music,	
Manchester	F
St Bede's College,	
Manchester	H

MERSEYSIDE

Kingsmead School, Wirral	F W Fl

MIDDLESEX

Harrow School, Harrow on the Hill	F

NORFOLK

Beeston Hall School, Cromer	F
Glebe House School, Hunstanton	W FI
Gresham's School, Holt	F
Hethersett Old Hall School, Norwich	F W FI
Langley Preparatory School & Nursery, Norwich	FI
Langley School, Norwich	F W
The New Eccles Hall School, Norwich	F W FI
Riddlesworth Hall, Diss	F W FI
Sacred Heart School, Swaffham	F W FI
Taverham Hall Preparatory School, Norwich	W FI

NORTHAMPTONSHIRE

Beachborough School, Brackley	FI
Bosworth Independent College, Northampton	F W H
Maidwell Hall School	F W
Oundle School, Nr Peterborough	F
Quinton House School, Northampton	H
Winchester House School, Brackley	F W FI

NORTHUMBERLAND

Longridge Towers School, Berwick-upon-Tweed	F W FI
Mowden Hall School, Stocksfield	F W

NOTTINGHAMSHIRE

Al Karam Secondary School, Retford	F FI
Ranby House School, Retford	F W FI
Trent College & The Elms, Nottingham	F W FI
Wellow House School, Newark	W FI
Worksop College, Worksop	F W FI

OXFORDSHIRE

Abacus College, Oxford	H
Abingdon School, Abingdon	F W
Cherwell College, Oxford	F W H
Cothill House Preparatory School, Abingdon	F
d'Overbroeck's College Oxford, Oxford	F H
Dragon School, Oxford	F
Greene's Tutorial College, Oxford	F W FI H
Headington School, Oxford	F W FI
Kingham Hill School, Chipping Norton	F W FI

Moulsford Preparatory School, Wallingford	W
The Oratory Preparatory School, Reading	F W FI
Oxford Tutorial College, Oxford	W FI H
Radley College, Abingdon	F
St Edward's School, Oxford	F
St Hugh's School, Faringdon	W FI
St. Clare's, Oxford, Oxford	F W FI
Shiplake College, Henley-on-Thames	F W
Sibford School, Banbury	F W FI
Summer Fields, Oxford	F
Tudor Hall School, Banbury	F
Wychwood School, Oxford	F W FI

RUTLAND

Oakham School, Oakham	F FI
Uppingham School, Uppingham	F

SHROPSHIRE

Adcote School for Girls, Shrewsbury	F W FI H
Bedstone College, Bucknell	F FI
Concord College, Shrewsbury	F
Ellesmere College, Ellesmere	F W FI
Moor Park School, Ludlow	F W FI
Moreton Hall School, Oswestry	F H
The Old Hall School, Telford	FI
Oswestry School, Oswestry	F W FI
Oswestry School Bellan House, Oswestry	FI
Packwood Haugh School, Shrewsbury	F
Prestfelde Preparatory School, Shrewsbury	W FI
Shrewsbury School, Shrewsbury	F
Wrekin College	F W FI

SOMERSET

All Hallows, Shepton Mallet	F FI
Bath Academy, Bath	F H
Bruton School for Girls, Bruton	F W FI
Chilton Cantelo School, Yeovil	F FI
Downside School, Bath	F
Hazlegrove, Yeovil	F W FI
King's Bruton and Hazlegrove, Bruton	F
King's College, Taunton	F
King's Hall, Taunton	F W FI
Millfield Preparatory School, Glastonbury	F
Millfield School, Street	F
The Park School, Yeovil	F W H
Perrott Hill School, Crewkerne	F W FI
Queen's College, Taunton	F FI
Queen's College Junior, Pre-Prep & Nursery Schools, Taunton	F
Taunton Preparatory School, Taunton	F W FI
Taunton School International, Taunton	F H
Taunton School Senior, Taunton	F
Wellington School, Wellington	F W FI

Wells Cathedral Junior School, Wells   F W Fl
Wells Cathedral School, Wells   F W Fl

BATH & NORTH EAST SOMERSET

Kingswood Preparatory School, Bath   F W Fl
Kingswood School, Bath   F W Fl
Prior Park College, Bath   F W Fl
The Royal High School, Bath, Bath   F W Fl

NORTH SOMERSET

Lancaster House School, Weston-Super-Mare   Fl
Sidcot School, Winscombe   F W Fl

STAFFORDSHIRE

Abbots Bromley School, Abbots Bromley   F W Fl
Abbotsholme School, Uttoxeter   F W Fl
Chase Academy, Cannock   F
Denstone College, Uttoxeter   F W Fl
Lichfield Cathedral School, Lichfield   F W Fl
Yarlet School, Stafford   Fl

SUFFOLK

Alexanders International School, Woodbridge   F
Barnardiston Hall Preparatory School,
    Haverhill   F W Fl
Brandeston Hall, The Preparatory School for
    Framlingham College, Brandeston   F W Fl
Culford School, Bury St Edmunds   F W Fl
Felixstowe International College, Felixstowe   F
Finborough School, Stowmarket   F W Fl
Framlingham College, Woodbridge   F W Fl
Ipswich School, Ipswich   F W Fl
Moreton Hall Preparatory School,
    Bury St Edmunds   F W Fl
Old Buckenham Hall School, Ipswich   F W
Orwell Park, Ipswich   F W Fl
The Royal Hospital School, Ipswich   F W Fl H
St George's School, Southwold   Fl
St Joseph's College, Ipswich   F W Fl H
Saint Felix School, Southwold   F W Fl
Stoke College, Sudbury   W Fl
Summerhill School, Leiston   F
Woodbridge School, Woodbridge   F W Fl

SURREY

ACS Cobham International School, Cobham   F W
Aldro School, Godalming   F W Fl

Amesbury, Hindhead   Fl
Bishopsgate School, Egham   W Fl
Box Hill School, Dorking   F W
Cambridge Tutors College, Croydon   H
Charterhouse, Godalming   F
City of London Freemen's School, Ashtead   F
Cranleigh School, Cranleigh   F
Duke of Kent School, Guildford   F W Fl
Edgeborough, Farnham   W Fl
Epsom College, Epsom   F W
Feltonfleet School, Cobham   W Fl
Frensham Heights School, Farnham   F Fl
Hall Grove School, Bagshot   W Fl
Hurtwood House, Dorking   F W
King Edward's School Witley, Godalming   F W Fl
Marymount International School,
    Kingston-upon-Thames   F W Fl H
Prior's Field School, Godalming   F W Fl
Reed's School, Cobham   F
Royal Alexandra and Albert School, Reigate   F
Royal Russell School, Croydon   F W Fl
The Royal School, Haslemere   F W Fl
St Catherine's School, Guildford   F W Fl
St Edmund's School, Hindhead   W Fl
St James Independent School for Boys (Senior),
    Ashford   W
St John's School, Leatherhead   F W
St Teresa's Preparatory School, Effingham   F W Fl
St Teresa's School, Dorking   F W Fl
TASIS The American School in England, Thorpe   F
Woodcote House School, Windlesham   F
Yehudi Menuhin School, Cobham   F Fl

EAST SUSSEX

Ashdown House School, Forest Row   F
Battle Abbey School, Battle   F W Fl
Bellerbys College, Brighton   F
Brighton College, Brighton   F W
Buckswood School, Hastings   F W
Eastbourne College, Eastbourne   F
Greenfields Independent Day and
    Boarding School, Forest Row   F W Fl H
Michael Hall (Steiner Waldorf School),
    Forest Row   F W Fl H
Moira House Girls School, Eastbourne   F W Fl
Moira House School, Eastbourne   F W Fl
Newlands School, Seaford   F W
Roedean School, Brighton   F Fl
St Andrew's School, Eastbourne   F W Fl
St Aubyns School, Brighton   W Fl
St Bede's Prep School, Eastbourne   F W Fl
St Bede's School, Hailsham   F W
St Leonards-Mayfield School, Mayfield   F W Fl
Stonelands School of Ballet & Theatre Arts,
    Hove   F Fl
Vinehall School, Robertsbridge   F Fl

WEST SUSSEX

Ardingly College, Haywards Heath	F W Fl
Ardingly College Junior School, Haywards Heath	Fl
Burgess Hill School for Girls, Burgess Hill	F Fl
Christ's Hospital, Horsham	F W
Copthorne Prep School, Copthorne	W Fl
Cottesmore School, Pease Pottage	F W Fl
Dorset House School, Pulborough	W Fl
Farlington School, Horsham	F W Fl
Great Ballard School, Chichester	W Fl
Great Walstead, Haywards Heath	W Fl
Handcross Park School, Haywards Heath	W Fl
Hurstpierpoint College, Hurstpierpoint	F W Fl
The Prebendal School, Chichester	F W Fl
Seaford College, Petworth	F W Fl
Slindon College, Arundel	F W Fl
Sompting Abbotts School, Sompting	W Fl
The Towers Convent School, Steyning	F W Fl
Westbourne House School, Chichester	F Fl
Windlesham House School	F
Worth School, Turners Hill	F

WARWICKSHIRE

Bilton Grange, Rugby	F W Fl
Rugby School, Rugby	F
Warwick School, Warwick	F W Fl

WEST MIDLANDS

Abbey College, Birmingham	Fl
Birchfield School, Wolverhampton	W
Elmhurst School for Dance, Birmingham	F
The Royal Wolverhampton Junior School, Wolverhampton	F
Tettenhall College, Wolverhampton	F W Fl

WILTSHIRE

Bishopstrow College	F
Chafyn Grove School, Salisbury	F Fl
Dauntsey's School, Devizes	F
The Godolphin School, Salisbury	F W Fl H
Leaden Hall School, Salisbury	F Fl
Marlborough College, Marlborough	F
Norman Court Preparatory School, Salisbury	F W Fl
Pinewood School, Shrivenham	F W Fl
Prior Park Preparatory School, Cricklade	F W Fl
St Mary's Calne, Calne	F
Salisbury Cathedral School, Salisbury	F Fl
Sandroyd School, Salisbury	F Fl
Stonar School	F W Fl
Warminster School, Warminster	F W Fl

WORCESTERSHIRE

Abberley Hall, Worcester	F Fl
The Abbey College, Malvern Wells	Fl
Bromsgrove Preparatory School, Bromsgrove	F W Fl
Bromsgrove School, Bromsgrove	F
The Downs, Malvern, Malvern	F W Fl
The Elms, Malvern	F Fl
Malvern St James, Great Malvern	F W Fl
Moffats School, Bewdley	F W Fl
Saint Michael's College, Tenbury Wells	F H

EAST RIDING OF YORKSHIRE

Pocklington School, Pocklington	F W

NORTH YORKSHIRE

Ampleforth College, York	F
Ashville College, Harrogate	F W Fl
Aysgarth Preparatory School, Bedale	F W Fl
Bootham School, York	F W Fl
Bramcote School, Scarborough	F W Fl
Cundall Manor School, York	F
Fyling Hall School, Whitby	F W Fl
Giggleswick Junior School, Settle	F Fl
Giggleswick School, Settle	F
Harrogate Ladies' College, Harrogate	F W Fl
Harrogate Language Academy, Harrogate	H
Harrogate Tutorial College, Harrogate	F W Fl H
Highfield Preparatory School, Harrogate	F W Fl
Lisvane, Scarborough College Junior School, Scarborough	F W
Malsis School, Near Skipton	F
The Mount School, York	F W Fl
Queen Ethelburga's College, York	F
Queen Mary's School, Thirsk	F W Fl
Read School, Selby	F W Fl
Ripon Cathedral Choir School, Ripon	F W Fl
St Martin's Ampleforth, York	F Fl
St Peter's School, York	F W Fl
Scarborough College & Lisvane School, Scarborough	F W Fl
Terrington Hall, York	F W Fl
Woodleigh School, Malton	F W Fl

WEST YORKSHIRE

Ackworth School, Pontefract	F W Fl
Bronte House School, Bradford	F W Fl
Fulneck School, Leeds	F W Fl
Rishworth School, Rishworth	F W Fl
Woodhouse Grove School, Apperley Bridge	F W Fl

NORTHERN IRELAND

COUNTY ANTRIM

Cabin Hill School, Belfast	FI
Campbell College, Belfast	F W FI
Hunterhouse College, Belfast	FI
Methodist College, Belfast	F
Victoria College Belfast, Belfast	F W FI

COUNTY ARMAGH

The Royal School ARMAGH, Armagh	F W FI

COUNTY DOWN

Rockport School, Holywood	F W FI

COUNTY TYRONE

The Royal School Dungannon, Dungannon	F W FI

SCOTLAND

ANGUS

Lathallan School, Montrose	F W FI

ARGYLL AND BUTE

Lomond School, Helensburgh	F H

CLACKMANNANSHIRE

Dollar Academy, Dollar	F W FI

FIFE

St Leonards School, St Andrews	F W FI

LOTHIAN

Basil Paterson Tutorial College, Edinburgh	H
Belhaven Hill, Dunbar	F
Cargilfield, Edinburgh	F W FI
The Edinburgh Academy, Edinburgh	FI
The Edinburgh Rudolf Steiner School, Edinburgh	FI
Fettes College, Edinburgh	F

George Watson's College, Edinburgh	H
Loretto Junior School, Musselburgh	F W FI
Loretto School, Musselburgh	F W FI
The Mary Erskine School, Edinburgh	F W
Merchiston Castle School, Edinburgh	F FI
St George's School for Girls, Edinburgh	F W FI
St Mary's Music School, Edinburgh	F
Stewart's Melville College, Edinburgh	F W FI

MORAYSHIRE

Gordonstoun School, Elgin	F W

PERTH AND KINROSS

Ardvreck School, Crieff	F
Glenalmond College, Perth	F
Kilgraston, Perth	F W FI
Queen Victoria School, Dunblane	F
Strathallan School, Perth	F

ROXBURGHSHIRE

St Mary's Preparatory School, Melrose	W FI

WALES

CARMARTHENSHIRE

Llandovery College, Llandovery	F W Fl
St Michael's School, Llanelli	F H

CONWY

St David's College, Llandudno	F W Fl

DENBIGHSHIRE

Howell's School, Denbigh	F W Fl
Ruthin School, Ruthin	F

MONMOUTHSHIRE

Haberdashers' Monmouth School For Girls, Monmouth	F W Fl
Monmouth School, Monmouth	F W Fl
St John's-on-the-Hill, Chepstow	F W Fl

POWYS

Christ College, Brecon	F W Fl

CONTINENTAL EUROPE

Aiglon College, Switzerland	F W	John F Kennedy International School	F
Chavagnes International College, CHAVAGNES-EN-PAILLERS, France	F W Fl	King's College Madrid, Madrid	F
Collège du Léman International School, Geneva	F W Fl	Le Rosey	F
Headfort	F W Fl	Mougins School	H
		St Columba's College	F

Religious Affiliation

The following index lists all schools specifying a particular denomination. However, it should be noted that this is intended as a guide only and that many of the schools listed also welcome children of other faiths. Schools which claim to be non- or inter-denominational are not listed. Parents should check precise details with individual schools. A full list of each school's entries elsewhere in the book is given in the main index at the back.

BUDDHIST

Dharma School, Brighton
Shi-Tennoji School In UK, Bury St Edmunds

CHRISTIAN

Abbey Gate School, Chester
Abingdon Preparatory School, Abingdon
Alderley Edge School for Girls, Alderley Edge
Aldro School, Godalming
All Saints School, Norwich
Allbrook Education Trust
Amberfield School, Ipswich
Ardvreck School, Crieff
The Ark School, Reading
Arnold Lodge School, Leamington Spa
Ashdell Preparatory School, Sheffield
Ashfold School, Aylesbury
Avon House, Woodford Green
Avondale School, Salisbury
Ballymoney Independent Christian School, Ballymoney
Bangor Independent Christian School, Bangor
Barn School, Much Hadham
Barnardiston Hall Preparatory School, Haverhill
Barnsley Christian School, Barnsley
The Beacon School, Amersham
Beechwood School, Whittlesord
Benedict House Preparatory School, Sidcup
Benty Heath School and Kindergarten, South Wirral
Berkhamsted School, Berkhamsted

Berkhamsted School, Berkhamsted
Bethany School, Cranbrook
Blundell's Preparatory School, Tiverton
Bowbrook House School, Pershore
Bradford Christian School, Bradford
Branch Christian School, Dewsbury
The Branch Christian School, Heckmondwike
Breckland Park School, Swaffham
Bromley High School GDST, Bromley
Broomwood Hall School
Brownberrie School, Leeds
Bushey Place School, Norwich
Carmel Christian School
Castle Court Preparatory School, Wimborne
Castle House School, Newport
Caterham Preparatory School, Caterham
The Cavendish School
Cedar School, London
Cedars Christian School, Rochester
The Cedars School, Aldermaston
Chard School, Chard
Chase Academy, Cannock
Chorcliffe School, Chorley
Christ the King School, Sale
Christian Fellowship School, Liverpool
Christian School (Takeley), Bishop's Stortford
Clifton Lodge Preparatory School
Combe Bank School, Sevenoaks
The Crescent School, Rugby
Croham Hurst School, South Croydon
The Daiglen School, Buckhurst Hill
Dale House School, Batley
Dame Alice Harpur School, Bedford
Danes Hill School, Leatherhead

Danesfield Manor School, Walton-on-Thames
Darvell School, Robertsbridge
Davenies School, Beaconsfield
Dean Close School, Cheltenham
Derby Grammar School, Derby
Derwent Lodge School for Girls, Tonbridge
Ditcham Park School, Petersfield
Dolphin School (Including Noah's Ark Nursery
    School), London
The Dolphin School, Exmouth
The Downs, Malvern, Malvern
Downham Prep School and Montessori Nursery,
    Kings Lynn
East London Christian Choir School
Edgbaston College, Birmingham
Emmanuel Christian School, Crosskeys
Emmanuel Christian School, Rochdale
Emmanuel Christian School, Oxford
Emmanuel School, Derby
Emmanuel School, Walsall
Emmanuel School, Exeter
Emmaus School, Trowbridge
Eversfield Preparatory School, Solihull
Eversley School, Southwold
Exeter Junior School, Exeter
Exeter School, Exeter
Felsted School, Felsted
Ffynone House School
Filgrave School, Newport Pagnell
Fosse Bank School, Tonbridge
Francis House Preparatory School, Tring
The Froebelian School, Leeds
Fulneck School, Leeds
Gatehouse School
Gateway Christian School, Ilkeston
Gems Bolitho School, Penzance
Ghyll Royd School, Ilkley
Glen Morven School, Aboyne
Glenarm College, Ilford
Godolphin Preparatory School, Salisbury
Gracefield Preparatory School, Fishponds
Grangewood Independent School
Great Walstead, Haywards Heath
Grey House Preparatory School, Hook
Guildford High School, Guildford
Hamilton College, Hamilton
Handsworth Christian School, Sheffield
Haslemere Preparatory School, Haslemere
Haylett Grange Preparatory School,
    Haverfordwest
Heath House Preparatory School
Heathfield School, Ascot
Hereford Cathedral School, Hereford
Herne Hill School
High Leas Education Centre, Lincoln
Highfield School, Liphook
Highway Christian School, London
Hill House School, Mayfield
Hillgrove School, Bangor

Holy Trinity School, Kidderminster
Honeybourne School, Birmingham
Horris Hill School, Newbury
Howell's School, Denbigh
Hydesville Tower School, Walsall
Immanuel School, Plymouth
Jack and Jill School, Hampton
Joseph Rayner Independent School, Audenshaw
King of Kings School, Manchester
King's School and Nursery, Plymouth
Kingdom Christian School, Kirkcaldy
Kingham Hill School, Chipping Norton
Kings Primary School, Southampton
Kingsfold Christian School, Preston
Kingsley Preparatory School, Solihull
Kingsmead School, Wirral
Kingston Grammar School, Kingston-upon-
    Thames
The King's School, Harpenden
The King's School, Nottingham
The King's School, Primary, Witney
The King's School Senior, Eastleigh
Kingsway School, East Grinstead
Kingsway School, Wigan
Knighton House, Blandford Forum
Kwabena Montessori School, Farnborough
La Sagesse School, Newcastle upon Tyne
Lady Barn House School, Cheadle
Lady Eden's School, London
The Lady Eleanor Holles School, Hampton
Lambs Christian School, Birmingham
Langley Manor School
Lea House School, Kidderminster
Leeds Christian School, Farnley
Leehurst Swan, Salisbury
Leicester Grammar School, Leicester
Lighthouse Christian School, Manchester
Lingfield Notre Dame School, Lingfield
Lisvane, Scarborough College Junior School,
    Scarborough
Littlefield School, Liphook
Lochinver House School, Potters Bar
Locksley Christian School, Manby
London Christian Learning Centre, London
Lorenden Preparatory School, Faversham
Luckley-Oakfield School, Wokingham
Lucton School, Leominster
The Lyceum
Mannafields Christian School, Edinburgh
Maranatha Christian School, Swindon
Marlin Montessori School, Berkhamsted
Mayfield Preparatory School, Walsall
Maypole House School, Alford
The Mead School, Tunbridge Wells
Meadowpark School and Nursery, Cricklade
Mereside Education Trust, Sale
Midland Oak School, Tipton
Monton Prep School with Montessori Nurseries,
    Eccles

Mount Lourdes Grammar School, Enniskillen
Mount Zion School, Eastville
Mountjoy House School, Huddersfield
Mourne Independent Christian School, Kilkeel
New Harvest Learning Centre, Salford
New Life Christian School, Croydon
Norfolk House Preparatory & Kids Corner Nursery,
    Sandbach
Norfolk House School, Birmingham
Northampton Christian School, Northampton
Northcote Lodge School
Norwich School, Norwich
The Octagon School, London
Paragon Christian Academy
The Park School, Yeovil
Perivale Study Centre
Phoenix School, Westoning
Plymouth College, Plymouth
The Pointer School
The Portsmouth Grammar School, Portsmouth
The Potters House School, Bury
The Preparatory School Lightcliffe, Halifax
Priory School, Shanklin
Promised Land Academy, London
Prospect School
The Rastrick Independent School, Brighouse
Red House School, Norton
Redcliffe School
Redemption Academy, Stevenage
Regius Christian School, Edinburgh
Richmond House School, Leeds
Ridgeway School, Maidenhead
River School, Worcester
Roundstone Preparatory School, Trowbridge
The Royal Hospital School, Ipswich
Sacred Heart Preparatory School,
    Chew Magna
Sceptre School, Dunstable
The School of the Lion, Gloucester
Sedbergh Junior School, Sedbergh
Sefton Park School, Stoke Poges
Shepherds Community School, London
Sherborne Preparatory School, Sherborne
Shobrooke House School, Crediton
Silchester Manor School, Taplow
Silfield School, Kings Lynn
Somerhill Pre-Preparatory School, Tonbridge
South Hills School, Salisbury
Spratton Hall, Northampton
Springfield Christian School
St Andrew's (Woking) School Trust, Woking
St Anne's Mixed High School, South Shields
St Aubyn's School, Woodford Green
St Christophers School, Totnes
St David's College, Llandudno
St David's School, Brecon
St Dominic's School, Stafford
St Faith's, Cambridge
St Francis' College, Letchworth Garden City

St George's School, Edgbaston, Birmingham
St Helen's College, Hillingdon
St Helen's School, Northwood
St Hilda's School, Westcliff-on-Sea
St John's Senior School, Enfield
St Joseph's College, Ipswich
St Lawrence College, Ramsgate
St Mary's Preparatory School, Lincoln
St Mary's Westbrook, Folkestone
St Mary's Westbrook, Folkestone
St Matthews School, Northampton
St Michael's School, Leigh-on-Sea
St Oswald's School, Alnwick
St Peter's School, Exmouth
St Piran's Preparatory School, Maidenhead
St Swithun's Junior School, Winchester
Stanway School, Dorking
Stonefield House, Lincoln
Stonehouse Nursery School, Leyland
Stoneygate College, Leicester
Stover School, Newton Abbot
Stretton House Pre-preparatory School,
    Knutsford
Sunflower Montessori School, Twickenham
Sunninghill Preparatory School, Dorchester
Tabernacle School
The Terrace School, Leamington Spa
Thames Christian College
Thomas's Kindergarten
Thorpe Hall School, Southend-on-Sea
Trent College & The Elms, Nottingham
Trinity School, Croydon
Trinity School, Stalybridge
Twickenham Preparatory School, Hampton
Victoria College, Jersey
Victory Academy, Leeds
Vine School, Southampton
Wakefield Tutorial Preparatory School, Leeds
Warlingham Park School, Croydon
Warwick Preparatory School, Warwick
Wellspring Christian School, Carlisle
West Buckland School, Barnstaple
West Hill Park School
Westmont School, Newport
Weston Green School, Thames Ditton
Westwing School, Thornbury
Wetherby Preparatory School
Wharfedale Montessori School, Skipton
White House Preparatory School, Wokingham
Willowfields School, Bradford
Windmill House Preparatory School,
    Uppingham
Woodford Green Preparatory School,
    Woodford Green
Worksop College, Worksop
Wyclif Independent Christian School,
    Machen
Yardley Court Preparatory School, Tonbridge
Yarm School, Yarm

CHRISTIAN SCIENCE

Claremont Fan Court School, Esher
Haberdashers' Aske's School for Girls, Elstree

CHURCH IN WALES

Agincourt School, Monmouth
Christ College, Brecon
Ffynone House School
Llandovery College, Llandovery
Lyndon School, Colwyn Bay
Monmouth School, Monmouth
The Cathedral School

CHURCH OF ENGLAND

The Abbey, Woodbridge
Abbey Gate College, Chester
The Abbey School, Reading
The Abbey School, Tewkesbury
Abbot's Hill School, Hemel Hempstead
Abbots Bromley School, Abbots Bromley
Abbots Junior Hill School, Hemel Hempstead
Abbotsbury School, Newton Abbot
Aberdour School, Tadworth
Abingdon School, Abingdon
The Acorn School, Nailsworth
Adcote School for Girls, Shrewsbury
Airthrie School, Cheltenham
Aldenham School, Elstree
Aldwickbury School, Harpenden
Alleyn Court Preparatory School,
    Southend-on-Sea
Alleyn's School
Allhallows College, Lyme Regis
Ambleside PNEU School, Cheam
Amesbury, Hindhead
Arden Lawn, Solihull
Ardingly College, Haywards Heath
Ardingly College Junior School, Haywards Heath
Arnold House School
Ashdown House School, Forest Row
The Atherley School, Southampton
Aymestrey School, Worcester
Aysgarth Preparatory School, Bedale
Ballard School, New Milton
Bancroft's School, Woodford Green
Barfield School and Nursery, Farnham
Beachborough School, Brackley
Bearwood College, Wokingham
Beaudesert Park School, Stroud
Bedford Preparatory School, Bedford
Bedford School, Bedford
Bedstone College, Bucknell
Beech Hall School, Macclesfield

Beechenhurst Preparatory School, Liverpool
Beechwood Park, St Albans
Beechwood Park School, St Albans
Beeston Hall School, Cromer
Bellerbys College, Wadhurst, Wadhurst
Benenden School, Cranbrook
Berkhampstead School, Cheltenham
Bilton Grange, Rugby
Birchfield School, Wolverhampton
Bloxham School, Banbury
The Blue Coat School, Birmingham
Blundell's School, Tiverton
Bodiam Manor School, Robertsbridge
Bow School, Durham
Bradfield College, Reading
Brambletye, East Grinstead
Bramcote Lorne School, Retford
Bramcote School, Scarborough
Bramcote School, Scarborough
Brandeston Hall, The Preparatory School for
    Framlingham College, Brandeston
Bredon School, Tewkesbury
Brentwood School, Brentwood
Brigg Preparatory School, Brigg
Brighton College, Brighton
Brighton College Pre-preparatory School, Brighton
Brighton College Prep School, Brighton
Bristol Cathedral School
Broadwater Manor School, Worthing
Brockhurst & Marlston House Pre-Preparatory
    School, Thatcham
Brockhurst and Marlston House Schools, Newbury
Bromsgrove Pre-preparatory and Nursery School,
    Bromsgrove
Bromsgrove Preparatory School, Bromsgrove
Bromsgrove School, Bromsgrove
Bronte School, Gravesend
Brookland Hall Golf Academy, Welshpool
Broomfield House School, Richmond
Bruern Abbey School, Oxford
Bryanston School, Blandford Forum
Buckingham College Preparatory School, Pinner
Cable House School, Woking
Caldicott School, Farnham Royal
Canford School, Wimborne
Casterton School, Kirkby Lonsdale
The Cathedral School, Lincoln
Cawston College, Norwich
Chafyn Grove School, Salisbury
Chandlings Manor School, Oxford
Charterhouse, Godalming
Cheam School, Newbury
Cheltenham College, Cheltenham
Cheltenham College Junior School, Cheltenham
Cheltenham College Junior School, Cheltenham
Chigwell School, Chigwell
Chigwell School, Chigwell
Chilton Cantelo School, Yeovil
The Chorister School, Durham

Christ Church Cathedral School, Oxford
Christ's Hospital, Horsham
Church High School, Newcastle upon Tyne,
    Newcastle upon Tyne
Claremont School, St Leonards-on-Sea
Clayesmore, Blandford Forum
Clayesmore Preparatory School, Blandford Forum
Clifton College
Clifton College Preparatory School
Colet Court
Colfe's School
Colston's Collegiate School
Conifers School, Midhurst
Coopersale Hall School, Epping
Copthorne Prep School, Copthorne
Cothill House Preparatory School, Abingdon
Cottesmore School, Pease Pottage
Coventry Prep School, Coventry
Cranford House School, Wallingford
Cranleigh Preparatory School, Cranleigh
Cranleigh School, Cranleigh
Croft House School, Blandford Forum
The Croft Preparatory School, Stratford-upon-Avon
Croftdown House Malvern Girls' Preparatory,
    Malvern
Cumnor House School, Haywards Heath
Cumnor House School, South Croydon
Cundall Manor School, York
Dair House School Trust Ltd, Farnham Royal
Dame Allan's Junior School, Newcastle upon Tyne
Daneshill School, Basingstoke
Dean Close Preparatory School, Cheltenham
Deepdene School, Hove
Denmead School, Hampton
Denstone College, Uttoxeter
Derby High School, Derby
The Dormer House PNEU School, Moreton-in-
    Marsh
Dorset House School, Pulborough
Dover College, Dover
Downe House, Thatcham
The Downs School, Wraxall
Downside Preparatory School, Purley
Duke of York's Royal Military School, Dover
Dulwich College
Dulwich College Preparatory School
Dulwich Preparatory School, Cranbrook,
    Cranbrook
Dumpton School, Wimborne
Dumpton School, Wimborne
Duncombe School, Hertford
Durham High School For Girls, Durham
Durham School, Durham
Durlston Court, New Milton
Eagle House, Sandhurst
Eastbourne College, Eastbourne
Eastbourne College, Eastbourne
Edenhurst School, Newcastle-under-Lyme
Edge Grove

Edgeborough, Farnham
Edgehill School, Newark
Elizabeth College, Guernsey
Ellesmere College, Ellesmere
Elmhurst School for Dance, Birmingham
The Elms, Malvern
Elmslie Girls' School, Blackpool
Elstree School, Reading
The Elvian School, Reading
Emanuel School
Emanuel School, London
Emscote Lawn School, Warwick
Epsom College, Epsom
Epsom College, Epsom
Eton College, Windsor
Eton End PNEU, Slough
Ewell Castle School, Epsom
Excell International School, Boston
Exeter Cathedral School, Exeter
Fairfield School, Backwell
Fairholme Preparatory School, St Asaph
Farlington School, Horsham
Felixstowe International College, Felixstowe
Felsted Preparatory School, Felsted
Feltonfleet School, Cobham
Fen School, Sleaford
Flexlands School, Woking
Fonthill Lodge, East Grinstead
Foremarke Hall, Derby
Forest Girls' School, London
Forest School
Forres Sandle Manor, Fordingbridge
Foxley Nursery School, Reading
Framlingham College, Woodbridge
Francis Holland School, Regent's Park NW1
Francis Holland School, Sloane Square SW1
Friern Barnet Grammar School, London
Gayhurst School, Gerrards Cross
Giggleswick School, Settle
Glebe House School, Hunstanton
The Godolphin School, Salisbury
Godstowe Preparatory School, High Wycombe
Great Ballard School, Chichester
Gresham's Prep School
Gresham's School, Holt
Haberdashers' Aske's Boys' School, Elstree
Haileybury, Hertford
Haileybury Junior School, Windsor
Hallfield School, Birmingham
The Hall School
Halstead Preparatory School, Woking
Hammond School, Chester
Hampden Manor School, Great Missenden
Hampshire Collegiate School, UCST, Romsey
Handcross Park School, Haywards Heath
Hanford School, Blandford Forum
Harrogate Ladies' College, Harrogate
Harrow School, Harrow on the Hill
Hatherop Castle School, Cirencester

Hazelwood School, Oxted
Hazlegrove, Yeovil
Headington School, Oxford
Heath Mount School, Hertford
Helvetia House School, Jersey
The Hereford Cathedral Junior School, Hereford
Hethersett Old Hall School, Norwich
Highfield Preparatory School, Harrogate
Highfield School, Liphook
Highgate Junior School, London
Highgate Pre-Preparatory School, London
Highgate School
Hilden Grange School, Tonbridge
Hilden Oaks School, Tonbridge
Hillcroft Preparatory School, Stowmarket
Hollington School, Ashford
Holme Grange School, Wokingham
Holme Park School, Kendal
Hordle House, Lymington
Hordle Walhampton School, Lymington
Hull Collegiate School, Anlaby
Hull Grammar School, Kingston-Upon-Hull
Hurstpierpoint College, Hurstpierpoint
Innellan House School, Pinner
Ipswich School, Ipswich
James Allen's Girls' School
James Allen's Preparatory School
The Jordans Nursery School, London
Junior King's Canterbury, Canterbury
The Junior School, Wellingborough School,
    Wellingborough
Kelly College, Tavistock
Kelly College Preparatory School, Tavistock
Keswick School, Keswick
King Edward's School, Birmingham
King Edward's School Witley, Godalming
King William's College, Castletown
King's Bruton and Hazlegrove, Bruton
King's Bruton Pre-Preparatory & Junior School,
    Yeovil
King's College, Taunton
King's College Junior School
King's College School
King's College School, Cambridge
King's Hall, Taunton
King's Hawford, Worcester
King's Preparatory School, Rochester
King's Rochester, Rochester
King's School Ely, Ely
The King's School, Canterbury
The King's School, Chester
The King's School, Gloucester
The King's School, Macclesfield
The King's School, Worcester
King's School Rochester, Rochester
Kingscote Pre-Preparatory School, Gerrards
    Cross
Kingshott School, Hitchin
Kingsland Grange, Shrewsbury

The Kingsley School, Leamington Spa
Knighton House, Blandford Forum
The Knoll School, Kidderminster
Lambrook, Bracknell
Lambrook, Bracknell
Lancing College, Lancing
Lancing College Preparatory School at Mowden,
    Hove
Landry School, Ingatestone
Lanesborough, Guildford
Lanherne Nursery and Junior School,
    Dawlish
Lavant House, Chichester
Laxton Junior School, Nr Peterborough
Laxton School, Peterborough
Leicester Grammar Junior School, Leicester
Leicester High School For Girls, Leicester
Leverets School, Stow on the Wold
Lichfield Cathedral School, Lichfield
The Littlemead School, Chichester
Liverpool College, Liverpool
Lockers Park, Hemel Hempstead
Lorne House, Retford
Ludgrove, Wokingham
Magdalen College School, Oxford
Maidwell Hall School
Malsis School, Near Skipton
Malvern College, Malvern
Malvern College Preparatory and Pre-Prep
    School, Malvern
Malvern St James, Great Malvern
Manor Independent School, Taunton
The Manor Preparatory School, Abingdon
Mansfield Infant College, Ilford
Margaret May Schools Ltd, Sevenoaks
Marlborough College, Marlborough
Marlborough House School, Hawkhurst
Marlston House School, Newbury
Meadowbrook Montessori School, Bracknell
Merchant Taylors' School, Northwood
Merton Court Preparatory School, Sidcup
Merton House, Chester
Micklefield School, Reigate
Milbourne Lodge School, Esher
Millbrook House School, Abingdon
Milton Abbey School, Blandford Forum
The Minster School, York
Moffats School, Bewdley
Moffats School, Bewdley
Monkton Prep, Bath
Monkton Senior School, Bath
Moorland School, Clitheroe
Morley Hall Preparatory School, Derby
Moulsford Preparatory School, Wallingford
Mount House School, Tavistock
Mowden Hall School, Stocksfield
Moyles Court School, Ringwood
The Mullberry Bush Nursery, Halesworth
Netherwood School, Saundersfoot

Nevill Holt School, Market Harborough
The New Beacon, Sevenoaks
New College School, Oxford
New Lodge School, Dorking
New School, Exeter
Norman Court Preparatory School, Salisbury
North Foreland Lodge School, Basingstoke
Northampton High School, Northampton
Northbourne Park School, Deal
Northwood Preparatory School, Rickmansworth
Oakham School, Oakham
Oakland Nursery School, Banstead
Oakwood School, Chichester
Old Buckenham Hall School, Ipswich
The Old Hall School, Telford
The Old Malthouse, Swanage
Old Palace of John Whitgift School, Croydon
The Old School, Beccles
Old Vicarage School, Richmond
Oriel Bank, Stockport
Orley Farm School, Harrow
Orley Farm School, Harrow
Oswestry School Bellan House, Oswestry
Oundle School, Nr Peterborough
Packwood Haugh School, Shrewsbury
Pangbourne College, Reading
Pangbourne College, Pangbourne
Papplewick School, Ascot
Park Hill School, Kingston-upon-Thames
Parkside School, Northampton
Parsons Mead, Ashtead
Peaslake School, Guildford
Pennthorpe School, Horsham
Perrott Hill School, Crewkerne
Peterborough & St Margaret's School, Stanmore
The Peterborough School, Peterborough
Pilgrims Pre-Preparatory School, Bedford
The Pilgrims' School, Winchester
Pinewood School, Shrivenham
Pipers Corner School, High Wycombe
Plumtree School, Nottingham
Pocklington School, Pocklington
The Prebendal School, Chichester
Prebendal School (Northgate House), Chichester
Prestfelde Preparatory School, Shrewsbury
Prestfelde Preparatory School, Shrewsbury
Prince's Mead School, Winchester
Prince's Mead School, Winchester
Princess Helena College, Hitchin
Putney Park School
Quainton Hall School, Harrow
Queen Anne's School
Queen Ethelburga's College, York
Queen Margaret's School, York
Queen Mary's School, Thirsk
Queen's College London, London
Queen's College Prep School
Radley College, Abingdon
Ranby House School, Retford

Rathdown School
Rathvilly School, Birmingham
Ravenscourt Theatre School
Read School, Selby
Reading Blue Coat School, Reading
Red House School, York
Reddiford, Pinner
Reed's School, Cobham
Reigate St Mary's Preparatory and Choir School,
   Reigate
Rendcomb College, Cirencester
Repton School, Derby
Riddlesworth Hall, Diss
Ripon Cathedral Choir School, Ripon
Rishworth School, Rishworth
Rock Hall School, Alnwick
Rodney School, Newark
Roedean School, Brighton
Rose Hill School, Wotton-under-Edge
Rose Hill Westonbirt School, Tetbury
Roselyon, Par
Rosemead School, Littlehampton
Rossall School, Fleetwood
Rossall School, Fleetwood
Rosslyn School, Birmingham
Roxeth Mead School, Harrow on the Hill
Royal Alexandra and Albert School, Reigate
Royal Russell School, Croydon
The Royal School, Haslemere
The Royal School For Girls, Haslemere
The Royal Wolverhampton Junior School,
   Wolverhampton
Rugby School, Rugby
Runton & Sutherland School, Cromer
Rushmoor School, Bedford
Rushmoor School, Bedford
Russell House School, Sevenoaks
Ryde School, Ryde
S. Anselm's School, Bakewell
Sackville School, Tonbridge
Saddleworth Preparatory School, Oldham
Saint Ronan's School, Hawkhurst
Salisbury Cathedral School, Salisbury
Salisbury Cathedral School, Salisbury
Sancton Wood School, Cambridge
Sanderstead Junior School, South Croydon
Sandroyd School, Salisbury
Sarum Hall
The School of St Clare, Penzance
Seaford College, Petworth
Sedbergh School, Sedbergh
Selwyn School, Gloucester
Shaw House School, Bradford
Sherborne Girls, Sherborne
Sherborne School, Sherborne
Shernold School, Maidstone
Sherrardswood School, Welwyn
Shiplake College, Henley-on-Thames
Shoreham College, Shoreham-by-Sea

Shrewsbury House School, Surbiton
Shrewsbury School, Shrewsbury
Sibton Park, Folkestone
Silchester House School, Maidenhead
Slapton Pre-Preparatory School, Towcester
Smallwood Manor Preparatory School, Uttoxeter
Snaresbrook College Preparatory School
Solefield School, Sevenoaks
Solihull School, Solihull
Sompting Abbotts School, Sompting
Southdown Nursery, Steyning
St Agnes PNEU School, Leeds
St Albans High School for Girls, St Albans
St Andrew's School, Woking
St Andrew's School, Reading
St Andrew's School, Eastbourne
St Andrew's Senior Girls' School, Harrow
St Aubyn's, Brighton
St Aubyns School, Brighton
St Bees School, St Bees
St Catherine's School, Guildford
St Christopher's School, Burnham-on-Sea
St Christopher's School
St Christopher's School, Epsom
St Christopher's School, Hove
St David's School, Purley
St Dunstan's Abbey Preparatory School, Plymouth
St Dunstan's Abbey School, Plymouth
St Dunstan's College
St Edmund's School, Hindhead
St Edmund's School Canterbury, Canterbury
St Edmunds Junior School, Canterbury
St Edward's School, Oxford
St Elphin's School, Matlock
St Francis Preparatory School, Drifield
St Francis School, Pewsey
St Gabriel's
St George's School, Windsor
St George's School, Ascot
St Helen & St Katharine, Abingdon
St Hilary's School, Alderley Edge
St Hilda's School, Whitby
St Hilda's School, Wakefield
St Hugh's School, Faringdon
St Hugh's School, Woodhall Spa
St Ives School, Haslemere
St James' School, Grimsby
St James's School, Malvern
St John's College School, Cambridge
St John's Northwood, Northwood
St John's School, Leatherhead
St John's-on-the-Hill, Chepstow
St Lawrence College Junior School, Ramsgate
St Margaret's School
St Margaret's School, Halstead
St Margaret's School, Exeter
St Margaret's School, Bushey
St Martin's Independent School, Crewkerne

St Martin's School, Northwood
St Martin's School, Bournemouth
St Mary's Calne, Calne
St Mary's Hall, Brighton
St Mary's Preparatory School, Tenbury Wells
St Mary's School, Wantage
St Mary's School, Gerrards Cross
St Michael's, Barnstaple
St Michael's School, Sevenoaks
St Neot's Preparatory School, Hook
St Nicholas' School, Fleet
St Olave's School (Junior of St Peter's), York
St Paul's Cathedral School
St Paul's School
St Peter's School, Kettering
St Peter's School, York
St Petroc's School, Bude
St Swithun's School, Winchester
St Wilfrid's Junior School, Exeter
St Wilfrid's School, Exeter
St Wystan's School, Repton
St Hilda's School, Harpenden
Stamford High School, Stamford
Stamford Junior School, Stamford
Stamford School, Stamford
Steephill Independent School, Longfield
Stepping Stones Nursery and Pre-Preparatory
    School, Marlborough
Stoke Brunswick, East Grinstead
Stoneygate School, Leicester
Stourbridge House School, Warminster
Stowe School, Buckingham
The Stroud School, Romsey
Stubbington House, Ascot
The Study School, New Malden
Summer Fields, Oxford
Sunderland High School, Sunderland
Sunningdale School, Sunningdale
Sunnyside School, Worcester
Surbiton High School, Kingston-upon-Thames
Surbiton Preparatory School, Surbiton
Sussex House School
Sutton Valence Preparatory School, Maidstone
Sutton Valence School, Sutton Valence
Swanbourne House School, Milton Keynes
Talbot Heath, Bournemouth
Temple Grove, Uckfield
Thomas's Kindergarten, Battersea
Thomas's Preparatory School
Thomas's Preparatory School Clapham
Thorpe House School, Gerrards Cross
Tockington Manor School, Tockington
Tonbridge School, Tonbridge
Trevor Roberts School
Truro High School, Truro
Tudor Hall School, Banbury
Twyford School, Winchester
Upfield Preparatory School Ltd, Stroud

Upper Chine School, Shanklin
Uppingham School, Uppingham
Upton House School, Windsor
Victoria Park Preparatory School, Shipley
Vinehall School, Robertsbridge
Wakefield Independent School, Wakefield
Warminster School, Warminster
Warwick School, Warwick
Wellesley House School, Broadstairs
Wellington College, Crowthorne
Wellington School, Wellington
Wells Cathedral Junior School, Wells
Wells Cathedral School, Wells
West Buckland Preparatory School, Barnstaple
West End School, Harrogate
Westbourne House School, Chichester
Westbrook Hay Preparatory School, Hemel
    Hempstead
Westminster Abbey Choir School
Westminster School, Westminster
Westminster Under School
Weston Favell Montessori Nursery School,
    Northampton
Westonbirt School, Tetbury
Wickham Court School, West Wickham
Widford Lodge, Chelmsford
Widford Lodge, Chelmsford
The Willow School, London
Wilton House School, Battle
Winchester College, Winchester
Winchester House School, Brackley
Winchester House School, Brackley
Windlesham House School
Windrush Valley School, Chipping Norton
Wisbech Grammar School, Wisbech
Witham Hall, Bourne
Wolborough Hill School, Newton Abbot
Wood Dene School, Norwich
Woodbridge School, Woodbridge
Woodleigh School, Malton
Wrekin College
Wroxall Abbey School, Warwick
Wycombe Abbey School, High Wycombe
Wykeham House School, Fareham
The Yarlet Schools, Stafford
Yateley Manor Preparatory School, Yateley
York College for Girls, York
York House School
Yorston Lodge School, Knutsford

CHURCH OF SCOTLAND

Butterstone School, Blairgowrie
The Glasgow Academy

EPISCOPALIAN

Glenalmond College, Perth
Glenalmond College, Perth
Hemdean House School, Reading

INTER-DENOMINATIONAL

Abacus College, Oxford
Abberley Hall, Worcester
Abbotsholme School, Uttoxeter
Aberlour House Preparatory School, Aberlour
The Albany College, London
Albemarle Independent College
Alder Bridge School, Reading
Alexanders International School, Woodbridge
Arbor Preparatory, Bury St Edmunds
Arnold School, Blackpool
Arts Educational Schools London
Ashdown School And Nursery, Jersey
Ashford School, Ashford
Ashgrove School, Bromley
Avalon Preparatory School, Wirral
Ayscoughfee Hall School, Spalding
Bablake Junior School, Coventry
Ballard School, New Milton
Bangor Grammar School, Bangor
Barnard Castle School, Barnard Castle
Basil Paterson College, Edinburgh
Bedford Modern School, Bedford
Bedford School Study Centre, Bedford
Beech House School, Rochdale
Bellerbys College, Mayfield, Wadhurst
Bentham Grammar School, Lancaster
Birkdale School, Sheffield
Bolton School (Boys' Division), Bolton
Boundary Oak School, Fareham
Bournemouth Collegiate Prep School, Poole
Bournemouth Collegiate School, Bournemouth
Bramdean School, Exeter
Briar School, Lowestoft
Bridge Lane Montessori School, London
Bristol Grammar School
Brooklands School & Little Brooklands Nursery,
    Stafford
Bryony School, Gillingham
The Buchan School, Castletown
Buckholme Towers, Poole
Buckingham College School, Harrow
Buckland School, Watchet
Burgess Hill School for Girls, Burgess Hill
Cabin Hill School, Belfast
Cannock School, Orpington
Cargilfield, Edinburgh
Channing Junior School
Channing School
Charters-Ancaster School GPDST, Bexhill-on-Sea

Chase School, Whickham
Cheltenham Ladies' College, Cheltenham
Cherubs Pre – School, Lee-on-the-Solent
Chetwynde School, Barrow-in-Furness
City of London Freemen's School, Ashtead
Claires Court Schools, The College, Maidenhead
Clewborough House Preparatory School,
    Camberley
Cliff School, Wakefield
Cobham Hall, Gravesend
The Cobham Montessori School, Cobham
Cokethorpe School, Witney
Colchester High School, Colchester
Collingwood School, Wallington
Convent Preparatory School, Gravesend
Coworth-Flexlands School, Woking
Craigclowan Preparatory School, Perth
Craigholme School
Craigievar School, Sunderland
Crawfordton House School, Thornhill
Croftinloan School, Pitlochry
Crosfields School, Reading
Dauntsey's School, Devizes
Davenport Lodge School, Coventry
Dean Grange Preparatory School, Huntingdon
Drayton House School, Guildford
The Drive School, Wolverhampton
Dulwich Montessori Nursery School, London
Eastcliffe School, Newcastle upon Tyne
Eaton Square School
Elliott-Clarke School, Liverpool
Eltham College
Eylesden Court Preparatory School, Maidstone
Falcon Manor, Towcester
The Falcons School for Boys
Fettes College, Edinburgh
Freddies (Reading) Limited, Reading
Froebel House School, Hull
Fulham Prep School (Pre-Prep)
Garden House Boys' School, London
Garden House School
Gateways School, Leeds
GEMS Hampshire School
GEMS Hampshire Schools, London
Gidea Park College, Romford
Giggleswick Junior School, Settle
Gosfield School, Halstead
Green Hill School, Evesham
Greycotes School GDST, Oxford
Grindon Hall Christian School, Sunderland
Grosvenor School, Nottingham
The Hall School, Wimbledon, London
The Hampshire Schools (Kensington Gardens),
    London
Hampton School, Hampton
Hanbury Prep School, Hanbury
Hawkesdown House School
Hereward House School
Hessle Mount School, Hessle

High Elms Manor School, Watford
High March School, Beaconsfield
The High School of Glasgow
Highfield School, Birkenhead
Highfield School, London
Hill House School, Doncaster
Holmewood House, Tunbridge Wells
Homefield School Senior & Preparatory,
    Christchurch
Howell's School, Llandaff GDST
Howsham Hall, York
Hutchesons' Grammar School
Joseph Rayner Independent School, Lancashire
Keil Junior School, Helensburgh
Keil School, Dumbarton
Kensington Prep School
Kew College, Richmond
King Edward VI High School for Girls,
    Birmingham
King Edward's Pre-Prep School, Bath
King's Ely International, Cambridge
King's House School, Richmond
Kingsbury Hill House, Marlborough
Kingswood House School, Epsom
The Knightsbridge Kindergarten, London
Ladymede, Aylesbury
Langdale Preparatory School, Blackpool
The Larks, Oxted
Lathallan School, Montrose
Leaden Hall School, Salisbury
Lincoln Minster School, Lincoln
Little Folk Montessori & Music Kindergarten,
    London
Lodge School, Purley
Longacre School, Guildford
Longridge Towers School, Berwick-upon-Tweed
Longwood School, Bushey
Lyonsdown School Trust Ltd, Barnet
Madingley Pre-Preparatory School, Cambridge
Maldon Court Preparatory School, Maldon
Manor House School, London
Manor Lodge School, Shenley
Merchiston Castle School, Edinburgh
The Mill School, Devizes
Millfield Preparatory School, Glastonbury
Millfield School, Street
Moira House Girls School, Eastbourne
Moira House School, Eastbourne
Montessori Pavilion School, London
Morrison's Academy, Crieff
Mount Carmel School, Ormskirk
The Mount School
Mrs Radcliffe's Montessori School, York
New Park School, St Andrews
New West Preston Manor Nursery School,
    Littlehampton
Newell House School, Sherborne
Newlands School, Seaford
Northfield School, Watford

Oakfield School, Woking
Oakhyrst Grange School, Caterham
Oaklands School, Loughton
Ockbrook School, Derby
Ormer House Preparatory School, Alderney
Orwell Park, Ipswich
Our Lady of Sion School, Worthing
Overstone Park School, Northampton
Oxford House School, Colchester
Paragon School, Prior Park College Junior, Bath
The Park School, Bournemouth
Penrhos College Junior School, Colwyn Bay
The Perse School, Cambridge
The Perse School for Girls, Cambridge
Pershore House School, Wirral
Pitsford School, Pitsford
Playdays Nursery/School and Montessori College,
    London
Plymouth College Prepratory School, Plymouth
Polam Hall, Darlington
Polwhele House School, Truro
Port Regis Preparatory School, Shaftesbury
Portora Royal School, Enniskillen
Pownall Hall School, Wilmslow
Priory Preparatory School, Banstead
Queen Elizabeth's Grammar School, Blackburn
Queen Elizabeth's Hospital
Queenswood, Hatfield
Ramillies Hall School, Cheadle
Rannoch School, Pitlochry
Rickmansworth PNEU School, Rickmansworth
Riverston School
Rockport School, Holywood
Rookesbury Park School, Portsmouth
Rose Hill School, Tunbridge Wells
Rydal Penrhos Senior School Girls' Division,
    Colwyn Bay
Scaitcliffe and Virginia Water Preparatory School,
    Egham
Scarborough College & Lisvane School,
    Scarborough
School of Jesus and Mary, Ipswich
Sevenoaks Preparatory School, Sevenoaks
Sevenoaks School, Sevenoaks
Shaftesbury Independent School, Purley
South Lee Preparatory School, Bury St Edmunds
Springfield Independent School, Ongar
St Albans School, St Albans
St Antony's Preparatory School, Sherborne
St Bede's Prep School, Eastbourne
St Bede's School, Hailsham
St Brandon's School, Clevedon
St David's College, West Wickham
St Denis and Cranley School, Edinburgh
St Dominic's Independent Junior School, Stoke-
    on-Trent
St George's School, Harpenden
St John's Preparatory School, Lichfield
St Joseph's In The Park, Hertford

St Margaret's School for Girls, Aberdeen
St Mary's Preparatory School, Melrose
St Michael's Preparatory School, Jersey
St Piran's School, Hayle
St Ursulas Convent School, Wigton
Stancliffe Hall, Matlock
Stockton House School, Fleet
Stonar School
Stormont, Potters Bar
Stretton School, Norwich
The Study Preparatory School
TCS Tutorial College, Harrow
Terra Nova School, Holmes Chapel
Terrington Hall, York
Tettenhall College, Wolverhampton
Thorngrove School, Newbury
Thornlow Preparatory School, Weymouth
Thornlow Senior School, Weymouth
Thorpe House School, Norwich
Tower College, Prescot
Tower House School, Paignton
Tring Park School for the Performing Arts, Tring
Trinity School, Teignmouth
Trinity School, Teignmouth
Walthamstow Hall, Sevenoaks
Wellow House School, Newark
West Dene School, Purley
West Lodge Preparatory School, Sidcup
Westbourne Preparatory School, Wallasey
Westerleigh & St Leonards College,
    St Leonards-on-Sea
Westfield School, Newcastle upon Tyne
Westholme School, Blackburn
Westville House Preparatory School, Ilkley
White House School, Seaton
Whitford Hall & Dodderhill School, Droitwich
Willington School
Willoughby Hall School, London
Wimbledon Common Preparatory School
Wispers School for Girls, Haslemere
Woodcote House School, Windlesham
Woodside Park International School, London
Wycliffe College, Stonehouse
Wycliffe College (Special Needs), Stonehouse
Wycliffe Preparatory School, Stonehouse
Yarrells School, Poole

JEWISH

Akiva School, London
Beis Hamedrash Elyon
Beis Malka Girls School, London
Beis Rochel D'Satmar Girls School
Bnois Jerusalem School, London
Carmel College, Wallingford
Gateshead Jewish High School for Girls,
    Gateshead
Gateshead Jewish Primary School, Gateshead

Getters Talmud Torah, London
Hasmonean Preparatory School, London
Hubert Jewish High School for Girls, Salford
Immanuel College, Bushey
Immanuel College, Bushey
Kerem House, London
Kerem School
London Jewish Girls' High School
Lubavitch House School (Junior Boys)
Lubavitch House Senior School for Girls, London
Manchester Jewish Grammar School, Prestwich
Mathilda Marks-Kennedy School, London
Mechinah Liyeshivah Zichron Moshe
Menorah Grammar School, Edgware
Naima Jewish Preparatory School
OYH Primary School, London
Pardes Grammar Boys' School
Side by Side Kids School, London
Talmud Torah Bobov Primary School
Talmud Torah Chinuch Norim, Salford
Talmud Torah Jewish School, London
Talmud Torah Machzikei Hadass, London
Talmud Torah Tiferes Shlomoh, London
Talmud Torah Torat Emet, London
Talmud Torah Yetev Lev, Salford
Tashbar of Edgware, Edgware
Tashbar School, Salford
Torah Academy, Hove
Yeshivah Ohr Torah School, Salford
Yesodey Hatorah Jewish School
Yetev Lev Day School for Boys

METHODIST

Ashdown Lodge, Apperley Bridge
Ashville College, Harrogate
Bronte House School, Bradford
Crowthorn School (NCH Action for Children),
    Bolton
Culford School, Bury St Edmunds
Culford School, Bury St Edmunds
Edgehill College, Bideford
Farringtons School, Chislehurst
Kent College, Canterbury
Kent College Infant & Junior School, Canterbury
Kent College Pembury, Tunbridge Wells
Kingsley School, Bideford
Kingswood Preparatory School, Bath
Kingswood School, Bath
The Leys School, Cambridge
Queen's College, Taunton
Queen's College Junior, Pre-Prep & Nursery
    Schools, Taunton
Rydal Penrhos Preparatory School, Colwyn Bay
Rydal Penrhos School, Colwyn Bay
Shebbear College, Beaworthy
St Crispin's School, Leicester
Truro School, Truro

Truro School Preparatory School, Truro
Woodhouse Grove School, Apperley Bridge

MUSLIM

Abu Bakr Independent School, Walsall
Adam Primary School, London
Afifah High School For Girls, Manchester
Al Hijrah School, Birmingham
Al Huda Girls School, Birmingham
Al Karam Secondary School, Retford
Al Mumin Primary School, Bradford
Al-Burhan Grammar School, Birmingham
Al-Furqaan Preparatory School, Dewsbury
Al-Furqan Community College, Birmingham
Al-Khair School, Croydon
Al-Mizan Primary & London East Academy
    Secondary & Sixth Form
Al-Muntada Islamic School
Amina Hatun Islamic School, London
Andalusia Academy Bristol
Azhar Academy, London
Balham Preparatory School
Balham Preparatory School, London
Birchfield Independent Girls School, Birmingham
Birmingham Muslim School, Birmingham
Bolton Muslim Girls School, Bolton
Brondesbury College For Boys
Copsewood School
Coventry Muslim School, Coventry
Crescent Community High School for Girls
Crystal Gardens, Bradford
Darul Arqam Educational Institute, Leicester
Darul Hadis Latifiah
Darul Uloom Dawatul Imaan, Bradford
Darul Uloom Islamic High School & College,
    Birmingham
Date Valley School, Mitcham
Gloucestershire Islamic Secondary School For
    Girls, Gloucester
Hanifah Infants Small School, Longsight
Imam Muhammad Zakariya School, Preston
Imam Zakaria Academy, London
IQRA School, Oxford
Islamia Girls High School, Huddersfield
Islamia Girls' School
Islamic Shakhsiyah Foundation, Slough
Islamic Shakhsiyah Foundation
Islamiyah School, Blackburn
Jamahiriya School
Jamea Al Kauthar, Lancaster
Jameah Islameah, Crowborough
Jamia Al-Hudaa Residential College, Mapperley
    Park
Jamia Islamia Birmingham, Birmingham
Jamiah Madaniyah Primary School
Jamiatul Uloom Al-Islamia, Luton
Jamiatul Ummah School, London

Jamiatul-Ilm Wal-Huda UK School, Blackburn
King Fahad Academy
London East Academy, London
London Islamic School
Madinatul Uloom Al Islamiya School, Kidderminster
Madni Girls School
Madni Muslim Girls' High School, Dewsbury
Madrasatul Imam Muhammad Zakariya, Bolton
Manchester Islamic High School, Manchester
Markazul Uloom, Blackburn
Mazahirul Uloom School, London
New Horizon Community School, Leeds
Noor Ul Islam Primary School
Paradise Primary School, Dewsbury
Preston Muslim Girls Secondary School, Preston
Quwwatt Ul Islam Girls School
Rabia Girls School, Luton
Rawdha Tul Uloom, Blackburn
Rochdale Girls School, Rochdale
Tawhid Boys School, Tawhid Educational Trust
Tayyibah Girls School
Tiny Tots Pre-School, Leicester
TTTY School, London
Zakaria Muslim Girls High School, Batley

NON-DENOMINATIONAL

The Abbey College, Malvern Wells
Abbey College, Manchester
The Abbey School, Torquay
Abbotsford Preparatory School, Manchester
Abbotsford School, Kenilworth
Abercorn School
Aberdeen Waldorf School, Aberdeen
Aberdour, Tadworth
Abinger Hammer Village School, Dorking
Acorn Independent College, Southall
ACS Cobham International School, Cobham
ACS Egham International School, Egham
ACS Hillingdon International School, Hillingdon
Akeley Wood Junior School, Milton Keynes
Akeley Wood School, Buckingham
Al-Sadiq and Al-Zahra Schools
Albyn School, Aberdeen
Alcuin School, Leeds
Alpha Preparatory School, Harrow
Altrincham Preparatory School, Altrincham
Amberley House School
Amberley School, Bexhill-on-Sea
The American School in London
Annemount Nursery School
Arden College, Southport
Arley House PNEU School, Loughborough
Arley House School, East Leake
Arts Educational Schools London – Sixth Form
Arundale Preparatory School, Pulborough
Ashbourne Independent Sixth Form College

Ashbourne Middle School
Ashbrooke House, Weston-Super-Mare
Ashton House School, Isleworth
Aston House School
Astwell Preparatory School, Birmingham
Atherton House School, Liverpool
Atholl School, Pinner
Attenborough Preparatory School, Nottingham
Avenue House School
Babington House School, Chislehurst
Bablake School, Coventry
Badminton School, Westbury-on-Trym
Bairnswood Nursery School, Scarborough
Barbara Speake Stage School
Barbourne Preparatory School and Cygnet Nursery, Worcester
Basil Paterson Tutorial College, Edinburgh
Bassett House School, London
Bath Academy, Bath
Bath High School GPDST, Bath
Batley Grammar School, Batley
Battle Abbey School, Battle
Beaconhurst School
Bedales Prep School, Dunhurst, Petersfield
Bedales School, Petersfield
Bedford High School for Girls, Bedford
Belfast Royal Academy, Belfast
Belhaven Hill, Dunbar
Bell Bedgebury International School, Cranbrook
Bellerbys College, Brighton
Belmont (Mill Hill Junior School), London
Belmont (Mill Hill Preparatory School)
Belmont Grosvenor School, Harrogate
Belmont Grosvenor School, Harrogate
Belmont House, Newton Mearns
The Belvedere School GDST, Liverpool
Bembridge School, Ryde
Bickley Park School, Bromley
Bickley Parva School, Bromley
Birkdale School for Hearing Impaired Children, Southport
Birkenhead High School GDST, Wirral
Birkenhead School, Wirral
Bishop's Stortford College, Bishop's Stortford
Bishop's Stortford College, Bishop's Stortford
Bishop's Stortford College Junior School, Bishop's Stortford
Bishopsgate School, Egham
Bishopstrow College
Blackheath High School GDST
Blackheath Preparatory School
Bloomsbury College, London
Bolton School (Girls' Division), Bolton
Box Hill School, Dorking
Brabyns School, Stockport
Brackenfield School, Harrogate
Bradford Girls' Grammar School, Bradford
Bradford Grammar School, Bradford
Braeside School for Girls, Buckhurst Hill

Bramley School, Tadworth
Brampton College
Brantwood School, Sheffield
Branwood Preparatory School, Eccles
Breaside Preparatory School, Bromley
Bricklehurst Manor Preparatory, Wadhurst
Bridgewater School, Manchester
Brighton and Hove High School GDST, Brighton
Bristol Steiner School
Broadhurst School
Broadmead Lower School, Bedford
Brockwood Park School, Bramdean
Brooke House College, Market Harborough
Brooke Priory School, Oakham
Broomham School, Hastings
Buckswood School, Hastings
Burwood Park School and College, Walton-on-Thames
Bury Grammar School Boys, Bury
Bury Grammar School Girls, Bury
Bury Lawn School, Flitwick
Bury Lawn School, Milton Keynes
Bute House Preparatory School for Girls
Buxlow Preparatory School, Wembley
Cambridge Centre for Sixth-form Studies, Cambridge
Cambridge Tutors College, Croydon
Cameron House School, Chelsea
Campbell College, Belfast
Canbury School, Kingston-upon-Thames
Canterbury Steiner School, Canterbury
The Cardiff Academy
The Carrdus School, Banbury
CATS College Cambridge, Cambridge
CATS College Canterbury, Canterbury
CATS College London
Cedar School, Street
Central Newcastle High School GDST, Newcastle upon Tyne
Cheadle Hulme School, Cheadle
Chelsea Independent College
The Chelsea Nursery School, London
Cherwell College, Oxford
Cheshunt Pre-preparatory School, Coventry
Chetham's School of Music, Manchester
Chetwynd House School, Sutton Coldfield
Chiltern House School, Thame
Chinthurst School, Tadworth
Chiswick and Bedford Park Preparatory School
Churchers College Junior School, Liphook
Churchers College Senior School
City of London School
City of London School for Girls
Claires Court School, Maidenhead
Claires Court Schools, Ridgeway, Maidenhead
Clarendon Cottage School, Eccles
Cleve House School
Clevedon House Preparatory School, Ilkley
Clevelands Preparatory School, Bolton

Clewborough House School, Frimley
Clifton Hall School, Edinburgh
Clifton High School
Clifton Preparatory School, York
College Saint-Pierre, Leigh-on-Sea
Collingham Independent GCSE and Sixth Form College
Colston's Girls' School
The Compass School, Haddington
Concord College, Shrewsbury
Connaught House
Cooley Primary School, Sixmilecross
Copthill School, Stamford
Corfton Hill Educational Establishment, London
Craig-y-Nos School, Bishoptston
Cranbrook, Ilford
Cranbrook School, Cranbrook
Cransley School, Northwich
Croft House School, Hexham
Crown House School, High Wycombe
Croydon High School GDST, South Croydon
Culcheth Hall, Altrincham
d'Overbroeck's College, Oxford
d'Overbroeck's College Oxford, Oxford
Dagfa House School, Nottingham
Daintry Hall Preparatory School, Congleton
Dallington School
Dame Bradbury's School, Saffron Walden
Davies Laing and Dick
Davies's College, London
Delrow House, Watford
Devonshire House Preparatory School
The Dixie Grammar Junior School, Nuneaton
The Dixie Grammar School, Market Bosworth
Dodderhill School, Droitwich Spa
Dollar Academy, Dollar
Dolphin School, Reading
The Dominie
Dorchester Preparatory and Independent Schools, Dorchester
Downsend Girls' Preparatory School, Leatherhead
Downsend School, Leatherhead
Downsend School – Ashtead Lodge, Ashtead
Downsend School – Epsom Lodge, Epsom
Downsend School – Leatherhead Lodge, Leatherhead
Downsend School – Leatherhead Lodge, Leatherhead
Dragon School, Oxford
Drumley House School, Ayr
The Duchy Grammar School, Truro
Duke of Kent School, Guildford
Dunedin School, Edinburgh
Dunottar School, Reigate
Durston House, London
Eagle House School – Sutton, Sutton
Ealing College Upper School
Ealing Independent College, Ealing
Ealing Montessori School, London

Eastbourne House School, Birmingham
Eastcourt Independent School, Ilford
Eaton House Belgravia, London
Eaton House The Manor Girls' School, London
Eaton House The Manor Nursery, London
Eaton House The Manor Pre-Preparatory, London
Eaton House The Manor Preparatory
Eaton House The Vale, London
Eccleston School, Birmingham
Eden Park School, Beckenham
Edgbaston High School for Girls, Birmingham
Edinburgh Academy Junior School, Edinburgh
The Edinburgh Academy, Edinburgh
The Edinburgh Rudolf Steiner School, Edinburgh
Elliott Park School, Sheerness
Elm Green Preparatory School, Chelmsford
Elm Tree House
Elmfield Rudolf Steiner School, Stourbridge
Elmhurst School, South Croydon
Elmwood Montessori School, London
Emberhurst, Esher
Emscote House School and Nursery, Leamington
    Spa
Essendene Lodge School, Caterham
Fairfield Preparatory School, Saxmundham
Fairfield Preparatory School, Loughborough
Fairstead House School, Newmarket
The Falcons School for Girls
Falkner House
Farleigh Further Education College (Frome),
    Frome
Farleigh Further Education College Swindon,
    Swindon
Farrowdale House Preparatory School, Oldham
Ferndale Preparatory School, Faringdon
Fine Arts College, London
Finton House School
Firth House Preparatory School, Littlehampton
Firwood Manor Prep School, Oldham
The Fold School, Hove
Forest Park School, Sale
Forest School, Altrincham
Fosse Way School, Leicester
Frensham Heights School, Farnham
Friars School, Ashford
Fulham Prep School (Prep Dept)
Fyling Hall School, Whitby
Gad's Hill School, Rochester
The Galloway Small School, Barnbarroch
Gask House School
Gateway School, Great Missenden
George Heriot's School, Edinburgh
George Watson's College, Edinburgh
Glaisdale School, Cheam
The Glasgow Academy Dairsie
Glebe House School, Rochdale
The Gleddings Preparatory School, Halifax
Glen House Montessori School, Hebden Bridge
Glendower Preparatory School

Glenesk School, Leatherhead
The Godolphin and Latymer School
Golders Hill School
Goodrington School, Hornchurch
Goodwyn School
Gordonstoun School, Elgin
Gower House School
Grainger Grammar School, Newcastle upon Tyne
Gramercy Hall School, Torbay
The Grammar School at Leeds, Leeds
Grange Park Preparatory School
The Grange School, Northwich
The Grantham Preparatory School, Grantham
Grantchester House, Esher
The Granville School, Sevenoaks
Grasscroft Independent School, Oldham
Great Houghton School, Northampton
Greenacre School for Girls, Banstead
Greenbank Preparatory School, Cheadle
Greenfield School, Woking
Greenfields Independent Day and Boarding
    School, Forest Row
Greenhayes Pre-Preparatory School, West
    Wickham
Greenholme School, Nottingham
Grittleton House School, Chippenham
Grove Independent School, Milton Keynes
Haberdashers' Monmouth School For Girls,
    Monmouth
Haberdashers' Redcap School, Hereford
Haddon Dene School, Broadstairs
Hall Grove School, Bagshot
Hall School Wimbledon (Junior School)
Hall School Wimbledon (Senior School)
Halliford School, Shepperton
Hampstead Hill Pre-Preparatory & Nursery
    School
Hampton Court House, East Molesey
Handel House Preparatory School, Gainsborough
Harecroft Hall School, Seascale
Harenc School Trust, Sidcup
Haresfoot Senior School, Berkhamsted
Harpenden Preparatory School, Harpenden
Harrogate Tutorial College, Harrogate
Hartlebury School, Kidderminster
Harvington School
Hawley Place School, Camberley
Hawley Place School, Camberley
The Hawthorns School, Redhill
Hazelhurst School For Girls, London
Heathcote School, Chelmsford
Heatherton House School, Amersham
Heathfield School, Kidderminster
Heathfield School, Pinner
Heathland College, Accrington
Heathside Preparatory School, Hampstead
Hendon Preparatory School, Hendon
Herington House School, Brentwood
Herries School, Maidenhead

Highclare School, Birmingham
Highfield Priory School, Preston
Highfield School, London
Highfield School, East Grinstead
Highfield School, Maidenhead
Highfields School, Newark
The Highlands School, Reading
Hill House International Junior School
Hill House St Mary's School, Doncaster
Hillcrest Grammar School, Stockport
The Hill Preparatory School, Westerham
Hillside School, Malvern
Hilltop Small School, St Leonards-on-Sea
Hipperholme Grammar School, Halifax
Hoe Bridge School, Woking
Holly Park Montessori School
Hollygirt School, Nottingham
Holmwood House, Colchester
Homefield School, Sutton
Homewood Pre-Preparatory School, St Albans
Hopelands School, Stonehouse
Horlers Pre-Preparatory School, Cambridge
Hornsby House School
Hounslow College, Feltham
Howe Green House School, Bishop's Stortford
Huddersfield Grammar School, Huddersfield
The Hulme Grammar School for Girls, Oldham
Hulme Hall Schools, Cheadle
Hulme Hall Schools (Junior School), Cheadle
Hunter Hall School, Penrith
Hunterhouse College, Belfast
The Hurlingham School
Hurst Lodge School, Ascot
Hurtwood House, Dorking
Hurworth House School, Darlington
Hyland House
Hylton Kindergarten & Pre-preparatory School,
    Exeter
Ibstock Place School
Inchkeith School and Nursery, Dunfermline
Ingleside PNEU School, Cirencester
International College, Sherborne School,
    Sherborne
International Community School
International School of Aberdeen, Aberdeen
The International School of Choueifat,
    Chippenham
International School of London
International School of London in Surrey, Woking
Ipswich High School GDST, Ipswich
The Italia Conti Academy of Theatre Arts
The John Lyon School, Harrow
Jordanhill School
The Junior School, Bishop's Stortford College,
    Bishop's Stortford
Justin Craig Education
Kayes' College, Huddersfield
Keble Preparatory School
Kelvinside Academy

Kenley Montessori School, London
Kew Green Preparatory School, Richmond
Kimbolton School, Huntingdon
The King Alfred School
King Edward VI School, Southampton
King Edward VII and Queen Mary School, Lytham
    St Annes
King Edward's Junior School, Bath
King Edward's School, Bath, Bath
King Henry VIII School, Coventry
King's High School, Warwick, Warwick
Kings Monkton School
Kings Monkton School and College, Cardiff
Kingswood College Trust, Ormskirk
Kirkham Grammar School, Preston
Kirkstone House School, Bourne
Knightsbridge School
Ladbroke Square Montessori School, London
The Ladies' College, Guernsey
Lady Lane Park School, Bingley
Lancaster House School, Weston-Super-Mare
Langley Preparatory School & Nursery, Norwich
Langley School, Norwich
Lansdowne College
Latymer Prep School
Latymer Upper School
Le Herisson
Leckford Place School, Oxford
Leeds Girls' High School, Leeds
Leicester Montessori School, Leicester
Lewes Old Grammar School, Lewes
Lime House School, Carlisle
Lion House School
Little Acorns Montessori School, Bushey
The Little Folks Lab, Stevenage
Littlegarth School, Colchester
Locksley Preparatory School, West Bridgford
Lomond School, Helensburgh
London Montessori Centre Ltd, London
Long Close School, Slough
Longacre Preparatory School, Nottingham
Lord Wandsworth College, Hook
Lord Wandsworth College, Hook
Loretto Junior School, Musselburgh
Loretto Junior School, Musselburgh
Loretto School, Musselburgh
Loughborough Grammar School, Loughborough
Loughborough High School, Loughborough
LVS Ascot, Ascot
Lycee Francais Charles de Gaulle
Lyndhurst House Preparatory School
Lyndhurst School, Camberley
Lynton Preparatory School, Scunthorpe
Lynton Preparatory School, Epsom
Macclesfield Preparatory School, Macclesfield
Maharishi School, Ormskirk
The Mall School, Twickenham
Maltman's Green School, Gerrards Cross
The Manchester Grammar School, Manchester

Manchester High School for Girls, Manchester
Mander Portman Woodward
Mander Portman Woodward, Birmingham
Manor House School, Ashby-de-la-Zouch
The Mary Erskine School, Edinburgh
The Maynard School, Exeter
Maria Montessori School Hampstead
Marycourt School, Gosport
Mayfield Preparatory School, Alton
Mayville High School, Southsea
McCaffreys School, London
McKee School of Education, Dance & Drama, Liverpool
Meoncross School, Fareham
Merchant Taylors' Boys' Schools, Liverpool
Merchant Taylors' Girls' School, Liverpool
The Merlin School
Methodist College, Belfast
Michael Hall (Steiner Waldorf School), Forest Row
Mill Hill School, London
Millfield Pre-Preparatory School, Glastonbury
Milton Keynes Preparatory School, Milton Keynes
The Montessori House
The Montessori House School, London
Montessori School, Lavenham
Moor Allerton School, Manchester
Moorfield School, Ilkley
Moorlands School, Leeds
Moorlands School, Luton
Moreton Hall School, Oswestry
Mortarboard Nursery School, Bracknell
Mostyn House School, South Wirral
Motcombe Grange School, Shaftesbury
Mount School, Huddersfield
Mount School, Bromsgrove
Mountford House School, Nottingham
The Mulberry House School
Nethercliffe School, Winchester
Netherleigh and Rossefield School, Bradford
Netherleigh School, Bradford
New College, Leamington Spa
New College and School, Cardiff
The New Eccles Hall School, Norwich
The New Small School (Bath), Bath
Newborough School, Liverpool
Newbridge Preparatory School, Wolverhampton
Newcastle School for Boys, Newcastle upon Tyne
Newcastle-under-Lyme School, Newcastle-under-Lyme
Newland House School, Twickenham
Newlands School, Seaford
Newlands School, Newcastle upon Tyne
Newton Prep
Norfolk House School
Norland Place School
Normanhurst School
North Bridge House Junior School
North Bridge House Lower Prep School

North Bridge House Nursery School
North Bridge House School Nursery and Prep, London
North Bridge House Senior School
North Cestrian Grammar School, Altrincham
North London Collegiate, Edgware
The North London International School, London
North London Rudolf Steiner School, Kings Langley
Northgate Preparatory, Rhyl
Northwood College, Northwood
Norwich High School for Girls GDST, Norwich
Notting Hill and Ealing High School GDST
Notting Hill Preparatory School
Nottingham High Junior School, Nottingham
Nottingham High School, Nottingham
Nottingham High School for Girls GDST, Nottingham
Oakfield Preparatory School
Oakleigh House School
The Old Vicarage School, Derby
The Oldham Hulme Grammar Schools, Oldham
Oldham Hulme Kindergarten, Oldham
Orchard House School
Oswestry Junior School, Oswestry
Oswestry School, Oswestry
Overndale School, Old Sodbury
Oxford High School GDST, Oxford
Oxford International College, Oxford
Oxford International Study Centre, Oxford
Oxford Tutorial College, Oxford
Padworth College, Reading
Paint Pots Montessori School Hyde Park, Hyde Park Crescent
Palmers Green High School
The Park School
Park School, Totnes
Park School for Girls, Ilford
Parkgate House School
Parkside Kindergarten and Preparatory School, Leighton Buzzard
Parkside School, Cobham
Pembridge Hall
The Phoenix School
Plymouth College, Plymouth
Polam School, Bedford
Portland Place School
Portsmouth High School GDST, Southsea
Primrose Independent School
Prior's Field School, Godalming
Priory Preparatory & Nursery School, Stamford
Prospect House School
The Purcell School, Bushey
Putney High School GDST
Queen Elizabeth Grammar School, Wakefield
Queen Mary School, Lytham
Queen Victoria School, Dunblane
Queen's Gate School
Queen's Park School, Oswestry

The Queen's School, Chester
Quinton House School, Northampton
Radlett Preparatory School, Radlett
Rainbow Montessori Junior School
Rainbow Montessori Nursery School, London
Ramshill School, Petersfield
Raphael Independent School, Hornchurch
Ravenscourt Park Preparatory School,
    Hammersmith
Ravenstone Day Nursery and Nursery School
Ravenstone Preparatory School
The Red Maids' School
Redehall Preparatory School, Horley
Redland High School for Girls
Reigate Grammar School, Reigate
RGS The Grange, Worcester
RGS Worcester & The Alice Ottley School,
    Worcester
The Richard Pate School, Cheltenham
Ringwood Waldorf School, Ringwood
Ripley Court School, Woking
River House Montessori School
Robert Gordon's College, Aberdeen
Robina Advantage, Marchington
The Roche School
Rokeby School, Kingston-upon-Thames
Rolfe's Montessori School, London
Rookwood School, Andover
Rosebrae School, Elgin
Rosemead Preparatory School
Rosemeade School, Huddersfield
Rossholme School, East Brent
Rougemont School
Rowan Preparatory School, Esher
The Rowans School
Rowden House School, Bromyard
Royal Ballet School
Royal Belfast Academical Institution, Belfast
Royal Caledonian Schools, Watford
Royal Grammar School, Guildford
Royal Grammar School, Newcastle upon Tyne
The Royal High School, Bath, Bath
The Royal Masonic School for Girls,
    Rickmansworth
The Royal School ARMAGH, Armagh
The Royal School Dungannon, Dungannon
The Royal School, Hampstead
Ruckleigh School, Solihull
Rudolf Steiner School, Kings Langley
Rudston Preparatory School, Rotherham
Rupert House, Henley-on-Thames
Rushmoor Independent School, Farnborough
Ruthin School, Ruthin
The Ryleys, Alderley Edge
Saint Felix School, Southwold
Saint Martin's School, Solihull
Saint Michael's College, Tenbury Wells
Salcombe Preparatory School
Salterford House School, Nottingham

Sandbach School, Sandbach
Sandhurst School, Worthing
Sands School, Ashburton
Saville House School, Mansfield
Scarisbrick Hall School, Ormskirk
Sea View Private School, Kirkcaldy
Seaton House School, Sutton
Sheffield High School GDST, Sheffield
Shepherd's Bush Day Nursery, London
Sherborne House School, Eastleigh
Sherfield School, Hook
Shrewsbury High School GDST, Shrewsbury
Sir William Perkins's School, Chertsey
Slindon College, Arundel
The Small School, Bideford
Somerville School, London
South Devon Steiner School, Dartington
South Hampstead High School
South London Montessori School, London
Southfields School, Sale
Springfield School, Worcester
St Andrew's, Wantage
St Andrew's School, Bedford
St Anne's High School, Bishop Auckland
St Anne's Preparatory School, Chelmsford
St Bernard's Preparatory School, Newton Abbot
St Catherine's Preparatory School, Stockport
St Catherine's School, Camberley
St Cedd's School, Chelmsford
St Christopher School, Letchworth Garden City
St Christopher's, wembley
St Christopher's School, Norwich
St Christopher's School, Beckenham
St Christopher's School
St Christopher's School, Wembley
St Clare's School, Porthcawl
St Colette's School, Cambridge
St Columba's School, Kilmacolm
St David's School, Ashford
St Edward's School, Reading
St Faith's at Ash School, Canterbury
St George's Preparatory School, Jersey
St George's School, Southwold
St George's School for Girls, Edinburgh
St Hilary's School, Godalming
St Hilda's School, Bushey
St Ia School, St Ives
St James Independent Junior School, Stockport
St James Independent School for Boys (Senior),
    Ashford
St James Independent Schools for Boys and Girls,
    London
St James Junior School
St James Senior Girls' School
St John's Preparatory School, Potters Bar
St John's Priory School, Banbury
St John's School, Porthcawl
St John's School, Billericay
St John's School, Porthcawl

St John's School, Sidmouth
St Johns Wood Pre-Preparatory School
St Joseph's School, Launceston
St Leonards – New Park, St Andrews
St Leonards School, St Andrews
St Martin's Preparatory School, Grimsby
St Martin's School
St Mary's Music School, Edinburgh
St Mary's School, Henley-on-Thames
St Mary's School, Colchester
St Michael's School, Llanelli
St Nicholas Nursery School, Folkestone
St Nicholas Preparatory School, London
St Nicholas School, Harlow
St Nicholas School
St Olave's Preparatory School
St Peter & St Paul School, Chesterfield
St Peter's Nursery School, Burgess Hill
St Serf's School, Edinburgh
St Winifred's School, Southampton
St. Clare's, Oxford, Oxford
Stafford Grammar School, Stafford
Staines Preparatory School, Staines
Stepping Stones Day Nursery School, Leeds
Stewart's Melville College, Edinburgh
Stockport Grammar School, Stockport
Stoke College, Sudbury
Stonelands School of Ballet & Theatre Arts, Hove
Stratford Preparatory School, Stratford-upon-Avon
Strathallan School, Perth
Streatham & Clapham High School
Streatham House School, Liverpool
Suffolk Country Courses, Bury St Edmunds
Sunny Bank Preparatory School, Burnley
Sunnymede School, Southport
Surrey College, Guildford
Sutton High School GDST, Sutton
Swan School for Boys, Salisbury
Syddal Park School, Stockport
Sydenham High School GDST
Sylvia Young Theatre School
TASIS The American School in England, Thorpe
Taunton Preparatory School, Taunton
Taunton School International, Taunton
Taunton School Senior, Taunton
Taverham Hall Preparatory School, Norwich
Tavistock & Summerhill School, Haywards Heath
Teesside High School, Eaglescliffe
Thetford Grammar School, Thetford
Toad Hall Montessori Nursery School, London
Toddlers and Mums Montessori, London
Tormead School, Guildford
Torwood House School, Redland
Tower Dene Preparatory School, Southport
Tower House, Barmouth
Tower House School
Town Close House Preparatory School, Norwich
Treffos School, Menai Bridge
Trent Fields Kindergarten, Nottingham

Trentvale Preparatory School, Keadby
Twycross House School, Atherstone
Unicorn School, Richmond
University College School
University College School Junior Branch
Upper Tooting Independent High School, London
Vernon Lodge Preparatory School, Brewood
Victoria College Belfast, Belfast
Victoria College Preparatory School, Jersey
The Village School
Virginia Water Preparatory School, Virginia Water
Wakefield Girls' High School, Wakefield
Waldorf School of South West London
Wallop School, Weybridge
Waverley House PNEU School, Nottingham
Waverley School, Wokingham
Wellington School, Ayr
West House School, Birmingham
Westbourne School, Sheffield
Westbourne School
Western College Preparatory School, Plymouth
Westminster Preparatory School, Westcliff-on-Sea
Westward Preparatory School, Walton-on-Thames
Westwood, Bushey Heath
Wetherby School
Wheelgate House School, Newquay
The White House Prep & Woodentops
   Kindergarten
White House School, Whitchurch
White House School, Stamford
Whitehall School, Huntingdon
Whitgift School, South Croydon
Whittingham School, London
William Hulme's Grammar School, Manchester
William Hulme's Preparatory Department,
   Manchester
Wimbledon High School GDST
Winbury School, Maidenhead
Windermere School, Windermere
Withington Girls' School, Manchester
Wolstanton Preparatory School, Newcastle-under-
   Lyme
Wolverhampton Grammar School,
   Wolverhampton
Woodford Prep & Nursery School, Stockport
Woodhill Preparatory School, Southampton
Woodlands School, Preston
Wychwood School, Oxford
Wylde Green College, Sutton Coldfield
Wynstones School, Gloucester
Yarm at Raventhorpe School, Darlington
Yehudi Menuhin School, Cobham
Young England Kindergarten, London

QUAKER

Ackworth School, Pontefract
Ackworth School, Pontefract

Ayton School, Great Ayton
Bootham Junior School, York
Bootham School, York
Friends' School, Lisburn
Friends' School
Leighton Park School, Reading
Sibford School, Banbury
Sidcot School, Winscombe
The Hall Pre-Preparatory School Sidcot,
    Winscombe
The Mount School, York
Tregelles, York

ROMAN CATHOLIC

The Abbey School, Westgate-on-Sea
All Hallows, Shepton Mallet
Alton Convent School, Alton
Ampleforth College, York
Ashbourne, London
Austin Friars School, Carlisle
Austin Friars St Monica's School, Carlisle
Barlborough Hall School, Chesterfield
Barlborough Hall School, Chesterfield
Barrow Hills School, Godalming
Beechwood Sacred Heart School, Tunbridge
    Wells
Besford Court School, Worcester
Bishop Challoner RC School, Bromley
Brigidine School Windsor, Windsor
Bury Catholic Preparatory School, Bury
Carleton House Preparatory School,
    Liverpool
Convent of Mercy, Guernsey
Convent Primary School, Rochdale
Crackley Hall School, Kenilworth
Cranmore School, Leatherhead
Donhead Prep School
Downside School, Bath
Farleigh School, Andover
Farleigh School, Andover
Farnborough Hill, Farnborough
FCJ Primary School, Jersey
Fernhill School, Glasgow
Grace Dieu Manor School, Leicester
Holy Cross Convent, Gerrards Cross
Holy Cross Junior School, Portsmouth
Holy Cross Preparatory School, Kingston upon
    Thames
Holy Trinity College, Bromley
Ilford Ursuline High School, Ilford
Ilford Ursuline Preparatory School, Ilford
Kilgraston, Perth
La Sagesse Convent, Romsey
Laleham Lea School, Purley
Leweston School, Sherborne
Loreto Grammar school, Altrincham
Loreto Preparatory School, Altrincham

Loyola Preparatory School, Buckhurst Hill
Marist Convent Independent Day School For Girls,
    London
The Marist preparatory school, Ascot
The Marist Senior School, Ascot
Marymount Convent School, Wallasey
Marymount International School, Kingston-upon-
    Thames
Moor Park School, Ludlow
More House School, London
Moreton Hall Preparatory School, Bury St
    Edmunds
Mount St Mary's College, Spinkhill
Mount St Mary's Convent School, Exeter
Mylnhurst Preparatory School & Nursery, Sheffield
New Hall School, Chelmsford
Notre Dame Preparatory School, Norwich
Notre Dame Preparatory School, Cobham
Notre Dame Senior School, Cobham
Oakhill College, Clitheroe
Oakwood School & Nursery, Purley
The Oratory Preparatory School, Reading
The Oratory Preparatory School, Reading
The Oratory School, Reading
Our Lady's Abingdon Junior School, Abingdon
Our Lady's Abingdon School, Abingdon
Our Lady's Convent Preparatory School, Kettering
Our Lady's Convent School, Cardiff
Our Lady's Convent School, Loughborough
Our Lady's Preparatory School, Crowthorne
Princethorpe College, Rugby
Princethorpe College, Rugby
Prior Park College, Bath
Prior Park Preparatory School, Cricklade
Priory School, Birmingham
Ratcliffe College, Leicester
Redcourt – St Anselms, Prenton
Rosecroft School Didsbury, Manchester
Runnymede St Edward's School, Liverpool
Rye St Antony School, Oxford
Sacred Heart R.C. Primary School, Wadhurst
Sacred Heart School, Swaffham
Salesian College, Farnborough
Sinclair House School, London
St Aloysius' College, Glasgow
St Ambrose College, Altrincham
St Ambrose Preparatory School, Altrincham
St Andrew's Preparatory School, Edenbridge
St Anne's Preparatory School, Sturry
St Anselm's College, Birkenhead
St Anthony's Montessori School, Sunderland
St Anthony's Preparatory School, London
St Anthonys School, Cinderford
St Augustine's Priory, Ealing
St Bede's College, Manchester
St Bede's School, Stafford
St Bede's School, Stafford
St Benedict's Junior School, London
St Benedict's School, Ealing

St Bernard's Preparatory School, Slough
St Brigid's School, Denbigh
St Catherine's School, Twickenham
St Christina's RC Preparatory School
St Clotilde's Senior School, Lechlade
St Columba's College, St Albans
St Dominic's Priory School, Stone
St Edmund's College, Ware
St Edmund's College & Prep School, Ware
St Edward's College, Liverpool
St Edward's School Cheltenham, Cheltenham
St George's College, Weybridge
St George's College Junior School, Weybridge
St George's College Junior School, Weybridge
St Gerard's School, Bangor
St John's Beaumont, Windsor
St John's College, Southsea
St John's Nursery School, Tadworth
St Joseph's College, Reading
St Joseph's College with The School of Jesus &
   Mar, Ipswich
St Joseph's Convent, Chesterfield
St Joseph's Convent School, Broadstairs
St Joseph's Convent School
St Joseph's Dominican Convent, Pulborough
St Joseph's Preparatory School, Gravesend
St Joseph's Preparatory School, Stoke-on-Trent
St Joseph's Preparatory School, Reading
St Joseph's Preparatory School, Wolverhampton
St Joseph's School, Kenilworth
St Joseph's School, Nottingham
St Joseph's School, Park Hill, Burnley
St Leonards-Mayfield School, Mayfield
St Margaret's School, Midhurst
St Margaret's School, Edinburgh
St Margaret's Senior School Convent of Mercy,
   Midhurst
St Martha's Senior School, Barnet
St Martin's Ampleforth, York
St Mary's, Worcester
St Mary's College, Liverpool
St Mary's College, Folkestone
St Mary's College, Southampton
St Mary's Hall, Clitheroe
St Mary's Hare Park School, Romford
St Mary's Hare Park School, Romford
St Mary's Junior School, Cambridge
St Mary's School Hampstead
St Mary's School, Ascot, Ascot
St Mary's School, Cambridge, Cambridge

St Mary's School, Dorset, Shaftesbury
St Michaels School, Newbury
St Monica's School, Carlisle
St Philip's School
St Philomena's Preparatory School, Frinton-on-Sea
St Pius X Preparatory School, Preston
St Richard's, Bromyard
St Richard's, Bromyard
St Teresa's Catholic Independent & Nursery
   School, Princes Risborough
St Teresa's Preparatory School, Effingham
St Teresa's School, Dorking
St Thomas Garnet's School, Bournemouth
St Ursula's High School, Westbury-on-Trym
St Winefride's Convent School, Shrewsbury
Stella Maris Junior School, Stockport
Stonyhurst College, Clitheroe
Stoodley Knowle School, Torquay
Thornton College Convent of Jesus and Mary,
   Milton Keynes
The Towers Convent School, Steyning
Upton Hall Convent School, Wirral
Ursuline College, Westgate-on-Sea
Ursuline Preparatory School
Ursuline Preparatory School, Brentwood
v, Godalming
Virgo Fidelis
Vita Et Pax Preparatory School
Westminster Cathedral Choir School
Winterfold House, Kidderminster
Winterfold House, Kidderminster
Woldingham School, Woldingham
Worth School, Turners Hill

SEVENTH DAY ADVENTIST

Dudley House School, Grantham
Fletewood School, Plymouth
The John Loughborough School, London
Newbold School, Bracknell
Stanborough School, Watford

UNITED REFORM CHURCH

Caterham School, Caterham
Silcoates School, Wakefield
Sunny Hill House School, Wakefield
The Firs School, Chester

Schools Registered with CReSTeD (Council for the Registration of Schools Teaching Dyslexic Pupils)

Registered charity number 1052103
Information provided by CReSTeD

CReSTeD (the Council for the Registration of Schools Teaching Dyslexic Pupils) produces a twice-yearly register of schools that provide for dyslexic children. The aim is to help parents and those who advise them to choose a school that has been approved to published criteria. CReSTeD was established in 1989 – its main supporters are the British Dyslexia Association and Dyslexia Action. Schools wishing to be included in the Register are visited by a CReSTeD consultant whose report is considered by the CReSTeD Council before registration can be finalized.

Consulting the Register should enable parents to decide which schools they wish to approach for further information. Dyslexic students have a variety of difficulties and so have a wide range of special needs. An equally wide range of teaching approaches is necessary. CReSTeD has therefore grouped schools together under four broad categories, which are designed to help parents match their child's needs to an appropriate philosophy and provision. The four categories of the schools are described below.

DYSLEXIA SPECIALIST PROVISION SCHOOLS – DSP and SPECIALIST PROVISION SCHOOLS – SP

The school is either established primarily to teach pupils with dyslexia or established to teach those with SpLD and associated difficulties. The curriculum and timetable are designed to meet specific needs in a holistic, coordinated manner with a significant number of staff qualified in teaching SpLD pupils.

DYSLEXIA UNIT – DU

The school has a designated unit or centre that provides specialist tuition on a small group or individual basis, according to need. The unit or centre is an adequately resourced teaching area under the management of a senior specialist teacher, who co-ordinates the work of other specialist teachers and ensures ongoing liaison with all mainstream teachers. This senior specialist teacher will probably have head of department status, and will certainly have significant input into the curriculum design and delivery.

SPECIALIST CLASSES – SC

Schools where dyslexic pupils are taught in separate classes within the school for some lessons, most probably English and Mathematics. These are taught by teachers with qualifications in teaching dyslexic pupils. These teachers are deemed responsible for communicating with the pupils' other subject teachers.

WITHDRAWAL SYSTEM – WS

Schools where dyslexic pupils are withdrawn from appropriately selected lessons for specialist tuition from a teacher qualified in teaching dyslexic pupils. There is ongoing communication between mainstream and specialist teachers.

Note: 'Qualified' means holding a BDA-recognized qualification in the teaching of dyslexic pupils.

The list below includes those schools registered with CReSTeD that are listed elsewhere in this Guide. For a full list of schools registered with CReSTeD, including specialist schools and maintained schools, contact CReSTeD on 01242 604852 or by e-mail at admin@crested.org.uk, or by writing to The Administrator, CReSTeD, Greygarth, Littleworth, Winchcombe, Cheltenham GL54 5BT. Alternatively, visit the website at www.crested.org.uk.

DYSLEXIA SPECIALIST PROVISION SCHOOLS & SPECIALIST PROVISION SCHOOLS

Abingdon House School, London W8
Appleford School, Salisbury
Blossom House School, London SW20
Brown's School, Orpington
Calder House School, Bath
Centre Academy, London SW11
Centre Academy, Suffolk
Chilton Tutorial School, Hants
The Dominie, London SW11
Fairley House School, London SW1P
Frewen College, Rye
Knowl Hill School, Pirbright
Mark College, Highbridge
The Moat School, London SW6
Moon Hall School, Dorking
Moon Hall College, Surrey
More House School, Surrey
Northease Manor School, Lewes
Nunnykirk Centre for Dyslexia, Morpeth
Shapwick School, Somerset
St David's College, Llandudno
Stanbridge Earls School, Hants
Sunnydown School, Caterham
Trinity School, Rochester
The Unicorn School, Abingdon

DYSLEXIA UNIT

Avon House, Woodford Green
Barnardiston Hall, Haverhill
Bethany School, Cranbrook
Bloxham School, Banbury
Bredon School, Tewkebury
Clayesmore School, Dorset
Clayesmore Preparatory School, Dorset
Clifton College Prep, Bristol
Cobham Hall, Gravesend

Danes Hill School, Leatherhead
DLD College, London
Ellesmere College,Ellesmere
Finborough School, Stowmarket
Fulneck School, Leeds
Holmewood House, Colchester
Hordle Walhampton School, Lymington
King's Bruton and Hazlegrove, Bruton
Kingham Hill School, Chipping Norton
Kingsley School, Devon
Kingswood House School, Surrey
Lavant School, West Sussex
Mayville High School, Hants
Millfield Preparatory School, Somerset
Moyles Court School, Hants
Newlands School, Sussex
Ramilies Hall School, Cheshire
Riddlesworth Hall Preparatory School, Norfolk
Scarsbrick Hall School, Lancs
Sidcot School, N Somerset
Slindon College, Sussex
St Bees School, Cumbria
Tettenhall College, W Midlands
Wycliffe College and Preparatory School, Gloucestershire

SPECIALIST CLASSES

Bruern Abbey School, Chesterton
St Crispin's School, Leicester

WITHDRAWAL SYSTEM

Kilgraston School, Perthshire
Leehurst Swan School, Salisbury
Manor House School, Surrey
Milton Abbey School, Dorset
Our Lady's Convent School, Leicestershire
Prior Park Preparatory School, Wiltshire
St John's School, Porthcawl
St Lawrence College, Kent
Thames Christian College, London SW11
Ysgol Rhydygors, Carmarthen

Provision for English as a Foreign Language

This index is intended as a general guide only and is compiled upon the basis of information given to Gabbitas by schools. Parents should note that there are wide variations in provision and are advised to contact individual schools for further details.

Schools listed below with a 'U' have a dedicated English language unit or offer intensive initial tuition for students whose first language is not English. Schools with no 'U' displayed offer one-to-one English language tuition, or arrange this tuition, according to need, for students whose first language is not English.

Parents may also wish to refer to the list of International Study Centres on page 32.

ENGLAND

BEDFORDSHIRE

Acorn School, Bedford
Bedford High School for Girls, Bedford
Bedford School, Bedford
Bedford School Study Centre, Bedford   U

BERKSHIRE

The Abbey School, Reading
The Ark School, Reading
Bearwood College, Wokingham   U
Bradfield College, Reading   U
Brockhurst & Marlston House Pre-Preparatory
    School, Thatcham
Brockhurst and Marlston House Schools,
    Newbury
The Cedars School, Aldermaston
Cheam School, Newbury   U
Claires Court School, Maidenhead
Claires Court Schools, The College, Maidenhead

Claires Court Schools, Ridgeway, Maidenhead
Dolphin School, Reading
Eagle House, Sandhurst
Elstree School, Reading
Heathfield School, Ascot   U
Highfield School, Maidenhead
Holme Grange School, Wokingham
Horris Hill School, Newbury
Hurst Lodge School, Ascot
Lambrook, Bracknell
Langley Manor School
Luckley-Oakfield School, Wokingham
Ludgrove, Wokingham
LVS Ascot, Ascot
Newbury Hall International School, Newbury   U
The Oratory School, Reading   U
Padworth College, Reading   U
Papplewick School, Ascot
Queen Anne's School   U
St Gabriel's
St George's School, Ascot
St John's Beaumont, Windsor   U

St Joseph's College, Reading
St Piran's Preparatory School, Maidenhead
Sunningdale School, Sunningdale
Upton House School, Windsor
Waverley School, Wokingham
Wellington College, Crowthorne
White House Preparatory School, Wokingham
Winbury School, Maidenhead

BRISTOL

Badminton School, Westbury-on-Trym
Bristol Grammar School
Clifton College   U
Clifton College Preparatory School   U
The Downs School, Wraxall
Gracefield Preparatory School, Fishponds
Queen Elizabeth's Hospital
The Red Maids' School
St Ursula's High School, Westbury-on-Trym   U
Tockington Manor School, Tockington   U
Torwood House School, Redland

BUCKINGHAMSHIRE

Akeley Wood School, Buckingham
The Beacon School, Amersham
Bury Lawn School, Milton Keynes
Caldicott School, Farnham Royal
Godstowe Preparatory School, High Wycombe   U
Grove Independent School, Milton Keynes
High March School, Beaconsfield
Kingscote Pre-Preparatory School, Gerrards
    Cross
Ladymede, Aylesbury
Maltman's Green School, Gerrards Cross
Milton Keynes Preparatory School, Milton Keynes
Pipers Corner School, High Wycombe
St Mary's School, Gerrards Cross
St Teresa's Catholic Independent & Nursery
    School, Princes Risborough
Stowe School, Buckingham   U
Swanbourne House School, Milton Keynes
Thornton College Convent of Jesus and Mary,
    Milton Keynes
Wycombe Abbey School, High Wycombe

CAMBRIDGESHIRE

Bellerbys College & Embassy CES Cambridge,
    Cambridge   U
Cambridge Centre for Sixth-form Studies,
    Cambridge   U
CATS College Cambridge, Cambridge   U
Kimbolton School, Huntingdon
King's School Ely, Ely   U

The Leys School, Cambridge   U
Madingley Pre-Preparatory School, Cambridge
MPW (Mander Portman Woodward), Cambridge U
The Perse School, Cambridge
The Peterborough School, Peterborough   U
St John's College School, Cambridge
St Mary's School, Cambridge, Cambridge   U
Sancton Wood School, Cambridge
Whitehall School, Huntingdon
Wisbech Grammar School, Wisbech

CHANNEL ISLANDS

St George's Preparatory School, Jersey

CHESHIRE

Abbey Gate School, Chester
Beech Hall School, Macclesfield
Cransley School, Northwich
The Firs School, Chester
Forest Park School, Sale
Greenbank Preparatory School, Cheadle
Hale Preparatory School, Altrincham   U
The King's School, Chester
Loreto Preparatory School, Altrincham
North Cestrian Grammar School, Altrincham
The Queen's School, Chester
The Ryleys, Alderley Edge
St Ambrose Preparatory School, Altrincham
Terra Nova School, Holmes Chapel
Wilmslow Preparatory School, Wilmslow

CORNWALL

Gems Bolitho School, Penzance   U
Highfields Private School, Redruth
St Piran's School, Hayle
Truro School, Truro

CUMBRIA

Casterton School, Kirkby Lonsdale
Chetwynde School, Barrow-in-Furness
Holme Park School, Kendal
Lime House School, Carlisle   U
St Bees School, St Bees   U
Sedbergh School, Sedbergh   U
Windermere School, Windermere   U

DERBYSHIRE

Derby Grammar School, Derby
Derby High School, Derby

Foremarke Hall, Derby
Mount St Mary's College, Spinkhill U
Repton School, Derby U
S. Anselm's School, Bakewell

DEVON

Blundell's School, Tiverton
Bramdean School, Exeter
Edgehill College, Bideford U
Exeter Cathedral School, Exeter
Exeter Tutorial College, Exeter U
Kelly College, Tavistock U
King's School and Nursery, Plymouth
KINGSLEY SCHOOL, Bideford U
The Maynard School, Exeter
Mount House School, Tavistock
Plymouth College, Plymouth U
Plymouth College Prepratory School, Plymouth
Stover School, Newton Abbot U
Shebbear College, Beaworthy U
South Devon Steiner School, Dartington
Tower House School, Paignton
Trinity School, Teignmouth U
West Buckland School, Barnstaple U

DORSET

Bournemouth Collegiate School, Bournemouth U
Bryanston School, Blandford Forum
Clayesmore, Blandford Forum
Clayesmore Preparatory School, Blandford Forum
International College, Sherborne School,
   Sherborne
Knighton House, Blandford Forum
Leweston School, Sherborne
Milton Abbey School, Blandford Forum U
Port Regis Preparatory School, Shaftesbury U
St Mary's School, Dorset, Shaftesbury
Sherborne Girls, Sherborne U
Sherborne School, Sherborne
Talbot Heath, Bournemouth
Yarrells School, Poole

COUNTY DURHAM

Barnard Castle School, Barnard Castle
Durham High School For Girls, Durham
Durham School, Durham
Polam Hall, Darlington U

ESSEX

Avon House, Woodford Green
Bancroft's School, Woodford Green

Braeside School for Girls, Buckhurst Hill
Brentwood School, Brentwood U
Chigwell School, Chigwell U
College Saint-Pierre, Leigh-on-Sea
Elm Green Preparatory School, Chelmsford U
Felsted School, Felsted U
Friends' School U
Gosfield School, Halstead
Holmwood House, Colchester
New Hall School, Chelmsford U
Oaklands School, Loughton
Park School for Girls, Ilford
Raphael Independent School, Hornchurch
St John's School, Billericay
St Mary's School, Colchester
Thorpe Hall School, Southend-on-Sea
Woodlands Schools, Brentwood

GLOUCESTERSHIRE

The Acorn School, Nailsworth
Airthrie School, Cheltenham
Bredon School, Tewkesbury
Cheltenham College, Cheltenham U
Cheltenham College Junior School, Cheltenham
Cheltenham Ladies' College, Cheltenham
Dean Close Preparatory School, Cheltenham U
Dean Close School, Cheltenham U
Hatherop Castle School, Cirencester
The King's School, Gloucester
Rendcomb College, Cirencester
Rose Hill School, Wotton-under-Edge
St Edward's School Cheltenham, Cheltenham
The School of the Lion, Gloucester
Westonbirt School, Tetbury U
Wycliffe College, Stonehouse U
Wycliffe Preparatory School, Stonehouse U
Wynstones School, Gloucester

SOUTH GLOUCESTERSHIRE

Silverhill School, Winterbourne

HAMPSHIRE

Ballard School, New Milton
Bedales Prep School, Dunhurst, Petersfield
Bedales School, Petersfield
Boundary Oak School, Fareham
Brockwood Park School, Bramdean U
Daneshill School, Basingstoke
Durlston Court, New Milton
Forres Sandle Manor, Fordingbridge
Glenhurst School, Havant
The Gregg School, Southampton
Grey House Preparatory School, Hook

Hampshire Collegiate School, UCST, Romsey
Highfield School, Liphook
Hordle Walhampton School, Lymington
Lord Wandsworth College, Hook
Mayville High School, Southsea   U
Portsmouth High School GDST, Southsea
Prince's Mead School, Winchester
Rookwood School, Andover
St John's College, Southsea
St Mary's College, Southampton
St Neot's Preparatory School, Hook
St Nicholas' School, Fleet
St Swithun's School, Winchester   U
St Winifred's School, Southampton
Stockton House School, Fleet
Sherborne House School, Eastleigh
Sherfield School, Hook
Twyford School, Winchester
Winchester College, Winchester
Woodhill School, Chandler's Ford
Wykeham House School, Fareham
Yateley Manor Preparatory School, Yateley

HEREFORDSHIRE

Hereford Cathedral School, Hereford
Lucton School, Leominster
St Richard's, Bromyard

HERTFORDSHIRE

Aldenham School, Elstree
Aldwickbury School, Harpenden
Beechwood Park School, St Albans
Berkhamsted School, Berkhamsted   U
Bishop's Stortford College, Bishop's Stortford
Bishop's Stortford College Junior School, Bishop's
    Stortford
Duncombe School, Hertford
Edge Grove
Francis House Preparatory School, Tring
Haileybury, Hertford
Haresfoot Preparatory School, Berkhamsted
High Elms Manor School, Watford
Howe Green House School, Bishop's Stortford
The Junior School, Bishop's Stortford College,
    Bishop's Stortford
Justin Craig Education
The King's School, Harpenden
Lockers Park, Hemel Hempstead
Queenswood, Hatfield   U
Rickmansworth PNEU School, Rickmansworth
The Royal Masonic School for Girls,
    Rickmansworth
St Albans High School for Girls, St Albans
St Christopher School, Letchworth Garden City
St Edmund's College & Prep School, Ware   U

St Francis' College, Letchworth Garden City   U
St Hilda's School, Bushey
St Margaret's School, Bushey
Stanborough School, Watford   U
Sherrardswood School, Welwyn
Tring Park School for the Performing Arts, Tring
York House School

ISLE OF MAN

King William's College, Castletown

ISLE OF WIGHT

Ryde School, Ryde

KENT

Ashford School, Ashford
Beechwood Sacred Heart School, Tunbridge
    Wells   U
Benenden School, Cranbrook
Bethany School, Cranbrook   U
Bishop Challoner RC School, Bromley
Bromley High School GDST, Bromley
CATS College Canterbury, Canterbury   U
Cobham Hall, Gravesend   U
Dover College, Dover   U
Dulwich Preparatory School, Cranbrook,
    Cranbrook
Farringtons School, Chislehurst   U
Fosse Bank School, Tonbridge
Holmewood House, Tunbridge Wells
Junior King's Canterbury, Canterbury   U
Kent College, Canterbury   U
Kent College Infant & Junior School,
    Canterbury   U
Kent College Pembury, Tunbridge Wells
King's Rochester, Rochester
Northbourne Park School, Deal   U
Rochester Independent College, Rochester   U
St Andrew's School, Rochester
St Christopher's School, Canterbury   U
St Edmund's School Canterbury, Canterbury
St Edmunds Junior School, Canterbury
St Joseph's Preparatory School, Gravesend
St Lawrence College, Ramsgate   U
St Lawrence College Junior School, Ramsgate
St Michael's School, Sevenoaks
Steephill Independent School, Longfield
Sevenoaks School, Sevenoaks
Sutton Valence School, Sutton Valence
Tonbridge School, Tonbridge
Walthamstow Hall, Sevenoaks
West Lodge Preparatory School, Sidcup
Wickham Court School, West Wickham

LANCASHIRE

Beech House School, Rochdale
The Bennett House School, Chorley
Bolton School (Girls' Division), Bolton
Clevelands Preparatory School, Bolton
Farrowdale House Preparatory School, Oldham
Kingswood College Trust, Ormskirk
Kirkham Grammar School, Preston
Langdale Preparatory School, Blackpool
Moorland School, Clitheroe
Queen Elizabeth's Grammar School, Blackburn
Rossall School, Fleetwood   U
Rossall School International Study Centre,
    Fleetwood   U
St Anne's College Grammar School, Lytham St
    Annes   U
St Mary's Hall, Clitheroe   U
Stonyhurst College, Clitheroe   U

LEICESTERSHIRE

Brooke House College, Market Harborough   U
Grace Dieu Manor School, Leicester
Leicester Grammar School, Leicester   U
Loughborough High School, Loughborough
Our Lady's Convent School, Loughborough
Ratcliffe College, Leicester   U
St Crispin's School, Leicester

LINCOLNSHIRE

Copthill School, Stamford
Dudley House School, Grantham
The Grantham Preparatory School, Grantham
Kirkstone House School, Bourne
Stamford High School, Stamford
Stamford Junior School, Stamford
Stamford School, Stamford

NORTH EAST LINCOLNSHIRE

St James' School, Grimsby   U

NORTH LINCOLNSHIRE

Trentvale Preparatory School, Keadby

LONDON

Abercorn School
Albemarle Independent College   U
Arnold House School

Ashbourne Middle School
Aston House School
Avenue House School
Bales College
Barbara Speake Stage School
Belmont (Mill Hill Preparatory School)
Blackheath High School GDST
Brampton College   U
Broomwood Hall School
Cameron House School, Chelsea
CATS College London   U
The Cavendish School
Channing School
Chelsea Independent College   U
City of London School
Colet Court
Collingham Independent GCSE and Sixth Form
    College
Connaught House
David Game College   U
Davies Laing and Dick   U
Devonshire House Preparatory School
Dolphin School (Including Noah's Ark Nursery
    School)
Donhead Prep School
Duff Miller
Dulwich College
Dulwich College Preparatory School
Ealing Independent College, Ealing
East London Christian Choir School   U
Eaton House Belgravia, London
Eaton House The Manor Pre-Preparatory, London
Eaton House The Manor Preparatory
Eaton House The Vale, London
Eaton Square School
Eridge House Preparatory
The Falcons School for Girls
Falkner House
Fine Arts College, London
Finton House School
Francis Holland School, Sloane Square SW1
Gatehouse School
GEMS Hampshire School
Goodwyn School
Grangewood Independent School
Great Beginnings Montessori School
Hall School Wimbledon (Junior School)
Hall School Wimbledon (Senior School)
Hawkesdown House School
Heath House Preparatory School
Heathside Preparatory School, Hampstead
Hendon Preparatory School, Hendon   U
Hill House International Junior School   U
Holland Park Pre-Preparatory School
Holly Park Montessori School
Ibstock Place School
International Community School   U
International School of London   U
Islamia Girls' School

James Allen's Preparatory School
Kerem School
The King Alfred School
Knightsbridge School
Lansdowne College
Le Herisson
Lion House School
The Lloyd Williamson School
Lyndhurst House Preparatory School
Mander Portman Woodward   U
The Merlin School
Mill Hill School
More House School, London
The Mount School   U
The Mulberry House School
Norland Place School
North Bridge House Senior School
North Bridge House Upper Prep School
The North London International School, London
Northcote Lodge School
Oakfield Preparatory School
Orchard House School
Parkgate House School
Portland Place School   U
Primrose Independent School
Prospect House School
Putney High School GDST
Putney Park School
Queen's College Prep School
Queen's Gate School
Rainbow Montessori Junior School
Ravenscourt Park Preparatory School,
    Hammersmith
Ravenstone Day Nursery and Nursery School
Redcliffe School
River House Montessori School
Riverston School
The Roche School
The Rowans School
The Royal School, Hampstead
St Augustine's Priory, Ealing
St Benedict's School, Ealing
St James Junior School
St James Senior Girls' School
St Johns Wood Pre-Preparatory School
St Margaret's School
St Martin's School
St Mary's School Hampstead
St Olave's Preparatory School
St Paul's Cathedral School
The Study Preparatory School
Southbank International School, Hampstead   U
Southbank International School, Kensington   U
Southbank International School, Westminster   U
Sylvia Young Theatre School
Thames Christian College   U
Thomas's Fulham
Thomas's Preparatory School   U
Tower House School

The Village School
Welsh School of London
Westminster School, Westminster
Westminster Tutors
Wetherby Preparatory School
The White House Prep & Woodentops
    Kindergarten
Willington School

GREATER MANCHESTER

Clarendon Cottage School, Eccles
St Bede's College, Manchester
Withington Girls' School, Manchester

MERSEYSIDE

Birkenhead School, Wirral
Kingsmead School, Wirral   U
Liverpool College, Liverpool
Merchant Taylors' Boys' Schools, Liverpool
Merchant Taylors' Girls' School, Liverpool
Runnymede St Edward's School, Liverpool
St Mary's College, Liverpool

MIDDLESEX

ACS Hillingdon International School, Hillingdon   U
Ashton House School, Isleworth
Buckingham College School, Harrow
Denmead School, Hampton
Halliford School, Shepperton
Hampton School, Hampton
Harrow School, Harrow on the Hill
Little Eden & Eden High SDA, Brentford
The Mall School, Twickenham
Northwood College, Northwood
St Catherine's School, Twickenham
St Christopher's School, Wembley
St Helen's College, Hillingdon
St Helen's School, Northwood
St Martin's School, Northwood
Staines Preparatory School, Staines
Twickenham Preparatory School, Hampton

NORFOLK

Beeston Hall School, Cromer
Gresham's School, Holt
Hethersett Old Hall School, Norwich   U
Langley School, Norwich   U
The New Eccles Hall School, Norwich   U
Norwich High School for Girls GDST, Norwich
Notre Dame Preparatory School, Norwich
Riddlesworth Hall, Diss   U

St Nicholas House Kindergarten & Prep School,
   North Walsham   U
Stretton School, Norwich
Taverham Hall Preparatory School, Norwich   U

NORTHAMPTONSHIRE

Bosworth Independent College, Northampton   U
Maidwell Hall School
Oundle School, Nr Peterborough
Pitsford School, Pitsford
Quinton House School, Northampton
Spratton Hall, Northampton

NORTHUMBERLAND

Longridge Towers School, Berwick-upon-Tweed

NOTTINGHAMSHIRE

Dagfa House School, Nottingham
Greenholme School, Nottingham
Grosvenor School, Nottingham
Highfields School, Newark
Ranby House School, Retford
Saville House School, Mansfield
Trent College & The Elms, Nottingham
Wellow House School, Newark
Worksop College, Worksop

OXFORDSHIRE

Abacus College, Oxford   U
Abingdon Preparatory School, Abingdon
Abingdon School, Abingdon
Cherwell College, Oxford
Christ Church Cathedral School, Oxford
Cokethorpe School, Witney
Cothill House Preparatory School, Abingdon
Cranford House School, Wallingford
d'Overbroeck's College Oxford, Oxford   U
Dragon School, Oxford
Greene's Tutorial College, Oxford
Headington School, Oxford
IQRA School, Oxford   U
Kingham Hill School, Chipping Norton   U
Leckford Place School, Oxford
The Manor Preparatory School, Abingdon
New College School, Oxford
The Oratory Preparatory School, Reading
Our Lady's Abingdon Junior School, Abingdon
Our Lady's Abingdon School, Abingdon
Oxford Tutorial College, Oxford   U
St Edward's School, Oxford
St Helen & St Katharine, Abingdon

St Hugh's School, Faringdon
St John's Priory School, Banbury
St Clare's, Oxford, Oxford   U
Shiplake College, Henley-on-Thames
Sibford School, Banbury   U
Summer Fields, Oxford
Tudor Hall School, Banbury
Wychwood School, Oxford

RUTLAND

Oakham School, Oakham
Uppingham School, Uppingham

SHROPSHIRE

Adcote School for Girls, Shrewsbury   U
Bedstone College, Bucknell   U
Castle House School, Newport
Concord College, Shrewsbury
Dower House School, Bridgnorth
Ellesmere College, Ellesmere   U
Kingsland Grange, Shrewsbury
Moor Park School, Ludlow
Moreton Hall School, Oswestry   U
Oswestry School, Oswestry   U
Packwood Haugh School, Shrewsbury
Prestfelde Preparatory School, Shrewsbury
St Winefride's Convent School, Shrewsbury
Shrewsbury High School GDST,
   Shrewsbury
Shrewsbury School, Shrewsbury
Wrekin College

SOMERSET

All Hallows, Shepton Mallet
Bath Academy, Bath   U
Bruton School for Girls, Bruton   U
Chard School, Chard
Chilton Cantelo School, Yeovil
Downside School, Bath
Hazlegrove, Yeovil
King's Bruton and Hazlegrove, Bruton
King's College, Taunton
King's Hall, Taunton
Millfield Preparatory School, Glastonbury U
Millfield School, Street   U
The Park School, Yeovil
Perrott Hill School, Crewkerne
Queen's College, Taunton   U
Queen's College Junior, Pre-Prep & Nursery
   Schools, Taunton
Taunton Preparatory School, Taunton   U
Taunton School International, Taunton   U
Taunton School Senior, Taunton   U

Wellington School, Wellington   U
Wells Cathedral School, Wells   U

Summerhill School, Leiston
Woodbridge School, Woodbridge   U

BATH & NORTH EAST SOMERSET

Kingswood Preparatory School, Bath
Kingswood School, Bath   U
Prior Park College, Bath
The Royal High School, Bath, Bath

NORTH SOMERSET

Sidcot School, Winscombe   U

STAFFORDSHIRE

Abbots Bromley School, Abbots Bromley
Abbotsholme School, Uttoxeter
Brooklands School & Little Brooklands Nursery,
    Stafford
Chase Academy, Cannock   U
Denstone College, Uttoxeter
Lichfield Cathedral School, Lichfield
Newcastle-under-Lyme School, Newcastle-under-
    Lyme
St Dominic's Independent Junior School, Stoke-
    on-Trent
St Dominic's School, Stafford
St Joseph's Preparatory School, Stoke-on-Trent

STOCKTON-ON-TEES

Teesside High School, Eaglescliffe

SUFFOLK

The Abbey, WOODBRIDGE
Alexanders International School, Woodbridge   U
Brandeston Hall, The Preparatory School for
    Framlingham College, Brandeston   U
Culford School, Bury St Edmunds
Fairstead House School, Newmarket
Felixstowe International College, Felixstowe   U
Framlingham College, Woodbridge
Ipswich School, Ipswich
Moreton Hall Preparatory School, Bury St
    Edmunds
Old Buckenham Hall School, Ipswich   U
Orwell Park, Ipswich
The Royal Hospital School, Ipswich   U
St Joseph's College, Ipswich   U
Saint Felix School, Southwold

SURREY

Aberdour, Tadworth
ACS Cobham International School,
    Cobham   U
ACS Egham International School, Egham   U
Aldro School, Godalming
Amesbury, Hindhead
Barrow Hills School, Godalming
Box Hill School, Dorking   U
Bramley School, Tadworth
Broomfield House School, Richmond
Cambridge Tutors College, Croydon   U
Charterhouse, Godalming
Chinthurst School, Tadworth
City of London Freemen's School, Ashtead
Claremont Fan Court School, Esher
Collingwood School, Wallington
Cranleigh School, Cranleigh
Cranmore School, Leatherhead
Croydon High School GDST, South Croydon
Cumnor House School, South Croydon
Downsend School, Leatherhead
Downsend School – Epsom Lodge, Epsom
Epsom College, Epsom
Ewell Castle School, Epsom
Feltonfleet School, Cobham
Frensham Heights School, Farnham   U
Grantchester House, Esher
Greenacre School for Girls, Banstead
Hampton Court House, East Molesey
Hawley Place School, Camberley
The Hawthorns School, Redhill
Hoe Bridge School, Woking
Homefield School, Sutton
Hurtwood House, Dorking   U
Kew College, Richmond
Kew Green Preparatory School, Richmond   U
King Edward's School Witley, Godalming   U
King's House School, Richmond
Kingston Grammar School, Kingston-upon-
    Thames
Kingswood House School, Epsom
Laleham Lea School, Purley
Longacre School, Guildford
Manor House School, Leatherhead
Marymount International School,
    Kingston-upon-Thames   U
New Life Christian School, Croydon
Notre Dame Preparatory School, Cobham
Old Palace of John Whitgift School, Croydon
Park Hill School, Kingston-upon-Thames
Prior's Field School, Godalming
Priory Preparatory School, Banstead
Redehall Preparatory School, Horley

Reigate St Mary's Preparatory and Choir School,
   Reigate
Ripley Court School, Woking
Royal Ballet School, Richmond
Royal Grammar School, Guildford
Royal Russell School, Croydon   U
The Royal School, Haslemere   U
St Catherine's School, Guildford
St David's School, Purley
St Hilary's School, Godalming
St James Independent School for Boys (Senior),
   Ashford
St John's School, Leatherhead   U
St Teresa's School, Dorking   U
The Study School, New Malden
Surbiton High School, Kingston-upon-Thames
Surbiton Preparatory School, Surbiton
Sutton High School GDST, Sutton
TASIS The American School in England,
   Thorpe   U
Trinity School, Croydon
Westbury House School, New Malden
Westward Preparatory School,
   Walton-on-Thames
Woodcote House School, Windlesham
Yehudi Menuhin School, Cobham   U

EAST SUSSEX

Ashdown House School, Forest Row
Battle Abbey School, Battle   U
Brighton College, Brighton   U
Brighton College Pre-preparatory School,
   Brighton
Brighton College Prep School, Brighton
Brighton Steiner School Limited,
   Brighton
Buckswood School, Hastings   U
Eastbourne College, Eastbourne
Greenfields Independent Day and Boarding
   School, Forest Row   U
Lancing College Preparatory School at Mowden,
   Hove
Michael Hall (Steiner Waldorf School),
   Forest Row   U
Moira House Girls School,
   Eastbourne   U
Moira House School, Eastbourne
Newlands School, Seaford   U
Roedean School, Brighton   U
St Andrew's School, Eastbourne   U
St Aubyns School, Brighton
St Bede's Prep School, Eastbourne
St Bede's School, Hailsham
St Leonards-Mayfield School, Mayfield   U
Stonelands School of Ballet & Theatre Arts, Hove
Vinehall School, Robertsbridge   U

WEST SUSSEX

Ardingly College, Haywards Heath
Ardingly College Junior School,
   Haywards Heath
Burgess Hill School for Girls, Burgess Hill
Cottesmore School, Pease Pottage
Dorset House School, Pulborough
Farlington School, Horsham   U
Great Ballard School, Chichester
Handcross Park School, Haywards Heath
Hurstpierpoint College, Hurstpierpoint
The Prebendal School, Chichester
Seaford College, Petworth
Slindon College, Arundel
The Towers Convent School, Steyning
Windlesham House School   U
Worth School, Turners Hill

TYNE AND WEAR

Central Newcastle High School GDST,
   Newcastle upon Tyne
Grindon Hall Christian School,
   Sunderland   U
The King's School, Tynemouth
Sunderland High School, Sunderland
Westfield School, Newcastle upon Tyne

WARWICKSHIRE

Arnold Lodge School, Leamington Spa
Bilton Grange, Rugby
The Kingsley School, Leamington Spa
Princethorpe College, Rugby
Rugby School, Rugby

WEST MIDLANDS

Al-Burhan Grammar School, Birmingham
Birchfield School, Wolverhampton
The Blue Coat School, Birmingham
Coventry Prep School, Coventry
Edgbaston High School for Girls,
   Birmingham
Eversfield Preparatory School, Solihull
Highclare School, Birmingham
Mander Portman Woodward, Birmingham
Priory School, Birmingham
St George's School, Edgbaston,
   Birmingham
Saint Martin's School, Solihull
Tettenhall College, Wolverhampton   U
Wolverhampton Grammar School,
   Wolverhampton

WILTSHIRE

Avondale School, Salisbury
Bishopstrow College   U
Chafyn Grove School, Salisbury
Dauntsey's School, Devizes
The Godolphin School, Salisbury
Grittleton House School, Chippenham
Marlborough College, Marlborough
Norman Court Preparatory School, Salisbury
Pinewood School, Shrivenham
Prior Park Preparatory School, Cricklade
St Margaret's Preparatory School, Calne
St Mary's Calne, Calne
Salisbury Cathedral School, Salisbury
Sandroyd School, Salisbury
Stonar School   U
Warminster School, Warminster   U

WORCESTERSHIRE

Abberley Hall, Worcester   U
The Abbey College, Malvern Wells   U
Bowbrook House School, Pershore
Bromsgrove Preparatory School, Bromsgrove   U
Bromsgrove School, Bromsgrove   U
The Downs, Malvern, Malvern
Green Hill School, Evesham
King's Hawford, Worcester
Malvern St James, Great Malvern   U
Moffats School, Bewdley
St Mary's, Worcester
Saint Michael's College, Tenbury Wells   U
Winterfold House, Kidderminster

EAST RIDING OF YORKSHIRE

Pocklington School, Pocklington

NORTH YORKSHIRE

Ampleforth College, York
Ashville College, Harrogate
Aysgarth Preparatory School, Bedale
Bootham School, York

Brackenfield School, Harrogate
Bramcote School, Scarborough
Fyling Hall School, Whitby
Giggleswick Junior School, Settle   U
Giggleswick School, Settle
Harrogate Ladies' College, Harrogate   U
Harrogate Language Academy, Harrogate   U
Harrogate Tutorial College, Harrogate   U
Malsis School, Near Skipton
The Mount School, York   U
Queen Ethelburga's College, York   U
Queen Mary's School, Thirsk
Read School, Selby
Ripon Cathedral Choir School, Ripon
St Martin's Ampleforth, York
Scarborough College & Lisvane School,
    Scarborough
Terrington Hall, York
Woodleigh School, Malton

SOUTH YORKSHIRE

Ashdell Preparatory School, Sheffield
Sheffield High School GDST, Sheffield
Westbourne School, Sheffield

WEST YORKSHIRE

Ackworth School, Pontefract   U
Batley Grammar School, Batley
Dale House School, Batley   U
The Froebelian School, Leeds
Fulneck School, Leeds   U
Gateways School, Leeds
Ghyll Royd School, Ilkley
The Gleddings Preparatory School, Halifax
Lady Lane Park School, Bingley
Moorlands School, Leeds
New Horizon Community School, Leeds
Queen Elizabeth Grammar School, Wakefield
The Rastrick Independent School, Brighouse
Rathbone Choices, Huddersfield
Richmond House School, Leeds
Rishworth School, Rishworth   U
Wakefield Independent School, Wakefield
Woodhouse Grove School, Apperley Bridge   U

NORTHERN IRELAND

COUNTY ANTRIM

Campbell College, Belfast   U
Victoria College Belfast, Belfast

COUNTY ARMAGH

The Royal School Armagh, Armagh   U

COUNTY DOWN

The Holywood Rudolf Steiner School, Holywood
Rockport School, Holywood

COUNTY TYRONE

The Royal School Dungannon, Dungannon   U

SCOTLAND

ABERDEENSHIRE

Albyn School, Aberdeen
International School of Aberdeen, Aberdeen   U
St Margaret's School for Girls, Aberdeen

SOUTH AYRSHIRE

Wellington School, Ayr

CLACKMANNANSHIRE

Dollar Academy, Dollar   U

FIFE

St Leonards School, St Andrews

GLASGOW

Craigholme School
Hutchesons' Grammar School
St Aloysius' College

LOTHIAN

Basil Paterson Tutorial College, Edinburgh   U
Belhaven Hill, Dunbar   U

Clifton Hall School, Edinburgh
The Edinburgh Rudolf Steiner School,
   Edinburgh   U
Fettes College, Edinburgh   U
George Watson's College, Edinburgh
Loretto Junior School, Musselburgh   U
Loretto School, Musselburgh   U
Merchiston Castle School, Edinburgh   U
St George's School for Girls, Edinburgh   U
St Serf's School, Edinburgh

MORAYSHIRE

Gordonstoun School, Elgin   U

PERTH AND KINROSS

Craigclowan Preparatory School, Perth
Glenalmond College, Perth
Kilgraston, Perth   U
Morrison's Academy, Crieff
Strathallan School, Perth   U

STIRLING

Beaconhurst School

WALES

BRIDGEND

St Clare's School, Porthcawl

CARDIFF

The Cardiff Academy
Howell's School, Llandaff GDST

Kings Monkton School
Westbourne School   U

CARMARTHENSHIRE

Llandovery College, Llandovery   U
St Michael's School, Llanelli

CONWY

St David's College, Llandudno

DENBIGHSHIRE

Howell's School, Denbigh   U
Ruthin School, Ruthin   U

GWYNEDD

Hillgrove School, Bangor

MONMOUTHSHIRE

Monmouth School, Monmouth
St John's-on-the-Hill, Chepstow

POWYS

Christ College, Brecon   U

SWANSEA

Craig-y-Nos School, Bishoptston

CONTINENTAL EUROPE

Aiglon College, Switzerland   U   John F. Kennedy International School   U
Chavagnes International College,   King's College Madrid, Madrid
   Chavagnes-en-Paillers, France   Mougins School   U
Headfort   U   St Columba's College

Schools in membership of the Constituent Associations of the Independent Schools Council

The schools listed below are all in membership of the Independent Schools Council in the UK. (Please note that ISC-accredited special schools and overseas schools are not included.) The constituent associations of the ISC include:

Association of Governing Bodies of Independent Schools (AGBIS)
The Girls' Schools Association (GSA)
The Headmasters' and Headmistresses' Conference (HMC)
The Independent Association of Prep Schools (IAPS)
The Independent Schools Association (ISA)
The Independent Schools' Bursars Association (ISBA)
The Society of Headmasters and Headmistresses of Independent Schools (SHMIS)

ENGLAND

BEDFORDSHIRE

Bedford High School for Girls, Bedford
Bedford Modern School, Bedford
Bedford School, Bedford
Dame Alice Harpur School, Bedford
Pilgrims Pre-Preparatory School, Bedford
Rushmoor School, Bedford
St Andrew's School, Bedford

BERKSHIRE

The Abbey School, Reading
Bradfield College, Reading
Brockhurst and Marlston House Schools, Newbury
Cheam School, Newbury
Downe House, Thatcham
Eagle House, Sandhurst
Elstree School, Reading
Eton End PNEU, Slough

Heathfield School, Ascot
Hemdean House School, Reading
Horris Hill School, Newbury
Hurst Lodge School, Ascot
Lambrook, Bracknell
Leighton Park School, Reading
Luckley-Oakfield School, Wokingham
The Oratory Preparatory School, Reading
The Oratory School, Reading
Padworth College, Reading
Pangbourne College, Pangbourne
Papplewick School, Ascot
Queen Anne's School, Reading
Reading Blue Coat School, Reading
Ridgeway School, Maidenhead
St Andrew's School, Reading
St Bernard's Preparatory School, Slough
St Gabriel's School, Newbury
St George's School, Windsor
St John's Beaumont, Windsor
St Joseph's Convent School, Reading
Sunningdale School, Sunningdale
Waverley School, Wokingham
Wellington College, Crowthorne
White House Preparatory School, Wokingham
Winbury School, Maidenhead

BRISTOL

Badminton School
Bristol Grammar School
Clifton College
Clifton College Pre-Prep – Butcombe
Clifton College Preparatory School
Clifton High School
Colston's Collegiate School
Colston's Girls' School
Colston's Lower School
Queen Elizabeth's Hospital
The Red Maids' School
Redland High School
St Ursula's High School
Tockington Manor School

BUCKINGHAMSHIRE

Ashfold School, Aylesbury
The Beacon School, Amersham
Caldicott School, Farnham Royal
Chesham Preparatory School, Chesham
Dair House School Trust Ltd, Farnham Royal
Davenies School, Beaconsfield
Gateway School, Great Missenden
Gayhurst School, Gerrards Cross
Heatherton House School, Amersham
High March School, Beaconsfield

Maltman's Green School, Gerrards Cross
Milton Keynes Preparatory School, Milton Keynes
Pipers Corner School, High Wycombe
St Mary's School, Gerrards Cross
St Teresa's Catholic Independent & Nursery
    School, Princes Risborough
Stowe School, Buckingham
Swanbourne House School, Milton Keynes
Thornton College Convent of Jesus and Mary,
    Milton Keynes
Thorpe House School, Gerrards Cross
Wycombe Abbey School, High Wycombe

CAMBRIDGESHIRE

CATS Cambridge
Cambridge Centre for Sixth-form Studies,
    Cambridge
Kings College, Cambridge
The King's School Ely, Ely
The Leys School, Cambridge
The Perse School, Cambridge
The Perse School for Girls, Cambridge
Peterborough High School, Peterborough
Sancton Wood School, Cambridge
St John's College School, Cambridge
St Mary's Junior School, Cambridge
St Mary's School, Cambridge

CHANNEL ISLANDS

Elizabeth College, Guernsey
The Ladies' College, Guernsey
St Michael's Preparatory School, Jersey
Victoria College, Jersey
Victoria College Preparatory School, Jersey

CHESHIRE

Abbey Gate College, Chester
Abbey Gate School, Chester
Alderley Edge School for Girls, Alderley Edge
Beech Hall School, Macclesfield
Cransley School, Northwich
The Firs School, Chester
The Grange School, Northwich
Hammond School, Chester
The King's School, Chester
The King's School, Macclesfield
Loreto Preparatory School, Altrincham
Pownall Hall School, Wilmslow
The Queen's School, Chester
Ramillies Hall School, Cheadle
Terra Nova School, Holmes Chapel
Wilmslow Preparatory School, Wilmslow

CORNWALL

Polwhele House School, Truro
Roselyon, Par
St Joseph's School, Launceston
Truro High School, Truro
Truro School, Truro

COUNTY DURHAM

Barnard Castle School, Barnard Castle
Durham High School for Girls, Durham
Durham School, Durham
Polam Hall, Darlington

CUMBRIA

Austin Friars St Monica's School, Carlisle
Chetwynde School, Barrow-in-Furness
Hunter Hall School, Penrith
Lime House School, Carlisle
St Bees School, St Bees
Sedbergh School, Sedbergh
Windermere St Anne's, Windermere

DERBYSHIRE

Derby Grammar School, Derby
Derby High School, Derby
Foremarke Hall School, Derby
Mount St Mary's College, Spinkhill
Ockbrook School, Derby
Repton School, Derby
St Anselm's School, Bakewell
St Peter and St Paul School, Chesterfield
St Wystan's School, Repton

DEVON

Blundell's Preparatory School, Tiverton
Blundell's School, Tiverton
Exeter Cathedral School, Exeter
Exeter School, Exeter
Kelly College, Tavistock
Kelly College Preparatory School, Tavistock
Mount House School, Tavistock
St Christopher's School, Totnes
St Dunstan's Abbey, Plymouth
St John's School, Sidmouth
St Margaret's School, Exeter
St Michael's, Barnstaple
St Peter's School, Exmouth
Shebbear College, Beaworthy
Stover School, Newton Abbot

Trinity School, Teignmouth
West Buckland School, Barnstaple

DORSET

Bryanston School, Blandford Forum
Canford School, Wimborne
Castle Court Preparatory School, Wimborne
Clayesmore Preparatory School, Blandford Forum
Clayesmore, Blandford Forum
Dumpton School, Wimborne
International College, Sherborne School, Sherborne
Knighton House, Blandford Forum
Leweston School, Sherbourne
Port Regis School, Shaftesbury
St Antony's Leweston Schools, Sherborne
St Mary's School, Shaftesbury
Sherborne Preparatory School, Sherborne
Sherborne School, Sherborne
Sherborne School for Girls, Sherborne
Sunninghill Preparatory School, Dorchester
Talbot Heath, Bournemouth
Thornlow Preparatory School, Weymouth
Uplands School, Poole
Wentworth College, Bournemouth
Yarrells School, Poole

ESSEX

Alleyn Court Preparatory School, Southend-on-Sea
Bancroft's School, Woodford Green
Braeside School for Girls, Buckhurst Hill
Brentwood School, Brentwood
Chigwell School, Chigwell
Colchester High School, Colchester
Coopersale Hall School, Epping
Crowstone Preparatory School, Westcliff-on-Sea
Dame Bradbury's School, Saffron Walden
Elm Green Preparatory School, Chelmsford
Felsted Preparatory School, Felsted
Felsted School, Felsted
Friends' School, Saffron Walden
Gidea Park College, Romford
Gosfield School, Halstead
Holmwood House, Colchester
Littlegarth School, Colchester
Loyola Preparatory School, Buckhurst Hill
Maldon Court Preparatory School, Maldon
New Hall School, Chelmsford
Oaklands School, Loughton
Park School for Girls, Ilford
St Anne's Preparatory School, Chelmsford
St Aubyn's School, Woodford Green
St Cedd's School, Chelmsford

St Hilda's School, Westcliff-on-Sea
St John's School, Billericay
St Margaret's School, Halstead
St Mary's School, Colchester
St Michael's School, Leigh-on-Sea
St Nicholas School, Harlow
St Philomena's Preparatory School, Frinton-on-Sea
Thorpe Hall School, Southend-on-Sea
Ursuline Preparatory School, Brentwood
Widford Lodge, Chelmsford
Woodford Green Preparatory School, Woodford Green
Woodlands Schools, Brentwood

GLOUCESTERSHIRE

Beaudesert Park School, Stroud
Berkhampstead School, Cheltenham
Bredon School, Tewkesbury
Cheltenham College, Cheltenham
Cheltenham College Junior School, Cheltenham
Cheltenham Dean Close School, Cheltenham
Cheltenham Ladies' College, Cheltenham
Hatherop Castle School, Cirencester
The King's School, Gloucester
Rendcomb College, Cirencester
The Richard Pate School, Cheltenham
Rose Hill School, Wotton-under-Edge
Westonbirt School, Tetbury
Wycliffe, Stonehouse
Wycliffe Preparatory School, Stonehouse

HAMPSHIRE

Alton Convent School, Alton
Ballard School, New Milton
Bedales School, Petersfield
Boundary Oak School, Fareham
Churchers College, Petersfield
Daneshill School, Basingstoke
Ditcham Park School, Petersfield
Dunhurst (Bedales Junior School), Petersfield
Farleigh School, Andover
Farnborough Hill, Farnborough
Forres Sandle Manor, Fordingbridge
The Gregg School, Southampton
Hampshire Collegiate School UCST, Romsey
Highfield School, Liphook
Hordle Walhampton School, Lymington
King Edward VI School, Southampton
Lord Wandsworth College, Hook
Mayville High School, Southsea
Moyles Court School, Ringwood
The Pilgrims' School, Winchester
The Portsmouth Grammar School, Portsmouth
Portsmouth High School GDST, Southsea
Prince's Mead School, Winchester

Rookesbury Park School, Portsmouth
Rookwood School, Andover
St John's College, Southsea
St Neot's School, Hook
St Nicholas' School, Fleet
St Swithun's School, Winchester
Salesian College, Farnborough
Sherborne House School, Eastleigh
Sherfield School, Hook
Stanbridge Earls School, Romsey
The Stroud School, Romsey
Twyford School, Winchester
West Hill Park, Fareham
Winchester College, Winchester
Wykeham House School, Fareham
Yateley Manor Preparatory School, Yateley

HEREFORDSHIRE

The Hereford Cathedral Junior School, Hereford
The Hereford Cathedral School, Hereford
Lucton School, Leominster

HERTFORDSHIRE

Abbot's Hill School, Hemel Hempstead
Aldenham School, Elstree
Aldwickbury School, Harpenden
Beechwood Park School, St Albans
Berkhamsted Collegiate Preparatory School, Berkhamsted
Berkhamsted Collegiate School, Berkhamsted
Bishop's Stortford College, Bishop's Stortford
CKHR Immanuel College, Bushey
Edge Grove, Aldenham
Egerton Rothesay School, Berkhamsted
Francis House Preparatory School, Tring
Haberdashers' Aske's Boys' School, Elstree
Haberdashers' Aske's School for Girls, Elstree
Haileybury, Hertford
Haresfoot Preparatory School, Berkhamsted
Heath Mount School, Hertford
Howe Green House School, Bishop's Stortford
Immanuel College, Bushey
Kingshott School, Hitchin
Lochinver House School, Potters Bar
Lockers Park, Hemel Hempstead
Lyonsdown School, New Barnet
Manor Lodge School, Shenley
Northwood Preparatory School, Rickmansworth
The Princess Helena College, Hitchin
The Purcell School, Bushey
Queenswood, Hatfield
The Royal Masonic School for Girls, Rickmansworth
St Albans High School for Girls, St Albans
St Albans School, St Albans

St Christopher School, Letchworth
St Columba's College, St Albans
St Edmund's College and St Hugh's School, Ware
St Francis' College, Letchworth Garden City
St Hilda's School, Bushey
St Hilda's School, Harpenden
St Joseph's in the Park, Hertingfordbury
St Margaret's School, Bushey
Sherrardswood School, Welwyn
Stanborough School, Watford
Stormont, Potters Bar
Tring Park School for the Performing Arts, Tring
Westbrook Hay Preparatory School, Hemel
    Hempstead

ISLE OF MAN

The Buchan School, Castletown
King William's College, Castletown

ISLE OF WIGHT

Ryde School, Ryde

KENT

Ashford School, Ashford
Babington House School, Chislehurst
Beechwood Sacred Heart School, Tunbridge
    Wells
Benenden School, Cranbrook
Bethany School, Cranbrook
Bickley Park School, Bromley
Bronte School, Gravesend
Combe Bank School, Nr Sevenoaks
Derwent Lodge School for Girls, Tonbridge
Dover College, Dover
Dulwich Preparatory School, Cranbrook
Farringtons School, Chislehurst
Fosse Bank School, Hildenborough
Gad's Hill School, Rochester
The Granville School, Sevenoaks
Harenc School Trust, Sidcup
Hilden Grange School, Tonbridge
Hilden Oaks School, Tonbridge
Junior King's School, Canterbury
The Junior School, St Lawrence College,
    Ramsgate
Kent College, Canterbury
Kent College Infant & Junior School, Canterbury
Kent College Pembury, Tunbridge Wells
King's Preparatory School, Rochester
The King's School, Canterbury
King's School Rochester, Rochester
Lorenden Preparatory School, Faversham
Marlborough House School, Hawkhurst

The Mead School, Turnbridge Wells
The New Beacon, Sevenoaks
Rochester Independent College, Rochester
Rose Hill School, Tunbridge Wells
Russell House School, Sevenoaks
Sackville School, Tonbridge
St Edmunds Junior School, Canterbury
St Edmund's School Canterbury, Canterbury
St Lawrence College, Ramsgate
St Michael's School, Sevenoaks
St Ronan's School, Hawkhurst
Sevenoaks Preparatory School, Sevenoaks
Sevenoaks School, Sevenoaks
Solefield School, Sevenoaks
Spring Grove School, Ashford
Steephill Independent School, Longfield
Sutton Valence Preparatory School, Maidstone
Sutton Valence School, Maidstone
Tonbridge School, Tonbridge
Walthamstow Hall, Sevenoaks
Wellesley House School, Broadstairs
Yardley Court, Tonbridge

LANCASHIRE

Arnold School, Blackpool
Highfield Priory School, Preston
The Hulme Grammar School for Girls, Oldham
King Edward VII and Queen Mary School, Lytham
    St Annes
Kirkham Grammar School, Preston
Moorland School, Clitheroe
The Oldham Hulme Grammar School, Oldham
Queen Elizabeth's Grammar School, Blackburn
Rossall Junior School, Fleetwood
Rossall School, Fleetwood
St Joseph's Convent School, Burnley
St Mary's Hall, Stonyhurst
St Pius X Preparatory School, Preston
Stonyhurst College, Clitheroe
Westholme School, Blackburn

LEICESTERSHIRE

Arley House PNEU School, Leicester
The Dixie Grammar School, Market Bosworth
Fairfield Preparatory School, Loughborough
Grace Dieu Manor School, Leicester
Leicester Grammar School, Leicester
Leicester High School for Girls, Leicester
Leicester Montessori Grammar School,
    Leicester
Loughborough Grammar School,
    Loughborough
Loughborough High School, Loughborough
Our Lady's Convent School, Loughborough
Ratcliffe College, Leicester

LINCOLNSHIRE

Ayscoughfee Hall School, Spalding
Copthill School, Stamford
Kirkstone House School, Bourne
Lincoln Minster School, Lincoln
St Hugh's School, Woodhall Spa
Stamford High School, Stamford
Stamford Junior School, Stamford
St James' School, Grimsby
St Martin's Preparatory School, Grimsby
Stamford School, Stamford Witham Hall, Bourne

LONDON

Abercorn School, NW8
Abingdon House School, W8
Alleyn's School, SE22
Arnold House School, NW8
Avenue House School, W13
Bassett House School, W10
Belmont (Mill Hill Preparatory School), NW7
Broomwood Hall Upper School, SW12
Bute House Preparatory School for Girls, W6
Cameron House School, SW3
The Cavendish School, NW1
Channing School, N6
City of London School, EC4
City of London School for Girls, EC2
Colfe's School, SE12
Davies, Laing & Dick College, W1
Devonshire House Preparatory School, NW3
Donhead Prep School, SW19
Dulwich College, SE21
Dulwich College Preparatory School, SE21
Eaton House, The Manor, SW4
Eaton House, The Vale, SW7
Eaton Square School, SW1
Eltham College, SE9
Emanuel School, SW11
The Falcons School for Boys, SW7
The Falcons School for Girls, W5
Fairley House School, SW1
Falkner House, SW7
Finton House School, SW17
Forest School, E17
Francis Holland School, Regent's Park, NW1
Francis Holland School, SW1
Garden House School, SW3
Gatehouse School, E2
Glendower Preparatory School, SW7
The Godolphin and Latymer School, W6
Grange Park Preparatory School, N21
Grangewood Independent School, E7
Harvington School, W5
Hawkesdown House School, W8
Hereward House School, NW3

Herne Hill School, SE24
Highgate School, N6
Ibstock Place School, SW15
The Italia Conti Academy of Theatre Arts, EC1
James Allen's Girls' School, SE22
James Allen's Preparatory School, SE22
Keble Preparatory School, N21
Kensington Prep School, SW6
The King Alfred School, NW11
King's College Junior School, SW19
King's College School, SW19
Knightsbridge School, SW1
Latymer Prep School, W6
Latymer Upper School, W6
Lyndhurst House Preparatory School, NW3
Mander Portman Woodward, SW7
Mill Hill School, NW7
The Moat School, SW6
More House, SW1
The Mount School, NW7
The Mulberry House School, NW2
Newton Prep School, SW8
Norland Place School, W11
Northcote Lodge School, SW11
The North London International School, N11
Notting Hill and Ealing High School GDST, W13
Oakfield Preparatory School, SE21
Orchard House School, W4
Palmers Green High School, N21
Pembridge Hall, W2
Portland Place School, W1
Prospect House School, SW15
Putney High School GDST, SW15
Putney Park School, SW15
Queen's College, W1
Queen's Gate School, SW7
Ravenscourt Park Preparatory School, W6
Redcliffe School, SW10
Riverston School, SE12
Rosemead Preparatory School, SE21
Royal Ballet School, WC2
The Royal School, Hampstead, NW3
St Anthony's Preparatory School, NW3
St Benedict's School, W5
St Christina's RC Preparatory School, NW8
St Christopher's School, NW3
St Dunstan's College, SE6
St James Independent School for Boys and Girls,
   W14
St James Independent School for Girls (Juniors),
   W14
St James Independent School for Senior Girls,
   W14
St Margaret's School, NW3
St Mary's School Hampstead, NW3
St Olave's Preparatory School, SE9
St Paul's Cathedral School, EC4
St Paul's Girls' School, W6
St Paul's Preparatory School, SW13

St Paul's School, SW13
South Hampstead High School, NW3
Southbank International School, Hampstead, NW3
Southbank International School, Kensington, W11
Southbank International School, Westminster, W1
Streatham and Clapham High School, SW16
Sussex House School, SW1
The Swaminarayan School, NW10
Sydenham High School GDST, SE26
Sylvia Young Theatre School, NW1
Tower House School, SW14
Trevor Roberts School, NW3
University College School, NW3
University College School Junior Branch, NW3
Ursuline Preparatory School, SW20
Virgo Fidelis, SE19
Vita et Pax School, N14
Westminster Abbey Choir School, SW1
Westminster Cathedral Choir School, SW1
Westminster School, SW1
Westminster Under School, SW1
Wimbledon High School GDST, SW19

GREATER MANCHESTER

Abbey College, Manchester
Abbotsford Preparatory School, Manchester
Chetham's School of Music, Manchester
The Manchester Grammar School, Manchester
Manchester High School for Girls, Manchester
Moor Allerton School, Manchester
St Bede's College, Manchester
Withington Girls' School, Manchester

MERSEYSIDE

The Belvedere School GDST, Liverpool
Birkenhead High School GDST, Wirral
Birkenhead School, Wirral
Carleton House Preparatory School, Liverpool
Kingsmead School, Wirral
Liverpool College, Liverpool
Merchant Taylors' Girls' School, Liverpool
Prenton Preparatory School, Wirral
Runnymede St Edward's School, Liverpool
St Mary's College, Liverpool
Sunnymede School, Southport
Tower College, Prescot

MIDDLESEX

ACS Hillingdon International School, Hillingdon
Alpha Preparatory School, Harrow
Ashton House School, Isleworth
Buckingham College School, Harrow
Denmead School, Hampton

Halliford School, Shepperton
Hampton School, Hampton
Harrow School, Harrow on the Hill
The John Lyon School, Harrow
The Lady Eleanor Holles School, Hampton
The Mall School, Twickenham
Merchant Taylors' School, Northwood
Newland House School, Twickenham
North London Collegiate, Edgware
Northwood College, Northwood
Orley Farm School, Harrow
Peterborough & St Margaret's School, Stanmore
Quainton Hall School, Harrow
Reddiford, Pinner
St Catherine's School, Twickenham
St Christopher's School, Wembley
St David's School, Ashford
St Helen's College, Hillingdon
St Helen's School, Northwood
St James Independent School for Boys (Senior),
    Twickenham
St John's Northwood, Northwood
St Martin's School, Northwood
Staines Preparatory School, Staines
Twickenham Preparatory School, Hampton

NORFOLK

Beeston Hall School, Cromer
Glebe House School, Hunstanton
Gresham's Preparatory School, Holt
Gresham's School, Holt
Hethersett Old Hall School, Norwich
Langley Preparatory School & Nursery, Norwich
Langley School, Norwich
The New Eccles Hall School, Norwich
Norwich High School for Girls GDST, Norwich
Norwich School, Norwich
Notre Dame Preparatory School, Norwich
Sacred Heart Convent School, Swaffham
St Nicholas House Kindergarten & Prep School,
    North Walsham
Taverham Hall Preparatory School, Norwich
Thetford Grammar School, Thetford
Town Close House Preparatory School, Norwich

NORTHAMPTONSHIRE

Beachborough School, Brackley
Great Houghton Preparatory School, Northampton
Laxton Junior School, Nr Peterborough
Maidwell Hall School, Northampton
Northampton High School, Northampton
Northamptonshire Grammar School, Pitsford
Oundle School, Nr Peterborough
St Peter's School, Kettering
Spratton Hall, Northampton

Wellingborough School, Wellingborough
Winchester House School, Brackley

NORTHUMBERLAND

Longridge Towers School, Berwick-upon-Tweed
Mowden Hall School, Stocksfield

NOTTINGHAMSHIRE

Dagfa House School, Nottingham
Grosvenor School, Nottingham
Highfields School, Newark
Nottingham High Junior School, Nottingham
Nottingham High School, Nottingham
Nottingham High School for Girls GDST,
    Nottingham
Ranby House School, Retford
St Joseph's School, Nottingham
Salterford House School, Nottingham
Wellow House School, Newark
Worksop College, Worksop

OXFORDSHIRE

Abingdon School, Abingdon
Bloxham School, Banbury
Bruern Abbey, Chesterton
The Carrdus School, Banbury
Chandlings Manor School, Oxford
Cokethorpe School, Witney
Cothill House Preparatory School, Abingdon
Cranford House School, Wallingford
d'Overbroeck's College, Oxford
Dragon School, Oxford
Ferndale Preparatory School, Faringdon
Headington School, Oxford
Kingham Hill School, Chipping Norton
The Manor Preparatory School, Abingdon
Moulsford Preparatory School, Wallingford
New College School, Oxford
Our Lady's Convent Senior School, Abingdon
Radley College, Abingdon
Rupert House, Henley-on-Thames
Rye St Antony School, Oxford
St Clare's, Oxford
St Edward's School, Oxford
St Hugh's School, Faringdon
The School of St Helen & St Katharine, Abingdon
Shiplake College, Henley-on-Thames
Sibford School, Banbury
Summer Fields, Oxford
Tudor Hall School, Banbury
Windrush Valley School, Chipping Norton
Wychwood School, Oxford

RUTLAND

Brooke Priory School, Oakham
Oakham School, Oakham
Uppingham School, Uppingham

SHROPSHIRE

Adcote School for Girls, Shrewsbury
Bedstone College, Bucknell
Castle House School, Newport
Concord College, Shrewsbury
Ellesmere College, Ellesmere
Moreton Hall School, Oswestry
The Old Hall School, Telford
Oswestry School, Oswestry
Packwood Haugh School, Shrewsbury
Prestfelde Preparatory School, Shrewsbury
St Winefride's Convent School, Shrewsbury
Shrewsbury High School GDST, Shrewsbury
Shrewsbury School, Shrewsbury
Wrekin College, Telford

SOMERSET

All Hallows, Shepton Mallet
Bruton School for Girls, Bruton
Chilton Cantelo School, Yeovil
Downside School, Bath
King Edward's School, Bath
King's College, Taunton
King's Hall, Taunton
King's Bruton and Hazlegrove, Bruton
Kingswood Preparatory School, Bath
Kingswood School, Bath
Millfield Preparatory School, Glastonbury
Millfield School, Street
Monkton Combe Junior School, Bath
Monkton Combe School, Bath
Paragon School, Bath
The Park School, Yeovil
Perrott Hill School, Crewkerne
Prior Park College, Bath
Queen's College, Taunton
Queen's College Junior, Pre-Prep & Nursery
    Schools, Taunton
The Royal High School, Bath
Sidcot School, Winscombe
Taunton Preparatory School, Taunton
Taunton School, Taunton
Wellington School, Wellington
Wells Cathedral Junior School, Wells
Wells Cathedral School, Wells

STAFFORDSHIRE

Abbots Bromley School for Girls, Abbots Bromley
Brooklands School, Stafford
Chase Academy, Cannock
Denstone College, Uttoxeter
Edenhurst School, Newcastle-under-Lyme
Lichfield Cathedral School, Lichfield
Maple Hayes School, Lichfield
Newcastle-under-Lyme School, Newcastle-under-Lyme
St Bede's School, Stafford
St Dominic's Priory School, Stone
St Dominic's School, Stafford
St Joseph's Preparatory School, Stoke-on-Trent
Stafford Grammar School, Stafford
Vernon Lodge Preparatory School, Brewood
Yarlet School, Stafford

STOCKTON-ON-TEES

Red House School, Norton
Teesside High School, Eaglescliffe

SUFFOLK

The Abbey, Woodbridge
Amberfield School, Ipswich
Barnardiston Hall Preparatory School, Haverhill
Brandeston Hall, The Prep School for
    Framlingham College, Brandeston
Culford School, Bury St Edmunds
Fairstead House School, Newmarket
Finborough School, Stowmarket
Framlingham College, Woodbridge
Framlingham College Preparatory School,
    Brandeston
Ipswich High School GDST, Ipswich
Ipswich Preparatory School, Ipswich
Ipswich School, Ipswich
Moreton Hall Preparatory School,
    Bury St Edmunds
Old Buckenham Hall School, Ipswich
Orwell Park, Ipswich
Royal Hospital School, Ipswich
Saint Felix School, Southwold
St Joseph's College, Ipswich
South Lee Preparatory School, Bury St Edmunds
Stoke College, Sudbury
Woodbridge School, Woodbridge

SURREY

Aberdour, Tadworth
ACS Cobham International School, Cobham
ACS Egham International School, Egham

Aldro School, Godalming
Amesbury, Hindhead
Barfield School, Farnham
Barrow Hills School, Godalming
Belmont School, Dorking
Bishopsgate School, Egham
Box Hill School, Dorking
Bramley School, Tadworth
Canbury School, Kingston upon Thames
Caterham Preparatory School, Caterham
Caterham School, Caterham
Charterhouse, Godalming
Chinthurst School, Tadworth
City of London Freemen's School, Ashtead
Claremont Fan Court School, Esher
Coworth-Flexlands School, Woking
Cranleigh Preparatory School, Cranleigh
Cranleigh School, Cranleigh
Cranmore School, Leatherhead
Cumnor House School, South Croydon
Danes Hill Preparatory School, Leatherhead
Duke of Kent School, Guildford
Dunottar School, Reigate
Edgeborough, Farnham
Epsom College, Epsom
Ewell Castle School, Epsom
Feltonfleet School, Cobham
Frensham Heights School, Farnham
Greenacre School for Girls, Banstead
Greenfield School, Woking
Guildford High School, Guildford
Hall Grove School, Bagshot
Halstead Preparatory School, Woking
Haslemere Preparatory School, Haslemere
The Hawthorns School, Redhill
Homefield School, Sutton
Hurtwood House, Dorking
King Edward's School Witley, Godalming
Kingston Grammar School, Kingston upon
    Thames
Kingswood House School, Epsom
Lanesborough, Guildford
Lingfield Notre Dame School, Lingfield
Longacre School, Guildford
Lyndhurst School, Camberley
Manor House School, Leatherhead
Marymount International School, Kingston upon
    Thames
Micklefield School, Reigate
Milbourne Lodge School, Esher
More House School, Farnham
Notre Dame Preparatory School, Cobham
Notre Dame Senior School, Cobham
Oakhyrst Grange School, Caterham
Parkside School, Cobham
Prior's Field School, Godalming
Priory Preparatory School, Banstead
Reed's School, Cobham
Reigate Grammar School, Reigate

Reigate St Mary's Preparatory and Choir School, Reigate
Rowan Preparatory School, Esher
Royal Grammar School, Guildford
The Royal School, Haslemere
Rydes Hill Preparatory School, Guildford
St Andrew's (Woking) School Trust, Woking
St Catherine's School, Guildford
St Christopher's School, Epsom
St David's School, Purley
St Edmund's School, Hindhead
St George's College, Weybridge
St George's College Junior School, Weybridge
St Hilary's School, Godalming
St Ives School, Haslemere
St John's School, Leatherhead
St Teresa's Preparatory School, Effingham
St Teresa's School, Dorking
Seaton House School, Sutton
Sir William Perkins's School, Chertsey
Surbiton High School, Kingston-upon-Thames
Surbiton Preparatory School, Surbiton
Sutton High School GDST, Sutton
Westward Preparatory School, Walton-on-Thames
Woldingham School, Woldingham
Woodcote House School, Windlesham
Yehudi Menuhin School, Cobham

EAST SUSSEX

Ashdown House School, Forest Row
Battle Abbey School, Battle
Bricklehurst Manor Preparatory, Wadhurst
Brighton and Hove High School GDST, Brighton
Brighton College, Brighton
Brighton College Prep School, Brighton
Eastbourne College, Eastbourne
Frewen College, Rye
Greenfields School, Forest Row
Lewes Old Grammar School, Lewes
Newland School, Seaford
Northease Manor, Lewes
Roedean School, Brighton
St Andrew's School, Eastbourne
St Aubyns School, Brighton
St Bede's Prep School, Eastbourne
St Bede's School, Hailsham
St Leonards-Mayfield School, Mayfield
St Mary's Hall, Brighton
Sacred Heart School, Wadhurst
Skippers Hill Manor Preparatory School, Mayfield
Vinehall School, Robertsbridge

WEST SUSSEX

Ardingly College, Haywards Heath
Ardingly College Junior School, Haywards Heath
Arundale Preparatory School, Pulborough
Brambletye, East Grinstead
Broadwater Manor School, Worthing
Burgess Hill School for Girls, Burgess Hill
Christ's Hospital, Horsham
Cottesmore School, Pease Pottage
Cumnor House School, Haywards Heath
Dorset House School, Pulborough
Farlington School, Horsham
Fonthill Lodge, East Grinstead
Great Ballard School, Chichester
Great Walstead, Haywards Heath
Handcross Park School, Haywards Heath
Hurstpierpoint College, Hurstpierpoint
Lancing College, Lancing
Lavant House, Chichester
Oakwood School, Chichester
Our Lady of Sion School, Worthing
The Prebendal School, Chichester
St Margaret's School Convent of Mercy, Midhurst
Seaford College, Petworth
Shoreham College, Shoreham-by-Sea
Slindon College, Arundel
Sompting Abbotts School, Sompting
Stoke Brunswick, East Grinstead
The Towers Convent School, Steyning
Westbourne House School, Chichester
Windlesham House School, Pulborough
Worth School, Turners Hill

TYNE AND WEAR

Argyle House School, Sunderland
Central Newcastle High School GDST, Newcastle upon Tyne
Dame Allan's Boys School, Newcastle upon Tyne
Dame Allan's Girls School, Newcastle upon Tyne
The King's School, Tynemouth
Newcastle Preparatory School, Newcastle upon Tyne
Royal Grammar School, Newcastle upon Tyne
Sunderland High School, Sunderland
Westfield School, Newcastle upon Tyne

WARWICKSHIRE

Arnold Lodge School, Leamington Spa
Bilton Grange, Rugby
The Crescent School, Rugby
The King's High School for Girls, Warwick
Princethorpe College, Rugby
Rugby School, Rugby
Stratford Preparatory School, Stratford-upon-Avon
Warwick Preparatory School, Warwick
Warwick School, Warwick

WEST MIDLANDS

Bablake Junior School, Coventry
Bablake School, Coventry
The Blue Coat School, Birmingham
Coventry Prep School, Coventry
Crackley Hall School, Kenilworth
Davenport Lodge School, Coventry
Edgbaston High School for Girls, Birmingham
Elmhurst School for Dance, Birmingham
Eversfield Preparatory School, Solihull
Hallfield School, Birmingham
King Edward VI High School for Girls, Birmingham
King Edward's School, Birmingham
King Henry VIII School, Coventry
Mayfield Preparatory School, Walsall
Newbridge Preparatory School, Wolverhampton
Norfolk House School, Birmingham
Priory School, Birmingham
The Royal Wolverhampton Junior School,
  Wolverhampton
The Royal Wolverhampton School,
  Wolverhampton
Ruckleigh School, Solihull
St George's School, Edgbaston, Birmingham
Saint Martin's School, Solihull
Solihull School, Solihull
Tettenhall College, Wolverhampton
West House School, Birmingham
Wolverhampton Grammar School, Wolverhampton

WILTSHIRE

Appleford School, Salisbury
Chafyn Grove School, Salisbury
Dauntsey's School, Devizes
The Godolphin School, Salisbury
Heywood Preparatory School, Corsham
Marlborough College, Marlborough
Norman Court, Salisbury
Pinewood School, Shrivenham
Prior Park Preparatory School, Cricklade
St Francis School, Pewsey
St Margaret's Preparatory School, Calne
St Mary's Calne, Calne
Salisbury Cathedral School, Salisbury
Sandroyd School, Salisbury
Warminster School, Warminster

WORCESTERSHIRE

Abberley Hall, Worcester
The Alice Ottley School, Worcester
Bowbrook House School, Pershore
Bromsgrove Preparatory School, Bromsgrove
Bromsgrove School, Bromsgrove

The Downs School, Malvern
The Elms, Malvern
Heathfield School, Kidderminster
Holy Trinity School, Kidderminster
King's Hawford, Worcester
The King's School, Worcester
The Knoll School, Kidderminster
Malvern College, Malvern
St James's School, Malvern
St Mary's Convent School, Worcester
Winterfold House, Kidderminster

EAST RIDING OF YORKSHIRE

Hull Collegiate School, Anlaby
Hymers College, Hull
Pocklington School, Pocklington

NORTH YORKSHIRE

Ampleforth College, York
Ashville College, Harrogate
Aysgarth Preparatory School, Bedale
Bramcote School, Scarborough
Clifton Preparatory School, York
Fyling Hall School, Whitby
Giggleswick School, Settle
Harrogate Ladies' College, Harrogate
The Minster School, York
The Mount School, York
Queen Ethelburga's College, York
Queen Margaret's School, York
Queen Mary's School, Thirsk
Read School, Selby
Ripon Cathedral Choir School, Ripon
St Peter's School, York
Scarborough College & Lisvane School,
  Scarborough
Terrington Hall, York
York St Olave's School (Junior of St Peter's), York

SOUTH YORKSHIRE

Ashdell Preparatory School, Sheffield
Birkdale School, Sheffield
Brantwood School, Sheffield
Mylnhurst Preparatory School & Nursery,
  Sheffield
Rudston Preparatory School, Rotherham
Sheffield High School GDST, Sheffield

WEST YORKSHIRE

Ackworth School, Pontefract
Batley Grammar School, Batley

Bradford Girls' Grammar School, Bradford
Bradford Grammar School, Bradford
Cliff School, Wakefield
Dale House School, Batley
The Froebelian School, Leeds
Fulneck School, Leeds
Gateways School, Leeds
The Grammar School at Leeds, Leeds
Hipperholme Grammar School, Halifax
Lady Lane Park School, Bingley

Moorfield School, Ilkley
Moorlands School, Leeds
Queen Elizabeth Grammar School, Wakefield
The Rastrick Independent School, Brighouse
Richmond House School, Leeds
Rishworth School, Rishworth
Silcoates School, Wakefield
Wakefield Girls' High School, Wakefield
Westville House Preparatory School, Ilkley
Woodhouse Grove School, Apperley Bridge

NORTHERN IRELAND

COUNTY ANTRIM

Belfast Royal Academy, Belfast
Campbell College, Belfast
Methodist College, Belfast
Royal Belfast Academical Institution, Belfast

COUNTY DOWN

Bangor Grammar School, Bangor
Rockport School, Holywood

COUNTY FERMANAGH

Portora Royal School, Enniskillen

COUNTY LONDONDERRY

Coleraine Academical Institution, Coleraine

COUNTY TYRONE

The Royal School Dungannon, Dungannon

SCOTLAND

ABERDEENSHIRE

Robert Gordon's College, Aberdeen
St Margaret's School for Girls, Aberdeen

ANGUS

High School of Dundee, Dundee
Lathallan School, Montrose

ARGYLL AND BUTE

Lomond School, Helensburgh

CLACKMANNANSHIRE

Dollar Academy, Dollar

FIFE

St Leonards School & VIth Form College,
   St Andrews

GLASGOW

Craigholme School, Glasgow
The Glasgow Academy, Glasgow
The High School of Glasgow, Glasgow
Hutchesons' Grammar School, Glasgow
Kelvinside Academy, Glasgow
St Aloysius Junior School, Glasgow

LOTHIAN

Belhaven Hill, Dunbar
Cargilfield, Edinburgh
Clifton Hall School, Edinburgh
The Edinburgh Academy, Edinburgh
Fettes College, Edinburgh

George Heriot's School, Edinburgh
George Watson's College, Edinburgh
The Mary Erskine School, Edinburgh
Merchiston Castle School, Edinburgh
St George's School for Girls, Edinburgh
St Margaret's School, Edinburgh
Stewart's Melville College, Edinburgh

MORAYSHIRE

Gordonstoun School, Elgin

PERTH AND KINROSS

Ardvreck School, Crieff
Craigclowan Preparatory School, Perth
Glenalmond College, Perth

Kilgraston, Perth
Morrison's Academy, Crieff
Strathallan School, Perth

RENFREWSHIRE

St Columba's School, Kilmacolm

ROXBURGHSHIRE

St Mary's Preparatory School, Melrose

STIRLING

Beaconhurst School, Bridge of Allan

WALES

CARDIFF

The Cathedral School, Cardiff
Howell's School, Llandaff GDST, Cardiff
Kings Monkton School, Cardiff
St John's College, Old St Mellors
Westbourne School, Cardiff

CARMARTHENSHIRE

Llandovery College, Llandovery
St Michael's School, Llanelli

CONWY

Lyndon Preparatory School, Colwyn Bay
Rydal Penrhos Senior School, Colwyn Bay
St David's College, Llandudno

DENBIGHSHIRE

Howell's School, Denbigh
Ruthin School, Ruthin

GWYNEDD

St Gerard's School, Bangor

MONMOUTHSHIRE

Haberdashers' Monmouth School for Girls,
    Monmouth
Monmouth School, Monmouth
St John's-on-the-Hill, Chepstow

NEWPORT

Rougemont School, Newport

POWYS

Christ College, Brecon

Educational associations and useful addresses

Allied Schools Agency Ltd
Suite 1, The Stables
Featherbed Court
Mixbury
Northants NN13 5RN
Tel: (01280) 847016
E-mail: z.foard@alliedschools.org.uk
Website: www.alliedschools.org.uk
General Manager: Michael Porter BA, MSc

The organization provides governance support to member schools and supports communication and exchange of best practice and ideas between school governors, heads, bursars and other staff. The Allied Schools include:

Barnardiston Hall
Canford School
Harrogate Ladies' College
The Old Hall School
Riddlesworth Hall
Rose Hill Westonbirt
St John's-on-the-hill, Chepstow
Stowe School
Westonbirt School
Wrekin College

The Association for the Education and Guardianship of International Students (AEGIS)
Tel/Fax: (01453) 755160
E-mail: secretary@aegisuk.net
Website: www.aegisuk.net
Secretary: Janet Bowman
Registered Charity No. 1111 384

The Association promotes best and legal practice in all areas of guardianship and the care of international students under 18 years of age, at school or college in the United Kingdom. All members, including school members, are required to adhere to the AEGIS Code of Practice and undertake to follow guidelines on caring for international students. Guardianship organizations are admitted to membership after a successful accreditation inspection.

Association of Governing Bodies of Independent Schools (AGBIS)

3 Codicote Road
Welwyn
Hertfordshire AL6 9LY
Tel: (01438) 840730
Fax: (0560) 3432632
E-mail: gensec@agbis.org.uk
Website: www.agbis.org.uk
General Secretary: Stuart Westley, MA

The aim of the Association is to advance education in independent schools, to promote good governance and administration in independent schools and to encourage cooperation between their governing bodies. For details please contact the General Secretary.

Association of Heads of Independent Schools

St Nicholas School
Redfields House, Redfields Lane
Church Crookham
Fleet
Hampshire GU52 0RF
Honorary Secretary: Mrs A V Whatmough

Membership of AHIS is open to the heads of girls' independent secondary schools and girls' co-educational junior independent schools that are accredited by the Independent Schools Council (see below).

Association of School and College Leaders (ASCL)

130 Regent Road
Leicester LE1 7PG
Tel: (0116) 299 1122
Fax: (0116) 299 1123
E-mail: info@ascl.org.uk
Website: www.ascl.org.uk
General Secretary: Dr J E Dunford

ASCL is the only professional association and trade union in Britain to speak exclusively for secondary school and college leaders, in both the independent and mainstream sectors. The Association has nearly 15,000 members including heads, deputy heads, assistant heads, bursars and business managers and others with school/college responsibility. ASCL has strong ties with the Headmasters' Conference and Girls' School Association and their members are automatically part of ASCL.

Benefits of ASCL membership include access to legal support and advice, a telephone hotline for guidance on urgent issues, personal support from regional field officers, regular publications and guidance on courses and conferences, and pension advice.

Association of Tutors

Sunnycroft
63 King Edward Road
Northampton NN1 5LY
Tel: (01604) 624171
Website: www.tutor.co.uk
Contact: Dr D J Cornelius

The professional body for independent private tutors. Members provide advice and individual tuition to students at all levels of education. The tutoring may be supplementary to full course provision or may be on a full course basis.

Boarding Schools' Association (BSA)

Grosvenor Gardens House
35–37 Grosvenor Gardens
London SW1W 0BS
Tel: (020) 7798 1580
Fax: (020) 7798 1581
E-mail: bsa@boarding.org.uk

Website: www.boarding.org.uk
National Director: Hilary Moriarty

The BSA has the twin objectives of promoting boarding education and developing quality boarding through high standards of pastoral care and boarding facilities.

A school can join the BSA only if it is a member of one of the constituent associations of the Independent Schools Council or, for state-maintained boarding schools, a member of SBSA (the State Boarding Schools Association). These two bodies require member schools to be regularly inspected by the Independent Schools Inspectorate (IS) or Ofsted. Parents and prospective pupils choosing a boarding school can therefore be assured that BSA member schools are committed to providing the best possible boarding environment for their pupils.

For further information about the BSA Professional Development Programme please contact Alex Thomson OBE, PGCE DipEd FCIPD MIFL, BSA Director of Training BSA, Tel: (020) 7798 1580.

British Accreditation Council

The Chief Executive
44 Bedford Row
London WC1R 4LL
Tel: (020) 7447 2554
Fax: (020) 7447 2555
E-mail: info@the-bac.org
Website: www.the-bac.org

BAC is a registered charity organization that was established in 1984 to act as the national accrediting body for independent further and higher education. A college accredited by BAC undergoes a thorough inspection every four years, which is followed up with an interim visit after two years. Accreditation means that a BAC college has achieved a satisfactory standard in the areas of health and safety provision, administration and staffing, the management of quality, student welfare, and teaching and learning. BAC also attempts to take action to intercede for students if a conflict arises between the student and the accredited college.

At present BAC accredits over 230 colleges in the UK and more than 25 overseas in 11 different countries: the Czech Republic, France, Spain, Pakistan, United Arab Emirates, Bulgaria, Greece, India, Mauritius, Germany and Switzerland.

British Association for Early Childhood Education (Early Education)

111 City View House
463 Bethnal Green Road
London E2 9QY
Tel: (020) 7739 7594
Fax: (020) 7613 5330

A charitable association that advises on the care and education of young children from birth to 8 years old. The Association also publishes booklets and organizes conferences for those interested in early childhood education.

British Dyslexia Association

Unit 8 Bracknell Beeches
Old Bracknell Lane
Bracknell RG12 7BW
Fax: (0118) 935 1927
E-mail: helpline@bdadyslexia.org.uk
Website: www.bdadyslexia.org.uk
Helpline/Information Service:
10am – 4pm Monday – Friday,
also 5pm – 7pm on Wednesdays.

Charity offering information and help to dyslexic people, their families, professionals and employees.

Children's Education Advisory Service

Trenchard Lines
Upavon
Pewsey
Wilts SN9 6BE
Tel: (01980) 618244
E-mail: enquiries@ceas.detsa.co.uk

To support Service families and entitled civilians in obtaining appropriate educational facilities for their children and to provide high quality, impartial advice on all aspects of education worldwide.

Choir Schools Association

Wolvesey
College Street
Winchester SO23 9ND
Tel: (01962) 890530
Fax: (01962) 869978
E-mail: info@choirschools.org.uk
Administrator: Susan Rees

An association of schools educating cathedral and collegiate boy and girl choristers. Membership comprises the following schools:

Bristol Cathedral School, Bristol
The Cathedral School, Llandaff
Chetham's School of Music, Manchester
The Chorister School, Durham
Christ Church Cathedral School, Oxford
Exeter Cathedral School, Exeter
Hereford Cathedral Junior School, Hereford
King's College School, Cambridge
King's Preparatory School, Rochester
The King's School, Ely

The King's School, Gloucester
The King's School, Worcester
Lanesborough, Guildford
Lichfield Cathedral School, Lichfield
Lincoln Minster School, Lincoln
Magdalen College School, Oxford
The Minster School, Southwell
The Minster School, York
New College School, Oxford
Norwich School, Norwich
The Pilgrim's School, Winchester
Polwhele House, Truro
The Prebendal School, Chichester
Reigate St Mary's Preparatory and Choir School, Reigate
Ripon Cathedral Choir School, Ripon
St Edmunds Junior School, Canterbury
St George's School, Windsor
St James's School, Grimsby
St John's College, Cardiff
St John's College School, Cambridge
St Mary's Music School, Edinburgh
St Paul's Cathedral School, London EC4
Salisbury Cathedral School, Salisbury
Wells Cathedral School, Wells
Westminster Abbey Choir School, London SW1
Westminster Cathedral Choir School, London SW1

Associate Members

Ampleforth College, Ampleforth, North Yorkshire
City of London School, London EC4
The King's School, Peterborough
The Oratory School, Reading
Portsmouth Grammar School, Portsmouth
Queen Elizabeth Grammar School, Wakefield
Runnymede St Edward's School, Liverpool
St Cedd's School, Chelmsford
St Edward's College, Liverpool
Warwick School, Warwick

Council for Independent Education (CIFE)

1 Knightsbridge Green
London SW1X 7NW
Tel: (020) 8767 8666
E-mail: enquiries@cife.org.uk
Website: www.cife.org.uk

CIFE, founded in 1973, is a professional association for independent colleges of further education which specialize in preparing students for GCSEs, A and AS levels and university entrance. In addition, some colleges offer English language tuition for students from abroad. The Association promotes good practice and adherence to strict standards of professional conduct and ethical propriety. Full membership is open to colleges which have been accredited either by the British Accreditation Council (BAC) or by the Independent Schools Council. All CIFE colleges, of which there are currently 17 spread throughout England, with concentrations in London, Oxford and Cambridge, have to abide by exacting codes of conduct and practice; and the character and presentation of their published exam results are subject to formal validation by the BACS. Further information and a list of colleges are available from the Secretary.

CReSTeD (Council for the Registration of Schools Teaching Dyslexic Pupils)

Greygarth, Littleworth
Winchcombe
Cheltenham GL54 5BT
Tel: (01242) 604 852
E-mail: admin@crested.org.uk
Website: www.crested.org.uk
Chairman: Brendan Wignall
Registered Charity No: 1052103

The CReSTeD Register is to help parents and those who advise them to choose schools for children with SpLD (dyslexia). Its main supporters are the British Dyslexia Association and Dyslexia Action which, with others, established CReSTeD to produce an authoritative list of schools, both maintained and independent, that have been through an established registration procedure, including a visit by the CReSTeD selected consultant.

Department for Children, Schools and Families

Sanctuary Buildings
Great Smith Street
London SW1P 3BT
Tel: (08700) 000 2288
Fax: (01928) 794 248
E-mail: info@dcsf.gsi.gov.uk
Website: www.dcsf.gov.uk

Dyslexia Action

Park House
Wick Road
Egham
Surrey TW20 0HH
Tel: (01784) 222300
Fax: (01784) 222333
E-mail: info@dyslexiaaction.org.uk
Website: www.dyslexiaaction.org.uk
Registered Charity No. 268502

Dyslexia Action is a national charity and the UK's leading provider of services and support for people with dyslexia and literacy difficulties. It specializes in providing assessments, teaching and training, as well as developing and distributing teaching materials and undertaking research. It has 26 centres and over 150 teaching locations around the UK and is committed to taking action to change the lives of those with dyslexia.

Gabbitas Educational Consultants

Norfolk House
30 Charles II Street
London SW1Y 4AE
Tel: (020) 7734 0161
Fax: (020) 7437 1764
E-mail: info@gabbitas.co.uk
Website: www.gabbitas.co.uk

Gabbitas offers independent, expert advice on all stages of education and careers:

- choice of independent schools and colleges;

- educational assessment services for parents concerned about their child's progress at school;

- sixth form options – A and AS level, International Baccalaureate and vocational courses;

- university and degree choices and UCAS applications;

- alternatives to university;

- careers assessment and guidance;

- extensive guidance for overseas students transferring into the British system;

- specialist services, including guardianship, for overseas students attending UK boarding schools.

Gabbitas also provides a full range of services for schools, including the appointment of heads and staff as well as consultancy on any aspects of school management and development.

The Girls' Day School Trust (GDST)

100 Rochester Row
London SW1P 1JP
Tel: (020) 7393 6666
Fax: (020) 7393 6789
E-mail: info@wes.gdst.net
Website: www.gdst.net
Registered Charity No. 306983

The GDST is one of the largest, longest-established and most successful groups of schools in the UK, with 4,000 staff and 20,000 students. As a charity that owns and runs a family of 26 schools in England and Wales, it reinvests all its income for the benefit of the pupils. With a long history of pioneering innovation in the education of girls, the GDST now also educates boys in some of its schools; has two co-educational Sixth Form Colleges; and is developing a selective group of prep schools, some of which are co-educational.

The wide-ranging curricular and extra-curricular opportunities available in GDST schools encourage creativity, articulate self-expression and enterprise in students who are prepared to participate fully in the challenges of 21st-century life.

Schools

The Belvedere Academy, Liverpool
Birkenhead High School, Birkenhead
Blackheath High School, London SE3
Brighton and Hove High School, Sussex
Bromley High School, Kent
Central Newcastle High School, Newcastle upon Tyne
Croydon High School, Croydon
Heathfield School, Pinner
Hilden Grange School, Tonbridge, Kent
Howell's School, Llandaff, Cardiff

Ipswich High School, Suffolk
Kensington Preparatory School,
   London SW6
Northampton High School,
   Northampton
Norwich High School for Girls, Norfolk
Notting Hill & Ealing High School,
   London W13
Nottingham High School for Girls,
   Nottingham
Oxford High School, Oxford
Portsmouth High School, Hampshire
Putney High School, London SW15
Royal High School, Bath
Sheffield High School, Sheffield
Shrewsbury High School, Shropshire
South Hampstead High School,
   London NW3
Streatham & Clapham High School,
   London SW16
Sutton High School, Surrey
Sydenham High School, London SE26
Wimbledon High School, London
   SW19

All GDST schools are non-denominational
day schools, and The Royal High School,
Bath, also takes boarders. The GDST's
small group of prep schools – Great
Houghton, The Hamlets, Hilden Grange
and Kensington – prepare pupils for entry
to other schools at 11 or 13. All other
schools in the group offer an 'all-through'
education, catering for pupils from ages
3 or 4 to 18, with thriving sixth forms and,
in many cases, nursery classes too.
   Howell's School in Cardiff and the
Royal High School in Bath have a
co-educational Sixth Form College,
and The Belvedere School in Liverpool
transferred from the independent sector
to Academy status and opened as
The Belvedere Academy in September
2007.

The Girls' Schools Association (GSA)
130 Regent Road
Leicester LE1 7PG
Tel: (0116) 254 1619
Fax: (0116) 255 3792
E-mail: office@gsa.uk.com
President: Mrs Jill Berry
Executive Director: Ms Sheila Cooper

GSA is the professional association
representing the heads of leading girls'
independent schools. Its aims are to
promote high standards of education for
girls; to inform and influence national
educational debate; raise awareness of
the benefits of single-sex education for
girls and to support members through
the provision of a broad range of services.
GSA also operates the MyDaughter
website – www.mydaughter.co.uk – the
first website dedicated to providing
information, expert opinion and lively
debate on all aspects of raising and
educating happy and fulfilled girls.

**The Headmasters' and Headmistresses'
Conference (HMC)**
12 The Point
Rockingham Road
Market Harborough
Leicestershire LE16 7QU
Tel: (01858) 469 059
Fax: (01858) 469 532
Membership Secretary: I Power
Secretary: G H Lucas

The Headmasters' and Headmistresses'
Conference (HMC) represents the
headteachers of some 250 leading
independent schools in the United
Kingdom and the Republic of Ireland.

IAPS (The Independent Association of Prep Schools)

11 Waterloo Place
Leamington Spa
Warwickshire CV32 5LA
Tel: (01926) 887833
Fax: (01926) 888014
E-mail: iaps@iaps.org.uk
Chief Executive: David Hanson

IAPS is a professional association for heads of independent prep schools in the UK and overseas. There are some 600 schools whose heads are in membership, accommodating over 150,000 children.

The Independent Schools Association (ISA)

1 Boys' British School
East Street
Saffron Walden
Essex CB10 1LS
Tel: (01799) 523619
Chief Executive: Neil Roskilly

There are approximately 300 schools in membership of ISA. These are all schools that have been accredited by the Independent Schools Council Inspection Service. This and the requirement that the school should be good of its kind are the criteria for membership. ISA represents schools with pupils throughout the age range. The majority of schools are day schools, but a significant number also have boarders. Membership of the Association enables heads to receive support from the Association in a number of ways and enables pupils to take part in many events organized by ISA.

The Independent Schools' Bursars Association (ISBA)

Unit 11–12, Manor Farm
Cliddesden, Basingstoke
Hants RG25 2JB
Tel: (01256) 330369
Fax: (01256) 330376
E-mail: office@theisba.org.uk
Website: www.theisba.org.uk
General Secretary: Mr Mike Lower

The ISBA, with over 1,000 schools in membership, aims to support and advance financial and operational performance in schools. The Association deals with ministers, civil servants, the media, the general public, a wide range of professional advisers and suppliers, and schools at a number of different levels including governors, heads and bursars. It works closely with the Independent Schools Council (ISC) and its other seven associations together with the Independent Schools Inspectorate (ISI) and the Boarding Schools Association (BSA). The ISBA's staff and Secretariat provide help and advice to schools, seek to keep ahead of regulatory change and promote the sharing of best practice.

The Independent Schools Careers Organisation (ISCO)

ISCO c/o Inspiring Futures
St George's House
Knoll Road
Camberley
Surrey GU15 3SY
Tel: (01276) 687525
E-mail: helpline@inspiringfutures.org.uk
Websites: www.isco.org.uk;
www.inspiringfutures.org.uk;
www.myfuturewise.org.uk;
www.expandinghorizons.info;
www.careerscope.org.uk

ISCO is the independent schools careers service from The Inspiring Futures Foundation. It is a not-for-profit organization established to help young people make informed decisions about higher education and career choices. It provides support to schools through its ISCO Membership and Information Service schemes and direct help and guidance to young people and their parents through the Futurewise scheme. This provides a range of career and higher education services, online and face-to-face, from enrolment to age 23. Services are delivered across the UK and internationally through a network of professionally qualified regional directors and regional advisers. Operations are supported centrally to ensure that up-to-date information is provided to members of the schemes through a range of resources, online services and the termly *Careerscope* magazine. The Expanding Horizons team organizes a range of unique development and career preparation opportunities for young people including InterActives, Insight courses and gap-year fairs.

Independent Schools Council (ISC)

St Vincent House
30 Orange Street
London WC2H 7HH
Tel: (020) 7766 7070
Fax: (020) 7766 7071
Chief Executive: David Lyscom

ISC is the umbrella body for the following associations:

The Association of Governing Bodies of Independent Schools (AGBIS), (COBIS)
The Girls' Schools Association (GSA)

The Headmasters' and Headmistresses' Conference (HMC)
The Independent Association of Prep Schools (IAPS)
The Independent Schools' Association (ISA)
The Independent Schools' Bursars Association (ISBA)
The Society of Headmasters and Headmistresses of Independent Schools (SHMIS), (COBIS)

The total membership of ISC comprises about 1,300 schools that are accredited by ISC and inspected on a six-year cycle by the Independent Schools Inspectorate (ISI) under arrangements agreed by the DCSF and OFSTED. ISC deals with matters of policy and other issues common to its members and when required speaks collectively on their behalf. It represents its members in discussions with the Department for Children, Schools and Families and with other organizations, and represents the collective view of members on independent education.

Independent Schools Examinations Board

The Pump House
16 Queen's Avenue
Christchurch BH23 1BZ
Tel: (01202) 487538
Fax: (01202) 473728
E-mail: enquiries@iseb.co.uk
Website: iseb.co.uk

Details of the Common Entrance examinations (see the section on Examinations and Qualifications) are available from the General Secretary at the address above.

The Round Square Schools
Braemar Lodge
Castle Hill
Hartley
Dartford
Kent DA3 7BH
Tel: (0147) 470 6927
Fax: (01737) 217133
E-mail: jane@roundsquare.org
Secretary: Mrs J Howson

An international group of schools that follow the principles of Kurt Hahn, founder of the Salem School in Germany and Gordonstoun in Scotland. There are now over 50 member schools in more than 12 countries: Australia, Canada, England, France, Germany, India, Japan, Kenya, Oman, Scotland, South Africa, Switzerland, Thailand and the United States. Member schools arrange regular exchange visits for pupils and undertake aid projects in India, Kenya, Eastern Europe and Thailand. All member schools uphold the five principles of outdoor adventure, community service, education for democracy, international understanding and environmental conservation. UK member schools are:

Abbotsholme, Uttoxeter (co-ed)
Box Hill, Dorking (co-ed)
Cobham Hall, Gravesend (girls)
Felsted School, Felsted (co-ed)
Gordonstoun, Elgin (co-ed)
Wellington College, Crowthorne
  (boys, girls in sixth form)
Westfield, Newcastle upon Tyne (girls)
Windermere St Anne's (co-ed)

SATIPS Professional Support and Training for Staff in Independent Schools
Cherry Trees
Stebbing
Great Dunmow
Essex CM6 3ST
Tel/Fax: (01371) 856823
E-mail: admin@satips.com
Website: www.satips.com
General Secretary: Alex Synge
Administrator: Mrs P M Harrison

SATIPS, founded in 1952, is a source of professional support and encouragement for staff in preparatory and other schools. We are now one of the foremost providers of subject-based and cross-curricular INSET courses for prep school and other staff. SATIPS is a registered charity. In 1993 the Society widened its appeal by changing its emphasis from purely preparatory school teachers to any school staff, especially those in independent schools. In particular, teachers who have pupils in Key Stages 1, 2 and 3 will find membership of SATIPS useful: we are particularly interested in making contact with colleagues in the maintained sector. The Society publishes 19 broadsheets each term in all subject areas and runs conferences (mostly one-day) at various venues during the year. We offer school and individual membership.

The Society of Heads
12 The Point
Rockingham Road
Market Harborough
Leicestershire LE16 7QU
Tel: (01858) 433760
Fax: (01858) 461413
E-mail: gensec@thesocietyofheads.org.uk

Website: www.thesocietyofheads.org.uk
General Secretary: Peter Bodkin

The Society of Heads comprises more than 100 independent schools. Within the membership there is a wide range of educational experience. Some schools are young, some have evolved from older foundations, some have behind them a long tradition of pioneer and specialist education; a number are at the leading edge of education in music, dance and the arts; and several are well known for their effective support for those with specific learning difficulties. The great majority are co-educational but we also have some boys' and girls' schools. Many have a strong boarding element, others are day only. Some have specific religious foundations and some are non-denominational. All offer a stimulating sixth-form experience.

Steiner Waldorf Schools Fellowship

Kidbrooke Park
Forest Row
East Sussex RH18 5JA
Tel: (01342) 822115
Fax: (01342) 826004
E-mail: info@swsf.org.uk
Website: www.steinerwaldorf.org.uk
Chairman: Christopher Clouder

The Steiner Waldorf Schools Fellowship represents the 32 autonomous Steiner Waldorf Schools and 45 Early Years Centres in the UK and Eire. There are now over 958 schools worldwide. Key characteristics of the education include:

- careful balance in the artistic, practical and intellectual content of the international Steiner Waldorf curriculum;

- co-educational from 3 to 19 years;

- shared Steiner Waldorf curriculum for all pupils;

- GCSE and A Level examinations;

- a broad education based on Steiner's approach to the holistic nature of the human being;

- cooperative school management;

- usually a variable parent payment scheme.

Steiner Waldorf education is rapidly gaining in popularity all over the world.

Woodard Schools (The Woodard Corporation)

High Street
Abbots Bromley
Rugeley
Staffordshire WS15 3BW
Tel: (01283) 840120
E-mail: jillshorthose@woodard.co.uk
Website: www.woodard.co.uk

The Woodard Corporation has 47 schools throughout the country, including 20 schools in the independent and maintained sectors that choose to be associated or affiliated. Woodard also sponsors four academies. All have an Anglican foundation and together they form the largest independent group of Church Schools in England and Wales.

Member schools

Abbots Bromley School for Girls, Abbots Bromley
Ardingly College, Haywards Heath
Ardingly College Prep School, Haywards Heath
Ardingly College Pre-Prep School, Haywards Heath

Bloxham School, Banbury
The Cathedral School, Cardiff
Denstone College, Uttoxeter
Ellesmere College, Ellesmere
Hurstpierpoint College, Hassocks
Hurstpierpoint College Prep School,
   Hassocks
King's College, Taunton
King's Hall School, Taunton
The King's School, Tynemouth
Lancing College, Lancing
Lancing College Prep School, Hove
Peterborough High School,
   Peterborough
Prestfelde School, Shrewsbury

Queen Mary's School, Thirsk
Roch House Prep School, Abbots
   Bromley
Smallwood Manor Prep School, Uttoxeter
St James' School, Great Grimsby
St Margaret's School, Exeter
Worksop College, Worksop
Worksop College Prep School, Retford

Associated schools (Independent)

Alderley Edge School for Girls, Alderley
   Edge
Derby High School, Derby
Exeter Cathedral School, Exeter
King's School, Rochester

Glossary of Abbreviations

ABRSM	Associated Board of the Royal Schools of Music
ADD	Attention Deficit Disorder
ADISR	Association des Directeurs d'Instituts de la Suisse Romande
AEB	Associated Examining Board
AGBIS	Association of Governing Bodies of Independent Schools
AHIS	Association of Heads of Independent Schools
ASCL	Association of School and College Leaders
AICE	Advanced International Certificate of Education
ANTC	Association of Nursery Training Colleges
ARCS	Accreditation, Review and Consultancy Service
AVDEP	Association Vaudoise des Ecoles Privees
BACIFHE	British Accreditation Council for Independent Further and Higher Education
BAGA	British Amateur Gymnastics Association
BAYS	British Association for the Advancement of Science
BHS	British Horse Society
BSA	Boarding Schools Association
CAE	Cambridge Certificate in Advanced English
CASE	Council for Advancement and Support of Education
CEE	Common Entrance Examination
CIFE	Council for Independent Further Education
COBIS	Council of British International Schools
CReSTeD	Council for the Registration of Schools Teaching Dyslexic Pupils
CSA	Choir Schools Association
DCSF	Department for Children, Schools and Families
ECIS	European Council for International Schools
EFL	English as a Foreign Language
ESL	English as a Second Language
ESOL	English for Speakers of Other Languages
EUK	English UK, language teaching association

FCE	Cambridge First Certificate in English
FOBISSEA	Federation of British International Schools in South-East Asia
FSEP	Federation Suisse des Ecoles Privees
GBA	Governing Bodies Association
GBGSA	Governing Bodies of Girls' Schools Association
GDST	Girls' Day School Trust
GSA	Girls' Schools Association
HAS	Head Teachers' Association of Scotland
HMC	Headmasters' and Headmistresses' Conference
IAPS	Independent Association of Prep Schools
IB	International Baccalaureate
IBO	International Baccalaureate Organisation
IBSCA	International Baccalaureate Schools and Colleges Association
IBTA	Independent Business Training Organisation
ICG	Independent Colleges Group
IGCSE	International General Certificate of Secondary Education
ISA	Independent Schools Association
ISBA	Independent Schools Bursars' Association
ISC	Independent Schools Council (formerly Independent Schools Joint Council or ISJC)
ISCIS	Independent Schools Council Information Service (formerly ISIS)
ISCO	Independent Schools Careers Organisation
ISI	Independent Schools Inspectorate
ISIS	Independent Schools Information Service
LAMDA	London Academy of Music and Dramatic Art
LISA	London International Schools Association
MSA	Middle States Association of Colleges and Schools (USA)
NABSS	National Association of British Schools in Spain
NAHT	National Association of Head Teachers
NAIS	National Association of Independent Schools
NE/SA	Near East/South Asia
NEAB	Northern Examinations and Assessment Board
NEASC	New England Association of Schools and Colleges
OFSTED	Office for Standards in Education
OUDLE	University of Oxford Delegacy of Local Examinations
PET	Cambridge Preliminary English Test
PSE	Personal and Social Education
RSA CLAIT	Computer Literacy and Information Technology
SATIPS	Society of Assistants Teaching in Preparatory Schools
SCIS	Scottish Council of Independent Schools
SGS	Scottish Girls' Schools
SHMIS	Society of Headmasters and Headmistresses of Independent Schools
SpLD	Specific Learning Difficulties
STABIS	State Boarding Schools Information Service
WJEC	Welsh Joint Education Committee

Abbreviations used to denote Special Needs provision are as follows:

Special needs support provided (independent mainstream schools)

Learning difficulties

CA Some children with special needs receive help from classroom assistants

RA There are currently very limited facilities for pupils with learning difficulties but reasonable adjustments can be made if necessary

SC Some children with special needs are taught in separate classes for specific subjects

SNU School has a dedicated Special Needs Unit, which provides specialist tuition on a one-to-one or small group basis by appropriately qualified teachers

WI There is no dedicated Special Needs Unit but some children with special needs are withdrawn individually from certain lessons for one-to-one tuition

Behavioural disorders/emotional and behavioural difficulties/challenging behaviour

CA Some children with behavioural problems receive help from classroom assistants

CO Trained counsellors available for pupils

RA There are currently very limited facilities for pupils with behavioural disorders but reasonable adjustments can be made if necessary

ST Behaviour management strategies identified in school's behaviour management policy

TS Staff trained in behaviour management available

Physical impairments/medical conditions

AT Adapted timetable for children with health problems

BL Materials can be provided in Braille

CA Some children receive help from classroom assistants

DS Signing by staff and pupils

HL Hearing loops available

IT Specialist IT provision available

RA There are currently very limited facilities for pupils with physical impairments or medical conditions but reasonable adjustments can be made if necessary

SL Stairlifts

SM Staff with medical training available

TW   Accessible toilet and washing facilities

W   School has wheelchair access (unspecified)

WA1   School is fully wheelchair accessible

WA2   Main teaching areas are wheelchair accessible

WA3   No permanent access for wheelchairs; temporary ramps available

Special needs

ADD   Attention Deficit Disorder
ADHD   Attention Deficit/Hyperactivity Disorder
ASD   Autistic Spectrum Disorder
ASP   Asperger's Syndrome
BESD   Behavioural, Emotional and Social Disorders
CB   Challenging Behaviour
CP   Cerebral Palsy
DOW   Down's Syndrome
DYC   Dyscalculia
DYP   Dyspraxia
DYS   Dyslexia
EPI   Epilepsy
HEA   Health Problems (eg heart defect, asthma)
HI   Hearing Impairment
IM   Impaired Mobility
MLD   Moderate Learning Difficulties
PMLD   Profound and Multiple Learning Difficulties
SLD   Severe Learning Difficulties
SP&LD   Speech and Language Difficulties
TOU   Tourette's Syndrome
VI   Visual Impairment
WU   Wheelchair User

Further Reading

Schools and Further Education

Schools for Special Needs 2013: The complete guide to special needs education in the United Kingdom
18th Edition: Gabbitas Educational Consultants and Kogan-Page
*The definitive guide to special needs education in the UK
£25.00   Paperback   ISBN 978 0 7494 6745 6   592 pages   2013

How to Pass Secondary School Selection Tests
Contains over 600 practice questions
Mike Bryon
*Ideal for 11+ common entrance & SATS
£8.99   Paperback   ISBN 978 0 7494 4217 0   224 pages   2004

Everything You Need to Know about Going to University
3rd Edition: Sally Longson
"comprehensive resource to help you make the right choices" – Mandy Telford, former National President, National Union of Students
£9.99   Paperback   ISBN 978 0 7494 3985 9   192 pages   2003

The Essential Guide to Paying for University
Effective funding strategies for parents and students
Catherine Dawson
£9.99   Paperback   ISBN 978 0 7494 5635 1   344 pages   2009

Educational Reference

British Qualifications
A complete guide to professional, vocational & academic qualifications in the United Kingdom
43rd Edition
"The single best one-volume reference on British educational awards in print" –
World Education News & Reviews
£64.99   Paperback   ISBN 978 0 7494 6743 2   2013

British Vocational Qualifications
A directory of vocational qualifications available in the United Kingdom
12th Edition
"Splendid... Every imaginable accessible procedure is packed into its pages" –
New Statesman
£40.00   Paperback   ISBN 978 0 7494 5881 2   408 pages   2010

Careers

The A–Z of Careers & Jobs
19th Edition: Susan Hodgson published in association with *The Times*
"The perfect starting point for students and school leavers" – *Education & Training*
£16.99   Paperback   ISBN 978 0 7494 6429 5   448 pages   2012

Also available:

Careers & Jobs in IT   David Yardley   £7.99   Paperback   ISBN 978 0 7494 4245 X
144 pages   2004
Careers & Jobs in the Police Service   Kim Clabby   £7.99
Paperback   ISBN 978 0 7494 4204 2   112 pages   2004
Careers & Jobs in Travel & Tourism   Verité Reily Collins   £7.99
Paperback   ISBN 978 0 7494 4205 0   112 pages   2004

What Next after School?
All you need to know about work, travel & study
10th Edition: Elizabeth Holmes, published in association with *The Times*
"A wealth of practical information about the world of work, training and
higher-education" – *Evening Standard*
£14.99   Paperback   ISBN 978 0 7494 6532 2   312 pages   2012

What Next after University?
Work, travel, education & life with a degree
2nd Edition: Simon Kent, published in association with *The Times*
"Covers everything from basic work, travel and education options and graduate
recruitment tests to finding a home and personal finance" – *Girl About Town*
£8.99   Paperback   ISBN 978 0 7494 4251 4   320 pages   2004

Job Applications

Great Answers to Tough Interview Questions
8th Edition: Martin Yate
"The best book on job-hunting" – *Financial Times*
£9.99   Paperback   ISBN 978 0 7494 6352 6   296 pages   2011

Ultimate CV
Write the perfect CV and get that job
3rd Edition: Martin Yate
*Over 100 samples of job-winning CVs
£14.99   Paperback   ISBN 0 978 0 7494 6404 2   2012

Ultimate Job Search Letters
Write the perfect letter and get that job
Martin Yate
£9.99   Paperback   ISBN 978 0 7494 5328 2   2008

Readymade Job Search Letters
Every type of letter for getting the job you want
4th Edition: Lynn Williams, published in association with *The Times*
"The first book I've seen which specifically deals with letters... A really useful resource"
– *Phoenix Journal*, Keele University
£8.99   Paperback   ISBN 978 0 7494 5322 0   224 pages   2008

Readymade CVs
Sample CVs for every type of job
4th Edition: Lynn Williams, published in association with *The Times*
"A resource book offering several ways to design your CV for a multitude of needs" –
All About Money Making
£12.99   Paperback   ISBN 978 0 7494 6505 6   248 pages   2012

Property

The Complete Guide to Buying & Selling Property
How to get the best deal on your home
2nd Edition: Sarah O'Grady
Published in association with the *Daily Express*
"Valuable, no-nonsense information" – *Ideal Home*
£8.99   Paperback   ISBN 978 0 7494 4194 4   240 pages   2004

The Complete Guide to Renovating & Improving Your Property
2nd Edition: Liz Hodgkinson
"Focuses on major renovation work, from obtaining planning permission to employing
and managing contractors" – *What Mortgage*
£10.99   Paperback   ISBN 978 0 7494 4870 7   224 pages   2007

Also available:

The Complete Guide to Buying Property Abroad
7th Edition: Liz Hodgkinson
£12.99   Paperback   ISBN 978 0 7494 5240 7   320 pages   2008

The Complete Guide to Buying Property in France
4th Edition: Charles Davey
£10.99   Paperback   ISBN 978 0 7494 4646 8   304 pages   2006

The Complete Guide to Buying Property in Italy
Barbara McMahon
£9.99   Paperback   ISBN 978 0 4794 4151 7   224 pages   2004

The Complete Guide to Buying Property in Portugal
Colin Barrow
£9.99   Paperback   ISBN 978 0 7494 4303 0   240 pages   2005

The Complete Guide to Buying Property in Spain
Charles Davey
£9.99   Paperback   ISBN 978 0 7494 4056 5   208 pages   2004

Personal Finance

A Complete Guide to Family Finance
Essential advice on everything from student loans to inheritance tax
Roderick Millar: published in association with the Daily Express
*Comprehensive and practical advice on everything you need to know about saving,
investing and insuring for the future
£12.99   Paperback   ISBN 978 0 7494 4203 3   368 pages   2004

How the Stock Market Works
A beginner's guide to investment
3rd Edition: Michael Becket and Yvette Essen
"Not just for investors, but for anyone who wishes to understand our financial system" –
Neil Collins, City Editor, *Daily Telegraph*
£9.99   Paperback   ISBN 978 0 7494 5689 4   208 pages   2009

How to Write Your Will
20th Edition: Marlene Garsia
"A practical and easy-to-read guide" – *Pensions World*
£9.99   Paperback   ISBN 978 0 7494 5995 6   208 pages   2010

Relocation

Working Abroad
The complete guide to overseas employment
31st Edition: Jonathan Reuvid
"Anyone involved in working abroad will quickly come to look upon this as their bible"
– *Personnel Today*
£12.99   Paperback   ISBN 978 0 7494 6111 9   320 pages   2010

Kogan Page publishes books on Business, Management, Marketing, HR, Training, Careers and Testing, Personal Finance, Property and more.

Visit our website for our full online catalogue: www.koganpage.com

5.11

Main Index

D

E

H

L

M

N

O

T

Z